ROAD ATLAS
GREAT BRITAIN

with special London Section

GEORGE PHILIP

CONTENTS

Key Map   1

Sectional Maps of Great Britain   2-64
General Scale 5 miles = 1 inch

Sectional Maps of Approaches to London   65-72
Scale ¾ inch = 1 mile

Sectional Maps of Central London   73-80
Scale 5 inches = 1 mile

Index to Sectional Maps of Great Britain   1-48

Index to Sectional Maps of Central London   49
and Approaches to London

The maps in this atlas are based upon the Ordnance Survey Map with the sanction of the Controller of Her Majesty's Stationery Office, Crown Copyright Reserved.

British Library Cataloguing in Publication Data
BP road atlas of Great Britain.
   1980
   1. Great Britain — road Maps
   I. Road atlas of Great Britain
   912'.41   G1812.21.P2
ISBN 0 540 05363 5
© 1980 George Philip & Son Ltd

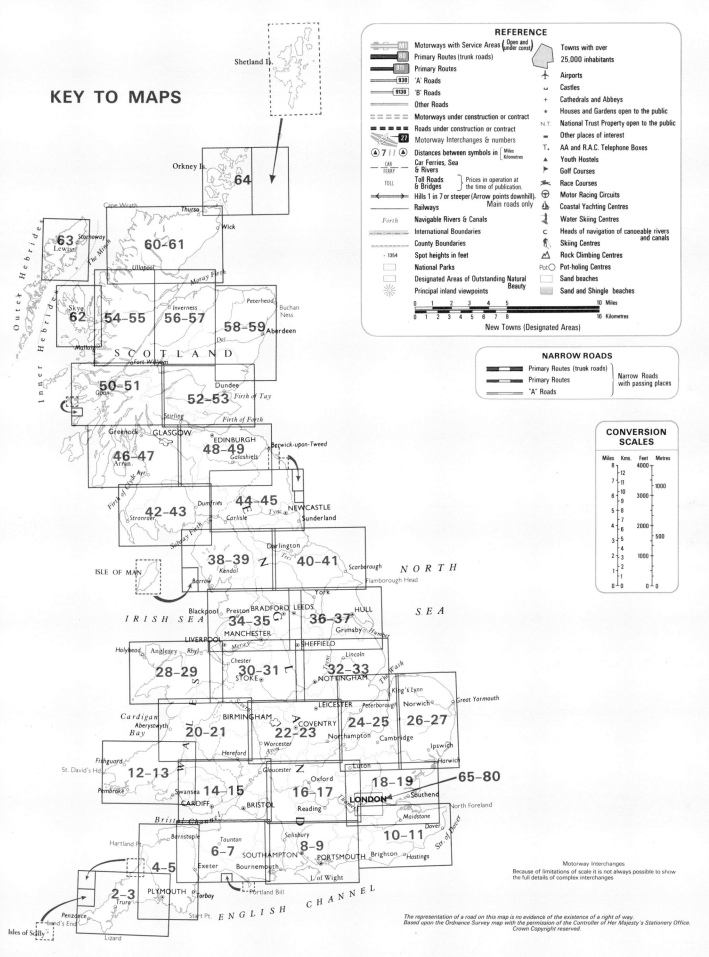

1

KEY TO MAPS

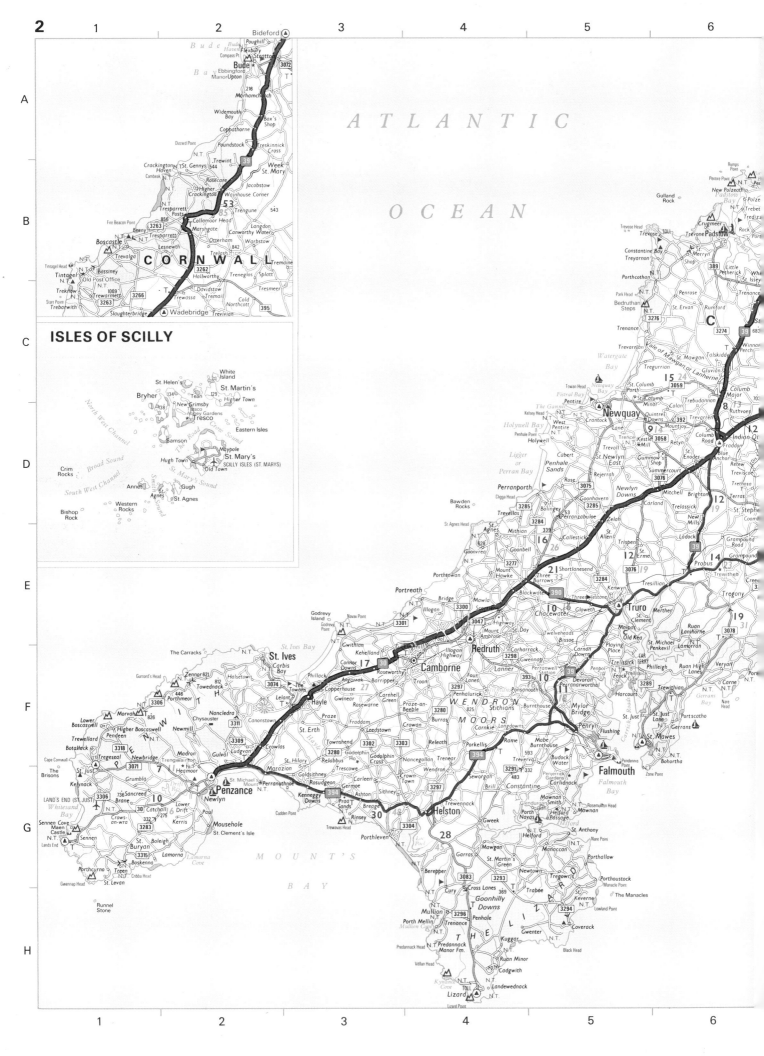

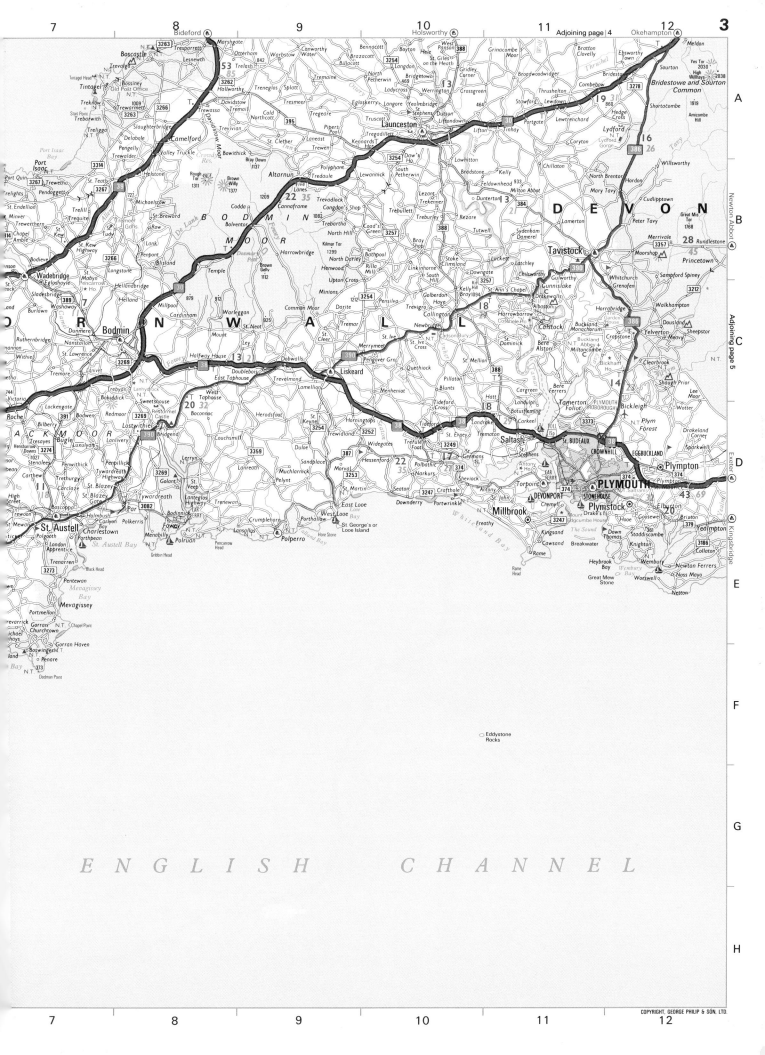

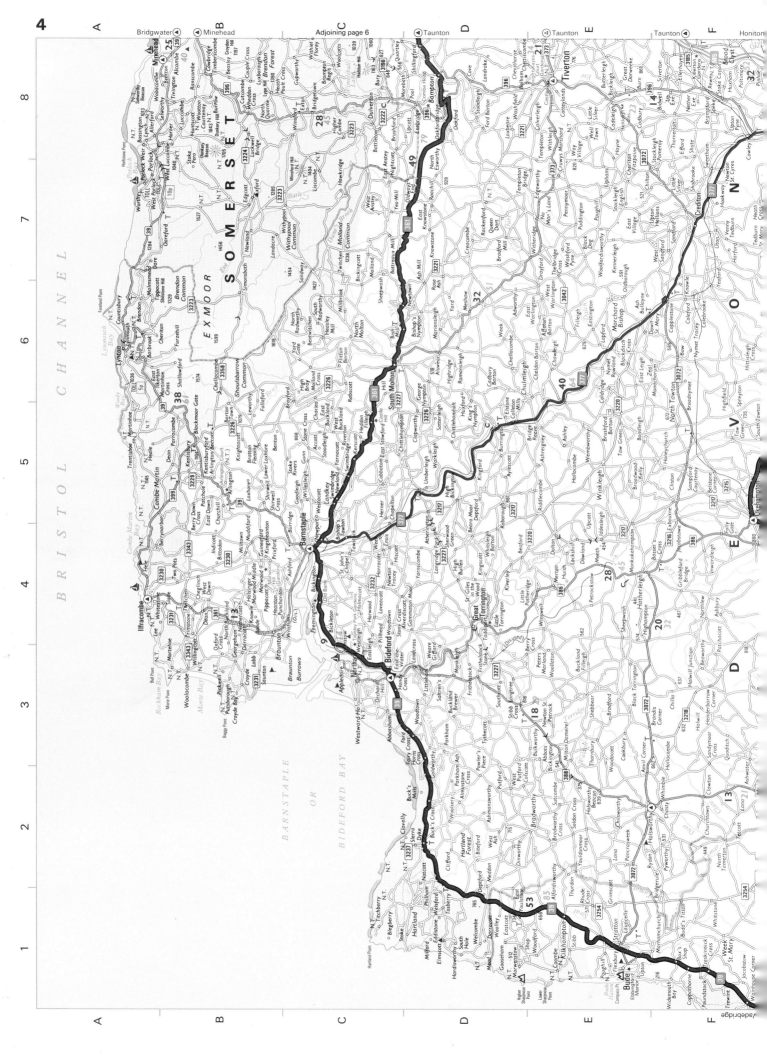

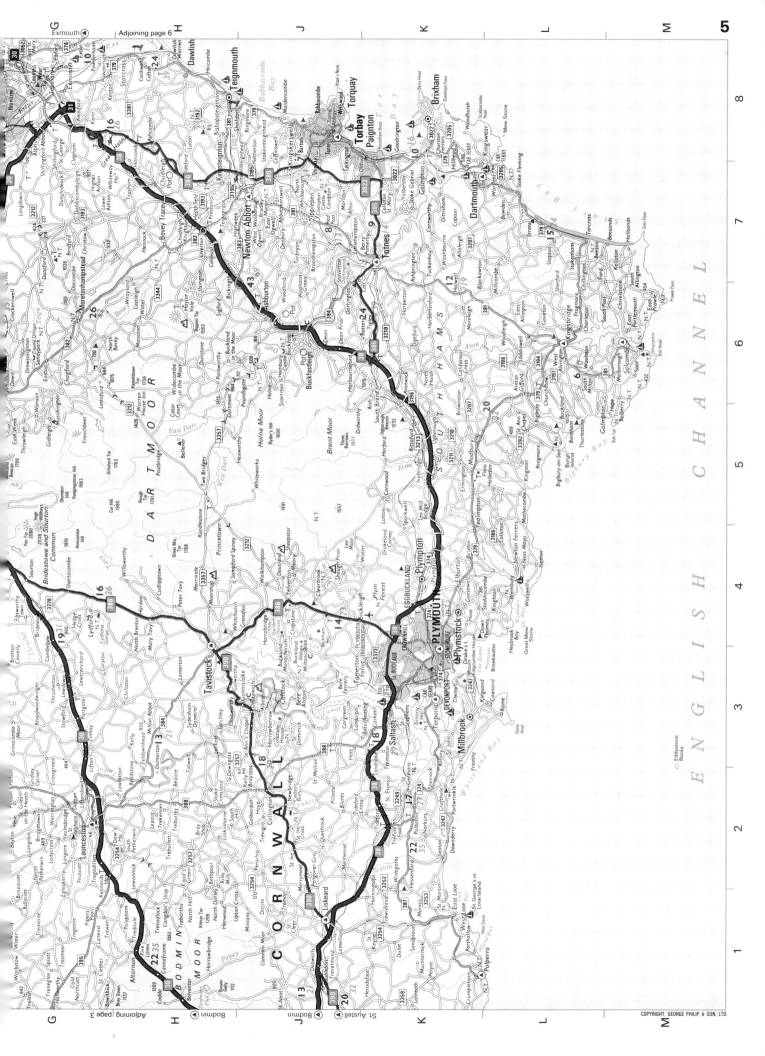

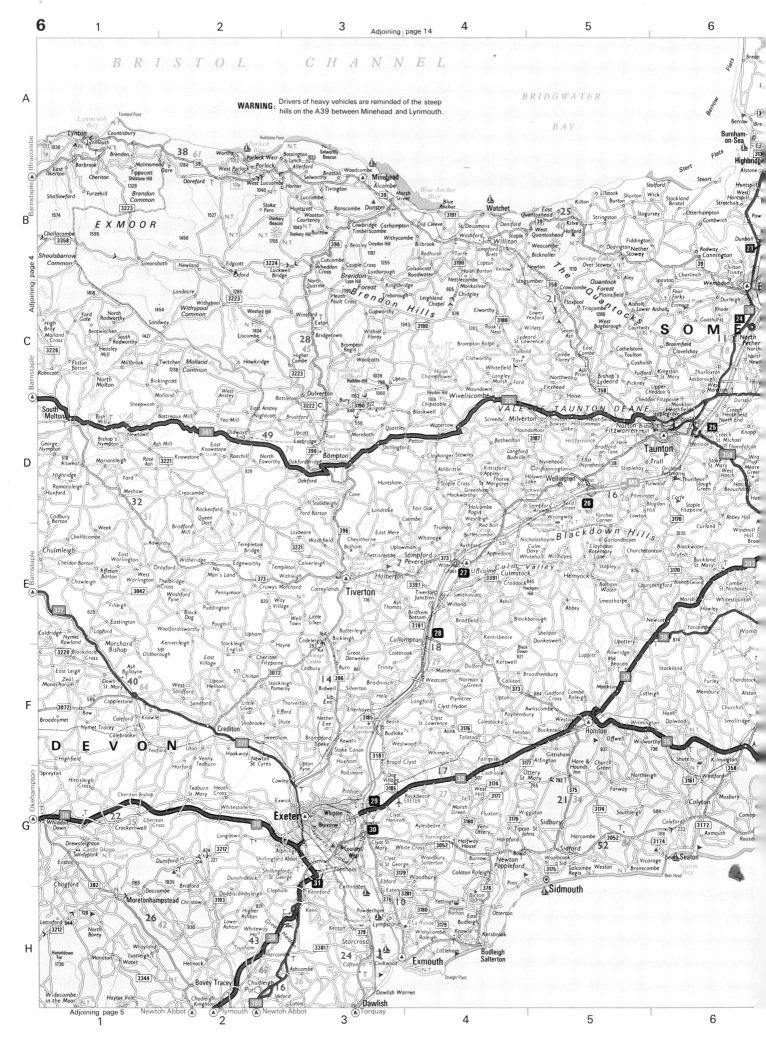

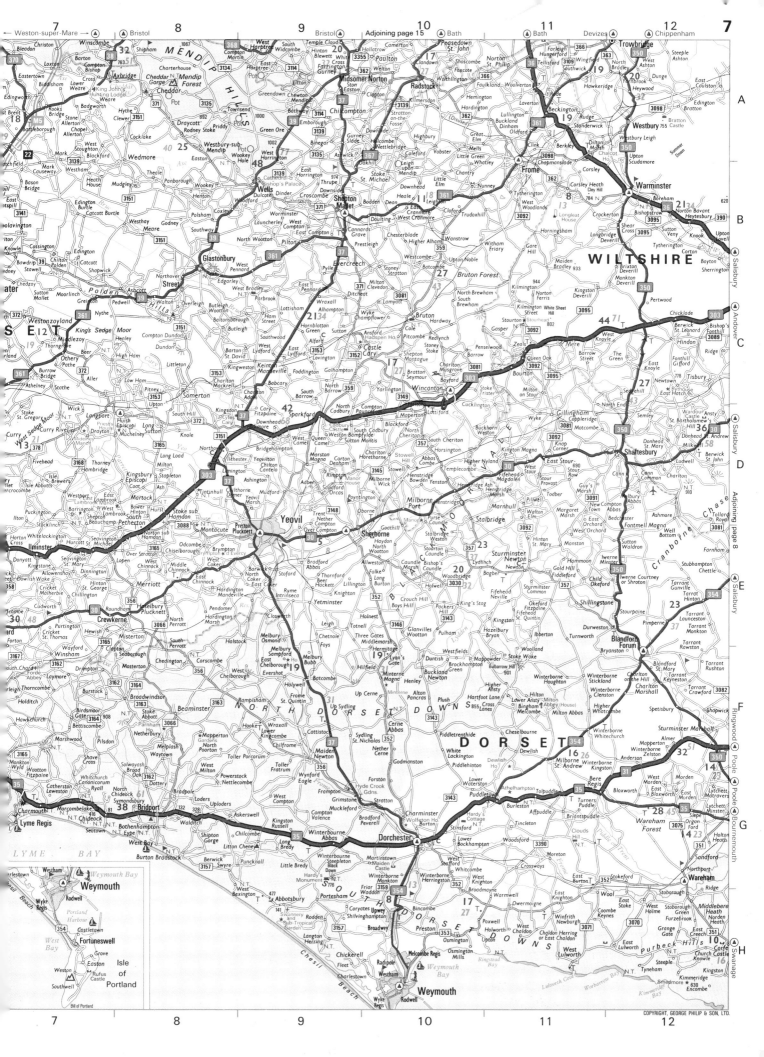

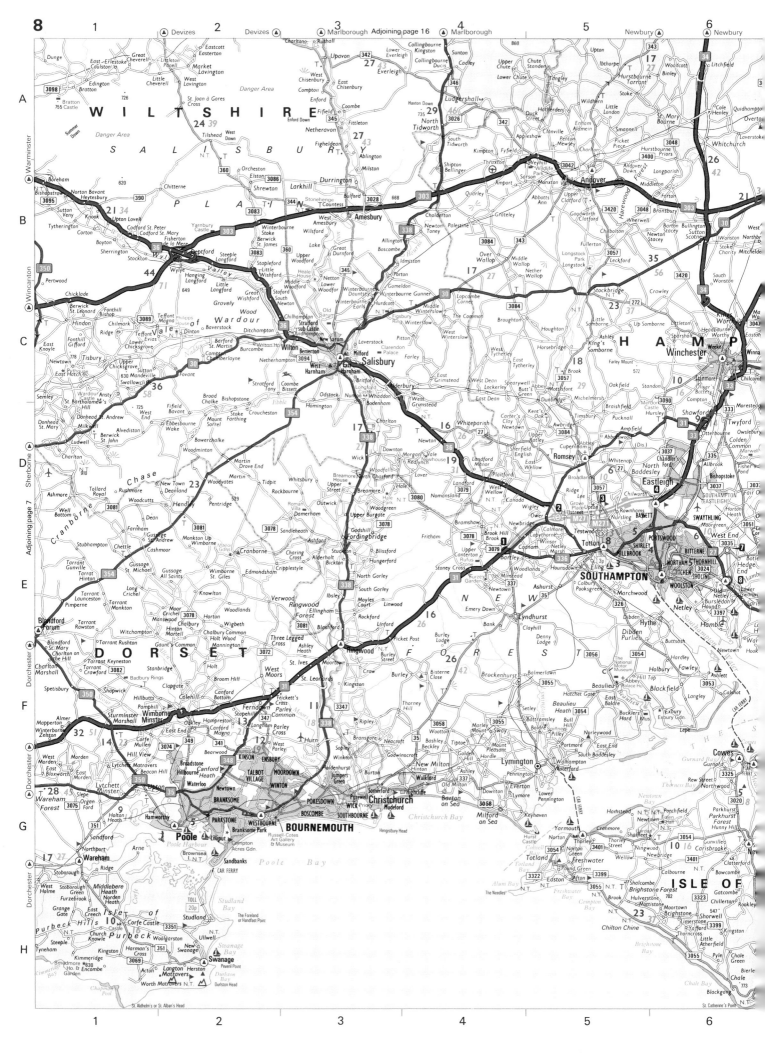

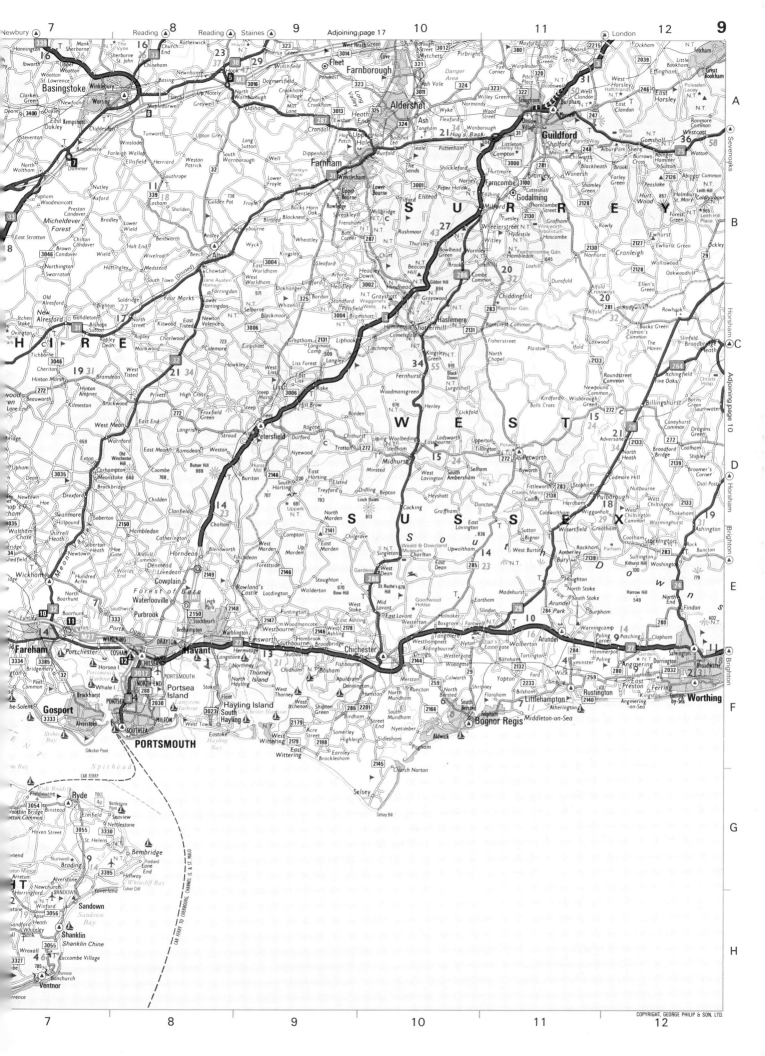

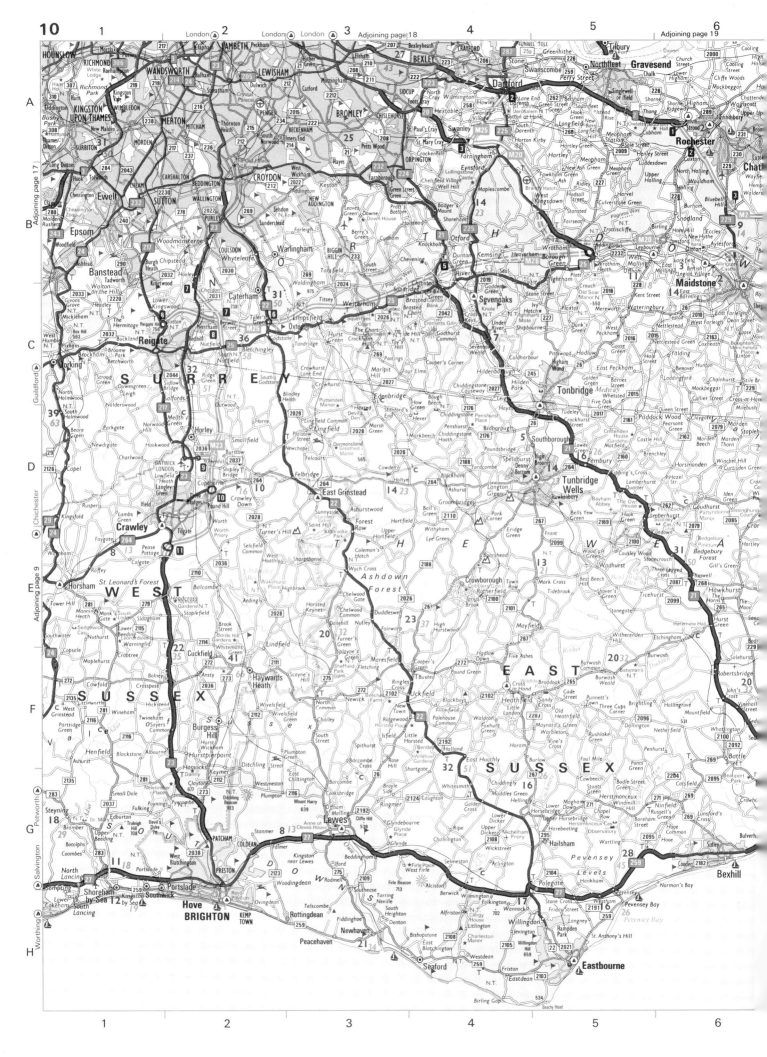

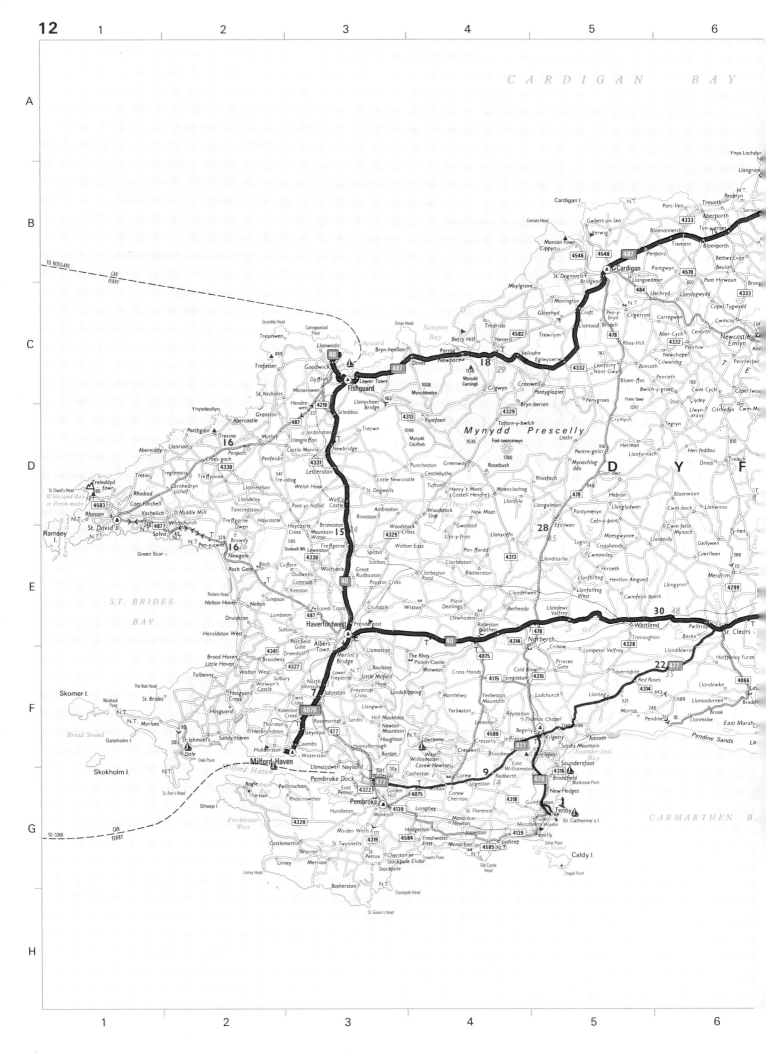

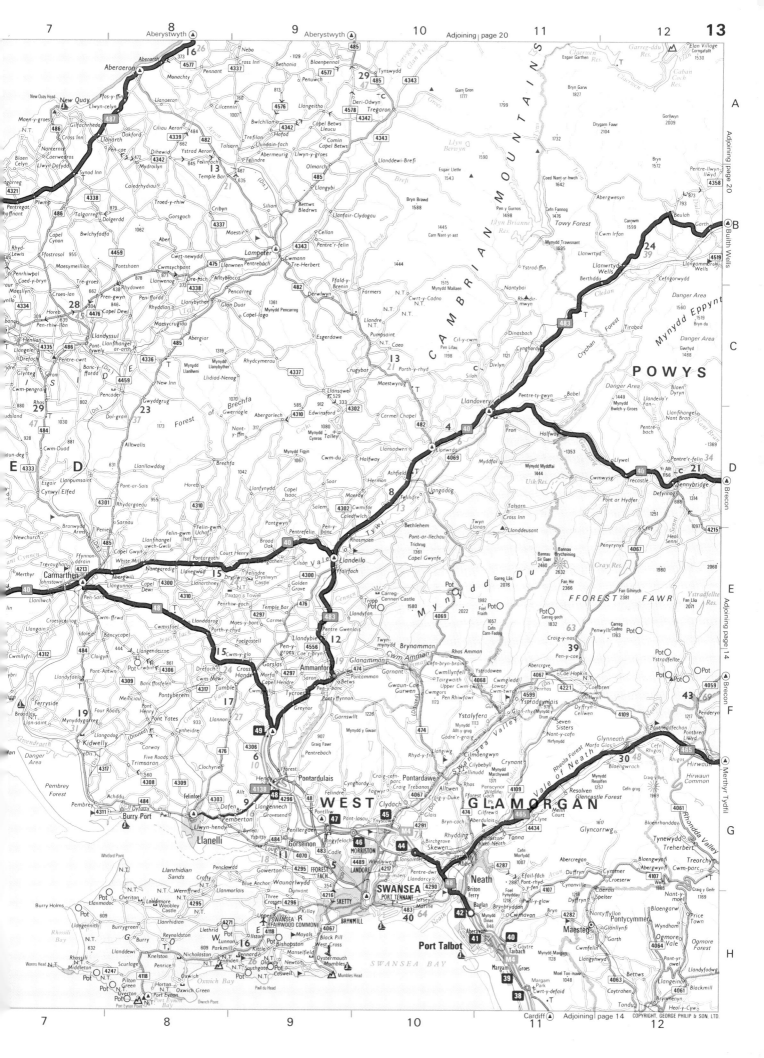

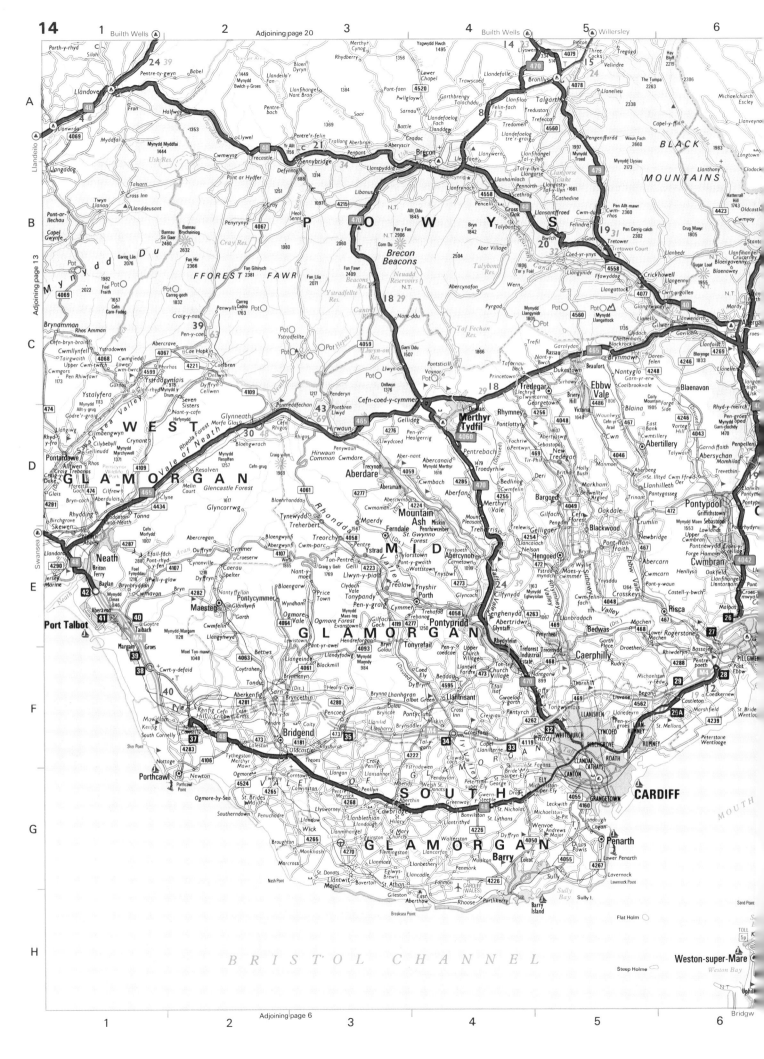

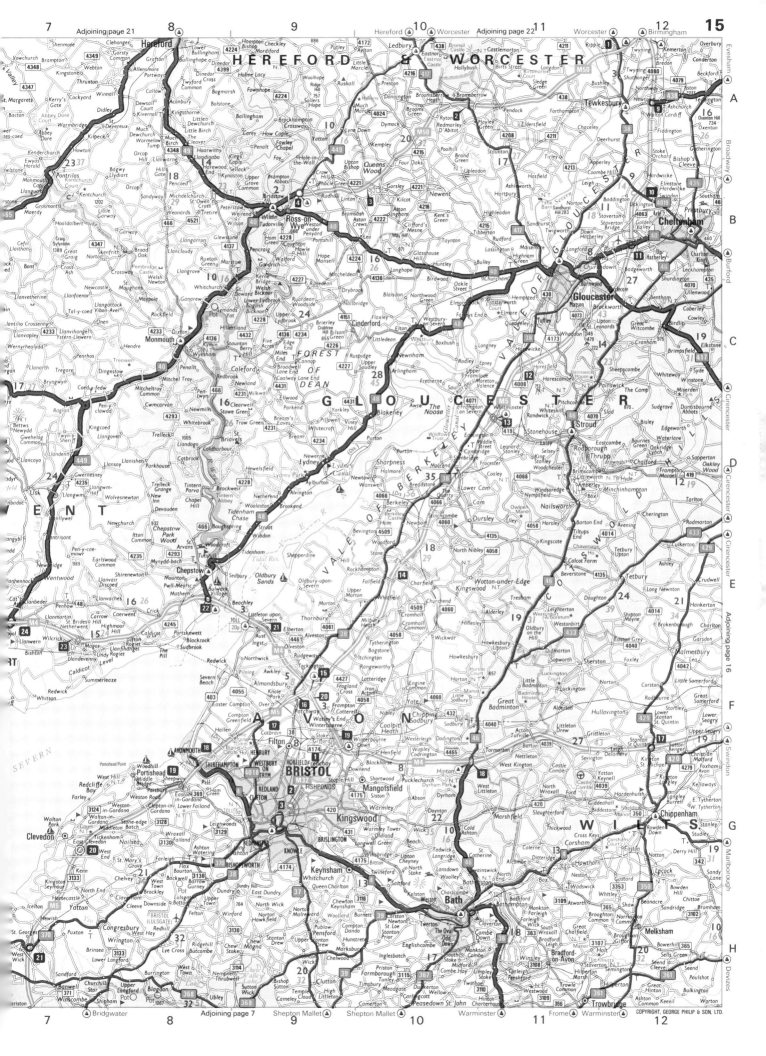

Adjoining page 22   Adjoining page 23

Adjoining page 15   Adjoining page 8

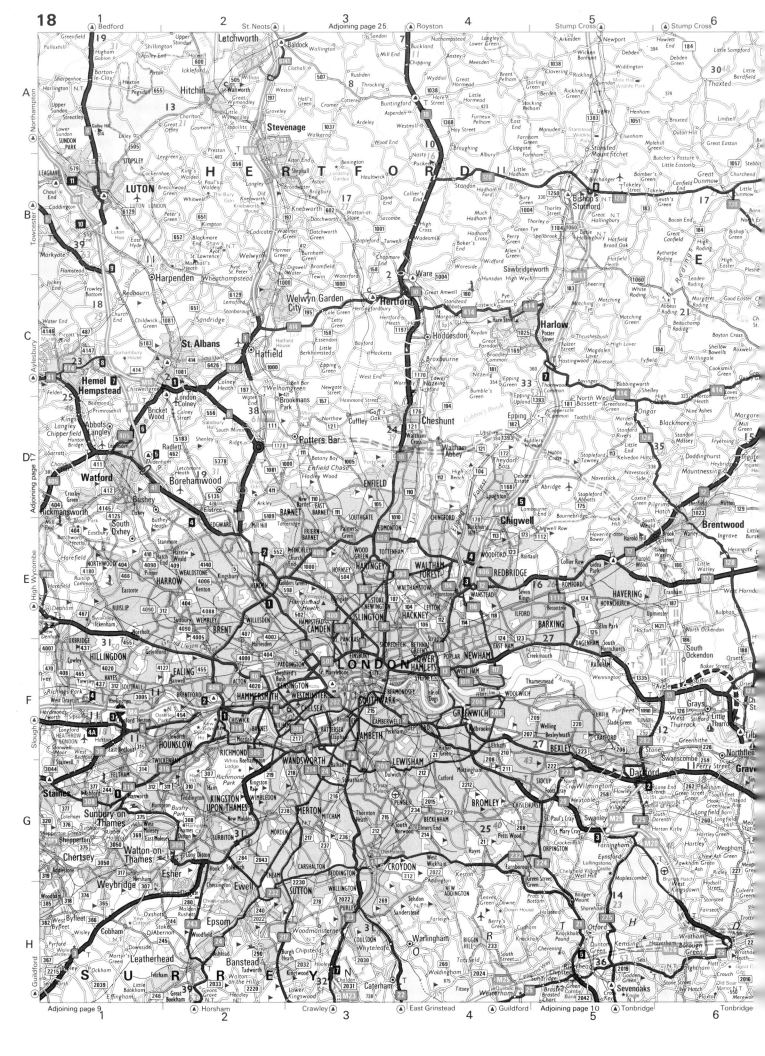

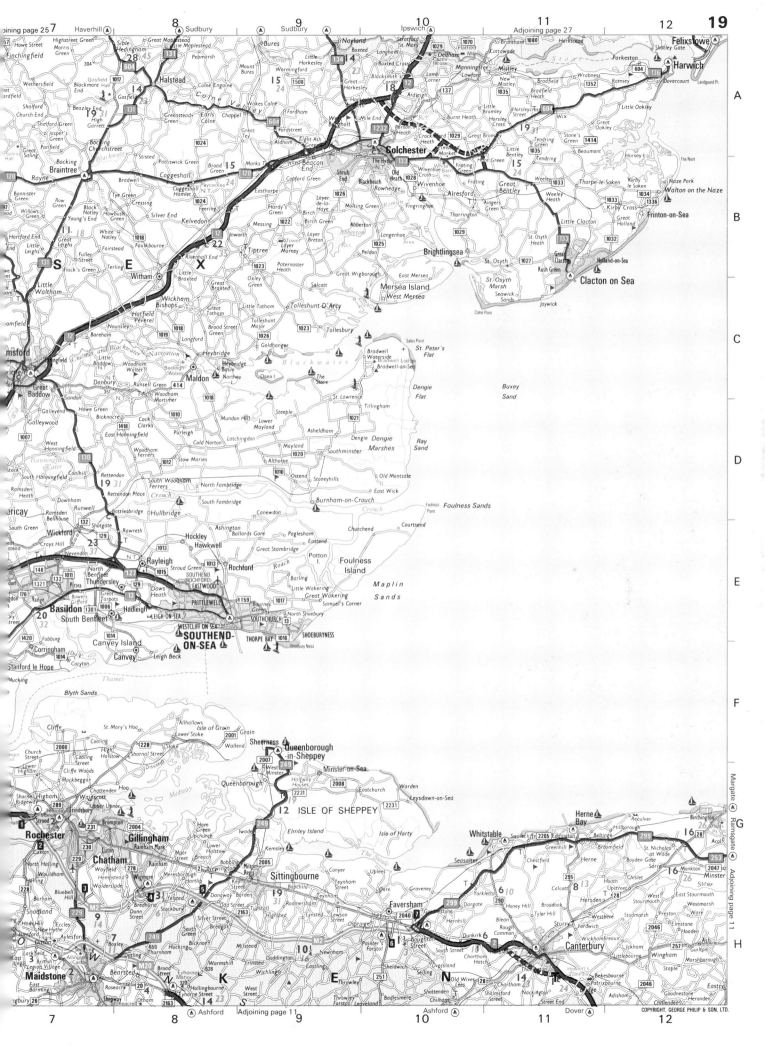

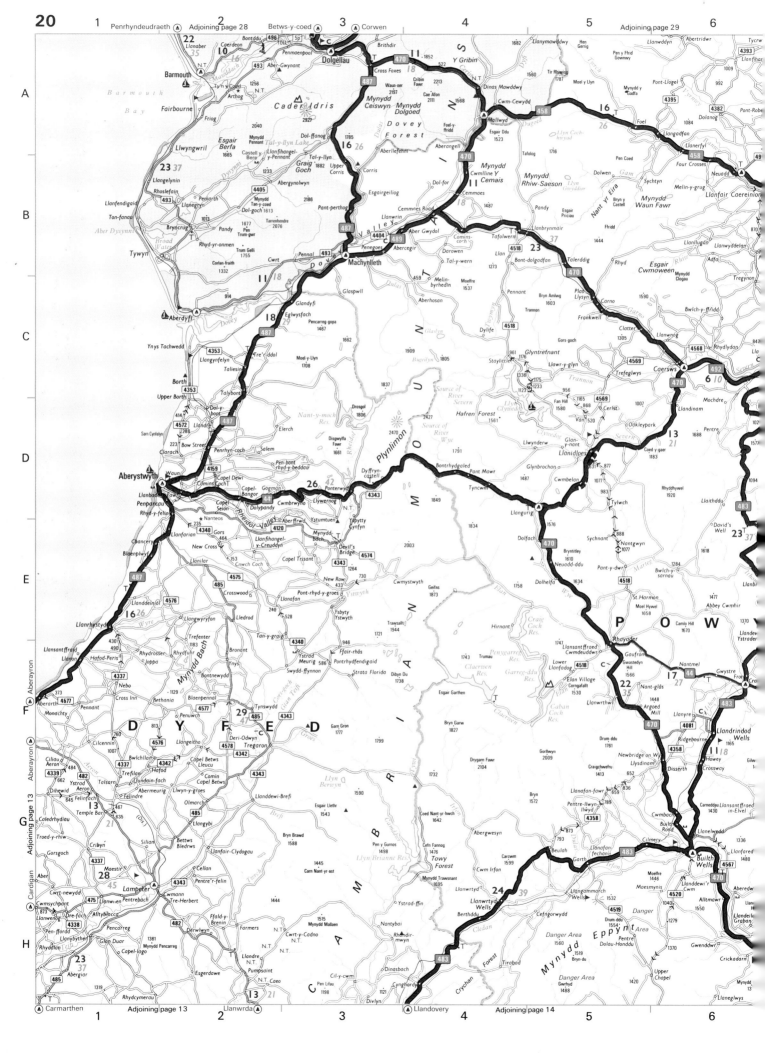

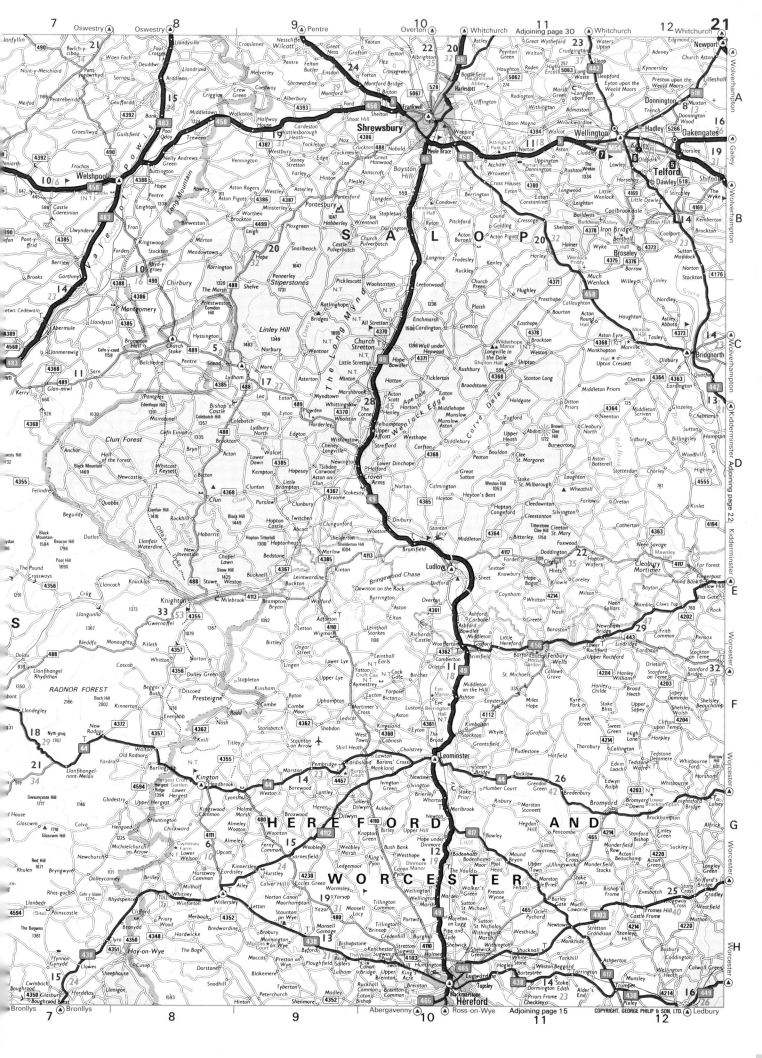

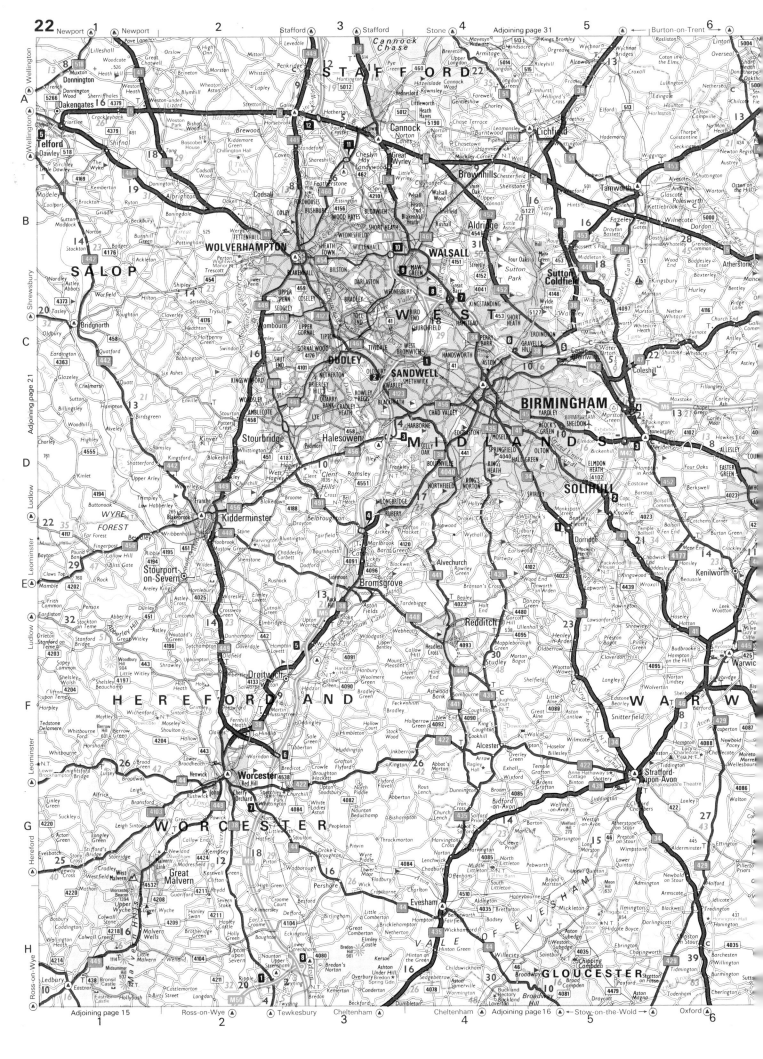

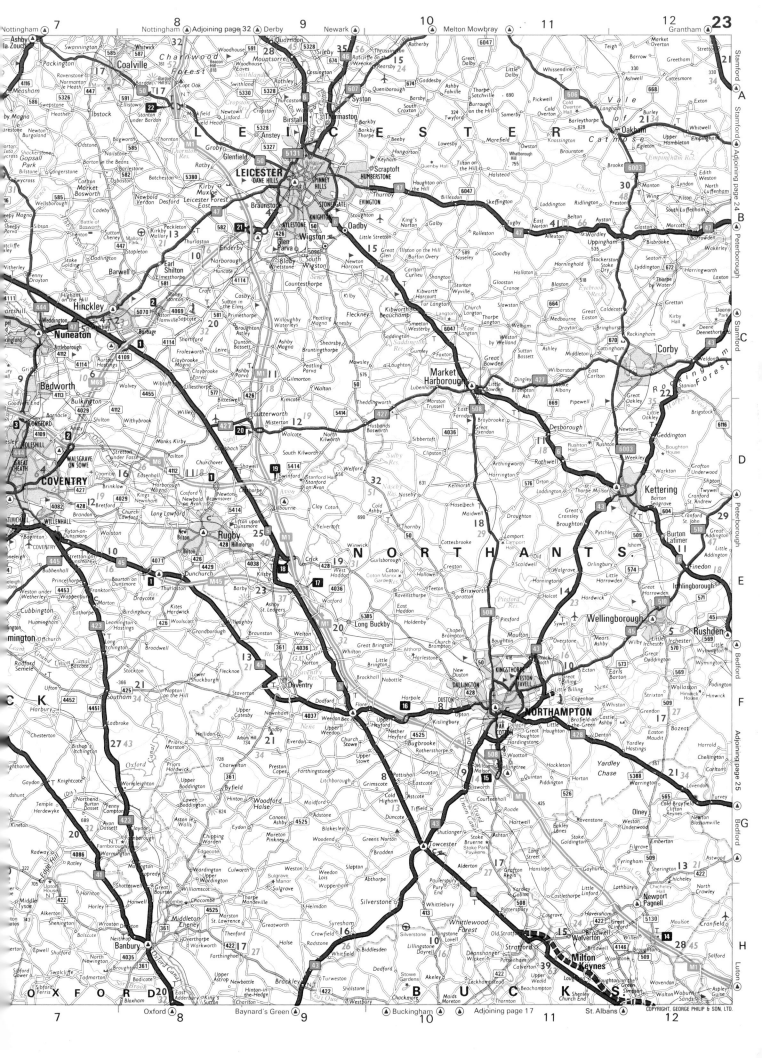

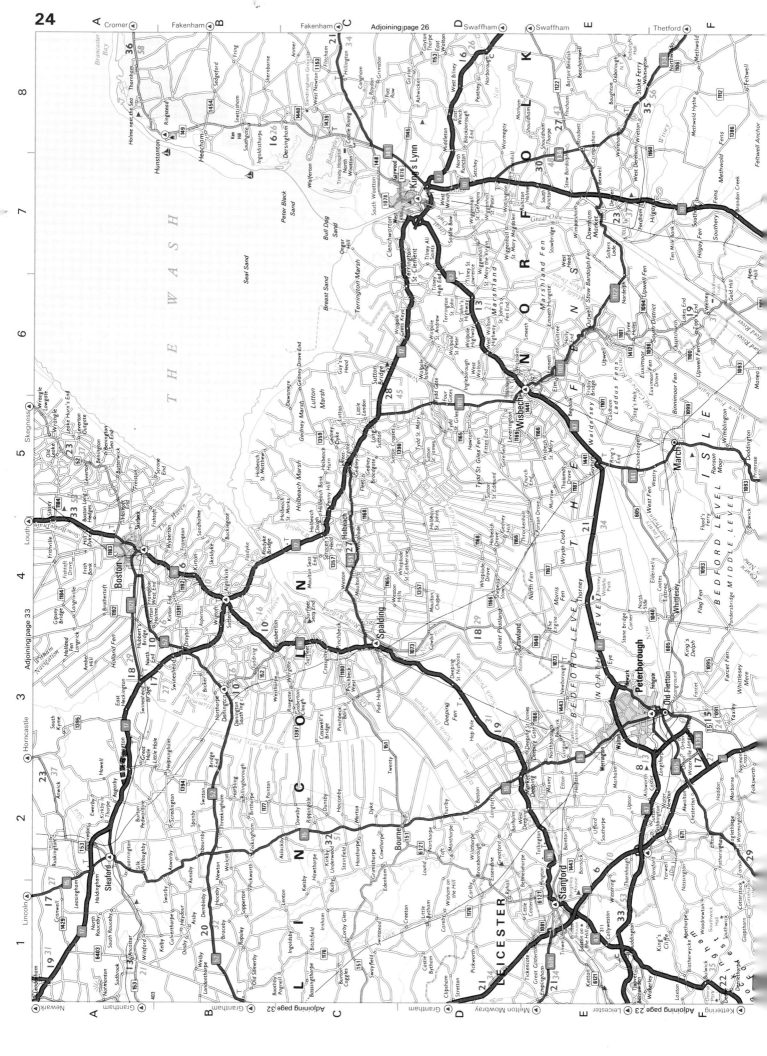

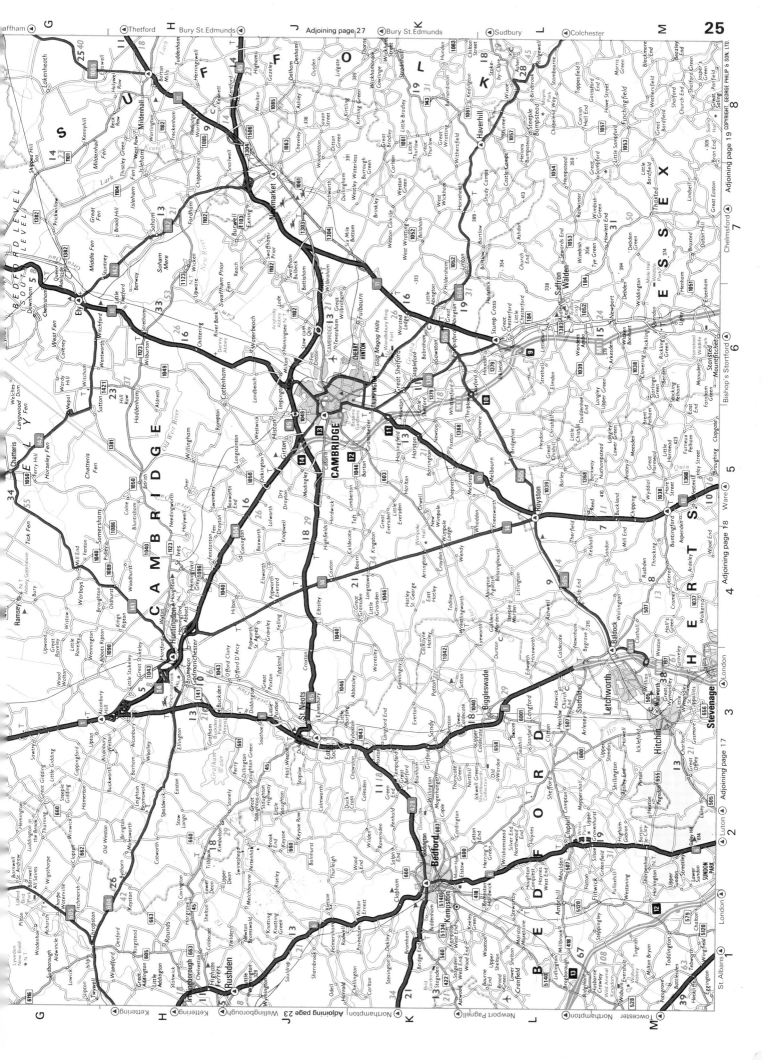

Adjoining page 24

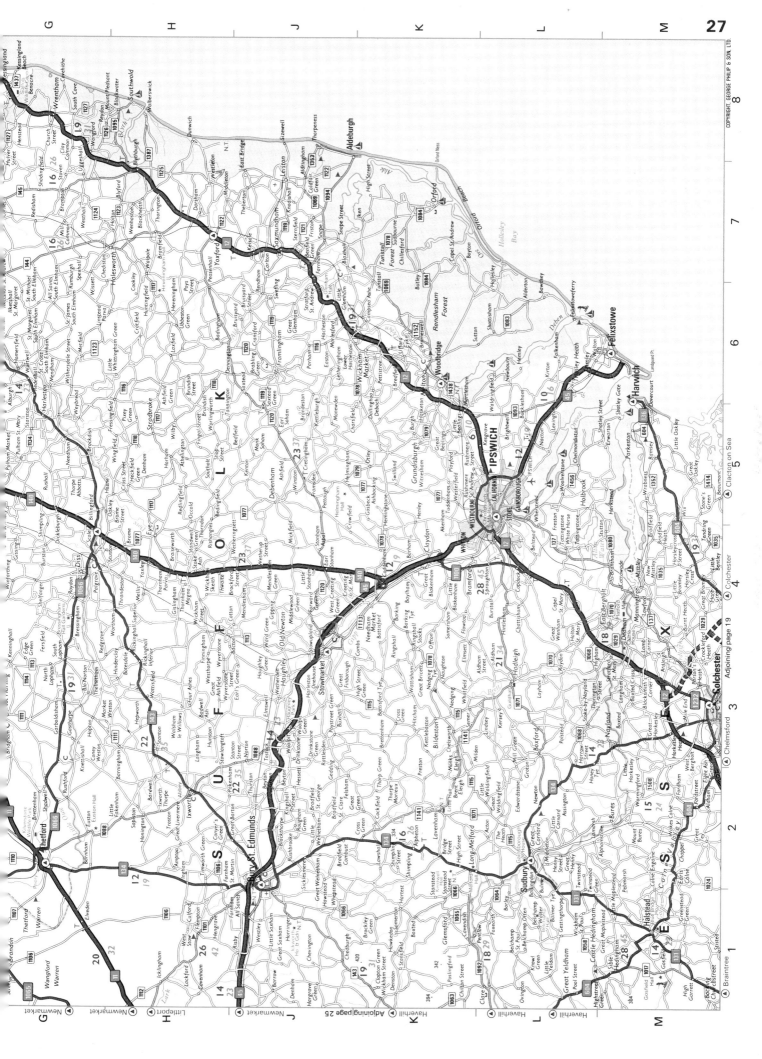

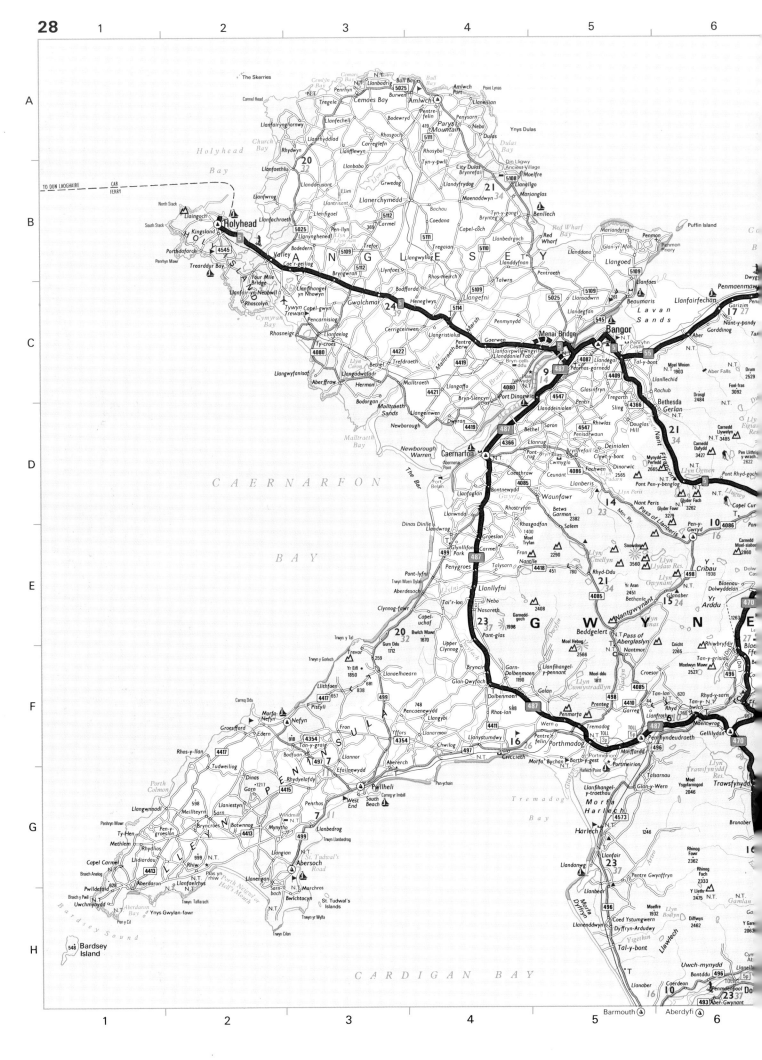

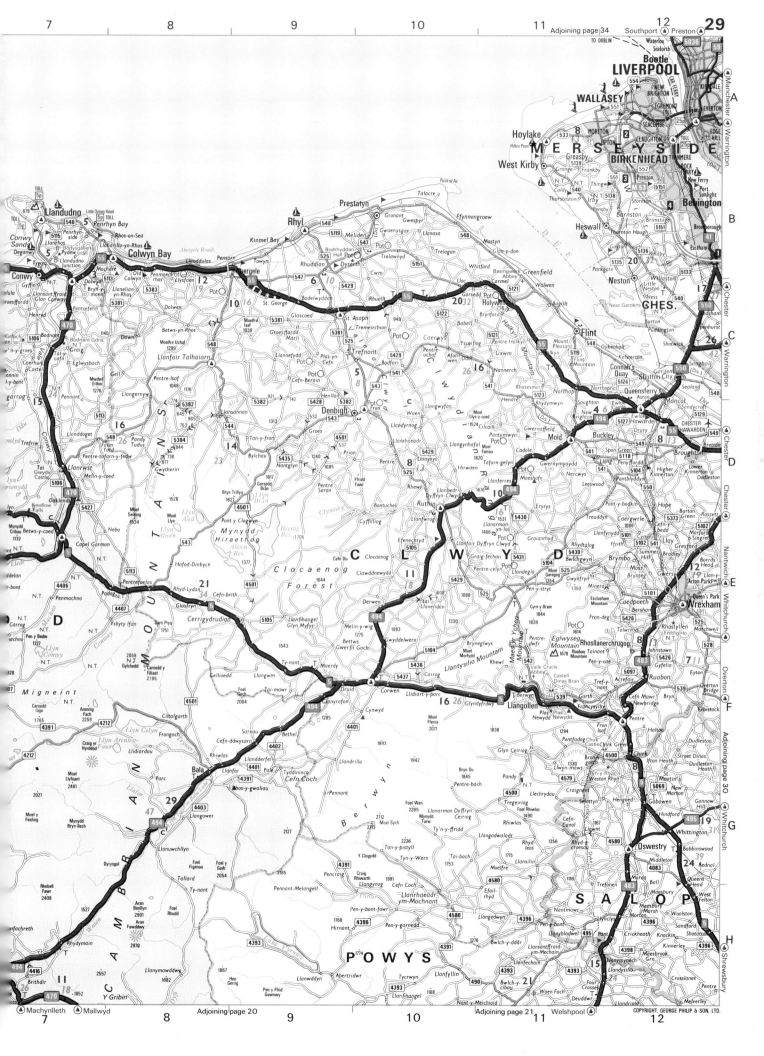

Adjoining page 34

Adjoining page 29

Adjoining page 21

MERSEYSIDE

CHESHIRE

CLWYD

POWYS

SALOP

LIVERPOOL
WALLASEY
BIRKENHEAD
Bebington
Hoylake
West Kirby
Heswall
Neston
Holywell
Flint
St Asaph
Mold
Buckley
Queensferry
Chester
Wrexham
Llangollen
Oswestry
Ruthin
Corwen
Ellesmere Port
Widnes
Runcorn
Warrington
Frodsham
Northwich
Winsford
Middlewich
Sandbach
Crewe
Nantwich
Whitchurch
Market Drayton
Newport
Ellesmere
Wem
Knutsford
Altrincham
Hale
Urmston
Irlam
St Helens
Prescot
Huyton
Newton-Le-Willows
Haydock
Wigan
Manchester
SALFORD

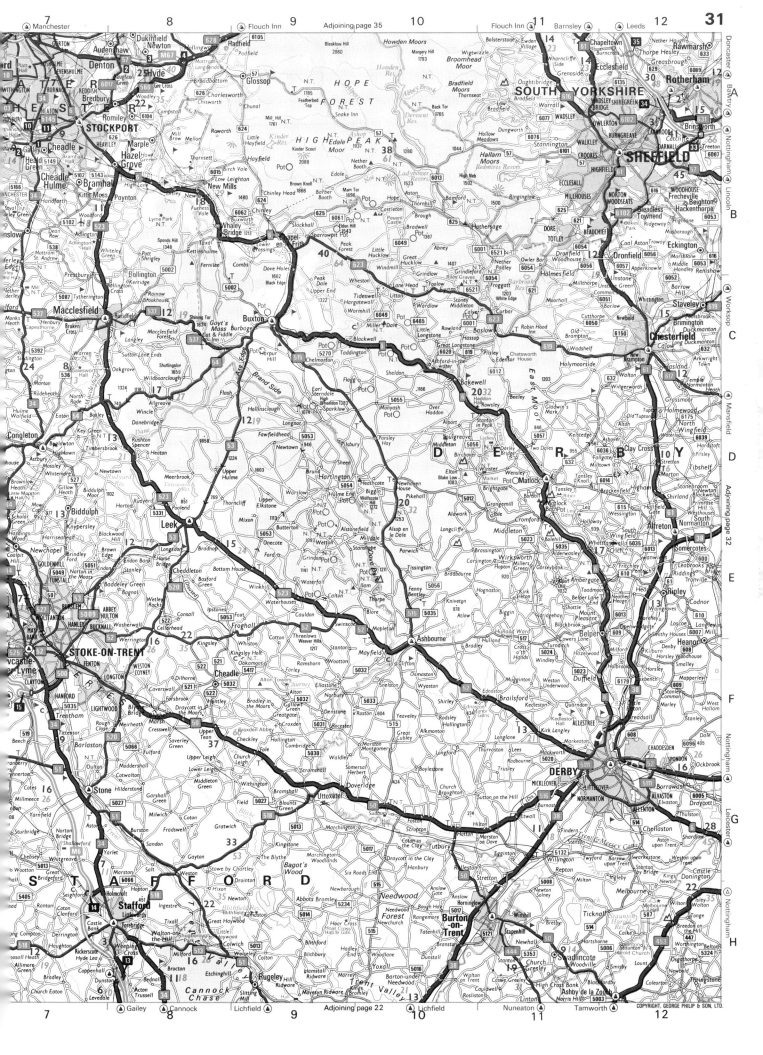

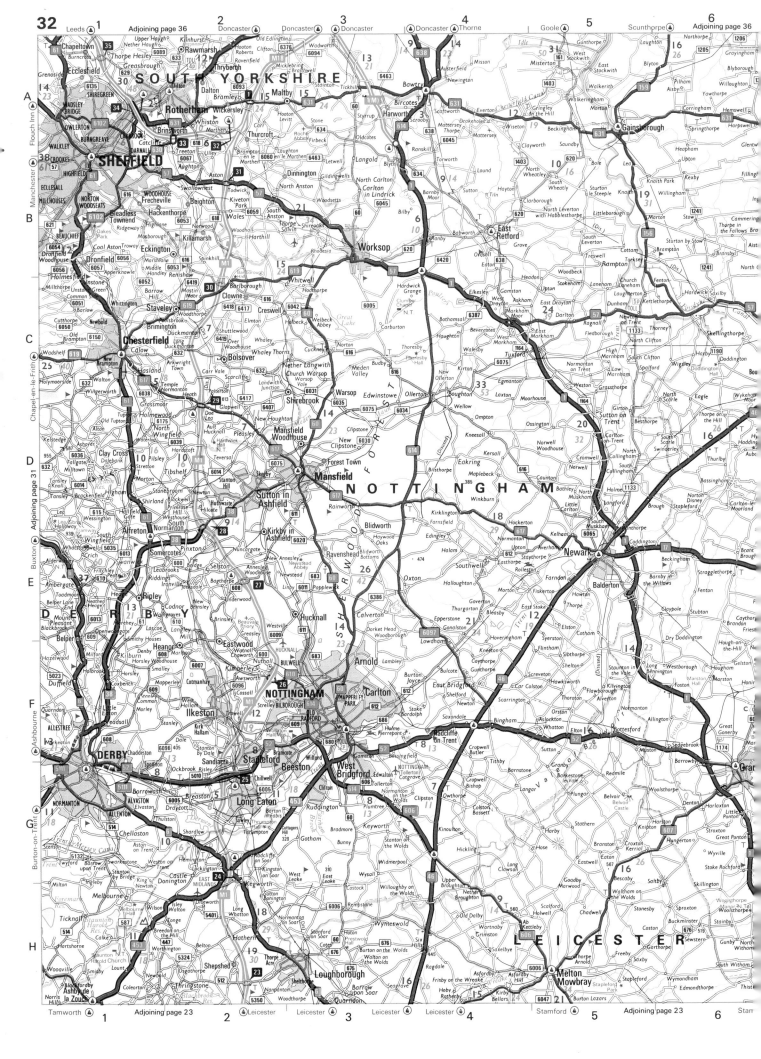

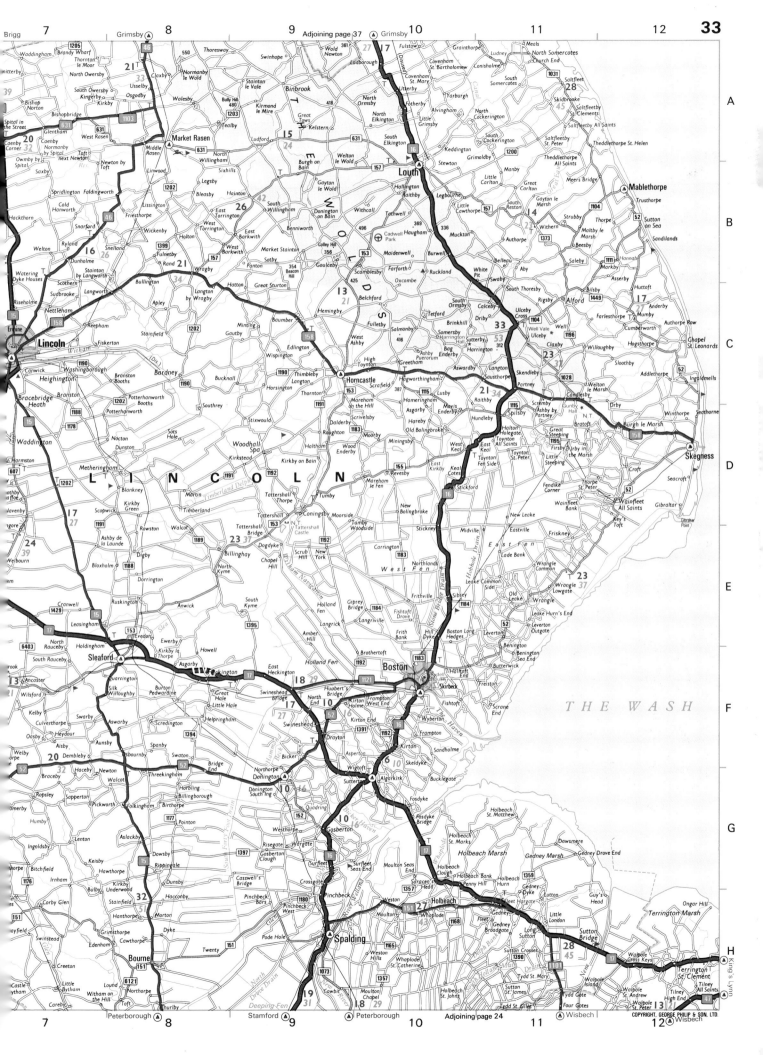

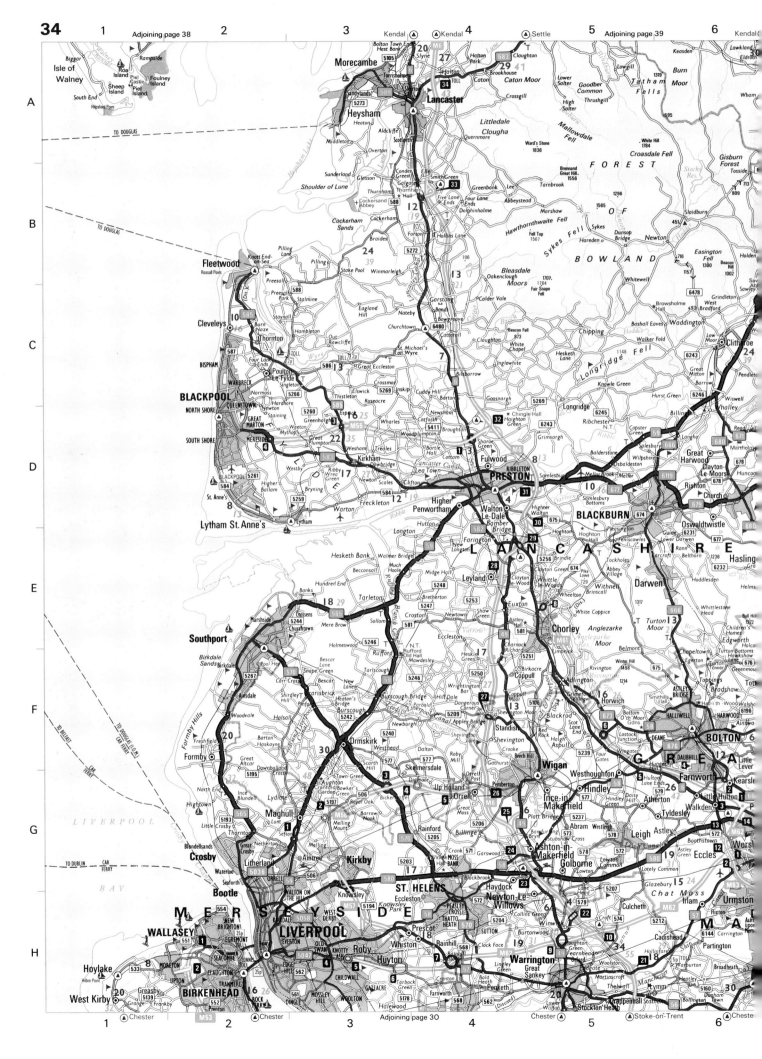

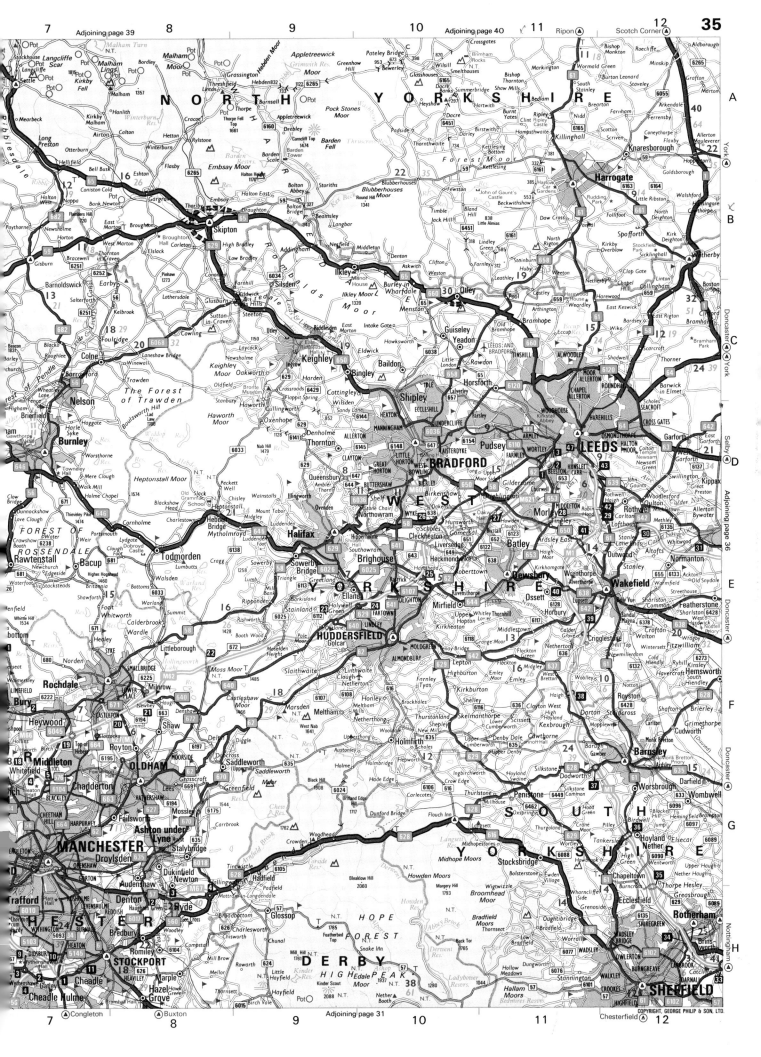

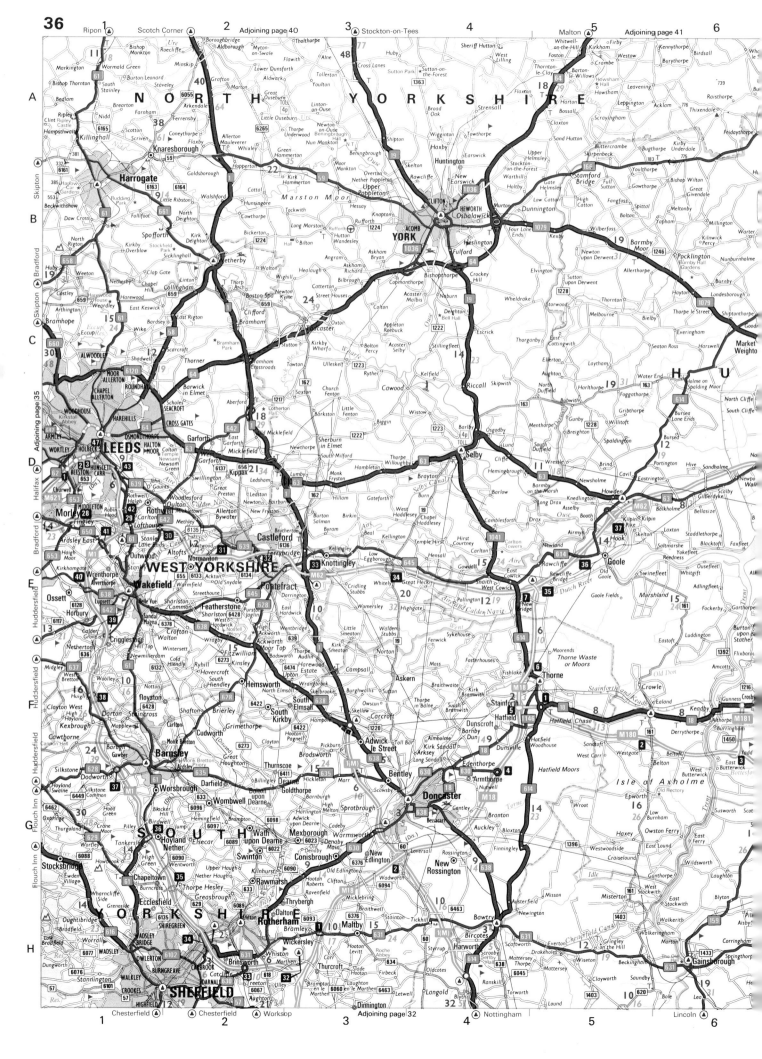

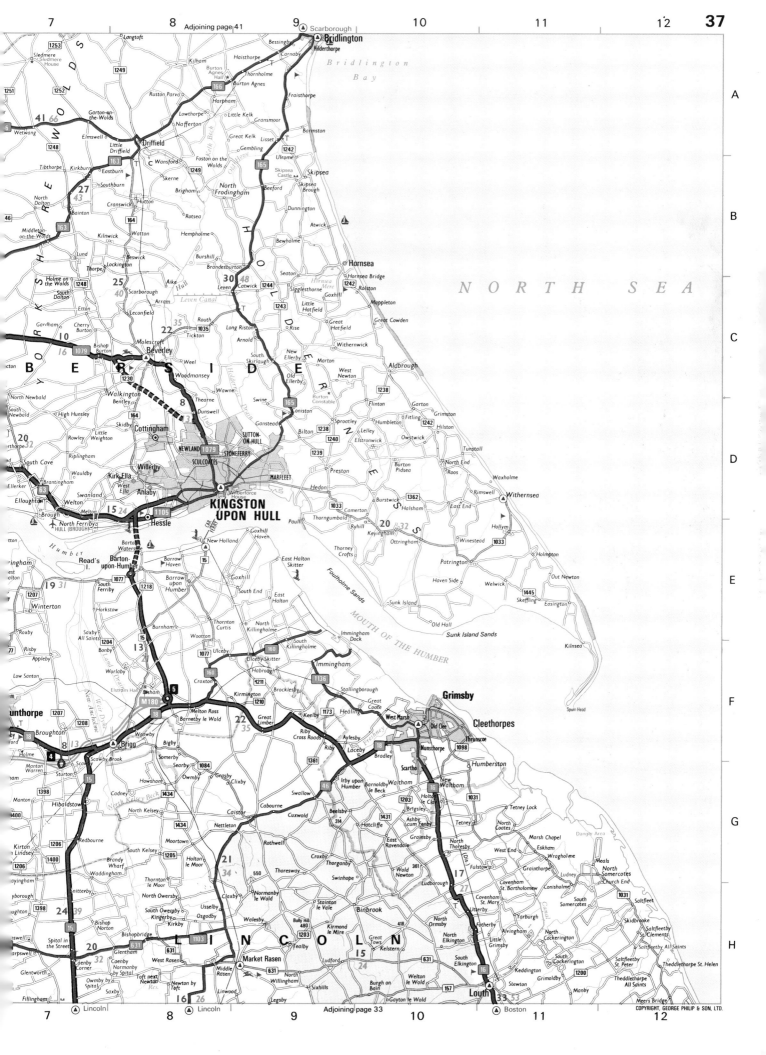

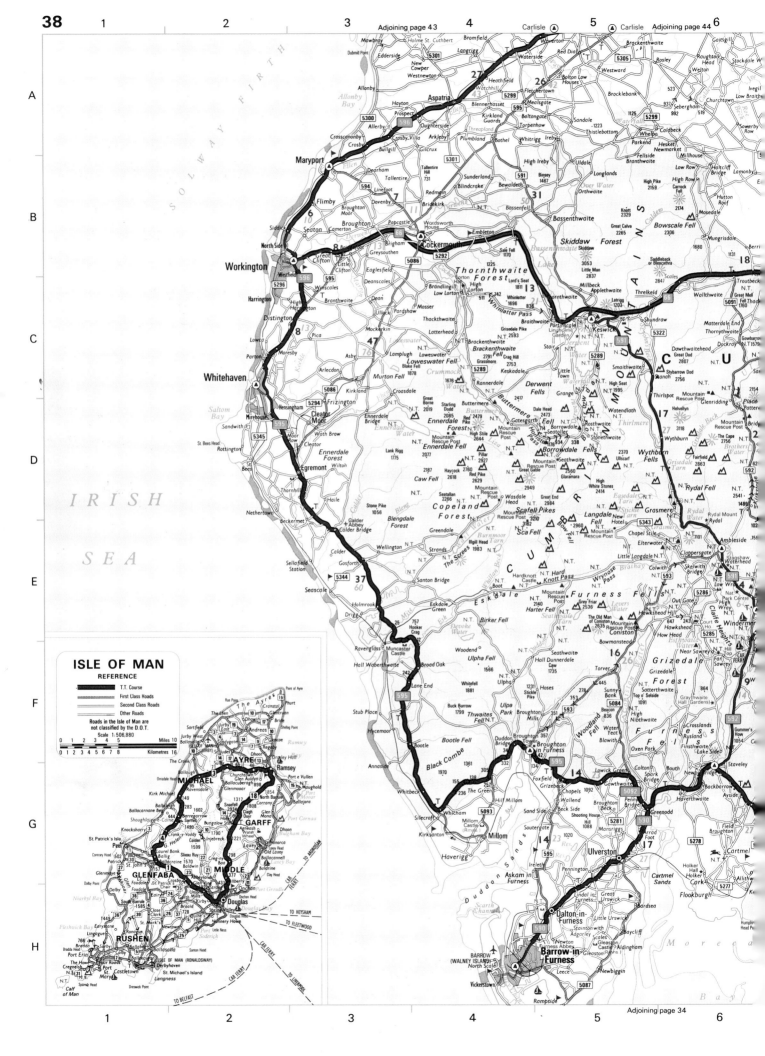

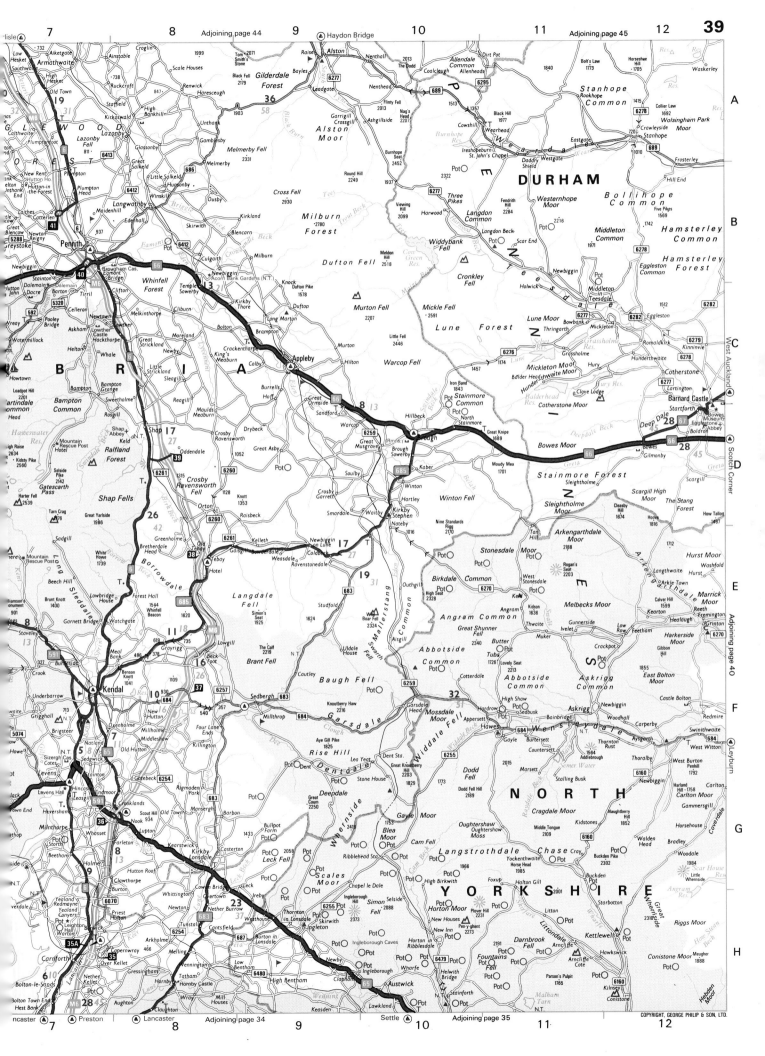

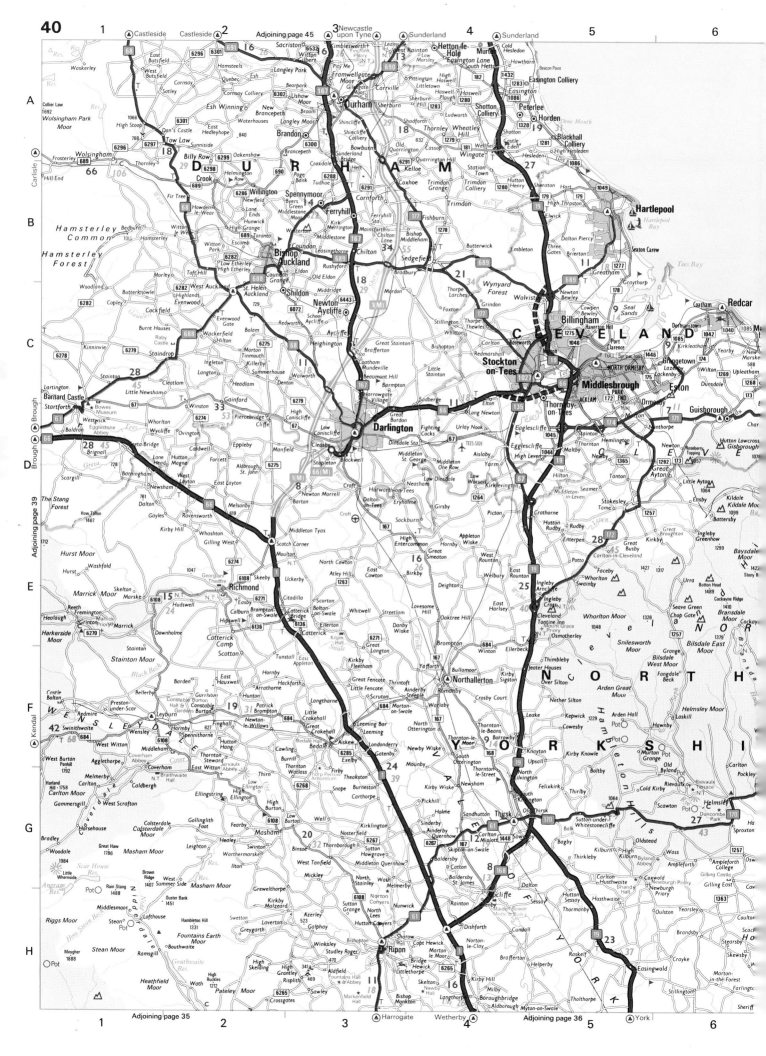

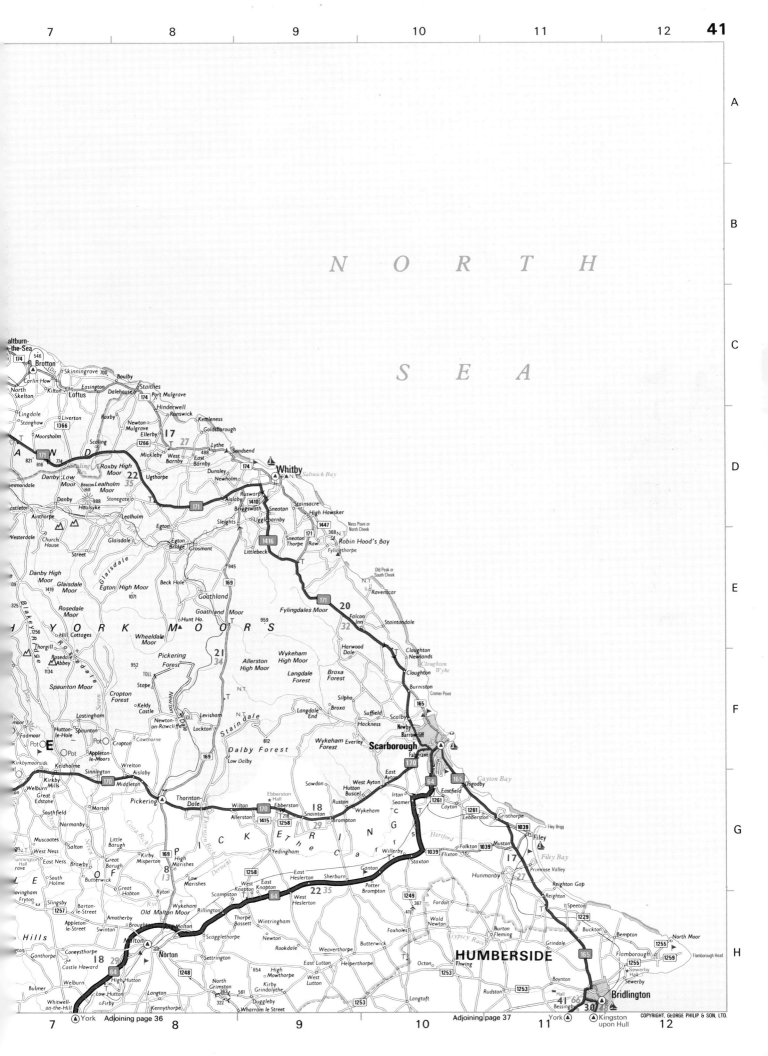

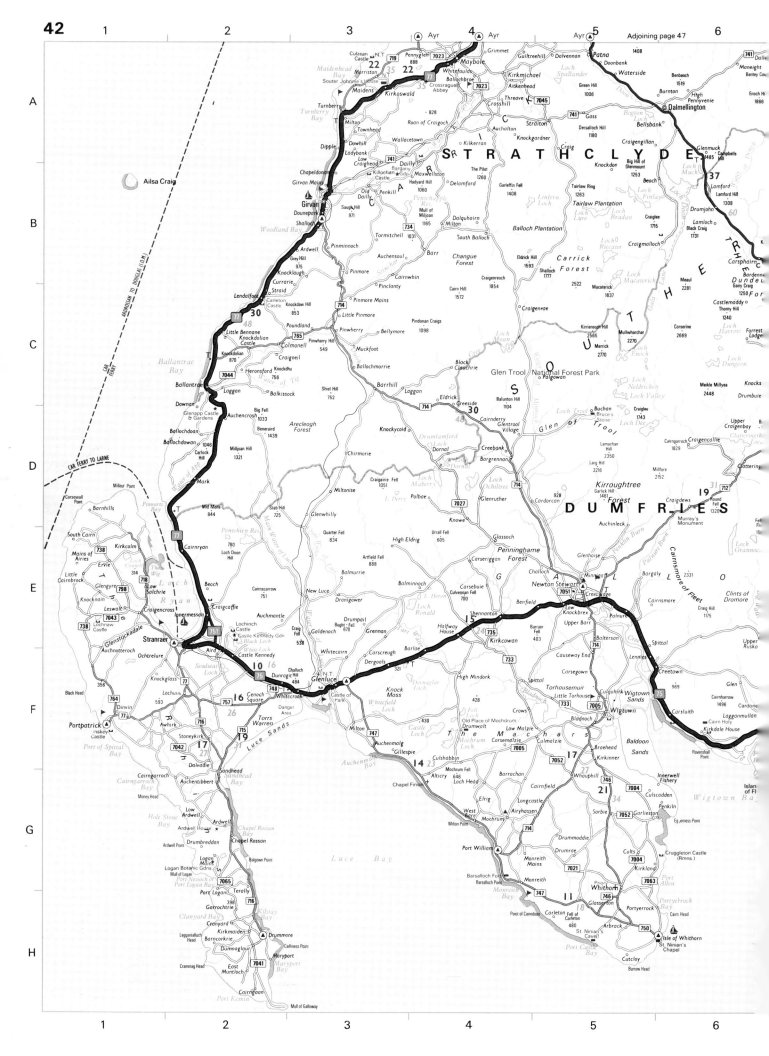

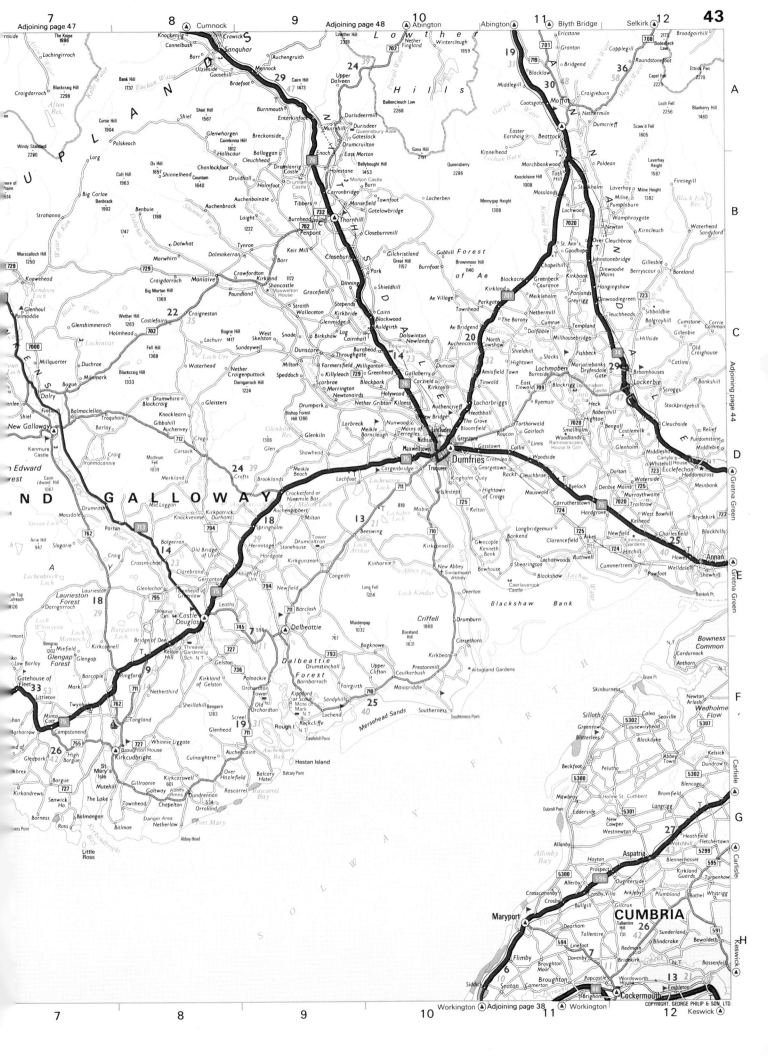

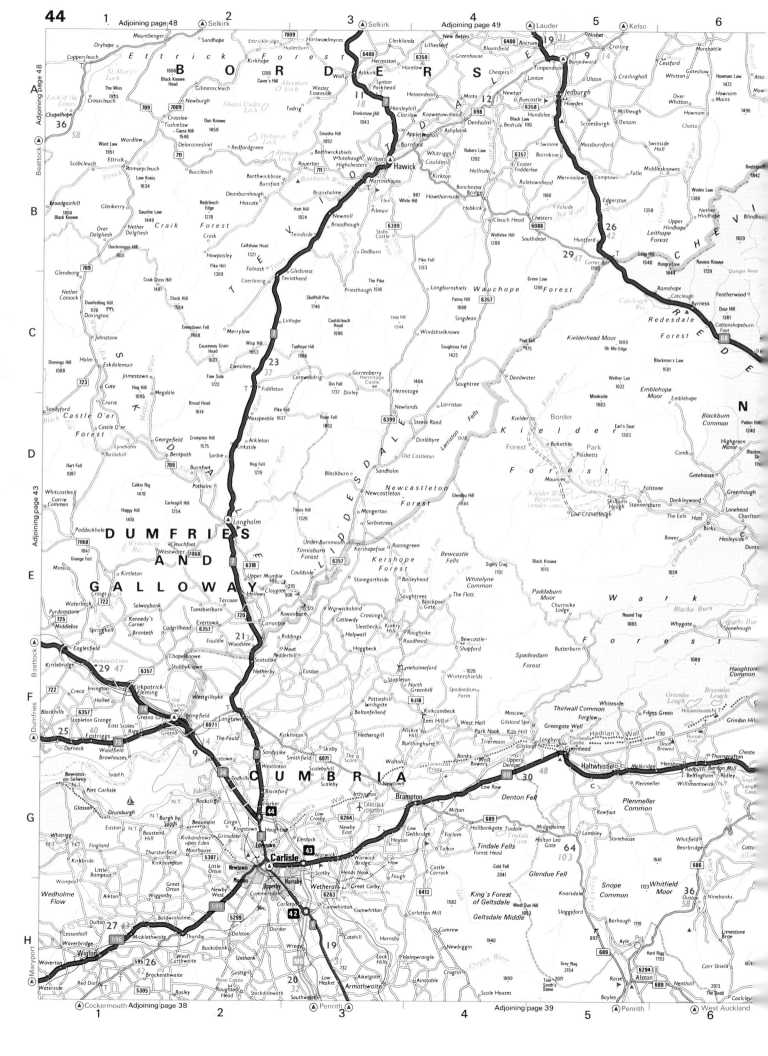

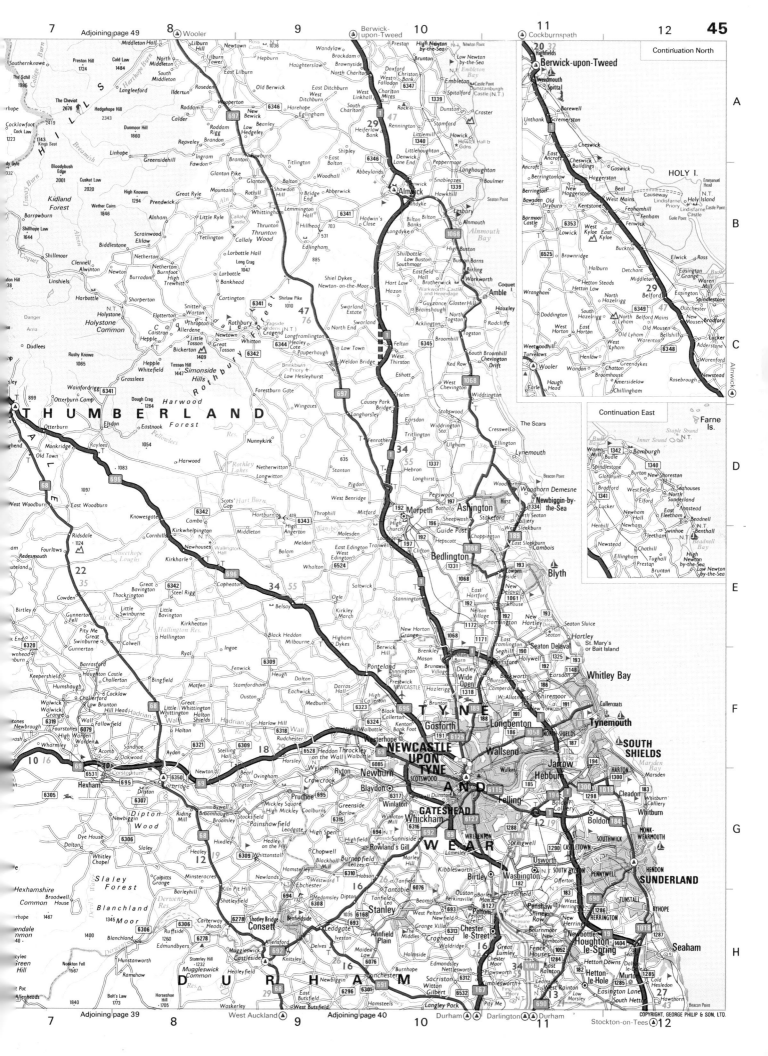

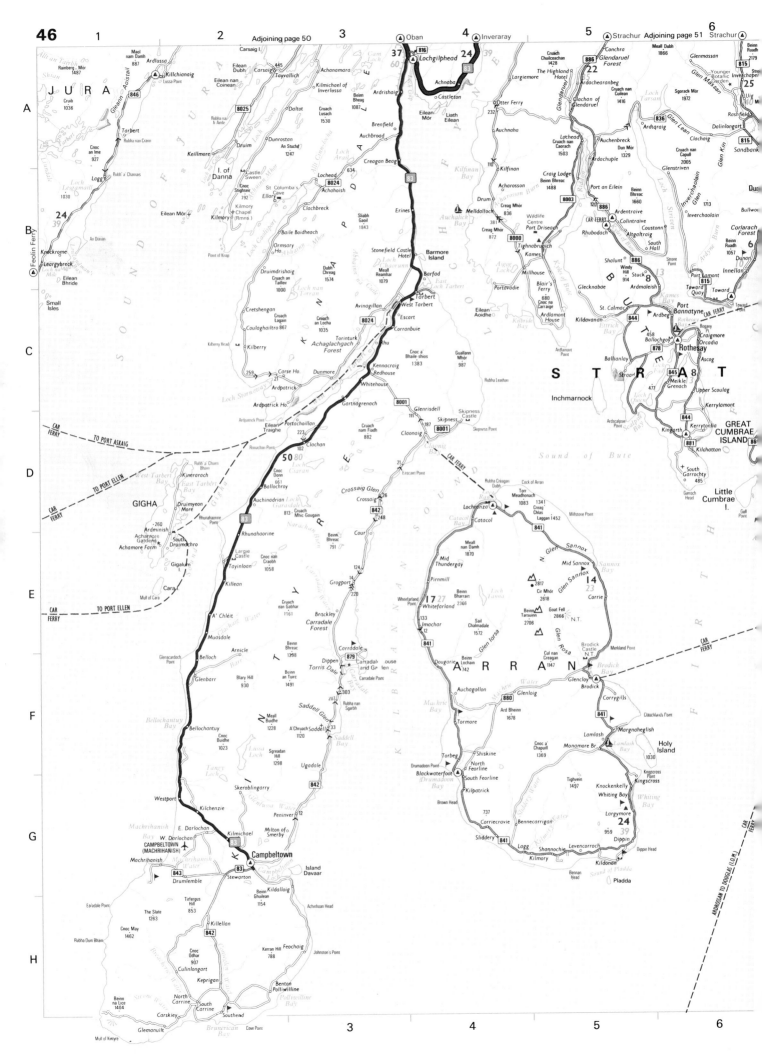

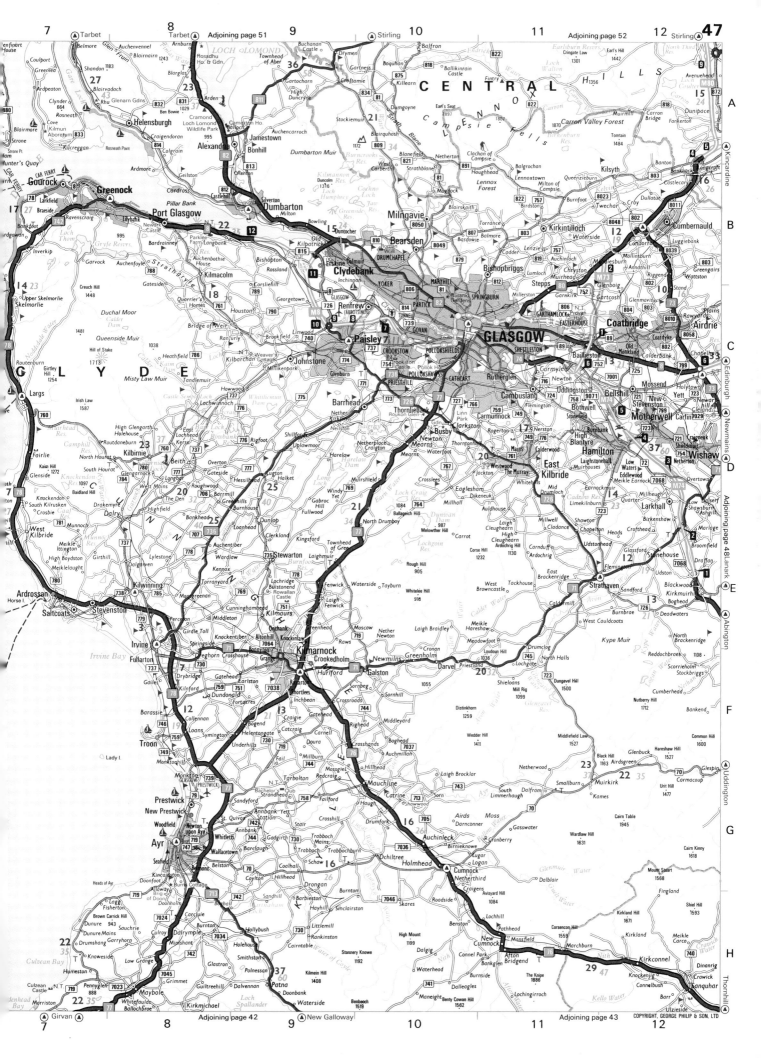

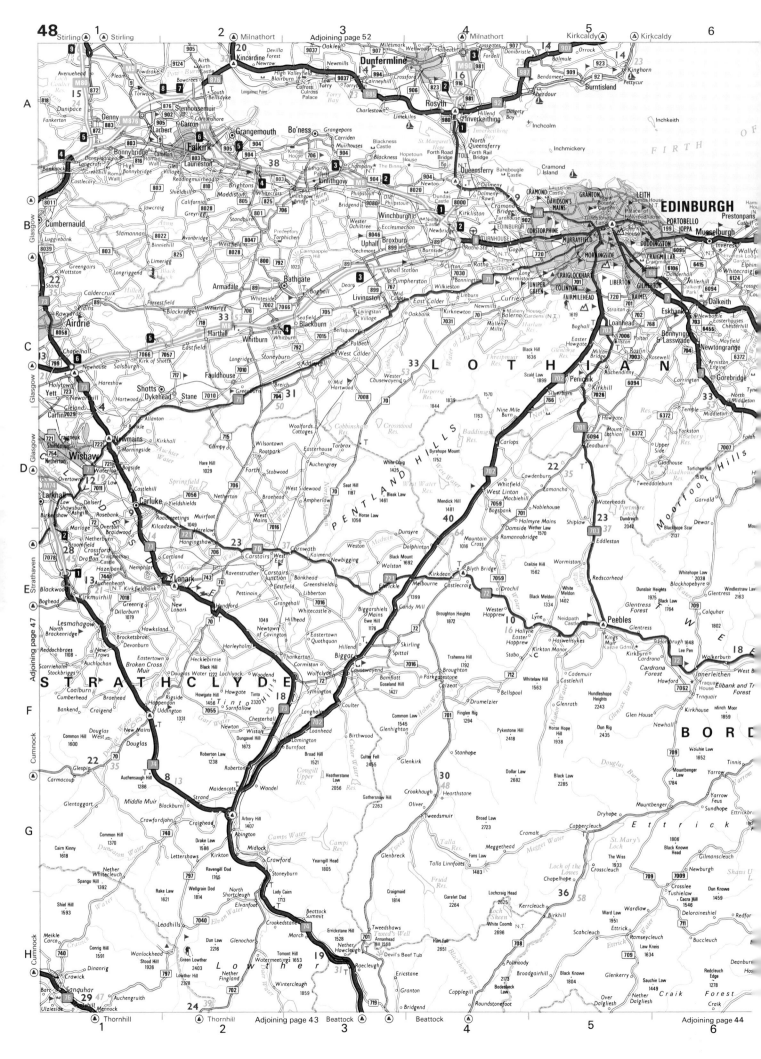

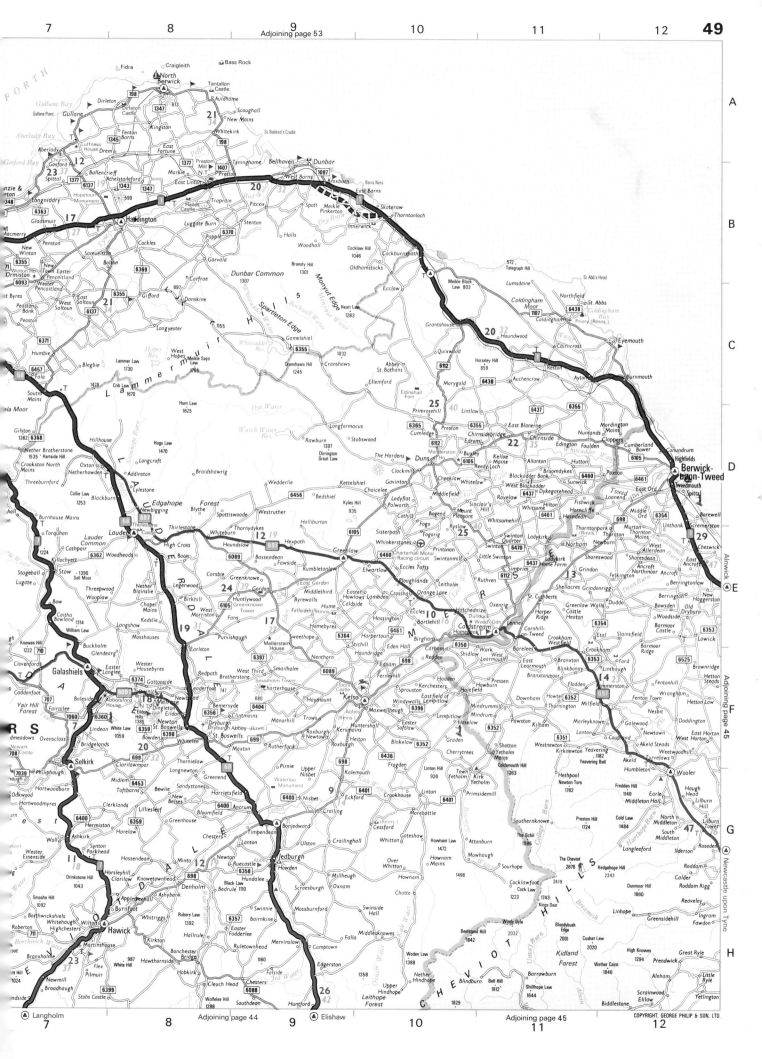

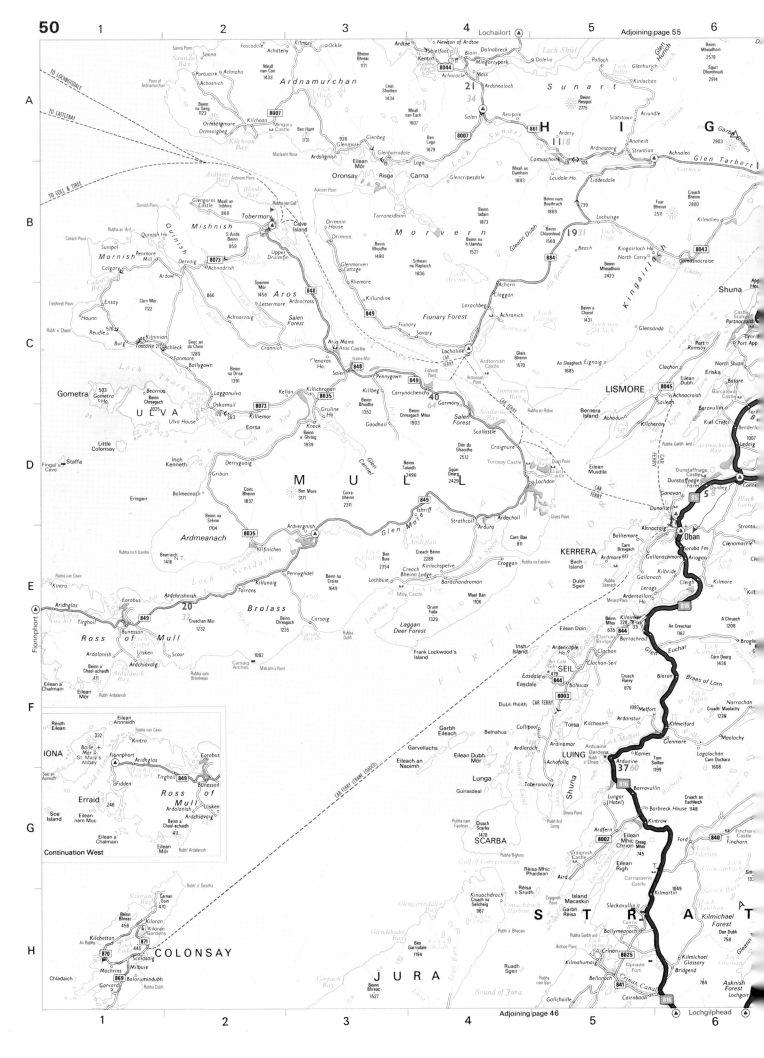

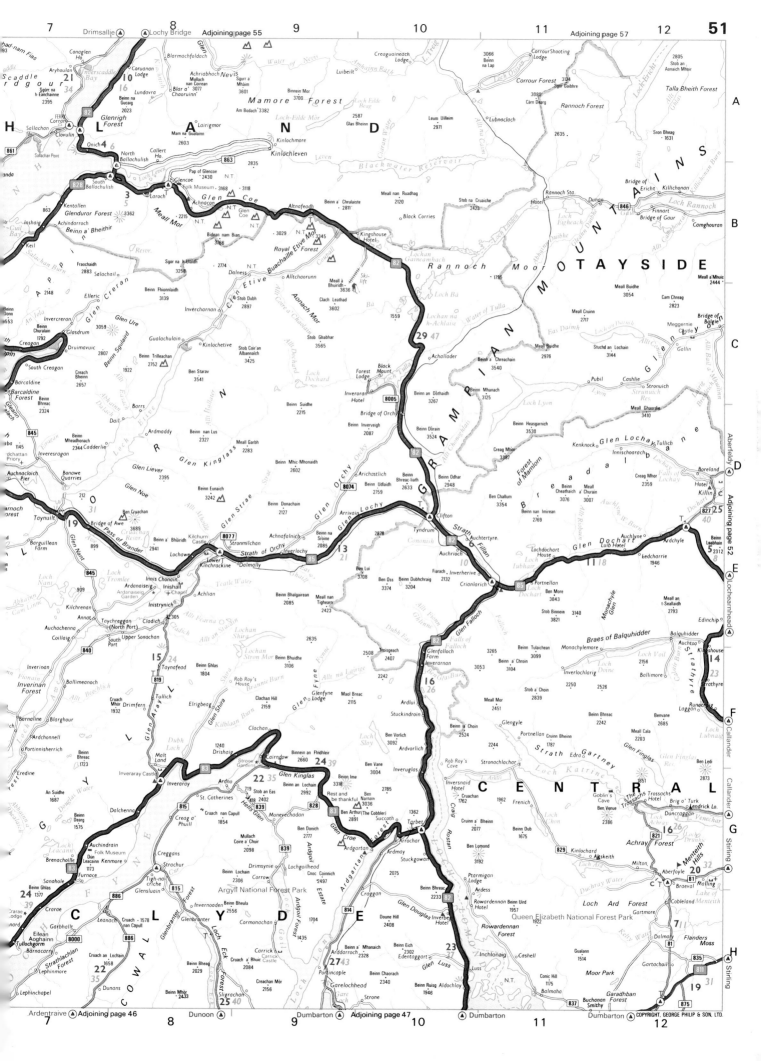

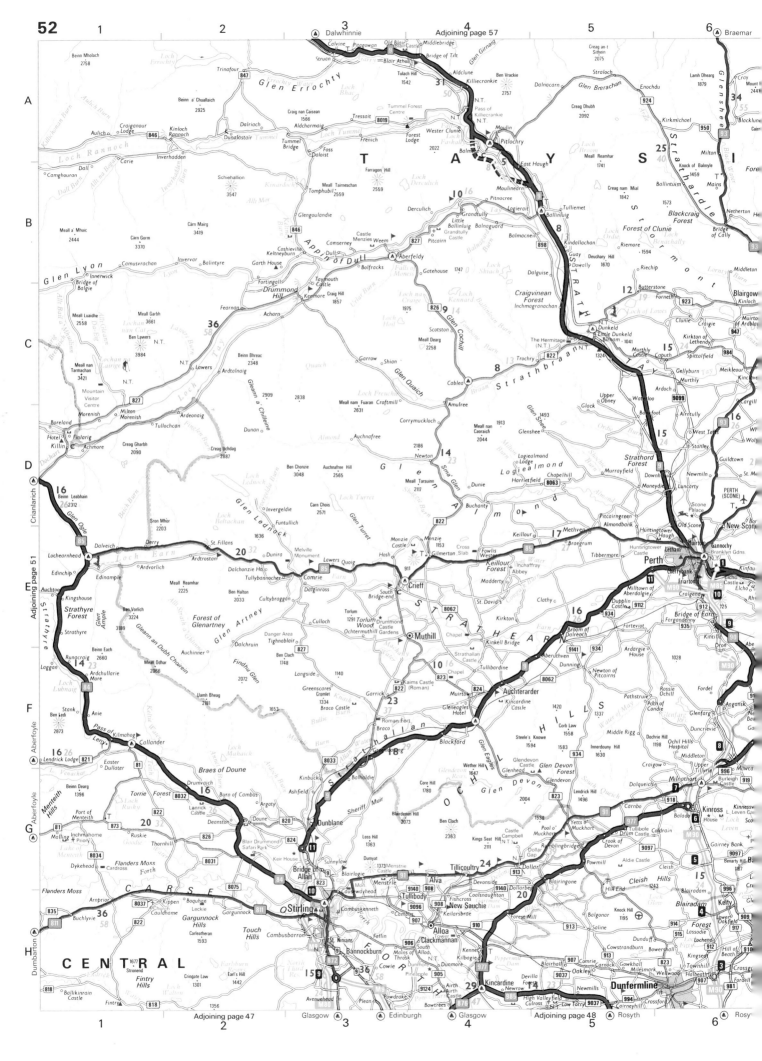

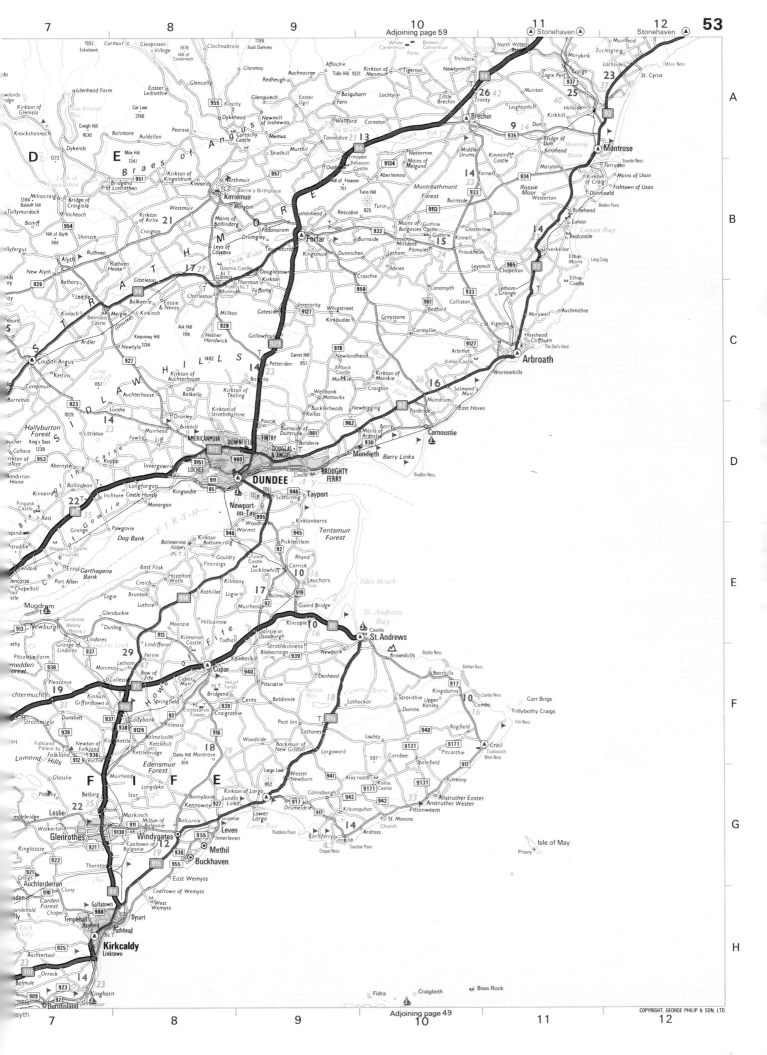

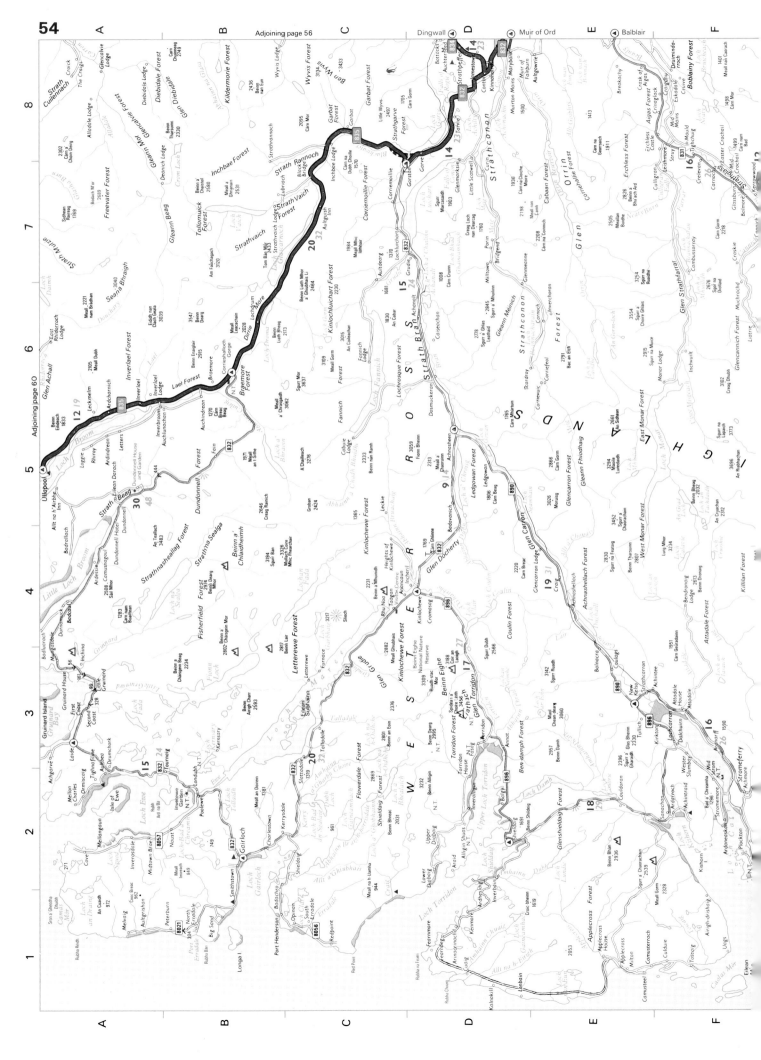

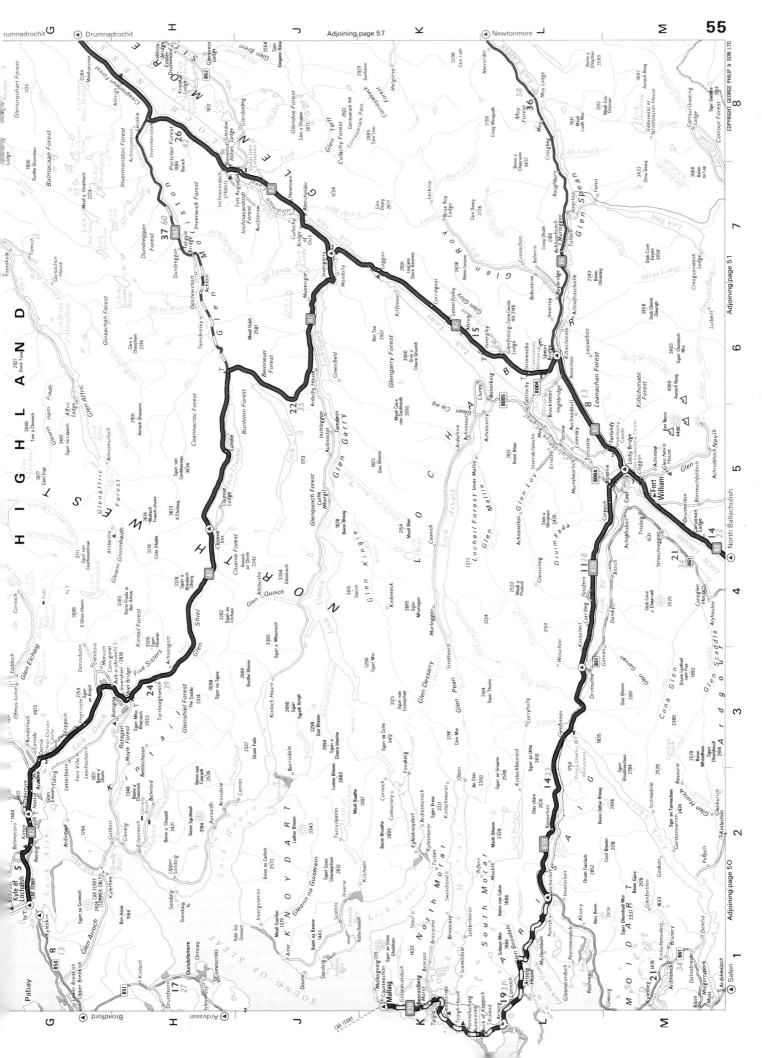

Adjoining page 58

Adjoining page 61

Adjoining page 60

Adjoining page 54

NORTH SEA

MORAY FIRTH

GRAMPIAN

Keith

Rhynie

Lossiemouth

Branderburgh

Burghead

Elgin

New Elgin

Forres

Nairn

Inverness (DALCROSS)

Dingwall

Beauly

Gorstan

Cannich

The Mound

Lairg

Dornoch

Portmahomack

Cromarty

Fortrose

Rosemarkie

BLACK ISLE

EASTER ROSS

Tarbat Ness

Whiteness Sands

Dornoch Sands

Bonar-bridge

Strathdearn Forest

Monaughty Forest

Darnaway Forest

Culbin Forest

Findon Forest

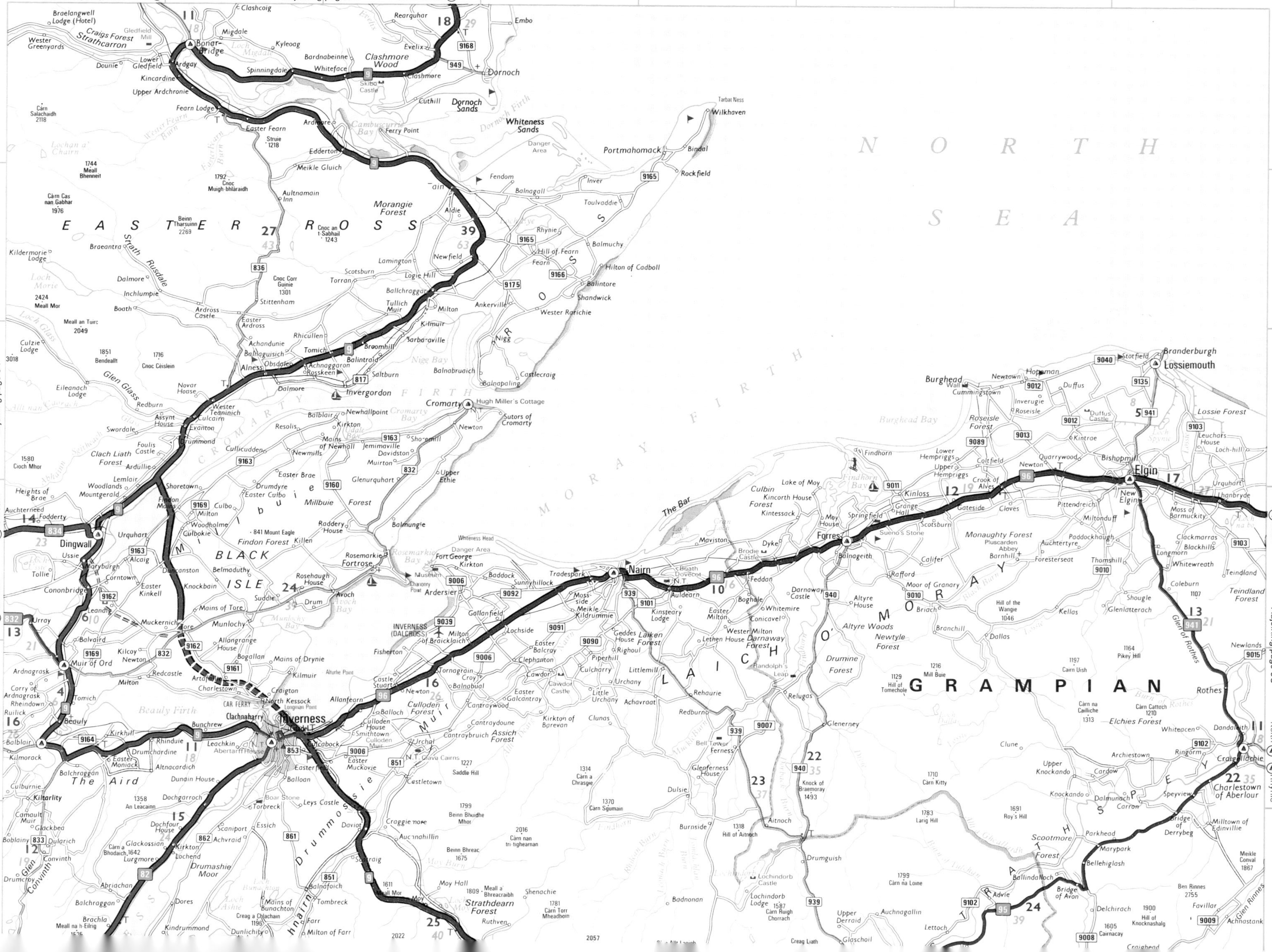

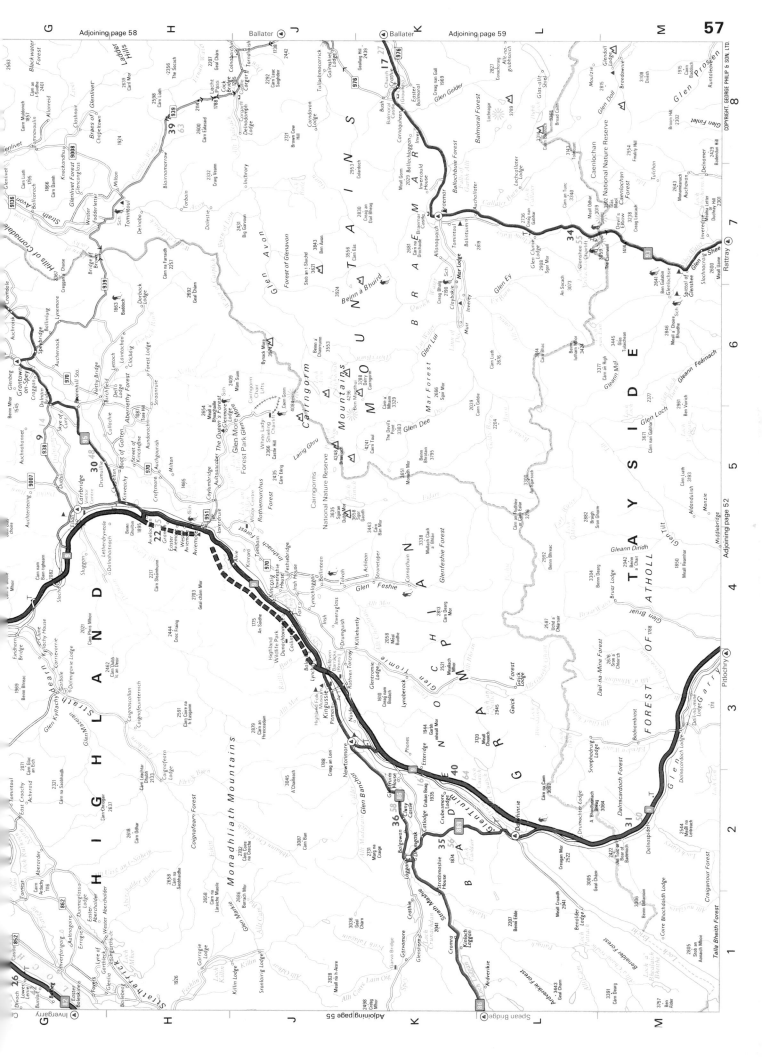

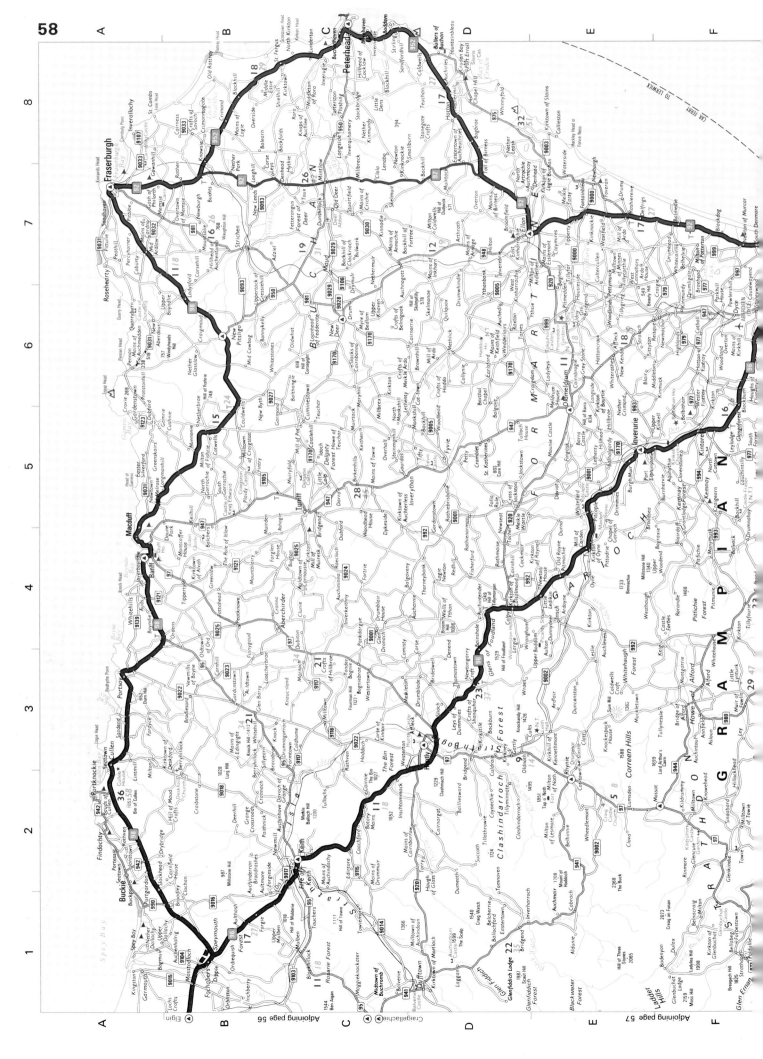

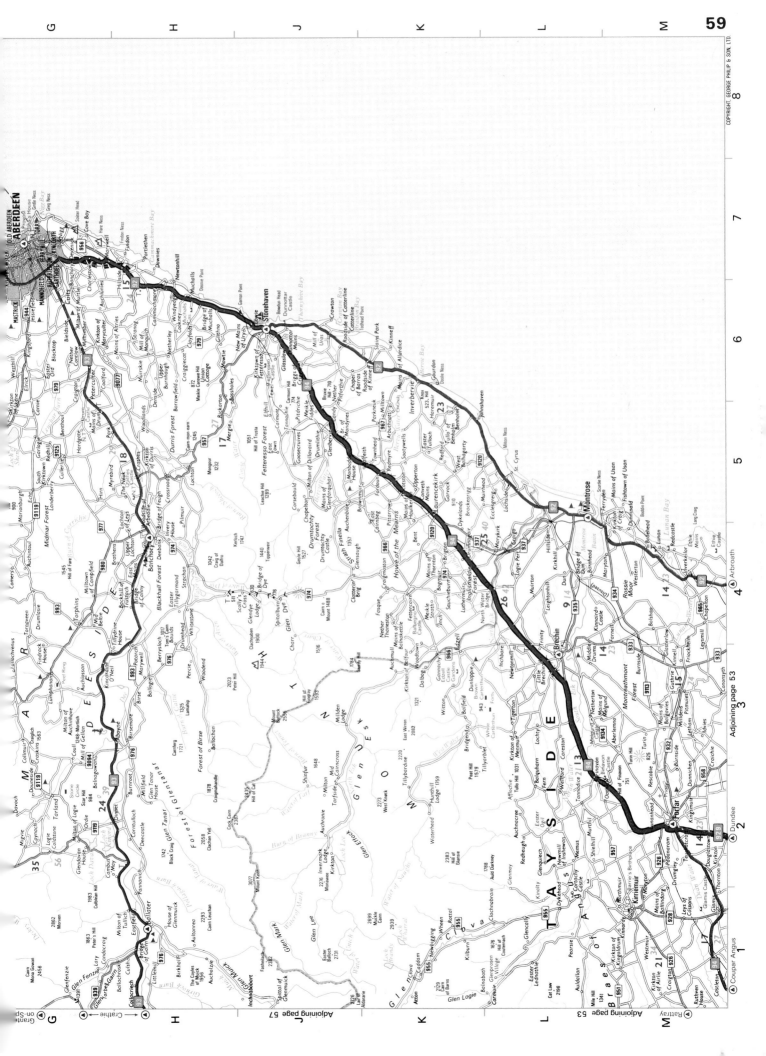

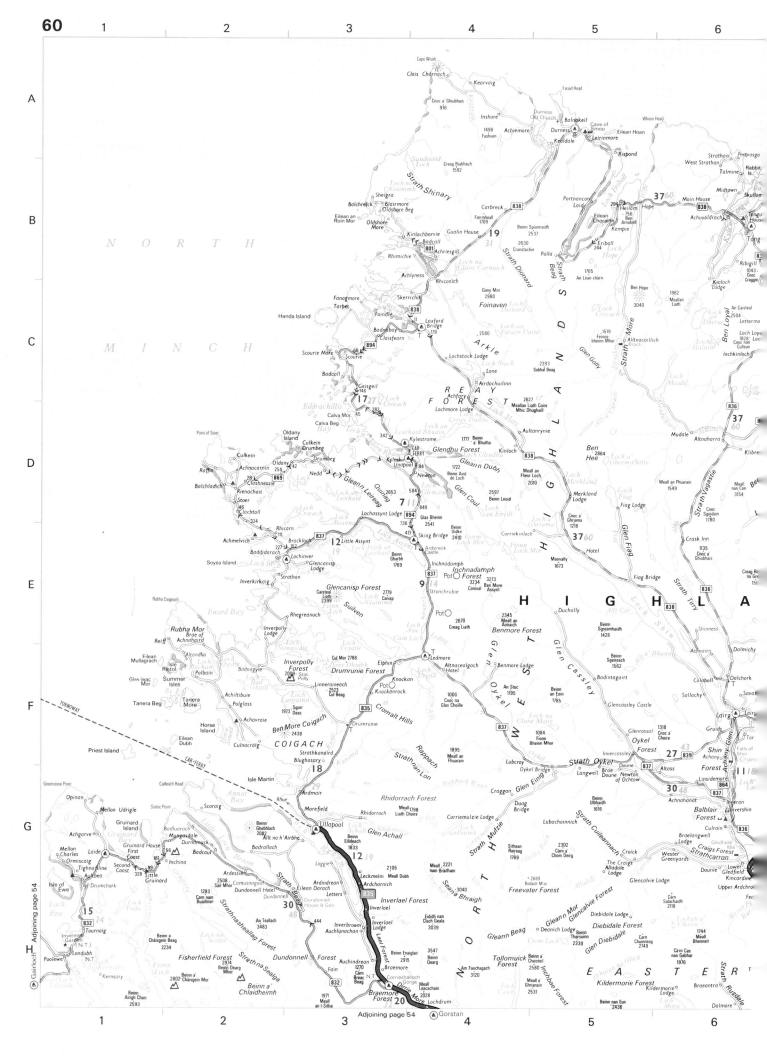

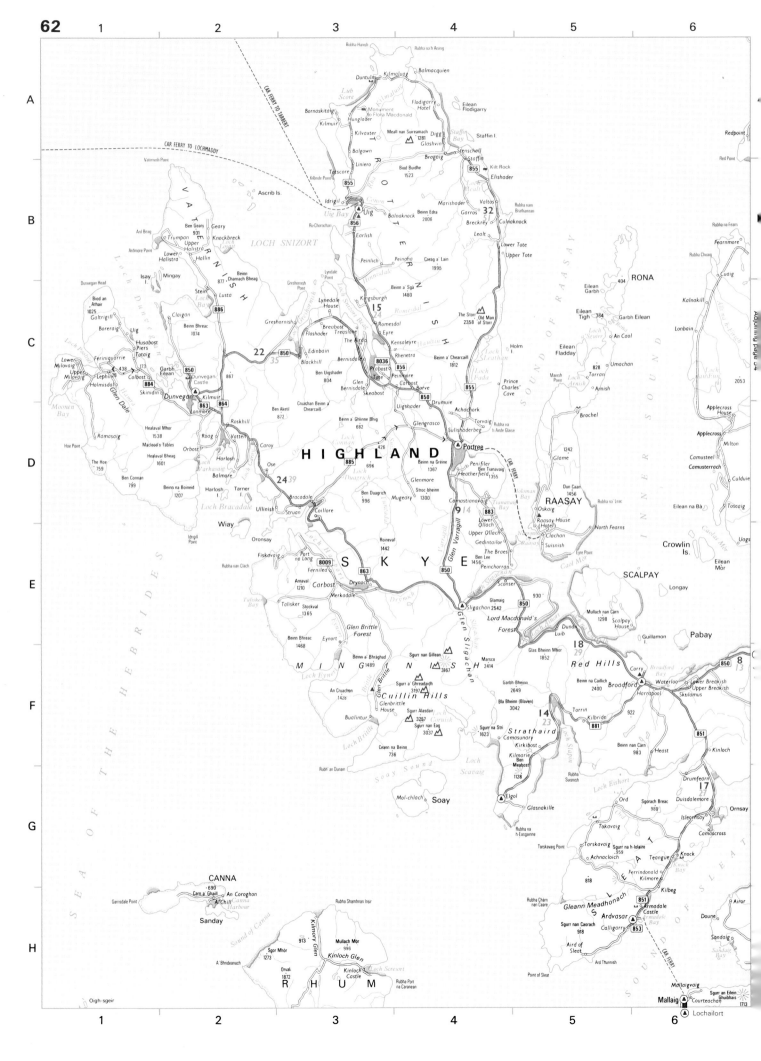

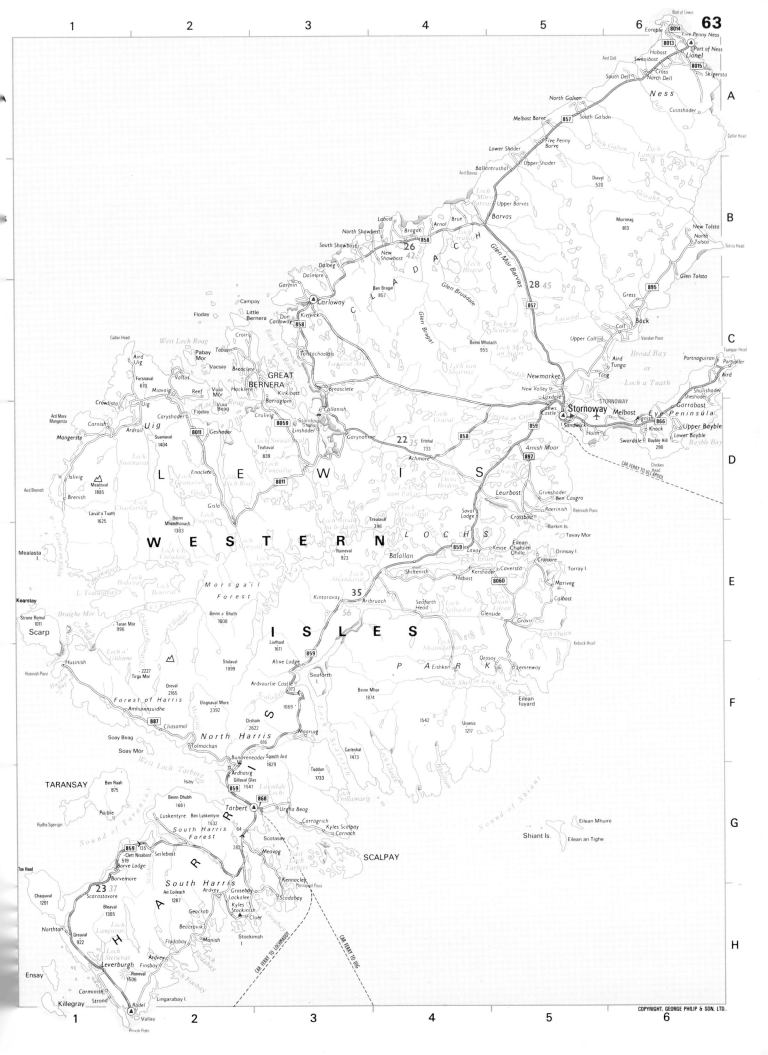

Butt of Lewis
Eoropie
8014
8013 Five Penny Ness
Port of Ness
Lionel
Habost
Swainbost 8015 Skigersta
Aird Dell Cross
South Dell North Dell

Ness

North Galson
857 South Galson Cuishader

Cellar Head

Melbost Borve
Lower Shader
Ballantrushal Upper Shader
Ard Barvas Five Penny Borve
North Shawbost
Labost Arnol Brue **Barvas**
Bragar
858 New Tolsta
North Tolsta

Loch Mòr Barvas
Diaval 520

B

Murneag 813

Tolsta Head

South Shawbost
Dalbeg New Shawbost **26** 42
Dalmore
Garinin Ben Bragar 857 Glen Mòr Barvas 28 45
Glen Bruadale 857
Glen Tolsta
895 Gress

Carloway
Little Bernera Dun Carloway
Campay Kirivick 858 Glen Bragar
Floday Croir
Tobson Tolstachaolais Beinn Mholach 955 Upper Coll Coll
Back
Breasclete Loch Mòr an Stairr Vatisker Point
C

Gallan Head Pabay Mòr Vacsay
Aird Uig Breaclete Kirkibost
Forsnaval 670 Reef Vuia Mòr GREAT BERNERA Callanish Newmarket New Valley Broad Bay or Loch a Tuath Tolsta Head
Crowlista Miavaig Vuia Beag Loch Roag Barraglom Crulivig Standing Laxdale Stornoway Tong Aird Tunga Portnaguiran Portvoller Aird
Ard More Mangersta Caryshader Floday Linshader Stones **STORNOWAY** Tumpan Head
Uig 8011 Geshader 8059 Lews Castle Melbost Shulishader Sheshader
Carnish Ardroil Suainaval Garynahine Garynahine 22 35 Eitshal 858 Sandwick 859 Agnish Garrabost
Mangersta 1404 Teahaval 839 733 Holm 866 Knock Upper Bayble
D Lower Bayble
Islivig Brenish Enaclete Achmore 897 Arnish Moor Swordale Bayble Hill 290 Bayble Bay
Ard Brenish Mealisval 1885 8011 Leurbost
Laival a Tuath 1625 Beinn Mheadhonach 1303 Gisla Loch Trealaval Grimshader Ben Casgro
Raernish Raernish Point

WESTERN Trealaval 396
Roineval 923 Soval Lodge Crossbost CAR FERRY TO ULLAPOOL
Mealasta I. **L E W I S** Barkin Is. Tavay Mòr
Kearstay 859 Laxay Keose Eilean Chaltuim Chille Orinsay I.
Stone Romul 1011 Balallan Kershader Caverstá Cromore Torray I.
Scarp Braighe Mòr Taran Mòr 996 Shiltenish Habost Mariveg
ISLES Kintaravay 35 Aribruach 8060 Calbost
Husinish Benn a Bhoth 1008 56 Seaforth Head Glenside Gravir
E
Husinish Point Loch Sgibacleit
Tirga Mòr 2227 Stulaval 1899 Liuthaid 1611 Kebock Head
Oreval Aline Lodge 859 Beinn Mhor 1874 Orosay I. Lemreway
Forest of Harris Uisgnaval More 2392 Ardvourlie Castle 473 Eishken 1069 Eilean luyard
Amhuinnsuidhe Clisham 2622 Seaforth Eilean
F 1542 Uisenis 1217
Cliasamol 887 Maaruig Carteshal 1473
Soay Beag Tolmachan North Harris 616 Toddun 1733
Soay Mòr Bunaveneadar Sgaoth Ard 1829
TARANSAY West Loch Tarbert Ardhasig Gillaval Glas 1547 Eilean Mhuire
Ben Raah 875 Isay 859 Uragh Beag Sound of Shiant
Paible 868 **Tarbert** Carragrich
Rudha Sgeirgin Luskentyre Ben Luskentyre 1532 Kyles Scalpay Shiant Is. Eilean an Tighe
G
Beinn Dhubh 1661 Scotasay Carnach
64
Toe Head 859 135 Seilebost Meavag **SCALPAY**
Chaipaval 1201 Clett Nisabost 519 Scadabay Plocrapool Point
23 37 Borve Lodge 282
Scarstavore Borvemore An Coileach 1267 Kennacley
Bleaval 1305 Ardvey Grosebay
Northton Greaval 922 Geocrab Lackalee Kyles Stockinish Cluer CAR FERRY TO LOCHMADDY
Loch Langavat **H** Beacravik Manish
Leverburgh Flodabay Stockinish I.
Ensay Ardvey Finsbay CAR FERRY TO UIG
Roneval 1506
Carminish
Killegray Strond Rodel
Vallay

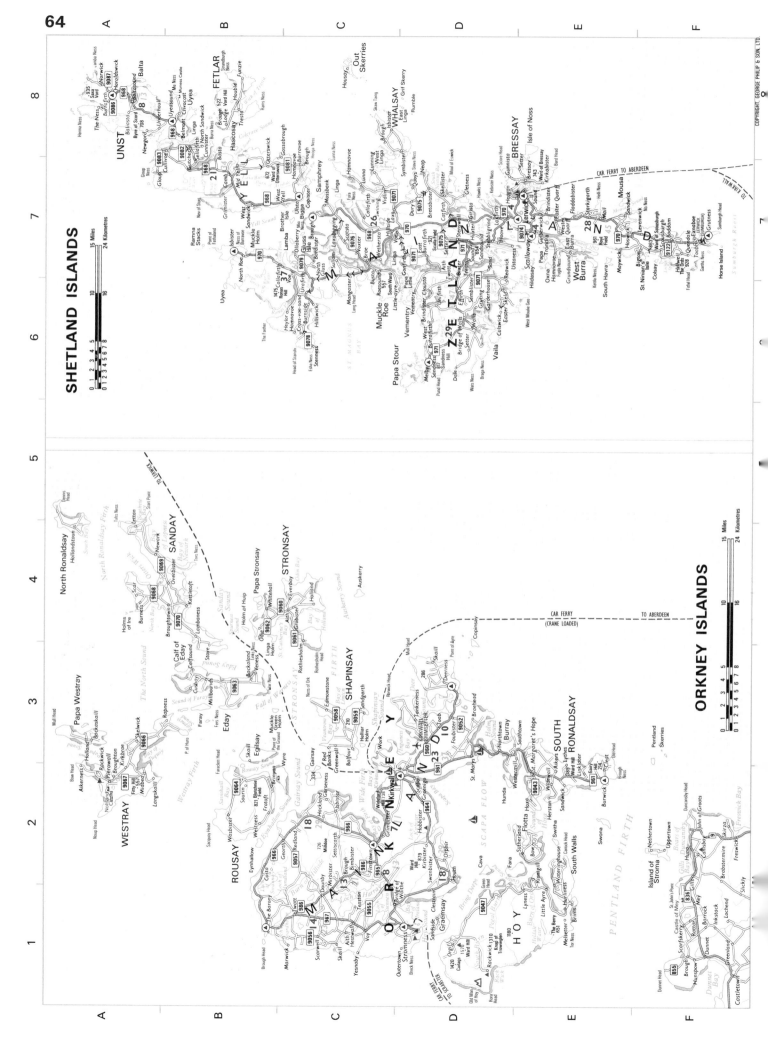

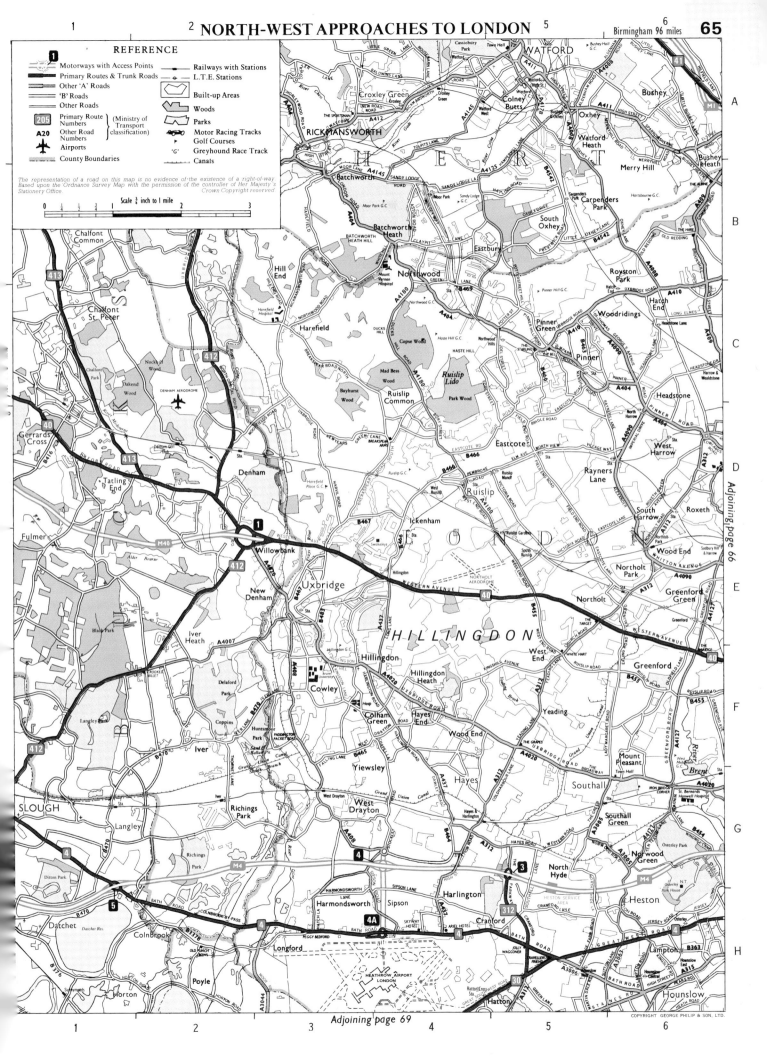

Adjoining page 66

Adjoining page 69

REFERENCE

Motorways with Access Points	Railways with Stations
Primary Routes & Trunk Roads	L.T.E. Stations
Other 'A' Roads	Built-up Areas
'B' Roads	Woods
Other Roads	Parks
205 Primary Route Numbers (Ministry of Transport classification)	Motor Racing Tracks
A20 Other Road Numbers	Golf Courses
Airports	'G' Greyhound Race Track
County Boundaries	Canals

The representation of a road on this map is no evidence of the existence of a right-of-way.
Based upon the Ordnance Survey Map with the permission of the controller of Her Majesty's Stationery Office. *Crown Copyright reserved*

Scale ¾ inch to 1 mile
0   ¼   ½   ¾   1   2   3

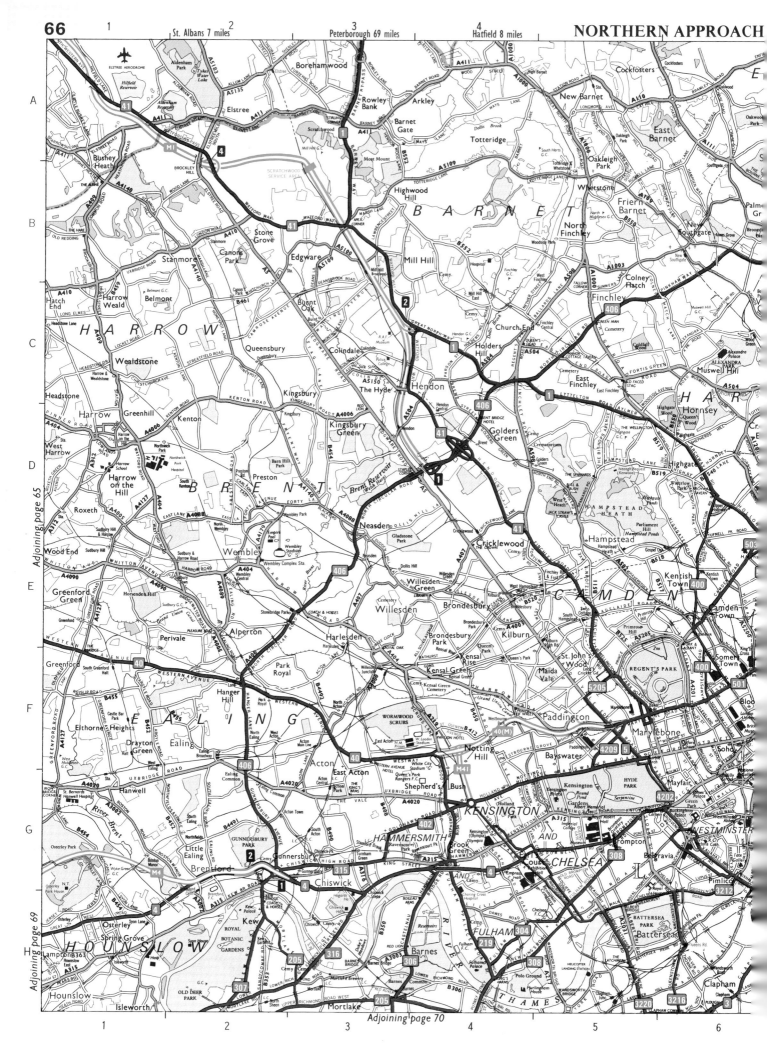

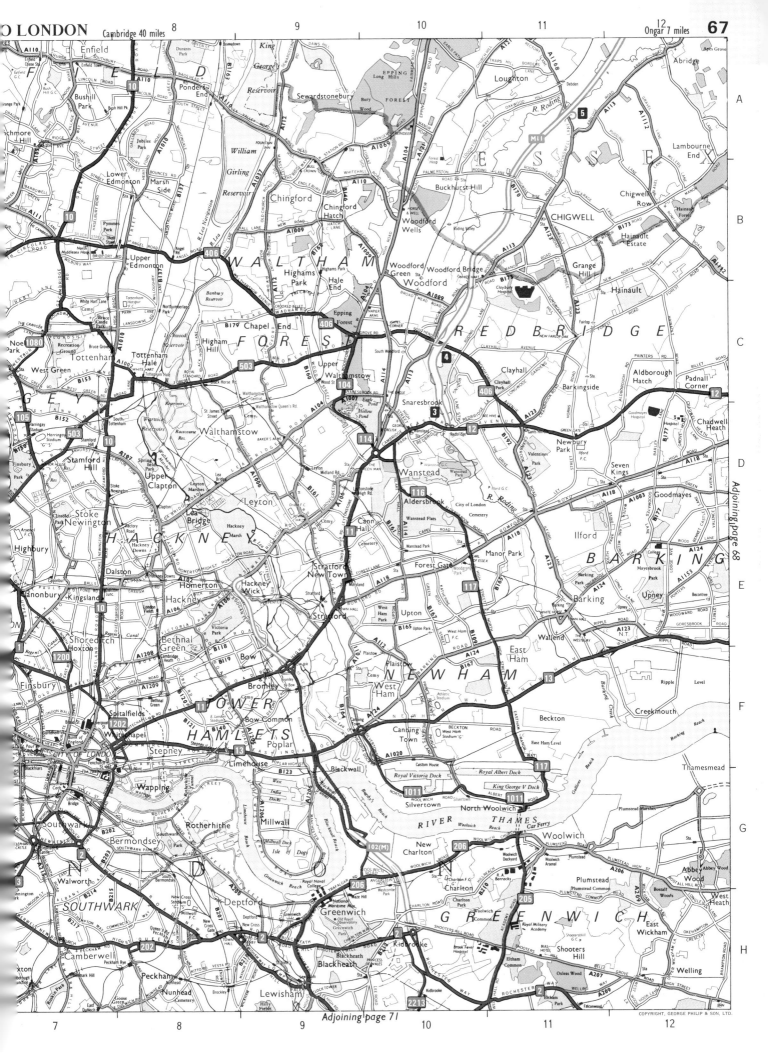

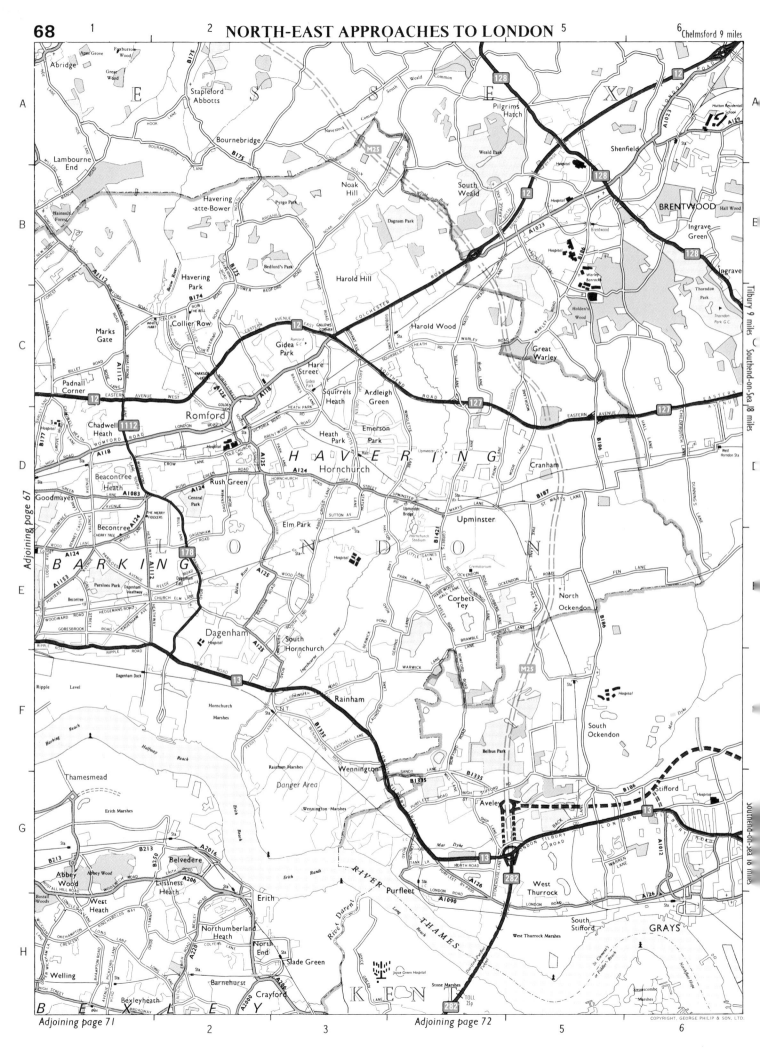

COPYRIGHT, GEORGE PHILIP & SON, LTD.

Adjoining page 67

Tilbury 9 miles Southend-on-Sea 18 miles

Southend-on-Sea 16 miles

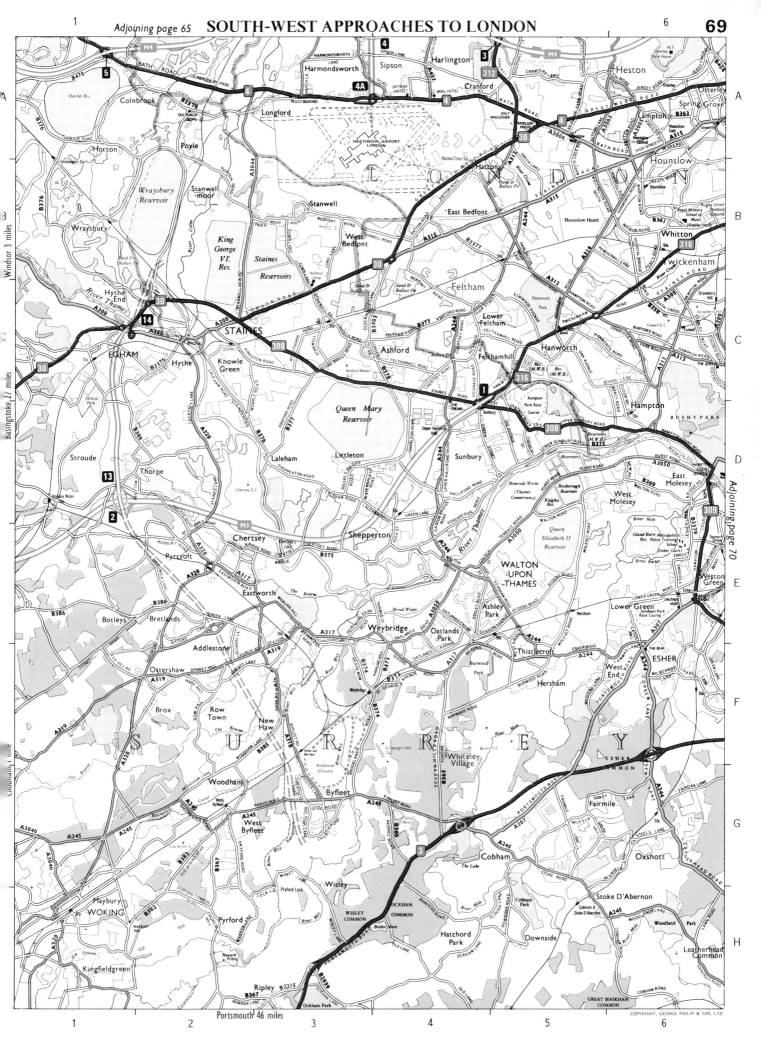

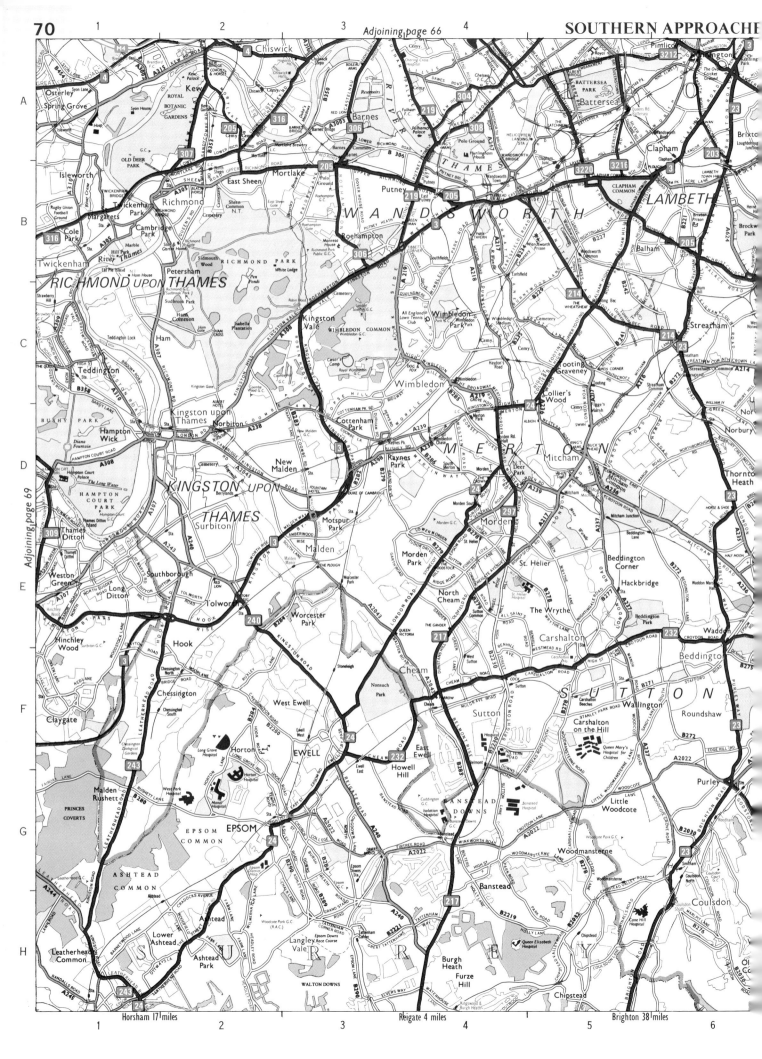

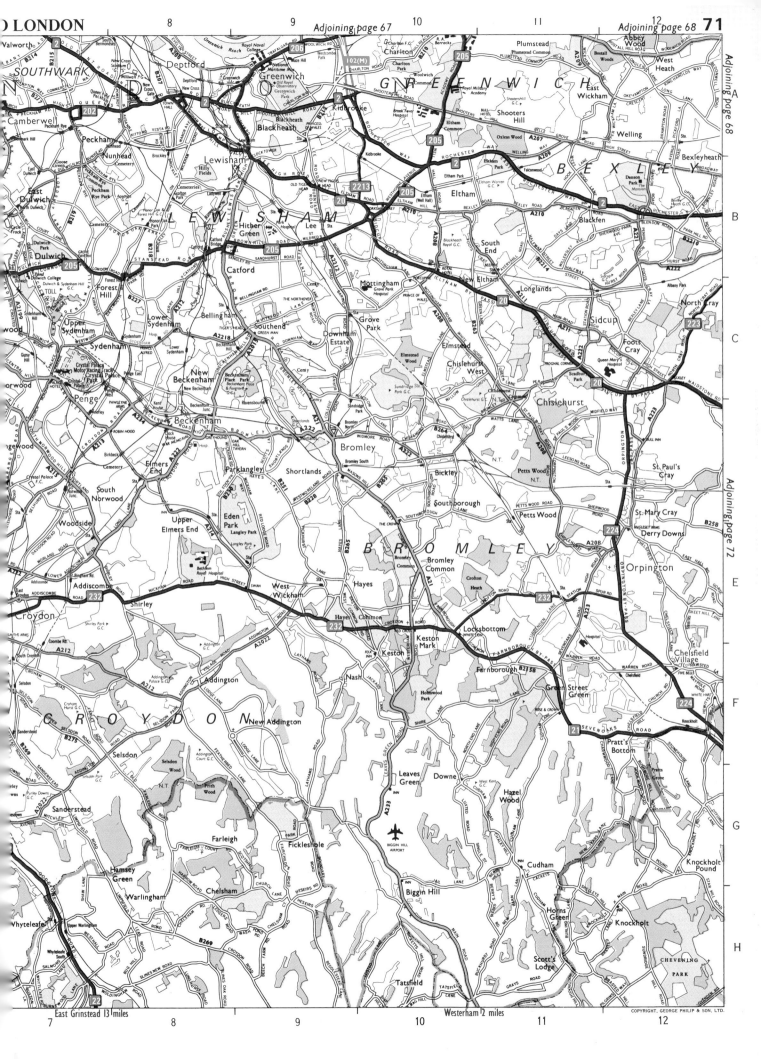

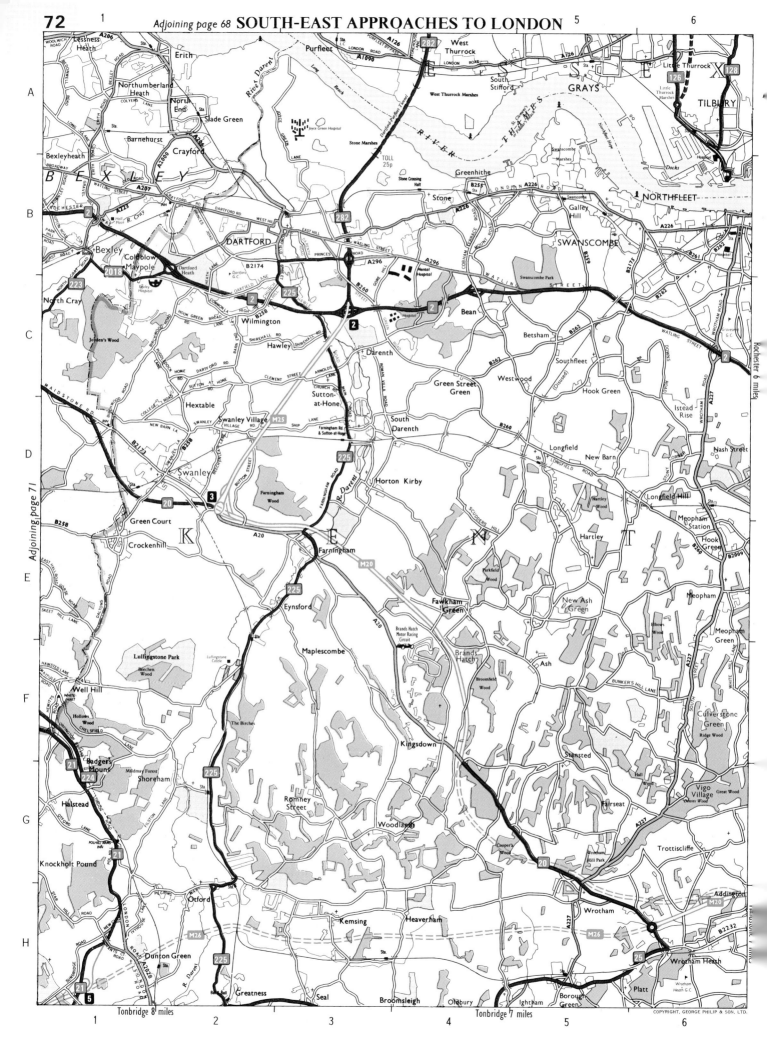

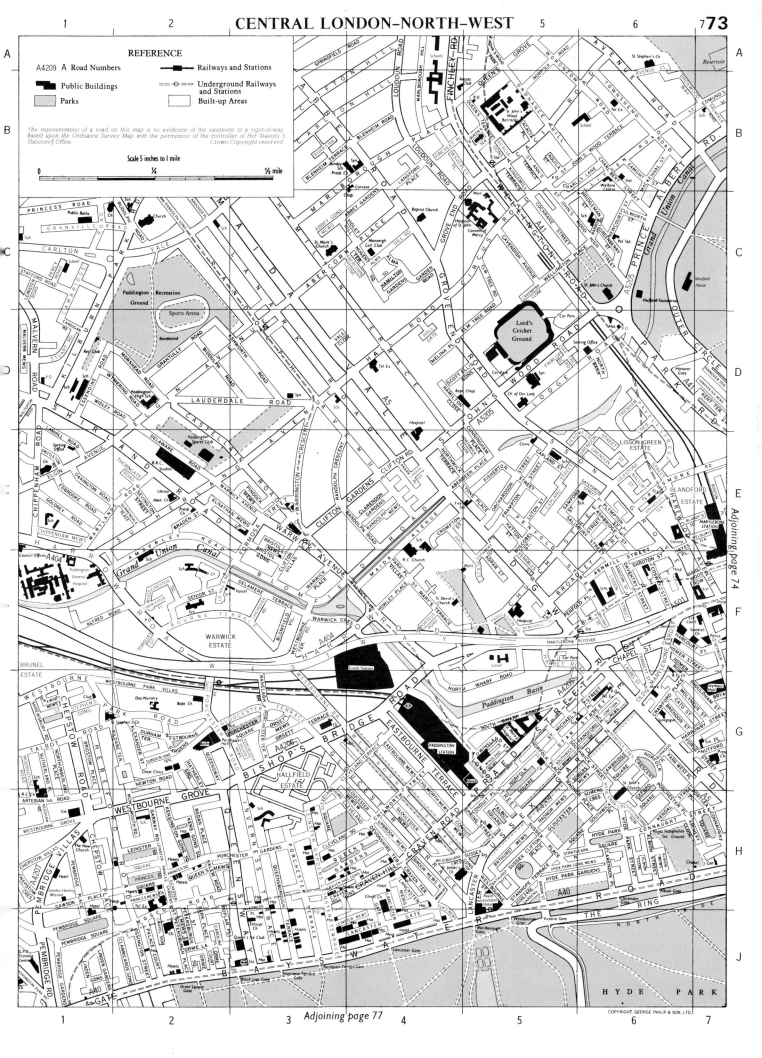

REFERENCE

A4209 A Road Numbers

Public Buildings

Parks

Railways and Stations

Underground Railways and Stations

Built-up Areas

The representation of a road on this map is no evidence of the existence of a right-of-way. Based upon the Ordnance Survey Map with the permission of the controller of Her Majesty's Stationery Office. Crown Copyright reserved.

Scale 5 inches to 1 mile

0   ¼   ½ mile

Adjoining page 74

COPYRIGHT. GEORGE PHILIP & SON. LTD.

HYDE PARK

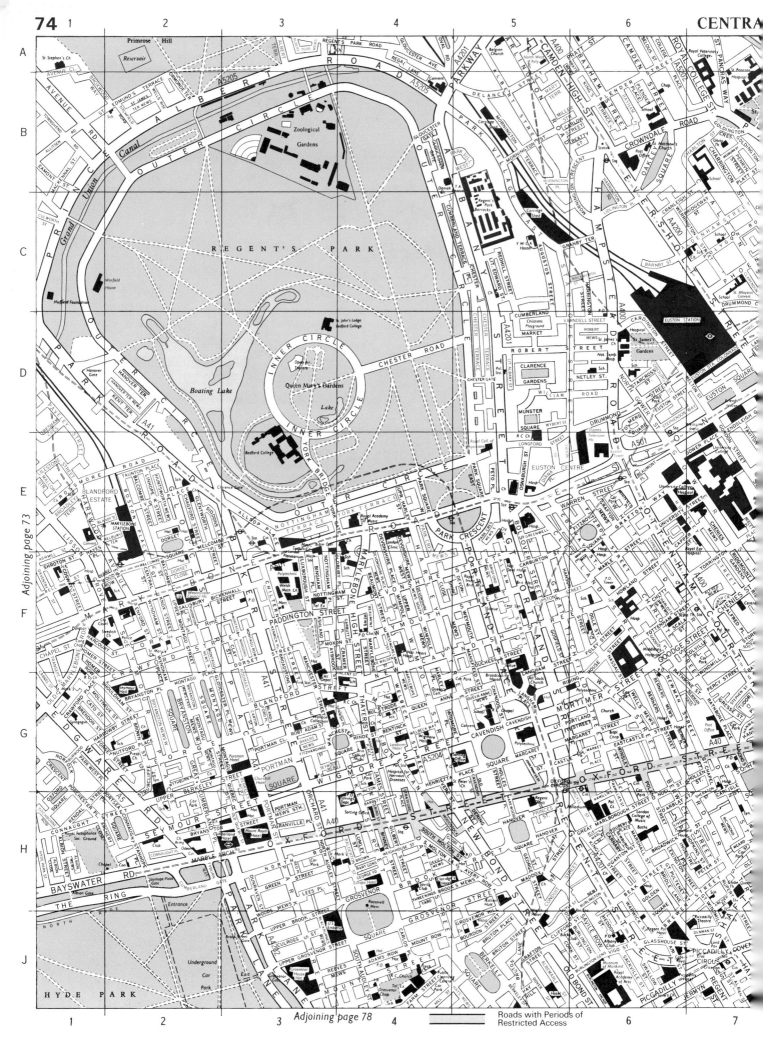

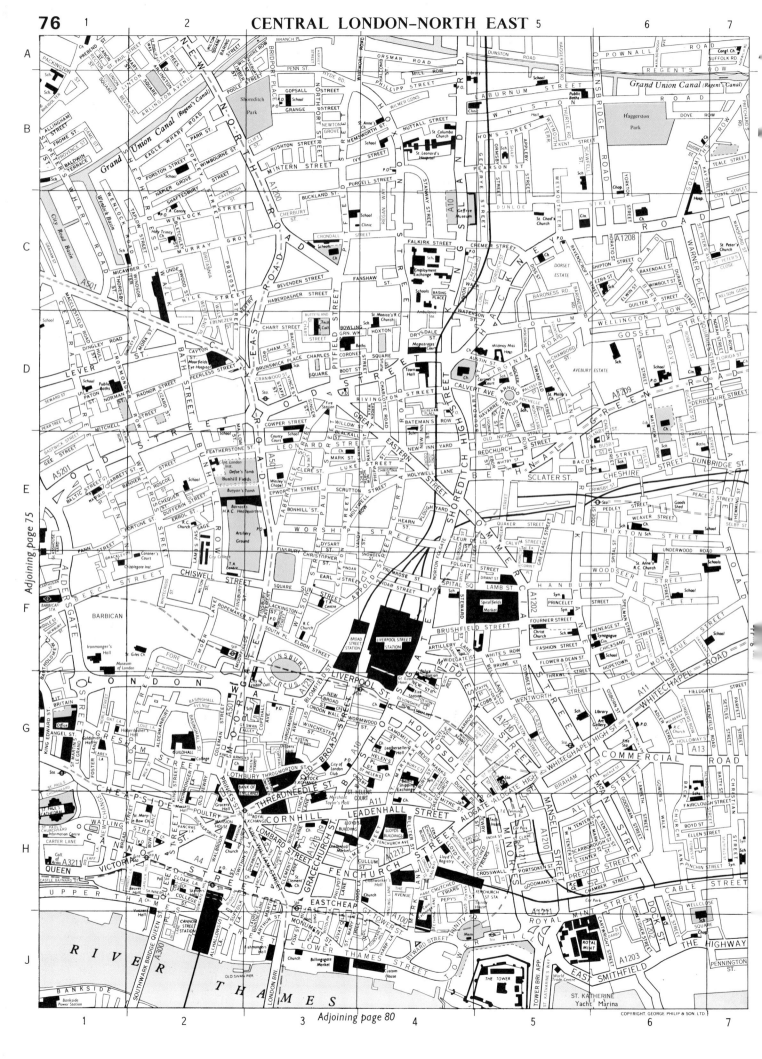

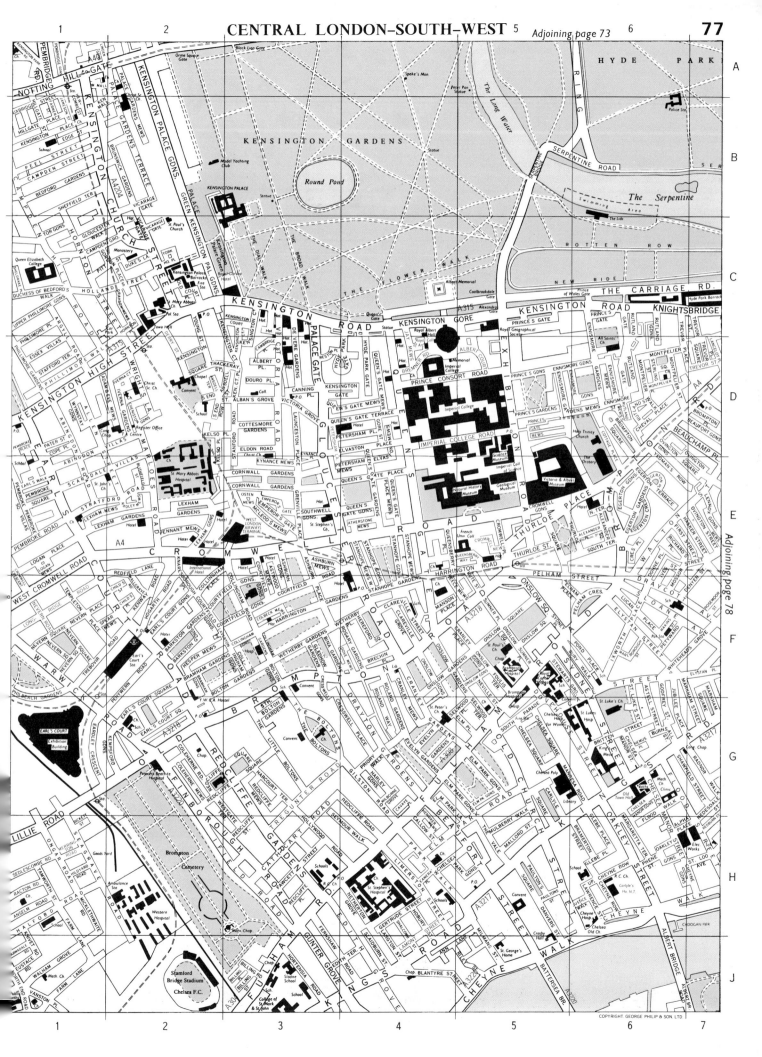

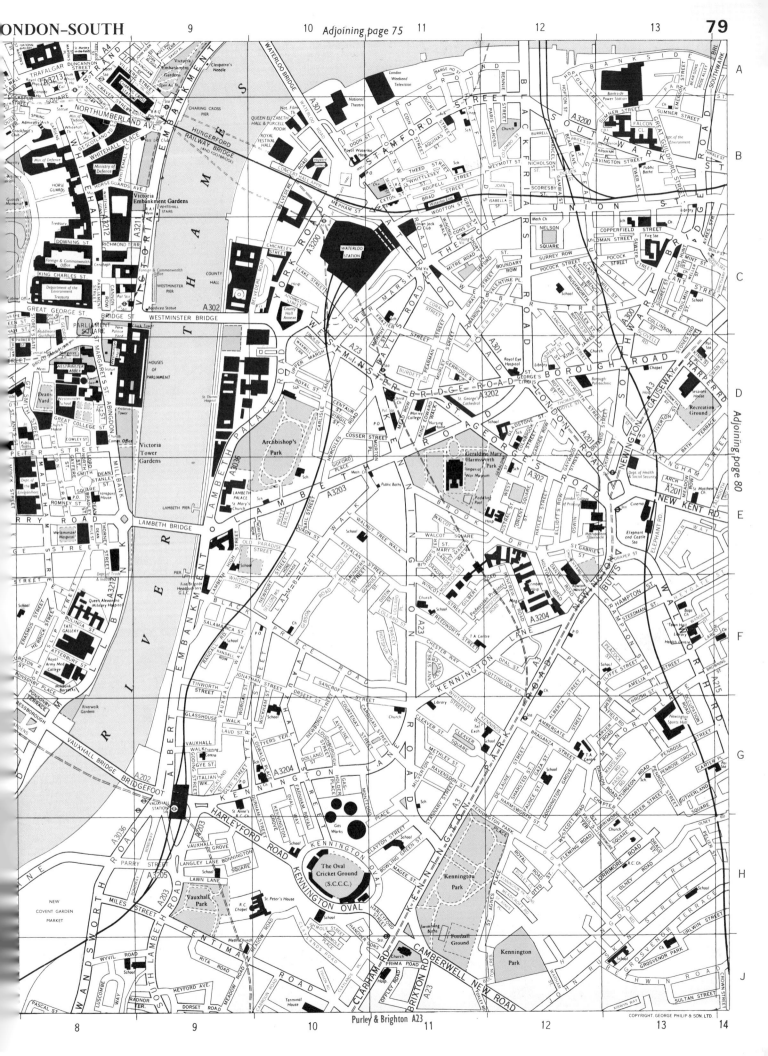

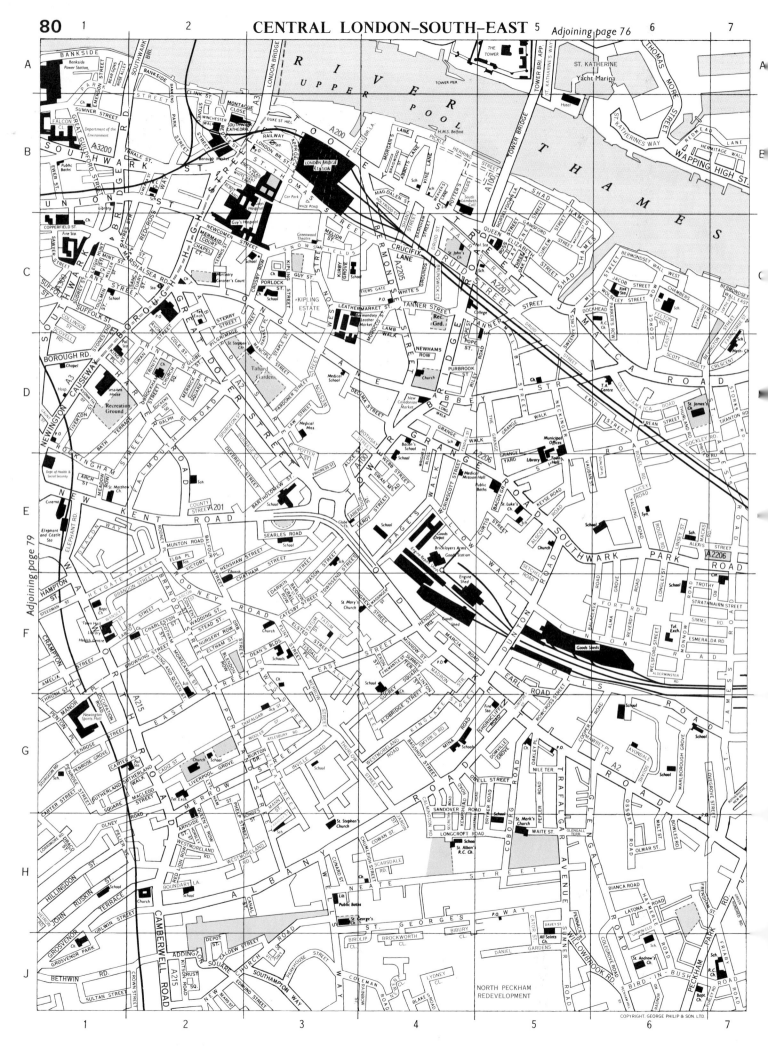

INDEX TO SECTIONAL MAP OF GREAT BRITAIN

ABBREVIATIONS

Beds. – *Bedfordshire*
Berks. – *Berkshire*
Bri. – *Bridge*
Bucks. – *Buckinghamshire*
Cambs. – *Cambridgeshire*
Cas. – *Castle*
Ches. – *Cheshire*
Cnr. – *Corner*
Co. – *County*
Com. – *Common*
Corn. – *Cornwall*
Cumb. – *Cumbria*
Derby. – *Derbyshire*
Dumf. & Gall. – *Dumfries & Galloway*
Dur. – *Durham*
E. – *East*
E. Sussex – *East Sussex*
Glos. – *Gloucestershire*
Gt. – *Great*
Grn. – *Green*
Hants. – *Hampshire*
Heref. & Worcs. – *Hereford & Worcester*
Hth. – *Heath*
Herts. – *Hertfordshire*
Ho. – *House*
Humber. – *Humberside*
I.o.M. – *Isle of Man*
I.o.W. – *Isle of Wight*
Junc. – *Junction*
L. – *Lake*
Lancs. – *Lancashire*
Leics. – *Leicestershire*
Lincs. – *Lincolnshire*
Lo. – *Lodge*
London – *Greater London*
Manchester – *Greater Manchester*
Mid Glam. – *Mid Glamorgan*
Norf. – *Norfolk*
N. – *North*
N. Yorks. – *North Yorkshire*
Northants. – *Northamptonshire*
Northumb. – *Northumberland*
Notts. – *Nottinghamshire*
Oxon. – *Oxfordshire*
Salop. – *Shropshire*
Som. – *Somerset*
S. – *South*
S. Glam. – *South Glamorgan*
S. Yorks. – *South Yorkshire*
Staffs. – *Staffordshire*
Sta. – *Station*
Suff. – *Suffolk*
Vill. – *Village*
War. – *Warwickshire*
W. – *West*
W. Glam. – *West Glamorgan*
W. Mid. – *West Midlands*
W. Sussex – *West Sussex*
W. Yorks. – *West Yorkshire*
W. Isles. – *Western Isles*
Wilts. – *Wiltshire*

32 Ab Kettleby **H 4**
7 Abbas Combe **D 10**
22 Abberley **E 1**
19 Abberton, Essex **B 10**
22 Abberton, Heref. & Worcs **G 3**
45 Abberwick **B 9**
18 Abbess Roding **C 6**
6 Abbey **E 5**
20 Abbey Cwmhir **E 6**
15 Abbey Dore **A 7**
6 Abbey Hill **D 6**
31 Abbey Hulton **E 7**
49 Abbey St. Bathans **C 10**
32 Abbey Town **F 12**
34 Abbey Village **E 5**
38 Abbeylands, I.o.M. **G 2**
45 Abbeylands, Northumb. **B 10**
34 Abbeystead **B 4**
4 Abbots Bickington **E 3**
31 Abbots Bromley **H 9**
17 Abbots Langley **D 11**
22 Abbot's Morton **G 4**
25 Abbots Ripton **G 3**
22 Abbot's Salford **G 4**
7 Abbotsbury **H 9**
4 Abbotsham **C 3**
5 Abbotskerswell **J 7**
25 Abbotsley **K 3**
8 Abbotswood **D 5**
8 Abbots Ann **B 5**
21 Abcott **E 9**
21 Abdon **D 11**
13 Aber, Dyfed **B 8**
28 Aber, Gwynedd **C 6**
13 Aberarth **A 8**
12 Aber-Cych **C 6**
20 Aber Gwydol **B 3**
28 Aber-Gwynant **H 6**
14 Aber Village **B 4**
13 Aberaeron **A 8**
14 Aberaman **D 3**
20 Aberangell **A 4**
57 Aberarder, Highland **G 2**
55 Aberarder, Highland **L 8**
52 Aberargie **F 6**
13 Aberavon **H 11**
13 Aber-banc **C 7**
14 Aberbeeg **D 5**
14 Aberbran **A 3**
14 Abercanaid **D 4**
14 Abercarn **E 5**
12 Abercastle **D 2**
20 Abercegir **B 4**
55 Aberchalder House **J 7**
58 Aberchirder **B 4**
14 Abercrave **C 2**
14 Abercregan **E 2**
14 Abercwmboi **D 3**
14 Abercynafon **C 4**
14 Abercynon **E 4**
14 Aberdare **D 3**
28 Aberdaron **H 1**
59 Aberdeen **G 7**
48 Aberdour **A 5**
13 Aberdulais **G 11**
20 Aberdyfi **C 2**
20 Aberedw **H 6**
12 Abereiddy **D 2**
28 Abererch **G 3**
14 Aberfan **D 4**
52 Aberfeldy **B 3**
28 Aberffraw **C 3**
36 Aberffrwd **E 2**
36 Aberford **C 2**
51 Aberfoyle **G 12**
14 Abergavenny **C 6**
29 Abergele **B 9**
13 Abergiar **C 8**
13 Abergorlech **D 9**
20 Abergwesyn **G 4**
13 Abergwili **E 8**
14 Abergwynfi **E 2**
20 Abergynolwyn **B 2**
20 Aberhosan **C 4**
14 Aberkenfig **F 2**
49 Aberlady **A 7**
53 Aberlemno **B 10**
20 Aberllefenni **A 3**
20 Abermeurig **G 1**
21 Abermule **C 7**
13 Abernant, Dyfed **E 7**
14 Aber-nant, Mid Glam. **D 3**
53 Abernethy **E 7**
53 Abernyte **D 7**
12 Aberporth **B 6**
28 Abersoch **G 3**
14 Abersychan **D 6**
14 Aberthin **G 3**
14 Abertillery **D 5**
14 Abertridwr, Mid Glam. **E 4**
29 Abertridwr, Powys **H 9**
14 Abertysswg **D 5**
52 Aberuthven **F 5**
14 Aberyscir **A 3**
20 Aberystwyth **D 2**
16 Abingdon **D 6**
9 Abinger **B 12**
9 Abinger Hammer **A 12**
48 Abington **G 2**
25 Abington Pigotts **L 4**
16 Ablington, Glos **C 2**
8 Ablington, Wilts. **A 3**
31 Abney **B 10**
59 Aboyne **H 3**
34 Abram **G 5**
56 Abriachan **F 1**
18 Abridge **D 5**
15 Abson **G 10**
23 Abthorpe **G 10**
33 Aby **B 11**
21 Acaster Malbis **C 4**
36 Acaster Selby **C 3**
4 Accott **C 5**
34 Accrington **D 6**
62 Achachork **D 4**
50 Achadun **D 5**
50 Achafolla **F 5**
46 Achahoish **B 3**
51 Achallader **C 10**
46 Achamore Farm **E 1**
54 Achanalt **D 6**
46 Achanamara **A 3**
46 Achandunie **C 2**
60 Achany **F 6**
55 Achaphubuil **M 5**
50 Acharacle **A 4**
50 Acharn, Highland **C 4**
52 Acharn, Tayside **C 2**
51 Acharole **C 11**
46 Acharosson **B 4**
50 Achateny **A 3**
58 Achath **F 5**
61 Achavanich **C 11**
56 Achavraat **E 5**
60 Achavraie **F 2**
13 Achddu **G 8**
61 Achentoul **D 8**
60 Achfary **C 4**
60 Achgarve **G 1**
60 Achiemore, Kyle of Durness, Highland **A 4**
61 Achiemore, Highland **B 9**
62 A'Chill **H 2**
60 Achiltibuie **F 2**
61 Achina **B 7**
51 Achindarroch **B 7**
55 Achintee, Highland **M 5**
54 Achintee, Highland **F 3**
54 Achintraid **F 2**
55 Achlain **H 6**
50 Achleck **C 1**
46 A'Chleit **E 2**
51 Achlian **E 8**
55 Achluachrach **L 7**
60 Achlyness **B 4**
60 Achmelvich **E 2**
52 Achmore, Central **D 1**
54 Achmore, Highland **F 2**
63 Achmore, W. Isles **D 4**
51 Achnaba, Strathclyde **D 7**
46 Achnaba, Strathclyde **A 4**
57 Achnabat **G 2**
60 Achnacarnin **D 2**
55 Achnacarry Ho. **L 5**
62 Achnacloich **G 5**
61 Achnaclyth **D 10**
51 Achnacon **B 8**
55 Achnaconeran **H 8**
50 Achnacraig **C 2**
50 Achnacroish **C 6**
50 Achnadrish **B 2**
51 Achnafalnich **E 9**
55 Achnafraschoille **L 6**
56 Achnaggaron **C 2**
50 Achnaha **A 2**
60 Achnahanat **G 6**
50 Achnalea **A 6**
61 Achnaluachrach **F 7**
55 Achnanellan **L 5**
60 Achnanerain **F 6**
55 Achnangart **H 3**
55 Achnasaul **K 5**
54 Achnasheen **D 5**
56 Achnastank **F 8**
50 Achosnich **A 2**
50 Achranich **C 4**
61 Achreamie **A 9**
51 Achriabhach **A 8**
60 Achriesgill **B 4**
61 Achrimsdale **F 9**
61 Achtoty **B 7**
25 Achurch **G 1**
60 Achuvoldrach **B 6**
61 Achvaich **G 7**
57 Achvraid, Highland **G 2**
56 Achvraid, Highland **F 2**
61 Ackergill **B 12**
40 Acklam, Cleveland **C 5**
36 Acklam, N. Yorks. **A 5**
22 Ackleton **B 1**
45 Acklington **C 10**
36 Ackton **E 2**
36 Ackworth Moor Top **F 2**
26 Acle **D 7**
22 Acock's Green **D 5**
11 Acol **A 11**
45 Acomb, Northumb. **F 7**
36 Acomb, N. Yorks. **B 4**
15 Aconbury **A 8**
34 Acre **E 6**
9 Acre Street **F 9**
29 Acrefair **F 12**
30 Acton, Cheshire **E 5**
8 Acton, Dorset **H 1**
18 Acton, London **F 2**
21 Acton, Salop **D 8**
27 Acton, Suffolk **L 2**
30 Acton Bridge **C 4**
21 Acton Beauchamp **G 12**
21 Acton Burnell **B 10**
21 Acton Green **G 12**
30 Acton Park **E 2**
21 Acton Pigott **B 11**
21 Acton Round **C 11**
21 Acton Scott **C 10**
31 Acton Trussell **H 8**
15 Acton Turville **F 11**
30 Adbaston **G 6**
7 Adber **D 9**
30 Adderley **F 5**
45 Adderstone **C 12**
48 Addiewell **C 3**
35 Addingham **B 9**
17 Addington, Bucks. **A 8**
10 Addington, Kent **B 5**
18 Addington, London **G 4**
49 Addinston **D 8**
17 Addlestone **H 11**
33 Addlethorpe **C 12**
30 Adeney **H 5**
20 Adfa **B 6**
21 Adforton **E 9**
11 Adisham **C 11**
16 Adlestrop **A 3**
36 Adlingfleet **E 6**
31 Adlington, Ches. **B 7**
34 Adlington, Lancs. **F 5**
21 Admaston, Salop. **A 11**
31 Admaston, Staffs. **H 9**
22 Admington **G 5**
17 Adstock **A 8**
23 Adstone **G 9**
9 Adversane **D 12**
56 Advie **F 7**
36 Adwick le Street **F 3**
36 Adwick upon Dearne **G 3**
4 Adworthy **D 6**
58 Adziel **B7**
43 Ae Bridgend **C 10**
43 Ae Village **C 10**
4 Affeton Barton **E 6**
58 Affleck, Grampian **D 3**
58 Affleck, Grampian **E 6**
7 Affpuddle **G 11**
55 Affric Lodge **G 5**
29 Afon-wen **C 10**
5 Afton, Devon **J 7**
8 Afton, I.o.W. **G 5**
47 Afton Bridgend **H 11**
40 Agglethorpe **F 1**
38 Agneash **G 2**
63 Aignish **D 6**
37 Aike **C 8**
64 Aikerness **A 2**
64 Aikers **E 2**
43 Aiket **E 11**
39 Aiketgate **A 7**
44 Aikton **H 1**
21 Ailey **G 9**
24 Ailsworth **F 2**
40 Ainderby Steeple **F 4**
19 Aingers Green **B 11**
34 Ainsdale **F 2**
39 Ainstable **A 7**
34 Ainsworth **F 6**
41 Ainthorpe **D 7**
34 Aintree **G 3**
42 Aird, Dumf & Gall. **F 2**
50 Aird, Strathclyde **G 5**
63 Aird, W. Isles **C 6**
62 Aird of Sleat **H 5**
63 Aird of Tunga **C 6**
63 Aird Uig **C 2**
60 Airdachuilinn **C 4**
47 Airdrie **C 12**
47 Airdsgreen **F 12**
54 Airigh-drishaig **F 1**
36 Airmyn **E 5**
52 Airntully **D 6**
55 Airor **J 1**
52 Airth **H 4**
35 Airton **A 7**
42 Airyhassen **G 4**
33 Aisby, Lincs. **F 7**
32 Aisby, Lincs. **A 6**
39 Aisgill **E 10**
5 Aish **K 6**
6 Aisholt **C 5**
40 Aiskew **F 3**
40 Aislaby, N. Yorks. **D 4**
41 Aislaby, N. Yorls. **G 8**
41 Aislaby, N. Yorks. **D 8**
32 Aisthorpe **B 6**
64 Aith, Orkney Is. **C 4**
64 Aith, Shetland Is. **D 7**
64 Aith Hestwall **C 1**
42 Aitkenhead **A 4**
56 Aitnoch **F 5**
49 Akeld **F 12**
49 Akeld Steads **F 12**
23 Akeley **H 10**
27 Akenham **K 5**
3 Albaston **C 11**
21 Alberbury **A 9**
12 Albert Town **E 3**
10 Albourn **F 1**
22 Albrighton, Salop, **B 2**
30 Albrighton, Salop. **H 4**
27 Alburgh **G 6**
27 Alburgh Street **G 5**
18 Albury, Herts. **B 4**
9 Albury, Surrey **A 12**
26 Alby Hill **B 5**
56 Alcaig **D 1**
22 Alcester **F 4**
10 Alciston **G 4**
6 Alcombe, Som. **B 3**
15 Alcombe, Wilts. **G 11**
25 Alconbury **H 3**
25 Alconbury Hill **G 3**
25 Alconbury Weston **H 3**
47 Aldandulish **M 5**
26 Aldborough, Norf. **B 5**
40 Aldborough, N. Yorks. **H 4**
16 Aldbourne **G 4**
37 Aldbrough, Humber. **C 10**
40 Aldbrough, N. Yorks. **D 2**
17 Aldbury **C 10**
52 Aldcharmaig **A 3**
34 Aldcliffe **A 3**
52 Aldclune **A 4**
27 Aldeburgh **J 8**
26 Aldeby **F 7**
18 Aldenham **D 1**
8 Alderbury **C 3**
26 Alderford **D 4**
15 Alderley **E 11**
31 Alderley Edge **B 7**
17 Aldermaston **H 7**
17 Aldermaston Wharf **G 7**
22 Alderminster **G 6**
21 Alder's End **H 11**
8 Alderholt **E 3**
9 Aldershot **A 10**
16 Alderton, Glos. **A 1**
23 Alderton, Northants **G 10**
30 Alderton, Salop **H 4**
27 Alderton, Suffolk **L 6**
15 Alderton, Wilts **F 11**
31 Alderwasley **E 11**
40 Aldfield **H 3**
30 Aldford **D 3**
19 Aldham, Essex **A 9**
27 Aldham, Suffolk **L 3**
27 Aldham Street **L 3**
56 Aldie **B 3**
9 Aldingbourne **F 10**
38 Aldingham **H 5**
22 Aldington **H 4**
11 Aldington Corner **D 9**
51 Aldochlay **H 10**
25 Aldreth **H 5**
22 Aldridge **B 4**
27 Aldringham **J 7**
16 Aldsworth **C 3**
58 Aldunie **E i**
31 Aldwark, Derby **D 10**
36 Aldwark, N. Yorks. **A 2**
9 Aldwick **F 10**
25 Aldwincle **G 1**
16 Aldworth **F 6**
47 Alexandria **A 9**
6 Aley **B 5**
4 Alfardisworthy **E 2**
6 Alfington **F 5**
9 Alfold **C 11**
9 Alfold Crossways **C 11**
58 Alford, Grampian **F 3**
33 Alford, Lincs. **C 11**
7 Alford, Somerset **C 9**
32 Alfreton **E 1**
22 Alfrick **G 1**
10 Alfriston **H 4**
24 Algarkirk **B 4**
7 Alhampton **C 9**
63 Aline Lodge **F 3**
55 Alisary **L 1**
36 Alkborough **E 6**
23 Alkerton **H 7**
11 Alkham **D 11**
30 Alkington **F 4**
31 Alkmonton **F 10**
27 All Saints, South Elmham **G 6**
21 All Stretton **C 10**
60 Alladale Lodge **G 5**
5 Allaleigh **K 7**
57 Allanaquoich **K 7**
56 Allanfearn **E 3**
56 Allangrange Ho. **E 2**
49 Allanton **D 11**
8 Allbrook **D 6**
16 All Cannings **H 2**
45 Allendale Town **G 7**
39 Allenheads **A 10**
18 Allen's Green **B 4**
45 Allensford **H 9**
15 Allensmore **A 8**
31 Allenton, Derby **G 12**
48 Allenton, Strathclyde **D 1**
7 Aller **C 7**
43 Allerby **H 11**
45 Allerdene **C 8**
6 Allerford **B 3**
41 Allerston **G 9**
36 Allerthorpe **B 5**
30 Allerton, Merseyside **B 3**
35 Allerton, W. Yorks. **D 10**
36 Allerton Bywater **D 2**
36 Allerton Mauleverer **A 2**
45 Allerwash **F 7**
22 Allesley **D 6**
31 Allestree **F 11**
23 Allexton **B 11**
31 Allgreave **D 8**
19 Allhallows **F 8**
54 Alligin Shuas **D 2**
31 Allimore Green **H 7**
32 Allington, Lincs. **F 6**
8 Allington, Wilts. **B 4**
16 Allington, Wilts. **H 2**
38 Allithwaite **G 6**
52 Alloa **H 4**
43 Allonby **G 11**
47 Alloway **H 8**
7 Allowenshay **E 7**
13 Allt **G 9**
55 Alltbeithe, Highland **G 4**
55 Alltneithe, Highland **J 4**
51 Alltchaorunn **B 9**
20 Alltmawr **H 6**
60 Alltnacaillich **C 5**
57 Allt-na-giubhsaich **L 8**
60 Allt na h'Airbhe **G 3**
60 Allton Dubh **F 2**
55 Alltsigh **H 8**
13 Alltwalis **D 8**
13 Alltwen **G 10**
13 Alltyblacca **B 8**

7 Allweston .... E 10
32 Alma Park Estate ...F 6
21 Almeley .... G 9
21 Almeley Wooton ...G 9
7 Almer .... F 12
36 Almholme .... F 4
30 Almington .... G 5
4 Alminstone Cross ..D 2
52 Almondbank .... E 5
15 Almondbury .... F 10
15 Almondsbury .... F 9
45 Alndyke .... B 10
36 Alne .... A 3
56 Alness .... C 2
45 Alnham .... B 8
45 Alnmouth .... B 10
45 Alnwick .... B 10
27 Alphamstone .... M 2
27 Alpheton .... K 2
5 Alphington .... G 8
31 Alport .... D 10
30 Alpraham .... D 4
19 Alresford .... B 10
22 Alrewas .... A 5
30 Alsager .... E 6
30 Alsagers Bank .... E 6
31 Alsop en le Dale .. E 10
44 Alston, Cumb. ....H 5
6 Alston, Devon .... F 6
16 Alstone, Glos. ....A 1
6 Alstone, Som. ....B 6
31 Alstonefield .... E 9
4 Alswear .... D 6
61 Altanduin .... E 8
3 Altarnun .... B 9
60 Altassmore .... G 6
46 Altgaltraig .... B 5
34 Altham .... D 6
19 Althorne .... D 9
36 Althorpe .... F 6
42 Alticry .... G 4
61 Altnabea .... E 16
61 Altnabreac Stn. ...C 9
56 Altnacardich .... E 1
60 Altnacealgach Hot..F 4
50 Altnacraig .... E 6
51 Altnafeadh .... B 9
60 Altnaharra .... D 6
35 Altofts .... E 12
32 Alton, Derby ....D 1
9 Alton, Hants. ....B 8
31 Alton, Staffs. ....F 9
16 Alton Barnes .... H 2
7 Alton Pancras ....F 10
16 Alton Priors .... H 2
47 Altonhill .... E 9
30 Altrincham .... A 6
55 Altrua .... K 6
51 Altskeith .... G 11
56 Alltyre House ....D 6
52 Alva .... G 4
30 Alvanley .... C 4
31 Alvaston .... G 12
22 Alvechurch .... E 4
22 Alvecote .... B 6
8 Alvediston .... D 1
22 Alveley .... D 1
4 Alverdiscott .... C 4
9 Alverstoke .... F 7
35 Alverthorpe .... E 11
32 Alverton .... F 5
16 Alvescot .... D 4
15 Alveston, Avon ....E 9
22 Alveston, War. ....F 6
9 Alverstone .... G 7
57 Alvie .... J 4
33 Alvingham .... A 10
15 Alvington .... D 9
24 Alwalton .... F 2
45 Alwinton .... B 7
35 Alwoodley .... C 11
53 Alyth .... B 7
33 Amber Hill .... E 9
15 Amberley, Glos. ..D 11
9 Amberley, W. Sussex
         E 11
31 Ambergate .... E 11
45 Amble .... C 11
22 Amblecote .... D 2
35 Ambler Thorn ....D 9
38 Ambleside .... E 6
12 Ambleston .... D 3
17 Ambrosden .... B 7
36 Amcotts .... F 6
53 Americanmuir ....D 8
17 Amersham .... D 10
17 Amersham Com. ..D 10
45 Amersidelaw .... C 12
8 Amesbury .... B 3
63 Amhuinnsuidhe ....F 2
22 Amington .... B 6
43 Amisfield Town ....C 11
28 Amlwch .... A 4
28 Amlwch Port .... A 4

13 Ammanford .... F 9
41 Amotherby .... H 7
8 Ampfield .... D 5
48 Ampherlaw .... D 3
40 Ampleforth .... G 6
40 Ampleforth Coll. ...G 6
16 Ampney Crucis ....D 2
16 Ampney St. Mary ...D 2
16 Ampney St. Peter ..D 2
8 Amport .... B 4
25 Ampthill .... L 1
27 Ampton .... H 2
12 Amroth .... F 5
52 Amulree .... C 4
62 An Caol .... C 5
62 An Coroghon .... H 2
50 Anaheilt .... A 5
54 Anancaun .... C 4
33 Ancaster .... F 7
21 Anchor .... D 7
49 Ancroft .... E 12
49 Ancroft Northmoor
         E 12
49 Ancrum .... G 9
33 Anderby .... C 12
7 Anderson .... F 12
30 Anderton .... C 5
8 Andover .... B 5
8 Andover Down .... B 5
16 Andoversford .... B 1
38 Andreas .... F 2
52 Angansk .... F 6
2 Angarrak .... F 3
16 Angle .... G 2
38 Anglers' Hotel ....D 3
28 Anglesey .... C 4
9 Angmering .... F 12
9 Angmering-on-Sea
         F 12
39 Angram, N. Yorks.
         E 11
36 Angram, N. Yorks.
         B 3
52 Anie .... F 1
56 Ankerville .... B 4
37 Anlaby .... D 8
24 Anmer .... C 8
8 Anna Valley .... B 5
43 Annan .... E 12
38 Annaside .... G 3
54 Annat, Highland ...D 3
51 Annat, Strathclyde
         E 7
47 Annathill .... B 12
47 Annbank .... G 9
47 Annbank Station ..G 9
32 Annesley Woodhouse
         E 2
58 Annfield .... F 3
45 Annfield Plain ....H 10
45 Annitsford .... F 11
21 Annscroft .... B 10
45 Annstead .... D 12
7 Ansford .... C 10
22 Ansley .... C 6
31 Anslow .... H 10
31 Anslow Gate .... H 10
9 Anstey, Hants. ....B 8
25 Anstey, Herts. ....M 5
23 Anstey, Leics. ....A 9
53 Anstruther Easter .G 10
53 Anstruther Wester .G 10
23 Ansty, War. .... D 7
10 Ansty, W. Sussex ..F 2
8 Ansty, Wilts. ....C 1
9 Anthill Common ..E 8
43 Anthorn .... F 12
26 Antingham .... B 6
3 Antony .... D 11
4 Anvil Corner .... E 2
33 Anwick .... E 8
42 Anwoth .... F 6
24 Apes Hall .... F 6
24 Apethorpe .... F 1
33 Apley .... C 8
32 Apperknowle .... B 1
15 Apperley .... B 11
39 Appersett .... F 10
50 Appin House .... C 6
39 Appleby, Cumbria ..C 9
37 Appleby, Humber. ..F 7
22 Appleby Magna ....A 6
22 Appleby Parva ....A 6
18 Appleby Street ....D 3
54 Applecross .... E 1
54 Applecross House ..E 1
4 Appledore, Devon ..C 3
6 Appledore, Devon ..E 4
11 Appledore, Kent ..E 8
11 Appledore Heath ..E 8
16 Appleford .... E 6
8 Appleshaw .... A 4
38 Applethwaite .... C 5
30 Appleton, Ches. ...B 5

40 Appleton, N. Yorks. E 4
16 Appleton, Oxon. ...D 5
36 Appleton Roebuck ..C 3
41 Appleton-le-Moors .F 7
41 Appleton-le-Street .H 7
49 Appletreehall .... H 8
41 Appletreewick ....A 9
6 Appley .... D 4
34 Appley Bridge .... F 4
9 Apse Heath .... H 7
18 Apsley End .... A 1
9 Apuldram .... F 9
58 Aquhythie .... F 5
54 Araid .... D 2
54 Aranarff .... F 3
59 Arbeadie .... H 4
53 Arbirlot .... C 10
17 Arborfield .... G 8
17 Arborfield Cross ...G 8
42 Arbrack .... H 5
53 Arbroath .... C 11
59 Arbuthnott .... K 5
56 Archiestown .... E 8
30 Arclid Green .... D 6
60 Archadail .... A 5
46 Ardachearanbeg ...A 5
50 Ardachoil .... D 4
46 Ardachuple .... A 5
55 Ardachvie .... K 5
50 Ardalanish .... F 1
51 Ardanaiseig .... E 8
54 Ardaneaskan .... F 2
50 Ardanstur .... F 5
52 Ardargie House ....A 5
54 Ardarie .... A 5
54 Ardarroch .... F 2
46 Ardbeg .... C 6
60 Ardcharnich .... G 3
50 Ardchiavaig .... F 1
51 Ardchonnell .... F 7
50 Ardchrishnish .... E 2
52 Ardchullarie More ..F 1
51 Ardchyle .... E 12
53 Ardcross .... G 10
51 Arddarroch .... H 9
21 Arddleen .... A 8
18 Ardeley .... A 3
55 Ardelve .... G 2
47 Arden .... A 8
40 Arden Hall .... F 5
46 Ardencaple Ho. ....F 5
22 Ardens Grafton ....C 4
50 Ardentallan Ho. ....E 5
46 Ardentraive .... B 6
50 Ardeonaig .... D 2
51 Ardess .... H 10
60 Ardessie .... G 2
50 Ardfern .... G 5
51 Ardgartan .... G 10
50 Ardgay .... B 7
47 Ardgowan .... B 7
63 Ardhasig .... G 2
54 Ardheslaig .... D 2
54 Ardinamar .... F 5
60 Ardindrean .... G 3
16 Ardingly .... E 2
16 Ardington .... E 5
55 Ardintoul .... G 2
49 Ardlair .... E 3
46 Ardlamont House ..C 5
50 Ardlarach .... F 5
23 Ardleigh .... M 3
53 Ardler .... C 7
16 Ardley .... A 6
31 Ardlui .... F 10
46 Ardlussa .... A 2
51 Ardmaddy .... D 8
46 Ardmair .... G 3
46 Ardmaleish .... C 6
51 Ardmay .... G 10
21 Ardminish .... E 2
55 Ardmolich .... M 1
61 Ardmore, Highland .H 7
50 Ardmore, Strathclyde
         E 5
47 Ardmore, Strathclyde
         B 8
50 Ardnacross .... C 3
47 Ardnadam .... A 7
56 Ardnagrask .... K 2
55 Ardnamurach .... K 2
50 Ardnastang .... A 5
47 Ardneil .... D 7
51 Ardno .... G 8
58 Ardo House .... E 7
52 Ardoch .... C 6
47 Ardochrig .... E 11
61 Ardochu .... F 7
53 Ardochy House ....J 6
50 Ardow .... B 2
58 Ardoyne .... E 4
46 Ardpatrick .... C 3
46 Ardpatrick House ..C 3
47 Ardpeaton .... A 7

46 Ardrishaig .... A 3
63 Ardröil .... D 1
56 Ardross Castle ....B 2
47 Ardrossan .... E 7
35 Ardsley .... G 12
35 Ardsley East .... E 11
45 Ardslignish .... A 3
52 Ardtalnaig .... C 2
46 Ardtaraig .... A 5
46 Ardtoe .... A 4
52 Ardtrostan .... E 2
50 Arduaine .... F 5
50 Ardullie .... C 1
50 Ardura .... E 4
62 Ardvasar .... H 5
50 Ardvergnish .... E 3
57 Ardverikie .... L 1
63 Ardvey,
  Loch Finsbay .....H 2
63 Ardvey,
  Loch Stockinish ..H 2
51 Ardvorlich,
  Strathclyde ......F 10
52 Ardvorlich, Tayside .E 1
63 Ardvourlie Castle ...F 3
52 Ardwell, Dumf. & Gall.
         G 2
42 Ardwell, Strathclyde
         B 3
22 Areley Kings .... E 2
9 Arford .... B 9
52 Argaty .... G 2
14 Argoed .... D 5
20 Argoed Mill .... F 5
63 Aribruach .... E 6
51 Arichastlich .... D 10
50 Aridhglas .... F 1
54 Arinacrinachd .... D 1
50 Ariogan .... E 6
55 Arisaig .... L 1
55 Arisaig House .... L 1
45 Ariundle .... A 5
36 Arkendale .... A 2
25 Arkesden .... M 6
39 Arkholme .... H 8
39 Arkle Town .... E 12
43 Arkleby .... H 12
54 Arkleton .... D 2
18 Arkley .... D 2
36 Arksey .... F 4
22 Arkwright Town ....C 2
15 Arle .... B 12
38 Arlecdon .... C 3
16 Arlesey .... L 3
21 Arleston .... A 12
30 Arley, Cheshire ....B 5
22 Arley, War. .... C 6
15 Arlingham .... C 10
4 Arlington, Devon ..B 5
10 Arlington, E. Sussex
         G 4
16 Arlington, Glos. ...C 2
4 Arlington Beccott ..B 5
61 Armadale, Highland
         B 8
48 Armadale, Lothian ..C 2
62 Armadale Castle ...H 6
39 Armathwaite .... A 7
39 Arminghall .... E 5
22 Armitage .... A 4
35 Armley .... D 11
22 Armscote .... H 6
25 Armston .... G 2
36 Armthorpe .... G 4
39 Arnburn .... A 8
39 Arncliffe .... H 11
39 Arncliffe Cote .... H 11
46 Arncroach .... G 10
8 Arne .... G 1
22 Arnesby .... C 9
46 Arnicle .... F 2
55 Arnisdale .... H 2
62 Arnish .... C 5
62 Arnisort .... C 3
48 Arniston Engine ...C 6
37 Arnol .... B 4
37 Arnold, Humber. ..C 9
32 Arnold, Notts. ....F 3
39 Arnprior .... H 1
39 Arnside .... G 7
50 Aros Mains .... C 3
8 Arrad Foot .... G 5
37 Arram .... C 8
40 Arrathorne .... F 2
25 Arreton .... G 7
25 Arrington .... K 4
51 Arrivain .... D 10
51 Arrochar .... G 10
22 Arrow .... F 4
56 Artafallie .... E 2
23 Arthington .... D 11
23 Arthingworth .... D 11
20 Arthog .... A 2

58 Arthrath .... D 7
9 Arundel .... E 11
51 Aryhoulan .... A 7
38 Asby .... C 3
37 Asby cum Fenby ...G 7
46 Ascog .... C 6
17 Ascot .... G 10
16 Ascott-under-
  Wychwood ......B 4
40 Asenby .... H 4
32 Asfordby .... H 4
32 Asfordby Hill .... H 4
33 Asgarby, Lincs. ...D 10
24 Asgarby, Lincs. ...A 2
11 Ash, Kent .... B 11
10 Ash, Kent .... B 5
7 Ash, Somerset ....D 8
9 Ash, Surrey .... A 10
4 Ash Bullayne .... E 6
23 Ash Green .... D 7
30 Ash Magna .... F 4
4 Ash Hill .... D 6
6 Ash Priors .... C 5
8 Ash Thomas .... E 3
4 Ash Vale .... A 10
16 Ashampstead .... F 6
27 Ashbacking .... K 5
31 Ashbourne .... F 10
6 Ashbrittle .... D 4
5 Ashburton .... J 6
4 Ashbury, Devon ..E 4
16 Ashbury, Oxon. ....F 4
37 Ashby .... F 7
33 Ashby by Partney ..D 11
33 Ashby de la Launde .E 7
31 Ashby de la Zouch .H 12
26 Ashby Dell .... F 5
23 Ashby Folville ....A 10
23 Ashby Magna .... C 9
23 Ashby Parva .... C 8
33 Ashby Puerorum ..C 10
23 Ashby St. Ledgers .E 9
26 Ashby St. Mary ...E 6
15 Ashchurch .... A 12
14 Ashcombe, Avon ..A 5
6 Ashcombe, Devon ..H 3
7 Ashcott .... C 8
47 Ashcraig .... C 7
17 Ashcroft .... F 8
25 Ashdon .... L 7
9 Ashe .... A 7
19 Asheldham .... D 9
25 Ashen .... L 8
17 Ashendon .... C 8
52 Ashfield, Central ..G 3
13 Ashfield, Dyfed ...D 10
27 Ashfield, Suffolk ..J 5
27 Ashfield Green ....H 6
4 Ashford, Devon ....C 4
8 Ashford, Hants. ....E 3
11 Ashford, Kent ....D 9
17 Ashford, Surrey ...G 11
21 Ashford Bowdler ..E 10
21 Ashford Carbonel .E 10
16 Ashford Hill .... H 6
31 Ashford-in-the-
  Water .... C 10
47 Ashgill .... D 12
39 Ashgillside .... A 10
4 Ashill, Devon .... E 4
26 Ashill, Norfolk ....E 2
6 Ashill, Somerset ..D 6
19 Ashington, Essex ..D 9
45 Ashington,
  Northumb. ......D 10
7 Ashington, Som. ..D 9
9 Ashington,
  W. Sussex ......E 12
49 Ashkirk .... G 7
8 Ashlett .... F 6
15 Ashleworth .... B 11
25 Ashley, Cambs. ....J 8
30 Ashley, Cheshire ..B 6
4 Ashley, Devon ....E 5
15 Ashley, Glos. .... E 12
8 Ashley, Hants. ....C 5
8 Ashley, Hants. ....G 4
11 Ashley, Kent .... C 11
23 Ashley, Northants. .C 11
30 Ashley, Staffs. ....F 6
17 Ashley Green .... D 10
8 Ashley Heath .... F 3
16 Ashmansworth ....H 5
4 Ashmansworthy ..D 2
7 Ashmore .... D 12
4 Ashreigney .... E 5
10 Ashtead .... B 1
30 Ashton, Cheshire ..C 4

2 Ashton, Cornwall ...G 3
21 Ashton, Heref. &
  Worcs. ....F 10
23 Ashton, Northants. G 11
25 Ashton, Northants. .G 2
15 Ashton Common ..H 12
16 Ashton Keynes ....E 2
34 Ashton-in-Makerfield
         G 5
22 Ashton under Hill ..H 3
35 Ashton under Lyne .G 8
34 Ashton-upon-
  Mersey ....H 6
15 Ashton Watering ..G 8
8 Ashurst, Hants. ...E 5
10 Ashurst, Kent ....D 4
10 Ashurst, W. Sussex .F 1
10 Ashurstwood .... D 3
4 Ashwater .... F 3
25 Ashwell, Herts. ....L 4
23 Ashwell, Leics. ...A 12
26 Ashwellthorpe .... F 4
7 Ashwick .... A 9
24 Ashwicken .... D 8
49 Ashybank .... H 8
38 Askam in Furness ..G 4
36 Askern .... F 3
9 Askerswell .... G 9
39 Askham .... C 7
36 Askham Bryan ....B 3
36 Askham Richard ...B 3
62 Asknish .... H 6
39 Askrigg .... F 11
35 Askwith .... B 10
26 Aslackby .... C 2
26 Aslacton .... F 4
32 Aslockton .... F 5
58 Asloun .... F 3
43 Aspatria .... G 12
18 Aspenden .... A 4
23 Aspley Guise .... H 12
17 Aspley Heath .... A 10
34 Aspull .... F 5
36 Asselby .... D 5
22 Asserby .... B 12
27 Assington .... L 2
56 Assynt House .... C 2
31 Astbury .... D 7
23 Astcote .... G 10
21 Asterley .... B 9
21 Asterton .... C 9
16 Asthall .... C 4
16 Asthall Leigh .... C 4
22 Astley, Heref. &
  Worcs. ....E 1
30 Astley, Salop. ......H 4
22 Astley, War. .... C 6
34 Astley Green .... G 6
17 Astley Bridge .... F 6
22 Astley Cross .... E 2
34 Astley Green .... G 6
17 Aston, Berks. ......F 9
30 Aston, Cheshire ...E 5
30 Aston, Cheshire ...B 10
29 Aston, Clwyd ......C 12
31 Aston, Derby ......B 10
21 Aston, Heref. &
  Worcs. ....E 10
21 Aston, Heref. &
  Worcs. ....F 10
18 Aston, Herts. ......B 3
16 Aston, Oxon. ......D 4
30 Aston, Salop. ......D 4
21 Aston, Salop. ......A 11
36 Aston, S. Yorks. ...B 2
31 Aston, Staffs. ......F 6
31 Aston, Staffs. ......G 7
22 Aston, W. Midlands .C 4
17 Aston Abbotts ....B 9
16 Aston Blank .... B 2
21 Aston Botterell ....D 11
22 Aston Cantlow ....F 5
17 Aston Clinton .... C 9
15 Aston Crews .... B 10
15 Aston Cross .... A 12
18 Aston End .... B 3
21 Aston Eyre .... C 12
22 Aston Fields .... E 3
23 Aston Flamville ....C 8
15 Aston Ingham ....B 10
30 Aston juxta Mondrum
         D 5
23 Aston le Walls .... D 9
16 Aston Magna .... A 3
21 Aston on Clun .... D 9
21 Aston Pigott .... B 9
21 Aston Rogers .... B 9
17 Aston Rowant .... D 8
17 Aston Sandford ....D 8
22 Aston Somerville ..H 4
22 Aston Subedge ....H 5
16 Aston Tirrold .... E 5
31 Aston upon Trent .G 12
16 Aston Upthorpe ....E 6

25 Astwick	L 3
25 Astwood	K 1
22 Astwood Bank	F 4
24 Aswarby	B 2
33 Aswardby	C 10
21 Atcham	B 11
27 Athelington	H 5
7 Athelney	C 7
49 Athelstaneford	B 8
4 Atherington, Devon	D 5
9 Atherington, W. Sussex	F 11
22 Atherstone	B6
22 Atherstone on Stour	G 5
34 Atherton	G 5
55 Athnamulloch	G 5
40 Atley Hill	E 3
31 Atlow	E 10
54 Attadale House	F 3
26 Attleborough, Norfolk	F 3
23 Attleborough, War.	C 7
26 Attlebridge	D 4
59 Atton	K 1
49 Attonburn	G 10
37 Atwick	B 9
15 Atworth	H 11
32 Aubourn	D 6
51 Auchachenna	E 7
46 Auchagallon	F 4
57 Auchallater	K 7
42 Auchalton	A 4
57 Auchavan	M 7
46 Auchbroad	A 3
58 Aucheldy	D 6
43 Auchenbainzie	B 9
59 Auchenblae	J 5
47 Auchenbothie Ho.	B 8
43 Auchenbrack	B 8
46 Auchenbreck	A 5
43 Auchencairn, Dumf. & Gall.	C 10
43 Auchencairn, Dumf. & Gall.	F 9
47 Auchencarroch	A 9
43 Auchencrieff	D 10
42 Auchencrosh	D 2
49 Auchencrow	C 11
48 Auchendinny	C 5
47 Auchenfoyle	B 8
43 Auchengibbert	D 9
48 Auchengray	D 3
43 Auchengruith	A 9
58 Auchenhairig	B 1
48 Auchenheath	E 1
42 Auchenmalg	F 3
42 Auchensoul	B 3
42 Auchentibbert	G 2
47 Auchentiber	E 8
47 Auchenvennel	A 8
43 Auchervey	D 8
57 Auchernack	G 6
57 Auchgourish	H 5
46 Auchinadrian	D 2
58 Auchinderran	B 2
51 Auchindrain	G 6
54 Auchindrean	B 6
58 Auchinhove	B 2
58 Auchininna	C 4
42 Auchinleck, Dumf. & Gall.	D 5
47 Auchinleck, Strathclyde	G 10
47 Auchinloch	B 11
52 Auchinner	F 2
58 Auchintender	F 3
59 Auchintoul, Grampian	G 4
58 Auchintoul, Grampian	F 3
58 Auchiries	D 8
58 Auchleven	E 4
48 Auchlochan	F 1
59 Auchlossan	G 3
60 Auchlunachan	H 3
59 Auchlunies	G 6
51 Auchlyne	E 12
58 Auchmacoy	D 7
42 Auchmantle	E 2
47 Auchmillan	F 10
53 Auchmithie	C 11
53 Auchmuirbridge	G 7
59 Auchmull	K 3
51 Auchnacloich Pier	D 7
59 Auchnacree	L 2
55 Auchnadaull	L 5
52 Auchnafree	D 3
56 Auchnagallin	F 6
58 Auchnagatt	G 7
46 Auchnaha	A 4
57 Auchnahannet	G 5
56 Auchnahillin	F 3
42 Auchnotteroch	F 1
59 Aucholzie	H 1
51 Auchrioch	E 10
57 Auchroisk	G 6
59 Auchronie	J 2
42 Auchtascailt	H 3
52 Auchterarder	F 4
53 Auchterhouse	C 8
53 Auchtermuchty	F 7
54 Auchterneed	D 8
53 Auchterteang	G 5
53 Auchtertool	H 7
51 Auchtertyre, Central	E 10
56 Auchtertye, Grampian	D 7
55 Auchtertyre, Highland	G 2
52 Auchtoo	E 1
61 Auckingill	B 12
36 Auckley	G 4
58 Auckmair	E 1
35 Audenshaw	G 8
30 Audlem	F 5
30 Audley	E 6
25 Audley End	L 6
58 Auds	A 4
36 Aughton, Humber.	C 5
34 Aughton, Lancs.	G 3
39 Aughton, Lancs.	H 8
32 Aughton, S. Yorks.	B 2
16 Aughton, Wilts.	H 3
53 Auldallan	A 8
54 Auldearn	D 5
21 Aulden	G 10
43 Auldgirth	C 10
49 Auldhame	A 8
47 Auldhouse	D 11
58 Auldtown	B 3
58 Auldtown of Carnousie	C 4
52 Aulich	A 1
32 Ault Hucknall	D 2
55 Ault-a-chrinn	H 3
60 Aultanrynie	D 4
54 Aultbea	G 1
54 Aultdearg	C 7
56 Aultfearn	E 1
54 Aultgowrie	E 8
54 Aultgrishan	A 1
54 Aultguish Inn	C 7
54 Aulthash	B 1
61 Aultiphurst	A 8
58 Aultmore	B 1
54 Aultnagoire	G 1
56 Aultnamain Inn	B 2
57 Aultnancaber	H 5
55 Aultnaslat	J 5
58 Aulton	E 3
54 Aultonrea	H 1
57 Aundorach	H 5
6 Aunk	F 4
24 Aunsby	B 1
15 Aust	E 9
17 Austenwood	E 10
58 Austerfield	H 4
35 Austonley	F 9
22 Austrey	B 6
35 Austwick	H 10
33 Authorpe	B 11
33 Authorpe Row	C 12
18 Avebury	G 2
18 Aveley	F 6
15 Avening	E 12
52 Avenuehead	H 3
32 Averham	E 5
5 Aveton Gifford	L 6
57 Avielochan	H 5
57 Aviemore	H 4
46 Avinagillan	C 3
16 Avington, Berks.	G 5
16 Avington, Hants.	C 7
56 Avoch	D 3
16 Avon, Co.	F 1
15 Avon	F 9
23 Avon Dassett	G 7
48 Avonbridge	B 2
15 Avonmouth	F 8
5 Avonwick	K 6
8 Awbridge	D 5
42 Awhirk	F 2
15 Awkley	F 9
6 Awliscombe	H 5
15 Awre	D 10
32 Awsworth	F 2
7 Axbridge	A 8
9 Axford, Hants.	B 7
16 Axford, Wilts.	G 3
6 Axminster	F 6
6 Axmouth	G 6
40 Aycliffe	C 3
45 Aydon	F 8
15 Aylburton	D 9
44 Ayle	H 5
6 Aylesbeare	G 4
17 Aylesbury	C 9
4 Aylescott	D 5
10 Aylesford	B 6
11 Aylsham	C 11
23 Aylestone	B 9
26 Aylmerton	B 5
26 Aylsham	C 5
15 Aylton	A 9
21 Aymestrey	F 9
16 Aynho	A 6
18 Ayot St. Lawrence	B 2
18 Ayot St. Peter	B 2
47 Ayr	G 8
39 Aysgarth	F 12
6 Ayshford	E 4
38 Ayside	G 6
23 Ayston	B 12
18 Aythorpe Roding	B 6
49 Ayton	C 11
40 Azerley	H 3
5 Babbacombe	J 8
30 Babbinswood	G 2
7 Babcary	C 9
13 Babel	C 11
29 Babell	C 11
7 Babington	A 10
25 Babraham	K 6
32 Babworth	B 4
63 Back	C 6
55 Back of Keppcoh	L 1
64 Backaland	B 3
64 Backaskaill	A 3
38 Backbarrow	G 6
58 Blackburn	D 3
12 Backe	E 6
58 Backfolds	B 8
30 Backford	C 3
30 Backford Cross	C 3
58 Backhill, Grampian	D 5
58 Backhill, Grampian	F 5
58 Backhill, Grampian	D 7
58 Backhill of Clackriach	C 7
58 Backhill of Fortree	D 7
59 Backhill of Trustach	H 4
61 Backies	F 8
53 Blackmuir of New Gilston	F 9
15 Backwell	G 8
45 Backworth	F 11
18 Bacon End	B 6
26 Baconsthorpe	B 4
15 Bacton, Heref. & Worcs.	A 7
26 Bacton, Norfolk	B 6
27 Bacton, Suffolk	J 3
35 Bacup	E 7
54 Badachro	B 2
60 Badagyle	F 2
61 Badanloch Lodge	A 8
54 Badavanich	D 5
16 Badbury	F 3
23 Badby	F 9
60 Badcall, Highland	G 2
60 Badcall, Highland	C 3
60 Badcall, Loch Inchard, Highland	B 4
31 Baddeley Green	E 8
22 Baddesley Ensor	B 6
60 Baddidarach	E 2
15 Baddington	B 12
56 Baddock	D 4
58 Badenyon	F 1
7 Badford Peverell	G 10
22 Badger	B 1
10 Badger's Mount	B 4
15 Badgeworth	B 12
7 Badgworth	A 7
55 Badicaul	G 1
27 Badingham	H 6
60 Badintagairt	F 5
11 Badlesmere	C 9
60 Badluchrach	G 2
60 Badnabay	C 3
60 Badnambiast	M 3
56 Badnonan	F 5
60 Badrallach	G 2
22 Badsey	H 4
9 Badshot Lea	A 10
36 Badsworth	F 2
27 Badwell Ash	H 3
33 Bag Enderby	C 10
7 Bagber	E 11
40 Bagby	G 5
16 Bagendon	C 1
29 Bagillt	C 11
23 Baginton	E 7
13 Baglan	H 10
30 Bagley	G 3
31 Bagnal	E 8
16 Bagnor	G 5
17 Bagshot, Surrey	H 10
16 Bagshot, Wilts.	H 4
15 Bagstone	F 10
26 Bagthorpe, Norf.	B 1
32 Bagthorpe, Notts.	E 2
23 Bagworth	A 8
15 Bagwy Llydiart	B 8
35 Baildon	C 10
46 Baile Boidheach	B 2
50 Baile Mor	F 11
57 Bailebeag	H 1
44 Baileyhead	E 3
44 Bailliehill	D 1
47 Baillieston	C 11
58 Bailliesward	D 2
39 Bainbridge	F 11
58 Bainshole	D 4
24 Bainton, Cambs.	E 2
37 Bainton, Humberside	B 7
44 Bairnkine	B 5
18 Baker Street	F 6
18 Baker's End	B 4
44 Bakethin	D 4
31 Bakewell	C 10
29 Bala	G 8
52 Balado	G 6
63 Balallan	E 4
56 Balalochan	B 1
50 Balarumindubh	H 1
57 Balavil	J 3
57 Balbeg	G 1
57 Balbeggie	D 6
58 Balbithan	F 5
56 Balblair, Highland	E 1
56 Balblair, Highland	C 3
43 Balcary	G 9
21 Balchedre	C 8
58 Balchers	A 4
60 Balchladich	D 2
56 Balchraggan	F 1
58 Balchreick	B 3
10 Balcombe	E 2
53 Balcurvie	G 8
9 Balder Head	C 11
40 Baldersby	G 4
40 Baldersby St. James	G 4
34 Balderstone	D 5
30 Balderton	A 5
53 Baldinnie	F 9
25 Baldock	M 3
53 Baldovie	D 9
38 Baldrine	G 2
38 Baldslow	G 7
38 Baldwin	G 2
44 Baldwinholme	H 2
30 Baldwins Gate	F 6
26 Bale	B 3
58 Balearn	B 8
48 Balerno	C 4
59 Balfeith	K 5
59 Balfield	K 3
64 Balfour	C 3
47 Balfron	A 10
58 Balgaveny	D 4
43 Balgerran	E 8
52 Balgonar	H 5
58 Balgove	D 6
57 Balgowan	K 2
62 Balgown	A 3
53 Balgray	C 9
43 Balgrayhill	C 12
47 Balgrochan	B 11
54 Balgy	D 2
52 Balhaldie	G 3
58 Balhalgardy	E 5
18 Balham	G 3
53 Balharry	C 7
64 Baliasta	A 8
61 Baligill	A 8
56 Balintore, Highland	B 4
53 Balintore, Tayside	A 7
56 Balintraid	C 3
57 Balintuim	K 7
52 Balintyre	B 2
53 Balkeerie	C 8
36 Balkholme	D 6
42 Balkissock	C 2
30 Ball	E 6
16 Ball Hill	H 5
38 Ballabeg	H 1
38 Ballacannell	G 2
38 Ballacarnane Beg	G 1
38 Ballachlaggan	H 4
59 Ballachrosk	H 1
51 Ballachulish Ho.	B 7
38 Ballacuberagh	G 2
43 Ballaggan	B 9
38 Ballajora	G 3
38 Ballakaigan	H 1
38 Ballaleigh	G 1
38 Ballantrae	C 2
63 Ballantrushal	B 5
19 Ballards Gore	E 9
38 Ballasalla, I.o.M.	F 2
38 Ballasalla, I.o.M.	H 1
59 Ballater	H 1
38 Ballaugh	G 2
56 Ballchraggan	B 3
57 Ballcorah	G 7
53 Ballechin	B 4
49 Ballencrieff	B 7
46 Ballianlay	C 5
58 Balliemore	E 5
38 Ballig	G 1
52 Balikinrain Castle	H 1
56 Ballimeanoch	F 7
51 Ballimore	F 12
56 Ballindalloch	F 7
58 Ballindean	D 7
27 Ballingdon	L 2
17 Ballinger Com.	D 10
15 Ballingham	A 9
59 Ballingry	G 6
56 Ballinlagg	F 6
57 Ballinluig, Highland	G 6
52 Ballinluig, Tayside	B 5
52 Ballintean	J 4
52 Ballintuim	B 6
42 Ballminnoch	E 4
56 Balloan	E 2
56 Balloch, Highland	E 3
47 Balloch, Strathclyde	A 9
59 Ballochan	H 3
42 Ballochbroe	A 4
42 Ballochdoan	D 2
42 Ballochdowan	D 2
53 Ballochford	D 1
46 Ballochgoy	C 6
42 Ballochmorrie	C 3
54 Ballochroy	D 2
59 Ballogie	H 3
9 Balls Cross	D 11
10 Ball's Green	D 4
50 Ballygown	C 2
50 Ballymeanoch	H 5
58 Balmacara	G 2
43 Balmaclellan	D 7
52 Balmacneil	B 5
58 Balmacolm	F 8
62 Balmacquien	A 4
43 Balmae	G 7
51 Balmaha	H 11
50 Balmaneach	D 2
43 Balmangan	G 7
58 Balmedie	F 7
53 Balmerino	E 8
8 Balmerlawn	F 5
56 Balmore, Highland	F 7
62 Balmore, Skye, Highland	D 2
47 Balmore, Strathclyde	B 11
52 Balmore, Tayside	A 4
53 Balmuchy	B 4
53 Balmule	H 7
53 Balmullo	E 9
56 Balmungie	D 3
42 Balmurrie	E 3
59 Balnaboth	K 1
56 Balnabruaich	C 3
56 Balnabual	E 3
61 Balnacoil Lodge	F 8
54 Balnacra	E 3
56 Balnacraig	F 1
56 Balnafoich	F 2
56 Balnagall	B 4
56 Balnageith	D 6
59 Balnagowan	G 2
54 Balnaguard	B 4
56 Balnaguisich	C 2
55 Balnain	G 8
60 Balnakeil	A 5
62 Balnaknock	B 3
56 Balnapaling	C 4
52 Balquhan	H 2
51 Balquhidder	E 12
22 Balsall	E 6
22 Balsall Common	D 6
23 Balscott	H 7
25 Balsham	K 7
64 Balsound	A 8
30 Balterley	E 6
42 Baltersan	E 5
58 Balthangie	C 6
7 Baltonsborough	C 8
50 Balure	C 6
50 Balvack	F 4
56 Balvaird	D 1
58 Balvenie	C 1
50 Balvicar	F 5
55 Balvraid, Highland	H 2
56 Balvraid, Highland	F 4
34 Bamber Bridge	E 4
18 Bamber's Green	B 6
45 Bamburgh	D 12
53 Bamff	B7
48 Bamflatt	F 3
31 Bamford	B 10
39 Bampton, Cumbria	C 7
6 Bampton, Devon	D 3
16 Bampton, Oxon.	D 4
39 Bampton Grange	C 7
55 Banavie	M 5
23 Banbury	H 8
21 Bancffosfelen	F 8
59 Banchory, Grampian	G 7
59 Banchory, Grampian	H 4
13 Bancycapel	E 7
12 Banc-y-felin	E 6
13 Banc-c-ffordd	C 7
53 Bandirran House	D 7
58 Banff	A 4
28 Bangor	C 5
30 Bangor-Is-coed	F 3
26 Banham	G 4
8 Bank, Hants.	E 4
21 Bank, Powys	A 8
35 Bank Newton	B 8
21 Bank Street	F 11
43 Bankend, Dumf. & Gall.	E 11
48 Bankend, Strathclyde	F 1
47 Bankfoot, Strathclyde	B 7
52 Bankfoot, Tayside	D 5
47 Bankglen	H 11
58 Bankhead, Grampian	F 6
59 Bankhead, Grampian	G 4
45 Bankhead, Northumb.	B 8
47 Bankhead, Strathclyde	D 8
48 Bankhead, Strathclyde	E 3
58 Banknock	B 12
44 Banks, Cumb.	F 4
34 Banks, Lancs.	E 3
43 Bankshill	C 12
26 Banningham	C 5
19 Bannister Green	B 7
52 Bannockburn	H 3
10 Banstead	B 1
5 Bantham	L 5
47 Banton	B 12
15 Banwell	H 7
11 Bapchild	B 8
50 Barachandroman	E 4
47 Barassie	F 8
50 Baravullin	D 6
56 Barbaraville	C 3
31 Barber Booth	B 9
47 Barbieston	H 9
39 Barbon	G 8
50 Barbreck House	G 5
4 Barbrook	A 6
23 Barby	E 9
51 Barcaldine	C 7
43 Barcaple	F 7
24 Barchesten	H 6
47 Barclaugh	G 9
43 Barclosh	E 9
10 Barcombe	G 3
10 Barcombe Cross	F 3
40 Barden	F 2
35 Barden Scale	A 9
42 Bardennoch	B 6
64 Bardister	C 7
61 Bardnabeinne	G 7
33 Bardney	C 8
23 Bardon	A 8
44 Bardon Mill	G 6
47 Bardowie	B 10
47 Bardrainney	B 8
38 Bardsea	H 5
35 Bardsey	C 12
27 Bardwell	H 2
49 Barelees	F 11
21 Barewood	G 9
46 Barfad	B 4
26 Barford, Norfolk	E 4
22 Barford, War.	F 6
16 Barford St. John	A 5
8 Barford St. Martin	C 2
16 Barford St. Michael	A 5
11 Barfreston	C 11
42 Bargaly	E 5
47 Barglas	A 8

14 Bargoed ....D 5
42 Bargrennan ......D 4
51 Barguillean Farm ..E 7
25 Barham, Cambs...H 2
11 Barham, Kent ....C 10
27 Barham, Suffolk ..K 4
43 Barharrow ....F 7
24 Barholm ....D 2
44 Barhough ....H 5
23 Barkby ....A 9
23 Barkby Thorpe ....A 9
32 Barkestone ......G 5
17 Barkham ....G 9
18 Barking, London ..E 5
27 Barking, Suffolk ..K 4
27 Barking Tye ......K 4
35 Barkisland ....E 9
32 Barkston, Lincs. ..G 5
36 Barkston, N. Yorks..D 3
25 Barkway ....M 5
42 Barlae ....F 4
31 Barlaston ....F 7
43 Barlay ....D 7
32 Barlborough ......C 2
36 Barlby ....D 4
23 Barlestone ....B 8
25 Barley, Herts. ....L 5
35 Barley, Lancs. ....C 7
45 Barley Mow ......H 11
45 Barleyhill ....H 8
23 Barleythorpe .....A 11
19 Barling ....E 9
32 Barlow, Derby ....C 1
36 Barlow, N. Yorks. .D 4
45 Barlow, Tyne &
   Wear ....G 9
36 Barmby Moor .....B 5
36 Barmby on the Marsh
   D 5
26 Barmer ....B 1
49 Barmoor Castle ..E 12
49 Barmoor Ridge ..E 12
20 Barmouth ....A 2
40 Barmpton ....C 3
37 Barmston ....A 9
43 Barmurrie ....D 7
51 Barnacarry ......H 7
24 Barnack ....E 2
23 Barnacle ....D 7
51 Barnaline ....F 7
39 Barnard Castle ..C 12
25 Barnardiston ....K 8
43 Barnbarroch .....F 9
36 Barnburgh ....G 3
26 Barnby ....F 8
36 Barnby Dun ......F 4
32 Barnby in the Willows
   E 6
32 Barnby Moor .....B 4
42 Barncorkrie .....H 2
18 Barnes ....F 2
10 Barness Street ...C 5
24 Barnet ....D 3
37 Barnetby le Wold ..F 8
26 Barney ....B 3
27 Barnham, Suffolk ..G 2
9 Barnham, W. Sussex
   F 11
26 Barnham Broom ...E 4
59 Barnhead ....L 4
56 Barnhill ....D 7
42 Barnhills ....D 1
40 Barningham, Dur. ..D 1
27 Barningham, Suff. .H 3
37 Barnoldby le Beck
   G 10
35 Barnoldswick ....C 7
9 Barns Green ....C 12
16 Barnsley, Glos. ..D 2
35 Barnsley, S. Yorks. .F 12
4 Barnstaple ......C 4
18 Barnston, Essex ..B 6
30 Barnston,
   Merseyside .....B 1
32 Barnstone ....G 4
22 Barnt Green .....E 4
30 Barnton ....C 5
25 Barnwell All Saints .G 2
25 Barnwell St. Andrew
   G 2
15 Barnwood ....C 11
21 Barons' Cross ...G 10
47 Barr, Dumf. & Gall.
   H 12
43 Barr, Dumf. & Gall..B 9
42 Barr, Strathclyde ..B 4
58 Barra Castle .....E 5
43 Barrachan ....G 4
50 Barrachrail ......E 5
63 Barraglom ....D 3
45 Barrasford ....F 7
50 Barravullin ......G 5
38 Barregaroow .....G 2
47 Barrhead ....D 10

42 Barrhill ....C 3
25 Barrington, Cambs. .K 5
7 Barrington, Som. ..D 7
2 Barripper ....F 3
55 Barrisdale ....J 3
47 Barrmill ....D 8
61 Barrock ....A 11
34 Barrow, Lancs. ...C 6
23 Barrow, Leics. ...A 12
21 Barrow, Salop. ...B 12
7 Barrow, Som. ....C 10
27 Barrow, Suffolk ...J 1
15 Barrow Gurney ...G 8
37 Barrow Haven ....E 8
32 Barrow Hill ......C 1
32 Barrow-in-Furness .H 5
34 Barrow Nook .....G 3
32 Barrow Street ...C 11
37 Barrow-upon-Humber
   E 8
32 Barrow-upon-Soar .H 3
31 Barrow-upon-Trent
   G 12
45 Barrowburn ......B 7
32 Barrowby ....G 6
41 Barrowcliff ......F 10
23 Barrowden ....B 12
35 Barrowford ......C 7
30 Barrows Green ...D 5
51 Barrs ....D 8
14 Barry, S. Glam. ...G 4
53 Barry, Tayside ...D 10
23 Barsby ....A 10
26 Barsham ....F 7
22 Barston ....D 5
21 Bartestree ....H 11
58 Barthol Chapel ..D 6
30 Barthomley ......E 6
34 Bartle Hall ......D 4
49 Bartlehill ....E 10
8 Bartley ....E 4
25 Bartlow ....L 7
7 Barton, Avon .....A 7
25 Barton, Cambs....K 5
30 Barton, Cheshire .D 4
39 Barton, Cumbria ..C 7
5 Barton, Devon .....J 8
16 Barton, Glos. ....B 2
34 Barton, Lancs. ....C 6
34 Barton, Lancs. ....F 2
40 Barton, N. Yorks...D 3
22 Barton, War. .....G 4
24 Barton Bendish ..E 8
26 Barton Common ..C 7
15 Barton End ......E 11
17 Barton Hartshorn ..A 7
32 Barton in Fabis ..G 2
23 Barton-in-the-Beans
   B 7
25 Barton-in-the-Clay .M 2
25 Barton Mills .....H 8
8 Barton-on-Sea ...G 4
16 Barton-on-the-Heath
   A 4
7 Barton St. David ...C 8
23 Barton Seagrave ..D 12
8 Barton Stacey ...B 6
4 Barton Town .....B 5
37 Barton Waterside ..E 8
41 Barton-le-Street ..H 7
36 Barton-le-Willows .A 5
31 Barton-under-
   Needwood ......H 10
37 Barton-upon-Humber
   E 8
35 Barugh ....F 11
63 Barvas ....B 5
25 Barway ....H 6
23 Barwell ....B 8
7 Barwick ....E 9
36 Barwick in Elmet ..C 2
30 Baschurch ....H 3
23 Basecote ....F 7
31 Basford Green ...E 8
34 Bashall Eaves ...C 6
8 Bashley ....F 4
17 Basildon, Berks. .F 7
19 Basildon, Essex ..E 7
9 Basing ....A 8
9 Basingstoke .....A 7
31 Baslow ....C 11
9 Bason Bridge ....B 7
14 Bassaleg ....F 6
49 Bassendean .....E 9
38 Bassenfell ....B 4
38 Bassenthwaite ...B 5
38 Bassenthwaite Lake
   Station ....B 4
4 Basset's Cross ...F 4
8 Bassett ....D 5
22 Bassett's Pole ...B 5
25 Bassingbourn ....L 4
32 Bassingfield .....F 3
32 Bassingham .....D 6

33 Bassingthorpe ....G 7
64 Basta ....B 7
24 Baston ....D 2
26 Bastwick ....D 7
18 Batchworth Heath ..E 1
7 Batcombe, Dorset ..F 9
7 Batcombe, Som. ..B 10
30 Bate Heath ......B 5
15 Bath ....H 10
15 Bathampton .....H 11
15 Bathealton ......D 4
15 Batheaston ......G 11
15 Bathford ....H 11
48 Bathgate ....B 3
32 Bathley ....D 5
15 Bathpool, Corn. ..B 10
6 Bathpool, Som. ..D 6
7 Bathway ....A 9
35 Batley ....E 11
16 Batsford ....A 3
40 Battersby ....D 6
18 Battersea ....F 3
27 Battisford ....K 4
27 Battisford Tye ...K 3
10 Battle, E. Sussex ..F 6
14 Battle, Powys ....A 3
7 Battleborough ....A 7
21 Battlefield ....A 10
19 Battlesbridge ....D 8
17 Battlesden ......A 10
4 Battleton ....C 3
8 Battramsley ......F 5
9 Batt's Corner ....B 9
26 Baubergh ....F 7
17 Baughurst ....H 7
9 Baulds ....H 4
16 Baulking ....E 4
33 Baumber ....C 9
6 Baunton ....D 1
8 Baverstock ......C 2
26 Bawburgh ....E 5
26 Bawdeswell ......C 3
7 Bawdrip ....B 7
27 Bawdsey ....L 6
53 Bawtry ....A 4
34 Baxenden ....E 6
22 Baxterley ....B 6
9 Baybridge ....D 7
38 Baycliff ....H 5
16 Baydon ....F 4
18 Bayford, Herts. ..C 3
7 Bayford, Som. ...C 10
39 Bayles ....A 9
7 Baylham ....K 4
16 Baynards' Green ..A 6
21 Bayston Hill .....B 10
21 Bayton ....E 12
15 Beach, Avon .....G 10
50 Beach, Highland ..B 5
23 Beachampton ....H 11
24 Beachamwell ....E 8
15 Beachley ....E 9
4 Beacon End ......A 9
8 Beacon Hill, Dor...G 1
9 Beacon Hill, Surrey
   B 10
17 Beacon's Bottom ..E 9
18 Beaconsfield .....E 10
63 Beacravik ....H 2
40 Beadlam ....G 6
45 Beadnell ....D 12
4 Beaford ....D 4
45 Beal, Northumb...B 12
36 Beal, N. Yorks. ...E 3
55 Bealachasan .....H 3
6 Beaminster ......F 8
45 Beamish ....H 10
35 Beamsley ....B 9
10 Bean ....A 5
15 Beanacre ....H 12
45 Beanley ....A 9
4 Beara Moor .....D 4
44 Bearbridge ......G 6
6 Beare ....F 3
10 Beare Green ....D 1
9 Bearl ....G 9
22 Bearley ....F 5
50 Bearnus ....C 1
6 Bearpark ....A 3
47 Bearsden ....B 10
11 Bearsted ....C 7
6 Bearwood ....F 2
6 Beasley ....B 3
43 Beattock ....A 11
27 Beattock Summit ..H 3
18 Beauchamp Roding .C 6
32 Beauchief ....B 1
8 Beaulieu ....F 5
56 Beauly ....E 1
14 Beaumaris ....C 5
44 Beaumont, Cumb. .G 2
19 Beaumont, Essex .A 11
40 Beaumont Hill ...C 3

22 Beausale ....E 6
9 Beauworth ....C 7
4 Beaworthy ....F 3
19 Beazley End .....A 7
30 Bebington ....B 2
45 Bebside ....E 11
26 Beccles ....F 7
34 Becconsall ......E 3
39 Beck Foot ....F 8
41 Beck Hole ....E 8
25 Beck Row ....H 8
38 Beck Side ....G 5
22 Beckbury ....B 1
18 Beckenham ......G 4
43 Beckfoot ....G 11
16 Beckford ....A 1
16 Beckhampton ....G 2
32 Beckingham, Lincs..A 4
32 Beckingham, Notts. .A 5
7 Beckington ......A 11
8 Beckley, Hants. ..F 4
16 Beckley, Oxon. ..C 6
11 Beckley, E. Sussex .F 7
35 Beckwithshaw ....B 11
18 Becontree ....E 5
17 Bedburn ....B 1
7 Bedchester .....D 12
14 Beddau ....F 4
28 Beddgelert ......E 5
10 Beddingham .....G 3
18 Beddington ......G 3
27 Bedfield ....J 5
25 Bedford ....K 2
25 Bedfordshire, Co. ..K 2
9 Bedhampton ......E 8
27 Bedingfield .....H 5
35 Bedlam ....A 11
45 Bedlington ......E 10
14 Bedlinog ....D 4
17 Bedmond ....D 11
31 Bednall ....H 8
49 Bedrule ....H 8
49 Bedshiel ....D 9
21 Bedstone ....E 9
14 Bedwas ....E 5
14 Bedwellty ....D 5
23 Bedworth ....C 7
23 Beeby ....A 10
9 Beech, Hants. ...B 8
31 Beech, Staffs. ...F 7
17 Beech Hill, Berks. ..H 8
39 Beech Hill, Cumb. .E 7
34 Beech Hill,
   Manchester ......F 4
16 Beechingstoke ...H 2
16 Beedon ....F 6
16 Beedon Hill ......F 6
37 Beeford ....B 9
31 Beeley ....C 11
37 Beelsby ....G 9
17 Beenham ....G 7
2 Beeny ....B 1
6 Beer, Devon .....G 6
7 Beer, Somerset ..C 7
7 Beer Hackett ....E 9
7 Beercrocombe ....D 7
7 Beesands ....M 7
33 Beesby ....B 11
5 Beeson ....L 7
25 Beeston, Beds. ...K 3
30 Beeston, Cheshire .D 4
26 Beeston, Norfolk ..D 2
32 Beeston, Notts. ..G 3
35 Beeston, W. Yorks.
   D 11
26 Beeston Regis ...A 5
43 Beeswing ....E 10
39 Beetham ....G 7
26 Beetley ....D 3
14 Began ....F 5
16 Begbroke ....C 5
26 Begdale ....E 6
12 Begelly ....F 5
21 Beggar's Bush ...F 8
26 Beguildy ....D 7
26 Beighton, Norf. ...E 7
32 Beighton, S. Yorks. .B 2
49 Beith ....D 8
11 Bekesbourne ....C 10
26 Belaugh ....D 6
22 Belbroughton ....D 3
27 Belchamp Otten ..L 1
27 Belchamp St. Paul..L 1
27 Belchamp Walter ..L 1
58 Belcherrie ....D 1
27 Belchford ....C 10
53 Belfarg ....G 7
45 Belford ....C 12
45 Belford Mains ...C 12
58 Belhelvie ....F 7
58 Belhinnie ....E 2
18 Bell Bar ....C 3

35 Bell Busk ....B 7
22 Bell Heath ......D 3
58 Bellabeg ....F 1
50 Bellanoch ....H 5
36 Bellasize ....D 6
35 Belle Vue ....E 12
33 Belleau ....B 11
40 Bellerby ....F 1
5 Bellever ....H 5
49 Bellhaven ....B 9
17 Bellingdon ......D 10
45 Bellingham ......E 7
46 Belloch ....F 2
46 Bellochantuy ....F 2
10 Bells Yew Green .D 5
42 Bellsbank ....A 5
45 Bellshill,
   Northumb. ......C 12
47 Bellshill, Strathclyde
   C 12
48 Bellspool ....F 4
48 Bellsquarry ......C 3
42 Bellymore ......C 3
56 Belmaduthy ......D 2
24 Belmesthorpe ....D 1
34 Belmont, Lancs. ..F 5
47 Belmont, Strathclyde
   G 8
64 Belmont, Shetland Is.
   B 8
47 Belmore ....A 7
58 Belnacraig ....F 1
3 Belowda ....D 7
31 Belper ....E 11
31 Belper Lane End ..E 11
45 Belsay ....E 9
27 Belstead ....L 4
27 Belston ....G 9
47 Belston ....G 9
4 Belstone ....F 5
4 Belstone Corner ..F 5
34 Belthorn ....E 6
11 Beltinge ....A 10
44 Beltingham ......G 6
32 Belton, Leics. ...H 2
23 Belton, Leics. ...B 11
36 Belton, Humber. ..F 6
32 Belton, Lincs. ...F 6
26 Belton, Norfolk ..E 8
32 Belvoir ....G 5
11 Bembridge ....G 8
49 Bemersyde ....F 8
8 Bemerton ....C 3
41 Bempton ....H 12
61 Ben Armine Lodge ..E 7
63 Ben Casgro .....D 5
27 Benacre ....G 8
57 Benalder Lodge ..L 1
43 Benbruie ....B 8
48 Bendameer ......A 5
54 Bendronaig Lodge .F 4
24 Benefield ....F 1
11 Benenden ....E 7
42 Benfield ....E 5
27 Benfield Green ...J 7
45 Benfieldside ....H 9
43 Bengall ....D 12
26 Bengate ....C 6
22 Bengeworth ......H 4
59 Benholm ....K 5
36 Beningbrough ....A 3
18 Benington, Herts. .B 3
33 Benington, Lincs. .E 11
33 Benington Sea End .F 11
28 Benllech ....B 4
46 Benmore ....A 6
60 Benmore Lodge ..F 4
5 Bennacott ....G 2
46 Bennecarrigan ...G 4
33 Benniworth ......B 9
10 Benover ....C 6
17 Benson ....E 7
47 Benston ....H 10
59 Bent ....K 4
45 Benthall,
   Northumb. ......D 12
21 Benthall, Salop. ..B 12
15 Bentham ....C 12
59 Benthoul ....G 5
9 Bentley, Hants. ..B 8
37 Bentley, Humber. .D 8
36 Bentley, S. Yorks. .G 3
22 Bentley, War. ....C 6
22 Bentley Heath ...D 5
4 Benton ....B 5
46 Benton Polliwilline .H 2
44 Bentpath ....D 2
24 Bentwick ....F 4
24 Bentwitchen ....C 6
9 Bentworth ......B 8
42 Beoch, Dumf. &
   Gall. ....E 2
42 Beoch, Strathclyde ..B 6
22 Beoley ....E 4

55 Beoraidberg .....K 1
9 Bepton ....D 10
18 Berden ....A 5
5 Bere Alston ......J 3
5 Bere Ferrers .....J 3
7 Bere Regis ......G 11
2 Berepper ....G 4
26 Bergh Apton .....E 6
17 Berinsfield ......E 7
17 Berkeley ....D 10
7 Berkley ....A 11
18 Berkhamstead ...C 10
28 Berkshire, Co. ...F 5
22 Berkswell ....D 6
18 Bermondsey .....F 3
27 Berners ....G 2
62 Bernisdale ......C 3
17 Berrick Salome ..E 7
61 Berriedale ......E 10
38 Berrier ....B 6
21 Berriew ....B 7
49 Berrington, Northumb.
   E 12
21 Berrington, Salop. .B 10
49 Berringtonlaw ...E 12
6 Berrow ....A 6
22 Berrow Green ...F 1
4 Berry Cross .....D 3
4 Berry Down Cross ..B 4
12 Berry Hill, Dyfed ..C 4
15 Berry Hill, Glos. ..C 9
5 Berry Pomeroy ..K 7
58 Berryhillock .....B 2
4 Berrynarbor .....A 4
18 Berry's Green ...H 4
43 Berryscaur ......C 7
59 Berrysloch ......H 3
29 Bersham ....E 11
20 Berthddu ....H 4
7 Berwick, Dorset ..G 8
10 Berwick, E. Sussex ..H 4
21 Berwick Bassett ..G 2
45 Berwick Hill ....F 10
8 Berwick St. James ..B 2
8 Berwick St. John ..C 2
7 Berwick St. Leonard
   C 12
49 Berwick-upon-Tweed
   D 12
29 Berwyn ....F 11
32 Bescaby ....G 5
34 Bescar ....F 3
22 Besford ....H 3
4 Bessacarr ......G 4
16 Bessels Green ...C 4
16 Bessels Leigh ...D 5
26 Bessingby ....A 9
26 Bessingham .....B 4
10 Best Beech Hill ..E 5
26 Besthorpe, Norf. .F 4
32 Besthorpe, Notts. .D 5
37 Beswick ....B 8
20 Betchworth .....C 1
20 Bethania, Dyfed ..F 1
28 Bethania, Gwynedd .F 6
28 Bethel, Gwynedd ..C 3
28 Bethel, Gwynedd ..D 5
29 Bethel, Gwynedd ..F 9
11 Bethersden ......D 8
12 Bethesda, Dyfed ..E 4
28 Bethesda, Gwynedd D 6
13 Bethlehem ......D 10
18 Bethnal Green ...F 3
30 Betley ....E 6
10 Betsham ....A 5
11 Betteshanger ...C 11
7 Bettiscombe .....F 7
30 Bettisfield ......G 3
30 Betton ....G 5
14 Bettws ....F 2
20 Bettws Bledrws ..G 2
12 Bettws Evan .....B 6
15 Bettws Newydd ...D 7
61 Bettyhill ....B 7
13 Betws ....F 9
21 Betws Cedewain ..C 7
28 Betws Garmon ...D 5
29 Betws Gwerfil Goch .F 9
29 Betws-y-coed ....E 7
29 Betws-yn-Rhos ...C 8
12 Beulah, Dyfed ...B 6
20 Beulah, Powys ...G 5
32 Bevercotes ......C 4
28 Beverley ....C 8
51 Beverstone ......E 11
15 Bevington ......E 10
38 Bewaldeth ....B 4
44 Bewcastle ......E 1
35 Bewerley ....A 10
37 Bewholme ....B 9
49 Bewlie ....G 6
10 Bexhill ....G 6
18 Bexley ....F 5

18 Bexleyheath ....F 5
24 Bexwell ....E 7
27 Beyton ....J 2
27 Beyton Green ....J 2
16 Bibury ....C 2
17 Bicester ....B 7
22 Bickenhill ....D 5
24 Bicker ....B 3
34 Bickerstaffe ....G 3
30 Bickerton, Ches. ....E 4
45 Bickerton, Northumb. ....C 8
36 Bickerton, N. Yorks. ....B 2
4 Bickingcott ....C 6
4 Bickington, Devon ....C 4
5 Bickington, Devon ...H 7
6 Bickleigh, Devon ...E 3
5 Bickleigh, Devon ...J 4
4 Bickleton ....C 4
30 Bickley Moss ....E 4
19 Bicknacre ....D 8
6 Bicknoller ....B 5
11 Bicknor ....B 7
8 Bickton, Hants. ....E 3
21 Bicton, Heref. & Worc. ....F 10
21 Bicton, Salop ....B 9
21 Bicton, Salop ...A 10
11 Biddenden ....D 7
11 Biddenden Green ...D 7
25 Biddenham ....K 1
15 Biddestone ....G 11
7 Biddisham ....A 7
23 Biddlesden ....H 9
45 Biddlestone ....B 8
31 Biddulph ....D 7
31 Biddulph Moor ...D 7
4 Bideford ....C 3
22 Bidford-on-Avon ..G 4
10 Bidorough ....D 4
6 Bidwell ....F 3
36 Bielby ....C 5
59 Bieldside ....G 6
8 Bierley, I.of Wight...H 6
35 Bierley, W. Yorks. ..D 10
17 Bierton ....C 9
43 Big Corlae ....B 7
54 Big Sand ....B 1
5 Bigbury ....L 5
5 Bigbury-on-Sea ...L 5
37 Bigby ....H 6
34 Biggar, Lancs. ....A 1
48 Biggar, Strathclyde ..F 3
48 Biggarshiels Mains ..E 3
31 Biggin, Derby ....E 11
31 Biggin, Derby ...D 10
36 Biggin, N. Yorks. ...D 3
18 Biggin Hill ....H 4
25 Biggleswade ....L 3
9 Bighton ....C 7
9 Bignor ....E 11
64 Bigton ....F 7
11 Bilberry ....D 7
32 Bilborough ....F 3
6 Bilbrook ....B 4
36 Bilbrough ....C 3
32 Bilby ....B 4
27 Bildeston ....K 3
3 Billacott ....A 9
19 Billericay ....D 7
32 Billesdon ....B 10
22 Billesley ....F 5
24 Billingborough ....B 2
34 Billinge ....G 4
27 Billingford ....G 5
26 Billingford ....C 3
40 Billingham ....C 5
33 Billinghay ....E 8
36 Billingley ....G 2
9 Billinghurst ....C 12
21 Billingsley ....D 12
17 Billington, Beds....B 10
34 Billington, Lancs...D 6
26 Billockby ....D 7
40 Billy Row ....A 2
34 Bilsborrow ....C 4
33 Bilsby ....C 11
9 Bilsham ....F 11
11 Bilsington ....E 9
15 Bilson Green ....C 9
32 Bilsthorpe ....D 4
48 Bilston, Lothian ..C 5
22 Bilston, W. Midlands
   B 3
23 Bilstone ....B 7
11 Bilting ....C 9
45 Bilton, Northumb. ..B 10
37 Bilton, Humber. ..D 9
36 Bilton, N. Yorks. ...B 3
23 Bilton, W. Midlands .E 8
45 Bilton Banks ....B 10
64 Bimbister ....C 2
37 Binbrook ....H 10

7 Bincombe ....H 10
61 Bindal ....H 9
7 Binegar ....A 9
17 Binfield ....G 9
17 Binfield Heath ....F 8
45 Bingfield ....F 8
32 Bingham ....F 4
7 Bingham's Melcombe
   F 11
35 Bingley ....C 10
26 Binham ....B 3
8 Binley ....A 6
48 Binniehill ....B 1
40 Binsoe ....G 3
9 Binstead ....G 7
9 Binsted ....B 9
22 Binton ....G 5
26 Bintree ....C 3
21 Binweston ....B 8
19 Birch, Essex ....B 9
35 Birch, Manchester ..F 7
19 Birch Green ....B 9
31 Birch Vale ....B 8
26 Bircham Newton ...B 1
26 Bircham Tofts ....B 1
18 Birchanger ....B 5
21 Bircher ....F 10
57 Birchfield ....G 5
14 Birchgrove, Cardiff,
   S. Glam. ....F 5
13 Birchgrove, W. Glam.
   G 10
11 Birchington ....A 11
31 Birchover ....D 10
32 Bircotes ....A 3
22 Bird End ....C 4
25 Birdbrook ....L 8
9 Birdham ....F 9
23 Birdingbury ....E 8
15 Birdlip ....C 12
36 Birdsall ....A 6
22 Birdsgreen ....D 1
7 Birdsmoor Gate ...F 7
47 Birdston ....B 11
35 Birdwell ....G 12
15 Birdwood ....B 10
49 Birgham ....E 10
34 Birkacre ....F 4
40 Birkby ....E 3
34 Birkdale ....F 2
30 Birkenhead ....A 2
58 Birkenhills ....C 5
47 Birkenshaw,
   Strathclyde .....D 12
35 Birkenshaw,
   W. Yorks........D 10
59 Birkhall ....H 1
49 Birkhill, Borders ...E 8
48 Birkhill, Borders ...H 5
51 Birkhill, Tayside ...D 8
36 Birkin ....D 3
44 Birks ....E 6
43 Birkshaw ....C 9
21 Birley ....G 10
10 Birling, Kent ....B 5
45 Birling, Northumb. B 10
22 Birlingham ....H 3
22 Birmingham ....D 5
52 Birnam ....G 3
47 Birnieknowe ....G 10
59 Birse ....H 3
59 Birsemore ....H 3
23 Birstall, Leics. ....A 9
35 Birstall, W. Yorks. .E 11
35 Birstwith ....A 11
24 Birthorpe ....B 2
48 Birthwood ....F 3
21 Birtley, Heref. &
   Worc. ....E 9
45 Birtley, Northumb...E 7
45 Birtley, Tyne &
   Wear ....G 11
15 Birts Street ....A 11
23 Bisbrooke ....B 12
4 Bish Mill ....C 6
17 Bisham ....F 9
21 Bishampton ....G 3
40 Bishop Auckland ...B 2
37 Bishop Burton ....C 7
40 Bishop Middleham ..B 3
40 Bishop Monkton ...H 3
33 Bishop Norton ....A 7
15 Bishop Sutton ....H 9
35 Bishop Thornton ..A 10
36 Bishop Wilton ....B 6
45 Bishopbridge ....A 7
47 Bishopbriggs ....B 11
56 Bishopmill ....C 8
11 Bishops Cannings ...H 2
21 Bishop's Castle ....D 8
7 Bishop's Caundle ..E 10
15 Bishop's Cleeve ....B 12
21 Bishop's Frome ...G 12
18 Bishop's Green ....B 6

6 Bishop's Hull ....D 5
23 Bishop's Itchington ..F 7
6 Bishop's Lydeard ...C 5
4 Bishop's Nympton ..D 6
30 Bishop's Offley ....G 6
18 Bishop's Stortford ...B 5
9 Bishop's Sutton ....C 7
22 Bishop's Tatchbrook
   F 6
4 Bishop's Tawton ....C 4
9 Bishop's Waltham ...D 7
22 Bishop's Wood ....A 2
11 Bishopsbourne ....C 10
11 Bishopsteignton ...H 8
8 Bishopstoke ....D 6
11 Bishopston ....H 9
17 Bishopstone, Bucks...C 9
10 Bishopstone,
   E. Sussex ....H 4
21 Bishopstone,
   Heref. & Worcs. ...H 9
8 Bishopstone, Wilts. ..C 2
16 Bishopstone, Wilts. .F 3
7 Bishopstrow ....B 11
6 Bishopswood ....E 6
15 Bishopsworth ....G 9
36 Bishopthorpe ....B 4
40 Bishopton, Dur. ....C 4
47 Bishopton,
   Strathclyde ....B 9
15 Bishpool ....E 7
15 Bishton ....F 7
15 Bisley, Glos. ....D 12
17 Bisley, Surrey .....H 10
34 Bispham ....C 2
2 Bissoe ....E 5
4 Bisterne Close ....F 4
33 Bitchfield ....G 7
4 Biteford ....D 2
4 Bittadon ....B 4
5 Bittaford ....K 5
26 Bittering Street ....D 2
21 Bitterley ....E 11
8 Bitterne ....E 6
23 Bitteswell ....D 8
17 Bix ....F 8
64 Bixter ....D 7
23 Blaby ....B 9
16 Black Bourton ....D 4
54 Black Bridge ....C 7
45 Black Callerton ....F 10
42 Black Clauchrie ....C 4
51 Black Corries ....B 10
50 Black Croft ....D 6
4 Black Dog ....E 7
45 Black Heddon ....E 9
51 Black Mount ....C 10
19 Black Notley ....B 7
13 Black Pill ....H 9
4 Black Torrington ....E 3
5 Blackacre ....C 11
49 Blackadder Bank ..D 11
5 Blackawton ....L 7
6 Blackborough ....E 4
24 Blackborough End ..D 8
10 Blackboys ....F 4
31 Blackbrook, Derby.
   E 11
34 Blackbrook,
   Merseyside ....G 4
30 Blackbrook, Staffs. ..F 6
49 Blackburn, Borders .D 8
44 Blackburn, Borders .D 3
58 Blackburn, Grampian
   F 6
34 Blackburn, Lancs. ..D 5
48 Blackburn, Lothian .C 3
48 Blackburn,
   Strathclyde ....G 2
43 Blackcraig ....D 8
4 Blackditch Cross ...E 6
52 Blackdog ....F 7
43 Blackdyke ....F 12
35 Blacker Hill ....G 12
18 Blackfield ....F 6
44 Blackford, Cumb....G 2
7 Blackford, Som. ....B 8
7 Blackford, Som. ...D 10
52 Blackford, Tayside ..F 4
31 Blackfordby ....H 11
8 Blackgang ....H 6
40 Blackhall Colliery ..A 5
45 Blackhall Mill ....G 9
11 Blackham ....D 4
49 Blackhaugh ....E 7
19 Blackheath, Essex ..B 10
27 Blackheath, Suff....H 7
9 Blackheath, Surrey
   B 11
22 Blackheath,
   W. Midlands ....D 3
58 Blackhill, Grampian .B 8
58 Blackhill, Grampian .C 8
62 Blackhill, Highland .C 3

58 Blackhilllock ....C 1
44 Blackhills, Dumf. &
   Gall. ....F 1
56 Blackhills, Grampian
   D 8
15 Blackhorse ....F 10
48 Blackhopebyre ....E 6
16 Blackland ....G 1
43 Blacklaw ....A 11
35 Blackley ....G 7
52 Blacklunans ....A 6
21 Blackmarstone ....H 10
14 Blackmill ....F 3
9 Blackmoor ....C 9
4 Blackmoor Gate ...B 5
25 Blackmore End,
   Essex ....M 8
18 Blackmore End,
   Hertfordshire ...B 2
48 Blackness ....A 3
9 Blacknest ....B 9
35 Blacko ....C 7
43 Blackpark ....C 10
34 Blackpool ....C 2
44 Blackpool Gate ....E 4
48 Blackridge ....C 2
43 Blackrigg ....C 11
14 Blackrock, Gwent ...C 5
15 Blackrock, Gwent ..E 8
34 Blackrod ....F 5
43 Blackshaw ....E 11
35 Blackshaw Head ...D 8
27 Blacksmith's Cnr. ..M 3
10 Blackstone ....F 1
17 Blackthorn ....B 7
27 Blackthorpe ....J 2
36 Blacktoft ....E 6
59 Blacktop ....G 6
2 Blackwater, Corn. ..E 4
17 Blackwater, Hants. .H 9
8 Blackwater, I.o.W. ..G 6
6 Blackwater, Som. ...E 6
27 Blackwater, Suff. ...H 8
58 Blackwater Lodge ..E 1
46 Blackwaterfoot ....G 4
31 Blackwell, Derby ..C 10
32 Blackwell, Derby ...D 2
40 Blackwell, Durham .D 3
6 Blackwell, Som. ....D 4
22 Blackwell, War. ....H 6
43 Blackwood, Dumf. &
   Gall. ....C 10
14 Blackwood, Gwent ..E 5
47 Blackwood,
   Strathclyde ....E 12
31 Blackwood Hill ....E 8
30 Blacon ....C 3
42 Bladnoch ....F 5
16 Bladon ....C 5
13 Blaen Celyn ....B 7
14 Blaen Dyryn ....A 3
12 Blaenannerch ....B 5
28 Blaennau-Dolwyddelan
   E 6
28 Blaenau Ffestiniog ..F 6
14 Blaenavon ....B 6
14 Blaenawey ....B 6
12 Blaen-ffos ....C 5
14 Blaengarw ....E 2
14 Blaengavenny ....B 6
14 Blaengwrach ....D 2
14 Blaengwynfi ....E 2
20 Blaenpennal ....F 2
20 Blaenplwyf ....E 2
12 Blaenporth ....B 6
12 Blaenwaun ....D 6
13 Blaen-y-Coed ....D 7
14 Blaerhondda ....D 3
6 Blagdon Hill ....D 5
15 Blagdon ....H 8
55 Blaich ....M 4
50 Blain ....A 4
14 Blaina ....D 5
58 Blair ....E 6
52 Blair Atholl ....A 4
52 Blair Drummond ...G 2
52 Blairadam ....H 6
48 Blairburn ....A 3
58 Blairdaff ....F 4
52 Blairgowrie ....C 6
52 Blairhall ....H 5
52 Blairingone ....G 5
52 Blairlogie ....G 3
60 Blairmore, Highland
   B 3
47 Blairmore,
   Strathclyde ....A 7
47 Blairnairn ....A 8
57 Blairnamarrow ....H 8
47 Blairquhosh ....A 10
46 Blair's Ferry ....H 8
47 Blairskaith ....B 10
47 Blairvadach ....A 7

15 Blaisdon ....C 10
22 Blakebrook ....D 2
22 Blakedown ....D 2
49 Blakelaw ....F 10
21 Blakemere ....H 9
15 Blakeney, Glos. ...D 10
26 Blakeney, Norfolk ..A 3
30 Blakenhall, Ches. ...E 6
22 Blakenhall,
   W. Midlands ....B 3
22 Blakenhall Heath ...B 4
22 Blakeshall ....D 2
23 Blakesley ....G 9
45 Blanchland ....H 8
35 Bland Hill ....B 10
7 Blandford Forum
   E 12
7 Blandford St. Mary
   F 12
47 Blanefield ....A 10
33 Blankney ....D 8
51 Blar a'Chaoruinn ...A 8
50 Blaran ....A 6
51 Blarghour ....F 7
55 Blarmachfoldach,
   Highland ....M 5
51 Blarmachfoldach,
   Highland ....A 8
60 Blarnaleyoch ....G 3
8 Blashford ....E 3
23 Blaston ....C 11
24 Blatherwycke ....F 1
38 Blawith ....F 5
27 Blaxhall ....J 7
36 Blaxton ....G 4
45 Blaydon ....G 10
33 Bleasby, Lincs. ....B 8
32 Bleasby, Notts. ....E 4
53 Blebocraigs ....F 9
21 Bleddfa ....F 7
16 Bledington ....B 3
17 Bledlow ....D 8
17 Bledlow Ridge ....D 9
4 Blegberry ....C 1
49 Blegbie ....C 7
58 Blencarn ....B 9
43 Blencogo ....G 12
9 Blendworth ....E 8
43 Blennerhasset ....G 12
16 Bletchingdon ....B 6
10 Bletchingley ....C 2
17 Bletchley, Bucks. ...A 9
30 Bletchley, Salop. ...G 5
12 Bletherston ....E 4
25 Bletsoe ....J 1
16 Blewbury ....F 6
26 Blickling ....C 5
32 Blidworth ....E 3
32 Blidworth Bottoms ..E 3
44 Blindburn ....B 6
38 Blindcrake ....B 4
10 Blindley Heath ....C 2
49 Blinkbonny ....F 11
22 Bliss Gate ....E 1
8 Blissford ....E 3
23 Blisworth ....G 10
31 Blithbury ....H 9
31 Blithford ....H 9
43 Blitterlees ....F 11
27 Blo Norton ....G 3
16 Blockley ....A 3
26 Blofield ....D 6
26 Blofield Corner ....D 6
43 Bloomfield, Dumf. &
   Gall. ....D 10
49 Bloomfield, Borders
   G 8
31 Blore ....E 10
31 Blounts Green ....G 9
16 Bloxham ....A 5
33 Bloxholm ....E 8
22 Bloxwich ....B 3
7 Bloxworth ....G 12
35 Blubberhouses ....B 10
2 Blue Anchor, Corn. .D 6
6 Blue Anchor, Som. ..B 4
13 Blue Anchor, W. Glam.
   G 9
10 Bluebell Hill ....B 6
60 Blughasary ....F 3
34 Blundellsands ....G 2
26 Blundeston ....F 8
25 Blunham ....K 3
16 Blunsdon St. Andrew
   E 2
22 Bluntington ....E 1
25 Bluntisham ....H 5
3 Blunts ....C 10
37 Blyborough ....H 7
27 Blyford ....H 7
22 Blymhill ....A 2

45 Blyth, Northumb. ..E 11
32 Blyth, Notts. ....B 3
48 Blyth Bridge ....E 4
31 Blyth Marsh ....F 8
27 Blythburgh ....H 7
31 Blythe Bridge ....E 4
31 Blythe Marsh ....F 8
36 Blyton ....H 6
53 Boarhills ....F 10
1 Boarhunt ....E 7
16 Boars Hill ....D 6
10 Boarshead ....E 4
17 Boarstall ....C 7
4 Boasley Cross ....F 4
57 Boat of Garten ....H 5
56 Boath ....B 1
11 Bobbing ....B 7
22 Bobbington ....C 2
56 Bobbingworth ....C 5
19 Bocking ....B 7
19 Bocking Churchstreet
   A 7
3 Boconnoc ....D 8
58 Boddam, Grampian
   C 8
64 Boddam, Shetland Is.
   F 7
7 Bodden ....B 10
28 Bodedern ....B 3
29 Bodelwyddan ....C 9
21 Bodenham, Heref.
   & Worcs. ...G 10
14 Bodenham, Wilts. ...D 3
21 Bodenham Moor ...G 11
28 Boderwryd ....A 3
29 Bodfari ....C 10
28 Bodffordd ....C 4
26 Bodham Street ....B 4
19 Bodiam ....E 6
23 Bodicote ....H 8
3 Bodieve ....B 7
3 Bodinnick ....D 8
10 Bodle Street Grn. ...G 5
3 Bodmin ....C 8
3 Bodnant ....C 7
26 Bodney ....E 1
12 Bodorgan ....C 3
11 Bodsham Green ....D 9
28 Boduan ....F 3
3 Bodwen ....D 7
56 Bogallan ....E 2
58 Bogbrae ....D 8
49 Bogend, Borders ...D 10
47 Bogend, Strathclyde .F 9
48 Boghall, Lothian ...C 5
48 Boghall, Lothian ...C 3
47 Boghall, Strathclyde H 9
58 Boghead, Grampian .E 7
47 Boghead, Strathclyde
   F 10
47 Boghead, Strathclyde
   E 12
56 Boghole ....D 5
43 Bognowe ....F 10
15 Bogmarsh ....A 8
59 Bogmuire, Grampian
   K 4
58 Bogmuir, Grampian
   A 1
58 Bogniebrae ....C 3
58 Bognor Regis ....F 11
58 Bograxie ....F 4
48 Bogsbank ....D 4
58 Bogside ....D 1
58 Bogton ....C 4
43 Bogue ....C 7
2 Bohortha ....F 6
55 Bohuntine ....L 7
3 Bokiddick ....C 7
2 Bolam, Durham. ...C 2
45 Bolam, Northumb. ..E 9
5 Bolberry ....M 6
4 Bold Heath ....A 4
45 Boldon Colliery ...G 11
8 Boldre ....F 5
5 Boldron ....D 1
32 Bole ....B 5
31 Bolehill ....E 11
2 Boleigh ....G 2
49 Boleside ....F 7
52 Bolfracks ....B 3
6 Bolham ....E 3
6 Bolham Water ....E 5
2 Bolingey ....D 5
58 Bollington, Ches. ...B 8
30 Bollington, Ches. ...B 6
31 Bollington Cross ....C 8
9 Bolney ....F 1
25 Bolnhurst ....J 2
53 Bolshan ....B 11
32 Bolsover ....C 2
35 Bolsterstone ....G 11
15 Bolstone ....A 8

40 Boltby ....F 5
17 Bolter End ....E 9
39 Bolton, Cumbria ....C 8
34 Bolton, Manchester .F 6
36 Bolton, Humber. ....B 5
49 Bolton, Lothian .....B 7
45 Bolton, Northumb. ..B 9
35 Bolton Abbey ......B 9
35 Bolton Bridge ......B 9
34 Bolton by Bowland .B 6
39 Bolton-le-Sands ....H 7
38 Bolton Low Houses .A 5
36 Bolton-on-Dearne .G 2
40 Bolton-on-Swale ..E 3
36 Bolton Percy ....C 3
39 Bolton Town End ..H 7
44 Boltonfellend ....F 3
3 Bolventor ....B 9
30 Bomere Heath ......E 9
60 Bonar Bridge ......G 6
51 Bonawe Quarries ..D 7
37 Bonby ....F 8
12 Boncath ....C 5
44 Bonchester Bridge .B 4
9 Bonchurch ....H 7
4 Bondleigh ....E 5
34 Bonds ....C 4
22 Bonehill ....B 5
48 Bo'ness ....A 3
52 Bonhard ....D 6
47 Bonhill ....A 9
22 Boningdale ....B 2
49 Bonjedward ....G 9
48 Bonkle ....D 1
48 Bonnington ....B 4
53 Bonnybank ....G 8
48 Bonnybridge ......A 1
58 Bonnykelly ....B 6
48 Bonnyrigg and
    Lasswade ......C 6
47 Bonnyton ....F 9
31 Bonsall ....D 11
15 Bont ....B 7
28 Bont Newydd .....F 6
28 Bontddu ....H 6
20 Bont-dolgadfan ..B 4
20 Bontnewydd, Dyfed .F 2
28 Bont-newydd,
    Gwynedd ......D 4
20 Bontrhydgaled .....D 4
29 Bontuchel ....D 10
14 Bonvilston ....G 4
13 Bon-y-maen ......G 10
4 Boode ....B 4
30 Booley ....H 4
39 Boon ....E 8
41 Boosbeck ....C 7
4 Boot ....F 1
36 Booth ....D 5
35 Booth Wood ....E 9
33 Boothby Graffoe ..D 7
33 Boothby Pagnell ....G 7
34 Boothtown ....G 6
38 Bootle, Cumbria ....F 4
34 Bootle, Merseyside .H 2
52 Boquhan, Central ..H 2
47 Boquhan, Central .A 10
21 Boraston ....E 11
7 Borden ....D 9
35 Bordley ....A 8
9 Bordon ....C 9
19 Boreham ....C 7
10 Boreham Street ....G 5
18 Borhamwood ......D 2
52 Boreland, Central ..D 1
43 Boreland, Dumf. &
    Gall. ....B 12
43 Boreland of Girthon ....F 7
62 Boreraig ....C 1
49 Borewell ....D 12
61 Borgie House ......B 7
43 Borgue, Dumf. & Gall. ....G 7
61 Borgue, Highland ..E 10
27 Borley ....L 1
62 Bornaskitaig ......A 3
43 Borness ....G 7
10 Borough Green .....B 5
40 Boroughbridge ....H 4
30 Borras Head ....E 2
61 Borrobol Lodge ....E 8
32 Borrowash ....G 1
40 Borrowby ....F 4
38 Borrowdale ....D 5
59 Borrowfield ....H 6
20 Borth ....C 2
44 Borthwickbrae ....B 2
44 Borthwickshiels ..B 2
28 Borth-y-gest ......F 5
62 Borve ....C 4
63 Borve Lodge ......G 1
63 Borvemore ....G 1
39 Borwick ....H 7

21 Bosbury ....H 12
3 Boscastle ....A 8
8 Boscombe, Dorset ..G 3
8 Boscombe, Wilts. ..B 3
3 Boscoppa ....D 7
9 Bosham ....F 9
12 Bosherston ....G 3
31 Bosley ....D 7
31 Bossall ....A 5
59 Bossholes ....H 6
5 Bossiney ....A 8
11 Bossingham .....C 10
3 Bossington ......A 3
30 Bostock Green ...C 5
24 Boston ....A 4
33 Boston Long Hedges
    ....E 10
36 Boston Spa ....C 2
3 Boswinger ....F 7
2 Botallack ....F 1
58 Botary Mains .....C 2
23 Botcheston ....B 8
23 Botesdale ....H 3
45 Bothal ....D 10
32 Bothamsall ....C 4
43 Bothel ....H 12
43 Bothenhampton ...G 8
47 Bothwell ....D 12
8 Botley, Bucks. ...D 10
8 Botley, Hants. ...E 6
16 Botley, Oxon. ....C 6
8 Botolph Claydon ..B 8
10 Botolphs ....G 1
54 Bottacks ....D 8
37 Bottesford, Humber.
    ....F 7
32 Bottesford, Leics. ..F 5
21 Bottisham ....J 6
16 Bottlesford ....H 2
31 Bottom House ....E 9
34 Bottom O'th'Moor .F 5
53 Bottomcraig ......E 8
35 Bottoms ....E 8
34 Botton Head ......A 5
38 Bottongate ....A 5
4 Bottreaux Mill ....C 7
31 Botusfleming ....D 11
28 Botwnnog ....G 2
10 Bough Beech ....C 4
21 Boughrood ....H 7
21 Boughrood Brest ..H 7
15 Boughspring ......E 9
23 Boughton, Norfolk .E 8
32 Boughton, Notts. ..C 4
11 Boughton Aluph ..C 9
23 Boughton ....E 11
11 Boughton Lees ....C 9
11 Boughton Malherbe .C 7
10 Boughton
    Monchelsea ......C 6
11 Boughton Street ..B 9
41 Boulby ....C 8
21 Bouldon ....D 11
45 Boulmer ....B 11
12 Boulston ....F 3
58 Boultenstone ......F 2
32 Boultham ....C 6
25 Bourn ....K 4
24 Bourne ....D 2
25 Bourne End, Beds. .L 1
17 Bourne End,
    Bucks. ....E 10
17 Bourne End,
    Herts. ....D 11
18 Bournebridge .....D 5
42 Bournemouth ....G 3
19 Bournes Green,
    Essex ....E 9
15 Bournes Green,
    Gloucestershire .D 12
22 Bournheath ....E 3
45 Bournmoor ....H 11
16 Bournville ....D 4
16 Bourton, Oxon. ...E 3
7 Bourton, Dorset ..C 11
21 Bourton, Salop. ..C 11
23 Bourton on Dunsmore
    ....E 8
16 Bourton-on-the-Hill
    ....A 3
16 Bourton-on-the-Water
    ....A 3
44 Boustead Hill .....G 1
38 Bouth ....G 5
40 Bouthwaite ....H 2
17 Boveney ....F 10
5 Boverton ....G 3
5 Bovey Tracey .....H 7
17 Bovingdon ....D 11
17 Bovingdon Green ..E 9
18 Bovinger ....C 5
49 Bow, Borders .....E 7

4 Bow, Devon ......F 6
64 Bow, Orkney Is. ...E 2
17 Bow Brickhill ....A 10
53 Bow of Fife ....F 8
20 Bow Street ....D 2
39 Bowbank ....C 11
40 Bowburn ....A 3
8 Bowcombe ....G 6
6 Bowd ....G 4
49 Bowden, Borders ..F 8
5 Bowden, Devon ...L 7
15 Bowden Hill ......H 12
39 Bowerdale ....E 9
30 Bowdon ....B 6
44 Bower ....E 6
7 Bower Hinton ....D 8
8 Bowerchalke ......D 2
15 Bowerhill ....H 12
61 Bowermadden ....B 11
31 Bowers ....G 7
19 Bowers Gifford ....E 7
52 Bowershall ....H 6
61 Bowertower ......B 11
39 Bowers ....D 12
34 Bowgreave ....C 4
6 Bowhill ....G 7
43 Bowhouse ....E 11
3 Bowithick ....A 9
34 Bowker's Green ...G 3
38 Bowland Bridge ...F 6
21 Bowley ....G 11
16 Bowlhead Green ..B 10
47 Bowling ....B 9
22 Bowling Green ....G 2
38 Bowmanstead .....F 5
44 Bowness-on-Solway G 1
38 Bowness-on-
    Windermere ....E 6
49 Bowsden ....E 12
61 Bowside Lodge ....B 8
48 Bowtrees ....A 2
15 Box, Glos. ....D 11
15 Box, Wilts. ......G 11
15 Boxbush ....C 10
16 Boxford, Berks. ...G 5
27 Boxford, Suffolk ..L 3
9 Boxgrove ....E 10
10 Boxley ....B 6
4 Box's Shop ....F 1
27 Boxted, Essex ....M 3
27 Boxted, Suffolk ....K 1
27 Boxted Cross .....M 3
25 Boxworth ....J 4
25 Boxworth End .....H 5
11 Boyden Gate ......B 11
31 Boylestone ......G 10
58 Boyndie ....A 4
41 Boynton ....H 11
7 Boys Hill ....E 10
5 Boyton, Cornwall ..G 2
27 Boyton, Suffolk ....K 7
8 Boyton, Wilts. ....B 1
18 Boyton Cross .....C 6
23 Bozeat ....F 12
38 Braaid ....H 2
27 Brabling Green ....J 6
11 Brabourne ....D 9
11 Brabourne Lees ....D 9
61 Brabstermire .....A 12
62 Bracadale ....D 3
24 Braceborough ....D 2
33 Bracebridge Heath ..C 7
33 Braceby ....G 7
35 Bracewell ....B 7
56 Brachla ....F 1
32 Brackenfield ......D 1
38 Brackenthwaite,
    Cumbria ....C 4
9 Bracklesham ......F 9
55 Brackletter ....L 6
23 Brackley, Northants.
    ....H 9
46 Brackley, Strathclyde
    ....E 3
60 Brackloch ....E 3
17 Bracknell ....G 9
52 Braco ....F 3
52 Bracobrae ....B 3
26 Bracon Ash ......E 5
55 Bracora ....K 1
55 Bracorina ....K 1
31 Bradbourne ......E 10
40 Bradbury ....B 3
38 Bradda ....H 1
23 Bradden ....G 10
17 Bradenham ....D 9
16 Bradenstoke ......F 1
17 Bradfield, Berks. ..G 7
6 Bradfield, Devon ..E 4
27 Bradfield, Essex ..M 4
35 Bradfield, S. Yorks.
    ....H 11
27 Bradfield Combust ..J 2
30 Bradfield Green ....D 5

27 Bradfield Heath ....M 4
27 Bradfield St. Clair ..J 2
27 Bradfield St. George .J 2
4 Bradford, Devon ...E 3
45 Bradford, Northumb.
    ....D 11
35 Bradford, W. Yorks.
    ....D 10
7 Bradford Abbas ...E 9
15 Bradford Leigh ...H 11
4 Bradford Mill .....D 7
15 Bradford-on-Avon
    ....H 11
6 Bradford-on-Tone ..D 5
9 Brading ....G 7
30 Bradley, Clwyd ....F 3
31 Bradley, Derby. ..F 10
9 Bradley, Hants. ....B 7
22 Bradley, Heref. &
    Worc. ....F 3
37 Bradley, Humber. .F 10
39 Bradley, N. Yorks. ..G 2
31 Bradley, Staffs. ...H 7
22 Bradley, W. Midlands
    ....C 3
30 Bradley Common ....F 4
22 Bradley Green .....F 3
31 Bradley in the Moors
    ....F 9
32 Bradmore ....G 3
7 Bradney ....B 7
6 Bradninch ....F 3
31 Bradnop ....E 8
7 Bradpole ....G 8
34 Bradshaw ....F 6
5 Bradstone ....H 3
30 Bradwall Green ....C 6
31 Bradwell, Derby. .B 10
19 Bradwell, Essex ....B 8
26 Bradwell, Suffolk ..E 8
23 Bradwell, Bucks. ..H 11
16 Bradwell Grove ...C 3
19 Bradwell-on-Sea ..C 10
19 Bradwell Waterside
    ....C 10
4 Bradworthy ......E 2
4 Bradworthy Cross ..E 2
64 Brae ....C 7
60 Brae Doune ......G 5
60 Brae of Achnahaird .E 2
55 Brae Roy Lodge ..K 7
56 Braeantra ....B 1
57 Braedownie .....M 8
43 Braefoot ....A 9
52 Braegrum ....E 5
58 Braehead, Grampian
    ....F 7
42 Braehead, Dumf. &
    Gall. ....F 5
64 Braehead, Orkney Is.
    ....D 3
48 Braehead, Strathclyde
    ....D 2
48 Braehead, Strathclyde
    ....F 1
53 Braehead, Tayside .B 11
61 Braehungie ....D 11
54 Braeintra ....F 2
60 Braelangwell Lodge
    (Hotel) ....G 6
57 Braemar ....K 7
61 Braemore, Highland
    ....D 10
54 Braemore, Highland
    ....B 6
47 Braeside ....B 7
51 Braeval ....G 12
40 Brafferton, Dur. ...C 3
40 Braverton, N. Yorks.
    ....H 4
23 Bradfield-on-the-
    Green ....F 11
63 Bragar ....B 4
18 Bragbury End .....B 3
50 Braglenbeg ....E 6
34 Braides ....B 3
49 Braidshawrig ......D 8
48 Braidwood ....E 1
31 Brailsford ....F 11
45 Braishaugh ....C 10
19 Braintree ....B 7
27 Braiseworth ......H 4
8 Braishfield ....D 5
38 Braithwaite, Cumb. .C 5
35 Braithwaite, S. Yorks.
    ....F 4
32 Braithwell ....A 3
10 Bramber ....G 1
32 Bramcote ....F 2
9 Bramdean ....C 7
26 Bramerton ....E 6
18 Bramfield, Herts. ..B 3
27 Bramfield, Suffolk ..H 7
27 Bramford ....K 4

31 Bramhall ....B 7
36 Bramham ....C 2
36 Bramham Crossroads
    ....C 2
35 Bramhope ....C 11
17 Bramley, Hants. ....H 7
9 Bramley, Surrey ..B 11
32 Bramley, S. Yorks. ..A 2
6 Brampford Speke ..F 3
25 Brampton, Cambs. ..H 3
44 Brampton, Cumb. ..G 4
39 Brampton, Cumb. ..C 9
15 Brampton, Heref. &
    Worc. ....A 7
32 Brampton, Lincs. ..B 6
35 Brampton, S. Yorks. G 2
27 Brampton, Suffolk .G 7
15 Brampton Abbots ..B 9
23 Brampton Ash ....C 11
21 Brampton Bryan ..E 9
32 Brampton en le
    Morthen ....A 2
31 Bramshall ....G 9
8 Bramshaw ....E 4
9 Bramshott ....C 9
18 Bran End ....A 6
50 Branault ....A 3
26 Brancaster ....A 1
26 Brancaster Staithe ..A 1
40 Brancepeth ......A 2
56 Branchill ....C 8
15 Brand Green ......B 10
56 Branderburgh ....C 8
37 Brandesburton ....D 9
27 Brandeston ....J 5
4 Brandis Corner ....E 3
26 Brandiston ....C 4
38 Brandingill ....C 4
40 Brandon, Durham ..A 3
32 Brandon, Lincs. ....E 6
45 Brandon, Northumb.
    ....A 8
27 Brandon, Suffolk ..G 1
23 Brandon, War. ....D 7
24 Brandon Creek ....F 7
26 Brandon Parva ....E 4
40 Brandsby ....H 6
37 Brandy Wharf ....G 8
8 Branksome ....G 2
8 Branksome Park ...G 2
6 Bransbury ....B 6
6 Branscombe ....G 5
22 Bransford ....G 1
8 Bransgore ....F 3
22 Branson's Cross ...E 4
32 Branston, Leics. ...G 5
33 Branston, Lincs. ...C 7
31 Branston, Staffs. ..H 10
33 Branston Booths ...C 7
9 Branstone ....H 7
32 Brant Broughton ..E 6
44 Branteth ....C 1
27 Brantham ....M 4
38 Branthwaite, Cumb. .C 3
38 Branthwaite, Cumb. .B 5
37 Brantingham ......D 7
45 Branton, Northumb. A 8
32 Branton, S. Yorks. ..G 4
44 Branxholme ......B 3
49 Branxton ....F 11
49 Branxtonmoor ....F 11
31 Brassington ......E 11
10 Brasted ....C 3
10 Brasted Chart .....C 3
59 Brathens ....H 4
33 Bratoft ....D 11
32 Brattleby ....B 6
6 Bratton, Somerset ..B 3
8 Bratton, Wilts. ....A 1
5 Bratton Clovelly ...G 3
4 Bratton Fleming ..B 5
7 Bratton Seymour ..C 10
18 Braughing ....A 4
23 Braunston, Leics. ..A 11
23 Braunston,
    Northants. ......E 9
23 Braunstone ....B 9
4 Braunton ....B 4
12 Brawby, Dyfed ....E 2
41 Brawby, N. Yorks. ..G 7
61 Brawlbin ....B 10
5 Bray ....F 10
3 Bray Shop ....B 10
17 Bray Wick ....F 9
23 Braybrooke ....D 11
4 Brayford ....C 6
36 Brayton ....D 4
62 Brazacott ....A 9
11 Breach ....B 7
26 Breachwood Green .B 2
63 Breaclete ....C 2
31 Breadsall ....F 12

15 Breadstone ....D 10
54 Breafield ....F 8
2 Breage ....G 3
54 Breakachy ....E 8
15 Bream ....D 9
8 Breamore ....D 3
15 Bream's Eaves ....D 9
6 Brean ....A 6
35 Brearton ....A 11
63 Breasclete ....C 3
32 Breaston ....G 2
13 Brechfa ....D 8
59 Brechin ....L 4
45 Breckonside ......A 9
62 Breckrey ....B 4
14 Brecon ....A 4
30 Bredbury ....H 8
11 Brede ....F 7
21 Bredenbury ....G 11
12 Bredfield ....K 6
11 Bredger ....B 7
11 Bredhurst ....B 7
22 Bredicot ....G 3
15 Bredon ....A 12
22 Bredon's Norton ..H 3
21 Bredwardine ......H 9
32 Breedon on the Hill .H 1
26 Breich ....C 2
36 Breighton ....D 5
21 Breinton ....H 10
21 Breinton Com. ...H 10
16 Bremhill ....G 1
51 Brenachoille ......G 7
10 Brenchley ....D 5
4 Brendon ....A 6
46 Brenfield ....A 3
26 Brenish ....D 1
45 Brenkley ....F 10
18 Brent ....E 2
27 Brent Eleigh ......K 2
6 Brent Knoll ....A 6
25 Brent Pelham ....M 5
18 Brentford ....F 2
26 Brentwood ....E 6
11 Brenzett ....E 8
22 Brereton ....A 4
30 Brereton Green ....D 6
30 Brereton Heath ....D 6
26 Bressay ....E 7
27 Bressingham ......G 4
64 Bretabister ....D 7
31 Bretby ....H 11
23 Bretford ....D 7
22 Bretforton ....H 4
39 Bretherdale Head ..E 8
34 Bretherton ....E 4
6 Brett ....B 4
27 Brettenham, Suff. ..K 3
27 Brettenhm, Norf. ...G 2
30 Bretton ....D 2
11 Brewer Street ....C 2
22 Brewood ....A 2
56 Briach ....D 6
22 Briantspuddle ....G 11
18 Bricket Wood .....D 1
22 Bricklehampton ...H 3
38 Bride ....F 2
38 Bridekirk ....B 4
12 Bridell ....C 5
5 Bridestowe ....G 4
58 Brideswell ....D 3
5 Bridford ....D 3
11 Bridge, Kent ......C 10
2 Bridge, Cornwall ..E 4
25 Bridge End, Beds. .K 1
24 Bridge End, Lincs. .B 2
45 Bridge End,
    Northumb. ......B 9
40 Bridge Hewick ....H 4
58 Bridge of Alford ...F 3
52 Bridge of Allan ...G 3
56 Bridge of Avon ....F 7
51 Bridge of Awe ....E 7
51 Bridge of Balgie,
    Perth ....C 12
53 Bridge of Brewlands
    ....A 7
57 Bridge of Brown ...G 7
52 Bridge of Cally ....B 6
54 Bridge of Canny ...H 4
53 Bridge of Craigisla .B 7
43 Bridge of Dee ....F 8
56 Bridge of Derrybeg .F 8
59 Bridge of Don ....F 7
59 Bridge of Dun ....L 4
59 Bridge of Dye ....J 4
52 Bridge of Earn ....E 6
51 Bridge of Ericht ..B 12
59 Bridge of Feugh ...H 4
61 Bridge of Forss ...A 10
59 Bridge of Gairn ...H 1
51 Bridge of Gaur ...B 12
53 Bridge of Lintrathen B 7
59 Bridge of Murchalls .H 6

51 Bridge of Orchy ...D 10
52 Bridge of Tilt ....A 4
64 Bridge of Waith ...D 1
64 Bridge of Walls ...D 6
47 Bridge of Weir ....C 9
4 Bridge Reeve ......E 5
21 Bridge Sollars ....H 9
27 Bridge Street .....K 2
30 Bridge Trafford ....C 3
25 Bridgefoot, Cambs. .L 5
38 Bridgefoot, Cumb. .B 3
7 Bridgehampton ....D 9
49 Bridgelands ......F 7
9 Bridgemary ....F 7
3 Bridgend, Corn. ..D 8
38 Bridgend, Cumbria .D 6
43 Bridgend, Dumf. &
　Gall. ....A 11
12 Bridgend, Dyfed ...B 5
53 Bridgend, Fife ....F 8
58 Bridgend, Grampian
　　　　　　　　　C 5
58 Bridgend, Grampian
　　　　　　　　　D 3
58 Bridgend, Grampian
　　　　　　　　　E 6
58 Bridgend, Grampian
　　　　　　　　　D 1
54 Bridgend, Highland .D 7
48 Bridgend, Lothian ..B 3
14 Bridgend, Mid Glam.
　　　　　　　　　F 2
50 Bridgend,
　Strathclyde .....H 6
59 Bridgend, Tayside ..K 3
4 Bridgerule ....F 1
21 Bridges ....C 9
3 Bridgetown, Corn.
　　　　　　　　　A 10
6 Bridgetown, Som. ..C 3
22 Bridgetown, Staffs. .A 3
27 Bridgham ....G 3
21 Bridgnorth ......C 12
7 Bridgwater ....B 6
41 Bridlington ......H 12
7 Bridport ....G 8
15 Bridstow ....B 9
35 Brierfield ....D 7
15 Brierley, Glos. ....C 9
21 Brierley, Heref. &
　Worc. ....G 10
36 Brierley, S. Yorks. ..F 2
22 Brierley Hill ......C 3
40 Brierton ....B 5
14 Briery Hill ....C 5
51 Brig o' Turk .....G 12
37 Brigg ....F 8
59 Briggs of Criggie ..J 6
41 Briggswath ....D 9
38 Brigham, Cumb. ...B 3
37 Brigham, Humber. ..B 8
35 Brighouse ....E 10
8 Brightstone ......H 6
16 Brighthampton ....D 5
31 Brightgate ......D 11
10 Brightling ....F 5
19 Brightlingsea .....B 10
2 Brighton, Corn. ...D 6
10 Brighton, E. Sussex .H 2
48 Brightons ....B 2
16 Brightwalton ......F 5
17 Brightwell, Oxon. ..E 7
27 Brightwell, Suffolk ..L 5
17 Brightwell Baldwin .E 7
40 Brignall ....D 1
37 Brigsley ....G 10
39 Brigsteer ....F 7
23 Brigstock ....D 12
17 Brill, Bucks. ......C 7
2 Brill, Cornwall ...G 4
21 Brilley ....G 8
12 Brimaston ....D 3
21 Brimfield ....F 10
32 Brimington ......C 1
15 Brimpsfield .....C 12
16 Brimpton ....H 6
64 Brims ....E 1
15 Brimscombe .....D 11
30 Brimstage ....B 2
57 Brin ....G 2
55 Brinacory ....K 1
36 Brind ....F 2
64 Brindister, Shetland Is.
　　　　　　　　　D 6
64 Brindister, Shetland Is.
　　　　　　　　　E 7
34 Brindle ....E 5
31 Brindley Ford .....E 7
22 Brineton ....A 2
23 Bringhurst ......C 11
25 Brington ....H 2
26 Briningham ....B 3
33 Brinkhill ....C 10
25 Brinkley ....K 7

23 Brinklow ....D 8
16 Brinkworth ......F 1
34 Brinscall ....E 5
15 Brinsea ....H 7
32 Brinsley ....E 2
21 Brinsop ....H 10
32 Brinsworth ....A 1
26 Brinton ....B 3
64 Brinyan ....B 2
26 Brisley ....C 3
15 Brislington ....G 9
11 Brissenden Green .D 8
15 Bristol ....G 9
26 Briston ....B 4
27 Britannia ....E 7
8 Britford ....C 3
29 Brithdir, Gwynedd .H 7
14 Brithdir, Mid Glam. .D 5
10 British Legion Village
　　　　　　　　　B 6
13 Briton Ferry ....G 10
17 Britwell Salome ...E 7
5 Brixham ....K 8
15 Brixton ....K 4
7 Brixton Deverill ..B 11
23 Brixworth ....E 10
16 Brize Norton .....C 4
16 Broad Blunsdon ..E 3
22 Broad Campden ...H 5
8 Broad Chalke ....C 2
6 Broad Clyst ......F 3
25 Broad Green, Beds. .L 1
19 Broad Green, Essex .B 8
22 Broad Green,
　Heref. & Worc. ..F 1
15 Broad Haven .....F 2
21 Broad Heath ....F 12
25 Broad Hill ....H 7
16 Broad Hinton .....F 2
16 Broad Laying .....H 5
22 Broad Marston ....G 5
38 Broad Oak, Cumb. .F 4
13 Broad Oak, Dyfed ..E 9
11 Broad Oak, E. Sussex
　　　　　　　　　F 7
15 Broad Oak, Heref. &
　Worc. ....B 8
36 Broad Oak, N. Yorks.
　　　　　　　　　B 4
11 Broad Street .....B 7
19 Broad Street Green .C 8
16 Broad Town ......F 2
35 Broadbottom .....H 8
9 Broadbridge .....E 9
9 Broadbridge Hth. .C 12
12 Broadfield ....G 5
62 Broadford ....F 5
8 Broadford Bri. ...D 12
48 Broadgairhill .....H 5
44 Broadhaugh ......B 3
61 Broadhaven .....C 12
30 Broadheath ......A 6
7 Broadhembury ....F 5
5 Broadhempston ...J 7
11 Broadland Row ...F 7
13 Broadlay ....F 7
58 Broadley ....B 1
18 Broadley Com. ....C 4
4 Broadmead ......D 7
49 Broadmeadows ....F 7
12 Broadmoor ......F 4
4 Broadnymet ......F 6
10 Broadoak, E. Sussex .F 5
11 Broadoak, Kent ..B 10
58 Broadrashes ......B 2
58 Broadsea ....E 5
11 Broadstairs .....A 12
8 Broadstone, Dorset .F 2
21 Broadstone, Salop. .C 11
16 Broadtown Lane ...F 2
22 Broadwas ....G 1
18 Broadwater, Herts. .B 2
9 Broadwater, W. Sussex
　　　　　　　　　F 12
12 Broadway, Dyfed ..F 6
12 Broadway, Dyfed ..F 2
22 Broadway, Heref.
　& Worc. ....H 4
6 Broadway, Som. ...E 6
16 Broadwell, Glos. ..A 3
16 Broadwell, Oxon. ..D 3
23 Broadwell, War. ...F 8
45 Broadwell House ...H 7
15 Broadwell Lane End
　　　　　　　　　C 9
7 Broadwey ....H 10
7 Broadwindsor ....F 1
4 Broadwood-Kelly ..E 5
5 Broadwoodwidger ..G 3
2 Brobury ....H 9
62 Brochel ....D 5
9 Brockbridge .....D 7
45 Brockdam ....A 9

27 Brockdish ....G 5
8 Brockenhurst .....F 4
48 Brocketsbrae .....E 1
27 Brockford Street ...J 4
23 Brockhall ....F 9
10 Brockham ....C 1
16 Brockhampton, Glos.
　　　　　　　　　B 1
15 Brockhampton,
　Heref. & Worc. ..A 9
7 Brockhampton Green
　　　　　　　　　F 10
35 Brockholes ......F 10
9 Brockhurst ....F 7
38 Brocklebank ......A 5
37 Brocklesby ....F 9
15 Brockley ....H 8
27 Brockley Green ...K 1
21 Brockton, Salop. ..B 1
21 Brockton, Salop. ..B 8
21 Brockton, Salop. ..C 11
15 Brockweir ....D 8
9 Brockwood ......D 7
15 Brockworth .....C 12
31 Brocton ....H 8
46 Brodick ....F 5
38 Brodiesord ....B 3
36 Brodsworth ......F 3
62 Brogaig ....A 4
30 Brogborough .....L 1
30 Broken Cross,
　Cheshire ....C 6
31 Broken Cross,
　Cheshire ....C 7
15 Brokenborough ...E 12
30 Bromborough .....B 2
27 Brome ....H 4
27 Brome Street .....H 5
27 Bromeswell ......K 6
64 Bromfield, Cumb. .G 12
21 Bromfield, Salop. ..E 10
25 Bromham, Beds. ...K 1
16 Bromham, Wilts. ..H 1
18 Bromley ....G 4
11 Bromley Green ...D 8
10 Brompton, Kent ..A 6
41 Brompton, N. Yorks.
　　　　　　　　　G 9
40 Brompton, N. Yorks.
　　　　　　　　　E 4
21 Brompton Hall ....C 8
40 Brompton-on-Swale
　　　　　　　　　E 2
6 Brompton Ralph ...C 4
6 Brompton Regis ...C 3
15 Bromsash ....B 9
38 Bromsberrow ....A 10
22 Bromsgrove ......E 3
30 Bromstead Heath ..H 6
21 Bromyard ....G 12
21 Bromyard Downs .G 12
28 Bronaber ....G 6
12 Bronant ....F 2
12 Brongest ....C 6
30 Bronington ......F 4
15 Bronllys ....A 5
13 Bronwydd Arms ...E 7
21 Bronydd ....H 8
21 Brook, Dyfed .....F 6
8 Brook, Hants. ....C 5
8 Brook, Hants. ....E 4
8 Brook, I.o.W. ....H 5
11 Brook, Kent .....D 9
9 Brook, Surrey ...B 12
9 Brook, Surrey ...B 10
25 Brook End ....J 2
16 Brook Hill ....E 4
18 Brook Street, Essex .E 6
10 Brook Street, W. Sussex
　　　　　　　　　E 2
23 Brooke, Leics. ...B 12
26 Brooke, Norfolk ...E 6
48 Brookend ....D 9
47 Brookfield ....C 9
31 Brookhouse, Ches. .C 8
34 Brookhouse, Lancs. .A 4
31 Brookhouse Green .D 7
11 Brookland ....D 8
43 Brooklands ......D 9
18 Brookmans Park ...D 2
21 Brooks ....C 7
21 Brookwood ......H 10
25 Broom, Beds. .....L 3
40 Broom, Durham ...A 3
22 Broom, War. .....G 4
8 Broom Hill ......F 2
52 Broom of Dalreoch .E 5
45 Broomdykes .....D 11
22 Broome,
　Heref. & Worcs. ..D 3
26 Broome, Norfolk ...F 6
21 Broome, Salop. ...D 9
10 Broome Park .....C 1
30 Broomedge ....B 5

9 Broomer's Crn. ..D 12
19 Broomfield, Essex ..C 7
58 Broomfield, Grampian
　　　　　　　　　D 7
11 Broomfield, Kent ..A 10
11 Broomfield, Kent ...C 7
6 Broomfield, Som. ..C 6
48 Broomfield, Strathclyde
　　　　　　　　　E 1
36 Broomfleet ....D 6
17 Broomhall ......G 10
45 Broomhaugh ......G 8
45 Broomhill, Northumb.
　　　　　　　　　C 10
56 Broomhill, Highland
　　　　　　　　　C 3
57 Broomhill Station .G 6
26 Broomholm ....B 6
45 Broomhouse .....C 11
43 Broomhouses ....C 12
45 Broomley ....G 8
15 Brooms Green ...A 10
15 Broomsberrow Heath
　　　　　　　　　A 10
61 Brora ....F 9
21 Broseley ....B 12
22 Brotheridge Green .H 2
49 Brotherstone ......F 9
33 Brothertoft ....F 10
36 Brotherton ....E 3
45 Brotherwick .....C 10
41 Brotton ....C 7
61 Broubster ....B 10
39 Brough, Cumbria .D 10
31 Brough, Derby. ...B 10
61 Brough, Highland .A 11
37 Brough, Humberside
　　　　　　　　　D 7
32 Brough, Notts. ....D 5
64 Brough, Orkney Is. .C 2
64 Brough, Whalasay,
　Shetland Is. .....C 8
64 Brough, Yell,
　Shetland Is. .....C 7
64 Brough, Zetland,
　Shetland Is. .....C 7
64 Brough Lodge ....B 8
39 Brough Sowerby ..D 10
30 Broughall ....F 4
23 Broughton, Bucks. .H 12
48 Broughton, Borders .F 1
25 Broughton, Cambs. .G 4
30 Broughton, Clwyd ..D 2
38 Broughton, Cumb. .B 3
8 Broughton, Hants. .C 4
37 Broughton, Humber. F 7
34 Broughton, Lancs. .B 4
14 Broughton, Mid Glam.
　　　　　　　　　G 2
23 Broughton, Northants.
　　　　　　　　　E 11
40 Broughton, N. Yorks.
　　　　　　　　　E 6
41 Broughton, N. Yorks.
　　　　　　　　　H 8
35 Broughton, N. Yorks.
　　　　　　　　　B 8
64 Broughton, Orkney Is.
　　　　　　　　　A 2
23 Broughton, Oxon. .H 7
23 Broughton Astley ..C 8
38 Broughton Beck ..G 5
15 Broughton Com. ..H 12
16 Broughton Foggs ..D 3
15 Broughton Gifford
　　　　　　　　　H 12
22 Broughton Hackett .G 3
38 Broughton in Furness
　　　　　　　　　F 5
38 Broughton Mills ..F 4
38 Broughton Moor ...B 3
64 Broughtown ....B 4
53 Broughty Ferry ...D 9
44 Browhouses ......G 1
9 Brown Candover ...B 7
31 Brown Edge ......E 7
58 Brownhill, Grampian
　　　　　　　　　D 6
30 Brownhill, Salop. ..H 3
53 Brownhills, Fife ..F 10
22 Brownhills, W.
　Midlands ....B 4
31 Brownlow Heath ...D 7
59 Brownmuir ......K 5
45 Brownridge ......B 11
15 Brown's Hill ....D 12
23 Brownsover ......D 8
45 Brownyside ......A 9
17 Brox ....H 11
41 Broxa ....G 9
18 Broxbourne ....C 4
49 Broxburn, Lothian ..B 9
48 Broxburn, Lothian ..B 4

18 Broxted ....A 6
30 Broxton ....E 3
21 Broxwood ....G 9
10 Broyle Side ......G 3
61 Bruan ....C 12
57 Bruar Lodge .....M 4
63 Brue ....B 4
30 Bruera ....D 3
16 Bruern Abbey .....B 4
27 Bruisyard ....J 6
27 Bruisyard Street ...J 6
36 Brumby ....F 6
31 Brund ....D 9
26 Brundhall ....E 6
27 Brundish ....H 5
27 Brundish Street ...H 6
55 Brunery ....M 1
45 Brunswick Village .F 10
23 Bruntingthorpe ...C 9
53 Brunton, Fife .....E 8
45 Brunton, Northumb.
　　　　　　　　　A 10
16 Brunton, Wilts. ....H 3
6 Brushford ....D 3
45 Brushford Barton ..E 5
7 Bruton ....C 10
7 Bryanston ......F 12
43 Brydekirk ....E 12
29 Brymbo ....E 12
7 Brympton ....E 8
29 Bryn, Clwyd ....F 12
13 Bryn, Dyfed .....G 9
34 Bryn, Manchester ..G 4
13 Bryn, W. Glam. ..H 11
21 Bryn, Salop. ......D 8
34 Bryn Gates ......G 5
14 Bryn Golau ......E 3
28 Bryn-Siencyn ....D 4
12 Brynamman .....F 10
12 Bryn-berian ......C 4
13 Brynbryddan .....H 11
14 Bryncethin ......F 2
28 Bryncir ....F 4
13 Bryn-coch ......G 10
28 Bryncroes ....G 2
20 Bryncrug ....B 2
29 Bryneglwys .....E 10
29 Brynford ....C 11
28 Bryngwran ......B 3
15 Bryngwyn, Gwent ..C 7
21 Bryngwyn, Powys .G 7
12 Bryn-henllan .....C 4
13 Brynhoffnant ......B 7
34 Bryning ....D 3
14 Brynmawr ....C 5
14 Brynmenyn ......F 2
13 Brynmill ....H 10
28 Bryn'refail ....D 5
14 Brynsadler ....F 3
29 Bryn-teg ....E 12
14 Bryn-y-Cae ......F 3
14 Bryn-y-gwenin ....C 6
29 Bryn-y-maen ......C 7
62 Bualintur ....F 3
23 Bubbenhall ......E 7
36 Bubwith ....C 5
48 Buccleuch ....H 6
42 Buchan ....D 5
47 Buchanan Castle ..A 9
51 Buchanan Smithy ..H 11
58 Buchanhaven .....C 8
52 Buchanty ....D 4
52 Buchlyvie ....H 1
58 Buchts ....B 7
44 Buckabank ......H 2
25 Buckden, Cambs. ..H 3
39 Buckden, N. Yorks.
　　　　　　　　　G 11
26 Buckenham ......E 6
6 Buckerell ....F 5
5 Buckfast ....J 6
5 Buckfastleigh .....J 6
53 Buckhaven ......D 9
49 Buckholm ....E 7
18 Buckhurst Hill ....E 4
58 Buckie ....A 2
17 Buckingham ......A 8
17 Buckinghamshire, Co.
　　　　　　　　　C 8
17 Buckland, Bucks. ..C 9
5 Buckland, Devon ..L 5
16 Buckland, Glos. ...A 2
25 Buckland, Herts. ..M 5
11 Buckland, Kent ..D 11
16 Buckland, Oxon. ..D 4
10 Buckland, Surrey ..C 1
4 Buckland Brewer ..D 3
17 Buckland Com. ....C 8
7 Buckland Dinham .A 11
4 Buckland Filleigh .E 3
5 Buckland in the Moor
　　　　　　　　　H 6
5 Buckland
　Monachorum ....J 4

7 Buckland Newton ..F 10
6 Buckland St. Mary ..E 6
24 Bucklegate ....B 4
53 Bucklerheads .....D 9
8 Bucklers Hard ....F 5
27 Bucklesham ......L 5
29 Buckley ....D 12
30 Bucklow Hill .....B 6
32 Buckminster .....H 6
16 Bucknall, Lincs. ...C 9
31 Bucknall, Staffs. ...E 7
16 Bucknell, Oxon. ...B 6
21 Bucknell, Salop. ...E 9
58 Buckpool ....A 2
4 Buck's Cross .....D 2
9 Bucks Green ....C 12
9 Bucks Horn Oak ..B 9
4 Buck's Mills ......D 2
7 Buckthorn Weston
　　　　　　　　　D 10
21 Buckton, Heref. &
　Worc. ....E 9
41 Buckton, Humberside
　　　　　　　　　H 11
45 Buckton, Northumb.
　　　　　　　　　B 12
25 Buckworth ....H 2
16 Buclebury ....G 6
22 Budbrooke ....F 6
32 Budby ....C 3
4 Budd's Titson ....F 1
4 Bude ....E 1
4 Budlake ....F 3
45 Budle ....D 12
6 Budleigh Salterton .H 4
2 Budock Water ....F 5
30 Buerton ....F 5
23 Bugbrooke ......F 10
31 Buglawton ....D 7
2 Bugle ....D 7
36 Bugthorpe ....A 5
21 Buildwas ....B 11
47 Builstonend ......E 9
20 Builth Road ......G 6
20 Builth Wells .....G 6
17 Bulbourne ......C 10
24 Bulby ....C 2
51 Bulcote ....F 2
30 Bulkeley ....E 4
23 Bulkington, War. ..D 7
15 Bulkington, Wilts. .H 12
4 Bulkworthy ......E 3
28 Bull Bay ....A 4
8 Bull Hill ....F 5
40 Bullamoor ....F 4
17 Bullbrook ....G 9
58 Bullers of Buchan .D 8
15 Bulley ....B 11
43 Bullgill ....H 11
15 Bullinghope .....A 8
8 Bullington, Hants. .B 6
33 Bullington, Lincs. .B 8
39 Bullpot Farm .....G 9
46 Bullwood ....B 6
27 Bulmer, Essex ...L 2
41 Bulmer, N. Yorks. .H 7
27 Bulmer Tye ......L 1
8 Bulphan ....E 6
10 Bulverhythe ......G 6
58 Bulwark ....C 7
48 Bulwark Village ..E 8
32 Bulwell ....F 3
24 Bulwick ....F 1
15 Bumble's Green ...C 4
55 Bunacaimb ....K 1
55 Bunarkaig ....L 6
63 Bunaveneadar ....F 2
30 Bunbury ....D 4
56 Bunchrew ....E 2
50 Bundalloch ......G 3
50 Bunessan ....E 1
38 Bungalow Station .G 2
26 Bungay ....G 1
57 Bunloit ....G 1
32 Bunny ....G 3
54 Buntait ....F 8
18 Buntingford ......A 4
26 Bunwell ....F 4
26 Bunwell Street ...F 4
31 Burbage, Derby ...C 9
23 Burbage, Leics. ...C 8
16 Burbage, Wilts. ...H 3
17 Burchett's Green ..F 9
7 Burcombe ......C 2
22 Burcot, Heref. &
　Worc. ....E 3
16 Burcot, Oxon. ....H 6
17 Burcott ....B 9
36 Burdale ....A 6
27 Bures ....M 2
16 Burford, Oxon. ...C 4
21 Burford, Salop. ..F 11
50 Burg ....C 1

10 Burgess Hill ....F 2
27 Burgh ....K 5
44 Burgh by Sands .....G 2
26 Burgh Castle ......E 8
10 Burgh Heath ....B 1
33 Burgh le Marsh ....D 12
58 Burgh Muir ....E 5
26 Burgh next Aylsham C 5
33 Burgh on Bain .....B 9
26 Burgh St. Margaret .D 7
26 Burgh St. Peter .....F 8
16 Burghclere ....H 6
56 Burghead ....C 7
17 Burghfield ....G 7
17 Burghfield Com.....G 7
21 Burghill ....H 10
36 Burghwallis ....F 3
10 Burham ....B 6
9 Buriton ....D 9
30 Burland ....E 5
3 Burlawn ....C 7
17 Burleigh ....G 10
6 Burlescombe ......E 4
7 Burleston ....G 11
8 Burley, Hants. ....F 3
23 Burley, Leics. .....A 12
21 Burley Gate ....H 11
35 Burley in Wharfdale C 10
8 Burley Lodge ......E 4
8 Burley Street ......F 3
30 Burleydam ....F 5
21 Burlingjobb ....G 8
10 Burlow ....F 4
30 Burlton ....H 3
11 Burmarsh ....E 9
22 Burmington ....H 6
5 Burn, Devon ......F 3
43 Burn, Dumf. & Gall. ....B 10
36 Burn, N. Yorks. ...D 4
34 Burn Naze ....C 2
52 Burn of Cambus ...G 2
35 Burnage ....H 7
31 Burnaston ....G 11
47 Burnbank ....D 11
47 Burnbrae ....E 12
36 Burnby ....C 6
35 Burncross ....G 12
39 Burneside ....F 7
64 Burness ....A 4
40 Burneston ....G 3
15 Burnett ....H 10
44 Burnfoot, Borders ..A 3
44 Burnfoot, Borders ..B 2
43 Burnfoot, Dumf. & Gall. ....B 10
44 Burnfoot, Dumf. & Gall. ....D 2
45 Burnfoot, Northumb. B 8
47 Burnfoot, Strathclyde B 11
32 Burngreave ....A 1
17 Burnham, Bucks. ..F 10
37 Burnham, Humberside E 8
17 Burnham Beeches ..B 4
26 Burnham Deepdale .A 1
18 Burnham Green ....B 3
26 Burnham Market ...A 1
26 Burnham Norton ..A 1
26 Burnham Overy ...A 1
26 Burnham Thorpe ..B 2
6 Burnham-on-Sea ..A 6
19 Burnham-on-Crouch D 9
58 Burnhaven ....C 8
43 Burnhead, Dumf. & Gall. ....C 10
43 Burnhead, Dumf. & Gall. ....B 9
58 Burnhervie ....F 5
22 Burnhill Green ....B 1
45 Burnhope ....H 10
47 Burnhouse ....D 8
49 Burnhouse Mains ..D 7
41 Burniston ....F 10
35 Burnley ....D 7
49 Burnmouth, Borders C 12
43 Burnmouth, Dumf. & Gall. ....A 9
45 Burnopfield ......G 10
59 Burnroot ....H 7
35 Burnsall ....A 9
43 Burnside, Dumf. & Gall. ....C 11
52 Burnside, Fife .....F 6
56 Burnside, Grampian F 5
48 Burnside, Lothian .B 4
64 Burnside, Shetland Is. C 6

47 Burnside, Strathclyde H 10
53 Burnside, Tayside ..B 9
53 Burnside of Dantrune ....D 9
19 Burnt Heath .....A 10
40 Burnt Houses .....C 2
35 Burnt Yates ....A 11
2 Burnthouse ....F 5
48 Burntisland ....A 5
47 Burnton, Strathclyde H 8
42 Burnton, Strathclyde A 6
47 Burnton, Strathclyde H 10
22 Burntwood ......A 4
9 Burpham, Surrey ..A 11
9 Burpham, W. Sussex E 11
45 Burradon, Northumb. B 8
45 Burradon, Tyne & Wear F 11
64 Burrafirth ....A 8
2 Burras ....F 4
64 Burravoe ....C 7
39 Burrells ....C 9
53 Burrelton ....C 7
4 Burridge, Devon ...C 4
9 Burridge, Hants. ...E 7
40 Burrill ....F 3
36 Burringham ....F 6
15 Burrington, Avon ..H 8
4 Burrington, Devon .D 5
21 Burrington, Heref. & Worc. ....E 10
25 Borrough Green ....K 7
23 Burrough on the Hill A 10
6 Burrow, Devon .....G 4
6 Burrow, Somerset ..B 3
7 Burrow Bridge ....C 7
17 Burrowhill ....H 10
9 Burrows Cross ....A 12
13 Burry ....H 8
13 Burry Port ....G 8
13 Burrygreen ....H 8
34 Burscough ....F 3
34 Burscough Bridge ..F 3
37 Bursea ....D 6
36 Bursea Lane Ends .D 6
37 Burshill ....B 8
8 Bursledon ....E 6
31 Burslem ....E 7
27 Burstall ....L 4
7 Burstock ....F 7
27 Burston, Norfolk ..G 4
31 Burston, Staffs. ...G 8
9 Burstow ....D 2
37 Burstwick ....D 10
39 Burtersett ....F 11
30 Burton, Cheshire ..D 4
39 Burton, Cumbria ..G 8
7 Burton, Dorset ....G 10
8 Burton, Dorset ....G 3
12 Burton, Dyfed .....F 3
33 Burton, Lincs. .....C 7
30 Burton, Merseyside .C 2
45 Burton, Northumb. D 12
6 Burton, Somerset ..B 5
15 Burton, Wilts. ....F 11
37 Burton Agnes .....A 9
7 Burton Bradstock ..G 8
33 Burton Coggles ...H 7
37 Burton Contable ..C 9
23 Burton Dassett ...G 7
41 Burton Fleming ...H 11
30 Burton Green, Clwyd D 2
22 Burton Green, W. Midlands ....E 6
23 Burton Hastings ...C 7
39 Burton in Lonsdale .H 9
32 Burton Joyce .....F 4
23 Burton Latimer ...E 12
32 Burton Lazars ....H 5
35 Burton Leonard ...A 12
32 Burton on the Wolds H 3
31 Burton-on-Trent ..H 10
23 Burton Overy .....B 10
24 Burton Pedwardine .A 2
37 Burton Pidsea ....D 10
36 Burton Salmon ...D 3
36 Burton upon Stather E 6
34 Burtonwood ......H 4
30 Burwardsley .....D 4
21 Burwarton ......D 11
10 Burwash ....F 5
10 Burwash Common ..F 5
10 Burwash Weald ...F 5

25 Burwell, Cambs. ....J 7
33 Burwell, Lincs. ....B 10
28 Burwen ....A 4
64 Burwick ....E 2
35 Bury, Cambs. .....G 4
35 Bury, Manchester ..F 7
6 Bury, Somerset ...C 3
9 Bury, W. Sussex ...E 11
18 Bury Green ......B 4
27 Bury St Edmunds ..J 2
36 Burythorpe ....A 6
47 Busby ....D 10
41 Buscel ....G 9
16 Buscot ....D 3
59 Bush ....L 5
21 Bush Bank ....G 10
27 Bush Green ......G 5
57 Bush ....K 8
22 Bushbury ....B 3
18 Bushey ....D 1
18 Bushey Heath .....E 2
15 Bushley ....A 11
16 Bushton ....F 2
64 Busta ....C 7
45 Buston Barns .....B 10
15 Butcher's Pasture ..B 6
15 Butcombe ....H 8
45 Buteland ....E 7
7 Butleigh ....C 8
7 Butleigh Wootton ..C 8
17 Butler's Cross .....C 9
22 Butlers Marston ...G 6
27 Butley ....K 7
30 Butt Green ....E 5
44 Butterburn ....F 5
36 Buttercrambe .....A 5
40 Butterknowle .....C 1
6 Butterleigh ......E 3
38 Buttermere, Cumb. .D 4
16 Buttermere, Wilts. .H 4
30 Butters Green ....E 6
35 Buttershaw ....D 10
52 Butterstone ......C 5
31 Butterton ....E 9
40 Butterwick, Dur. ...B 4
24 Butterwick, Lincs. ..A 5
41 Butterwick, N. Yorks. H 10
41 Butterwick, N. Yorks. G 7
21 Buttington ....B 8
23 Buttock's Booth ...F 11
22 Buttonoak ....D 1
5 Butt's Green ......C 4
8 Buttsash ....E 6
27 Buxhall ....J 3
49 Buxley ....D 10
10 Buxted ....F 4
31 Buxton, Derby ....C 9
26 Buxton, Norfolk ...C 5
26 Buxton Heath ....C 5
14 Bwlch ....B 5
29 Bwlchgwyn ....E 11
29 Bwlchllan ....F 1
28 Bwlchtocyn ......H 3
29 Bwlch-y-cibau ...H 11
29 Bwlch-y-ddâr ....H 11
13 Bwlchyfadfa .....B 8
20 Bwlch-y-ffridd ...C 6
12 Bwlch-y-groes ...C 6
20 Bwlch-y-sarnau ..E 6
43 Byeloch ....D 11
40 Byers Green .....B 2
23 Byfield ....G 8
17 Byfleet ....H 11
21 Byford ....H 9
25 Bygrave ....L 4
61 Bylbster ....B 11
30 Bylchau ....D 9
30 Byley ....C 6
13 Bynea ....G 9
49 Byrewalls ....E 9
44 Byrness ....C 6
25 Bythorn ....H 2
21 Byton ....F 9
45 Bywell ....G 8
9 Byworth ....D 11

2 Cadgwith ....H 4
53 Cadham ....G 7
34 Cadishead ....H 6
13 Cadle ....G 9
16 Cadley, Wilts. ....G 3
8 Cadley, Wilts. .....A 4
17 Cadmore End .....E 8
8 Cadnam ....E 5
37 Cadney ....G 8
29 Cadole ....D 11
13 Cadoxton-Juxta-Neath G 11
60 Cadubh ....G 3
14 Cae Hopkin ......C 2
28 Caeathraw ....D 4
28 Cae-lwyn-grydd ...C 3
33 Caenby ....A 7
33 Caenby Corner ...A 7
14 Caeo ....C 10
12 Caer Farchell ....D 1
14 Caerau ....E 2
13 Cae'r-bryn ....F 9
28 Caerdeon ....H 6
12 Caerleon ....E 6
12 Caerleon ....E 6
28 Caernarvon ......D 4
14 Caerphilly ....F 5
20 Caersws ....C 6
13 Caerwedros ......A 7
15 Caerwent ....E 8
29 Caerwys ....C 10
57 Caggan ....H 4
43 Cairn ....C 10
50 Cairnbaan ....H 5
58 Cairnbrogie ......E 6
49 Cairncross ......C 11
42 Cairnderry ......D 4
51 Cairndow ....F 9
58 Cairness ....B 8
48 Cairneyhill ......A 3
42 Cairnfield ....G 5
58 Cairnfield House ..B 2
42 Cairngaan ....H 2
42 Cairngarroch ....G 1
42 Cairnsmore .....E 5
47 Cairntable ....H 9
42 Cairnwhin ......B 3
54 Caiseachan ......D 6
26 Caister-on-Sea ...D 8
37 Caistor ....G 9
26 Caistor St. Edmund .E 5
45 Caistron ....C 8
49 Caitha Bowland ...E 7
63 Calbost ....E 5
8 Calbourne ......G 6
33 Calceby ....C 11
22 Calchems Corner ..E 6
15 Calcot Farm .....E 11
17 Calcot Row .....G 7
56 Calcots Station ...C 8
11 Calcott ....B 10
38 Caldbeck ....A 6
40 Caldbergh ....G 1
25 Caldecote, Beds. ..L 3
25 Caldecote, Cambs. .K 4
25 Caldecote, Cambs. .G 2
23 Caldecott, Leics. ..C 12
25 Caldecott, Northants H 1
38 Calder, Cumb. .....E 3
49 Calder, Northumb. G 12
38 Calder Bridge ....E 3
35 Calder Grove ....E 11
61 Calder Mains ....B 10
34 Calder Vale ......C 4
47 Calderbank ......C 12
35 Calderbrook .....E 8
48 Caldercruix ......C 1
47 Caldermill ......E 11
47 Calderwood .....D 11
15 Caldicot ....E 8
49 Caldside ....E 9
40 Caldwell ....D 2
30 Caldy ....B 1
13 Caledfwlch .....D 10
13 Caledrhydiau ....B 8
64 Calfsound ....B 3
50 Calgary ....B 1
56 Califer ....D 6
48 California, Central .B 2
26 California, Norf. ...D 8
27 California, Suff. ...L 5
5 California Cross ..K 6
31 Calke ....H 12

45 Callaly ....B 9
52 Callander ....F 1
63 Callanish ....D 3
51 Callert House .....A 8
2 Callestick ....E 5
62 Calligarry ....H 5
15 Callington ....C 10
15 Callow ....A 8
22 Callow End ....G 2
22 Callow Hill, Heref. & Worcs. ....E 1
22 Callow Hill, Heref. & Worcs. ....F 4
16 Callow Hill, Wilts. .F 1
17 Callowhill ....G 11
21 Callows Grave ....F 11
16 Calmore ....E 5
16 Calmsden ....C 1
16 Calne ....G 1
32 Calow ....C 1
8 Calshot ....F 6
3 Calstock ....C 11
16 Calstone Wellington G 1
26 Calthorpe ....B 5
39 Calthwaite ......A 7
35 Calton, N. Yorks. ..A 8
31 Calton, Staffs. ....E 9
30 Calveley ....D 4
31 Calver ....C 11
21 Calver Hill ......G 9
30 Calverhall ......F 5
6 Calverleigh .....E 3
35 Calverley ....C 10
23 Calverton, Bucks. .H 11
32 Calverton, Notts. ..E 3
58 Calvine ....A 3
43 Calvo ....F 12
15 Cam ....D 10
62 Camascross .....G 6
54 Camasine ....A 5
50 Camasnacroise ...B 6
54 Camasterach .....E 1
54 Camastianavaig ..D 4
62 Camasunary .....F 4
64 Camb ....B 7
11 Camber ....F 8
17 Camberley ....H 9
16 Camberwell ......F 3
36 Camblesforth ....D 4
53 Cambo, Fife ......F 10
45 Cambo, Northumb. .D 8
45 Cambois ....E 11
2 Camborne ....F 4
25 Cambridge, Cambs. J 5
15 Cambridge, Glos. .D 10
25 Cambridgeshire Co. K 5
52 Cambus ....H 3
59 Cambus o'May ...G 2
52 Cambusbarron ...H 3
52 Cambuskenneth ..H 3
47 Cambuslang .....C 11
52 Cambusmore Lo. ..G 8
61 Cambussorray ....F 7
18 Camden ....E 3
18 Cameley ....H 9
2 Camelford ....A 8
48 Camelon ....A 2
9 Camelsdale ......C 10
56 Camerory ....F 4
18 Camerton, Avon ..A 10
38 Camerton, Cumb. .B 3
57 Camghouran ......B 1
55 Camisky ....L 5
59 Cammachmore ...H 6
26 Cammeringham ...B 6
56 Campbelltown or Ardersier ....D 3
46 Campbeltown ....G 2
45 Camperdown .....F 11
53 Campmuir ....C 7
25 Camps Green ....L 7
36 Campsall ....F 3
27 Campsey Ash ....K 6
12 Campton ....L 2
44 Camptown ....B 5
12 Camrose ....E 3
52 Camserney ......B 3
61 Camster ....C 11
55 Camus-luinie .....G 3
54 Camusteel ....E 1
52 Camusvrachan ...B 1
4 Canada ....D 4
59 Candacraig ......G 1
58 Candacraig House ..F 1
49 Candlesby ....D 11
59 Candy ....J 5
48 Candyburn ....E 3
48 Cane End ....F 8
19 Canewdon ....D 9
18 Canfield End .....B 6
8 Canford Bottom ..F 2

8 Canford Magna .....F 2
61 Canisbay ....A 12
7 Cann ....D 12
7 Cann Common ...D 12
3 Cannaframe ......B 9
7 Cannards Grave ..B 9
54 Canncih ....F 7
6 Cannington ....B 6
22 Cannock ....A 3
22 Cannock Wood ...A 4
15 Cannop ....C 9
21 Canon Bridge .....H 10
21 Canon Pyon ......G 10
44 Canonbie ....E 2
23 Canons Ashby ....G 9
2 Canonstown ......F 2
11 Canterbury ......B 10
26 Cantley, Norfolk ...E 7
36 Cantley, S. Yorks. ..A 4
14 Canton ....G 5
56 Cantraybruich ....E 3
56 Cantraydoune ....E 3
56 Cantraywood ....E 3
39 Cantsfield ....H 8
19 Canvey ....F 8
33 Canwick ....C 7
2 Canworthy Water ..B 2
55 Caol ....M 5
55 Caonich ....K 4
10 Capel ....D 1
20 Capel-Bangor ....D 2
20 Capel Betws Lleucu .G 2
28 Capel Carmel ....G 1
28 Capel Curig ......D 6
13 Capel Cynon .....B 7
13 Capel Dewi, Dyfed .E 8
20 Capel Dewi, Dyfed .D 2
13 Capel Dewi, Dyfed .C 8
29 Capel Garmon ....E 7
13 Capel Gwyn .....E 8
13 Capel Gwynfe ....E 10
13 Capel Hendre ....F 9
13 Capel Isaac ......D 9
12 Capel Iwan ......C 6
11 Capel le Ferne ...D 11
14 Capel Llanilterne ..F 4
27 Capel St. Andrew ..K 7
27 Capel St. Mary ...L 4
20 Capel Seion ......D 2
20 Capel Trisant .....E 3
12 Capel Tygwydd ...C 6
28 Capel-côch ......B 4
13 Capel-gwyn ......C 3
13 Capel-Iago ......C 9
28 Capel-uchaf .....E 4
29 Capelulo ....C 7
14 Capel-y-ffin .....A 6
30 Capenhurst ......C 2
39 Capenwray ......H 8
45 Capheaton ......E 8
56 Cappercleuch ....G 5
48 Capplegill ....H 4
5 Capton, Devon ...K 7
6 Capton, Somerset .B 4
52 Caputh ....C 6
32 Car Colston ......F 4
2 Carbis Bay ....F 2
62 Carbost, Skye ....E 3
62 Carbost, Skye ....C 4
60 Carbreck ....B 4
32 Carbrook ....A 1
26 Carbrooke ....E 3
32 Carburton ....C 3
3 Carclaze ....D 7
47 Carcluie ....H 8
36 Carcroft ....F 3
53 Cardenden ....H 7
21 Cardeston ....A 9
14 Cardiff ....G 5
12 Cardigan ....B 5
25 Cardington, Bedfordshire ....K 2
21 Cardington, Salop. .C 10
3 Cardinham ......C 8
42 Cardorcan ....D 5
56 Cardow ....E 7
48 Cardrona ....F 6
47 Cardross ....B 8
43 Cardurnock ......F 12
24 Careby ....D 1
59 Careston ....L 3
12 Carew ....G 4
12 Carew Cheriton ...G 4
12 Carew Newton ...F 4
44 Carewoodrig .....C 3
15 Carey ....A 9
47 Carfin ....D 12
3 Carfrae ....G 4
43 Cargenbridge ....D 10
52 Cargill ....C 6
44 Cargo ....G 2
3 Cargreen ....C 11
49 Carham ....F 10
6 Carhampton ......B 3

2 Carharrack ....F 4
52 Carie ....A 1
8 Carisbrooke ....G 6
38 Cark ....G 6
3 Carkeel ....D 11
2 Carland ....D 5
44 Carlatton Mill ....H 4
24 Carlby ....D 2
35 Carlecotes ....G 10
2 Carleen ....G 3
44 Carleton, Cumb. ....H 3
42 Carleton, Dumf. & Gall. ....H 5
35 Carleton, N. Yorks. ....B 8
26 Ca:letonForehoe ....E 4
26 Carleton Rode ....E 4
2 Carlidnack ....G 5
41 Carlin How ....C 7
15 Carlingcott ....H 10
44 Carlisle ....G 2
48 Carlops ....D 4
63 Carlyon Bay ....C 3
25 Carlton, Beds. ....K 1
25 Carlton, Cambs. ....K 7
40 Carlton, Cleveland ....C 4
23 Carlton, Leics. ....B 7
40 Carlton, N. Yorks. ....E 5
40 Carlton, N. Yorks. ....F 6
40 Carlton, N. Yorks. ....G 1
36 Carlton, N. Yorks. ....E 4
32 Carlton, Notts. ....F 3
35 Carlton, S. Yorks. ....F 12
27 Carlton, Suffolk ....J 7
36 Carlton, W. Yorks. ....D 1
26 Carlton, Colville ....F 8
23 Carlton Curlieu ....B 10
40 Carlton Husthwaite ....G 5
32 Carlton in Lindrick ....B 3
40 Carlton Miniott ....G 4
32 Carlton Scroop ....F 6
32 Carlton-le-Moorland ....D 6
32 Carlton-on-Trent ....D 5
48 Carluke ....D 1
3 Carlyon Bay ....D 7
48 Carmacoup ....G 1
13 Carmarthen ....E 7
29 Carmel, Clwyd ....C 11
13 Carmel, Dyfed ....E 9
28 Carmel, Gwynedd ....E 4
28 Carmel, Gwynedd ....B 5
13 Carmel Chapel ....D 10
38 Carmel Fell ....F 6
63 Carminish ....H 1
59 Carmont ....J 5
47 Carmunnock ....D 11
47 Carmyle ....C 11
53 Carmyllie ....C 10
37 Carnaby ....A 9
55 Carnach, Highland ....L 1
55 Carnach, Highland ....G 4
63 Carnach, W. Isles ....G 3
55 Carnachuin ....K 4
57 Carnaquheen ....K 8
53 Carnbee ....F 10
52 Carnbo ....G 5
55 Carndu ....G 3
47 Carnduff ....E 11
2 Carne ....F 6
47 Carnell ....F 9
14 Carnetown ....E 4
39 Carnforth ....H 7
55 Carn-gorm ....G 3
12 Carnhedryn Uchaf ....D 2
2 Carnhell Green ....F 3
63 Carnish ....D 1
2 Carnkie ....F 4
20 Carno ....C 5
55 Carnoch, Highland ....K 2
54 Carnoch, Highland ....F 7
54 Carnoch, Highland ....H 6
52 Carnock ....H 5
2 Carnon Downs ....F 5
53 Carnoustie ....D 10
48 Carnwath ....E 3
29 Carog ....E 7
39 Carperby ....F 12
32 Carr ....A 2
34 Carr Cross ....F 3
44 Carr Shield ....H 6
32 Carr Vale ....C 2
46 Carradale ....E 3
63 Carragrich ....G 3
57 Carrbridge ....G 5
35 Carrbrook ....G 8
28 Carreglefn ....A 3
12 Carregwen ....C 6
53 Carrick, Fife ....E 9
51 Carrick, Strathclyde ....H 9
48 Carriden ....A 3
34 Carrington, Manchester ....H 6
33 Carrington, Lincs. ....E 10

48 Carrington, Lothian ....C 6
29 Carrog ....F 10
48 Carron, Central ....A 2
56 Carron, Grampian ....E 8
48 Carron Bridge ....A 12
43 Carronbridge ....B 9
48 Carronshore ....A 2
47 Carrot ....E 10
15 Carrow Hill ....E 7
43 Carrutherstown ....D 11
40 Carrville ....A 3
46 Carsaig, Strathclyde ....A 2
50 Carsaig, Strathclyde ....E 3
43 Carscreugh ....F 3
46 Carse House ....C 2
42 Carsebuie ....E 4
42 Carsegown ....F 5
42 Carseriggan ....E 4
43 Carsethorn ....F 10
18 Carshalton ....G 3
31 Carsington ....E 11
46 Carskiey ....H 2
42 Carsluith ....F 6
48 Carstairs ....E 2
48 Carstairs Junction ....E 2
49 Carterhaugh ....G 7
8 Carter's Clay ....D 4
16 Carterton ....C 4
45 Carterway Heads ....H 8
3 Carthew ....D 7
40 Carthorpe ....G 3
45 Cartington ....C 8
48 Cartland ....E 1
38 Cartmel ....G 6
13 Carway ....F 8
7 Cary Fitzpaine ....D 9
63 Caryshader ....D 2
43 Carzield ....C 10
21 Cascob ....F 8
51 Cashell ....H 11
51 Cashlie ....C 12
8 Cashmoor ....E 1
16 Cassey Compton ....C 1
16 Cassington, Oxon ....C 5
7 Cassington, Som. ....B 7
40 Cassop Colliery ....A 4
24 Casswell's Bridge ....C 3
14 Castell-y-bwch ....E 6
39 Casterton ....G 8
26 Castle Acre ....D 1
23 Castle Ashby ....F 11
31 Castle Bank ....H 7
39 Castle Bolton ....F 12
22 Castle Bromwich ....C 5
24 Castle Bytham ....D 1
21 Castle Caereinion ....B 7
25 Castle Camps ....L 7
44 Castle Carrock ....G 4
7 Castle Cary ....C 10
15 Castle Combe ....F 11
32 Castle Donnington ....G 2
43 Castle Douglas ....E 8
16 Castle Eaton ....E 2
40 Castle Eden ....A 4
58 Castle Forbes ....F 4
21 Castle Frome ....H 12
17 Castle Green ....H 10
31 Castle Gresley ....H 11
49 Castle Heaton ....E 11
27 Castle Hedingham ....L 1
10 Castle Hill ....D 6
41 Castle Howard ....H 7
53 Castle Huntly ....D 8
42 Castle Kennedy ....F 2
12 Castle Morris ....D 3
44 Castle O'er ....D 1
21 Castle Pulverbatch ....B 9
24 Castle Rising ....C 8
56 Castle Stuart ....E 3
12 Castlebythe ....D 4
47 Castlecary ....B 12
48 Castlecraig, Borders ....E 4
56 Castlecraig, Highland ....C 4
43 Castlefairn ....C 8
36 Castleford ....E 2
48 Castlehill, Borders ....F 5
58 Castlehill, Grampian ....C 5
47 Castlehill, Strathclyde ....B 9
48 Castlehill, Strathclyde ....D 1
42 Castlemaddy ....C 6
12 Castlemartin ....G 3
43 Castlemilk ....D 12
15 Castlemorton ....A 11
45 Castleside ....H 9
23 Castlethorpe ....H 11
44 Castleton, Borders ....D 3
31 Castleton, Derby ....B 10
35 Castleton, Manchester ....F 7

14 Castleton, Gwent ....F 6
41 Castleton, N. Yorks. ....D 7
46 Castleton, Strathclyde ....A 4
53 Castleton, Tayside ....C 8
7 Castletown, Dorset ....H 7
61 Castletown, Highland ....A 11
56 Castletown, Highland ....E 3
38 Castletown, I.o.M. ....H 1
45 Castletown, Tyne & Wear ....G 11
35 Castley ....C 11
26 Caston ....F 2
24 Castor ....F 2
43 Castramont ....E 7
13 Caswell ....H 9
31 Cat and Fiddle Inn ....C 8
46 Catacol ....D 4
15 Catbrain ....F 9
15 Catbrook ....D 8
2 Catchall ....G 2
32 Catcliffe ....A 2
7 Catcott ....B 7
7 Catcott Burtle ....B 7
47 Catcraig ....F 9
10 Caterham ....C 2
26 Catfield ....C 7
64 Catfirth ....D 7
18 Catford ....G 4
34 Catforth ....D 4
14 Cathays ....F 5
47 Cathcart ....C 10
14 Cathedine ....B 5
7 Catherington ....E 8
7 Catherston Leweston ....G 7
21 Catherton ....E 12
49 Cathpair ....E 7
43 Catlins ....C 12
57 Catlodge ....K 2
44 Catlowdy ....E 3
16 Catmore ....F 5
34 Caton ....A 4
5 Cator Court ....H 5
47 Catrine ....G 10
15 Cat's Ash ....E 7
10 Catsfield ....G 6
22 Catshill ....E 3
36 Cattal ....B 2
27 Cattawade ....M 4
34 Catterall ....C 4
40 Catterick ....E 3
40 Catterick Bridge ....E 3
40 Catterick Camp ....E 2
39 Catterlen ....B 7
59 Catterline ....J 6
36 Catterton ....C 3
9 Catteshall ....B 11
23 Catthorpe ....D 9
7 Cattistock ....F 9
26 Catton, Norfolk ....D 5
44 Catton, Northumb. ....G 6
40 Catton, N. Yorks ....G 4
37 Catwick ....C 9
25 Catworth ....H 2
16 Caulcott ....B 6
52 Cauldhame ....H 1
44 Cauldmill ....B 4
31 Cauldon ....E 9
58 Cauldwells ....B 5
43 Caulkerbush ....F 10
7 Caundle Marsh ....E 1
22 Caunsall ....D 2
32 Caunton ....D 5
58 Causewayend, Grampian ....F 7
48 Causewayend, Strathclyde ....F 3
52 Causewayhead, Central ....H 3
43 Causewayhead, Cumb. ....F 12
45 Causey Park Bri. ....D 10
39 Cautley ....F 9
27 Cavendish ....K 1
27 Cavenham ....H 1
17 Caversfield ....B 7
17 Caversham ....G 8
31 Caverswall ....F 8
36 Cavil ....D 5
56 Cawdor ....E 4
3 Cawsand ....E 11
26 Cawston ....C 4
11 Cawthorn ....F 8
35 Cawthorne ....F 11
24 Cawthorpe ....C 2
36 Cawood ....C 3
40 Cawton ....G 6
25 Caxton ....J 4

21 Caynham ....E 11
32 Caythorpe, Lincs. ....E 6
32 Caythorpe, Notts. ....F 4
41 Cayton ....G 10
61 Ceann-na-coille ....C 7
29 Cefn-Berain ....C 9
15 Cefn-Canol ....G 11
29 Cefn Coch ....G 10
14 Cefn Cribbwr ....F 2
14 Cefn Cross ....F 2
21 Cefn Einion ....D 8
14 Cefn Fforest ....D 5
29 Cefn Mawr ....F 12
14 Cefn Rhigos ....D 2
29 Cefn-brith ....E 8
13 Cefn-bryn-brain ....F 10
14 Cefn-coed-y-cymmer ....C 3
29 Cefn-ddwysarn ....F 9
20 Cefngorwydd ....H 5
29 Cefn-y-bedd ....E 12
12 Cefn-y-pant ....D 5
13 Cellan ....B 9
31 Cellarhead ....E 8
39 Celleron ....C 7
28 Cemaes Bay ....A 3
20 Cemmaes ....B 4
20 Cemmaes Road ....B 4
12 Cenarth ....C 6
53 Ceres ....F 9
20 Cerist ....D 5
7 Cerne Abbas ....F 10
16 Cerney Wick ....E 2
28 Cerrigceinwen ....C 4
29 Cerrigydrudion ....E 9
26 Cess ....D 7
49 Cessford ....G 10
28 Ceunant ....C 4
15 Chaceley ....A 11
2 Chacewater ....E 5
23 Chackmore ....A 8
22 Chad Valley ....D 4
22 Chadbury ....G 4
35 Chadderton ....G 7
31 Chaddesden ....F 12
23 Chaddesley Corbett ....E 2
16 Chaddleworth ....F 5
16 Chadlington ....B 4
23 Chadshunt ....G 7
32 Chadwell ....H 5
18 Chadwell St. Mary ....F 6
22 Chadwick End ....E 5
7 Chaffcombe ....E 7
5 Chagford ....G 6
10 Chailey ....F 3
24 Chainbridge ....E 5
10 Chainhurst ....C 6
8 Chalbury ....E 2
8 Chalbury Com. ....E 2
10 Chaldon ....C 2
7 Chaldon Herring or East Chaldon ....H 11
8 Chale ....H 6
8 Chale Green ....H 6
17 Chalfont St. Giles ....E 10
17 Chalfont St. Peter ....E 11
15 Chalford ....D 12
17 Chalford Com. ....E 11
17 Chalgrove ....D 7
10 Chalk ....A 5
4 Challacombe, Devon ....B 6
4 Challacombe, Devon ....D 6
42 Challoch ....E 5
10 Challock Lees ....C 8
17 Chalton, Beds. ....B 11
9 Chalton, Hants. ....E 8
10 Chalvey ....F 10
10 Chalvington ....G 4
48 Champany ....B 3
20 Chancery ....E 1
17 Chandler's Cross ....D 11
8 Chandler's Ford ....D 6
43 Chanlockfoot ....B 8
7 Chantry ....B 10
53 Chapel ....H 7
7 Chapel Allerton ....B 8
35 Chapel Allerton ....C 11
3 Chapel Amble ....B 7
28 Chapel Brampton ....E 10
23 Chapel Chorlton ....F 6
24 Chapel End ....C 7
22 Chapel Green ....D 6
36 Chapel Haddlesey ....D 4
58 Chapel Hill, Grampian ....D 8
15 Chapel Hill, Gwent ....D 8
33 Chapel Hill, Lincs. ....E 9
35 Chapel Hill, N. Yorks. ....C 12
21 Chapel Lawn ....E 8

39 Chapel le Dale ....G 9
49 Chapel Mains ....E 8
59 Chapel of Barras ....J 6
58 Chapel of Garioch ....E 5
42 Chapel Rossan ....G 2
16 Chapel Row, Berks. ....G 6
10 Chapel Row, E. Sussex ....G 5
33 Chapel St. Leonards ....C 12
38 Chapel Stile ....E 5
25 Chapeland Way ....L 8
42 Chapeldonan ....B 3
31 Chapel-en-le-Frith ....B 9
47 Chapelhall ....C 12
43 Chapelhill, Dumf. & Gall. ....B 11
53 Chapelhill, Tayside ....E 7
52 Chapelhill, Tayside ....D 5
48 Chapelhope ....G 5
44 Chapelknowe ....F 2
38 Chapels ....G 5
4 Chapelton, Devon ....C 5
43 Chapelton, Dumf. & Gall. ....G 8
59 Chapelton, Grampian ....J 5
57 Chapelton, Grampian ....H 5
47 Chapelton, Highland ....E 11
53 Chapelton, Tayside ....B 11
57 Chapeltown, Grampian ....G 8
34 Chapeltown, Lancs. ....F 6
35 Chapeltown, S. Yorks. ....G 12
5 Chapmans Well ....G 2
7 Chapmanslade ....B 11
18 Chapmore End ....B 3
19 Chappel ....A 9
7 Chard ....E 7
6 Chardstock ....F 6
15 Charfield ....E 10
11 Charing ....C 8
8 Charing Cross ....E 3
11 Charing Heath ....C 8
22 Charingworth ....H 5
16 Charlbury ....B 5
15 Charlcombe ....H 10
16 Charlcutt ....G 1
22 Charlecote ....F 6
4 Charles ....C 6
43 Charlesfield ....E 12
53 Charleston ....C 8
59 Charlestown, Grampian ....G 7
8 Charlestown, Corn. ....E 7
7 Charlestown, Dorset ....H 9
48 Charlestown, Fife ....A 3
54 Charlestown, Highland ....B 2
56 Charlestown, Highland ....E 2
35 Charlestown, W. Yorks. ....D 8
56 Charlestown of Aberlour ....E 8
35 Charlesworth ....H 9
5 Charleton ....L 6
6 Charlinch ....B 6
18 Charlton, Herts. ....A 2
40 Charlton, Cleveland ....D 6
44 Charlton, Northumb. ....D 6
16 Charlton, Oxon ....A 6
9 Charlton, W. Sussex ....E 10
8 Charlton, Wilts. ....A 3
8 Charlton, Wilts. ....D 3
16 Charlton, Wilts. ....H 2
7 Charlton, Wilts. ....D 12
16 Charlton, Wilts. ....E 1
22 Charlton, Heref. & Worc. ....H 4
16 Charlton Abbots ....B 1
7 Charlton Adam ....C 9
7 Charlton Horethorne ....D 10
16 Charlton Kings ....B 1
7 Charlton Mackrell ....C 8
7 Charlton Marshall ....F 12
45 Charlton Mires ....A 10
7 Charlton Musgrove ....C 10
16 Charlton-on-Otmoor ....C 6
7 Charlton-on-the-Hill ....F 12
9 Charlwood, Hants. ....C 8

10 Charlwood, Surrey ....D 1
7 Charminster ....G 10
7 Charmouth ....G 7
17 Charndon ....B 7
16 Charney Bassett ....E 5
34 Charnock Richard ....F 4
27 Charsfield ....J 5
11 Chart Sutton ....C 7
17 Charter Alley ....H 7
49 Charterhouse, Borders ....F 9
7 Charterhouse, Som. ....A 8
16 Charterville Allotments ....C 4
11 Chartham ....C 9
11 Chartham Hatch ....B 9
8 Charton ....A 5
17 Chartridge ....D 10
23 Charwelton ....G 8
22 Chase Terrace ....A 4
22 Chasetown ....A 4
16 Chastleton ....A 3
4 Chasty ....F 2
34 Chatburn ....C 6
30 Chatcull ....G 6
10 Chatham ....B 6
45 Chathill ....E 12
10 Chattenden ....A 6
25 Chatteris ....G 5
27 Chattisham ....L 4
45 Chatton ....C 12
17 Chaul End ....B 11
4 Chawleigh ....E 6
25 Chawston ....K 3
9 Chawton ....B 8
31 Cheadle, Manchester ....A 7
31 Cheadle, Staffs. ....F 8
31 Cheadle Hulme ....B 7
18 Cheam ....G 2
17 Cheapside ....G 10
17 Chearsley ....C 8
31 Chebsey ....G 7
17 Checkendon ....F 7
30 Checkley, Cheshire ....F 6
21 Checkley, Heref. & Worc. ....H 11
31 Checkley, Staffs. ....F 7
27 Chedburgh ....J 1
7 Cheddar ....A 8
30 Cheddington ....B 10
31 Cheddleton ....E 8
6 Cheddon Fitzpaine ....C 6
26 Chedgrave ....E 7
7 Chedington ....F 8
27 Chediston ....G 7
16 Chedworth ....C 2
7 Chedzoy ....B 7
49 Cheeklaw ....D 10
35 Cheetham Hill ....C 7
4 Cheglinch ....B 4
4 Cheldon Barton ....C 7
31 Chelford ....C 7
31 Chellaston ....G 12
25 Chellington ....K 1
22 Chelmarsh ....C 1
27 Chelmondiston ....L 5
31 Chelmorton ....C 7
19 Chelmsford ....C 7
18 Chelsea ....F 3
18 Chelsfield Village ....G 5
27 Chelsworth ....K 3
15 Cheltenham, Glos. ....B 12
14 Cheltenham, Gwent ....C 5
25 Chelveston ....H 1
15 Chelvey ....G 8
15 Chelwood ....H 9
10 Chelwood Com. ....E 3
10 Chelwood Gate ....E 3
21 Cheney Longville ....D 9
17 Chenies ....D 11
15 Chepstow ....E 8
16 Cherhill ....G 1
15 Cherington, Glos. ....D 12
22 Cherington, War. ....H 6
9 Cheriton, Hants. ....C 5
11 Cheriton, Kent ....D 11
4 Cheriton, Som. ....A 6
13 Cheriton, W. Glam. ....H 8
5 Cheriton Bishop ....F 6
5 Cheriton Cross ....G 6
6 CheritonFitzpaine ....F 2
12 Cheriton or Stackpole Elidor ....G 3
30 Cherrington ....H 5
37 Cherry Burton ....C 7
25 Cherry Hinton ....K 6
22 Cherry Orchard ....E 6
52 Cherrybank ....E 6
49 Cherrytrees ....F 10
17 Chertsey ....G 11
7 Cheselbourne ....F 11
17 Chesham ....D 10
17 Chesham Bois ....D 10

30 Cheshire, Co. ......D 5
18 Cheshunt ....D 4
22 Cheslyn Hay ......A 3
18 Chessington ....H 2
30 Chester ....D 3
45 Chester Moor .....H 11
7 Chesterblade .....B 10
32 Chesterfield ....C 1
22 Chesterfield ....B 4
48 Chesterhall ....F 2
48 Chesterhill ....C 6
45 Chester-le-Street ..H 11
44 Chesters, Borders ..B 5
49 Chesters, Borders ..G 8
24 Chesterton, Cambs. .F 2
16 Chesterton, Oxon ..B 6
31 Chesterton, Staffs. .E 7
23 ChestertonGreen ...F 7
44 Chesterwood ......F 6
11 Chestfield ....B 10
30 Cheswardine ......G 6
45 Cheswick ....A 11
45 Cheswick Bldgs. ..A 11
7 Chetnole ....E 9
6 Chettiscombe .....E 3
25 Chettisham ....G 6
8 Chettle ....E 1
21 Chetton ....C 12
30 Chetwynd Aston ..H 6
30 Chetwynd Park ....H 6
25 Cheveley ....J 8
10 Chevening ....B 4
27 Chevington ....J 1
45 Chevington Drift ..C 11
6 Chevithorne ......E 3
15 Chew Magna ......H 9
15 Chew Stoke ....H 9
15 Chewton Keynsham .H 9
7 Chewton Mendip ..A 9
23 Chicheley ....G 12
9 Chichester ....F 10
7 Chickerell ....H 9
7 Chicklade ....C 12
21 Chickward ....G 8
9 Chidden ....D 8
9 Chiddingfold .....C 11
10 Chiddingly ....G 4
10 Chiddingstone ....D 4
10 Chiddingstone
     Causeway ....C 4
10 Chiddingstone Hoath
                  D 4
7 Chideock ....G 7
6 Chidgley ....C 4
9 Chidham ....F 9
16 Chieveley ....G 5
18 Chignall St. James ..C 6
18 Chignall Smealy ...C 6
18 Chigwell ....E 4
18 Chigwell Row .....E 5
8 Chilbolton ....B 5
8 Chilcomb ....C 6
7 Chilcombe ....G 9
7 Chilcompton ......A 9
22 Chilcote ....A 6
18 Child Okeford ....E 11
30 Childer Thornton ..B 2
34 Children's Homes ..E 6
16 Childrey ....E 5
30 Child's Ercall ....H 5
22 Childswickham ....H 4
30 Childwall ....A 3
18 Childwick Green ...C 1
7 Chilfrome ....F 9
9 Chilgrove ....E 9
11 Chilham ....C 9
8 Chilhampton ......C 3
5 Chilla ....F 3
5 Chillaton ....H 3
11 Chillenden ......C 11
8 Chillerton ....H 6
27 Chillesford ......K 7
45 Chillingham ......C 12
5 Chillington, Devon ..L 7
7 Chillington,
     Somerset ....E 7
32 Chillwell ....G 2
8 Chilmark ....C 1
16 Chilson ....B 4
3 Chilsworthy, Corn. .B 11
4 Chilsworthy, Devon .E 2
7 Chilthorne Domer ..D 8
17 Chilton, Bucks. ....C 8
4 Chilton, Devon ....E 7
16 Chilton, Oxon ....F 6
40 Chilton, Durham ..B 3
9 Chilton Candover ..B 7
17 Chilton Cantelo ...D 9
16 ChiltonFoliat .....G 4
40 Chilton Lane ......B 3
7 Chilton Polden ...B 7
27 Chilton Street ....K 1
6 Chilton Trinity ...B 6
8 Chilworth, Hants. ..D 5

9 Chilworth, Surrey .A 11
16 Chimney ....D 4
9 Chineham ....A 8
18 Chingford ....E 4
31 Chinley ....B 9
31 Chinley Head .....B 9
17 Chinnor ....D 8
30 Chipnall ....G 6
25 Chippenham, Cambs.
                  H 8
15 Chippenham, Wilts.
                  G 12
17 Chipperfield ......D 11
25 Chipping, Herts. ..M 5
34 Chipping, Lancs....C 5
22 Chipping Campden .H 5
16 Chipping Norton ..B 4
15 Chipping Sodbury .F 10
23 Chipping Warden ...G 8
6 Chipstable ....D 4
10 Chipstead, Kent ..B 4
10 Chipstead, Surrey ..B 2
21 Chirbury ....C 8
29 Chirk ....F 12
29 Chirk Green ......F 12
42 Chirmorie ....D 3
49 Chirnside ....D 11
49 Chirnsidebridge ..D 11
16 Chirton ....H 2
16 Chisbury ....G 4
7 Chiselborough .....E 8
16 Chiseldon ....F 3
17 Chislehampton ...D 7
18 Chislehurst ......G 4
11 Chislet ....B 11
35 Chisley ....D 9
18 Chiswell Green ...C 1
18 Chiswick ....C 2
35 Chisworth ....H 8
11 Chitcombe ....F 7
9 Chithurst ....D 9
25 Chittering ....H 6
16 Chitterne ....B 2
4 Chittlehamholt ....D 5
4 Chittlehampton ...C 5
15 Chittoe ....H 12
5 Chivelstone ......M 6
17 Chobham ....H 10
49 Choicelee ....D 10
8 Cholderton ....B 4
17 Cholesbury ....C 10
45 Chollerford ....F 7
45 Chollerton ....F 7
17 Cholsey ....E 7
21 Cholstrey ....F 10
40 Chop Gate ....E 6
45 Choppington .....E 10
44 Chopwell ....G 9
30 Chorley, Cheshire ..E 4
34 Chorley, Lancs. ...E 5
21 Chorley, Salop. ...D 12
22 Chorley, Staffs. ...A 4
17 Chorleywood .....E 11
30 Chorlton ....E 6
35 Chorlton cum Hardy
                  H 7
30 Chorlton Lane .....E 3
25 Chrishall ....L 5
24 Christchurch, Cambs.
                  F 6
8 Christchurch, Dorset
                  G 3
15 Christchurch, Gwent
                  E 7
16 Christian Malford ...F 1
30 Christleton ....D 3
17 Christmas Com. ...E 8
7 Christon ....A 2
45 Christon Bank ....A 10
5 Christow ....G 7
9 Christ's Hospital ..C 12
47 Chryston ....B 11
5 Chudleigh ....H 7
5 Chudleigh Knighton
                  H 7
4 Chulmleigh ....E 6
35 Chunal ....H 9
34 Church ....D 6
30 Church Aston .....H 6
23 Church Brampton .E 10
31 Church Broughton
                  G 10
9 Church Crookham ..A 9
31 Church Eaton .....H 7
25 Church End, Beds. ..L 3
19 Church End, Essex ..A 7
25 Church End, Essex ..L 7
17 Church End, Hants. .H 7
17 Church End;
     Hertfordshire ...C 12
37 Church End, Lincs. G 12
18 Church End,
     London ....E 3
24 Church End, Norf. ..E 5

22 Church End, War. ..C 6
16 Church End, Wilts. ..F 1
16 Church Enstone ....B 5
36 Church Fenton ....C 3
6 Church Green .....G 5
31 Church Gresley ...H 11
16 Church Hanborough
                  C 5
30 Church Hill ....D 5
22 Church Honeybourne
                  H 5
41 Church House ......E 7
41 Church Houses ....E 7
8 Church Knowle ....H 1
32 Church Laneham ...C 5
23 Church Langton ...C 10
23 Church Lawford ...D 8
31 Church Lawton ....E 7
31 Church Leigh ......G 8
22 Church Lench .....G 4
30 Church Minshull ...D 5
21 Church Preen ....C 11
21 Church Pulverbatch .B 9
21 Church Stoke .....C 8
23 Church Stowe .....F 9
10 Church Street, Kent
                  A 6
27 Church Street, Suffolk
                  G 8
21 Church Stretton ...C 10
39 Church Town ......F 7
14 Church Village .....F 4
32 Church Warsop ....C 3
15 Churcham ....B 11
15 Churchdown ......B 12
15 Churchend, Avon ..E 10
18 Churchend, Essex ..B 6
19 Churchend, Essex .E 10
22 Churchfield ....C 4
15 Churchill, Avon....H 7
4 Churchill, Devon ...B 5
6 Churchill, Devon ...F 6
22 Churchill, Heref. &
     Worc. ....G 3
16 Churchill, Oxon ...B 4
22 Churchill, Salop. ...D 2
6 Churchingford .....E 5
23 Churchover ....D 8
6 Churchstanton .....E 5
5 Churchstow ......L 6
38 Churchtown, Cumb.
                  A 6
4 Churchtown, Dev. ..F 2
38 Churchtown, I. o. M.
                  G 2
34 Churchtown, Lancs. C 4
34 Churchtown,
     Merseyside ......E 3
44 Churnsike Lodge ..E 5
5 Churston Ferrers ..K 8
9 Churt ....B 10
30 Churton ....E 3
35 Churwell ....D 11
8 Chute Standen ....A 5
28 Chwilog ....F 4
29 Cilcain ....D 11
13 Cilcennin ....A 8
13 Cilfrew ....G 11
14 Cilfynydd ....E 4
12 Cilgerran ....C 5
12 Cilgwyn ....C 4
13 Ciliau Aeron ......A 8
13 Cilmaengwyn .....F 10
50 Cilmalieu ....B 6
21 Cilmery ....G 5
12 Cilrhedyn ....D 6
13 Cilsan ....E 9
29 Ciltalgarth ....F 8
12 Cilwendeg ....C 6
13 Cilybebyll ....F 10
13 Cil-y-cwm ....C 11
15 Cinderford ....C 10
12 Cippyn ....B 5
16 Cirencester ....D 1
40 Citadilla ....E 2
28 City Dulas ....B 4
57 Clach Bharraig ...J 5
57 Clachaig, Highland .H 6
46 Clachaig, Strathclyde
                  A 6
62 Clachan, Highland ..E 5
50 Clachan, Strathclyde
                  C 6
50 Clachan, Strathclyde
                  F 5
51 Clachan, Strathclyde
                  F 9
46 Clachan, Strathclyde
                  D 3
52 Clachan, Tayside ...A 3
47 Clachan of Campsie
                  A 11
46 Clachan of Glendaruel
                  A 5

35 Clayton, W. Yorks.
                  D 10
34 Clayton Green .....E 5
35 Clayton West ....F 11
34 Clayton-le-Moors ..D 6
34 Clayton-le-Woods ..E 4
32 Clayworth ....A 4
45 Cleadon ....G 12
5 Clearbrook ....J 4
15 Clearwell ....D 9
40 Cleasby ....D 3
64 Cleat ....E 2
40 Cleatlam ....C 1
38 Cleator ....D 3
38 Cleator Moor .....D 3
35 Cleckheaton ......E 10
21 Clee St. Margaret .D 11
21 Cleedownton .....D 11
21 Cleehill ....E 11
21 Cleestanton ......D 11
37 Cleethorpes ......F 10
21 Cleeton St. Mary ..E 11
15 Cleeve, Avon ......H 8
17 Cleeve, Oxon .....F 7
16 Cleeve Hill ....A 1
22 Cleeve Prior ......G 4
15 Clehonger ....A 8
50 Cleigh ....E 6
52 Cleish ....G 6
48 Cleland ....D 1
50 Clenamacrie ......E 6
16 Clench Common ...H 3
24 Clenchwarton .....C 7
45 Clennell ....B 7
22 Clent ....D 3
21 Cleobury Mortimer E 12
21 Cleobury North ...D 11
56 Clephanton ....E 4
47 Clerkland ....E 9
21 Clerklands ....G 7
64 Clestran ....D 1
44 Cleuch Head .....D 8
43 Cleuchbrae ......D 11
44 Cleuchfoot ....E 2
43 Cleuchhead ......B 9
43 Cleuchheads .....C 12
43 Cleuchside ....D 12
16 Clevancy ....G 2
15 Clevedon ....G 7
40 Cleveland, Co. ....C 5
40 Cleveland Tontine Inn
                  E 5
34 Cleveleys ....C 2
16 Cleverton ....F 1
14 Clevis ....G 2
7 Clewer ....A 8
26 Cley-next-the-Sea ..A 3
12 Cliasamol ....F 2
39 Cliburn ....C 8
9 Cliddesden ....A 7
50 Cliff ....A 4
11 Cliff End ....G 7
10 Cliff Woods ......D 8
53 Cliffburn ....C 11
19 Cliffe, Kent ....F 7
36 Cliffe, N. Yorks. ...D 4
36 Cliffe, N. Yorks. ...D 2
4 Clifford, Devon ...D 2
21 Clifford, Heref. &
     Worc. ....H 8
36 Clifford, W. Yorks. .C 2
22 Clifford Chambers .G 5
11 Clifford's Mesne ..B 10
11 Cliffsend ....B 12
15 Clifton, Avon .....G 9
51 Clifton, Central ..D 10
39 Clifton, Cumbria ...C 8
31 Clifton, Derby ...F 10
22 Clifton, Heref. &
     Worc. ....G 2
34 Clifton, Lancs. ....D 4
48 Clifton, Lothian ...B 4
35 Cliton, N. Yorks. ..B 10
36 Clifton, N. Yorks. ..B 4
45 Clifton, Northumb. E 10
32 Clifton, Notts. ....G 3
16 Clifton, Oxon .....A 6
36 Clifton, S. Yorks. ..B 5
22 Clifton Campville ..A 6
16 Clifton Hampden ..E 6
23 Clifton Reynes ...G 12
23 Clifton upon
     Dunsmore ....D 8
21 Clifton upon Teme .F 12
11 Cliftonville ......A 12
9 Climping ....F 11
48 Climpy ....D 2
7 Clink ....A 11
35 Clint ....A 11
26 Clint Green ....D 3
48 Clintmains ....F 8
26 Clippesby ....D 7
37 Clipsham ....D 1

4 Clipston, Devon ...F 5
23 Clipston, Northants
                  D 10
32 Clipston, Notts. ...G 3
32 Clipstone ....D 3
34 Clitheroe ....C 6
30 Clive ....H 4
64 Clivocast ....B 8
37 Clixby ....G 8
29 Clocaenog ....E 10
58 Clochan ....B 1
13 Clochyrie ....F 8
30 Clock Face ....A 4
49 Clockmill ....D 10
14 Clodock ....B 6
7 Cloford ....B 10
13 Cloigyn ....F 8
58 Clola ....C 7
25 Clophill ....L 2
25 Clopton ....G 2
27 Clopton Green ....K 1
38 Close Clark ....B 9
43 Closeburn ....B 9
43 Closeburnmill .....B 10
7 Closworth ....E 9
25 Clothall ....M 4
40 Clotherholme ......H 3
30 Clotton ....D 4
35 Clough ....F 9
35 Clough Foot ......E 8
41 Cloughton ....F 10
41 Cloughton Newlands
                  F 10
64 Clousta ....D 6
58 Colva, Grampian ...E 2
52 Clova, Tayside ....K 1
39 Clove Lodge .....C 11
4 Clovelly ....D 2
49 Clovenfords ......F 7
58 Clovenstone ......F 5
56 Cloves ....D 7
51 Clovulin ....A 7
35 Clow Bridge ......D 7
32 Clowne ....C 2
55 Cluanie Inn ....H 4
55 Cluanie Lodge ...H 5
21 Cluddley ....A 11
63 Cluer ....H 2
21 Clun ....D 8
56 Clunas ....E 4
21 Clunbury ....D 9
56 Clune ....E 7
55 Clunes ....K 6
21 Clungunford ......E 9
58 Clunie, Grampian ..C 4
52 Clunie, Tayside ....C 6
21 Clunton ....D 9
53 Cluny ....H 7
57 Cluny Castle .....K 2
15 Clutton, Avon ....H 9
30 Clutton, Cheshire ..E 3
29 Clwyd, Co. ......E 10
13 Clydach, Gwent ...C 5
13 Clydach, W. Glam.
                  G 10
14 Clydach Vale .....C 6
47 Clydebank ....B 10
12 Clydey ....C 6
16 Clyffe Pypard .....F 2
47 Clynder ....A 7
12 Clynderwen ....E 5
13 Clyne ....G 11
61 Clynekirkton ......F 8
61 Clynelish ....F 8
28 Clynnog-fawr .....E 4
21 Clyro ....H 7
6 Clyst Honiton ....G 3
6 Clyst Hydon ......G 3
6 Clyst St. George ..G 3
6 Clyst St. Lawrence .F 4
6 Clyst St. Mary ....G 3
28 Clwyt-y-bont ......D 5
20 Cnwch Coch ......E 2
58 Coachford ....C 4
3 Coad's Green .....B 10
32 Coal Ashton ......B 1
21 Coalbrookdale ....B 12
14 Coalbrookvale ....C 5
48 Coalburn ....F 1
45 Coalburns ....G 9
39 Coalcleugh ....A 10
15 Coaley ....D 11
59 Coalford ....C 6
47 Coalhall ....G 9
19 Coalhill ....D 7
15 Coalpit Heath ....F 10
31 Coalpit Hill ......E 7
21 Coalport ....B 12
52 Coalsnaughton ....H 4
53 Coaltown of Balgonie
                  G 8
53 Coaltown of Wemyss
                  H 8
23 Coalville ....A 8

15 Coalway Lane End ..C 9
7 Coat ....D 8
47 Coatbridge ......C 12
47 Coatdyke ....C 12
16 Coate, Wilts. ......H 2
16 Coate, Wilts. ....F 3
24 Coates, Cambs. ....F 4
16 Coates, Glos. ....D 1
9 Coates, W. Sussex .D 11
40 Coatham ....C 6
40 Coatham Mundeville
    C 3
43 Coatsgate ....A 11
4 Cobbaton ....C 5
15 Coberley ....C 12
10 Cobham, Kent ....A 5
17 Cobham, Surrey ..H 11
51 Cobleland ....H 12
21 Cobnash ....F 10
58 Coburty ....A 7
57 Cock Bridge ......H 8
19 Cock Clarks ......D 8
21 Cock Gate ......F 10
40 Cockayne ....E 6
25 Cockayne Hatley ..K 4
49 Cockburnspath ....B 10
49 Cockenzie and
    Port Seton ......B 7
34 Cockerham ......B 3
38 Cockermouth ......B 4
18 Cockernhoe Green ..B 1
40 Cockfield, Durham .C 2
27 Cockfield, Suffolk ..K 2
9 Cocking ....D 10
5 Cockington ......J 8
7 Cocklake ....A 8
45 Cocklaw ....F 7
49 Cocklawfoot ......G 11
49 Cockles ....B 8
26 Cockley Clet ......D 4
58 Cockmuir ....D 4
17 Cockpole Green ....F 9
30 Cockshutt ....G 3
26 Cockthorpe ......A 3
6 Cockwood ......H 3
15 Cockyard ....A 7
3 Codda ....B 9
27 Coddenham ......K 4
30 Coddington, Ches. ..E 3
21 Coddington, Heref. &
    Worc. ....H 12
32 Coddington, Notts...E 5
8 Codford St. Mary ...B 1
8 Codford St. Peter ...B 1
18 Codicote ....B 2
9 Codmore Hill .....D 12
32 Codnor ....E 1
15 Codrington ......F 10
22 Codsall ....B 2
22 Codsall Wood ....B 2
14 Coed Ely ....F 4
15 Coed Morgan .....C 7
28 Coed Ystumgwern ..H 5
28 Coedana ....B 5
14 Coedkernew ......F 6
29 Coedpoeth ......E 12
21 Coedway ....A 9
13 Coed-y-bryn ......A 7
14 Coed-y-fedw ......C 7
14 Coed-yr-ynys ......B 5
14 Coelbren ....C 2
6 Coffinswell ......J 8
6 Cofton ....H 3
22 Cofton Hacket ....E 3
1 Cogan ....G 5
23 Cogenhoe ......F 11
19 Coggeshall ......B 8
19 Coggeshall Hamlet ..B 8
57 Coignafearn Lo.....H 2
57 Coignafeuinternich .H 3
57 Coignascallan ......H 3
59 Coilacreich ......H 1
57 Coilintuie ......J 6
51 Coillaig ....E 7
55 Coille Mhorgil ....J 5
62 Coillore ....D 3
55 Coiltry ....J 7
57 Coire Bhachdaidh
    Lodge ....M 1
14 Coity ....F 3
60 Colaboll ....F 6
2 Colan ....D 6
6 Colaton Raleigh ...G 4
62 Colbost ....C 1
40 Colburn ....E 2
18 Colbury ....E 5
39 Colby, Cumbria ....C 9
38 Colby, I.o.M.......H 1
26 Colby, Norfolk ....B 5
19 Colchester ......A 10
14 Colcot ....G 4
16 Cold Ash ....A 5
23 Cold Ashby ......D 10
15 Cold Ashton ......G 10

12 Cold Blow ....F 5
23 Cold Brayfield ....G 12
33 Cold Hanworth ....B 7
30 Cold Hatton ......H 5
35 Cold Hesleden ....H 12
35 Cold Hiendly .....F 12
21 Cold Higham .....G 10
40 Cold Kirby ......G 5
3 Cold Northcott ....A 9
19 Cold Norton ......D 8
23 Cold Overton ....A 11
39 Coldbeck ....E 9
60 Coldbackie ......B 6
10 Coldean ....G 2
5 Coldeast ....H 7
6 Colden Common ..D 6
27 Coldfair Green .....J 7
24 Coldham ....E 5
15 Coldharbour, Glos. .D 8
10 Coldharbour, Kent ..C 4
58 Coldhome ....C 3
49 Coldingham ......C 11
12 Coldrain ....G 6
11 Coldred ....C 11
4 Coldridge ......C 9
49 Coldstream ......E 11
9 Coldwaltham .....D 11
58 Coldwells ....D 8
58 Coldwells Croft ....E 3
7 Cole ....C 10
18 Cole Green ......C 3
8 Cole Henley ......A 6
21 Colebatch ......D 8
6 Colebrook ......F 3
4 Colebrooke ......F 6
56 Coleburn ....D 8
37 Coleby, Humber. ..E 7
33 Coleby, Lincs. ....D 7
4 Coleford, Devon ...F 6
15 Coleford, Glos. ....C 9
7 Coleford, Som. ....A 10
8 Colehill ....F 2
10 Coleman's Hatch ..E 3
9 Colemere ....G 3
9 Colemore ....C 8
32 Coleorton ......H 1
8 Colerne ....G 11
16 Colesbourne ......C 1
16 Coleshill, Oxon ....E 3
22 Coleshill, War. ....C 5
6 Colestocks ......F 4
10 Colgate ....E 1
47 Colgrain ....A 8
53 Colinsburgh ......G 9
48 Colinton ....C 5
46 Colintraive ......B 5
26 Colkirk ....C 2
63 Coll ....C 6
53 Collace ....D 7
64 Collafirth ......C 7
2 Collamoor Head ...B 2
5 Collaton ....L 4
5 Collaton St. Mary ..K 7
47 Collenan ....F 8
53 Collessie ....F 7
4 Colleton Mills ....D 5
18 Collier Row ......E 5
10 Collier Street ....C 6
18 Collier's End ......B 4
58 Collieston ......D 8
43 Collin ....D 11
8 Collingbourne Ducis
    A 4
8 Collingbourne
    Kingston ....A 4
35 Collingham ......C 12
21 Collington ......F 12
23 Collingtree ......G 11
34 Collins Green ....H 4
53 Colliston ....C 10
6 Colliton ....F 4
59 Collmuir ....G 3
58 Collynie ....D 6
24 Collyweston ......E 1
42 Colmonell ......C 3
25 Colmworth ......J 2
16 Coln Rogers ......C 2
16 Coln St. Aldwyn ...D 2
16 Coln St. Dennis ...C 2
57 Colnabaichin ......H 8
17 Colnbrook ......F 11
25 Colne, Cambs. ....H 5
35 Colne, Lancs......C 7
27 Colne Engaine ....M 2
26 Colney ....E 5
18 Colney Heath ....C 2
18 Colney Street ....D 2
45 Colpitts Grange ..G 8
58 Colpy ....D 4
48 Colquhar ....E 6
4 Colscott ....D 2
40 Colsterdale ......G 2

32 Colsterworth ......H 6
32 Colston Bassett ....G 4
56 Coltfield ....C 7
26 Coltishall ......D 6
38 Colton, Cumbria ..G 5
26 Colton, Norfolk ...D 4
36 Colton, N. Yorks. ..C 3
31 Colton, Staffs. ....H 9
35 Colton, W. Yorks. ..D 12
21 Colva ....G 7
22 Colwall Green .....H 1
22 Colwall Stone ....H 1
45 Colwell ....E 8
31 Colwich ....H 8
14 Colwinston ......G 3
38 Colwith ....E 5
9 Colworth ....F 10
29 Colwyn Bay ......B 8
6 Colyford ....G 6
6 Colyton ....G 6
44 Comb ....D 6
16 Combe, Berks. ....H 5
21 Combe, Heref. &
    Worc. ....F 9
16 Combe, Oxon ....C 5
9 Combe Common ..B 10
21 Combe Moor ......F 9
6 Combe Florey ....C 5
4 Combe Martin ....A 5
6 Combe Raleigh ....F 5
6 Combe St. Nicholas .C 4
5 Combebow ......G 4
5 Combeinteignhead ..J 8
30 Comberbach ......C 5
25 Comberton, Cambs. .K 5
21 Comberton, Heref. &
    Worc. ....F 10
6 Combpyne ......G 6
31 Combridge ......F 9
22 Combrook ......G 6
31 Combs, Derby ....B 9
27 Combs, Suffolk ...K 3
14 Combwich ......B 6
59 Comers ....G 4
20 Comin Capel Betws .G 2
20 Comins-coch Dyfed .D 2
20 Comins-coch Powys .B 4
58 Comisty ....C 3
14 Common Coed-y-paen
    D 6
32 Common Side ....C 1
41 Commondale ....D 7
3 Common Moor ....C 9
31 Commonside ....F 11
31 Compstall ......A 8
43 Compstonend ....F 7
16 Compton, Berks. ..H 5
5 Compton, Devon ...J 7
8 Compton, Hants. ..C 6
9 Compton, Surrey ..A 11
9 Compton, W. Sussex
    E 9
8 Compton, Wilts. ...A 3
7 Compton Abbas ..D 12
16 Compton Abdale ..C 2
16 Compton Bassett ..G 1
16 Compton Beauchamp
    E 4
7 Compton Bishop ..A 7
8 Compton
    Chamberlayne ....C 2
15 Compton Dando ...H 9
7 Compton Dundon ..C 8
15 Compton Greenfield
    F 9
7 Compton Martin ..A 8
7 Compton Pauncefoot
    D 10
7 Compton Valence ..G 9
52 Comrie, Fife ......H 5
52 Comrie, Tayside ...B 3
51 Conaglen House ...A 7
46 Conchra ....A 5
34 Conder Green ....B 3
16 Condicote ......A 3
47 Condorrat ......B 12
21 Condover ......B 10
27 Coney Weston ....G 3
9 Coneyhurst Com...D 12
41 Coneysthorpe ....H 7
35 Coneythorpe ....A 12
58 Confunderland .....F 3
31 Congdon's Shop ..B 10
43 Congeith ....E 9
23 Congerstone ......B 7
24 Congham ....C 8
31 Congleton ......D 7
28 Congl-y-wal ......F 6
15 Congresbury ......H 9
56 Conicavel ......D 5
33 Coningsby ......D 9
25 Conington, Cambs. .J 4
25 Conington, Cambs. .H 5
36 Conisbrough ......G 3

37 Conisholme ......H 11
38 Coniston, Cumbria ..E 5
37 Coniston, Humber. .D 9
33 Coniston Cold ....H 12
39 Conistone ......H 12
29 Connah's Quay ....C 12
50 Connel ....D 6
47 Connel Park ......H 11
47 Connelbush ......H 12
2 Connor Downs ....F 3
56 Cononbridge .....D 1
35 Cononley ....B 8
53 Cononsyth ......C 10
31 Consall ....E 8
45 Consett ....H 9
38 Constable Burton ..F 2
2 Constantine ......G 4
2 Constantine Bay ...B 6
54 Contin ....D 8
56 Contullich ......C 2
49 Conundrum ......D 12
59 Conveth Mains ....K 5
56 Convinth ....F 1
29 Conwy ....B 7
11 Conyer ....B 8
27 Conyer's Green ....H 2
10 Cooden ....G 6
4 Cookbury ....E 3
17 Cookham ....F 10
17 Cookham Dean ....F 9
17 Cookham Rise ....F 9
22 Cookhill ....F 4
22 Cookley, Heref. &
    Worc. ....D 2
27 Cookley, Suffolk ...H 6
17 Cookley Green ....E 8
17 Cookney ....H 6
10 Cooksbridge ......G 3
18 Cooksmill Green ...C 6
10 Coolham ....D 12
10 Cooling, Kent ....A 6
19 Cooling, Kent ....F 7
10 Cooling Street ....A 6
2 Coombe, Cornwall .D 6
4 Coombe, Cornwall ..E 1
8 Coombe, Devon ...D 4
8 Coombe, Wilts. ...A 3
8 Coombe Bissett ...C 3
15 Coombe Down ....H 11
15 Coombe Hay .....H 10
15 Coombe Hill ....B 12
15 Coombe Keynes ..H 11
10 Coombes ....G 1
7 Coombs ....F 4
56 Cooperhill ......D 6
10 Cooper's Corner ...C 4
7 Cooper's Green ...F 4
18 Coopersale Com. ..D 5
9 Cootham ....E 12
27 Copdock ....L 4
8 Copford Green ....B 9
64 Copister ....C 7
15 Cople ....K 2
40 Copley ....C 1
36 Copmanthorpe ....B 3
2 Coppathorne ......A 2
31 Coppenhall ......H 7
2 Copperhouse ......F 3
25 Coppingford ......G 3
4 Copplestone ......F 6
34 Coppull ....F 4
34 Coppull Moor ....F 4
10 Copsale ....F 1
15 Copster Green ....D 5
22 Copt Heath .....D 5
40 Copt Hewick .....H 4
10 Copt Oak ....A 8
10 Copthorne ......D 2
26 Copy's Green .....B 2
8 Copythorne ......E 5
45 Corbridge ......G 8
23 Corby ....C 12
23 Corby Glen ......H 7
21 Coreley ....E 11
17 Cores End ......E 10
8 Corfe ....D 6
8 Corfe Castle ......H 1
8 Corfe Mullen ....F 1
31 Corfton ....D 10
9 Corhampton ......D 7
22 Cork's Pond ......D 5
22 Corley ....D 6
22 Corley Ash ......C 6
22 Corley Moor ....D 6
48 Cormiston ......F 3
51 Cormonachan ......H 9
22 Cormuir ....A 8
57 Corndavon Lodge ..J 8
40 Cornforth ......B 3
40 Cornhill ....B 3
49 Cornhill-on-Tweed
    E 11

45 Cornhills ....E 8
35 Cornholme ......D 8
25 Cornish Hall End ...L 8
40 Cornsay ....A 2
40 Cornsay Colliery ...A 2
56 Corntown, Mid Glam.
    G 3
56 Corntown, Highland
    D 1
59 Corntulloch ......H 2
3 Cornwall, County ..C 8
16 Cornwell ....A 4
5 Cornwood ......K 5
5 Cornworthy ......K 7
55 Corpach ....M 5
26 Corpusty ....C 4
51 Corran, Highland ..A 7
55 Corran, Highland ...J 2
46 Corranbuie ......C 3
38 Corrany ....G 2
55 Corribeg ....L 4
55 Corrie ....E 5
43 Corrie Common ...C 12
46 Corriecravie ......G 4
60 Corriemulzie Lo. ...G 4
57 Corrievorrie ......G 3
54 Corrieviuc ......E 6
55 Corrimony ......G 7
19 Corringham, Essex .F 7
32 Corringham, Lincs. .A 6
2 Corris ....B 3
51 Corrour Shooting
    Lodge ....A 11
51 Corrow ....G 9
62 Corry ....F 6
56 Corry of Ardnagrask
    E 1
46 Corrygills ......F 5
55 Corryhully ......L 3
46 Corrykinloch ......E 5
52 Corrymuckloch ...D 4
50 Corrynachenchy ...C 4
49 Corsbie ....E 8
7 Corscombe ......F 8
58 Corse, Grampian ..D 3
58 Corse, Grampian ..B 7
59 Corse House .....G 3
58 Corse of Kinnoir ...C 3
58 Corsebauld ......J 5
58 Corsehill ....B 7
42 Corsemalzie ......C 3
15 Corhsam ....G 11
59 Corsindae ......G 4
7 Corsley ....B 11
7 Corsley Heath ....B 11
47 Corsliehill ......C 9
43 Corsock ....D 8
15 Corston, Avon ....H 10
15 Corston, Wilts. ...F 12
48 Corstorphine ......B 5
26 Corton, Suffolk ...F 8
8 Corton, Wilts. ....B 1
7 Corton Denham ...D 9
51 Coruanan Lodge ..A 8
29 Corwen ....F 10
7 Coryates ....H 9
5 Coryton, Devon ...G 3
19 Coryton, Essex ....F 7
22 Cosby ....C 9
22 Coseley ....C 3
23 Cosgrove ......H 11
9 Cosham ....F 8
12 Cosheston ......G 3
52 Coshieville ......B 3
32 Cossall ....F 2
23 Cossington, Leics. ..A 9
14 Cossington, Som. ..B 2
26 Costessey ......D 5
32 Costock ....H 3
32 Coston, Leics. ....H 6
26 Coston, Norfolk ...E 4
44 Cote ....C 1
30 Cotebrook ......D 4
44 Cotehill ....H 3
31 Cotes, Cumbria ...F 7
31 Cotes, Staffs. ....G 7
32 Cotesbach ......D 8
58 Cothall ....F 6
23 Cotham ....E 5
6 Cothelstone ......C 5
39 Cotherstone ......C 12
16 Cothill, Oxon ....D 6
10 Cothill, Borders ...D 10
6 Cotleigh ....F 5
32 Cotmanhay ......F 2
25 Coton, Cambs. ...J 5
23 Coton, Northants. ..E 10
31 Coton, Staffs. ....H 7
31 Coton, Staffs. ......G 8

31 Coton Clanford ...H 7
31 Coton in the Clay ..G 10
22 Coton in the Elms ..A 6
3 Cott ....K 6
34 Cottam, Lancs. ....D 4
32 Cottam, Notts. ....B 5
56 Cottartown ......F 6
25 Cottenham ......H 5
39 Cotterdale ......F 10
18 Cottered ....A 3
24 Cotterstock ......F 1
23 Cottesbrooke ....E 10
23 Cottesmore ......A 12
6 Cotteylands ......E 3
37 Cottingham,
    Humberside .....D 8
23 Cottingham,
    Northants. ......C 11
35 Cottingley ......C 9
17 Cottisford ......A 7
31 Cotton, Derby .....F 9
27 Cotton, Suffolk ...J 4
25 Cotton End ......L 2
58 Cot-town, Grampian E 2
58 Cot-town, Grampian
    D 6
31 Cotwalton ......G 8
58 Cotwells ....B 5
3 Couchsmill ......D 8
15 Coughton, Heref. &
    Worc. ....B 9
22 Coughton, War. ...F 4
46 Coulaghailtro ....C 2
54 Coulags ....E 3
54 Couldoran ......E 2
54 Coulin Lodge ....D 4
59 Coull ....G 3
47 Coulport ....A 7
18 Coulsdon ......H 3
8 Coulston ....A 1
48 Coulter ....F 3
40 Coulton ....H 6
21 Cound ....B 11
40 Coundon, Durham .B 3
22 Coundon, W. Midlands
    D 6
40 Coundon Grange ..B 2
39 Countersett ....F 11
23 Counthesthorpe ...C 9
8 Countess ....B 3
6 Countess Wear ...G 3
4 Countisbury ......A 6
53 Coupar Angus ....C 7
49 Coupland ......F 12
6 Couple Cross ....B 3
46 Cour ....E 3
43 Courance ......C 11
17 Court Corner ....H 7
13 Court Henry ......E 9
55 Courteachan ......K 1
23 Courteenhall ....G 11
19 Courtsend ......E 10
5 Courtway ....C 6
48 Cousland ....C 6
10 Cousleywood ....E 5
46 Coustonn ......B 6
5 Cove, Devon .....D 3
9 Cove, Hampshire .A 10
54 Cove, Highland ...A 2
47 Cove, Strathclyde ..A 7
59 Cove Bay ....G 7
27 Covehithe ......G 8
22 Coven ....A 3
25 Coveney ....G 6
37 Covenham St.
    Bartholomew ...H 11
37 Covenham St. Mary
    H 11
23 Coventry ......D 7
2 Coverack ......H 5
40 Coverham ......F 1
25 Covington ......H 2
22 Cow Honeybourne ..H 5
39 Cowan Bridge ....G 8
10 Cowbeech ......G 5
24 Cowbit ....D 4
14 Cowbridge, S. Glam.
    G 3
6 Cowbridge, Som. ..B 3
10 Cowden, Kent ....D 3
45 Cowden, Northumb. E 7
52 Cowdenbeath ....H 6
48 Cowdenburn ....D 5
8 Cowes ....F 6
40 Cowesby ....F 5
10 Cowfold ....F 1
52 Cowie, Central ...H 3
59 Cowie, Grampian ..J 6
45 Cowpen ....E 11
40 Cowpen Bewley ..C 5
31 Cowers Lane ....E 11
10 Cowley, Devon ...G 3
15 Cowley, Glos. ...C 12
18 Cowley, London ...F 1

16 Cowley, Oxon ......D 6
40 Cowling. N. Yorks. ..F 3
35 Cowling. N. Yorks. ..C 8
25 Cowlinge ....K 8
9 Cowplain ....E 8
39 Cowshill ....A 10
52 Cowstrandburn ......H 5
36 Cowthorpe ....B 2
17 Cox Green ....F 9
30 Coxbank ....F 5
31 Coxbench ....F 12
10 Coxheath ....C 6
11 Coxhill ....C 11
40 Coxhoe ....B 3
7 Coxley ....B 8
18 Coxtie Green .....D 5
40 Coxwold ....G 5
14 Coychurch ....F 3
47 Coylton ....G 9
57 Coylumbridge ......H 5
59 Coynach ....G 2
58 Coynachie ....D 2
14 Coytrahen ....F 2
54 Cozae Lodge ....F 6
22 Crabbs Cross ......F 4
10 Crabtree ....F 1
61 Crackaig ....F 9
39 Crackenthorpe .....C 9
2 Crackington Haven
                    B 2
22 Crackley ....E 6
22 Crackley Bank .....A 1
39 Crackpot ....E 12
35 Cracoe ....A 8
6 Craddock ....E 4
22 Cradley ....G 1
22 Cradley Heath .....D 3
14 Cradoc ....A 3
3 Crafthole ....D 10
45 Cragend ....C 9
35 Cragg ....E 8
57 Craggan, Highland ..G 6
60 Craggan, Highland ..G 4
51 Craggan, Strathclyde
                    H 10
56 Craggiemore ....F 3
45 Craghead ....H 10
58 Craibstone, Grampian
                    F 6
58 Craibstone, Grampian
                    B 2
53 Craichie ....B 10
43 Craig, Dumf. & Gall.
                    D 7
43 Craig, Dumf. & Gall.
                    E 8
54 Craig, Highland ....E 4
42 Craig, Strathcylde ..A 5
46 Craig Lodge ....B 5
14 Craig Penllyn .....F 3
13 Craig Trebanos ....G 10
52 Craiganour Lodge ..A 1
55 Craigard ....J 7
55 Craigbeg ....L 8
42 Craigcaffie ....E 2
13 Craig-cefn-parc ...G 10
58 Craigdam ....E 6
43 Craigdarrcoh, Dumf. &
   Gall. ....C 8
43 Craigdarroch,
   Strathclyde ....A 7
42 Craigdews ....D 6
54 Craigdhu ....F 8
58 Craigearn ....F 5
56 Craigellachie .....E 8
42 Craigencallie .....D 6
42 Craigencross ......E 1
48 Craigend, Strathclyde
                    F 1
52 Craigend, Tayside ..E 6
47 Craigendoran ......A 8
42 Craigengillan .....A 5
42 Craigenrae ....C 4
47 Craigens ....G 10
59 Craiggiecat ....H 6
56 Craighead, Grampian
                    G 2
48 Craighead, Strathclyde
                    G 2
58 Craigie, Grampian .F 6
47 Craigie, Strathclyde .F 9
52 Craigie, Tayside ....C 6
43 Craigieburn ....A 11
48 Craiglockhart .....B 5
42 Craimalloch ....B 5
58 Craigmaud ....B 6
46 Craigmore ....C 6
59 Craigmoston ....K 4
30 Craignant ....G 1
42 Craigneil ....C 2
43 Craigneston ....C 8
47 Craigneuk ....D 12
50 Craignure ....D 4
59 Craigo ....L 4

52 Craigow ....F 6
53 Craigrothie ....F 8
53 Craigs ....G 7
59 Craigton, Grampian
                    G 6
54 Craigton, Highland ..F 3
56 Craigton, Highland .E 2
47 Craigton, Strathclyde
                    D 10
53 Craigton, Tayside ..C 10
53 Craigton, Tayside ...B 8
61 Craigtown ....B 9
13 Craig-y-Duke .....G 10
14 Craig-y-nos ....C 2
44 Craik ....B 2
53 Crail ....F 11
49 Crailing ....G 9
49 Crailinghall ......G 9
36 Craiselound ....G 5
48 Cramalt ....G 5
36 Crambe ....A 5
45 Cramlington ....E 11
48 Cramond ....B 5
48 Cramond Bridge ....B 4
55 Cranachan ....L 7
30 Cranage ....C 6
31 Cranberry ....G 7
58 Cranbog ....F 7
8 Cranborne ....E 2
17 Cranbourne ....G 10
10 Cranbrook ....D 6
10 Cranbrook Com. ....D 6
35 Crane Moor ....G 11
25 Cranfield ....L 1
18 Cranford ....F 1
23 Cranford St. Andrew
                    D 12
23 Cranford St. John .D 12
15 Cranham, Glos. ...C 12
18 Cranham, London ..E 6
34 Crank ....G 4
9 Cranleigh ....B 12
8 Cranmore ....G 5
58 Cranna ....B 4
58 Crannach ....B 2
50 Crannich ....C 2
23 Cranoe ....C 11
27 Cransford ....J 6
49 Cranshaws ....C 9
38 Cranstal ....F 2
37 Cranswick ....B 8
2 Crantock ....D 5
33 Cranwell ....E 7
26 Cranwich ....F 1
26 Cranworth ....E 3
42 Cranyard ....H 2
5 Crapstone ....J 4
51 Crarae ....H 7
60 Crask Inn ....E 6
54 Crask of Aigas ....E 8
54 Craskie ....F 7
59 Craskins ....G 3
45 Craster ....A 10
27 Cratfield ....H 6
59 Crathes ....H 5
57 Crathie ....K 1
40 Crathorne ....D 5
21 Craven Arms ......D 10
45 Crawcrook ....G 9
48 Crawford ....G 2
48 Crawfordjohn ......G 2
43 Crawfordton ....B 9
47 Crawick ....H 12
8 Crawley, Hants. ...C 6
16 Crawley, Oxon ...C 4
10 Crawley, W. Sussex .D 1
10 Crawley Down ....D 2
39 Crawleyside ......A 12
35 Crawshaw Booth ..E 7
59 Crawton ....J 6
39 Cray, N. Yorks. ..G 11
14 Cray, Powys ....B 2
18 Crayford ....F 5
40 Crayke ....H 6
19 Crays Hill ....E 7
17 Cray's Pond ....F 7
17 Crazies Hill ......F 9
50 Creach Bheinn Lodge
                    E 4
4 Creacombe ....D 7
51 Creag a' Phuill ...G 8
51 Creagan ....C 7
46 Creagan Beag ......A 3
51 Creaguaineach Lo. .A 10
23 Creaton ....E 10
44 Creca ....F 1
21 Credenhill ....H 10
4 Crediton ....F 7
42 Creebank ....D 4
42 Creebridge ....E 5
6 Creech Heathfield .D 6
6 Creech St. Michael .D 6
2 Creed ....E 6
18 Creekmouth ....F 5

42 Creeside ....C 4
27 Creeting St. Mary ..J 4
24 Creeton ....D 1
42 Creetown ....F 6
21 Cregerina ....G 7
51 Creggans ....G 8
38 Cregneish ....H 1
38 Creg-ny-Baa ......G 2
53 Creich ....E 8
14 Creigiau ....F 4
54 Crelevan ....F 7
3 Cremyll ....D 11
21 Cressage ....B 11
12 Cresselly ....F 4
17 Cressex ....E 9
19 Cressing ....B 8
12 Cresswell, Dyfed ..F 4
45 Cresswell, Northumb.
                    D 11
31 Cresswell, Staffs. ...F 8
32 Creswell ....C 2
21 Cretingham ....J 5
46 Cretshengan ....C 2
21 Crew Green ....A 8
23 Crewe, Cheshire ...E 3
30 Crewe, Cheshire ...E 6
7 Crewkerne ....E 7
51 Crainlarich ....E 11
13 Cribyn ....B 8
28 Criccieth ....F 4
32 Crich, Derby .....E 12
48 Crichton ....C 6
15 Crick, Gwent ......E 8
23 Crick, Northants. ..E 9
20 Crickadarn ....H 6
7 Cricket Malherbie ..E 7
7 Cricket St. Thomas ..E 7
30 Crickheath ....H 2
14 Crickhowell ....B 5
16 Cricklade ....E 2
18 Cricklewood ....E 2
36 Cridling Stubbs ...E 3
52 Crieff ....E 3
21 Criggan ....A 8
35 Crigglestone .....E 11
58 Crimond ....B 8
58 Crimonmogate ......B 8
24 Crimplesham ....E 7
54 Crinaglack ....F 8
50 Crinan ....H 5
26 Cringleford ....E 3
12 Crinow ....F 5
6 Cripplestyle ......E 3
10 Cripp's Corner ....F 6
38 Croasdale ....C 3
7 Crock Street ......E 7
10 Crockenhill ....A 4
5 Crockernwell ......G 6
7 Crockerton ....B 11
43 Crocket or Ninemile
   Bar ....D 9
36 Crockey Hill ......B 4
10 Crockham Hill .....C 3
10 Crockhurst Street ..D 5
19 Crockleford Hth. ..A 10
21 Crockmeole ....A 9
14 Croes-Hywel ....C 6
14 Croeserw ....E 2
12 Croes-goch ....D 2
13 Croes-Ian ....C 7
14 Croes-y-ceiliog ...E 6
13 Croesyceiliog .....E 7
14 Croes-y-mwyalch ...E 6
12 Croft, Dyfed ......C 5
23 Croft, Leics. ......C 8
34 Croft, Merseyside ..H 5
33 Croft, Lincs. .....D 12
36 Croft, N. Yorks. ...D 3
47 Croftamie ....A 9
47 Crofthead ....E 12
52 Croftmill ....C 3
57 Croftmore ....H 5
57 Crofthaven ....H 5
36 Crofton, W. Yorks. E 12
16 Crofton, Wilts. ...H 4
43 Crofts ....D 8
58 Crofts of Belnagoak .C 6
58 Crofts of Haddo ..D 6
58 Crofts of Hillbrae ...C 3
58 Crofts of Meikle Ardo
                    D 6
58 Crofts of Savoch ....B 8
58 Crofts of Shanquhar D 3
13 Crofty ....G 8
50 Croggan ....E 4
55 Croglin ....A 9
43 Crogo ....D 8
60 Croick ....G 5
13 Croir ....C 2
56 Cromarty ....C 3
54 Cromasag ....D 4
58 Cromblet ....D 5
57 Cromdale ....G 6
28 Cromer, Herts. ....A 3

26 Cromer, Norfolk ...A 5
31 Cromford ....E 11
15 Cromhall ....E 10
15 Cromhall Com. ....E 10
65 Cromore ....E 5
57 Cromra ....K 1
32 Cromwell ....D 5
47 Cronan ....E 10
47 Cronberry ....G 11
9 Crondall ....A 9
38 Cronk-y-Voddy ....G 2
30 Cronton ....A 4
39 Crook, Cumbria ...F 7
40 Crook, Durham ....B 2
56 Crook of Alves ....D 7
52 Crook of Devon ...G 5
34 Crooke ....F 4
47 Crookedholm ......F 9
48 Crookedstane ......H 2
31 Crookes ....B 1
16 Crookham, Berks. ..H 6
49 Crookham, Northumb.
                    F 11
9 Crookham Village ..A 9
49 Crookham Westfield
                    F 11
48 Crookhaugh ....G 4
49 Crookhouse ....G 10
39 Crooklands ....G 8
47 Crookston ....C 10
49 Crookston North
   Mains ....D 7
22 Croome Court .....H 2
23 Cropredy ....G 8
32 Cropston ....A 9
22 Cropthorne ....H 3
41 Cropton ....F 8
32 Cropwell Bishop ..G 4
32 Cropwell Butler ..F 4
43 Crosbie ....G 9
43 Crosby, Cumb. ...H 11
38 Crosby, I.o.M. ....G 2
35 Crosby, Humber. ..F 5
34 Crosby, Merseyside .G 2
40 Crosby Court .....F 4
39 Crosby Garrett ...D 9
39 Crosby Ravensworth
                    D 8
43 Crosby Villa .....H 11
7 Croscombe ....B 9
7 Cross ....A 7
10 Cross Ash ....B 7
10 Cross-at-Hand ....C 6
20 Cross Foxes ......A 3
35 Cross Gates ......D 12
15 Cross Green ......K 2
15 Cross Hands, Avon .F 9
13 Cross Hnads, Dyfed .F 9
12 Cross Hands, Dyfed .F 4
35 Cross Hills ....C 9
21 Cross Houses .....B 11
14 Cross in Hand ....F 4
13 Cross Inn, Dyfed ..A 7
13 Cross Inn, Dyfed ..A 9
13 Cross Inn, Dyfed ..D 11
14 Cross Inn, Mid Glam
                    F 4
10 Cross Keys, Kent ...C 4
15 Cross Keys, Wilts. .G 11
2 Cross Lanes, Corn. .G 4
30 Cross Lanes, Clwyd .F 2
7 Cross Lanes, Dorset
                    F 11
36 Cross Lanes, N. Yorks.
                    A 3
63 Cross North Dell ..A 6
14 Cross Oak ....B 4
58 Cross of Jackson ..D 5
31 Cross o'th' Hands .F 11
27 Cross Street ......H 5
46 Crossaig ....D 3
63 Crossbost ....D 5
43 Crosscanonby ....H 11
48 Crossleuch ....G 5
26 Crossdale Street ..B 5
34 Crossens ....E 3
48 Crossford, Fife ...A 3
48 Crossford, Strathclyde
                    E 1
24 Crossgate ....C 3
48 Crossgatehall ....C 6
52 Crossgates, Fife ..H 6
40 Crossgates, N. Yorks.
                    H 2
20 Crossgates, Powys ...F 6
55 Crossgill, Cumb. ..A 9
34 Crossgill, Lancs. ..A 4
5 Crossgreen, Devon .G 3
21 Crossgreen, Salop .A 10
49 Crosshall ....E 10
12 Crosshands, Dyfed .E 5
47 Crosshands, Strathclyde
                    F 9
52 Crosshill, Fife ...G 6

42 Crosshill, Strathcylde
                    A 4
47 Crosshill, Strathclyde
                    G 9
47 Crosshouse ....F 9
44 Crossings ....E 3
14 Crosskeys ....E 5
61 Crosskirk ....A 10
38 Crosslands ....F 6
30 Crosslanes ......H 2
48 Crosslee ....G 6
47 Crosslees ....D 10
43 Crossmichael .....E 8
34 Crossmor ....C 3
10 Crosspost ....F 1
59 Crossroads, Grampian
                    H 5
47 Crossroads, Strathclyde
                    F 9
35 Crossroads, W. Yorks.
                    C 9
64 Cross-voe-sand ....C 6
15 Crossway, Heref. &
   Worc. ....A 9
15 Crossway, Gwent ..B 5
20 Crossway, Powys ..G 6
22 Crossway Green ...E 2
7 Crossways ....G 11
12 Crosswell ....C 5
20 Crosswood ....E 2
34 Croston ....E 4
26 Crostwick ....D 6
10 Crouch ....C 5
21 Crouch Hill ......E 10
8 Croucheston ......D 2
16 Croughton ....A 6
58 Crovie ....A 5
8 Crow ....F 3
35 Crow Edge ....G 10
15 Crow Hill ....B 9
2 Crowan ....F 4
10 Crowborough .....E 4
20 Crowborough Town .E 4
6 Crowcombe ....C 5
35 Crowden ....G 9
17 Crowell ....D 8
23 Crowfield, Northants.
                    H 9
27 Crowfield, Suffolk .J 5
10 Crowhurst, E. Sussex
                    G 6
10 Crowhurst, Surrey ..C 3
10 Crowhurst Lane End
                    C 3
24 Crowland ....D 3
2 Crowlas ....F 2
22 Crowle, Heref. &
   Worc. ....G 3
36 Crowle, Humber. ..F 5
63 Crowlista ....D 1
17 Crowmarsh Gifford .E 7
2 Crown Town ......G 3
5 Crownhill ....K 4
26 Crownthorpe ......E 4
42 Crows ....F 3
2 Crows-an-wra .....G 1
17 Crowthorne ....H 9
30 Crowton ....C 4
22 Croxall ....A 5
37 Croxby ....G 9
40 Croxdale ....B 3
31 Croxden ....F 9
17 Croxley Green ...E 11
25 Croxton, Cambs. ...J 3
37 Croxton, Humber. ..F 8
26 Croxton, Norfolk ..G 2
30 Croxton, Staffs. ...G 6
32 Croxton Kerrial ..G 5
56 Croy, Highland ....E 4
47 Croy, Strathclyde ..B 12
4 Croyde ....B 3
4 Croyde Bay ....B 3
25 Croydon, Cambs. ..K 4
18 Croydon, London ..C 3
57 Crubenmore Lo. ...K 2
58 Cruden Bay ....D 8
30 Crudgington ....H 5
16 Crudwell ....E 1
21 Crug ....E 1
21 Crugmeer ....B 6
13 Crugybar ....C 10
54 Cruive ....F 8
63 Crulivig ....D 3
14 Crumlin ....D 5
3 Crumplehorn .....E 9
12 Crundale, Dyfed ..E 3
11 Crundale, Kent ...C 9
44 Crurie ....D 1
22 Cruwys Morchard ..E 2
16 Crux Easton ......H 5
13 Crwbin ....F 8
17 Cryers Hill ......D 9
14 Crymmych ....D 5
13 Crynant ....F 11

54 Cuaig ....D 1
23 Cubbington ....E 7
2 Cubert ....D 5
17 Cublington ....B 9
10 Cuckfield ....F 2
7 Cucklington .....D 10
32 Cuckney ....C 3
17 Cuddesdon ....D 7
17 Cuddington, Bucks. ..C 8
30 Cuddington, Ches. ..C 4
30 Cuddington Heath ..F 2
34 Cuddy Hill ....C 4
18 Cudham ....H 4
5 Cudlipptown ......H 4
7 Cudworth, Som. ...E 7
36 Cudworth, S. Yorks. .F 2
12 Cuffern ....E 2
18 Cuffley ....D 3
63 Cuiashader ....A 6
54 Culaneilan ....D 4
56 Culbo ....D 2
56 Culbokie ....D 2
56 Culburnie ....E 1
56 Culcabock ....E 2
56 Culcairn ....C 2
56 Culcharry ....E 4
34 Culcheth ....H 5
56 Culcraggie ....C 2
52 Culdees ....F 4
58 Culdrain ....D 3
54 Culduie ....F 1
27 Culford ....H 1
39 Culgaith ....B 8
16 Culham ....D 6
46 Culinlongart .....H 2
60 Culkein ....D 2
60 Culkein Drumbeg ..D 3
15 Culkerton ....E 12
57 Cullachie ....G 5
58 Cullen ....A 3
45 Cullercoats .....F 12
59 Cullerlie ....G 5
56 Cullicudden ......C 2
54 Culligran ....F 7
35 Cullingworth .....D 9
50 Cullipool ....F 5
64 Cullivoe ....B 8
52 Culloch ....E 3
55 Cullochy ....J 7
56 Culloden House ...E 4
6 Cullompton ....E 4
6 Culm Davy ....E 5
61 Culmaily ....G 8
42 Culmalzie ....F 5
21 Culmington ......D 10
6 Culmstock ....E 4
60 Culnacraig ....F 2
43 Culnaightrie ......E 8
62 Culnaknock ....B 4
42 Culquhirk ....F 5
48 Culrain ....G 6
47 Culroy ....H 8
42 Culscadden ....F 6
59 Culsh ....H 1
54 Culshabbin ....F 4
64 Culswick ....D 6
58 Cultercullen .....E 7
42 Cults, Dumf. & Gall.
                    G 5
58 Cults, Grampian ...D 3
59 Cults, Grampian ...G 6
52 Cultybraggan ....F 3
10 Culverstone Green .B 5
57 Culverthorpe .....F 7
23 Culworth ....G 9
56 Culzie Lodge .....C 1
49 Cumberland Bower
                    D 12
47 Cumbernauld ....B 12
33 Cumberworth ....C 12
38 Cumbria, Co. .....C 6
47 Cuminestown .....C 5
49 Cumledge ....D 10
44 Cummersdale .....H 2
48 Cummertrees ....E 12
56 Cummingstown ...C 7
47 Cumnock ....G 10
16 Cumnor ....D 5
44 Cumrew ....H 4
43 Cumrue ....C 11
32 Cumstone ....C 12
44 Cumwhinton ......H 3
44 Cumwhitton ......H 3
14 Cundall ....H 4
47 Cunninghamhead ..F 9
64 Cunnister ....B 7
52 Cupar ....F 8
53 Cupar Muir ......F 8
8 Cupernnam ....D 5
31 Curbar ....C 11
16 Curbridge, Oxon ..D 7
9 Curdbridge, Hants. .E 7

22 Curdworth ....C 5
54 Curin ....D 7
6 Curland ....E 6
42 Currarie ....B 2
16 Curridge ....G 6
48 Currie ....C 4
7 Curry Mallet ....D 7
7 Curry Rivel .....D 7
10 Curtisden Green ..D 6
2 Cury ....G 4
58 Cushnie ....B 5
6 Cushuish ....C 5
21 Cusop ....H 8
64 Cusvie ....B 3
42 Cutcloy ....H 5
6 Cutcombe ....B 3
61 Cuthill, Highland ..H 8
48 Cuthill, Lothian ..B 6
22 Cutnall Green ...E 2
16 Cutsdean ....A 2
31 Cutthorpe ....C 11
17 Cuxham ....E 7
10 Cuxton ....A 6
37 Cuxwold ....G 9
29 Cwm, Clwyd .....C 10
14 Cwm, Gwent ......D 5
20 Cwm-Cewydd ......A 4
12 Cwm Cych ....C 6
13 Cwm-Duad ....D 7
14 Cwm Ffrwd Oer ...D 6
20 Cwm Irfon ....G 4
13 Cwm-Mawr ....F 8
12 Cwm-Morgan ......D 6
29 Cwm-Penmachno ...E 7
14 Cwmaman ....D 3
14 Cwmann ....B 9
13 Cwmavon ....H 11
12 Cwm-bach, Dyfed ..D 6
14 Cwm-bach, Mid. Glam.
        D 4
20 Cwm-bach, Powys ..G 6
21 Cwm-bach, Powys ..H 7
20 Cwmbelan ....D 5
14 Cwmbran ....E 6
20 Cwmbrwyno ....D 3
14 Cwmcarn ....E 5
15 Cwmcarvan ....D 8
12 Cwmcoy ....C 6
14 Cwmdare ....D 3
13 Cwm-du, Dyfed ...D 9
14 Cwm-du, Powys ...B 5
14 Cwmfelin, Mid Glam.
        D 4
14 Cwmfelin, Mid Glam.
        E 2
12 Cwmfelin Boeth ...E 5
14 Cwmfelin-fach ...E 5
12 Cwmfelin-Mynach ..E 6
13 Cwm-ffrwd ....E 7
13 Cwmgiedd ....C 1
13 Cwmgors ....F 10
13 Cwmgwili ....F 9
13 Cwmifor ....D 10
13 Cwmisfael ....E 8
20 Cwmlline ....B 4
13 Cwmllyfri ....F 7
13 Cwmllynfell .....F 10
12 Cwmmiles ....E 5
14 Cwm-parc ....E 3
13 Cwm-pengraig ....C 7
14 Cwm-rhos ....B 5
13 Cwmsychpant .....B 8
14 Cwmtillery ......D 5
14 Cwmwysg ....A 2
13 Cwm-y-glo ....F 9
14 Cwmyoy ....B 6
20 Cwmystwyth ......E 3
20 Cwrt ....B 2
13 Cwrt-newydd .....B 8
13 Cwrt-y-Cadno ....C 10
14 Cwrt-y-defaid ...F 1
14 Cwrt-y-gollen ...C 6
28 Cwym-y-glo ......D 5
29 Cyffilliog ......D 10
14 Cymmer, Mid Glam. E 3
14 Cymmer, W. Glam. .E 2
14 Cyncoed ....F 5
13 Cynghordy, Dyfed .C 11
13 Cynghordy, W. Glam.
        G 10
13 Cynheidre ....F 8
14 Cynonville ......E 2
29 Cynwyd ....F 10
13 Cynwyl Elfed ....D 7
35 Dacre Banks .....A 10
23 Dadford ....H 10
23 Dadlington ......B 7
13 Dafen ....G 8
18 Dagenham ....F 5
16 Daglingworth ....D 1
17 Dagnall ....C 10
13 Dail ....D 8
42 Dailly ....B 3
57 Dail-na-mine Lo...M 3

53 Dairsie or Osnaburgh
        E 9
34 Daisy Hill ......G 5
51 Dalavich ....F 7
43 Dalbeattie ......E 9
63 Dalbeg ....B 3
47 Dalblair ....G 11
59 Dalbog ....K 3
38 Dalby ....H 1
61 Dalchalm ....F 9
51 Dalchenna ....G 8
52 Dalchonzie ......E 2
60 Dalchork ....F 6
55 Dalchreichart ...H 7
52 Dalchruin ....E 2
54 Dalchuirn ....F 3
56 Dalcross Station .E 3
33 Dalderby ....D 9
32 Dale, Derby .....F 2
12 Dale, Dyfed .....F 2
64 Dale, Shetland Is..D 6
39 Dale Head ....D 7
41 Dalehouse ....C 8
50 Dalelia ....A 5
57 Dalestie ....H 7
43 Dalfibble ....C 11
47 Dalfram ....G 11
47 Dalgarven ....E 8
48 Dalgety Bay .....A 4
47 Dalgig ....H 10
52 Dalginross ......E 3
52 Dalguise ....B 5
61 Dalhalvaig ......B 9
25 Dalham ....J 8
46 Dalinlongart ....A 6
48 Dalkeith ....C 6
52 Dall ....B 1
56 Dallas ....D 7
47 Dalleagles ......H 10
27 Dallinghoo ......K 5
10 Dallington, E. Sussex
        F 5
23 Dallington, Northants.
        F 10
39 Dalmain Dacre ...C 7
43 Dalmakerran .....B 8
51 Dalmally ....E 9
42 Dalmellington ...A 6
48 Dalmeny ....B 4
48 Dalmeny Rows ....B 4
60 Dalmichy ....F 6
57 Dalmigavie ......H 3
57 Dalmigavie Lodge ..G 3
56 Dalmore, Highland ..C 2
56 Dalmore, Highland .B 1
63 Dalmore, W. Isles .B 3
47 Dalmuir ....B 10
56 Dalmunach ....E 8
50 Dalnabreck ......A 4
57 Dalnacardoch Lo..M 3
52 Dalnacarn ....A 5
57 Dalnahaitnach ...H 3
61 Dalnamain ....G 7
57 Dalnaspidal .....M 2
61 Dalnawillan Lo. ..C 10
51 Dalness ....B 9
61 Dalnessie ....E 7
52 Daloist ....A 3
52 Dalqueich ....G 6
42 Dalquhairn ......B 4
61 Dalreavoch ......F 7
52 Dalriach ....A 2
43 Dalry, Dumf. & Gall.
        D 12
47 Dalry, Strathclyde ..D 8
47 Dalrymple ....H 8
48 Dalserf ....D 1
44 Dalston ....H 2
43 Dalswinton ......C 10
43 Dalton, Dumf. & Gall.
        D 12
34 Dalton, Lancs. ...F 4
45 Dalton, Northumb..F 9
45 Dalton, Northumb. .G 7
40 Dalton, N. Yorks...G 4
40 Dalton, N. Yorks...D 1
32 Dalton, S. Yorks. .A 2
40 Dalton Piercy ...B 5
38 Dalton-in-Furness .H 5
45 Dalton-le-Dale ..H 12
40 Dalton-on-Tees ..D 3
46 Daltot ....A 3
42 Dalvadie ....F 2
52 Dalveich ....E 1
47 Dalvennan ....H 9
61 Dalvina Lodge ...C 7
43 Dalwhat ....B 8
57 Dalwhinnie ......L 2
6 Dalwood ....F 6
8 Damerham ....D 3
26 Damgate ....E 7
42 Damnaglaur ......H 2
48 Damside ....D 4
11 Danaway borden ..B 7

19 Danbury ....C 8
41 Danby ....D 7
40 Danby Wiske .....E 3
56 Dandaleith ......E 8
48 Danderhall ......B 6
18 Dane End ....B 3
23 Dane Hills ......B 9
31 Danebridge ......D 8
10 Danehill ....E 3
34 Dangerous Corner ..F 4
40 Dan's Corner ....A 1
22 Danzey Green ....E 5
14 Daren—felen .....C 5
10 Darenth ....A 4
30 Daresbury ....B 4
36 Darfield ....G 2
11 Dargate ....B 9
45 Dargues ....D 7
3 Darite ....C 9
22 Darlaston ....C 3
35 Darley ....A 10
31 Darley Bridge ...D 11
22 Darlingscott ....H 6
40 Darlington ......D 3
30 Darliston ....G 4
32 Darlton ....C 5
32 Darnall ....A 1
56 Darnaway Castle ..D 5
47 Darnconner ....G 10
43 Darngarroch .....E 7
49 Darnick ....F 8
20 Darowen ....B 4
58 Darra ....C 5
4 Darracott, Corn ..D 1
4 Darracott, Devon ..B 3
45 Darras Hall .....F 9
36 Darrington ......E 3
27 Darsham ....H 7
10 Dartford ....A 4
5 Dartington ......J 6
5 Dartmeet ....H 5
5 Dartmouth ....K 7
35 Darton ....F 11
47 Darvel ....F 10
34 Darwen ....E 6
17 Datchet ....F 10
23 Datchworth ......B 3
18 Datchworth Green ..B 3
34 Daubill ....F 6
16 Dauntsey ....F 1
16 Dauntsey Green ..F 1
16 Dauntsey Lock ...F 1
30 Davenham ....C 5
23 Daventry ....F 9
20 David's Well ....E 6
48 Davidson's Mains .B 5
56 Davidston ....C 3
3 Davidstow ....A 8
6 Davington ....C 1
58 Daviot, Grampian ..E 5
6 Daviot, Highland ..F 3
17 Davis Street,....G 9
58 Davoch of Grange .C 2
35 Daw Cross ....B 11
21 Dawesgreen ......C 1
21 Dawley ....B 12
52 Dawley Bank .....B 12
21 Dawley Magna ....B 12
5 Dawlish ....H 8
7 Dawlish Wake ....E 7
7 Dawlish Warren ..H 3
29 Dawn ....C 8
19 Daws Heath ......C 8
3 Daw's House ....A 10
24 Dawsmere ....C 5
16 Dawthwaitehead ..C 6
16 Daylesford ......B 3
44 Deadwater ....C 4
42 Deadwaters ......E 12
11 Deal ....C 12
38 Dean, Cumb ......C 3
4 Dean, Devon .....B 4
4 Dean, Devon .....B 5
5 Dean, Devon .....J 6
8 Dean, Dorset ....D 1
7 Dean, Hants .....D 7
7 Dean, Somerset ..B 10
5 Dean Prior ......J 6
31 Dean Row ....B 7
10 Dean Street .....C 6
44 Deanburnhaugh ...B 2
7 Deane ....A 7
60 Deanich Lodge ...H 5
38 Deanscales ......C 3
23 Deanshanger Hill .H 11
50 Deanston ....G 2
38 Dearham ....B 3
27 Debach ....K 5
25 Debden, Essex ...M 7
18 Debden Estate ...D 4
25 Debden Green ....M 7
27 Debenham ....J 5

48 Dechmont ....B 3
16 Deddington ......A 6
27 Dedham ....M 4
59 Deebank ....H 4
59 Deecastle ....H 2
23 Deene ....C 12
23 Deenethorpe ....F 1
17 Deepcut ....H 10
24 Deeping Gate ....E 3
24 Deeping St. James .E 3
24 Deeping St. Nicholas
        D 3
58 Deerhill ....B 2
15 Deerhurst ....A 11
64 Deerness ....D 3
8 Defford ....H 3
14 Defynnog ....B 2
7 Deganwy ....B 7
40 Deighton, N.Yorks. .E 4
35 Deighton, W.Yorks.
        E 10
36 Deighton ....C 4
28 Deiniolen ....D 5
3 Delabole ....A 8
30 Delamere ....C 4
42 Delamford ....B 4
56 Delchirach ......F 7
58 Delfrigs ....E 7
57 Dell Lodge ......H 6
56 Delliefure ......F 6
56 Delnabo ....H 7
57 Delnadamph Lo ...J 8
21 Delph ....F 8
45 Delves ....H 9
25 Dembleby ....B 1
36 Denaby ....G 3
36 Denaby Main .....G 3
43 Denbie Mains ....D 11
29 Denbigh ....D 10
28 Denby ....F 1
32 Denby ....F 1
35 Denby Dale ......F 11
16 Denchworth ......E 5
30 Denend ....D 3
25 Denford ....H 1
19 Dengie ....D 9
27 Denham, Bucks ...E 11
27 Denham, Suffolk ..H 5
27 Denham, Suffolk ..J 1
58 Denhead, Fife ...F 9
58 Denhead, Grampian
        B 7
58 Denhead, Grampian
        E 7
49 Denholm ....G 8
35 Denholme ....D 9
9 Denmead ....E 8
27 Dennington ......H 6
48 Denny ....A 1
10 Denny Bottom ...D 4
8 Denny Lodge .....E 5
48 Dennyloanhead ...A 1
35 Denshaw ....F 8
59 Denside ....H 5
27 Denston ....K 1
31 Denstone ....F 9
39 Dent ....F 9
39 Dent Station ....F 10
25 Denton, Cambs ...G 2
40 Denton, Durham ..C 2
10 Denton, E.Sussex ...H 3
11 Denton, Kent ...C 11
32 Denton, Lincs ...G 6
35 Denton, Manchester
        H 8
27 Denton, Norfolk ..G 6
35 Denton, N. Yorks .B 10
23 Denton, Northants .F 11
17 Denton, Oxon ....D 7
24 Denver ....E 7
45 Denwick ....B 10
45 Denwick Lane End
        A 10
26 Deopham ....E 3
26 Deopham Green ...F 3
4 Deptford, Devon ...D 5
4 Deptford, Devon ..D 1
18 Deptford, London..F 4
8 Deptford, Wilts ..B 2
31 Derby ....G 11
38 Derbyhaven ......H 1
32 Derbyshire, Co ...D11
52 Derculich ....B 4
42 Dergoals ....F 3
14 Deri ....D 5
20 Deri—Odwyn .....F 2
52 Derry ....E 1
15 Derry Hill ......G 12
50 Derryguaig ......D 2
11 Derringstone ....C 10
31 Derrington ......H 7
36 Derrythorpe .....F 6

24 Dersingham ......C 8
50 Dervaig ....B 2
29 Derwen ....E 10
13 Derwlwyn ....C 9
23 Desborough .....D 11
23 Desford ....F 2
45 Detchant ....B 12
11 Detling ....B 7
29 Deuddwr ....H 11
15 Devauden ....D 8
59 Devenick ....G 7
20 Devil's Bridge ..E 3
16 Devizes ....H 1
14 Devon, County ...F 5
48 Devonburn ....E 1
3 Devonport ....D 11
52 Devonside ....G 4
2 Devoran ....F 5
48 Dewar ....D 6
7 Dewlish ....F 11
15 Dewsall Court ...A 8
35 Dewsbury ....E 11
38 Dhoon ....G 2
38 Dhoor ....F 2
38 Dhowin ....F 2
9 Dial Post ....D 12
8 Dibden ....E 5
8 Dibden Purlieu ..E 5
27 Dickleburgh .....G 4
16 Didbrook ....A 2
16 Didcot ....E 6
25 Diddington ......J 3
21 Diddlebury ......D 10
15 Didley ....A 7
9 Didling ....D 10
15 Didmarton ......F 11
35 Didsbury ....H 7
33 Digby ....E 8
62 Digg ....A 4
35 Diggle ....F 9
34 Digmoor ....G 4
18 Digswell Water ..B 3
13 Dihewid ....B 2
47 Dikeneuk ....D 11
26 Dilham ....C 6
31 Dilhorne ....F 8
48 Dillarburn ......E 1
25 Dillington ......J 2
45 Dilston ....G 8
7 Dilton Marsh ....A 11
21 Dilwyn ....G 9
48 Dinanrig ....H 1
12 Dinas, Dyfed ....D 6
12 Dinas, Dyfed ....C 4
28 Dinas, Gwynedd ..G 3
20 Dinas Mawddwy ..A 4
14 Dinas Powis .....G 5
13 Dinasbach ....C 11
7 Dinder ....B 9
15 Dinedor ....A 8
15 Dinedor Cross ...A 8
15 Dingestow ....C 7
30 Dingle ....B 2
49 Dingleton ....F 8
23 Dingley ....C 11
56 Dingwall ....D 1
44 Dinlabyre ....D 4
44 Dinley ....C 3
59 Dinnet ....H 2
43 Dinning ....C 9
45 Dinnington,
        Northumb. .F 10
7 Dinnington, Som. ..E 7
28 Dinorwic ....D 5
40 Dinsdale Station ..D 4
17 Dinton, Bucks ...C 8
8 Dinton, Wilts ...C 2
42 Dinvin ....F 1
43 Dinwoodie Mains ..C 11
43 Dinwoodiegreen ..C 11
4 Dinworthy ....D 2
46 Dippen ....F 3
9 Dippenhall ......A 9
46 Dippin ....G 5
58 Dipple, Grampian .B 1
42 Dipple, Strathclyde .A 3
5 Diptford ....K 6
45 Dipton ....H 9
49 Dirleton ....A 8
21 Discoed ....F 8
32 Diseworth ....H 2
40 Dishforth ....H 4
31 Disley ....B 8
27 Diss ....G 4
20 Disserth ....G 6
38 Distington ......C 2
8 Ditchampton ....C 2
7 Ditcheat ....C 9
26 Ditchingham .....F 6
10 Ditchling ....F 2
15 Ditteridge .....G 11
5 Dittisham ....K 7

30 Ditton, Cheshire ..B 3
10 Ditton, Kent ....B 6
25 DittonGreen .....J 8
21 Ditton Priors ...D 11
57 Divach ....G 1
13 Divlyn ....C 11
16 Dixton, Glos ....A 1
15 Dixton, Gwent ...C 8
35 Dobcross ....F 8
3 Dobwalls ....C 9
5 Doccombe ....G 6
56 Dochfour House ..F 2
56 Dochgarroch .....F 2
26 Docking ....B 1
21 Docklow ....G 11
38 Dockray ....C 6
44 Dodburn ....B 3
18 Doddinghurst ....D 6
24 Doddington, Cambs.
        F 5
11 Doddington, Kent .B 8
32 Doddington, Lincs. .C 6
49 Doddington,
        Northumb. ...F 12
21 Doddington, Salop.
        E 11
22 Dodford, Heref.
        and Worc ......E 3
23 Dodford,Northants. .F 9
15 Dodington, Avon ..F 10
6 Dodington, Som ..B 5
30 Dodleston ....D 2
35 Dodworth ....G 11
32 Doe Lea ....D 2
4 DogVillage ......G 3
33 Dogdyke ....E 9
9 Dogmersfield ....A 9
20 Dolanog ....A 5
14 Dolau, Mid.Glam. .F 3
21 Dolau, Powys ....F 7
28 Dolbenmaen .....F 4
20 Dolfach ....E 5
20 Dol-ffanog ......A 3
20 Dol-for, Powys ...B 4
20 Dol-for, Powys ...D 6
29 Dolgarrog ....C 7
28 Dolgellau ....H 6
13 Dolgerdd ....B 7
20 Dol-goch ....B 2
13 Dol-gran ....D 8
20 Dolhelfa ....E 5
61 Doll ....F 8
52 Dollar ....G 4
52 Dollarbeg ....G 4
21 Dolley Green ....F 8
21 Dolleycanney ....G 7
34 Dolphinholme ....B 4
48 Dolphinton ......E 4
4 Dolton ....E 4
29 Dolwen, Clwyd ...C 8
20 Dolwen, Powys ...B 5
29 Dolwyd ....B 7
29 Dolwyddelan .....E 7
20 Dol-y-bont ......D 2
20 Dolypandy ....D 2
36 Doncaster ....G 4
8 Donhead St. Andrew
        D 1
7 Donhead St. Mary .D 12
52 Donibristle .....H 6
6 Doniford ....B 4
24 Donington, Lincs .B 3
22 Donington, Salop .A 6
33 Donington on Bain .B 9
24 Donington South Ing
        B 3
22 Donisthorpe .....A 6
17 Donkey Town ....H 10
4 Donkleywood ....D 6
16 Donnington, Berks. G 6
16 Donnington, Glos .A 3
15 Donnington,Heref.
        and Worc. ....A 10
21 Donnington,Salop.
        B 11
21 Donnington, Salop.
        A 12
9 Donnington, W.Sussex
        F 10
21 Donnington Wood
        A 12
7 Donyatt ....E 7
47 Doonbank ....H 9
47 Doonfoot ....G 8
47 Doonholm ....H 8
57 Dorback Lodge ...H 6
7 Dorchester, Dorset
        G 10
17 Dorchester, Oxon .E 7
26 Dordon ....B 6
31 Dore ....B 11
56 Dores ....F 2
32 Dorket Head .....E 3

10 Dorking C1
10 Dormans Land D3
40 Dormanstown C6
21 Dormington H11
17 Dorney F10
55 Dornie G3
61 Dornoch G8
44 Dornock F1
61 Dorrery B10
22 Dorridge E5
33 Dorrington, Lincs ...E8
21 Dorrington, Salop. .B10
21 Dorset, County ...F10
22 Dorsington G5
21 Dorstone H8
17 Dorton C7
55 Dorusduain G3
54 Dosmuckeran D6
22 Dosthill B6
7 Dottery G8
3 Doublebois C9
15 Doughton E12
38 Douglas, I.o.M. H2
48 Douglas,Strathclyde
F1
53 Douglas& Angus ..D9
28 Douglas Hill D5
48 Douglas Water ...F2
48 Douglas West F1
53 Douglastown B9
46 Dougrie F4
7 Doulting B10
64 Dounby C1
52 Doune, Central G2
55 Doune, Highland ..J1
42 Dounepark B3
59 Douneside G2
60 Dounie G6
58 Dounie Park B4
47 Doura F9
5 Dousland J4
31 Dove Holes B9
38 Dovenby B3
11 Dover D12
27 Dovercourt M6
22 Doverdale F2
31 Doveridge G9
52 Dowally B5
34 Dowbridge D3
16 Dowdeswell B1
42 Dowhill A3
14 Dowlais D4
4 Dowland E4
16 Down Ampney D2
15 Down Hatherley ..B11
4 Down St. Mary ...E6
5 Down Thomas L4
56 Downan, Grampian .F7
42 Downan, Strathclyde
C2
3 Downderry D10
18 Downe H4
15 Downend, Avon ...G9
16 Downend, Berks ...G6
9 Downend, I.o.W. ...G7
53 Downfield D8
3 Downgate B10
25 Downham, Cambs. .G6
19 Downham, Essex ...D7
34 Downham, Lancs ..C6
49 Downham, Northumb.
F11
24 Downham Market ..E7
7 Downhead, Som ...D9
7 Downhead, Som ...B10
52 Downhill D6
34 Downholland Cross .F2
40 Downholme E1
59 Downies H7
17 Downley E9
7 Downside, Som ...A10
7 Downside, Som B9
15 Downside, Avon ...H8
17 Downside, Surrey .H12
8 Downton, Hants ..G4
8 Downton, Wilts ...D3
21 Donton on the Rock
E9
24 Dowsby D3
45 Doxford A10
15 Doynton G10
14 Draethen F5
48 Draffan E1
9 Dragons Green D12
5 Drakeland Corner .K4
47 Drakemyre D8
22 Drake's Broughton .G4
22 Drakes Cross F2
3 Drakewalls C11
42 Dranigower E3
23 Draughton, Northants
D11
35 Draughton, N.Yorks.
B9

36 Drax D5
16 Draycot Foliat ...F3
23 Draycote E8
32 Draycott, Derby ..G2
16 Draycott, Glos ...A3
7 Draycott, Som ...A8
31 Draycott in the Clay
G10
31 Draycott in the Moors
F8
4 Drayford E6
9 Drayton, Hants ...E8
23 Drayton, Leics ...C11
24 Drayton, Lincs ...B4
26 Drayton, Norfolk ..D5
16 Drayton, Oxon ...E6
23 Drayton, Oxon ...H8
22 Drayton, Salop ...F8
7 Drayton, Som ...D7
22 Drayton Bassett ...B5
17 Drayton Beauchamp
C10
17 Drayton Parslow ...A9
17 Drayton St. Leonard
D7
35 Drebley A9
12 Dreenhill F3
13 Dre-fach, Dyfed ..B8
13 Drefach, Dyfed ...C7
13 Drefach, Dyfed ...F8
47 Dreghorn F8
11 Drellingore N11
49 Drem A8
5 Drewsteignton ...G6
33 Driby C11
16 Driffield, Glos ...D2
37 Driffield, Humber. .A8
38 Drigg E3
35 Drighlington D11
51 Drimfern F8
58 Drimmies E5
50 Drimnin B3
50 Drimnin House ...B3
7 Drimpton F7
55 Drimsallie L3
51 Drimsynie G9
27 Drinkstone J3
27 Drinkstone Green ..J3
51 Drishaig F8
48 Drochil E4
31 Drointon G9
22 Droitwich F2
52 Dron F6
32 Dronfield B1
31 Dronfield Woodhouse
B11
47 Drongan G9
53 Dronley D8
14 Drope G4
9 Droxford D7
29 Druid F9
43 Druidhall B9
59 Druidsdale J6
12 Druidston E2
46 Druim A2
55 Druimarbin M5
51 Druimavuic C7
54 Druimdhu D5
46 Druimdrishaig ...B2
54 Druimindarroch ...F8
46 Druimyeon More ..D2
58 Drum, Grampian ..C6
56 Drum, Highland ...D2
46 Drum, Strathclyde .B4
52 Drum, Tayside ...G5
60 Drumbeg D3
58 Drumblade D3
58 Drumblair House ..C4
42 Drumbreddan G2
42 Drumbuie,
Dumf. & Gall. C6
55 Drumbuie, Highland G2
44 Drumburgh G1
43 Drumburn E10
47 Drumchapel B10
56 Drumchardine E1
14 Drumclog E11
43 Drumcoltran E9
56 Drumcroy F1
47 Drumcruilton A9
58 Drumdaig F3
56 Drumdyre D2
53 Drumeldrie G9
48 Drumelzier F4
62 Drumfearn E5
43 Drumfork G10
57 Drumgask K2
53 Drumgley B9
56 Drumguish, Highland
F6
57 Drumguish, Highland
J4
59 Drumhead, Grampian
H4

58 Drumhead, Grampian
F7
42 Drumjohn B6
43 Drumlanrig Castle .B9
59 Drumlasie G4
46 Drumlemble G2
58 Drumligair F6
59 Drumlithie J5
42 Drummoddie G5
56 Drummond C2
42 Drummore H2
57 Drumnadrochit ...G1
59 Drumnagair K4
58 Drumnagorrach ...B3
44 Drumnahoy F4
42 Drumpail E3
43 Drumpark D9
42 Drumrae G5
43 Drumrash D7
60 Drumrunie Lodge ..F3
47 Drumshang H7
43 Drumstinchall ...F9
59 Drumtochty Castle .J4
62 Drumuie D4
57 Drumuillie G5
52 Drumvaich G2
42 Drumwalt F4
58 Drumwhindle D7
43 Drumwhirn D8
29 Drury D12
32 Dry Doddington ...F6
25 Dry Drayton J5
19 Dry Street E7
39 Drybeck D9
58 Drybridge Grampian
A2
47 Drybridge Strathclyde
F8
15 Drybrook C9
49 Dryburgh F8
43 Dryfesdale Gate ...C11
48 Dryhope C9
47 Drymen A9
58 Drymuir C6
62 Drynoch E3
60 Duag Bridge G4
58 Dubford, Grampian
C5
58 Dubford, Grampian
A5
58 Dubiton C4
60 Duchally E5
43 Duchrae C7
8 Duck Street A5
30 Duckington E4
16 Ducklington G4
32 Duckmanton C2
25 Duck's Cross K2
25 Duddenhoe End ...L6
48 Duddingston B6
24 Duddington E1
10 Duddleswell E3
49 Duddo E12
30 Duddon D4
38 Duddon Bridge ...F4
30 Dudleston F2
30 Dudleston Heath ..F2
45 Dudley, Northants. .F10
22 Dudley, W.Midlands
C3
12 Dudwells E3
31 Duffield F11
14 Duffryn E2
58 Dufftown D1
56 Duffus C7
33 Dufton C9
41 Duggleby H9
62 Duisdalemore G6
55 Duisky M4
14 Dukestown C5
35 Dukinfield G8
56 Dularich F1
28 Dulas A4
58 Dulax F1
7 Dulcote B9
6 Dulford F4
52 Dull B3
47 Dullatur B12
21 Dullingham J7
57 Dulnain Bridge ...G5
25 Duloe, Beds. J3
3 Duloe, Cornwall ..D9
56 Dulsie E5
6 Dulverton C3
18 Dulwich G3
47 Dumbarton B9
16 Dumbleton A3
58 Dumcrieff A11
58 Dumeath D2
43 Dumfries A10
47 Dumgoyne A10
9 Dummer B7
59 Dun L4

63 Dun Carloway C3
57 Dunachtonmore J4
56 Dunain House E2
52 Dunalastair A2
46 Dunan, Strathclyde .B6
52 Dunan, Tayside ...D2
51 Dunan, Tayside ...B11
62 Dunan, Skye E5
51 Dunans H7
49 Dunbar B9
61 Dunbeath D11
52 Dunblane G3
53 Dunbog E7
6 Dunboll B6
8 Dunbridge C5
61 Duncansby Head ...A12
58 Duncanston,
Grampian E3
56 Duncanston,
Highland D2
6 Dunchideock G2
23 Dunchurch E8
23 Duncote G10
43 Duncow C10
52 Duncraggan G12
54 Duncraig Castle ...F2
52 Duncrievie F6
9 Duncton D11
53 Dundee D9
47 Dundon C8
53 Dundonald, Fife ..H7
47 Dundonald,
Strathclyde F8
60 Dundonnell Hotel ..H2
60 Dundonnell House .H3
43 Dundrennan G8
55 Dundreggan H7
43 Dundrennan G8
5 Dundry H8
52 Dunduff H6
59 Dunecht G5
48 Dunfermline A4
35 Dunford Bridge ...G10
7 Dunge A12
32 Dunham C5
30 Dunham Town B6
30 Dunham-on-the-Hill
C3
22 Dunhampton E2
33 Dunholme B7
52 Dunie D4
53 Dunino F10
48 Dunipace A1
52 Dunira E2
52 Dunkeld C5
15 Dunkerton H10
6 Dunkeswell E5
11 Dunkirk B9
5 Dunk's Green C5
59 Dunlappie K3
22 Dunley E1
56 Dunlichity Lodge ..F2
47 Dunlop D9
57 Dunmaglass Lodge .G2
7 Dunmere C7
52 Dunmore, Central .H4
46 Dunmore,
Strathclyde C3
11 Dunn Street B7
61 Dunnet A11
53 Dunnichen B10
53 Dunninald B11
52 Dunning F5
37 Dunnington,
Humberside B9
36 Dunnington, N. Yorks.
B4
22 Dunnington, War ..G4
35 Dunnockshaw D7
59 Dunnottar Mains ..J6
58 Dunnydeer E4
50 Dunollie D6
46 Dunoon B6
53 Dunotter G9
42 Dunragit F2
46 Dunrostan A2
49 Duns D10
16 Duns Tew A5
24 Dunsby C2
43 Dunscore C9
36 Dunscroft F4
40 Dunsdale D2
17 Dunsden Green ...F8
9 Dunsfold B11
5 Dunsford G7
53 Dunshelt F7
58 Dunshillock C7
17 Dunsley D9
17 Dunsmore D9
34 Dunsop Bridge ...B5
15 Dunstable B11
50 Dunstaffnage Fm ..D6
31 Dunstall H10
6 Dunster B3

33 Dunston, Lincs D8
26 Dunston, Norfolk ...E5
45 Dunston, Northumb.
A10
31 Dunston, Staffs ...H8
45 Dunston, Tyne & Wear
G10
5 Dunstone H6
36 Dunsville F4
37 Dunswell D8
48 Dunsyre E3
44 Dunterley E6
5 Dunterton H2
16 Duntisbourne Abbots
C1
16 Duntisbourne Rouse
D1
7 Duntish F10
47 Duntocher B9
25 Dunton, Beds L3
17 Dunton, Bucks ...B9
26 Dunton, Norfolk ..C2
23 Dunton Bassett ...C9
10 Dunton Green B4
18 Dunton Wayletts ..E6
62 Duntulm A3
47 Dunure H7
47 Dunure Mains H7
13 Dunvant H9
62 Dunvegan C2
27 Dunwich H8
52 Dupplin Castle ...E5
44 Durdar H2
40 Durham A3
43 Durisdeer A10
43 Durisdeermill ...A9
6 Durleigh C6
16 Durley, Wilts ...H3
8 Durley, Hants ...D6
9 Durley Street ...D7
60 Durnamuck G2
60 Durness A5
58 Durno E5
9 Durrington, W.Sussex
F12
8 Durrington, Wilts. .B3
15 Dursley D10
6 Durston C6
7 Durweston E11
64 Dury D7
23 Duston F10
57 Duthil G5
21 Dutlas E7
18 Duton Hill A6
7 Dutson A10
30 Dutton B4
25 Duxford L6
28 Dwygyfylchi C7
28 Dwyran D4
58 Dyce F6
58 Dye House G7
13 Dyfatty G8
12 Dyfed, Co D6
57 Dyffryn, Dyfed ...E6
12 Dyffryn, Dyfed ...C3
14 Dyffryn, Mid. Glam.
F4
14 Dyffryn, S. Glam .G4
14 Dyffryn, W. Glam. .E2
28 Dyffryn-Ardudwy ..H5
14 Dyffryn Cellwen ...C2
20 Dyffryn-castell ...D3
4 Dyke, Devon D2
24 Dyke, Lincs C2
56 Dyke, Grampian ...D5
49 Dykegatehead D11
52 Dykehead, Central .G1
48 Dykehead, Strathclyde
C2
59 Dykehead, Tayside .L1
59 Dykelands K5
53 Dykends A7
58 Dykeside C5
54 Dylife C4
11 Dymchurch E9
15 Dymock A10
15 Dyrham G10
53 Dysart H8
58 Dyserth B10
45 Eachwick F9
34 Eagland Hill C3
40 Eagle D6
40 Eaglescliffe Junc .D4
38 Eaglesfield, Cumb .B3
44 Eaglesfield,
Dumf. & Gall. F1
47 Eaglesham D10
24 Eaglethorpe F2
38 Eairy H1
23 Eakley Lanes G11
32 Eakring D4
36 Ealand F6
18 Ealing F2
39 Eamont Bridge ...B7

35 Earby C8
34 Earcroft E6
21 Eardington C12
21 Eardisland F9
21 Eardisley G8
21 Eardiston, Heref.
& Worc. F12
30 Eardiston, Salop ..H2
25 Earith H5
23 Earl Shilton B8
27 Earl Soham J5
31 Earl Sterndale ...C9
27 Earl Stonham J4
49 Earle G12
7 Earley G8
26 Earlham E5
62 Earlish B3
23 Earls Barton F12
19 Earls Colne A8
22 Earl's Croome ...H2
27 Earl's Green J3
22 Earlsdon D6
53 Earlsferry G9
21 Earlsford D6
49 Earlston, Borders .F8
47 Earlston, Strathclyde
F9
22 Earlswood E5
15 Earlswood Com. ...E8
9 Earnley F5
47 Earnockmuir D11
45 Earsdon, Northumb.
F11
45 Earsdon, Tyne & Wear
F11
26 Earsham A4
36 Earswick A4
9 Eartham E10
38 Earystane H1
40 Easby, N. Yorks. ..D6
40 Easby, N. Yorks. ..E2
50 Easdale F5
9 Easebourne D10
23 Easenhall D8
11 Eashing B11
17 Easington, Bucks. .C8
41 Easington, Cleveland
D7
40 Easington, Dur. ...A4
37 Easington, Humberside
E11
45 Easington, Northumb.
C12
17 Easington, Oxon. ..D7
40 Easington Colliery .A4
45 Easington Grange .B12
45 Easington Lane ..H12
40 Easingwold H5
11 Easole Street ...C11
53 Eassie & Nevay ...C8
14 East Aberthaw ...H4
16 East Adderbury ...A6
5 East Allington ...L6
45 East Ancroft A11
4 East Anstey C7
9 East Ashling E9
58 East Auchronie ...F6
41 East Ayton G10
14 East Bank D5
33 East Barkwith ...B9
10 East Barming C6
41 East Barnby D8
18 East Barnet D3
49 East Barns B9
26 East Barsham B2
26 East Beckham B5
18 East Bedfont F1
27 East Bergholt ...M4
26 East Bilney D3
49 East Blanerne ...D11
10 East Blatchington .H4
7 East Bloxworth ...G12
45 East Boldon G11
8 East Boldre F5
45 East Bolton A9
47 East Brackenridge .E11
26 East Bradenham ...C3
7 East Brent A7
27 East Bridge J7
32 East Bridgford ...F4
45 East Brunton F10
4 East Buckland ...C5
6 East Budleigh ...H4
64 East Burra E7
64 East Burrafirth ..D7
7 East Burton G11
40 East Butsfield ...A1
36 East Butterwick ..G6
59 East Cairnbeg ...K5
48 East Calder C4
26 East Carleton ...E5
23 East Carlton C11
16 East Challow E5
7 East Chelborough ..F9

10 East Chiltington ...G 3
7 East Chinnock ....E 8
8 East Chisenbury ...A 3
9 East Clandon .....A 12
17 East Claydon ....B 8
15 East Clevedon ....G 7
7 East Coker ......E 9
6 East Combe .....C 5
7 East Compton ....B 9
36 East Cottingwith ...C 5
8 East Cowes .....F 6
36 East Cowick .....E 4
40 East Cowton .....C 5
45 East Cramlington ..E 11
7 East Cranmore ....B 10
8 East Creech ......H 1
57 East Croachy .....G 2
46 East Darlochan ....G 2
8 East Dean, Hants ...C 4
9 East Dean, W. Sussex
E 10
26 East Dereham ....D 3
45 East Ditchburn ....A 9
4 East Down ....B 5
32 East Drayton .....C 5
15 East Dundry .....H 9
45 East Edington .....E 10
15 East End, Avon ...G 8
8 East End, Dorset ...F 2
16 East End, Hants. ...H 5
9 East End, Hants. ...D 8
8 East End, Hants. ...F 5
18 East End Herts ....A 4
37 East End, Humber. D 10
11 East End, Kent ....E 7
26 East End, Norfolk ..D 8
16 East End, Oxon ....C 5
8 East Erlestoke ....A 1
10 East Farleigh .....C 6
23 East Farndon .....D 10
36 East Ferry ......G 6
45 East Fleetham ....D 12
53 East Flisk ......E 3
49 East Fortune .....A 8
36 East Garforth ....D 2
16 East Garston .....F 5
16 East Ginge ......E 5
49 East Gordon .....E 9
16 East Grafton .....H 4
8 East Grimstead ...C 4
10 East Grinstead ...D 3
11 East Guldeford ...F 8
23 East Haddon .....E 10
16 East Hagbourne ...E 6
37 East Halton ......E 9
37 East Halton Skitter .E 9
18 East Ham ....F 4
16 East Hanney .....E 5
19 East Hanningfield ..D 7
36 East Hardwick ....E 2
27 East Harling .....G 3
40 East Harlsey .....E 4
8 East Harnham ....C 3
7 East Harptree ....A 9
45 East Hartford ....E 11
9 East Harting .....D 9
7 East Hatch .....C 12
25 East Hatley ......K 4
52 East Haugh ......B 4
40 East Hauxwell ....F 2
53 East Haven ......D 10
24 East Heckington ...A 3
40 East Hedleyhope ..A 2
16 East Hendred .....E 5
41 East Heslerton ....G 9
10 East Hoathly .....F 4
7 East Horrington ...B 9
9 East Horsley .....A 12
45 East Horton .....C 11
7 East Huntspill ....B 7
17 East Hyde ......B 12
4 East Ilkerton ....A 6
16 East Ilsley ......F 6
33 East Keal ......D 11
16 East Kennett .....G 2
35 East Keswick .....C 12
47 East Kilbride .....B 2
58 East Kinharrachie ..D 7
33 East Kirby ......D 10
41 East Knapton ....G 9
7 East Knighton ....H 11
4 East Knowstone ...D 7
7 East Knoyle .....C 12
7 East Lambrook ...D 7
11 East Langdon ....C 12
23 East Langton .....C 10
61 East Langwell ....F 7
9 East Lavant .....E 10
40 East Layton .....D 2
32 East Leake ......H 3
4 East Leigh ....E 6
49 East Learmouth ...F 11
26 East Lexham .....D 2
45 East Lilburn ....A 8

49 East Linton ......B 8
9 East Liss ......C 9
47 East Lockhead ....D 8
3 East Looe ......D 9
36 East Lound ......G 6
9 East Lovington ...E 10
7 East Lulworth ....H 12
41 East Lutton .....H 9
59 East Mains ......H 4
10 East Malling .....B 6
9 East Marden .....E 9
32 East Markham ....C 5
35 East Marton .....B 8
9 East Meon ......D 8
8 East Mere ......E 3
19 East Mersea .....C 10
17 East Molesey .....G 12
7 East Mordon .....C 2
43 East Morton, Dumf. &
Gall. ....B 9
35 East Morton,
W. Yorks. ......C 9
42 East Muntloch ....H 2
41 East Ness ......G 9
23 East Norton .....B 11
6 East Nynehead ...D 5
9 East Oakley ......A 7
5 East Ogwell .....J 7
7 East Orchard ....D 11
49 East Ord ......D 12
5 East Panson .....G 2
10 East Peckham ....C 5
12 East Pennar .....G 3
7 East Pennard ....C 9
52 East Plean ......H 3
26 East Poringland ...E 6
5 East Portlemouth ..M 6
5 East Prawle .....M 6
9 East Preston .....F 12
6 East Quantoxhead .B 5
45 East Rainton .....H 11
37 East Ravendale ...G 10
26 East Raynham ....C 2
32 East Retford .....B 4
35 East Rigton .....C 12
40 East Rounton ....E 4
26 East Rudham .....C 1
26 East Runton .....A 5
26 East Ruston .....C 6
49 East Saltoun .....C 7
44 East Scales ......F 1
16 East Shefford ....G 5
45 East Sleekburn ...E 11
26 East Somerton ...D 8
36 East Stockwith ...H 6
7 East Stoke, Dorset
H 12
32 East Stoke, Notts. ...E 5
7 East Stour ......D 11
11 East Stourmouth ..B 11
4 East Stowford ....C 5
9 East Stratton ....B 7
11 East Studdal ....C 11
10 East Sussex, Co ...F 5
3 East Taphouse ....C 9
19 East Tilbury .....F 7
43 East Tinwald .....C 11
9 East Tistead .....C 8
33 East Torrington ...B 8
59 East Town ......J 5
26 East Tuddenham ..D 4
8 East Tytherley ....C 4
16 East Tytherton ...G 1
4 East Village .....E 7
24 East Walton .....D 8
4 East Warlington ...E 6
5 East Week ......G 5
8 East Wellow .....D 5
53 East Wemyss .....G 8
48 East Whitburn ....C 2
19 East Wick ......D 10
12 East Williamston ..F 4
24 East Winch ......D 8
9 East Wittering ...F 9
40 East Witton .....G 2
45 East Woodburn ...D 7
16 East Woodhay ...H 5
9 East Worldham ...B 9
26 East Wretham ....F 2
4 East Youlstone ...D 1
10 Eastbourne .....H 5
37 Eastburn ......B 7
16 Eastbury, Herts. ...E 1
16 Eastbury, Berks. ...F 4
11 Eastchurch ......A 8
15 Eastcombe ......D 12
18 Eastcote, London ..E 1
23 Eastcote, Northants
G 10
22 Eastcote, W. Midlands
D 5
4 Eastcott, Devon ..D 1
8 Eastcott, Wilts. ...A 2

16 Eastcourt, Wilts. ...H 3
16 Eastcourt, Wilts. ....E 1
10 Eastdean ......H 4
19 Eastend ......E 9
56 Easter Ardross ....B 2
58 Easter Aucharnie ..D 4
57 Easter Aviemore ..H 4
56 Easter Balcroy ....E 4
57 Easter Balmoral ...K 8
57 Easter Boleskine ..G 1
56 Easter Brae .....C 2
15 Easter Compton ...F 9
54 Easter Crochail ...E 3
56 Easter Culbo .....D 2
59 Easter Davoch ....G 2
55 Easter Drummond .H 8
52 Easter Dullater ....F 1
43 Easter Earshaig ...A 11
61 Easter Fearn .....H 7
44 Easter Fodderlee ..B 4
56 Easter Galcantray ..E 4
22 Easter Green .....D 6
48 Easter Happrew ...E 4
48 Easter Howgate ...C 5
49 Easter Howlaws ...E 10
56 Easter Kinkell ....D 1
49 Easter Langlee .....F 8
53 Easter Lednathie ..A 8
56 Easter Milton ....D 5
56 Easter Moniack ...E 1
56 Easter Muckovie ..E 3
59 Easter Ord ......G 6
64 Easter Quarff ......E 7
58 Easter Silverford ..A 5
64 Easter Skeld .....D 6
54 Easter Slumbay ....F 3
49 Easter Softlaw ...F 10
48 Easter Stanhope ..F 4
59 Easter Tillygarmond
H 4
59 Easter Tulloch ....K 5
56 Easterfield ......E 3
9 Eastergate ......F 11
47 Fasterhouse,
Strathclyde ......C 11
48 Easterhouse,
Strathclyde ......D 3
8 Easterton ....A 2
58 Eastertown, Grampian
D 1
48 Eastertown,
Strathclyde ......F 2
48 Eastertown,
Strathclyde ......E 3
48 Eastertown,
Strathclyde ......G 1
7 Eastertown, Som. ...A 7
58 Eastertown of
Auchleuchries ....D 8
59 Eastfield, Grampian
H 1
41 Eastfield, N. Yorks
G 10
48 Eastfield, Strathclyde
C 2
48 Eastfield, Strathclyde
E 2
45 Eastfield Hall ....B 10
49 Eastfield of Lempitlaw
F 10
39 Eastgate, Dur. ...A 11
26 Eastgate, Norfolk ..C 4
30 Eastham ......B 2
17 Easthampstead ...G 9
17 Eastheath ......G 9
4 East-the-Water ...C 3
21 Easthope ......C 11
19 Easthorpe, Essex ..B 8
32 Easthorpe, Notts. ..E 4
48 Easthouses ......C 6
4 Eastington, Devon ..E 6
15 Eastington, Glos. ..D 11
16 Eastington, Glos ...C 2
16 Eastleach Martin ..D 3
16 Eastleach Turville ..D 3
4 Eastleigh, Devon ..C 4
8 Eastleigh, Hants. ..D 6
11 Eastling ......B 8
45 Eastnook ......D 8
15 Eastnor ......A 10
36 Eastoft ......E 6
9 Eastoke ......F 8
25 Easton, Cambs. ...H 2
44 Easton, Cumb. ...G 1
44 Easton, Cumb. ...F 3
5 Easton, Devon ....H 7
8 Easton, Dorset ...H 7
8 Easton, Hants. ...C 6
8 Easton, I.o.W. ...G 6
32 Easton, Leics. ...G 6
26 Easton, Norfolk ...D 4
7 Easton, Somerset ..A 8
27 Easton, Suffolk ...J 6
15 Easton, Wilts. ...G 12

15 Easton Grey ......E 12
15 Easton-in-Gordano
G 8
23 Easton Maudit ....F 12
16 Easton Royal .....H 3
24 Eastrea ......F 4
44 Eastriggs ....F 1
36 Eastrington .....D 5
11 Eastry ......C 11
33 Eastville ......E 11
32 Eastwell ......G 5
15 Eastwick ......C 4
19 Eastwood, Essex ..E 8
32 Eastwood, Notts ...F 2
30 Eaton, Cheshire ...D 4
31 Eaton, Cheshire ...D 7
32 Eaton, Leics. ....B 4
32 Eaton, Leics. ....G 5
26 Eaton, Norfolk ...E 5
16 Eaton, Oxon. ....D 5
21 Eaton, Salop ....C 9
21 Eaton, Salop. .....C 10
21 Eaton Bishop ....H 10
17 Eaton Bray .....B 10
21 Eaton Constantine .B 11
16 Eaton Green .....B 10
16 Eaton Hastings ...D 4
25 Eaton Soçon ....J 3
30 Eaton upon Tern ..H 5
41 Ebberston ......G 9
8 Ebbesbourne Wake .D 2
14 Ebbw Vale .....C 5
45 Ebchester ......G 9
15 Ebdon ......H 7
8 Ebford ......G 3
15 Ebley ......D 11
22 Ebrington ......H 5
5 Ebsworthy Town ..G 4
16 Ecchinswell ......H 6
49 Ecclaw ......C 10
43 Ecclefechan .....D 12
49 Eccles, Borders ...E 10
10 Eccles, Kent .....B 6
34 Eccles, Manchester .G 6
21 Eccles Green .....H 9
26 Eccles Road .....F 3
49 Eccles Tofts .....E 10
32 Ecclesall ......B 1
35 Ecclesfield ......H 12
59 Ecclesgreig ......L 5
31 Eccleshall ......G 7
35 Eccleshill ......D 10
48 Ecclesmachan ....B 3
30 Eccleston, Ches. ..D 3
34 Eccleston, Lancs. ..E 4
34 Eccleston, Merseyside
H 4
34 Eccleston Green ..E 4
35 Eccup ......C 11
59 Echt ......G 5
49 Eckford ......G 9
22 Eckington ......H 3
23 Ecton ......F 11
31 Edale ......B 9
10 Edburton ......G 11
43 Edderside ......G 11
61 Edderton ......H 7
16 Eddington, Berks. ..G 4
11 Eddington, Kent ..A 10
4 Eddiston ......D 1
48 Eddleston ......E 5
47 Eddlewood ......D 12
10 Eden Hall ......F 10
10 Edenbridge ......C 3
35 Edenfield ......E 7
39 Edenhall ......B 8
24 Edenham ......C 5
31 Edensor ......C 11
52 Edentaggart .....H 10
36 Edenthorpe ......F 4
44 Edentown ......G 2
28 Edern ......F 2
7 Edgarley ......C 8
22 Edgbaston ......D 4
17 Edgcott, Bucks. ...B 8
6 Edgcott, Som. ...B 2
21 Edge ......B 9
15 Edge End ......C 9
30 Edge Green, Ches. .E 3
27 Edge Green, Norf. .G 3
30 Edge Hill ......A 2
30 Edgebottom ......H 4
26 Edgefield ......B 4
26 Edgefield Green ..B 6
44 Edgerston ......B 5
44 Edges Green .....F 5
35 Edgeside ......E 7
15 Edgeworth ......D 12
4 Edgeworthy ......E 7
30 Edgmond ......H 6
30 Edgmond Marsh ..H 6
21 Edgton ......D 9

18 Edgware ......E 2
34 Edgworth ......E 6
52 Edinample ......E 1
62 Edinbain ......C 3
48 Edinburgh ......B 5
52 Edinchip ......E 1
22 Edingale ......A 6
9 Edingley ......E 4
26 Edingthorpe ......B 6
49 Edington, Borders
D 11
7 Edington, Som. ...B 7
8 Edington, Wilts. ..A 1
7 Edington Burtle ...B 7
7 Edingworth ......A 7
58 Edintore ......C 2
23 Edith Weston .....B 12
6 Edithmead ......A 6
17 Edlesborough ....B 10
21 Edlingham ......B 9
33 Edlington ......C 9
8 Edmondsham ....E 2
45 Edmondsley ......H 10
32 Edmondthorpe ....H 6
64 Edmonstone ......C 3
18 Edmonton ......E 3
45 Edmundbyers ....H 8
29 Ednam ......F 10
51 Edra ......F 11
49 Edrom ......D 11
30 Edstaston ......G 4
22 Edstone ......F 5
21 Edvin Loach .....G 12
32 Edwalton ......G 3
21 Edwardstone .....L 2
13 Edwinsford ......D 9
32 Edwinstowe ......D 3
25 Edworth ......L 3
21 Edwyn Ralph ....G 12
32 Edzell ......K 3
14 Efail Isaf ......F 4
13 Efail-fâch ......G 11
13 Efailnewydd .....G 3
29 Efail-rhyd ......H 11
12 Efailwen ......D 5
29 Efenechtyd ......E 10
21 Effingham ......A 12
64 Effirth ......D 6
4 Efford ......F 8
11 Egerton, Kent ......C 8
34 Egerton, Manchester
F 6
5 Egg Buckland ....K 4
17 Eggington ......B 10
40 Egglescliffe ......D 4
39 Eggleston ......C 12
17 Egham ......G 11
23 Egleton ......A 12
45 Eglingham ......A 9
3 Egloshayle ......C 7
3 Egloskerry ......A 9
14 Eglwys-Brewis ...G 3
29 Eglwysbach ......C 7
21 Eglwysfach ......C 3
12 Eglwyswrw ......C 5
32 Egmanton ......C 4
38 Egremont, Cumb. .D 3
30 Egremont,
Merseyside ......A 2
41 Egton ......D 8
41 Egton Bridge .....E 8
17 Egypt ......F 10
13 Eight Ash Green ..A 9
50 Eignaig ......C 5
57 Eil ......H 4
57 Eilanreach ......H 2
49 Eildon ......F 8
60 Eilean Darach ....H 3
56 Eileanach Lodge ..C 1
63 Eishken ......F 4
20 Elan Village ......F 5
5 Elberton ......E 9
5 Elburton ......K 4
52 Elcho ......E 6
52 Elcombe ......F 2
24 Eldernell ......F 4
15 Eldersfield ......A 11
40 Eldon ......B 3
42 Eldrick ......C 4
35 Eldroth ......A 6
35 Eldwick ......C 10
20 Elerch ......D 2
45 Elford, Northumb. D 12
22 Elford, Staffs. ...A 5
56 Elgin ......C 8
62 Elgol ......G 4
11 Elham ......D 10
52 Elie ......G 9
45 Elilaw ......B 8
8 Eling ......E 5
62 Elishader ......C 4
45 Elishaw ......D 7
32 Elkesley ......C 4

16 Elkstone ....C 1
57 Ellan ......G 5
35 Elland ......E 10
46 Ellary ......B 2
31 Ellastone ......F 9
34 Ellel ......B 4
49 Ellemford ......C 10
31 Ellenhall ......G 7
9 Ellen's Green ....C 12
40 Ellerbeck ......E 4
41 Ellerby ......D 8
30 Ellerdine Heath ...H 5
6 Ellerhayes ......F 3
51 Elleric ......C 7
37 Ellerker ......D 7
36 Ellerton, Humber. .C 5
40 Ellerton, N. Yorks. .E 3
30 Ellerton, Salop ...H 6
17 Ellesborough .....C 9
30 Ellesmere ......G 2
30 Ellesmere Port ...C 3
8 Ellingham, Hants. .E 3
26 Ellingham, Norf. ..F 6
45 Ellingham, Northumb.
E 12
40 Ellingstring ......G 2
25 Ellington, Cambs. .H 3
45 Ellington, Northumb.
D 11
9 Ellisfield ......B 8
23 Ellistown ......A 8
58 Ellon ......D 7
38 Ellonby ......B 6
37 Elloughton ......D 7
15 Ellwood ......C 9
24 Elm ......E 6
18 Elm Park ......E 5
22 Elmbridge ......E 2
25 Elmdon, Essex .....L 6
22 Elmdon,
W. Midlands ....D 5
22 Elmdon Heath ....D 5
18 Elmers End .....G 4
23 Elmesthorpe ....C 8
9 Elmfield ......G 7
22 Elmhurst ......A 5
22 Elmley Castle ....H 3
22 Elmley Lovett ....E 2
15 Elmore ......C 11
15 Elmore Back .....C 10
4 Elmscott ......D 1
27 Elmsett ......K 3
19 Elmstead Market ..B 10
11 Elmstone ......B 11
15 Elmstone Hardwicke
B 12
37 Elmswell, Humber. .A 7
27 Elmswell, Suffolk ..J 3
32 Elmton ......C 2
60 Elphin ......F 3
48 Elphinstone ......B 6
59 Elrick ......G 6
42 Elrig ......G 4
51 Elrigbeag ......F 8
45 Elsdon ......D 7
35 Elsecar ......G 12
18 Elsenham ......A 5
16 Elsfield ......C 6
37 Elsham ......F 8
26 Elsing ......D 4
35 Elslack ......B 8
30 Elson ......G 2
48 Elsrickle ......E 3
9 Elstead ......B 10
9 Elsted ......D 9
32 Elston, Notts. ...E 5
8 Elston, Wilts. ...B 2
4 Elstone ......D 5
37 Elstonwick ......D 10
25 Elstow ......K 2
18 Elstree ......D 2
34 Elswick ......C 3
25 Elsworth ......J 4
38 Elterwater ......E 5
18 Eltham ......F 4
25 Eltisley ......J 4
24 Elton, Cambs. ...F 2
30 Elton, Cheshire ...C 3
40 Elton, Cleveland ....C 4
31 Elton, Derby ....D 10
15 Elton, Glos. ....C 10
21 Elton, Heref. &
Worc. ......E 10
32 Elton, Notts. ....F 5
48 Elvanfoot ......H 2
31 Elvaston ......G 12
27 Elveden ......G 1
11 Elvington, Kent ..C 11
36 Elvington, N. Yorks
B 5
49 Elwartlaw ......E 10
40 Elwick, Cleveland ..B 5
45 Elwick, Northumb.
B 12

30 Elworth ....D 6
6 Elworthy ....C 4
25 Ely, Cambs. ......G 6
14 Ely, S. Glam. .....G 5
23 Emberton ....G 12
44 Emblehope ....D 6
38 Embleton, Cumb. ..B 4
40 Embleton, Dur .....B 4
45 Embleton, Northumb.
       A 10
61 Embo ....G 8
35 Embsay ....B 8
8 Emery Down ......E 4
35 Emley ....F 11
35 Emley Moor ....F 11
17 Emmbrook ....G 8
17 Emmington ....D 8
24 Emneth ....E 6
24 Emneth Hungate ..E 6
23 Empingham ....A 12
9 Empshott ....C 9
9 Emsworth ....E 9
63 Enaclete ....D 2
16 Enborne ....G 5
16 Enborne Row .....H 5
21 Enchmarsh ....C 10
7 Encombe ....H 12
23 Enderby ....B 8
39 Endmoor ....G 7
31 Endon ....E 7
31 Endon Bank ......E 8
18 Enfield ....D 3
8 Enford ....A 3
15 Engine Common ...F 10
17 Englefield ....G 7
17 Englefield Green ..G 10
15 English Bicknor ....C 9
30 English Frankton ..G 3
15 Englishcombe .....H 10
8 Enham Alamein ...A 5
6 Enmore ....C 6
38 Ennerdale Bridge ..D 3
43 Enoch ....B 9
52 Enochdu ....A 5
50 Ensay ....C 1
8 Ensbury ....F 2
21 Ensdon ....A 9
4 Ensis ....C 4
16 Enstone ....B 5
43 Enterkinfoot ......A 9
40 Enterpen ....E 5
22 Enville ....C 2
50 Eorabus ....E 1
63 Eoropie ....A 6
15 Epney ....C 11
32 Epperstone ....E 4
18 Epping ....D 4
18 Epping Green .....C 3
18 Epping Green .....C 4
18 Epping Upland ....C 4
40 Eppleby ....D 2
10 Epsom ....B 1
23 Epwell ....H 7
36 Epworth ....G 5
29 Erbistock ....F 12
55 Erbusaig ....G 1
54 Erchless Castle ...E 8
22 Erdington ....C 5
51 Eredine ....G 7
60 Eriboll ....B 5
48 Ericstane ....H 3
10 Eridge Green .....E 4
46 Erines ....B 4
25 Eriswell ....G 8
18 Erith ....F 5
33 Ermine ....C 7
5 Ermington ....K 5
26 Erpingham ....B 5
55 Errocht ....L 5
57 Errogie ....G 1
53 Errol ....E 7
47 Erskine ....B 9
42 Ervie ....E 1
27 Erwarton ....M 5
20 Erwood ....H 6
40 Eryholme ....D 3
29 Eryrys ....D 11
46 Escart ....C 3
40 Escomb ....B 2
36 Escrick ....C 4
13 Esgair ....D 7
20 Esgairgeiliog .....B 3
13 Esgerdawe ....C 9
40 Esh ....A 2
40 Esh Winning .....A 2
17 Esher ....H 12
45 Eshott ....C 10
35 Eshton ....B 8
54 Eskadale ....F 8
48 Eskbank ....C 6
38 Eskdale Green ....E 4
44 Eskdalemuir ......C 1
37 Eskham ....G 11
34 Esprick ....D 3

24 Essendine ....D 1
18 Essendon ....C 3
19 Essex, Co ....C 7
56 Essich ....F 2
22 Essington ....B 3
40 Eston ....C 6
49 Etal ....E 11
16 Etchilhampton ....H 2
16 Etchingham ....E 6
11 Etchinghill, Kent ..D 10
31 Etchinghill, Staffs ...H 8
17 Eton ....F 10
17 Eton Wick ....F 10
57 Etteridge ....K 3
22 Ettington ....G 6
24 Etton, Cambs. ....E 2
37 Etton, Humberside .C 7
48 Ettrick ....H 5
48 Ettrickbridge End ..G 6
31 Etwall ....G 11
27 Euston ....G 2
24 Euximoor Drove ..F 6
34 Euxton ....E 4
14 Evanstown ....E 3
56 Evanton ....C 2
33 Evedon ....E 8
61 Evelix ....G 7
21 Evenjobb ....F 8
17 Evenley ....A 7
16 Evenlode ....A 3
40 Evenwood ....C 2
40 Evenwood Gate ...C 2
64 Everbay ....C 4
7 Evercreech ....B 9
23 Everdon ....F 9
36 Everingham ......C 6
8 Everleigh ....A 3
41 Everley ....F 10
25 Eversholt ....M 1
7 Evershot ....F 9
17 Eversley ....H 8
17 Eversley Cross ....H 9
37 Everthorpe ....D 7
25 Everton, Beds ....K 3
8 Everton, Hants ....G 4
30 Everton, Merseyside A 2
32 Everton, Notts ....A 4
44 Evertown ....E 2
21 Evesbatch ....H 12
22 Evesham ....H 4
23 Evington ....B 10
35 Ewden Village ....G 11
10 Ewell ....B 1
11 Ewell Minnis .....D 11
17 Ewelme ....E 7
16 Ewen ....D 1
14 Ewenny ....G 2
33 Ewerby ....E 8
44 Eweslees ....C 2
11 Ewhurst, E.Sussex .F 7
9 Ewhurst, Surrey ..B 12
9 Ewhurst Green ...B 12
29 Ewloe ....D 12
4 Eworthy ....F 3
9 Ewshot ....A 9
15 Ewyas Harold .....B 7
4 Exbourne ....F 5
8 Exbury ....F 6
6 Exebridge ....D 3
6 Exelby ....F 3
6 Exeter ....G 3
6 Exford ....B 2
22 Exhall ....G 4
17 Exlade Street .....F 7
4 Exminster ....G 3
4 Exmouth ....H 4
64 Exnaboe ....F 7
25 Exning ....J 7
6 Exton, Devon .....H 3
9 Exton, Hants .....D 7
23 Exton, Leics. .....A 12
6 Exton, Somerset ...C 3
6 Exwick ....G 3
31 Eyam ....C 10
23 Eydon ....G 9
21 Eye, Cambs. ......E 3
21 Eye, Heref. &
     Worc. ....F 10
27 Eye, Suffolk ......H 4
49 Eyemouth ....C 12
25 Eyeworth ....L 4
11 Eyhorne Street ...C 7
27 Eyke ....K 6
25 Eynesbury ....J 3
10 Eynsford ....B 4
16 Eynsham ....C 5
7 Eype ....G 8
62 Eyre ....C 3
11 Eythorne ....C 11
29 Eyton, Clwyd ....F 12
21 Eyton, Heref. &
     Worc. ....F 10
21 Eyton, Salop .....D 9
30 Eyton, Salop .....H 3

21 Eyton upon the Weald
     Moors ....A 12
16 Faccombe ....H 5
40 Faceby ....E 5
28 Fachwen ....D 5
35 Facit ....E 7
30 Faddiley ....E 4
55 Faddoch ....G 3
41 Fadmoor ....F 7
31 Fagginton ....G 11
13 Fagwyr ....G 10
47 Fail ....F 9
15 Failand ....G 8
47 Failford ....G 9
35 Failsworth ....G 8
54 Fain ....B 5
6 Fair Oak, Devon ..D 4
8 Fair Oak, Hants ...D 6
17 Fair Oak Green ...H 7
20 Fairbourne ....A 2
36 Fairburn ....D 2
22 Fairfield, Heref. &
     Worc. ....H 4
22 Fairfield, Heref. &
     Worc. ....E 3
16 Fairford ....D 3
43 Fairgirth ....F 9
47 Fairlie ....D 7
11 Fairlight ....G 7
11 Fairlight Cove ....G 7
6 Fairmile ....F 4
48 Fairmilehead .....C 5
49 Fairnilee ....F 7
30 Fairoak ....G 6
10 Fairseat ....B 5
19 Fairstead, Essex ..B 7
26 Fairstead, Norfolk .C 6
10 Fairwarp ....E 4
4 Fairy Cross ......D 3
26 Fakenham ....C 2
49 Fala ....C 7
48 Falahill ....D 6
41 Falcon Inn ....E 10
33 Faldingworth .....B 8
15 Falfield ....E 10
27 Falkenham ....L 6
48 Falkirk ....A 2
53 Falkland ....F 7
44 Falla ....B 5
32 Fallgate ....D 1
52 Fallin ....H 3
47 Fallowfield ......F 7
49 Fallsidehill ......E 9
10 Falmer ....G 2
2 Falmouth ....F 5
44 Falnash ....B 2
41 Falsgrave ....F 10
44 Falstone ....D 5
60 Fanagmore ....C 3
40 Fangdale Beck ....F 6
36 Fangfoss ....B 5
50 Fanmore ....C 2
54 Fannich Lodge ...C 6
9 Fans ....E 9
17 Far Bletchley ....A 9
23 Far Cotton ....F 11
38 Far Sawrey ....F 6
24 Farcet ....E 11
21 Farden ....E 11
22 Fareham ....F 7
22 Farewell ....A 4
33 Farforth ....B 10
44 Farglow ....F 5
16 Faringdon ....E 4
34 Farington ....E 4
44 Farlam ....G 4
15 Farleigh, Avon ....G 8
10 Farleigh, Surrey ...B 3
7 Farleigh Hungerford
       A 11
9 Farleigh Wallop ...A 8
15 Farleigh Wick ....H 11
33 Farlesthorpe .....C 11
39 Farleton ....G 8
15 Farley, Avon .....G 7
31 Farley, Cheshire ...F 9
21 Farley, Salop .....B 9
8 Farley, Wiltshire ...C 4
9 Farley Green .....B 12
17 Farley Hill ......H 8
15 Farleys End ......C 11
40 Farlington ....H 6
21 Farlow ....D 11
29 Farm Yard ....D 7
15 Farmborough .....H 10
16 Farmcote ....A 2
13 Farmers ....C 10
43 Farmersfield .....C 9
16 Farmington ......C 2
16 Farmoor ....C 5
58 Farmtown ....C 3
16 Farnborough, Berks. F 5
9 Farnborough, Hants.
       A 10

18 Farnborough, London
       G 4
23 Farnborough, War.
       G 8
17 Farnborough Green .H 9
9 Farncombe ....B 11
30 Farndon, Clwyd ...E 3
32 Farndon, Notts ....E 5
53 Farnell ....B 11
8 Farnham, Dorset ..E 1
19 Farnham, Essex ...A 5
35 Farnham, N.Yorks .A 12
27 Farnham, Suffolk ..J 7
9 Farnham, Surrey ..B 9
17 Farnham Com ....F 10
18 Farnham Green ...A 5
17 Farnham Royal ...F 10
35 Farnhill ....C 9
16 Farningdon ....G 4
10 Farningham ......A 4
35 Farnley, N.Yorks .B 11
35 Farnley, W.Yorks .D 11
35 Farnley Tyas .....F 10
30 Farnworth, Ches. .B 4
34 Farnworth, Manchester
       G 6
56 Farr, Highland ....F 2
57 Farr, Highland ....J 4
61 Farr, Highland ....B 7
56 Farr House ....F 2
9 Farringdon ....C 8
7 Farrington Gurney .A 9
35 Farsley ....D 10
23 Farthinghoe .....H 8
11 Farthingloe ......D 11
23 Farthingstone ....G 9
35 Fartown ....E 10
6 Farway ....G 5
54 Fasag ....D 3
50 Fasakdale ....A 2
55 Fasnakyle ....G 7
59 Fasque ....K 4
55 Fassfern ....L 4
45 Fatfield ....H 11
58 Fattahead ....B 4
48 Faugh ....G 3
48 Fauldhouse ......C 2
44 Fauldie ....F 2
30 Faulsgreen ......G 4
11 Faversham ....B 9
56 Favillar ....F 8
45 Fawdon ....B 8
31 Fawfieldhead .....D 9
10 Fawkham Green ..B 5
16 Fawler ....B 5
16 Fawley, Berks. ...F 5
17 Fawley, Bucks. ...E 8
8 Fawley, Hants ....F 6
15 Fawley Chapel ...A 9
49 Fawside ....E 9
36 Faxfleet ....E 6
3 Faygate ....E 1
22 Fazeley ....B 5
40 Fearby ....G 2
56 Fearn ....B 4
60 Fearn Lodge .....H 6
52 Fearnan ....C 2
54 Fearnbeg ....D 1
30 Fearnhead ....A 5
54 Fearnmore ....D 1
22 Featherstone, Staffs.
       B 3
36 Featherstone,
     W. Yorks. ....E 2
44 Featherwood .....C 6
11 Feckenham ....F 4
56 Feddan ....D 5
19 Feering ....B 8
27 Feetham ....E 12
10 Felbridge ....D 3
26 Felbrigg ....B 5
17 Felcourt ....D 3
5 Feldownhead .....H 2
17 Felden ....D 11
12 Felin-Wnda ......B 6
20 Felindre, Dyfed ...G 1
13 Felindre, Dyfed ...D 10
13 Felindre, Dyfed ...G 9
13 Felindre, Dyfed ...E 9
13 Felindre, Powys ...D 7
14 Felindre, Powys ...B 5
13 Felinfach, Dyfed ..A 8
13 Felin-fach, Powys ..A 4
13 Felinfoel ....G 8
13 Felin-gwm Isaf ...E 8
13 Felin-gwm Uchaf ..E 8
40 Felixkirk ....G 5
27 Felixstowe ....M 6
27 Felixstoweferry ...L 6
49 Felkington ....E 12
45 Felling ....G 11

38 Fellside ....B 5
25 Felmersham ......J 1
26 Felmingham ......C 6
9 Felpham ....F 11
27 Felsham ....J 2
19 Felstead ....B 7
18 Feltham ....G 1
26 Felthorpe ....D 5
21 Felton, Heref. &
     Worc. ....G 11
45 Felton, Northumb. .C 10
15 Felton, Somerset ...H 8
21 Felton Butler .....A 9
24 Feltwell ....F 8
25 Fen Drayton ......H 4
22 Fen End ....E 6
35 Fenay Bridge ....F 10
35 Fence ....C 7
45 Fence Houses ....H 11
33 Fendike Corner ..D 11
56 Fendom ....B 4
24 Fengate ....B 12
45 Fenham ....B 12
34 Feniscowles .....E 5
6 Feniton ....F 4
31 Fenny Bentley ....E 10
23 Fenny Compton ..G 7
23 Fenny Drayton ...B 7
17 Fenny Stratford ..A 10
45 Fenrother ....D 10
25 Fenstanton ......H 4
25 Fenton, Cambs. ...G 4
32 Fenton, Lincs. ...C 6
32 Fenton, Notts. ...E 6
31 Fenton, Staffs. ...F 7
49 Fenton Barns .....A 8
45 Fenton Town .....F 12
49 Fentonhill ....F 12
45 Fenwick, Northumb.
       F 9
45 Fenwick, Northumb.
       B 12
36 Fenwick, N. Yorks ..E 4
47 Fenwick, Strathclyde
       E 9
46 Feochaig ....H 3
2 Feock ....F 5
62 Ferindonald ....G 6
54 Feriniquarrie .....C 1
50 Ferlochan ....D 6
55 Fern ....L 2
55 Fern Villa ....G 3
14 Ferndale ....E 3
8 Ferndown ....F 2
49 Ferneyhill ....F 10
16 Fernham ....E 4
10 Fernhill ....D 2
22 Fernhill Heath ...F 2
9 Fernhurst ....C 10
53 Fernie ....F 8
62 Fernilea ....E 3
31 Fernilee ....B 8
21 Ferny Common ...G 9
35 Ferrensby ....A 12
9 Ferring ....F 12
65 Ferry Hill ....G 5
36 Ferrybridge ......E 3
53 Ferryden ....B 12
40 Ferryhill, Durham ..B 3
59 Ferryhill, Grampian
       G 7
40 Ferryhill Station ...B 3
13 Ferryside ....F 7
61 Ferrytown ....H 7
26 Fersfield ....G 4
55 Fersit ....L 7
57 Feshiebridge .....J 4
11 Fetcham ....H 12
58 Fetterangus .....C 7
59 Fettercairn ......K 4
35 Fewston ....B 10
13 Ffairfach ....E 9
20 Ffair-rhôs ....F 3
13 Ffaid-y-Brenin ...C 9
14 Ffawyddog ....B 5
28 Ffestiniog ....F 6
29 Ffordd-las, Gwynedd
       C 7
21 Fforddlas, Powys ..H 7
13 Fforest ....G 9
13 Fforest fach ......G 9
13 Fforest Goch .....G 10
13 Ffostrasol ....B 7
13 Ffos-y-ffin ....A 8
29 Ffrith ....E 12
13 Ffynnon Gynydd ..H 7
13 Ffynnon-ddrain ...E 7
13 Ffynnongroew ....B 10
60 Fiag Bridge ......E 5
60 Fiag Lodge ....D 5
50 Fidden ....E 5
12 Fiddington, Glos ..A 12
6 Fiddington, Som ..B 5

7 Fiddleford ....E 11
18 Fiddlers Hamlet ...D 5
44 Fiddleton ....C 2
31 Field ....G 9
38 Field Broughton ..G 6
26 Field Dalling .....B 3
23 Field Head ....A 8
47 Fieldhead ....D 11
53 Fife, County .....G 7
58 Fife of Keith .....C 2
       D 11
7 Fifehead Magdalen
       D 11
7 Fifehead Neville ..E 11
7 Fifehead St. Quinton
       E 11
17 Fifield, Berks. ...F 10
16 Fifield, Glos. .....B 3
8 Fifield, Wilts. ....A 3
8 Fifield Bavant ....D 2
8 Figheldean ......A 3
40 Fighting Cocks ...D 4
26 Filby ....D 8
41 Filey ....G 11
23 Filgrave ....G 12
40 Filkins ....D 3
4 Filleigh, Devon ...E 6
4 Filleigh, Devon ...C 5
32 Fillingham ......B 6
22 Fillongley ....C 6
15 Filton ....F 9
37 Fimber ....A 7
59 Finavon ....L 2
24 Fincham ....E 8
9 Finchampstead ...H 9
50 Fincharn ....G 6
9 Finchdean ....E 9
25 Finchingfield ....M 8
18 Finchley ....E 3
53 Fincraigs ....E 8
31 Findern ....G 11
56 Findhorn ....C 6
57 Findhorn Bridge ..G 4
58 Findochty ....A 2
59 Findon, Grampian ..H 7
9 Findon, W.Sussex .E 12
56 Findon Mains ....D 2
59 Findrack House ...G 3
23 Finedon ....E 12
27 Fingal Street .....H 5
58 Fingask, Grampian .E 5
52 Fingask, Tayside ...E 6
21 Fingerpost ....E 11
17 Fingest ....E 8
40 Finghall ....F 2
44 Fingland, Cumb. ..G 1
47 Fingland, Dumf. &
     Gall. ....H 12
11 Finglesham .....C 12
19 Fingringhoe .....B 10
55 Finiskaig ....K 2
52 Finlarig ....D 1
17 Finmere ....A 7
55 Finnart ....B 12
43 Finniegill ....B 12
27 Finningham .....H 3
36 Finningley ......G 4
58 Finnygaud ....B 3
63 Finsbay ....H 2
18 Finsbury ....E 3
22 Finstall ....E 3
38 Finsthwaite .....F 6
16 Finstock ....C 4
64 Finstown ....C 2
43 Fintloch ....D 7
47 Fintry, Central ...A 11
58 Fintry, Grampian ..B 5
53 Fintry, Tayside ...D 9
50 Fionnphort ......F 1
40 Fir Tree ....B 2
32 Firbeck ....A 3
41 Firby, N.Yorks ...H 7
40 Firby, N.Yorks ...G 3
33 Firsby ....D 11
60 First Coast ......G 1
36 Fishlake ....F 4
43 Fishbeck ....C 11
9 Fishbourne, I.o. W. .G 7
9 Fishbourne, W.Sussex
       F 10
40 Fishburn ....B 4
52 Fishcross ....H 4
58 Fisherford ......D 4
9 Fisher's Pond ....D 6
9 Fisherstreet .....C 11
56 Fisherton, Highland
       E 3
47 Fisherton,
     Strathclyde .....H 7
8 Fisherton de la Mere
       B 2
12 Fishguard ....C 3
15 Fishponds ....G 9
35 Fishpool, Manchester
       F 7

32 Fishpool, Notts E 3
24 Fishtoft A 5
33 Fishtoft Drive E 10
53 Fishtown of Usan B 12
49 Fishwick D 11
62 Fiskavaig E 2
33 Fiskerton, Lincs C 7
32 Fiskerton, Notts E 4
37 Fitling D 10
24 Fitten End D 5
8 Fittleton A 3
9 Fittleworth D 11
30 Fitz H 3
6 Fitzhead C 5
36 Fitzwilliam F 2
50 Fiunary C 3
15 Five Acres C 9
10 Five Ashes F 4
34 Five Lane Ends B 4
3 Five Lanes B 9
10 Five Oak Green D 5
9 Five Oaks C 12
63 Five Penny Borve A 5
63 Five Penny Ness A 6
13 Five Roads F 8
30 Fivecrosses C 4
7 Fivehead D 7
19 Flack's Green B 7
17 Flackwell Heath E 9
22 Fladbury G 3
64 Fladdabister E 7
31 Flagg C 10
41 Flamborough H 2
17 Flamstead C 11
9 Flansham F 11
35 Flappit Spring C 9
35 Flasby B 8
31 Flash C 8
17 Flaunden D 11
32 Flawborough F 5
36 Flawith A 3
15 Flax Bourton G 8
35 Flaxby A 12
15 Flaxley C 10
6 Flaxpool C 5
36 Flaxton A 4
23 Fleckney C 10
23 Flecknoe F 8
7 Fleet, Dorset H 9
9 Fleet, Hants A 9
9 Fleet, Hants F 8
24 Fleet, Lincs C 5
33 Fleet Hargate H 11
45 Fleetham E 12
34 Fleetwood B 2
14 Flemingston G 3
47 Flemington, Strathclyde C 11
47 Flemington, Strathclyde E 12
27 Flempton H 1
38 Fletchertown A 4
10 Fletching F 3
4 Flexbury E 1
9 Flexford A 10
38 Flimby B 3
10 Flimwell E 6
29 Flint C 11
29 Flint Mountain C 11
32 Flintham F 5
37 Flinton D 10
24 Flitcham C 8
25 Flitton L 2
4 Flitton Barton C 6
25 Flitwick M 1
36 Flixborough F 6
34 Flixton, Manchester H 6
41 Flixton, N. Yorks G 10
27 Flixton, Suffolk G 6
35 Flockton F 11
35 Flockton Green F 11
49 Flodden F 11
63 Flodabay H 2
62 Flodigarry Hotel A 4
24 Flood's Ferry F 5
38 Flookburgh H 6
26 Flordon F 5
23 Flore F 9
45 Flotterton C 8
35 Flouch Inn G 10
27 Flowton K 4
2 Flushing, Cornwall F 5
58 Flushing, Grampian C 8
6 Fluxton G 4
22 Flyford Flavell G 3
19 Fobbing E 7
58 Fochabers B 1
14 Fochriw D 4
36 Fockerby E 6
56 Fodderty D 1
7 Foddington C 9
20 Foel A 5
13 Foelgastell E 9
53 Foffarty C 9
36 Foggathorpe C 5
49 Fogo D 10
49 Fogorig E 10
60 Foindle C 3
53 Folda A 7
31 Fole F 9
23 Foleshill D 7
7 Folke E 10
11 Folkestone E 11
24 Folkingham B 2
10 Folkington H 4
24 Folksworth F 2
41 Folkton G 10
58 Folla Rule D 5
35 Follifoot B 12
4 Folly Gate F 4
9 Folly Hill A 9
14 Fonmon G 4
8 Fonthill Bishop C 1
7 Fonthill Gifford C 12
7 Fontmell Magna E 12
9 Fontwell E 10
31 Foolow C 10
18 Foots Cray G 5
58 Forbestown F 1
6 Forches Corner D 5
17 Ford, Bucks C 8
5 Ford, Devon L 7
4 Ford, Devon D 3
16 Ford, Glos. A 2
49 Ford, Northumb. F 12
21 Ford, Salop A 9
6 Ford, Somerset C 4
31 Ford, Staffs E 9
50 Ford, Strathclyde G 6
9 Ford, W. Sussex F 11
15 Ford, Wilts G 11
6 Ford Barton D 3
19 Ford End B 7
6 Ford Street D 5
10 Fordcombe D 4
52 Fordel F 6
52 Fordell H 6
21 Forden B 8
25 Fordham, Cambridgeshire H 7
19 Fordham, Essex A 9
24 Fordham, Norfolk E 7
22 Fordhouses B 3
8 Fordingbridge E 3
41 Fordon H 10
59 Fordoun K 5
19 Fordstreet A 9
16 Fordwells C 4
11 Fordwich B 10
58 Fordyce A 3
31 Forebridge H 8
9 Forest Green B 12
39 Forest Hall E 8
44 Forest Head G 4
17 Forest Hill C 7
51 Forest Lo., Highland C 10
57 Forest Lo., Highland H 6
52 Forest Lo., Tayside A 4
52 Forest Mill H 4
10 Forest Row D 3
32 Forest Town D 3
45 Forestburn Gate C 9
56 Foresterseat D 7
9 Forestside E 9
53 Forfar B 9
52 Forgandenny E 6
14 Forge Hammer E 6
14 Forge Side D 6
58 Forgie B 1
58 Forgieside B 1
58 Forglen House B 4
34 Formby F 2
26 Forncett End F 4
26 Forncett St. Mary F 4
26 Forncett St. Peter F 5
52 Forneth C 6
27 Fornham All Saints J 1
27 Fornham St. Martin H 2
56 Forres D 6
48 Forrestfield C 1
31 Forsbrook F 8
61 Forse D 11
61 Forse House D 11
61 Forsinain C 9
61 Forsinard C 9
61 Forsinard Station C 8
7 Forston G 10
55 Fort Augustus J 7
56 Fort George D 3
55 Fort William M 5
47 Fortacres F 9
52 Forteviot E 5
48 Forth D 2
15 Forthampton A 11
52 Fortingall B 2
8 Forton, Hants B 6
34 Forton, Lancs B 4
21 Forton, Salop A 9
7 Forton, Somerset E 7
30 Forton, Staffs H 6
58 Fortrie C 4
56 Fortrose D 3
7 Fortuneswell H 7
17 Forty Green E 10
25 Forty Feet Bridge G 4
27 Forward Green J 4
16 Fosbury H 4
24 Fosdyke B 4
24 Fosdyke Bridge B 4
52 Foss A 3
16 Fossebridge C 2
18 Foster Street C 5
36 Fosterhouses F 4
31 Foston, Derby G 10
32 Foston, Lincs F 6
36 Foston, N. Yorks A 5
37 Foston on the Wolds B 8
33 Fotherby A 10
24 Fotheringhay F 2
64 Foubister D 3
10 Foul Mile F 5
49 Foulden, Borders D 11
26 Foulden, Norfolk E 1
56 Foulis Castle C 1
35 Foulridge C 7
26 Foulsham C 3
58 Fountainbleau, Grampian D 8
58 Fountainbleau, Grampian E 7
49 Fountainhall D 7
27 Four Ashes H 3
28 Four Crosses, Gwynedd F 3
29 Four Crosses, Powys H 12
20 Four Crosses, Powys B 6
22 Four Crosses, Staffs. A 3
10 Four Elms C 3
6 Four Forks C 6
34 Four Gate F 5
24 Four Gates D 5
30 Four Lane Ends, Ches. D 4
39 Four Lane Ends, Cumbria F 8
34 Four Lane Ends, Lancashire B 4
34 Four Lane Ends, Lancashire C 2
36 Four Lane Ends, N. Yorks B 4
2 Four Lanes F 4
9 Four Marks C 8
28 Four Mile Bridge B 2
11 Four Oaks, E. Sussex F 7
15 Four Oaks, Glos B 10
22 Four Oaks, W. Midlands D 6
22 Four Oaks, W.Midlands B 4
13 Four Roads, Dyfed F 8
38 Four Roads, I.o.M. H 1
10 Four Throws E 6
30 Fourlanes End D 6
45 Fourlaws E 7
45 Fourstones F 7
6 Fovant C 2
58 Foveran E 7
3 Fowey D 8
58 Fowlershill F 7
10 Fowlhall C 6
53 Fowlis D 8
52 Fowlis Wester E 4
52 Fowlmere L 5
15 Fownhope A 9
9 Fox Corner A 11
17 Fox Lane H 9
7 Foxcote A 10
38 Foxdale H 1
27 Foxearth L 1
38 Foxfield G 5
16 Foxham F 1
3 Foxhole D 7
41 Foxholes H 10
10 Foxhunt Green F 4
26 Foxley, Norfolk C 3
15 Foxley, Wilts F 12
31 Foxt E 9
25 Foxton, Cambs K 5
40 Foxton, Durham C 4
23 Foxton, Leics C 10
39 Foxup G 11
30 Foxwist Green C 5
21 Foxwood E 11
15 Foy A 9
57 Foyers G 1
7 Foys E 9
2 Fraddam F 3
2 Fraddon D 6
22 Fradley A 5
31 Fradswell G 8
37 Fraisthorpe A 9
7 Framfield F 4
26 Framingham Earl E 6
26 Framingham Pigot E 6
27 Framlingham J 6
7 Frampton, Dorset G 9
24 Frampton, Lincs B 4
15 Frampton Cotterell F 9
15 Frampton Mansell D 12
15 Frampton on Severn D 10
24 Frampton West End B 4
27 Framsden J 5
40 Framwellgate Moor A 3
22 Franche D 2
30 Frandley B 5
30 Frankby B 1
22 Frankley D 3
21 Frank's Bridge G 7
23 Frankton E 7
20 Frankwell, Powys C 5
21 Frankwell, Salop A 10
10 Frant E 5
58 Fraserburgh A 7
19 Frating B 10
19 Frating Green B 10
3 Freathy D 11
32 Frecheville B 1
25 Freckenham H 8
34 Freckleton D 3
32 Freeby H 5
16 Freeland C 5
26 Freethorpe E 7
26 Freethorpe Com. E 7
24 Freiston A 5
4 Fremington, Devon C 4
40 Fremington, N. Yorks E 1
15 Frenchay F 9
5 Frenchbeer G 5
51 Frenich, Central G 11
52 Frenich, Tayside A 3
9 Frensham B 9
61 Fresgoe A 9
34 Freshfield F 2
8 Freshwater G 5
12 Freshwater East G 4
27 Fressingfield H 5
61 Freswick A 12
15 Fretherne C 10
26 Frettenham D 5
53 Freuchie F 7
12 Freystrop Cross F 3
7 Friar Waddon H 10
52 Friarton E 6
24 Friday Bridge E 6
10 Friday Street H 5
36 Fridaythorpe A 6
18 Friern Barnet E 3
33 Friesthorpe B 8
32 Frieston E 6
17 Frieth E 9
16 Frilford D 5
16 Frilsham G 6
17 Frimley H 9
17 Frimley Green H 10
10 Frindsbury A 6
24 Fring B 8
17 Fringford A 7
11 Frinsted B 7
19 Frinton B 12
53 Friockheim B 10
20 Friog A 2
32 Frisby on the Wreake H 4
33 Friskney E 11
10 Friston, E.Sussex H 4
27 Friston, Suffolk J 7
32 Fritchley E 1
33 Frith Bank E 10
21 Frith Common E 12
8 Fritham E 4
4 Frithelstock D 3
4 Frithelstock Stone D 3
17 Frithsden C 11
33 Frithville E 10
11 Frittenden D 7
26 Fritton, Norfolk F 5
26 Fritton, Norfolk E 7
16 Fritwell A 6
38 Frizington D 3
15 Frocester D 11
21 Frochas B 7
21 Frodesley B 10
37 Frodingham F 7
30 Frodsham B 4
49 Frogden G 10
31 Froggatt C 11
31 Froghall E 9
15 Frogland Cross F 9
5 Frogmore, Devon L 6
17 Frogmore, Hants H 9
23 Frolesworth C 8
7 Frome B 11
7 Frome St. Quintin F 9
21 Fromes Hill H 12
29 Fron, Clwyd D 10
13 Fron, Dyfed D 11
28 Fron, Gwynedd E 4
28 Fron, Gwynedd F 3
21 Fron, Powys B 8
20 Fron, Powys F 6
29 Fron Isaf F 12
29 Froncysyllte F 12
29 Fron-deg E 12
29 Frongoch F 8
28 Fron-oleu G 6
39 Frosterley A 12
64 Frotoft B 2
16 Froxfield G 4
9 Froxfield Green D 8
9 Froyle B 9
18 Fryerning D 6
41 Fryton H 7
32 Fulbeck E 6
25 Fulbourn K 6
16 Fulbrook C 4
36 Fulford, N. Yorks B 4
6 Fulford, Somerset C 5
31 Fulford, Staffs F 8
18 Fulham F 2
10 Fulking G 1
36 Full Sutton B 5
4 Fullaford B 6
47 Fullarton F 8
19 Fuller Street B 7
30 Fuller's Moor E 4
8 Fullerton B 5
33 Fulletby C 10
47 Fullwood D 9
17 Fulmer F 10
26 Fulmodestone B 3
33 Fulnetby B 8
37 Fulstow G 11
34 Fulwood, Lancs D 4
6 Fulwood, Som D 5
9 Funtington E 9
9 Funtley E 7
52 Funtullich D 2
64 Funzie B 8
6 Furley F 6
54 Furnace, Highland C 3
51 Furnace, Strathclyde G 7
22 Furnace End C 6
10 Furner's Green E 3
36 Furness E 5
31 Furness Vale B 8
18 Furneux Pelham A 4
17 Furze Platt F 9
7 Furzebrook H 12
4 Furzehill B 6
6 Fyfett E 6
18 Fyfield, Essex C 6
16 Fyfield, Glos. D 3
8 Fyfield, Hants A 4
16 Fyfield, Oxon D 5
16 Fyfield, Wilts G 2
41 Fyling Thorpe E 9
58 Fyvie D 5
47 Gabroc Hill D 9
23 Gaddesby A 10
47 Gadgirth G 9
14 Gaer B 5
28 Gaerwen C 4
16 Gagingwell B 5
57 Gaick Lodge L 3
47 Gailes F 8
22 Gailey A 3
40 Gainford C 2
32 Gainsborough, Lincs. A 5
27 Gainsborough, Suff. L 5
25 Gainsford End L 8
43 Gairloch, Dumf. & Gall. D 11
59 Gairloch, Grampian G 5
54 Gairloch, Highland B 2
55 Gairlochy L 6
52 Gairney Bank G 6
57 Gairnshiel Lodge J 8
39 Gaisgill E 8
44 Gaitsgill H 2
48 Galalaw E 3
49 Galashiels F 7
23 Galby B 10
42 Galdenoch E 3
49 Galewood F 12
34 Galgate B 4
7 Galhampton C 9
43 Gallaberry C 10
50 Gallanach E 5
50 Gallanachmore E 5
53 Gallatown H 7
50 Gallchoille H 5
22 Galley Common C 6
19 Galleyend D 7
19 Galleywood D 7
51 Gallin C 12
53 Gallowfauld C 9
22 Gallows Green, Heref. & Worc. F 3
31 Gallows Green, Staffs. F 9
55 Galltair G 2
5 Galmpton, Devon K 7
5 Galmpton, Devon M 6
40 Galphay H 3
47 Galston F 10
62 Galtrigill C 1
43 Galtway G 8
39 Gamblesby A 8
25 Gamlingay K 3
4 Gammaton Moor D 4
40 Gammersgill G 1
58 Gamrie A 5
32 Gamston, Notts C 4
32 Gamston, Notts F 3
15 Ganarew C 8
50 Ganavan D 6
28 Ganllwyd H 6
59 Gannachy K 3
52 Gannochy E 6
30 Gannow Hill G 2
37 Ganstead D 9
41 Ganthorpe H 7
41 Ganton G 10
50 Gaodhail D 3
54 Garbat C 8
51 Garbhallt H 7
27 Garboldisham G 3
57 Garbole G 3
29 Garden City C 12
58 Gardenstown A 5
64 Garderhouse D 6
37 Gardham C 7
7 Gare Hill B 11
51 Garelochhead H 9
16 Garford E 5
36 Garforth D 2
35 Gargrave B 8
52 Gargunnock H 2
63 Garinin C 3
28 Garizim C 6
42 Garlieston G 5
11 Garlinge Green C 9
59 Garlogie G 5
58 Garmond B 5
50 Garmony D 4
58 Garmouth A 1
28 Garn G 2
28 Garn-Dolbenmaen F 4
13 Garnant F 10
14 Garndiffaith D 6
39 Garnett Bridge E 7
47 Garnkirk C 11
14 Garnlydan C 5
13 Garnswllt F 9
14 Garn-yr-erw C 5
63 Garrabost D 6
57 Garragie H 1
2 Garras G 4
28 Garreg F 5
52 Garrick F 3
39 Garrigill A 9
40 Garriston F 2
43 Garroch C 7
42 Garrochtrie H 2
62 Garros B 4
52 Garrow C 3
47 Garryhorn H 8
39 Garsdale Head F 10
16 Garsdon E 1
31 Garshall Green G 8
17 Garsington D 7
34 Garstang C 4
30 Garston B 3
34 Garswood G 4
51 Gartachoil H 12
47 Gartcosh C 11
29 Garth, Clwyd. F 11
38 Garth, I.o.M. H 2
14 Garth, Mid.Glam. E 2
20 Garth, Powys G 5
52 Garth House B 2
14 Garth Place E 5
47 Garthamlock C 11
14 Garthbrengy A 4
59 Garthdee G 7
21 Garthmyl C 7
36 Garthorpe, Humber. E 6
32 Garthorpe, Leics H 5
58 Gartly D 3
51 Gartmore H 12

46 Gartnagrenach ....C 3
47 Gartness ....A 10
47 Gartocharn ......A 9
37 Garton ....D 10
37 Garton-on-the-Wolds
A 7
61 Gartymore ......E 9
48 Garvald, Borders ...D 6
49 Garvald, Lothian ..B 8
57 Garvamore ......K 1
55 Garvan ....M 3
50 Garvard ....H 1
54 Garve ....D 8
26 Garvestone ......E 3
47 Garvock, Strathclyde
B 7
59 Garvock, Tayside ...K 5
15 Garway ....B 8
63 Garynahine .....D 3
58 Gash of Philorth ...A 7
55 Gaskan ....M 2
7 Gaspar ....C 11
42 Gass ....A 5
43 Gasstown ....D 10
47 Gasswater ......G 11
15 Gastard ....G 12
27 Gasthorpe ......G 3
8 Gatcombe ......H 6
36 Gate Helmsley ...B 5
30 Gateacre ....A 3
39 Gatebeck ....G 8
36 Gateforth ......D 3
47 Gatehead ....F 9
44 Gatehouse, Northumb.
D 6
52 Gatehouse, Tayside .B 4
43 Gatehouse of Fleet .F 7
43 Gatelawbridge ....B 10
26 Gateley ....C 3
40 Gatenby ....F 3
38 Gatesgarth .....D 4
49 Gateshaw ....G 10
45 Gateshead ......G 10
30 Gatesheath .....D 3
52 Gateside, Fife .....F 6
56 Gateside, Grampian
D 7
47 Gateside, Strathclyde
D 8
47 Gateside, Strathclyde
B 8
53 Gateside, Tayside ..C 9
43 Gateslack ......A 10
34 Gathurst ....F 4
31 Gatley ....A 7
10 Gatton ....C 3
49 Gattonside ......F 8
20 Gaufron ....F 5
53 Gauldry ....E 8
24 Gaultree ....E 6
8 Gaunt's Common ..F 2
33 Gautby ....C 9
49 Gavinton ....D 10
58 Gawanhill ......A 8
35 Gawber ....F 11
17 Gawcott ....A 8
38 Gawthwaite .....G 5
23 Gaydon ....G 7
23 Gayhurst ....G 11
39 Gayle ....F 11
40 Gayles ....D 1
30 Gayton, Merseyside
B 1
24 Gayton, Norfolk ....D 8
23 Gayton, Northants.
G 10
31 Gayton, Staffs ...G 8
33 Gayton le Marsh ..B 11
33 Gayton le Wold ...B 9
24 Gayton Thorpe ....D 8
24 Gaywood ....C 7
25 Gazeley ....J 8
62 Geary ....B 2
56 Geddes House ...D 4
27 Gedding ....J 2
23 Geddington .....D 12
62 Gedintailor .....E 4
24 Gedney ....C 5
24 Gedney Broadgate ..C 5
24 Gedney Drove End .C 6
24 Gedney Dyke ....C 5
24 Gedney Hill .....D 4
35 Gee Cross ......H 8
60 Geisgeil ....C 3
26 Geldeston ......F 7
29 Gell ....C 8
29 Gelli ....E 3
14 Gellideg ....D 3
14 Gelligaer ....E 5
28 Gellilydan ......F 6
13 Gellinudd ....G 10
29 Gellioedd ....F 8
52 Gellyburn ......C 6
43 Gelston ....F 8

37 Gembling ....A 9
42 Genoch Square ....F 2
22 Gentleshaw .....A 4
63 Geocrab ....H 2
17 George Green ...F 11
4 George Nympton ...D 6
44 Georgefield .....D 1
4 Georgeham ......B 3
43 Georgetown, Dumf.
& Gall. ....D 10
14 Georgetown, Gwent
C 5
47 Georgetown,
Strathclyde ......C 9
61 Georgmas Junction
Station ....B 11
64 Georth ....C 2
28 Gerlan ....C 6
4 Germansweek ....F 3
2 Germoe ....G 3
2 Gerrans ....F 6
43 Gerranton ......E 8
17 Gerrards Cross ...E 11
63 Geshader ....D 2
17 Gestingthorpe ...L 1
21 Geuffordd ......A 7
43 Gibbshill ....D 8
33 Gibraltar ....D 12
15 Giddeahall .....G 11
18 Gidea Park .....E 5
5 Gidleigh ....G 5
49 Gifford ....C 8
53 Giffordtown ....F 7
35 Giggleswick ....A 7
36 Gilberdyke .....D 6
43 Gilchristland ...B 10
49 Gilchriston .....C 7
43 Gilcrux ....H 12
35 Gildersome .....D 11
32 Gildingwells ....B 3
40 Gilesgate Moor ...A 3
14 Gileston ....H 3
14 Gilfach ....D 5
14 Gilfach Goch ....E 3
13 Gilfachrheda ....A 7
41 Gillamoor ......F 7
43 Gillenbie ....C 12
43 Gillesbie ....B 12
42 Gillespie ....F 3
40 Gilling East ....G 6
40 Gilling West ....E 2
7 Gillingham, Dorset
D 11
11 Gillingham, Kent ..A 7
26 Gillingham, Norfolk
F 7
61 Gillock ....B 11
31 Gillow Heath ....D 7
43 Gillroanie ......G 8
61 Gills ....A 12
5 Gill's Green .....A 6
48 Gilmanscleuch ...G 6
48 Gilmerton, Lothian .C 5
52 Gilmerton, Tayside .B 4
39 Gilmonby ....D 12
23 Gilmorton ......C 9
44 Gilsland ....F 5
44 Gilsland Spa ....F 5
49 Gilston ....D 7
14 Gilwern ....C 6
26 Gimingham .....B 6
27 Gipping ....J 4
33 Gipsey Bridge ...E 10
47 Girdle Toll .....E 8
64 Girlsta ....D 7
40 Girsby ....D 4
25 Girtford ....K 3
32 Girthill ....E 7
43 Girthon ....F 7
25 Girton, Cambs ....J 5
32 Girton, Notts ....D 5
42 Girvan ....B 9
42 Girvan Mains ...B 3
35 Gisburn ....B 7
63 Gisla ....D 2
26 Gisleham ....F 8
27 Gislingham .....H 4
27 Gissing ....G 4
5 Gittisham ....F 5
10 Givons Grove ...C 1
52 Glack ....D 5
56 Glackbea ....F 1
56 Glackossian ....F 2
11 Gladdish ....C 7
21 Gladestry ......G 7
48 Gladhouse ......D 6
49 Gladsmuir .....B 7
31 Gladwin's Mark ..D 11
33 Glais ....G 10
41 Glaisdale ......E 8
43 Glaisters ....D 8
53 Glamis ....B 8
13 Glan Duar ......C 8
28 Glan-Dwyfach ...F 4

28 Glanaber ....E 6
13 Glanamman ....F 10
26 Glandford ......B 3
14 Glandwr ....D 5
14 Glan-dwr ....D 5
12 Glandyfi ....C 3
14 Glangrwyney ....C 5
14 Glanllynfi ......E 2
21 Glan-miwl ......C 7
12 Glanryd ....D 5
14 Glan-ryd, Dyfed ..D 5
14 Glan-ryd, Powys ...C 1
45 Glanton ....B 9
45 Glanton Pike ....B 9
7 Glanvilles Wootton
E 10
29 Glan-y-don .....B 11
20 Glan-y-nant ....D 5
21 Glanyrafon .....F 9
28 Glan-y-Wern ....G 5
24 Glapthorn ......F 1
12 Glapwell ....D 2
57 Glas-allt Shiel ...L 8
21 Glasbury ....H 7
14 Glaschoil ....F 6
38 Glascoe ....F 2
29 Glascoed ....C 9
57 Glascoforest ....F 5
22 Glascote ....B 6
21 Glascwm ....G 7
14 Glasdrum ....C 7
21 Glasfryn ....E 8
47 Glasgow ....C 10
44 Glashvin ....A 4
28 Glasinfryn ......C 5
59 Glaslaw ....J 6
55 Glasnacardoch,
Highland ....L 1
55 Glasnacardoch,
Highland ....K 1
62 Glasnakille .....G 5
20 Glaspwll ....C 3
54 Glassburn ......F 7
42 Glasserton .....H 5
47 Glassford ....E 12
15 Glasshouse Hill ...B 8
35 Glasshouses ....A 10
53 Glasslie ....G 7
43 Glassoch ....E 4
44 Glasson, Cumb ....G 1
34 Glasson, Lancs ...B 3
29 Glassonby ....A 8
53 Glasterlaw .....B 10
23 Glaston ....B 12
9 Glastonbury ....B 8
47 Glastron ....H 8
25 Glatton ....G 2
34 Glazebury ......G 5
21 Glazely ....D 12
32 Gleadless Townend .B 1
38 Gleaston ....H 5
46 Glecknabae .....C 5
43 Gledpark ....F 7
44 Gledsnest ......B 3
46 Glemanuilt .....H 1
27 Glemsford ......K 1
42 Glen, Dumf. & Gall.
F 6
43 Glen, Dumf. & Gall.
D 9
58 Glen, Grampian ...D 2
52 Glen, Tayside ....E 6
58 Glen Barry ......B 3
58 Glen Auldyn ....G 2
58 Glen Bernisdale ...C 3
50 Glen Borrodale ...A 3
57 Glen Clunie Lodge .L 7
54 Glen Dronoch ...C 4
48 Glen House .....F 6
38 Glen Mona ......G 2
55 Glen Nevis House .M 5
23 Glen Parva ......B 9
59 Glen Tanar House .H 2
58 Glen Tolsta .....B 6
58 Glen Village ....B 2
38 Glen Vine ......G 2
50 Glenancross ....K 1
50 Glenaros House ...C 3
46 Glenbarr ....F 2
58 Glenbeg, Grampian .B 2
50 Glenbeg, Highland .A 3
59 Glenbervie .....J 5
46 Glenboig ....C 12
51 Glenbranter ....H 8
48 Glenbreck ......G 3
58 Glenbrein Lodge ..H 8
62 Glenbrittle House .F 3
58 Glenbuchat Lodge .F 1
47 Glenbuck ....C 9
47 Glenburn ....C 9
59 Glencally ......L 1
60 Glencalvie Lodge .G 5
60 Glencanisp Lodge .E 3
43 Glencaple ......E 10

54 Glencarron Lodge ..E 4
53 Glencarse ......E 7
60 Glencassley Castle .F 5
46 Glencloy ....F 5
51 Glencoe ....B 8
57 Glenconglass ...G 7
52 Glencraig ....H 6
50 Glencripesdale ...B 4
58 Glencuie ....F 2
59 Glendavan House .G 2
49 Glendearg, Borders
F 8
44 Glendearg, Dumf.
& Gall. ....C 1
52 Glendevon ......G 5
55 Glendoe Lodge ...H 8
55 Glendoebeg .....J 8
53 Glendoik ....E 7
57 Glendoll Lodge ..M 8
53 Glenduckie .....E 7
59 Glendye Lodge ...J 4
52 Gleneagles Hotel ..F 4
56 Gleneig ....H 2
56 Glenerney ......E 6
51 Glenfalloch Farm .F 10
53 Glenfarg ....F 6
59 Glenfenzie ......G 1
56 Glenferness House .E 5
58 Glenfiddich Lodge .D 1
23 Glenfield ....B 9
47 Glenfinart House ..A 7
55 Glenfinnan ......L 3
55 Glenfintaig Lodge .L 6
51 Glenfyne Lodge ...F 9
52 Glenfoot ....F 6
55 Glenforslan ....M 1
51 Glengap ....F 7
47 Glengarnock ....D 8
52 Glengoulandie ...B 3
62 Glengrasco ......D 4
55 Glengyle ....F 11
42 Glengyre ....E 1
43 Glenhead, Dumf. &
Gall. ....F 8
52 Glenhead, Tayside ..G 4
53 Glenhead Farm ...A 7
51 Glenhighton .....F 4
42 Glenhoise ......E 5
43 Glenholm ......D 12
43 Glenhoul ....C 7
50 Glenhurich ......A 5
48 Glenkerry ......H 5
51 Glenkiln ....D 9
58 Glenkindie ......F 2
48 Glenkirk ....F 3
58 Glenlatterach ...D 7
43 Glenlee ....D 7
57 Glenlia ....H 1
57 Glenlochar .....E 8
57 Glenlochsie ....M 6
46 Glenloig ....F 4
42 Glenluce ....F 3
54 Glenmarksie ....D 7
46 Glenmassan .....A 6
38 Glenmaye ....G 1
54 Glenmeanne ....D 7
43 Glenmidge ......C 9
38 Glenmooar ......G 2
50 Glenmore, Highland
A 3
62 Glenmore, Highland
D 4
50 Glenmore, Strathclyde
F 6
57 Glenmore Lodge ..H 5
50 Glenmorven Cott. .B 3
42 Glenmuck ......A 6
48 Glenochar ......H 2
57 Glenquiech .....L 2
48 Glenrath ....F 5
38 Glenridding .....D 6
46 Glenrisdell .....D 4
60 Glenrossal ......F 5
53 Glenrothes .....G 7
54 Glenruther .....D 4
50 Glensanda ......C 5
59 Glensaugh ......J 4
43 Glenshee ....D 5
43 Glenshimmeroch ...C 7
57 Glenshirra Lodge .K i
47 Glenside, Strathclyde
D 7
63 Glenside, W.Isles ..E 5
51 Glensluain .....H 8
55 Glensulaig ......L 4
61 Glentaggart .....G 1
33 Glentham ......A 7
48 Glentress, Borders ..E 6
48 Glentress, Borders ..E 6
57 Glentromie Lodge .K 3
42 Glentrool Village ..D 4
57 Glentruan ....F 2
57 Glentruim House .K 2

32 Glentworth ......A 6
56 Glenurquhart ....C 3
43 Glenwhargen ....A 8
42 Glenwhilly .....D 3
48 Glespin ....G 1
64 Gletness ....D 7
15 Glewstone ......B 9
24 Glinton ....E 3
59 Glithno ....H 6
23 Glooston ....C 11
35 Glossop ....H 9
45 Gloster Hill ....C 10
15 Gloucester ......C 11
15 Gloucestershire, Co.
D 10
64 Gloup ....A 7
2 Gloweth ....E 5
35 Glusburn ....C 8
61 Glutt Lodge ....D 9
2 Gluvian ....C 6
16 Glympton ......B 5
29 Glyn ....D 7
12 Glyn-Arthen ....B 6
29 Glyn Ceiriog ...F 11
20 Glynbrochan ....D 5
14 Glyncoch ....E 4
14 Glyncorrwg .....D 2
14 Glynde ....G 3
10 Glyndebourne ...G 3
29 Glyndyfrdwy ....F 10
28 Glynllifon Park ...E 4
14 Glynneath ......D 2
14 Glyntaff ....E 4
13 Glynteg ....C 7
31 Gnosall ....H 7
31 Gnosall Heath ...H 7
23 Goadby ....B 11
32 Goadby Marwood ..H 5
11 Goat Lees ......C 9
16 Goatacre ....F 1
7 Goathill ....E 10
41 Goathland ......E 8
6 Goathurst ......C 6
10 Goathurst Com ...C 4
60 Gobernuisgach Lo. .C 5
30 Gobowen ....G 2
9 Godalming .....B 11
11 Goddard's Green ..E 7
10 Godden Green ...C 4
6 Godford Cross ...F 5
25 Godmanchester ...H 3
5 Godmanstone ...F 10
11 Godmersham ...C 9
7 Godney ....B 8
2 Godolphin Cross ..F 3
13 Godre'r-graig ...F 11
8 Godshill, Hants ...E 3
9 Godshill, I.o.W. ...H 7
10 Godstone ....C 2
6 Godwinscroft ...F 3
14 Goetre ....D 6
18 Goff's Oak ......D 3
48 Gogar ....B 4
20 Gogfnan ....D 2
28 Golan ....F 5
3 Golant ....D 8
23 Golberdon .....C 10
34 Golborne ....G 5
35 Golcar ....D 7
24 Gold Hill, Cambs ..F 6
7 Gold Hill, Dorset ..E 11
15 Goldcliff ....F 7
16 Golden Balls ....D 6
10 Golden Cross ...G 4
10 Golden Green ...G 5
13 Golden Grove ...E 9
12 Golden Hill, Dyfed .G 3
8 Golden Hill, Hants. .F 4
9 Golden Pot ......B 8
15 Golden Valley ...B 12
31 Goldenhill .....E 7
18 Golders Green ...E 3
19 Goldhanger .....C 9
21 Golding ....B 11
25 Goldington .....K 2
41 Goldsborough,
N.Yorks. ....D 8
36 Goldsborough,
N.Yorks ....B 2
2 Goldsithney ....G 3
30 Goldstone ......G 6
36 Goldthorpe .....G 3
4 Goldworthy .....D 3
56 Gollanfield ....D 4
40 Gollinglith Foot ..G 2
4 Golsoncott .....B 4
61 Golspie ....G 8
61 Golval ....B 9
48 Gomeldon ......C 3
48 Gomersal ....E 10
50 Gometra House ..C 1
19 Gomshall ....A 12
32 Gonalston .....E 4
64 Gonfirth ....D 7

18 Good Easter ......D 6
26 Gooderstone .....E 1
43 Goodhope ......B 11
4 Goodleigh ......C 5
36 Goodmanham ...C 5
11 Goodnestone, Kent
C 11
11 Goodnestone, Kent ..B 9
15 Goodrich ....B 9
9 Goodrington ....K 8
12 Goodwick ......C 3
8 Goodworth Clatford
C 11
23 Goodyers End ...D 7
36 Goole ....E 5
36 Goole Fields ....E 5
2 Goonbell ....E 4
2 Goonhavern ....D 5
59 Goose Green ....C 5
59 Goosecruives ...J 5
4 Gooseham ......D 1
43 Goosehill ......A 8
5 Goosewell ......K 4
16 Goosey ....E 4
34 Goosnargh .....C 4
30 Goostrey ....C 6
22 Gorcott Hill .....E 4
28 Gorddinog ......C 6
49 Gordon ....E 9
61 Gordonbush ....F 8
58 Gordonstown,
Grampian ....D 5
58 Gordonstown,
Grampian ....B 3
48 Gorebridge .....C 6
24 Gorefield ......D 5
17 Goring ....F 7
9 Goring-by-Sea ..F 12
17 Goring Heath ...F 7
26 Gorleston on Sea ..E 8
22 Gornalwood ....C 3
3 Gorran Churchtown
E 7
3 Gorran Haven ...E 7
44 Gorrenberry ....C 3
14 Gors ....E 2
16 Gorse Hill ......E 3
29 Gorsedd ....C 10
13 Gorseinon ......G 9
64 Gorseness .....B 11
31 Gorseybank ....E 11
13 Gorsgoch ......B 8
13 Gorslas ....F 9
15 Gorsley ....B 9
54 Gorstan ....D 7
55 Gorstanvorran ..M 2
30 Gorstella ......D 2
22 Gorsty Common ..A 8
35 Gorton ....G 7
27 Gosbeck ....K 5
23 Gosberton .....B 3
24 Gosberton Clough ..C 3
32 Gosfield ....M 1
21 Gosford ....F 10
49 Gosford House ...B 7
38 Gosforth, Cumb ..E 3
45 Gosforth, Tyne &
Wear ....F 10
18 Gosmore ....A 2
9 Gosport ....F 7
64 Gossabrough ....C 8
45 Goswick ....B 12
32 Gotham ....G 3
16 Gotherington ...A 1
10 Goudhurst ......D 6
33 Goulceby ....B 9
47 Gourock ....B 7
55 Gourdas ....C 5
59 Gourdon ....K 6
47 Govan ....C 10
32 Goverton ....E 4
5 Goveton ....L 6
14 Govilon ....C 6
38 Gowdall ....D 1
13 Gowerton ......G 9
52 Gowkhall ......H 5
36 Gowthorpe .....B 5
37 Goxhill, Humber. ..E 9
37 Goxhill, Humber. ..C 9
37 Goxhill Haven ...E 9
13 Goytre ....H 11
43 Gracefield ......C 9
9 Graffham, Cambs ..D 10
25 Grafham, Cambs ..H 3
9 Grafham, Surrey ..B 11
15 Grafton, Heref.&
Worc ....A 8
21 Grafton, Heref.&
Worc ....F 11
16 Grafton, Oxon ...D 4
30 Grafton, Salop ...H 3
36 Grafton, N.Yorks ..A 2

22 Grafton Flyford .... G 3
23 Grafton Regis .... G 11
23 Grafton Underwood .... D 12
11 Grafty Green .... C 7
29 Graianrhyd .... E 11
29 Graig .... C 7
29 Graig-fechan .... E 10
48 Graigmillar .... B 6
19 Grain .... F 9
37 Grainsby .... G 10
37 Grainthorpe .... G 11
2 Grampound .... E 6
2 Grampound Road .... E 6
17 Granborough .... B 8
32 Granby .... G 5
23 Grandborough .... E 8
52 Grandtully .... B 4
34 Grane .... E 6
38 Grange, Cumb. .... C 5
53 Grange, Fife .... F 10
30 Grange, Merseyside .... B 1
40 Grange, N. Yorks. .... F 6
47 Grange, Strathclyde .... F 9
53 Grange, Tayside .... E 7
58 Grange Crossroads .... B 2
7 Grange Gate .... H 12
56 Grange Hall .... D 6
35 Grange Moor .... E 11
53 Grange of Lindores .... E 7
45 Grange Villa .... H 10
48 Grangehall .... E 2
31 Grangemill .... D 11
48 Grangemouth .... A 2
38 Grange-over-Sands .... G 6
48 Grangepans .... A 3
40 Grangetown, Cleveland .... C 6
14 Grangetown, S. Glam. .... G 5
57 Granish .... H 5
37 Gransmoor .... A 9
12 Granston .... D 2
25 Grantchester .... K 5
32 Grantham .... G 6
58 Grantlodge .... F 5
48 Granton, Dumf. & Gall. .... H 3
48 Granton, Lothian .... B 5
57 Granton-on-Spey .... G 6
21 Grantsfield .... F 10
49 Grantshouse .... C 10
30 Grappenhall .... B 5
37 Grasby .... G 8
38 Grasmere .... D 6
35 Grasscroft .... G 8
30 Grassendale .... B 3
39 Grassholme .... C 11
35 Grassington .... A 9
45 Grasslees .... C 8
32 Grassmoor .... D 1
32 Grassthorpe .... C 5
8 Grateley .... B 4
31 Gratwich .... G 9
25 Graveley, Cambs. .... J 4
18 Graveley, Herts. .... A 2
22 Gravelly Hill .... C 5
11 Graveney .... B 9
10 Gravesend .... A 5
63 Gravir .... E 5
37 Grayingham .... G 7
39 Grayrigg .... E 8
18 Grays .... F 6
9 Grayshott .... C 10
9 Grayswood .... C 10
40 Graythorp .... B 5
17 Grazeley .... G 8
36 Greasbrough .... H 2
30 Greasby .... B 1
32 Greasley .... E 2
25 Great Abington .... K 6
25 Great Addington .... H 1
22 Great Alne .... F 5
34 Great Altcar .... F 2
18 Great Amwell .... C 4
39 Great Asby .... D 9
27 Great Ashfield .... H 3
40 Great Ayton .... D 6
19 Great Baddow .... C 7
15 Great Badminton .... F 11
25 Great Bardfield .... M 8
25 Great Barford .... K 2
22 Great Barr .... C 4
16 Great Barrington .... C 3
30 Great Barrow .... C 3
27 Great Barton .... J 2
41 Great Barugh .... G 7
45 Great Bavington .... E 8
27 Great Bealings .... K 5
6 Great Bedwyn .... H 4
9 Great Bentley .... B 11
23 Great Billing .... F 11
26 Great Bircham .... B 1
27 Great Blakenham .... K 4
39 Great Blencow .... B 7
30 Great Bolas .... H 5
9 Great Bookham .... A 12
23 Great Bourton .... H 8
23 Great Bowden .... C 11
25 Great Bradley .... K 8
19 Great Braxted .... G 8
27 Great Bricett .... K 3
17 Great Brickhill .... A 10
31 Great Bridgeford .... G 7
23 Great Brington .... F 10
19 Great Bromley .... A 10
30 Great Budworth .... B 5
40 Great Burdon .... B 5
19 Great Burstead .... E 7
40 Great Busby .... E 5
18 Great Canfield .... B 6
33 Great Carlton .... B 11
24 Great Casterton .... E 1
15 Great Chalfield .... H 11
11 Great Chart .... D 8
22 Great Chatwell .... A 1
25 Great Chesterfield .... L 6
8 Great Cheverall .... A 1
25 Great Chishill .... L 5
19 Great Clacton .... B 11
38 Great Clifton .... B 3
37 Great Coate .... F 10
22 Great Comberton .... H 3
44 Great Corby .... H 3
27 Great Cornard .... L 2
37 Great Cowden .... C 10
16 Great Coxwell .... E 4
40 Great Crakehall .... F 3
23 Great Cransley .... D 11
26 Great Cressingham .... E 1
34 Great Crosby .... G 2
31 Great Cubley .... F 10
23 Great Dalby .... A 10
23 Gt. Doddington .... F 12
6 Great Dorweeke .... F 3
15 Great Doward .... C 9
26 Great Dunham .... D 2
18 Great Dunmow .... B 6
8 Great Durnford .... B 3
18 Great Easton, Essex .... A 6
23 Great Easton, Leics. .... C 11
34 Great Eccleston .... C 3
41 Great Edstone .... G 7
26 Great Ellingham .... F 3
7 Great Elm .... A 10
25 Great Eversden .... K 5
40 Great Fencote .... F 3
27 Great Finborough .... J 3
26 Great Fransham .... D 2
17 Great Gaddesden .... C 11
25 Great Gidding .... G 2
36 Great Givendale .... B 6
27 Great Glenham .... J 6
23 Great Glen .... B 10
32 Great Gonerby .... F 6
15 Great Graig .... B 7
25 Great Gransden .... K 4
26 Great Green, Norf. .... F 6
27 Great Green, Suff. .... K 2
41 Great Habton .... G 8
24 Great Hale .... A 2
18 Great Hallingbury .... B 5
21 Great Hanwood .... B 10
23 Great Harrowden .... E 12
34 Great Harwood .... D 6
17 Great Haseley .... D 7
37 Great Hatfield .... C 9
31 Great Haywood .... H 8
23 Great Heath .... D 7
36 Great Heck .... E 4
27 Great Henny .... L 2
15 Great Hinton .... H 12
26 Great Hockham .... F 2
19 Great Holland .... B 12
27 Great Horkesley .... M 3
25 Great Hormead .... M 5
35 Great Horton .... D 10
17 Great Horwood .... A 8
23 Great Houghton, Northants .... F 11
36 Great Houghton, S. Yorks. .... F 2
31 Great Hucklow .... B 10
37 Great Kelk .... A 8
17 Great Kimble .... D 9
17 Great Kingshill .... D 9
40 Great Langton .... F 3
19 Great Leighs .... B 7
37 Great Limber .... F 9
23 Great Linford .... H 12
27 Great Livermere .... H 2
31 Great Longstone .... C 10
45 Great Lumley .... H 11
22 Great Malvern .... G 2
27 Great Maplestead .... M 1
34 Great Marton .... D 2
26 Great Massingham .... C 1
26 Great Melton .... E 4
17 Great Milton .... D 7
17 Great Missenden .... D 10
34 Great Mitton .... C 6
11 Great Mongeham .... C 12
34 Great Moss .... G 4
39 Great Musgrave .... D 10
30 Great Ness .... H 3
19 Great Oakley, Essex .... A 11
23 Great Oakley, Northants .... D 12
18 Great Offley .... A 1
39 Great Ormside .... C 9
44 Great Orton .... H 2
36 Great Ouseburn .... A 2
23 Great Oxendon .... D 10
18 Great Oxney Grn. .... C 6
26 Great Palgrave .... D 1
18 Great Parndon .... C 4
25 Great Paxton .... J 3
34 Great Plumpton .... D 3
26 Great Plumstead .... D 6
32 Great Ponton .... G 6
36 Great Preston .... D 2
25 Great Raveley .... G 4
16 Great Rissington .... B 3
16 Great Rollright .... A 4
12 Great Rudbaxton .... E 3
26 Great Ryburgh .... C 3
45 Great Ryle .... B 8
19 Great Saling .... A 7
39 Great Salkeld .... B 8
25 Great Sampford .... L 7
30 Great Sankey .... A 4
30 Great Saughall .... C 2
27 Great Saxham .... J 1
16 Great Shefford .... G 5
25 Great Shelford .... K 6
40 Great Smeaton .... E 4
26 Great Snoring .... B 2
16 Great Somerford .... F 1
30 Great Soudley .... G 6
40 Great Stainton .... C 3
19 Great Stambridge .... E 9
25 Great Staughton .... J 2
33 Great Steeping .... D 11
11 Great Stonar .... B 12
39 Great Strickland .... C 8
25 Great Stukeley .... H 3
33 Great Sturton .... C 9
30 Gt. Sutton, Ches. .... C 2
21 Gt. Sutton, Salop. .... D 10
45 Great Swinburne .... E 7
19 Great Tarpots .... E 7
16 Great Tew .... A 5
19 Great Tey .... A 9
25 Great Thurlow .... K 8
4 Great Torrington .... D 4
45 Great Tosson .... C 8
19 Great Totham .... C 8
38 Great Urswick .... H 5
19 Great Wakering .... E 9
27 Great Waldingfield .... L 2
26 Great Walsingham .... B 2
19 Great Waltham .... C 7
18 Great Warley .... E 6
16 Great Washbourne .... A 1
27 Great Welnetham .... J 2
27 Great Wenham .... L 4
45 Great Whittington .... F 8
19 Great Whigborough .... B 9
25 Great Wilbraham .... J 6
8 Great Wishford .... C 2
15 Great Witcombe .... C 12
22 Great Witley .... E 1
16 Great Wolford .... A 3
23 Great Woolstone .... H 12
25 Great Wratting .... K 8
18 Great Wymondley .... A 2
22 Great Wyrley .... A 3
30 Great Wytheford .... H 4
26 Great Yarmouth .... E 8
27 Great Yeldham .... L 1
18 Greater London, Co. .... F 3
35 Greater Manchester, Co. .... G 7
24 Greatford .... D 2
31 Greatgate .... F 9
40 Greatham, Cleveland .... B 5
9 Greatham, Hants. .... C 9
9 Greatham, W. Sussex .... E 11
11 Greatstone-on-Sea .... F 9
23 Greatworth .... H 9
25 Green End .... K 2
36 Green Hammerton .... A 2
7 Green Ore .... A 9
10 Green Street Green .... A 5
19 Green Tye .... B 4
34 Greenbank .... B 4
43 Greenbeck .... C 11
48 Greenburn .... C 2
38 Greendale .... E 4
7 Greendown .... A 9
45 Greendykes .... C 12
49 Greenend .... G 8
25 Greenfield, Beds. .... M 2
29 Greenfield, Clwyd .... B 11
55 Greenfield, Highland .... J 6
35 Greenfield, Manchester .... G 8
17 Greenfield, Oxon. .... E 8
18 Greenford .... F 1
48 Greengairs .... B 1
44 Greengate Well .... F 5
34 Greenhalgh .... D 3
16 Greenham, Berks. .... H 6
6 Greenham, Som. .... D 4
44 Greenhaugh .... D 6
43 Greenhead, Dumf. & Gal. .... C 10
44 Greenhead, Northumb. .... F 5
47 Greenhead, Strathclyde .... E 9
48 Greenhill, Central .... B 1
11 Greenhill, Kent .... A 10
47 Greenhills .... D 8
10 Greenhithe .... A 5
47 Greenholm .... F 10
39 Greenholme .... E 8
49 Greenhouse .... G 8
35 Greenhow Hill .... A 9
64 Greenigo .... D 2
49 Greenknowe .... E 9
61 Greenland .... A 11
17 Greenlands .... F 8
49 Greenlaw, Borders .... E 9
58 Greenlaw, Grampian .... B 4
49 Greenlaw Walls .... E 12
43 Greenlea, Dumf. & Gal. .... D 11
47 Greenlea, Dumf. & Gal. .... A 7
52 Greenloaning .... F 3
34 Greenmount .... F 6
47 Greenock .... B 8
38 Greenodd .... G 5
48 Greenrig .... E 1
43 Greenrow .... F 11
23 Greens Norton .... G 10
32 Greenscares .... F 3
48 Greenshields .... E 3
45 Greenside .... G 9
45 Greensidehill .... A 8
58 Greenskairs .... A 5
19 Greenstead Green .... A 8
18 Greensted Green .... D 5
64 Greenwall .... C 3
12 Greenway, Dyfed .... D 4
14 Greenway, S. Glam. .... G 4
18 Greenwich .... F 4
16 Greet .... A 1
21 Greete .... E 11
23 Greetham, Leics. .... A 12
33 Greetham, Lincs. .... C 10
35 Greetland .... E 9
7 Greinton .... C 7
23 Grendon, N'thants .... F 12
22 Grendon, War. .... B 6
22 Grendon Common .... B 6
21 Grendon Green .... G 11
17 Grendon Underwood .... B 8
42 Grennan .... E 3
5 Grenofen .... J 4
35 Grenoside .... H 11
30 Gresford .... E 2
26 Gresham .... B 5
62 Greshornish .... C 3
63 Gress .... C 6
26 Gressenhall .... D 3
26 Gressenhall Grn. .... D 3
39 Gressingham .... H 8
30 Grestey Green .... E 6
40 Greta Bridge .... D 1
44 Gretna .... F 2
44 Gretna Green .... F 1
16 Gretton, Glos. .... A 1
23 Gretton, N'thants .... C 12
21 Gretton, Salop. .... C 10
40 Grewelthorpe .... G 2
58 Grey Stone .... E 6
40 Greygarth .... H 2
13 Greynor .... F 9
48 Greyrigg, Central .... B 2
43 Greyrigg, Dumf. & Gall. .... C 11
38 Greysouthen .... B 3
39 Greystoke, Cumb. .... B 7
53 Greystoke, Tayside .... C 10
43 Greystone .... D 10
9 Greywell .... A 8
4 Gribbleford Bridge .... F 4
36 Gribthorpe .... D 5
50 Gribun .... D 2
5 Gridley Corner .... G 2
23 Griff .... C 7
14 Griffithstown .... D 6
39 Grigghall .... F 7
64 Grimbister .... C 2
34 Grimeford Village .... F 5
36 Grimethorpe .... F 2
22 Grimley .... F 2
47 Grimmet .... H 8
33 Grimoldby .... A 11
34 Grimsargh .... D 5
37 Grimsby .... F 10
23 Grimscote .... G 10
4 Grimscott .... E 1
63 Grimshader .... D 5
24 Grimsthorpe .... C 2
37 Grimston, Humber. .... D 10
32 Grimston, Leics. .... H 4
24 Grimston, Norfolk .... C 8
7 Grimstone .... G 9
5 Grinacombe Moor .... G 3
41 Grindale .... H 11
22 Grindle .... B 1
31 Grindleford .... B 11
34 Grindleton .... C 6
30 Grindley Brook .... F 4
31 Grindlow .... B 10
40 Grindon, Cleveland .... C 4
44 Grindon, Northumb. .... F 6
49 Grindon, Northumb. .... E 11
31 Grindon, Staffs. .... E 9
44 Grindon Hill .... F 6
49 Grindonrigg .... E 11
32 Gringley on the Hill .... A 4
44 Grinsdale .... G 2
30 Grinshill .... H 4
40 Grinton .... E 1
41 Gristhorpe .... G 11
26 Griston .... E 2
16 Grittenham .... F 1
15 Grittleton .... F 11
38 Grizebeck .... G 5
38 Grizedale .... F 6
64 Grobister .... C 4
23 Groby .... A 8
29 Groes, Clwyd .... D 9
13 Groes, W. Glam. .... H 11
14 Groesfaen .... F 4
28 Groesffordd .... F 2
29 Groesffordd .... C 7
29 Groesffordd Marli .... C 9
21 Groesllwyd .... A 7
28 Groeslon, Gwynedd .... C 3
28 Groeslon, Gwynedd .... E 4
46 Grogport .... E 3
29 Gronant .... B 10
10 Groombridge .... D 4
63 Grosebay .... H 2
15 Grosmont, Gwent .... B 7
41 Grosmont, N. Yorks. .... E 8
27 Groton .... L 2
7 Grove, Dorset .... H 7
16 Grove, Oxon. .... E 5
32 Grove, Notts. .... B 4
13 Grovesend .... G 9
54 Grudie .... D 7
60 Gruids .... F 6
60 Gruinard House .... G 1
62 Grula .... E 3
50 Gruline House .... D 3
2 Grumbla .... G 1
27 Grundisburgh .... K 5
64 Grundsound .... E 7
64 Gruting .... D 6
64 Grutness .... F 7
28 Grwedog .... B 3
51 Gualachulain .... C 8
60 Gualin House .... B 4
53 Guard Bridge .... E 9
22 Guarlford .... H 2
52 Guay .... B 5
43 Gubhill .... B 10
11 Guestling Green .... G 7
11 Guestling Icklesham .... F 7
26 Guestwick .... C 3
34 Guide .... E 6
45 Guide Post .... E 10
25 Guilden Morden .... L 4
30 Guilden Sutton .... C 3
9 Guildford .... A 11
53 Guildtown .... D 6
23 Guilsborough .... E 10
21 Guilsfield .... A 8
11 Guilton .... B 11
47 Guiltreehill .... H 8
4 Guineaford .... B 4
55 Guisachan House .... G 7
40 Guisborough .... D 6
35 Guiseley .... C 10
26 Guist .... C 3
16 Guiting Power .... B 2
64 Gulberwick .... E 7
49 Gullane .... A 7
2 Gulval .... F 2
5 Gulworthy .... H 3
12 Gumfreston .... G 4
23 Gumley .... C 10
2 Gummow's Shop .... D 6
36 Gunby, Humber. .... D 5
32 Gunby, Lincs. .... H 6
9 Gundleton .... C 7
4 Gunn .... C 5
39 Gunnerside .... E 11
45 Gunnerton .... F 7
45 Gunnerton Fell .... E 7
36 Gunness .... F 6
3 Gunnislake .... C 11
64 Gunnista .... D 7
36 Gunthorpe, Humber. .... G 6
26 Gunthorpe, Norf. .... B 3
32 Gunthorpe, Notts. .... F 4
8 Gunville .... G 6
6 Gupworthy .... C 3
8 Gurnard .... F 6
7 Gurney Slade .... A 9
14 Gurnos .... C 1
8 Gussage All Saints .... E 2
8 Gussage St. Andrew .... E 1
8 Gussage St. Michael .... E 1
11 Guston .... D 11
64 Gutcher .... B 8
53 Guthrie .... B 10
24 Guy's Head .... C 6
7 Guy's Marsh .... D 11
24 Guyhirn .... E 5
45 Guyzance .... C 10
14 Gwaelod-y-garth .... F 4
29 Gwaenysgor .... B 10
28 Gwalchmai .... C 3
12 Gwastad .... D 4
13 Gwaun-cae-Gurwen .... F 10
12 Gwbert-on-Sea .... B 5
2 Gweek .... G 4
15 Gwehelog Com. .... D 7
20 Gwenddwr .... H 6
2 Gwennap .... F 4
14 Gwent, Co. .... D 6
2 Gwenter .... H 4
29 Gwernaffield .... D 11
21 Gwernaffel .... E 8
15 Gwernesney .... D 7
13 Gwernogle .... D 8
29 Gwernymynydd .... D 11
14 Gwern-y-Steeple .... G 4
30 Gwersyllt .... E 2
29 Gwespyr .... B 10
2 Gwinear .... F 3
2 Gwithian .... F 3
29 Gwddelwern .... F 10
13 Gwyddgrug .... C 8
29 Gwynfryn .... E 11
28 Gwynedd, Co. .... E 5
20 Gwystre .... F 6
29 Gwytherin .... D 8
29 Gyfelia .... F 12
29 Gyffin .... C 7
29 Gyffylliog .... D 10
21 Habberley .... B 9
63 Habost, W. Isles .... E 4
63 Habost, W. Isles .... A 6
37 Habrough .... F 9
24 Hacconby .... C 2
24 Haceby .... B 1
27 Hacheston .... J 6
32 Hackenthorpe .... B 1
18 Hacketts .... C 3
26 Hackford .... E 3
40 Hackforth .... F 3
64 Hackland .... C 2
63 Hacklete .... C 2
23 Hackleton .... G 11
41 Hackness .... F 10
18 Hackney .... E 4
33 Hackthorn .... B 7
39 Hackthorpe .... C 7
18 Hacton .... E 5
49 Hadden .... F 10
17 Haddenham, Bucks. .... C 8
25 Haddenham, Cambs. .... H 6
49 Haddington, Lothian .... B 8
32 Haddington, Lincs. .... D 6
26 Haddiscoe .... F 7
58 Haddoch .... C 3

24 Haddon ....F 2
35 Hade Edge ....G 10
22 Hademore ....A 5
35 Hadfield ....G 9
18 Hadham Cross ....B 4
18 Hadham Ford ......B 4
19 Hadleigh, Essex ...E 8
27 Hadleigh, Suffolk ..L 3
21 Hadley ....A 12
31 Hadley End ....H 10
18 Hadley Wood ......D 3
10 Hadlow ....C 5
10 Hadlow Down .....F 4
30 Hadnall ....H 4
25 Hadstock ....L 7
45 Hadwin's Close ...B 10
22 Hadzor ....F 3
11 Haffenden Quarter .D 7
20 Hafod ....G 1
29 Hafod-Dinbych ...E 8
20 Hafod-Peris ....F 1
35 Haggate ....D 7
44 Haggbeck ....F 3
45 Haggerston ......B 11
21 Hagley, Heref. &
   Worcs. ....H 11
22 Hagley, Heref. &
   Worcs. ....D 3
33 Hagworthingham ..C 10
34 Haigh, Manchester ..F 5
35 Haigh, S. Yorks. ...F 11
35 Haigh Moor ......E 11
34 Haighton Green ...D 4
25 Hail Weston ....J 3
38 Haile ....D 3
18 Hailey, Herts. ....C 4
16 Hailey, Oxon. .....C 4
10 Hailsham ....G 5
18 Hainault ....E 4
26 Hainford ....D 5
33 Hainton ....B 9
37 Haisthorpe ....A 9
32 Halam ....E 4
52 Halbeath ....H 6
6 Halberton ....E 3
61 Halcro ....B 11
30 Hale, Cheshire ....B 3
30 Hale, Manchester ..B 6
8 Hale, Hants. ......D 3
9 Hale, Surrey .....A 10
30 Hale Cliff ....B 3
10 Hale Street ....C 5
30 Halebarns ....B 6
26 Hales, Norfolk ....F 7
30 Hales, Staffs. .....G 6
22 Halesowen ....D 3
'27 Halesworth ....H 7
30 Halewood ....B 3
22 Halfrod, War. .....H 6
21 Halford, Salop. ..D 10
12 Halfpenny Furze ..F 6
22 Halfpenny Green ...C 2
16 Halfway, Berks. ...G 5
13 Halfway, Dyfed ..D 11
13 Halfway, Dyfed ..D 10
3 Halfway House,
   Cornwall ....C 8
6 Halfway House,
   Devon ....G 4
21 Halfway House,
   Salop. ....A 9
42 Halfway House,
   Dumf. & Gall. ....E 4
11 Halfway Houses ...A 8
35 Halifax ....E 9
47 Halket ....D 9
61 Halkirk ....B 10
29 Halkyn ....C 11
47 Hall ....D 9
38 Hall Dunnerdale ...F 5
22 Hall Green ....D 5
47 Hall of Carnduff ..E 11
21 Hall of the Forest ..D 7
38 Hall Waberthwaite ..F 3
10 Halland ....F 4
23 Hallaton ....B 11
7 Hallatrow ....A 10
44 Hallbankgate ......G 4
15 Hallen ....F 8
32 Hallfield Gate ....D 1
49 Halliburton ......D 9
62 Hallin ....B 2
10 Halling ....B 6
33 Hallington, Lincs. .B 10
45 Hallington, Northumb.
            E 8
34 Halliwell ....F 6
32 Halloughton ....E 4
22 Hallow ....F 2
44 Hallrule ....B 4
49 Halls ....B 9
18 Hall's Green ......A 3
5 Hallsands ....M 7
43 Hallscaur ....B 8

24 Halltoft End ......A 5
49 Halltree ....D 7
3 Hallworthy ....A 9
48 Hallyne ....E 5
30 Halmer End ....E 6
15 Halmore ....D 10
48 Halmyre Mains ...D 4
9 Halnaker ....E 10
34 Halsall ....F 2
23 Halse, Northants. ..H 9
6 Halse, Somerset ..C 5
37 Halsham ....D 10
4 Halsinger ....B 4
27 Halstead, Essex ...M 1
10 Halstead, Kent ....B 4
23 Halstead, Leics. ..B 11
7 Halstock ....E 8
38 Haltcliff Bridge ...B 6
33 Haltham ....D 9
17 Halton, Bucks. ....C 9
30 Halton, Cheshire ..B 4
29 Halton, Clwyd ...F 12
34 Halton, Lancs. ....A 4
45 Halton, Northumb. .B 7
35 Halton East ....B 9
39 Halton, Gill .....G 11
33 Halton Holegate ..D 11
44 Halton Lea Gate ..G 5
35 Halton Moor ....D 12
34 Halton Park ....A 4
11 Halton Shields ....F 8
35 Halton West ....B 7
44 Haltwhistle ....C 5
26 Halvergate ....E 7
5 Halwell ....K 6
4 Halwill ....F 3
4 Halwill Junction ..F 3
6 Ham, Devon ......F 6
15 Ham, Glos. ......D 10
11 Ham, Kent ....C 12
18 Ham, London .....G 2
16 Ham, Wilts. ....H 4
15 Ham Green, Avon .G 8
22 Ham Green,
   Heref. & Worcs. ...F 4
11 Ham Green, Kent ..A 7
10 Ham Hill ....B 6
11 Ham Street, Kent ..E 8
7 Ham Street, Som. ..C 9
3 Hamble ....E 6
17 Hambledon ....E 8
9 Hambledon, Hants. .E 8
9 Hambledon, Surrey
            B 11
34 Hambleton, Lancs. ..C 3
36 Hambleton, N. Yorks.
            D 3
7 Hambridge ....D 7
8 Hambrook ....E 9
33 Hameringham ....C 10
25 Hamerton ....G 2
47 Hamilton ....D 12
9 Hammer ....C 10
9 Hammerpot ....F 11
18 Hammersmith .....F 2
22 Hammerwich ......A 4
7 Hammoon ....E 11
64 Hamnavoe, W. Burra
            E 7
64 Hamnavoe, Yell ...C 7
64 Hamnavoe, Zetland .C 6
64 Hamnavoe, Zetland .C 7
10 Hampden ....H 5
17 Hampden Row ....D 9
16 Hampnett ....C 9
36 Hampole ....F 3
8 Hampreston ....F 2
8 Hampshire, Co. ....C 6
18 Hampstead ....E 3
16 Hampstead Norris ..F 6
35 Hampsthwaite ...A 11
22 Hampton, Heref. &
   Worcs. ....H 4
18 Hampton, London .G 1
22 Hampton, Salop. ..D 1
15 Hampton Bishop ...A 9
30 Hampton Heath ...E 4
22 Hampton in Arden .D 5
22 Hampton Lovett ...F 2
22 Hampton Lucy .....F 6
22 Hampton on the Hill
            F 6
16 Hampton Poyle ....C 6
31 Hamstall Ridware ..H 9
8 Hamstead, I. o. W. ..G 5
22 Hamstead,
   W. Midlands .....B 3
16 Hamstead Marshall .H 5
40 Hamsteels ....A 2
40 Hamsterley, Dur. ..B 1
45 Hamsterley, Dur. ..G 9
8 Hamworthy ....G 1
31 Hanbury, Staffs. ..G 10

22 Hanbury, Heref. &
   Worcs. ....F 3
30 Handbridge ....D 3
10 Handcross ....E 2
31 Handforth ....B 7
30 Handley, Cheshire .D 3
8 Handley, Dorset ...D 2
22 Handsacre ....A 4
22 Handsworth ....C 4
17 Handy Cross, Bucks.
           E 9
4 Handy Cross, Devon
           C 3
31 Hanford ....F 7
8 Hanging Langford ..B 2
43 Hangingshaw,
   Dumf. & Gall. ...C 11
48 Hangingshaw,
   Strathclyde ......E 2
30 Hankelow ....F 5
16 Hankerton ....E 1
10 Hankham ....G 5
31 Hanley ....E 7
22 Hanley Castle .....H 2
21 Hanley Childe ....F 12
22 Hanley Swan ......H 2
22 Hanley William ..F 12
35 Hanlith ....A 8
30 Hanmer ....F 3
9 Hannington, Hants. .A 7
23 Hannington,
   Northants. ......E 11
16 Hannington, Wilts. .E 3
16 Hannington Wick ..E 3
23 Hanslope ....G 11
24 Hanthorpe ....C 2
18 Hanwell, London ..F 2
23 Hanwell, Oxon. ...H 8
26 Hanworth, Lond. ..G 1
26 Hanworth, Norf. ..B 5
48 Happendon ....F 1
26 Happisburgh ......B 7
26 Happisburgh Com. .C 7
30 Hapsford ....C 3
34 Hapton, Lancs. ...D 6
26 Hapton, Norfolk ..F 5
6 Harberton ....K 6
5 Harbertonford ....K 6
11 Harbledown ......B 10
22 Harborne ....D 4
23 Harborough Magna .D 8
45 Harbottle ....C 7
5 Harbourneford ....J 6
22 Harbury ....G 4
32 Harby, Leics. .....G 5
32 Harby, Notts. .....C 6
6 Harcombe, Devon .H 2
6 Harcombe, Devon .G 5
2 Harcourt ....F 5
35 Harden ....G 9
15 Hardenhuish ....G 12
43 Hardgate, Dumf. &
   Gall. ....E 9
59 Hardgate, Grampian
           G 5
43 Hardgrove ....D 11
9 Hardham ....D 11
34 Hardhorn ....C 2
26 Hardingham ......E 3
31 Hardings Wood ...E 7
23 Hardingstone ....F 11
31 Hardington
   Mandeville ......E 8
7 Hardington Marsh .E 8
4 Hardisworthy .....D 4
8 Hardley ....F 6
26 Hardley Street ....E 7
18 Hardmonsworth ...F 1
39 Hardrow ....F 11
32 Hardstoft ....D 2
7 Hardway ....C 10
18 Hardwick, Bucks. .B 9
25 Hardwick, Cambs. .J 5
32 Hardwick, Lincs. .C 6
26 Hardwick, Norf. ..F 5
23 Hardwick, Northants.
          E 11
16 Hardwick, Oxon. ..D 5
17 Hardwick, Oxon. ..A 7
32 Hardwick Grange ..C 4
15 Hardwicke, Glos. .B 12
15 Hardwicke, Glos. .C 11
21 Hardwicke, Heref. &
   Worcs. ....H 8
19 Hardy's Green .....B 9
6 Hare & Hounds Inn .G 5
17 Hare Green ....F 9
19 Hare Hatch ....F 9
18 Hare Street, Essex ..C 4
18 Hare Street, Herts. ..A 4
10 Harebeating ....G 5
33 Hareby ....D 10
34 Hareden ....B 5

18 Harefield ....E 1
17 Harefield Moor ...E 11
35 Harehills ....D 11
49 Harehope ....A 9
48 Harelaw, Strathclyde
           G 8
49 Harelaw, Borders ..G 8
           E 2
47 Harelaw, Strathclyde
           D 9
59 Haremuir ....K 5
39 Haresceugh ....A 8
15 Harescombe ......C 11
15 Haresfield ......C 11
48 Hareshaw ....C 1
35 Harewood ....C 12
11 Harewood End .....B 8
36 Harewood Estate ...F 3
4 Harford, Devon ...F 7
5 Harford, Devon ...K 5
26 Hargate ....F 4
31 Hargatewall ......C 9
25 Hargrave, Ches. ...D 3
25 Hargrave, Northants.
           H 1
27 Hargrave Green ....J 1
18 Haringey ....E 3
18 Harker ....G 2
27 Harkstead ....M 5
22 Harlaston ....A 5
58 Harlaw House .....E 5
32 Harlaxton ....G 6
35 Harle Syke ....D 7
28 Harlech ....H 5
18 Harlescott ......A 10
18 Harlesden ....F 2
27 Harleston, Norf. ..G 5
27 Harleston, Suffolk ..J 3
23 Harlestone ....F 10
21 Harley ....B 11
48 Harleyholm ....F 2
25 Harlington, Beds. .M 1
36 Harlington, Lond. ..F 1
36 Harlington, S. Yorks.
           G 3
25 Harlosh ....D 2
18 Harlow ....C 5
45 Harlow Hill ....F 9
45 Harlthorpe ....C 5
25 Harlton ....K 5
8 Harman's Cross ...H 1
40 Harmby ....F 2
28 Harmer Green .....B 3
30 Harmerhill ....H 3
31 Harmston ....D 7
16 Harnhill ....D 2
18 Harold Hill ....E 5
64 Haroldston West ...E 2
64 Haroldswick ......A 8
40 Harome ....G 6
27 Harpenden ....C 12
49 Harper Ridge ....E 11
49 Harpertoun ......E 10
6 Harpford ....G 4
37 Harpham ....A 8
21 Harpley, Heref. &
   Worcs. ....F 12
26 Harpley, Norfolk ...C 1
23 Harpole ....F 10
17 Harpsden ....F 8
32 Harpswell ....A 6
31 Harpur Hill ....C 9
35 Harpurhey ....G 7
64 Harra ....B 7
44 Harraby ....H 3
62 Harrapool ....F 6
52 Harrietfield ......D 5
11 Harrietsfield .....G 9
11 Harrietsham ......C 7
38 Harrington, Cumb. .C 2
33 Harrington, Lincs. .C 10
23 Harrington,
   Northants. ......D 11
23 Harringworth ....B 12
31 Harriseahead ......E 7
35 Harrogate ....B 12
23 Harrold ....E 2
18 Harrow ....E 2
27 Harrow Street ....L 3
18 Harrow Weald ....E 2
3 Harrowbarrow ...C 11
3 Harrowbridge .....B 9
40 Harrowgate Village .C 3
25 Harston, Cambs. ..K 5
32 Harston, Leics. ...G 5
36 Harswell ....C 6
40 Hart ....B 5
45 Hart Law ....D 9
45 Hartburn ....D 9
27 Hartest ....K 1
10 Hartfoot Lane ...F 11
25 Hartford, Cambs. .H 4
30 Hartford, Ches. ...C 5
19 Hartford End .....B 7

17 Hartfordbridge .....H 8
30 Harthill, Cheshire ..E 4
32 Harthill, S. Yorks. ..B 2
48 Harthill, Strathclyde
           C 2
31 Hartington ....D 9
4 Hartland ....D 1
22 Hartlebury ....E 2
40 Hartlepool ....B 5
39 Hartley, Cumbria ..D 10
10 Hartley, Kent .....A 5
10 Hartley, Kent .....E 6
45 Hartley, Northumb.
           E 11
10 Hartley Green .....A 5
17 Hartley Wespall ...H 8
17 Hartley Wintney ...H 8
11 Hartlip ....B 7
36 Harton, N. Yorks. ..A 5
21 Harton, Salop ...D 10
45 Harton, Tyne &
   Wear ....G 12
15 Hartpury ....B 11
35 Hartshead ....E 10
23 Hartshill ....C 7
31 Hartshorne ......H 11
48 Hartside ....F 2
38 Hartsop ....D 6
17 Hartwell, Bucks. ...C 9
23 Hartwell, Northants.
          G 11
35 Hartwith ....A 11
48 Hartwood ....C 1
49 Hartwoodburn ....G 7
49 Hartwoodmyres ...G 7
10 Harvel ....B 5
22 Harvington ....G 4
22 Harvington Cross ..G 4
30 Harwarton ....G 2
16 Harwell ....E 6
27 Harwich ....M 6
39 Harwood, Dur. ..B 10
34 Harwood,
   Manchester ......F 6
45 Harwood, Northumb.
           D 8
41 Harwood Dale .....F 9
32 Harworth ....A 3
9 Hascombe ......B 11
23 Haselbech ......D 10
7 Haselbury Plucknett
           E 8
22 Haseley ....E 6
22 Haselor ....F 5
15 Hasfield ....B 11
12 Hasguard ....F 2
12 Hasguard Cross ...F 2
34 Haskayne ....F 2
27 Hasketon ....K 5
32 Hasland ....C 1
9 Haslemere ....C 10
34 Haslingden ....E 6
25 Haslingfield ......K 5
30 Haslington ....E 6
30 Hassall ....D 6
30 Hassall Green ....D 6
11 Hassell Street ....C 9
49 Hassendean ......G 8
26 Hassingham ......E 6
49 Hassington ....E 10
10 Hassocks ....F 2
31 Hassop ....C 10
61 Hastigrow ....B 11
11 Hastingleigh .....D 9
11 Hastings ....G 7
18 Hastingwood .....C 5
17 Hastoe ....C 10
40 Haswell ....A 4
40 Haswell Plough ...A 4
48 Haswellsykes .....E 5
9 Hatch ....A 8
10 Hatch Beauchamp .D 6
18 Hatch End ....E 1
6 Hatch Green ......D 6
46 Hatchednize .....E 10
8 Hatchet Gate .....F 5
30 Hatchmere ....C 4
37 Hatcliffe ....G 10
21 Hatfield, Heref. &
   Worcs. ....F 11
21 Hatfield, Heref. &
   Worcs. ....G 2
18 Hatfield, Herts. ...C 2
36 Hatfield, S. Yorks. .G 3
18 Hatfield Broad Oak
           B 5
18 Hatfield Heath ....B 5
19 Hatfield Peverel ...C 8
36 Hatfield Woodhouse
           F 5
16 Hatford ....E 4
28 Hatherden ....A 5
4 Hatherleigh ......E 4
16 Hatherop ....D 3

31 Hathersage ....B 10
35 Hathershaw ....G 8
30 Hatherton, Ches. ..E 5
22 Hatherton, Staffs. ..A 3
25 Hatley St. George ..K 4
3 Hatt ....C 11
9 Hattingley ....B 8
30 Hatton, Cheshire ..B 4
31 Hatton, Derby ...G 10
58 Hatton, Grampian ..D 8
33 Hatton, Lincs. ....C 9
18 Hatton, London ....F 1
21 Hatton, Salop. ...C 10
22 Hatton, War. ......E 6
58 Hatton Fintray ....F 6
30 Hatton Heath .....D 3
58 Hattoncrook ......E 6
18 Haultweek ....B 3
50 Haunn ....A 1
22 Haunton ....A 6
9 Hauxley ....C 11
25 Hauxton ....K 5
35 Haugh, Manchester .F 8
47 Haugh, Strathclyde
           G 10
49 Haugh Head ......G 12
58 Haugh of Glass ...D 2
43 Haugh of Urr .....E 9
33 Haugham ....B 10
47 Haughhead ......B 11
27 Haughley ....J 3
22 Haughley Green ...J 3
58 Haughs of Clinterty .F 6
45 Haughterslaw .....A 9
32 Haughton, Notts. ..C 4
21 Haughton, Salop. .A 11
21 Haughton, Salop. .C 12
30 Haughton, Salop. ..G 2
31 Haughton, Staffs. ..H 7
45 Haughton Castle ...F 7
35 Haughton Green ..H 8
30 Haughton Moss ...E 4
9 Havant ....F 8
21 Haven ....G 9
37 Haven Side ....E 10
9 Haven Street .....G 7
36 Havercroft ....F 2
12 Haverfordwest ....E 3
25 Haverhill ....L 8
38 Haverigg ....G 4
18 Havering ....E 5
18 Havering-atte-Bower
           E 5
18 Havering's Grove ..D 6
23 Haversham ......H 11
38 Haverthwaite .....G 6
40 Haverton Hill .....C 5
29 Hawarden ....D 12
19 Hawbush Green ...B 8
13 Hawen ....B 7
39 Hawes ....F 11
22 Hawford ....F 2
44 Hawick ....B 3
31 Hawk Green ......B 8
7 Hawkchurch ......F 7
27 Hawkedon ....K 1
10 Hawkenbury ......D 5
7 Hawkeridge .....A 11
22 Hawkes End ....D 6
15 Hawkesbury .....F 10
15 Hawkesbury Upton
           F 11
45 Hawkhill ....B 10
10 Hawkhurst ....E 6
9 Hawkley ....C 8
6 Hawkridge ....C 2
34 Hawkshaw Lane ...F 6
38 Hawkshead ....E 6
38 Hawkshead Hill ...E 6
32 Hawksland ....A 1
39 Hawkswick ......H 12
32 Hawksworth, Notts. .E 5
35 Hawksworth,
   W. Yorks. ....C 10
18 Hawkwell ....E 8
10 Hawley, Hants. ...A 9
17 Hawley, Kent .....A 9
16 Hawling ....B 2
40 Hawnby ....F 2
35 Haworth ....D 9
27 Hawstead ....J 1
40 Hawthorn, Dur. ...A 4
15 Hawthorn, Wilts. ..A 5
44 Hawthornside .....B 4
24 Hawthorpe ....C 2
32 Hawton ....E 5
36 Haxby ....A 4
36 Haxey ....G 5
10 Haxted ....D 3
21 Hay-on-Wye .....H 8
18 Hay Street ....A 4
12 Haycastle ....D 2
12 Haycastle Cross ...D 3
34 Haydock ....G 4

7 Haydon, Dorset E 10
45 Haydon, Northumb. F 7
45 Haydon Bridge G 7
16 Haydon Wick E 2
3 Haye C 10
18 Hayes, Kent G 4
18 Hayes, London F 1
31 Hayfield, Derby B 9
53 Hayfield, Fife H 7
47 Hayhill H 9
2 Hayle F 3
9 Hayling Island F 8
49 Haymount F 9
6 Hayne F 2
25 Haynes L 2
25 Haynes West End L 2
10 Haysden D 4
53 Hayshead C 11
43 Hayton, Cumb. G 11
44 Hayton, Cumb. G 3
59 Hayton, Grampian G 7
36 Hayton, Humber. C 6
32 Hayton, Notts. B 4
21 Hayton's Bent D 10
5 Haytor Vale H 6
10 Hayward's Heath F 2
32 Haywood Oaks E 3
31 Hazel Grove B 8
48 Hazelbank E 1
7 Hazelbury Bryan E 11
17 Hazeley H 8
22 Hazelslade A 4
53 Hazelton Walls E 8
31 Hazelwood F 11
17 Hazlemere E 10
45 Hazlerigg F 10
16 Hazleton B 2
45 Hazon C 10
24 Heacham B 8
8 Headbourne Worthy C 6
21 Headbrook G 8
11 Headcorn D 7
16 Headington C 6
40 Headlam C 2
22 Headless Cross F 4
9 Headley, Hants. C 9
16 Headley, Hants. H 6
10 Headley, Surrey C 1
9 Headley Down B 10
32 Headon C 5
47 Heads E 12
44 Heads Nook G 3
32 Heage E 1
39 Healaugh, N. Yorks. E 12
36 Healaugh, N. Yorks. B 3
31 Heald Green B 7
4 Heale, Devon A 5
7 Heale, Somerset B 10
35 Healey, Lancs. E 7
45 Healey, Nothumb. G 8
40 Healey, N. Yorks. G 2
45 Healey Cote C 9
45 Healeyfield H 9
37 Healing F 10
2 Heamor G 2
32 Heanor F 2
4 Heanton Punchardon B 4
32 Heapham A 6
48 Hearthstane G 4
4 Heasley Mill C 6
62 Heast F 6
32 Heath C 2
17 Heath and Reach A 10
4 Heath Cross F 7
17 Heath End, Berks. H 7
9 Heath End, Surrey A 10
22 Heath End, W. Midlands B 4
22 Heath Hayes A 4
22 Heath Hill A 1
7 Heath House B 7
6 Heath Pault Cross C 3
22 Heath Town B 3
31 Heathcote D 10
23 Heather A 7
62 Heatherfield D 4
52 Heatheryhaugh B 6
43 Heathfield, Cumb. G 12
5 Heathfield, Devon H 7
10 Heathfield, East Sussex F 4
6 Heathfield, Som. D 5
47 Heathfield, Strathclyde C 8
43 Heathhall D 10
22 Heathton C 2
30 Heatley A 5
34 Heaton, Lancs. A 3
35 Heaton, Manchester H 7
31 Heaton, Staffs. D 8
35 Heaton, W. Yorks. D 10
34 Heaton's Bridge F 3
10 Heaverham B 4
31 Heaviley A 7
6 Heavitree G 3
45 Hebburn G 11
35 Hebden A 9
35 Hebden Bridge D 8
30 Hebden Green D 5
12 Hebron, Dyfed D 5
45 Hebron, Northumb. D 10
43 Heck D 11
17 Heckfield H 8
27 Heckfield Green H 5
24 Heckington A 2
48 Hecklebirnie F 2
35 Heckmondwike E 10
16 Heddington G 1
16 Heddington Wick G 1
4 Heddon C 5
45 Heddon on the Wall F 9
26 Hedenham F 6
5 Hedge Cross G 4
8 Hedge End E 6
17 Hedgerley E 10
6 Hedging C 6
45 Hedley on the Hill G 9
22 Hednesford A 3
37 Hedon D 9
17 Hedsor E 10
21 Hedgon Hill G 11
45 Heiferlaw Bank A 10
40 Heighington, Dur. C 3
33 Heighington, Lincs. C 7
56 Heights of Brae D 1
54 Heights of Kinlochewe C 4
60 Heilam B 5
49 Heiton F 9
6 Hele, Devon F 3
4 Hele, Devon A 4
5 Hele, Devon G 2
6 Hele, Somerset D 5
4 Hele Lane E 7
47 Helensburgh A 8
47 Helentongate F 9
2 Helford G 5
2 Helford Passage G 5
26 Helhoughton C 2
25 Helions Bumpstead L 7
3 Helland C 8
3 Hellandbridge C 8
26 Hellesdon D 5
23 Hellidon F 8
35 Hellifield B 7
10 Helling G 4
26 Hellington E 6
45 Helm C 10
23 Helmdon H 9
27 Helmingham J 5
40 Helmington Row B 2
61 Helmsdale E 10
34 Helmshore E 6
40 Helmsley G 6
40 Helperby H 5
41 Helperthorpe H 9
24 Helpringham B 2
24 Helpston E 2
30 Helsby C 3
2 Helston G 4
3 Helstone B 8
39 Helton C 7
39 Helwith Bridge H 10
17 Hemel Hempstead D 11
36 Hemingbrough D 4
33 Hemingby C 9
36 Hemongfield G 2
25 Hemingford Abbots H 4
25 Hemingford Grey H 4
27 Hemingstone K 5
32 Hemington, Leics. G 2
25 Hemington, Northants. G 2
7 Hemington, Som. A 10
27 Hemley L 6
40 Hemlington D 5
22 Hempholme B 8
26 Hempnall F 5
26 Hempnall Green F 5
25 Hempstead, Essex L 7
10 Hempstead, Kent B 6
26 Hempstead, Norf. B 4
15 Hempsted C 11
26 Hempton, Norfolk C 2
16 Hempton, Oxon. A 5
26 Hemsby D 8
32 Hemswell A 6
36 Hemsworth F 2
6 Hemyock E 5
15 Henbury, Avon F 9
31 Henbury, Ches. C 7
4 Henderbarrow Corner F 3
18 Hendon, London E 2
45 Hendon, Tyne & Wear G 12
15 Hendre C 8
14 Hendreforgan E 3
12 Hendre-wen D 3
13 Hendy G 9
28 Heneglwys C 4
12 Hen-feddau D 6
15 Henfield, Avon F 10
10 Henfield, W. Sussex F 1
11 Hengherst D 8
14 Hengoed, Mid Glam. E 5
21 Hengoed, Powys G 8
30 Hengoed, Salop. G 2
27 Hengrave H 1
18 Henham A 5
45 Henhill E 12
21 Heniarth B 7
6 Henlade D 6
45 Henlaw C 11
7 Henley, Dorset F 10
21 Henley, Salop. D 10
7 Henley, Somerset C 8
27 Henley, Suffolk K 5
9 Henley, W. Sussex D 10
22 Henley-in-Arden E 5
17 Henley-on-Thames F 8
10 Henley Street A 5
29 Henllan, Clwyd C 9
13 Henllan, Dyfed C 7
12 Henllan Amgoed E 5
14 Henllys E 6
25 Henlow L 3
5 Hennock H 7
27 Henny Street L 2
29 Henryd C 7
12 Henry's Moat D 4
36 Hensall E 4
41 Henshaw G 6
38 Hensingham D 2
27 Henstead G 8
7 Henstridge D 10
7 Henstridge Ash D 10
7 Henstridge Bowden D 10
17 Henton, Oxon. D 8
7 Henton, Som. B 8
7 Henstridge Marsh D 11
22 Henwick G 2
3 Henwood B 9
64 Heogan D 7
14 Heol Senni B 3
13 Heol-las G 10
14 Heol-y-Cyw F 3
45 Hepburn A 9
45 Hepple C 8
45 Hepple Whitefield C 8
45 Hepscott E 10
35 Hepstonstall D 8
27 Hepworth, Suff. H 3
35 Hepworth, W. Yorks. F 10
12 Herbrandston F 2
21 Hereford H 10
22 Hereford & Worcester, Co. F 2
48 Heriot D 6
49 Heriot Station D 7
49 Hermiston G 8
16 Hermitage, Berks. G 6
44 Hermitage, Borders C 3
7 Hermitage, Dorset F 10
44 Hermitage, Dumf. & Gall. E 9
9 Hermitage, W. Sussex F 9
13 Hermon, Dyfed D 10
12 Hermon, Dyfed D 5
28 Hermon, Gwynedd C 3
11 Herne B 10
11 Herne Bay A 10
4 Herner C 5
11 Hernhill B 9
3 Herodsfoot D 9
11 Heronden C 11
18 Herongate E 6
42 Heronsford C 2
17 Heronsgate E 11
9 Herriard B 8
26 Herringfleet F 8
25 Herring's Green L 2
25 Herringswell H 8
45 Herrington H 11
11 Hersden B 10
17 Hersham H 12
10 Herstmonceux G 5
8 Herston, Dorset H 2
64 Herston, Orkney Is. E 2
18 Hertford C 3
18 Hertford Heath C 3
18 Hertfordshire, Co. B 2
18 Hertingfordbury C 3
38 Hesket Newmarket A 6
34 Hesketh Bank E 3
34 Hesketh Lane C 5
34 Heskin Green F 4
40 Hesleden A 4
44 Hesleyside E 6
36 Heslington B 4
36 Hessay B 3
3 Hessenford D 10
27 Hessett J 2
47 Hessilhead D 9
37 Hessle E 8
34 Hest Bank A 3
18 Heston F 1
30 Heswall B 1
17 Hethe A 7
26 Hethersett E 5
44 Hethersgill F 3
49 Hethpool G 11
40 Hett B 3
35 Hetton A 8
45 Hetton Downs H 11
45 Hetton Law C 11
45 Hetton Steads B 11
45 Hetton-le-Hole H 11
45 Heugh F 9
58 Heugh-head F 1
27 Heveningham H 6
10 Hever D 4
39 Heversham G 7
26 Hevingham C 5
15 Hewelsfield D 9
15 Hewish, Avon H 7
7 Hewish, Somerset E 7
36 Heworth B 4
45 Hexham G 7
49 Hexpath E 9
10 Hextable A 4
5 Hexworthy H 5
19 Heybridge, Essex C 8
18 Heybridge, Essex D 6
19 Heydridge Basin C 8
5 Heybrook Bay L 4
25 Heydon, Cambs. L 5
26 Heydon, Norfolk C 4
33 Heydour F 7
34 Heysham A 3
35 Heyshaw A 10
9 Heyshott D 10
8 Heytesbury B 1
16 Heythrop A 4
35 Heywood Manchester F 7
7 Heywood, Wilts. A 12
37 Hibaldstow G 7
36 Hickleton G 3
26 Hickling, Norfolk C 7
32 Hickling, Notts. G 4
26 Hickling Green C 7
22 Hidcote Boyce H 5
36 High Ackworth E 2
45 High Angerton E 9
39 High Bankhill A 8
18 High Beach D 4
39 High Bentham H 9
4 High Bickington D 5
39 High Birkwith G 10
47 High Blantyre D 11
48 High Bonnybridge B 1
43 High Borgue F 7
47 High Boydston E 7
35 High Bradley B 9
4 High Bray C 6
10 High Brooms D 5
4 High Bullen D 4
40 High Burton G 2
45 High Buston B 10
45 High Callerton F 10
36 High Catton B 5
45 High Church E 10
47 High Cleughearn E 11
16 High Cogges C 5
40 High Coniscliffe D 3
49 High Cross, Borders E 8
9 High Cross, Hants. C 8
18 High Cross, Herts. B 4
47 High Cross, Strathclyde E 9
31 High Cross Bank H 11
47 High Duncryne A 9
18 High Easter B 6
42 High Eldrig E 3
40 High Ellington G 2
40 High Entercommon E 4
21 High Ercall A 11
40 High Etherley B 2
19 High Garrett A 7
47 High Glengarth D 8
40 High Grange B 2
40 High Grantley H 3
22 High Green, Heref. & Worcs. H 2
26 High Green, Norf. E 4
35 High Green, S. Yorks. G 12
11 High Halden D 8
10 High Halstow A 6
7 High Ham C 8
38 High Harrington C 3
40 High Haswell A 4
30 High Hatton H 5
41 High Hawsker D 9
39 High Hesket A 7
40 High Hesleden A 5
35 High Hoyland F 11
37 High Hursley D 7
10 High Hurstwood E 4
41 High Hutton H 8
38 High Ireby B 5
40 High Kilburn G 5
31 High Lane, Manchester B 8
21 High Lane, Heref. & Worcs. F 12
18 High Laver C 5
30 High Legh B 5
40 High Leven D 5
15 High Littleton H 9
38 High Lorton C 4
41 High Marishes G 8
32 High Marnham C 5
36 High Melton G 3
45 High Mickley G 9
42 High Mindork F 4
41 High Mowthorpe H 9
38 High Newton G 6
45 High Newton by-the-Sea E 12
38 High Nibthwaite F 5
30 High Offley H 6
18 High Ongar D 5
22 High Onn A 2
42 High Pennyvenie A 6
18 High Roding B 6
38 High Row B 6
34 High Salter A 5
39 High Shaw F 11
40 High Skelding H 2
45 High Spen G 9
40 High Stoop A 1
3 High Street, Corn. D 7
27 High Street, Suff. K 7
27 High Street, Suff. K 2
27 High Street Green K 3
40 High Throston B 5
33 High Toynton C 10
45 High Trewhitt B 8
48 High Valleyfield A 3
45 High Warden F 7
38 High Wray E 6
18 High Wych C 5
17 High Wycombe E 9
32 Higham, Derby D 1
10 Higham, Kent A 6
35 Higham, Lancs. D 7
25 Higham, Suffolk J 8
27 Higham, Suffolk L 3
45 Higham Dykes E 9
25 Higham Ferrers H 1
25 Higham Gobion M 2
23 Higham on the Hill C 7
10 Higham Wood C 5
4 Highampton E 4
55 Highbridge, Highland L 6
6 Highbridge, Som. B 6
10 Highbrook E 2
35 Highburton F 10
7 Highbury A 10
44 Highchesters B 3
16 Highclere H 5
8 Highcliffe G 4
7 Higher Alham B 10
7 Higher Ansty F 11
6 Higher Ashton H 2
34 Higher Ballam D 2
2 Higher Boscaswell F 1
6 Higher Combe C 3
2 Higher Crackington B 2
30 Higher Heath G 4
29 Higher Kinnerton D 11
7 Higher Nyland D 10
34 Higher Penwortham D 4
2 Higher Town C 2
30 Higher Walton, Ches. B 4
34 Higher Walton, Lancs. D 5
7 Higher Whatcombe F 11
30 Higher Whitley B 5
30 Higher Wych F 3
4 Highfield, Devon F 6
32 Highfield, S. Yorks. B 1
47 Highfield, Strathclyde D 8
45 Highfield, Tyne & Wear G 9
25 Highfields, Cambs. J 5
49 Highfields, Northumb. D 12
18 Highgate, London E 3
36 Highgate, N. Yorks. E 4
44 Highgreen Manor D 6
40 Highlands, Dur. C 2
58 Highlands, Grampian F 6
32 Highlane B 1
15 Highleadon B 11
9 Highleigh F 9
22 Highley D 1
17 Highmoor Cross F 8
15 Highmoor Hill E 8
15 Highnam Green B 11
4 Highridge D 6
11 Highsted B 8
27 Highstreet Green M 1
27 Hightae D 11
31 Hightown, Ches. D 7
43 Hightown, Dumf. & Gall. C 11
34 Hightown, Merseyside G 2
43 Hightown of Craigs D 11
2 Highway, Corn. E 4
16 Highway, Wilts. G 2
5 Highweek J 7
16 Highworth E 3
26 Hilborough E 1
32 Hilcote D 2
16 Hilcott H 2
10 Hilden Park C 4
10 Hildenborough C 4
25 Hildersham K 6
31 Hilderstone G 8
37 Hilderthorpe A 9
7 Hilfield F 9
24 Hilgay F 7
15 Hill, Avon E 9
4 Hill, Devon E 9
22 Hill, W. Midlands B 5
9 Hill Brow D 9
41 Hill Cottages E 7
34 Hill Dale F 4
33 Hill Dyke E 10
39 Hill End, Dur. B 12
52 Hill End, Fife H 5
15 Hill Gate B 8
9 Hill Head, Hants. F 7
45 Hill Head, Northumb. F 7
38 Hill Millom G 4
12 Hill Mountain F 3
52 Hill of Beath H 6
56 Hill of Fearn B 4
58 Hill of Maud Crofts B 2
31 Hill Ridware H 9
25 Hill Row H 5
8 Hill Top, Hants F 5
35 Hill Top, W. Yorks. F 12
8 Hill View F 1
36 Hillam D 3
39 Hillbeck D 10
38 Hillberry G 2
11 Hillborough A 10
8 Hillbourne G 2
58 Hillbrae E 5
8 Hillbutts F 1
53 Hillcairnie E 8
6 Hillcommon D 5
48 Hillend, Fife A 4
48 Hillend, Strathclyde E 3
15 Hillersland C 9
17 Hillesden A 8
15 Hillesley E 11
6 Hillfarance D 5
5 Hillhead, Devon K 8
43 Hillhead, Dumf. & Gall. B 8
58 Hillhead, Grampian E 5
45 Hillhead, Northumb. B 9
47 Hillhead, Strathclyde F 10
47 Hillhead, Strathclyde G 9
48 Hillhead, Strathclyde E 3
58 Hillhead of Auchentumb B 7
58 Hillhead of Cocklaw C 8
49 Hillhouse D 7
22 Hilliard's Cross A 5
18 Hillingdon F 1
24 Hillington C 8
23 Hillmorton E 8
59 Hillockhead, Grampian G 1
58 Hillockhead, Grampian F 2

9 Hillpound ....D 7
43 Hillside, Dumf. &
   Gall. ....C 12
59 Hillside, Grampian .H 7
64 Hillside, Shetlands ..C 7
59 Hillside, Tayside ....L 4
8 Hillstreet ....D 5
64 Hillswick ....C 6
9 Hillway ....G 8
64 Hillwell ....F 7
16 Hilmarton ....G 1
15 Hilperton ....H 12
15 Hilperton Marsh ..H 11
9 Hilsea ....F 8
37 Hilston ....D 10
25 Hilton ....J 4
49 Hilton, Borders ...D 11
40 Hilton, Cleveland ..D 5
39 Hilton, Cumbria ...C 9
31 Hilton, Derby .....G 11
7 Hilton, Dorset ....F 11
40 Hilton, Durham ....C 2
58 Hilton, Grampian ..D 7
22 Hilton, Salop ....C 1
56 Hilton of Cadboll ..B 4
22 Himbleton ....F 3
22 Himley ....C 2
39 Hincaster ....G 7
16 Hinchwick ....A 2
23 Hinckley ....C 7
27 Hinderclay ....H 3
41 Hinderwell ....D 8
30 Hindford ....G 2
9 Hindhead ....C 10
34 Hindley, Manchester
   ....G 5
45 Hindley, Northumb. G 8
34 Hindley Green ....G 5
22 Hindlip ....F 2
26 Hindolveston ....C 3
7 Hindon ....C 12
26 Hindringham ....B 3
26 Hingham ....E 3
30 Hinstock ....H 5
27 Hintlesham ....L 4
15 Hinton, Avon .....G 10
8 Hinton, Hants. ....G 4
21 Hinton, Heref. &
   Worcs. ....H 9
23 Hinton, Northants. .G 8
21 Hinton, Salop. .....B 9
9 Hinton Ampner ....C 7
7 Hinton Blewett ....A 9
15 Hinton Charterhouse
   ....H 11
22 Hinton Green ......H 4
23 Hinton-in-the-Hedge
   ....H 9
9 Hinton Marsh .....C 7
8 Hinton Martell ....E 2
22 Hinton on the Green
   ....H 4
16 Hinton Parva .....F 3
7 Hinton St. George .E 7
7 Hinton St. Mary ..E 11
16 Hinton Waldrist ...D 5
21 Hints, Salop. ....E 11
22 Hints, Staffs. ....B 5
23 Hinwick ....F 12
11 Hinxhill ....D 9
25 Hinxton ....L 6
25 Hinxworth ....L 3
35 Hipperholme ......E 10
40 Hipswell ....E 2
12 Hiraeth ....E 5
59 Hirn ....G 5
29 Hirnant, Powys ....H 10
20 Hirnant, Powys ....E 4
45 Hirst ....D 11
36 Hirst Courtney ....E 4
29 Hirwaen ....D 10
14 Hirwaun ....D 3
4 Hiscott ....C 4
25 Histon ....J 5
27 Hitcham ....K 3
43 Hitchill ....E 12
18 Hitchin ....A 2
18 Hither Green ......F 4
4 Hittisleigh Cross ..F 6
36 Hive ....D 6
31 Hixon ....H 8
11 Hoaden ....B 11
31 Hoaldalbert ....B 7
31 Hoar Cross ....H 10
15 Hoarwithy ....A 8
11 Hoath ....B 10
21 Hobarris ....E 8
64 Hobbister ....D 2
18 Hobbs Cross ....D 5
44 Hobkirk ....B 4
45 Hobson ....G 10
32 Hoby ....H 4
26 Hockering ....D 4
32 Hockerton ....E 4

19 Hockley ....E 8
22 Hockley Heath ....E 5
17 Hockliffe ....A 10
25 Hockwold cum Wilton
   ....G 8
6 Hockworthy ....D 4
18 Hoddesdon ....C 4
34 Hoddlesden ....E 6
43 Hoddomcross .....D 12
12 Hodgeston ....G 4
30 Hodnet ....G 5
10 Hodsoll Street .....B 5
36 Hodson ....F 3
32 Hodthorpe ....C 3
9 Hoe, Hampshire ...D 7
26 Hoe, Norfolk ......D 3
9 Hoe Gate ....E 8
39 Hoff ....C 9
17 Hoggeston ....B 9
34 Hoghton ....E 5
31 Hognaston ....E 11
33 Hogsthorpe ....C 12
24 Holbeach ....C 5
24 Holbeach Bank ....C 5
24 Holbeach Clough ..C 4
24 Holbeach Drove ...D 4
24 Holbeach Hurn ....C 5
24 Holbeach St. Johns .C 4
24 Holbeach St. Marks .C 5
24 Holbeach St. Matthew
   ....B 5
32 Holbeck, Notts. ...C 3
35 Holbeck, W. Yorks.
   ....D 11
22 Holberrow Green ..F 4
5 Holbeton ....L 5
31 Holbrook, Derby .F 12
27 Holbrook, Suffolk .L 5
8 Holbury ....F 6
45 Holburn ....B 11
5 Holcombe, Devon ..H 8
34 Holcombe,
   Manchester ....E 6
7 Holcombe, Som. ..A 10
34 Holcombe Brook ..F 6
6 Holcombe Rogus ..D 4
23 Holcot ....E 11
34 Holden ....B 6
23 Holdenby ....E 10
8 Holdenhurst ....G 3
21 Holdgate ....C 11
33 Holdingham ....E 7
7 Holditch ....F 7
49 Holefield ....F 10
47 Holehouse,
   Strathclyde ....H 9
47 Holehouse,
   Strathclyde ....D 8
15 Hole-in-the-Wall ...A 9
43 Holestane ....B 9
6 Holford ....B 5
38 Holker ....G 6
26 Holkham ....A 2
4 Hollacombe ....F 2
64 Holland, Papa Westray
   Orkney Is. ....A 3
64 Holland, Stronsay,
   Orkney, Is. ....C 4
33 Holland Fen ....E 9
19 Holland-on-Sea ..B 11
64 Hollandstoun ......A 4
44 Hollee ....F 1
27 Hollesley ....L 6
11 Hollingbourne .....C 7
10 Hollingrove ....F 6
31 Hollington, Derby F 10
10 Hollington, E. Sussex
   ....G 6
31 Hollington, Staffs. .F 9
35 Hollingworth ......G 8
35 Hollins ....F 7
30 Hollins Green .....A 5
34 Hollins Lane ......B 4
31 Hollinsclough .....D 9
4 Hollocombe ....E 5
22 Hollow Court ......F 3
31 Hollow Meadows ..A 11
31 Holloway ....E 11
23 Hollowell ....E 10
44 Hollows ....E 2
31 Holly Bush, Clwyd .F 3
14 Holly Bush, Gwent .D 5
24 Holly End ....E 6
21 Holly Green ....H 2
15 Hollybush, Heref. &
   Worcs. ....A 10
47 Hollybush,
   Strathclyde ....H 9
31 Hollym ....E 11
22 Hollywood ....D 4
44 Holm, Dumf. & Gall.
   ....C 1
63 Holm, W. Isles ...D 5
43 Holm St. Cuthbert .G 12

4 Holmacott ....C 4
35 Holmbridge ......F 10
9 Holmbury St. Mary
   ....B 12
3 Holmbush ....D 7
31 Holmcroft ....H 8
25 Holme, Cambs. ...G 3
39 Holme, Cumbria ..G 7
37 Holme, Humber. ...F 7
40 Holme, N. Yorks. ..G 4
32 Holme, Notts. .....D 5
35 Holme, W. Yorks. ..F 9
35 Holme Chapel .....D 7
26 Holme Hale ....E 2
15 Holme Lacy ....A 9
21 Holme Marsh ......G 9
24 Holme next the Sea .A 8
37 Holme on the Wolds C 7
32 Holme Pierrepont ..F 3
36 Holm upon Spalding
   Moor ....C 6
21 Holmer ....H 10
17 Holmer Green ....D 10
30 Holmes Chapel ....C 6
31 Holmesfield ....B 11
34 Holmeswood ....E 3
32 Holmewood ....D 2
35 Holmfirth ....F 10
43 Holmfoot ....B 9
47 Holmhead ....G 10
62 Holmisdal ....C 1
37 Holmpton ....E 11
38 Holmrook ....E 3
45 Holmside ....H 10
44 Holmwrangle ....H 4
5 Holne ....J 6
4 Holsworthy ....F 2
4 Holsworthy Beacon .E 2
30 Holt, Clwyd ....E 3
8 Holt, Dorset ......F 2
26 Holt, Norfolk .....B 4
15 Holt, Wilts. ......H 11
22 Holts, Heref. &
   Worcs. ....F 2
9 Holt End, Hants. ..B 8
22 Holt End, Heref. &
   Worcs. ....E 4
22 Holt Heath ....F 2
8 Holt Wood ....E 2
36 Holtby ....B 4
33 Holton, Lincs. ....B 8
17 Holton, Oxon. .....G 7
7 Holton, Som. ....D 10
27 Holton, Suffolk ...H 7
8 Holton Heath .....G 1
37 Holton le Clay ...G 10
37 Holton le Moor ...G 8
27 Holton St. Mary ...L 4
10 Holtye ....D 3
7 Holwell, Dorset ..H 10
18 Holwell, Herts. ...A 2
32 Holwell, Leics. ...H 5
16 Holwell, Oxon. ....C 3
29 Holwick ....C 11
7 Holworth ....H 11
22 Holy Cross ....D 3
45 Holy Island ......B 12
9 Holybourne ....B 9
28 Holyhead ....B 2
31 Holymoorside ....C 11
17 Holyport ....F 10
45 Holystone ....C 8
47 Holytown ....C 12
25 Holywell, Cambs. ..H 4
29 Holywell, Clwyd ..C 11
2 Holywell, Corn. ...D 5
44 Holywell, Cumb. ..E 3
7 Holywell, Dorset ..F 2
45 Holywell, Northumb.
   ....F 11
35 Holywell Green ...E 10
6 Holywell Lake .....D 5
25 Holywell Row .....H 8
43 Holywood ....C 10
15 Hom Green ....B 9
49 Homebank ....E 10
49 Homebyres ....E 9
21 Homer ....B 11
27 Homersfield ......G 6
8 Homington ....D 3
11 Honey Hill ....B 10
16 Honey Street ......H 2
27 Honey Tye ....L 2
12 Honeyborough .....F 2
4 Honeychurch ......F 5
22 Honiley ....E 6
26 Honing ....C 6
26 Honingham ....D 4
32 Honington, Lincs. ..E 6
27 Honington, Suff. ..H 2
22 Honington, War. ..H 6
6 Honiton ....F 5
35 Honley ....F 10
10 Hoo ....A 6

22 Hoobrook ....E 2
35 Hood Green ......G 11
5 Hooe, Devon ......K 4
10 Hooe, E. Sussex ..G 6
10 Hooe Common .....G 6
12 Hook, Dyfed ......F 3
9 Hook, Hants. ......A 8
36 Hook, Humber. ....E 5
18 Hook, London .....G 2
16 Hook, Wilts. ......A 8
10 Hook Green, Kent .A 5
10 Hook Green, Kent ..D 5
16 Hook Norton ......A 4
7 Hooke ....F 9
30 Hookgate ....G 6
4 Hookway ....F 7
10 Hookwood ....D 2
30 Hoole ....C 3
31 Hooley ....B 2
30 Hooton ....B 2
32 Hooton Levitt .....A 2
31 Hooton Pagnell ...F 3
36 Hooton Roberts ...G 3
64 Hoove ....D 7
5 Hop Pole ....D 3
31 Hope, Derby .....B 10
5 Hope, Devon .....M 5
29 Hope, Clwyd ....D 12
60 Hope, Highland ...B 5
21 Hope, Powys ......B 8
21 Hope, Salop. .....B 10
21 Hope Bagot .....E 11
21 Hope Bowdler ...C 10
24 Hope Mansell .....A 9
21 Hope under Dinmore
   ....G 10
56 Hopeman ....C 7
21 Hopesay ....D 9
36 Hopperton ....B 2
16 Hopton, Derby ...E 11
31 Hopton, Salop. ...G 4
31 Hopton, Staffs. ...H 8
26 Hopton, Suffolk ...E 8
27 Hopton, Suffolk ...G 3
21 Hopton Cangeford
   ....D 11
21 Hopton Castle ....E 9
21 Hopton Wafers ..E 11
21 Hoptonheath ......E 9
22 Hopwas ....B 5
22 Hopwood ....E 4
10 Horam ....F 4
24 Horbling ....B 2
35 Horbury ....E 11
40 Horden ....A 5
21 Horderley ....D 9
4 Hordle ....F 4
30 Hordley ....G 2
5 Hordon ....H 4
13 Horeb, Dyfed .....C 7
13 Horeb, Dyfed .....D 8
15 Horfield ....F 9
21 Horham ....H 5
19 Horkesley Heath ..A 9
37 Horkstow ....E 7
22 Horley, Oxon. ....H 7
10 Horley, Surrey ...D 2
7 Hornblotton Grn. ..C 9
39 Hornby, Lancs. ...H 8
40 Hornby, N. Yorks. ..F 2
40 Hornby, N. Yorks. ..E 4
33 Horncastle ....C 9
18 Hornchurch ....E 5
49 Horncliffe ....D 11
49 Horndean, Borders
   ....D 11
9 Horndean, Hants. ..E 8
18 Horndon on the Hill
   ....F 6
10 Horne ....D 2
6 Horner ....B 3
26 Horning ....D 6
23 Horninghold .....B 11
31 Horninglow ......H 10
25 Horningsea ....J 6
7 Horningsham .....B 11
26 Horningtoft ......C 2
3 Horningtops .....D 9
4 Horns Cross, Devon
   ....D 3
11 Horns Cross,
   E. Sussex ....F 7
32 Hornsby ....H 3
37 Hornsea ....B 9
37 Hornsea Bridge ...B 9
18 Hornsey ....A 3
23 Hornton ....H 7
5 Horrabridge ......J 4
21 Horringer ....J 1
9 Horringford ......H 7
48 Horsburgh ....E 6
31 Horse Bridge .....E 8
8 Horsebridge ......C 5
22 Horsebrook ....A 2

15 Horsecastle ......H 7
21 Horsehay ....B 12
25 Horseheath ....K 7
39 Horsehouse ......G 12
17 Horsell ....H 10
30 Horseman's Grn. ..F 3
17 Horsenden ....D 9
26 Horsey ....C 8
26 Horsford ....D 5
35 Horsforth ....C 11
22 Horsham, Heref. &
   Worcs. ....F 1
10 Horsham, W. Sussex
   ....E 1
26 Horsham St. Faith .D 5
33 Horsington, Lincs. .C 9
7 Horsington, Som. .D 10
32 Horsley, Derby ....F 1
15 Horsley, Glos. ....E 11
45 Horsley, Northumb. .C 7
45 Horsley, Northumb. .F 9
19 Horsley Cross ....A 11
32 Horsley Woodhouse .F 1
19 Horsleycross St. ..A 11
49 Horsleyhill ....G 8
10 Horsmonden ....D 6
17 Horspath ....D 7
26 Horstead ....D 5
10 Horsted Keynes ...E 3
15 Horton, Avon ....F 10
21 Horton, Bucks. ..B 10
17 Horton, Bucks. ..F 11
8 Horton, Dorset ....E 2
35 Horton, Lancs. ....B 7
23 Horton, Northants.
   ....G 11
6 Horton, Somerset ..E 6
31 Horton, Staffs. ...D 8
16 Horton, Wilts. ....H 2
13 Horton, W. Glam. .H 8
7 Horton Cross .....E 7
30 Horton Green .....E 3
8 Horton Heath .....D 6
39 Horton in Ribblesdale
   ....H 10
10 Horton Kirby .....A 4
34 Horwich ....F 5
4 Horwood ....C 4
44 Hoscote ....B 2
32 Hose ....G 5
49 Hoselaw ....F 10
38 Hoses ....F 5
64 Hoswick ....E 7
37 Hotham ....D 7
11 Hothfield ....D 8
32 Hoton ....H 3
44 Hott ....D 6
64 Houbie ....B 8
30 Hough ....E 6
30 Hough Green ......B 3
32 Hough-on-the-Hill ..F 6
32 Hougham ....F 6
25 Houghton, Cambs. .H 4
44 Houghton, Cumb. ..G 2
12 Houghton, Dyfed ..F 3
8 Houghton, Hants. ..C 5
9 Houghton, W. Sussex
   ....E 11
25 Houghton Conquest .L 2
30 Houghton Green ...A 5
17 Houghton Regis ..B 11
45 Houghton-le-Spring
   ....H 11
23 Houghton on the Hill
   ....B 10
41 Houlsyke ....D 7
8 Hound ....D 6
17 Hound Green .....H 8
49 Houndridge ......F 10
49 Houndslow ....E 9
6 Houndsmoor ......D 5
49 Houndwood ......C 11
8 Hounsdown ....E 5
18 Hounslow ....F 2
64 Housay ....C 8
59 House of Glenmuick
   ....H 1
58 Housieside ....E 6
47 Houston ....C 9
61 Houstry ....D 10
61 Hove ....H 2
32 Hoveringham ......E 4
26 Hoveton ....D 6
37 Hovingham ....H 7
44 How ....G 3
16 How Caple ....A 9
10 How Green ....C 4
38 How Head ....E 6
45 Howbrook ....G 11
49 Howburn ....F 10
49 Howden, Borders ..G 9
36 Howden, Humber. ..D 5
35 Howden Clough ..D 11
40 Howden-le-Wear ..B 2

39 Howe, Cumbria ....F 5
61 Howe, Highland ...B 12
26 Howe, Norfolk .....E 6
19 Howe Green ....D 7
58 Howe of Teucher ..C 5
19 Howe Street, Essex .B 7
25 Howe Street, Essex .M 8
33 Howell ....F 8
43 Howes ....E 12
20 Howey ....F 6
48 Howford ....F 6
48 Howgate, Lothian ..D 5
48 Howgate, Strathclyde
   ....F 2
45 Howick ....A 10
16 Howle ....H 5
15 Howle Hill ....B 9
25 Howlett End ......M 7
6 Howley ....E 6
49 Howliston ....D 7
49 Hownam ....G 10
49 Hownam Mains ..G 10
44 Howpasley ....B 2
37 Howsham, Humber. G 8
36 Howsham, N. Yorks.
   ....A 5
49 Howtel ....F 11
64 Howth ....D 2
15 Howton ....A 7
39 Howtown ....C 7
47 Howwood ....C 9
64 Hoxa ....E 2
27 Hoxne ....G 5
30 Hoylake ....A 5
35 Hoylake Nether ...G 12
35 Hoylake Swaine ...G 11
15 Hubberston ....F 2
24 Hubbert's Bridge ..A 4
36 Huby, N. Yorks. ....A 3
35 Huby, N. Yorks. ..B 11
15 Hucclecote ....C 12
11 Hucking ....B 7
32 Hucknall ....E 3
35 Huddersfield ......E 10
22 Huddington ....F 3
40 Hudswell ....A 2
36 Huggate ....B 6
2 Hugh Town ....D 2
17 Hughenden Valley ..D 9
21 Hughley ....C 11
4 Huish, Devon .....E 4
16 Huish, Wilts. .....H 2
6 Huish Barton ......B 4
6 Huish Champflower .C 4
7 Huish Episcopi ....B 9
17 Hulcott ....B 9
31 Hulland ....F 11
31 Hulland Ward ....E 11
15 Hullavington .....F 12
19 Hullbridge ....D 8
31 Hulme End ....D 9
31 Hulme Walfield ...D 7
34 Hulton Lane Ends .G 6
27 Hulver Street .....G 8
8 Hulverstone ......H 5
37 Humber Court ...G 11
37 Humberside, Co. ...C 7
37 Humberston .....G 10
37 Humberstone ....B 10
49 Humbie ....C 7
37 Humbleton, Humber.
   ....D 10
49 Humbleton,
   Northumb. ....G 12
49 Hume ....E 9
47 Humeston ....H 7
45 Humshaugh ....F 7
61 Huna ....A 12
34 Huncoat ....D 6
23 Huncote ....B 8
49 Hundalee ....G 9
39 Hunderthwaite ...C 12
33 Hundleby ....D 11
12 Hundleton ....G 3
25 Hundon ....K 8
9 Hundred Acres ....E 7
34 Hundred End ......E 3
21 Hundred House ...G 7
23 Hungarton ....A 10
34 Hunger Hill ....F 5
16 Hungerford, Berks. .G 4
8 Hungerford, Hants. .E 3
16 Hungerford Newton G 5
32 Hungerton ....F 6
62 Hunglader ....A 3
63 Hunisish ....F 1
41 Hunmanby ....G 11
23 Hunningham ......E 7
21 Hunny Hill ....G 6
18 Hunsdon ....C 4
36 Hunsingore ....B 2
35 Hunslett Carr ...D 11
35 Hunsonby ....B 8
61 Hunspow ....A 11

24 Hunstanton ......B 8
45 Hunstanworth ....H 8
27 Hunston, Suffolk ..H 3
9 Hunston, W. Sussex F 10
15 Hunstrete ....H 9
35 Hunsworth ......D 10
22 Hunt End ....F 4
41 Hunt Ho ....E 7
47 Hunter's Quay ....B 7
49 Huntershall .....F 10
47 Hunterston Works ..D 7
44 Huntford ....B 5
59 Hunthill Lodge ...K 2
25 Huntingdon, Cambs. H 3
22 Huntingdon, Staffs. .A 3
27 Huntingfield ......H 6
21 Huntington,
    Heref. & Worcs. ..G 8
21 Huntington,
    Heref. & Worcs. .H 10
36 Huntington, N. Yorks. B 4
52 Huntingtower Haugh E 5
15 Huntley, Glos. ...B 10
31 Huntley, Staffs. ...F 8
58 Huntly ....D 3
49 Huntlywood ......E 9
10 Hunton, Kent .....C 6
40 Hunton, N. Yorks. ..F 2
17 Hunton Bridge ...D 11
30 Hunt's Cross ......B 3
6 Huntscott ....B 3
6 Huntsham ....D 3
6 Huntspill ....B 6
7 Huntworth ....C 7
40 Hunwick ....B 2
26 Hunworth ....B 4
7 Hurcott ....E 7
40 Hurdcott ....C 3
17 Hurley, Berks. ....F 9
22 Hurley, War. ......C 9
47 Hurlford ....F 9
64 Hurliness ....E 1
8 Hurn ....F 3
31 Hursdfield ....C 8
8 Hursley ....D 6
17 Hurst, Berks......G 9
35 Hurst, Manchester ..G 8
40 Hurst, N. Yorks. ..E 1
7 Hurst, Somerset ...D 8
10 Hurst Green,
    E. Sussex ......E 6
34 Hurst Green, Lancs. .C 6
10 Hurst Green, Surrey C 3
10 Hurst Wickham ...F 2
8 Hurstbourne Priors .A 6
8 Hurstbourne Tarrant A 5
21 Hurstley ....G 9
10 Hurstpierpoint ....F 2
21 Hurstway Com......G 8
40 Hurtmore ....B 11
40 Hurworth ....D 3
39 Hury ....C 11
62 Husabost Piers ....C 1
23 Husbands Bosworth D 10
25 Husborne Crawley ..L 1
40 Husthwaite ....H 5
32 Huthwaite ....D 2
49 Hutlertown ......G 7
33 Huttoft ....C 12
15 Hutton, Avon .....H 7
49 Hutton, Borders ..D 11
39 Hutton, Cumb. ....C 7
18 Hutton, Essex ....D 6
37 Hutton, Humber. ..B 8
34 Hutton, Lancs. ...D 4
41 Hutton Buscel ....G 9
40 Hutton Conyers ..H 3
39 Hutton End ....A 7
40 Hutton Hang ......F 2
40 Hutton Henry .....B 4
39 Hutton-in-the-Forest B 7
39 Hutton John ......C 7
41 Hutton-le-Hole ...F 7
40 Hutton Lowcross ..D 6
40 Hutton Magna ....D 2
38 Hutton Roof, Cumb. B 6
39 Hutton Roof, Cumbria G 8
40 Hutton Rudby ....E 5
40 Hutton Sessay ....H 5
36 Hutton Wandesley ..B 3
4 Huxford ....D 6
6 Huxham ....F 3
30 Huxley ....D 4
64 Huxter ....D 7

30 Huyton ....A 3
38 Hycemoor ....F 3
15 Hyde, Glos. ......D 12
35 Hyde, Manchester ..H 8
17 Hyde Heath ......D 10
31 Hyde Lea ....H 7
9 Hydestile ....B 11
38 Hydro ....F 2
48 Hyndford ....E 2
21 Hyssington ....C 8
8 Hythe, Hants. ....E 5
11 Hythe, Kent ......E 10
7 Hythe, Somerset ..A 8
17 Hythe End ....G 11
58 Hythie ....C 7
58 Ianstown ....A 2
7 Ibberton ....E 11
31 Ible ....D 11
8 Ibsley ....E 3
23 Ibstock ....A 7
17 Ibstone ....E 8
8 Ibthorpe ....A 5
9 Ibworth ....A 7
15 Icelton ....H 7
26 Ickburgh ....F 1
18 Ickenham ....E 1
17 Ickford ....C 7
11 Ickham ....B 11
18 Ickleford ....A 2
25 Ickleton ....L 6
27 Icklingham ......H 1
25 Ickwell Green ...L 3
16 Icomb ....B 3
16 Idbury ....B 3
4 Iddesleigh ......E 4
2 Ide ....G 2
10 Ide Hill ....C 4
5 Ideford ....H 8
11 Iden ....F 8
10 Iden Green, Kent ..D 6
11 Iden Green, Kent ..E 7
35 Idle ....C 10
22 Idlicote ....H 6
13 Idole ....E 7
31 Idridgehay ......E 11
62 Idrigil ....B 3
16 Idstone ....F 4
53 Idvies ....B 10
10 Ifield ....D 1
9 Ifold ....C 11
10 Iford ....G 3
15 Ifton ....E 8
30 Ifton Heath .....G 2
30 Ightfield ....F 5
10 Ightham ....B 5
27 Iken ....K 7
31 Ilam ....E 10
7 Ilchester ....D 8
49 Ilderton ....G 12
18 Ilford ....E 4
4 Ilfracombe ......A 4
32 Ilkeston ....F 2
27 Ilketshall St. Andrew G 6
27 Ilketshall St. Margaret G 2
35 Ilkley ....B 9
35 Illingworth .....D 9
22 Illey ....D 3
2 Illogan ....E 4
2 Illogan Highway ..E 4
23 Illston on the Hill ..B 10
17 Ilmer ....D 8
22 Ilmington ....H 5
7 Ilminster ....E 7
5 Ilsington ....H 5
11 Ilston ....H 9
40 Ilton, N. Yorks. ..G 2
7 Ilton, Somerset ..D 7
46 Imachar ....E 6
37 Immingham ......F 9
37 Immingham Dock ..F 9
25 Impington ....J 5
55 Inbhireala or
    Strathossian Ho. .M 8
30 Ince ....C 3
34 Ince Blundell ....G 2
34 Ince-in-Makerfield ..G 2
59 Inch ....K 4
54 Inchbae Lodge ...C 8
59 Inchbare ....L 3
47 Inchbean ....F 9
58 Inchberry ....B 1
53 Incheoch ....B 7
60 Inchina ....G 2
47 Inchinnan ....B 9
60 Inchkinloch .....C 6
55 Inchlaggan ......J 5
56 Inchlumpie .....B 1
59 Inchnabobart ....J 1
55 Inchnacardoch (Hotel) H 7
60 Inchnadamph ....E 4

57 Inchrory ....J 7
53 Inchture ....D 7
54 Inchvuilt ....F 6
52 Inchyra ....E 6
2 Indian Queens ...D 6
4 Indicott ....B 4
18 Ingatestone ......D 6
35 Ingbirchworth ...G 10
31 Ingestre ....H 8
32 Ingham, Lincs. ...B 6
26 Ingham, Norfolk ..C 7
27 Ingham, Suffolk ..H 2
24 Ingleborough, Norfolk D 6
39 Ingleborough,
    N. Yorks. ......H 10
31 Ingleby ....G 12
40 Ingleby Arncliffe ..E 5
40 Ingleby Cross ....E 5
40 Ingleby Greenhow ..E 6
15 Inglesbatch .....H 10
16 Inglesham ....D 3
40 Ingleton, Durham .C 2
39 Ingleton, N. Yorks. .H 9
34 Inglewhite ....C 4
45 Ingoe ....F 8
33 Ingoldmells .....C 12
33 Ingoldsby ....G 7
24 Ingoldsthorpe ...B 8
45 Ingram ....A 8
18 Ingrave ....E 6
35 Ingrow ....C 9
39 Ings ....E 7
15 Ingst ....E 9
26 Ingworth ....C 5
51 Inistrynich ......A 8
38 Injebreck ....G 2
22 Inkberrow ....F 4
16 Inkpen ....H 4
61 Inkstack ....A 11
46 Inellan ....B 6
48 Innerleithen .....F 6
53 Innerleven ......G 8
42 Innermessan .....E 2
42 Innerwell Fishery ..G 6
49 Innerwick, Lothian B 10
52 Innerwick, Tayside ..B 1
51 Innis Chonain ....E 8
51 Innischoarach ...D 12
58 Insch ....E 4
58 Inschtammack ...C 2
57 Insh ....J 4
57 Insh House ......J 4
51 Inshaig ....B 7
60 Inshore ....A 4
34 Inskip ....C 3
4 Instow ....C 3
35 Intake Gate .....C 10
57 Inver, Grampian ..K 8
56 Inver, Highland ..B 4
52 Inver, Tayside ...C 5
54 Inver Alligin ....D 2
55 Inver Mallie .....K 5
55 Inverailort ......L 1
58 Inverallochy .....A 8
60 Inveran ....G 8
51 Inverarnan ......F 10
54 Inverasdale .....A 2
53 Inverarity ....C 9
51 Inverarnan ......F 10
54 Inverbain ....D 2
51 Inverbeg Hotel ..H 10
59 Inverbervie .....K 6
60 Inverboyndie ....A 4
60 Inverbroom ......H 3
57 Invercauld House ..K 7
46 Inverchaolain ...B 6
46 Inverchapel .....A 6
54 Invercharnan ....C 8
54 Inverchoran .....E 6
51 Invercreran .....C 7
57 Inverdruie ......H 5
58 Inverebrie ......D 7
57 Inveredrie ......M 7
57 Invereshie House ..J 4
48 Inveresk ....B 6
51 Inveresragan ....D 7
57 Inverewe House ..B 2
57 Inverey ....K 6
57 Inverfarigaig ....G 1
57 Invergarry ....J 7
52 Invergeldie .....D 2
55 Invergloy ....L 6
57 Invergordon .....D 3
53 Invergowrie .....D 8
55 Inverguseran .....J 1
55 Inverhadden .....A 2
58 Inverharroch ....D 1
51 Inverherive .....E 10
55 Inverie ....J 1
51 Inverinan ....F 7
55 Inverinate ......G 3
53 Inverkeilor ......B 11

48 Inverkeithing ....A 4
58 Inverkeithny .....C 4
47 Inverkip ....B 7
60 Inverkirkaig .....E 2
60 Inverlael ....H 3
60 Inverlael Lodge ..H 3
51 Inverlair ....L 7
51 Inverlochlarig ...F 11
51 Inverlochy ......E 9
55 Invermark Lodge ..J 2
55 Invermoriston ...H 8
58 Invernan House ..F 1
56 Invernaver ......B 7
56 Inverness ....E 2
58 Invernetie ......C 8
58 Inveroran Hotel ..C 10
60 Inverpolly Lodge ..E 2
55 Inverroy ....L 6
50 Inversanda ......B 7
51 Invershiel ......H 3
60 Invershin ....G 6
60 Invershin Station ..G 6
55 Inverskilavulin ..L 5
51 Inversnaid Hotel ..G 10
58 Inverugie, Grampian C 8
56 Inverugie, Grampian C 7
51 Inveruglas ......G 10
57 Inveruglass ......J 4
58 Inverurie ....E 5
58 Invervar ....B 2
59 Invery House ....H 4
58 Inverwick ....C 5
4 Inwardleigh .....F 4
19 Inworth ....B 8
9 Iping ....D 10
18 Ipplepen ....J 7
18 Ippollits ....A 2
27 Ipsden ....F 7
31 Ipstones ....E 8
27 Ipswich ....L 5
33 Irby ....B 6
33 Irby in the Marsh .D 11
37 Irby Upon Humber .G 9
39 Irchester ....E 12
39 Ireby ....H 9
38 Ireleth ....G 5
39 Ireshopeburn ....A 11
55 Irine ....L 1
34 Irlam ....H 6
31 Irnham ....G 7
15 Iron Acton ....F 10
21 Iron Bridge .....B 12
22 Iron Cross ......G 4
60 Ironmacannie ...D 7
32 Ironville ....E 2
26 Irstead ....C 7
44 Irthington ......G 3
39 Irthlingborough ..E 12
44 Irton ....G 10
47 Irvine ....E 8
44 Irvington ....F 1
61 Isauld ....A 9
64 Isbister, Orkney ..C 2
64 Isbister, Zetland ..B 7
64 Isbister, Zetland ..C 8
10 Isfield ....F 3
23 Isham ....E 12
50 Ishriff ....D 4
7 Isle Abbots .....D 7
7 Isle Brewers ....D 7
18 Isle of Dogs .....F 4
42 Isle of Whithorn ..H 6
25 Isleham ....H 7
62 Isleornsay ......G 6
43 Islesteps ....D 10
18 Isleworth ....F 2
32 Isley Walton ....H 2
18 Islington ....E 3
25 Islip, Northants. ..G 1
16 Islip, Oxon. .....C 6
63 Islivig ....D 1
8 Itchen ....E 6
7 Itchen Abbas ...C 7
9 Itchen Stoke ....C 7
9 Itchingfield ....C 12
9 Itchington ......F 10
26 Itteringham .....C 4
15 Itton Common ...E 8
18 Ivegill ....A 6
39 Ivelet ....E 11
17 Iver ....F 11
17 Iver Heath ......F 11
45 Iveston ....H 9
17 Ivinghoe ....B 10
17 Ivinghoe Aston ..B 10
21 Ivington ....G 10
21 Ivington Green ..G 10
10 Ivy Hatch ....C 5
5 Ivybridge ....K 5
11 Ivychurch ......E 9

11 Iwade ....A 7
7 Iwerne Courtney or
    Shroton ....E 12
7 Iwerne Minster ..E 12
27 Ixworth ....H 2
27 Ixworth Thorpe ..H 2
35 Jack Hill ....B 10
32 Jacksdale ....E 2
58 Jackstown ....D 5
47 Jackton ....D 10
4 Jacobstow ....B 2
4 Jacobstowe ......F 5
9 Jacobswell ......A 11
12 Jameston ....G 4
44 Jamestown, Dumf. &
    Gall. ....C 1
54 Jamestown, Highland D 8
47 Jamestown,
    Strathclyde ....A 9
61 Janetstown .....D 11
45 Jarrow ....F 11
10 Jarvis Brook ....E 4
19 Jasper's Green ..A 7
48 Jawcraig ....B 1
19 Jaywick Sands ..C 11
17 Jealott's Hill ...G 9
40 Jeater Houses ...F 4
49 Jedburgh ....G 9
12 Jeffreston ......F 4
56 Jemimaville .....C 3
13 Jersey Marine ..H 10
59 Jessiefield .....G 6
17 Jevington ....H 4
17 Jockey End ......C 11
30 Jodrell Bank ....C 6
35 John O'Gaunts ..D 12
61 John o'Groats ...A 12
38 Johnby ....B 6
10 John's Cross ....F 6
59 Johnshaven .....K 6
12 Johnston ....F 3
44 Johnstone, Dumf. &
    Gall. ....C 1
47 Johnstone,
    Strathclyde .....C 9
43 Johnstonebridge ..B 11
29 Johnstown, Clwyd .F 12
13 Johnstown, Dyfed .E 7
20 Joppa, Dyfed ....F 1
48 Joppa, Lothian ..B 6
17 Jordans ....E 10
12 Jordanston ......D 3
19 Jordons ....E 8
35 Jump ....G 12
8 Jumpers Green ..G 3
48 Juniper Green ...B 5
38 Jurby East ......F 2
38 Jurby West ......F 2
44 Justicetown .....G 2
35 Kaber ....D 10
58 Kaecloch ....C 4
48 Kaimes ....C 5
49 Kalemouth ......G 9
54 Kalnakill ....D 1
46 Kames, Strathclyde ..B 5
50 Kames, Strathclyde ..F 5
47 Kames, Strathclyde G 11
36 Keadby ....F 6
33 Keal Cotes ......D 10
34 Kearsley ....G 6
39 Kearstwick ......G 8
39 Kearton ....E 12
60 Kearvaig ....A 4
39 Keasden ....H 9
33 Keddington .....A 10
31 Kedington ......K 8
31 Kedleston ....F 11
49 Kedslie ....E 8
37 Keelby ....F 9
25 Keeley Green ....L 1
45 Keepershield ....F 7
15 Keeston ....E 3
15 Keevil ....H 12
32 Kegworth ....G 2
2 Kehelland ....F 3
58 Keig ....F 3
35 Keighley ....C 9
51 Keil ....B 7
56 Keilarsbrae ....H 4
58 Keilhill ....B 5
46 Keillmore ....A 2
52 Keillour ....E 5
7 Keinton Mandeville ..C 3
43 Keir Mill ....B 9
24 Keisby ....F 1
61 Keiss ....B 12
58 Keith ....C 2
58 Keithen ....C 4
35 Kelbrook ....C 8
33 Kelby ....F 7
39 Keld, Cumbria ..D 8

39 Keld, N. Yorks. ..E 11
41 Keldholme ....F 7
41 Keldy Castle .....F 8
36 Kelfield ....C 4
32 Kelham ....E 5
43 Kelhead ....E 12
50 Kellan ....C 3
56 Kellas, Grampian ..D 7
53 Kellas, Tayside ..D 9
5 Kellaton ....M 7
16 Kellaways ....G 1
39 Kelleth ....E 9
21 Kelling ....A 4
36 Kellingley ......E 3
36 Kellington ......E 3
40 Kelloe ....B 4
49 Kelloe Mains ...D 11
5 Kelly ....H 3
3 Kelly Bray ......C 10
23 Kelmarsh ....D 10
16 Kelmscot ....D 3
27 Kelsale ....J 7
30 Kelsall ....C 4
30 Kelsall Hill .....C 4
25 Kelshall ....L 4
43 Kelsick ....F 12
49 Kelso ....F 10
31 Kelstedge ....D 11
33 Kelstern ....A 9
29 Kelsterton .....C 12
15 Kelston ....H 10
43 Kelton ....D 10
43 Kelton Hill .....F 8
52 Kelty ....H 6
19 Kelvedon ....B 8
18 Kelvedon Hatch ..D 6
2 Kelynack ....G 1
53 Kemback ....F 9
22 Kemberton ......B 1
16 Kemble ....D 1
22 Kemerton ....H 3
15 Kemeys Commander D 7
58 Kemnay ....F 5
10 Kemp Town ......H 2
60 Kempie ....B 5
15 Kempley ....A 10
22 Kempsey ....G 2
16 Kempsford ....D 3
9 Kempshott ....A 7
25 Kempston ....A 1
25 Kempston Hardwick L 1
25 Kempston West End K 1
21 Kempton ....D 9
10 Kemsing ....B 4
11 Kemsley ....A 8
11 Kenardington ...E 8
21 Kenchester Sugwas H 10
16 Kencot ....D 4
39 Kendal ....F 7
21 Kenderchurch ...A 7
14 Kenfig ....F 1
14 Kenfig Hill ......F 2
22 Kenilworth ......E 6
51 Kenknock ....D 11
21 Kenley ....B 11
54 Kenmore, Highland .D 1
51 Kenmore, Strathclyde G 8
52 Kenmore, Tayside ..C 3
15 Kenn, Avon ......G 7
6 Kenn, Devon .....H 3
63 Kennacley ......C 3
46 Kennacraig ......C 3
55 Kennards House ..A 10
44 Kennedy's Corner ..E 1
2 Kenneggy Downs ..G 3
4 Kennerleigh .....E 7
52 Kennet ....H 4
43 Kenneth Bank ...E 10
25 Kennett ....H 8
6 Kennford ....G 3
27 Kenninghall .....G 3
11 Kennington, Kent .D 9
18 Kennington, London F 3
16 Kennington, Oxon. .D 6
53 Kennoway ....E 8
47 Kennox ....E 8
25 Kennyhill ....H 8
36 Kennythorpe ....A 6
62 Kensaleyre ......C 3
18 Kensington ......F 3
17 Kensworth ......B 11
17 Kensworth Com. ..B 11
11 Kentl County ....C 5
10 Kent Street .....C 5
51 Kentallen ....B 7
21 Kentchurch .....B 7
25 Kentford ....J 8
6 Kentisbeare .....E 4
4 Kentisbury ......B 5

4 Kentisburyford ....B 5
39 Kentmere ....E 7
6 Kenton, Devon ....H 3
18 Kenton, London ...E 2
27 Kenton, Suffolk ...J 5
45 Kenton Bank Foot .F 10
50 Kentra ....A 4
38 Kents Bank ....H 6
15 Kent's Green .....B 10
8 Kent's Oak ....D 5
45 Kentstone ....B 11
30 Kenwick ....G 3
2 Kenwyn ....E 5
60 Keoldale ....A 5
63 Keose ....E 5
55 Keppcoh ....G 3
46 Keprigan ....H 2
40 Kepwick ....F 5
49 Kerchesters ......F 10
23 Keresley ....D 7
15 Kerne Bridge .....B 9
48 Kerrcleuch ....H 5
31 Kerridge ....C 8
2 Kerris ....G 2
54 Kerrowwood ....F 7
21 Kerry ....C 7
46 Kerrylamont ......D 6
15 Kerry's Gate .....A 7
54 Kerrysdale ....B 2
46 Kerrytonlia ......D 6
32 Kersall ....D 4
6 Kersbrooke ....H 4
4 Kerscott ....C 5
47 Kerse ....D 8
27 Kersey ....L 3
63 Kershader ....E 4
44 Kershopefoot .....E 3
49 Kersmains ....F 9
22 Kershaw ....H 3
6 Kerswell ....F 4
22 Kerswell Green ...G 2
27 Kesgrave ....L 5
38 Keskadale ....C 4
27 Kessingland ......G 8
27 Kessingland Beach ..G 8
2 Kestle Mill ......D 5
18 Keston ....G 4
38 Keswick, Cumb. ...C 5
26 Keswick, Norfolk ..B 6
26 Keswick, Norfolk ...E 5
21 Ketley ....A 12
49 Kettelshiel ......D 9
23 Kettering ....D 12
26 Ketteringham .....E 5
53 Kettins ....C 7
27 Kettlebaston .....K 3
53 Kettlebridge .....F 8
22 Kettlebrook ......B 6
27 Kettlebrugh ......J 5
53 Kettlehill ....F 8
41 Kettleness ....D 8
31 Kettleshulme .....B 8
35 Kettlesing ....B 11
35 Kettlesing Bottom .A 11
26 Kettlestone ......B 3
32 Kettlethorpe .....C 6
64 Kettletoft ....B 4
39 Kettlewell ....H 11
24 Ketton ....E 1
18 Kew ....F 2
14 Kewstoke ....H 6
35 Kexbrough ....F 11
32 Kexby, Lincs. ....B 5
36 Kexby, N. Yorks. ..B 5
31 Key Green ....D 7
11 Key Street ....B 7
23 Keyham ....B 10
8 Keyhaven ....D 5
37 Keyingham ....E 10
10 Keymer ....F 2
9 Keynsham ....G 9
33 Key's Toft ....D 12
25 Keysoe ....J 2
25 Keysoe Roe ....J 2
25 Keyston ....H 1
45 Kibblesworth .....G 10
23 Kibworth Beauchamp
...........C 10
23 Kibworth Harcourt
...........C 10
18 Kidbrooke ....F 4
22 Kiddemore Green ..A 2
22 Kidderminster ....D 2
16 Kiddington ....B 5
16 Kidlington ....C 6
17 Kidmore End ......F 8
30 Kidnal ....E 3
58 Kidrummy ....F 2
31 Kidsgrove ....E 7
39 Kidstones ....G 11
13 Kidwelly ....F 7
50 Kiel Crofts ......D 6
44 Kielder ....D 4
52 Kilbagie ....H 4

47 Kilbarchan ....C 9
62 Kilbeg ....H 6
46 Kilberry ....C 2
47 Kilbirnie ....D 8
50 Kilbride ....E 6
62 Kilbride, Highland ..F 5
50 Kilbride, Strathclyde
...........E 6
32 Kilburn, Derby ...F 1
40 Kilburn, N. Yorks. .G 5
59 Kilburn, Tayside ...K 1
23 Kilby ....C 9
48 Kilcadzow ....D 2
50 Kilchattan,
Strathclyde ....H 1
46 Kilchattan,
Strathclyde ......D 6
46 Kilchenzie ....G 2
50 Kilcheran ....E 5
50 Kilchoan, Highland .A 2
55 Kilchoan, Highland .K 2
50 Kilchoan, Strathclyde
...........F 5
51 Kilchrenan ....E 7
53 Kilconquhar ......G 9
15 Kilcot ....B 10
56 Kilcoy ....E 1
47 Kilcreggan ....A 7
40 Kildale ....D 6
46 Kildalloig ....G 4
46 Kildavanan ....C 5
56 Kildermorie Lodge .B 1
46 Kildonan, Arran ...G 5
61 Kildonan, Highland
...........E 9
61 Kildonan Lodge ...E 9
42 Kildrochat House ...F 2
35 Kildwick ....C 9
46 Kilfinan ....B 4
55 Kilfinnan ....K 6
12 Kilgetty ....F 5
37 Kilham, Humber. ..A 8
49 Kilham, Northumb.
...........F 11
42 Kilkerran ....A 4
4 Kilkhampton ......E 1
32 Killamarsh ....B 2
13 Killay ....H 9
50 Killbeg ....C 3
46 Killchianaig .....A 1
46 Killean ....E 2
47 Killearn ....A 10
46 Killellan ....H 2
56 Killen ....D 2
40 Killerby ....C 2
42 Killern ....F 6
51 Killichonan ......B 12
50 Killichronan .....C 3
55 Killiechanate ....L 6
52 Killiecrankie ....A 4
57 Killiehuntly .....K 4
50 Killiemor ....D 2
55 Killilan ....G 3
61 Killimster ....B 12
52 Killin ....D 1
57 Killin Lodge .....J 1
35 Killinghall ......A 11
39 Killington ....F 8
49 Killochyett ......E 7
50 Killunaig ....E 2
50 Killundine ....C 3
43 Killyleoch ....C 9
47 Kilmacolm ....B 8
50 Kilmahumaig ......H 5
62 Kilmaluag ....A 4
53 Kilmany ....E 8
62 Kilmarie ....F 5
47 Kilmarnock ....F 9
53 Kilmaron Castle ..E 8
54 Kilmartin ....H 5
47 Kilmaurs ....E 9
50 Kilmelford ....F 6
7 Kilmersdon ....A 10
9 Kilmeston ....D 7
46 Kilmichael ....G 2
50 Kilmichael Glassary
...........H 6
46 Kilmichael of
Inverlussa ....A 3
6 Kilmington, Devon .F 6
7 Kilmington, Wilts. .C 11
7 Kilmington Street ..C 11
56 Kilmorack ....E 1
62 Kilmore, Highland .G 6
50 Kilmore, Strathclyde
...........E 6
46 Kilmory, Arran ...G 4
50 Kilmory, Highland .A 3
46 Kilmory, Strathclyde
...........B 2
61 Kilmote ....F 9
62 Kilmuir, Highland .A 3
62 Kilmuir, Highland .C 2
56 Kilmuir, Highland .B 3

56 Kilmuir, Highland ..E 2
46 Kilmun ....A 6
17 Kiln Green ....F 9
44 Kiln Hill ....F 4
45 Kiln Pit Hill ....H 8
10 Kilndown ....E 6
43 Kilness ....D 10
47 Kilnford ....F 8
36 Kilnhurst ....G 2
50 Kilninian ....C 1
50 Kilninver ....E 5
37 Kilnsea ....F 11
39 Kilnsey ....H 12
37 Kilnwick ....B 7
36 Kilnwick Percy ...B 6
46 Kiloran ....H 1
46 Kilpatrick ....G 4
15 Kilpeck ....A 7
61 Kilphedir ....E 9
36 Kilpin ....D 5
36 Kilpin Pike ......D 5
53 Kilrenny ....G 10
23 Kilsby ....E 9
53 Kilspindie ....E 7
48 Kilsyth ....B 12
41 Kilton, Cleveland .C 7
6 Kilton, Somerset ..B 5
6 Kilvaxter ....A 3
6 Kilve ....B 5
32 Kilvington ....F 5
47 Kilwinning ....E 8
26 Kimberley, Norf. ..E 4
32 Kimberley, Notts. .F 2
17 Kimble Wick ......C 9
45 Kimblesworth .....H 11
25 Kimbolton, Cambs. .H 2
21 Kimbolton,
Heref. & Worcs. .F 10
23 Kimcote ....C 9
7 Kimmeridge ......H 12
49 Kimmerston ....F 12
8 Kimpton, Hants. ..A 4
18 Kimpton, Herts. ..B 2
61 Kinbrace ....D 8
55 Kinbreack ....K 4
52 Kinbuck ....G 3
47 Kincaidston ......G 8
53 Kincaple ....E 9
52 Kincardine, Fife ..H 4
60 Kincardine, Highland
...........G 6
59 Kincardine O'Neil ..G 3
52 Kinclaven ....C 6
59 Kincorth ....G 7
56 Kincorth House ...D 6
57 Kincraig ....J 4
52 Kindallachan .....B 5
56 Kindrummond .....F 2
46 Kinerarach ....D 2
16 Kineton, Glos. ...B 2
23 Kineton, War. ....G 7
52 Kinfauns ....E 6
15 King Stanley .....D 11
50 Kingairloch Ho. ..B 6
46 Kingarth ....D 6
15 Kincoed ....D 7
33 Kingerby ....A 7
4 Kingford ....D 5
16 Kingham ....B 3
50 Kingharair ....C 2
43 Kingholm Quay ...D 10
48 Kinghorn ....A 5
53 Kinglassie ....G 7
58 Kingoodie, Grampian
...........E 6
53 Kingoodie, Tayside .D 8
21 King's Acre ......H 10
31 Kings Bromley ....F 1
15 Kings Caple ......A 9
24 King's Cliffe ....F 1
22 King's Coughton ..F 4
22 Kings Heath ......D 4
17 Kings Langley ....D 11
24 King's Lynn ......D 7
39 King's Meaburn ...C 8
48 Kings Muir ....E 5
23 King's Norton, Leics.
...........B 10
22 King's Norton,
W. Midlands .....D 4
4 King's Nympton ...D 6
21 King's Pyon ......G 10
25 Kings Ripton .....H 4
8 King's Samborne ..C 5
7 King's Stag ....E 10
16 King's Sutton ....A 6
18 King's Walden ....B 2
11 Kings Wood ....C 6
8 Kings Worth ......C 6
3 Kingsand ....E 11
58 Kingsbarns ......F 10
5 Kingsbridge, Devon .L 6
6 Kingsbridge, Som. .C 3
62 Kingsburgh ....C 3

18 Kingsbury, London .E 2
22 Kingsbury, War. ...C 6
7 Kingsbury Episcopi .D 8
16 Kingsclere ....H 6
5 Kingscote ....E 11
4 Kingscott ....D 4
46 Kingscross ....G 5
7 Kingsdon ....D 8
11 Kingsdown ....C 12
22 Kingseat ....H 6
17 Kinsey ....C 4
10 Kingsfold ....D 1
59 Kingsford, Grampian
...........G 6
22 Kingsford, Heref &
Worcs. ....D 2
47 Kingsford, Strathclyde
...........E 9
27 Kingshall Street ..J 2
4 Kingsheanton .....B 4
52 Kingshouse ....E 1
51 Kinghouse Hotel ..B 10
5 Kingskerswell ....J 7
53 Kingskettle ......F 8
28 Kingsland, Gwynedd
...........B 2
21 Kingsland, Heref. &
Worcs. ....F 10
30 Kingsley, Ches. ..C 4
9 Kingsley, Hants. ..B 9
31 Kingsley, Staffs. ..F 8
22 Kingsley Green ...C 10
31 Kingsley Holt ....F 9
53 Kingsmuir ....B 9
11 Kingsnorth ....D 9
22 Kingstanding .....C 4
5 Kingsteignton ....H 7
15 Kingsthorne ......A 8
23 Kingsthorpe .....F 11
25 Kingston, Cambs. ..K 4
5 Kingston, Devon ..L 5
7 Kingston, Dorset ..E 11
8 Kingston, Dorset ..H 1
58 Kingston, Grampian
...........A 1
8 Kingston, Hants. ..F 3
8 Kingston, I.o.W. ...H 6
11 Kingston, Kent ...C 10
49 Kingston, Lothian ..A 8
9 Kingston, W. Sussex
...........F 12
16 Kingston Bagpuize .D 5
17 Kingston Blount ...D 8
10 Kingston by Sea ...H 1
7 Kingston Deverill .C 11
16 Kingston Lisle ...E 4
10 Kingston near Lewes
...........G 3
32 Kingston on Soar ..G 2
7 Kingston Russell ..G 9
6 Kingston St Mary ..C 6
15 Kingston Seymour ..H 7
37 Kingston upon Hull .D 8
18 Kingston upon Thames
...........G 2
18 Kingston Vale ....G 2
15 Kingstone, Heref. &
Worcs. ....A 7
7 Kingstone, Som. ...E 7
31 Kingstone, Staffs. .G 9
44 Kingstown ....G 2
5 Kingswear ....K 7
22 Kingswinford .....C 2
15 Kingswood, Avon ..G 9
17 Kingswood, Bucks. .B 8
21 Kingswood, Glos. .E 10
21 Kingswood, Powys ..B 8
10 Kingswood, Surrey .B 1
22 Kingswood, War. ...E 5
21 Kingswood Com. ...G 8
21 Kington, Heref. &
Worcs. ....G 8
22 Kington, Heref. &
Worcs. ....G 3
15 Kington Langley .G 12
7 Kington Magna ...D 11
15 Kington St. Michael
...........F 12
57 Kingussie ....J 3
7 Kingweston ......C 8
43 Kinharvie ....E 10
52 Kinkell Bridge ...E 4
58 Kinknockie,
Grampian ....C 7
58 Kinknockie,
Grampian ....E 7
44 Kinkry Hill ......E 3
31 Kinlet ....D 1
53 Kinloch, Fife ....F 7
62 Kinloch, Highland .F 6
60 Kinloch, Highland .D 4
52 Kinloch, Tayside ..C 6
53 Kinloch, Tayside ..C 7
62 Kinloch Castle ...H 3

55 Kinloch Hourn .....J 3
57 Kinloch Laggan ...K 1
60 Kinloch Lodge ....B 6
52 Kinloch Rannoch ..A 2
50 Kinlochan ....A 5
51 Kinlochard ......G 11
55 Kinlochbeoraid ...L 2
60 Kinlochbervie ....B 3
55 Kinlocheil ....L 4
51 Kinlochetive .....C 8
54 Kinlochewe ......D 4
51 Kinlochleven .....A 9
55 Kinlochmoidart ...M 1
55 Kinlochmorar ....K 2
51 Kinlochmore .....A 9
55 Kinlochnanuagh ...L 1
50 Kinlochspelve ....E 4
55 Kinloid ....L 1
56 Kinloss ....D 6
29 Kinmel Bay ....B 9
58 Kinmuck ....F 6
58 Kinnadie ....C 7
54 Kinnahaird ....D 8
59 Kinnaid Castle ...L 4
53 Kinnaird ....D 7
59 Kinneff ....K 6
43 Kinnelhead ......B 11
53 Kinnell ....B 10
30 Kinnerley ....H 2
21 Kinnersley, Heref. &
Worcs. ....G 9
22 Kinnersley, Heref. &
Worcs. ....H 2
52 Kinnesswood .....G 6
40 Kinninvie ....C 1
53 Kinnordy ....B 8
32 Kinoulton ....G 4
57 Kinrara ....J 4
52 Kinross ....G 6
53 Kinrossie ....D 7
21 Kinsham ....F 9
36 Kinsley ....F 2
8 Kinson ....F 2
56 Kinsteary Lodge ..D 5
63 Kintaravay ....E 3
16 Kintbury ....G 5
56 Kintessack ....D 6
52 Kintillo ....E 6
59 Kintocher ,......G 3
30 Kinton, Salop. ...H 2
58 Kintore ....F 5
50 Kintra ....F 1
56 Kintrae ....C 7
50 Kintraw ....G 5
50 Kinuachdrach .....H 4
57 Kinveachy ....H 5
22 Kinver ....D 2
36 Kippax ....D 2
52 Kippen ....H 1
43 Kippford or Scaur .F 9
10 Kipping's Cross ...D 5
64 Kirbister ....D 2
38 Kirby ....H 2
26 Kirby Bedon ......E 6
32 Kirby Bellars ....H 4
26 Kirby Cane ......F 7
19 Kirby Cross ......B 12
41 Kirby Grindalythe .H 9
40 Kirby Hill, N. Yorks.
...........E 2
40 Kirby Hill, N. Yorks.
...........H 4
40 Kirby Knowle ....F 5
19 Kirby le Soken ...B 12
41 Kirby Misperton ..G 8
23 Kirby Muxloe .....B 8
35 Kirby Overblow ..B 12
26 Kirby Row ....F 7
40 Kirby Sigston ....F 4
36 Kirby Underdale ..A 6
40 Kirby Wiske ......G 4
9 Kirdford ....C 11
63 Kirivick ....C 3
61 Kirk ....B 11
36 Kirk Bramwith ...F 4
35 Kirk Deighton ...B 12
37 Kirk Ella ....D 8
32 Kirk Hallam ......F 2
36 Kirk Hammerton ..B 3
31 Kirk Ireton ......E 11
31 Kirk Langley ....F 11
40 Kirk Merrington ..B 3
38 Kirk Michael .....G 1
48 Kirk of Shotts ...C 1
36 Kirk Sandall ....F 4
36 Kirk Smeaton .....E 3
49 Kirk Yetholm ....G 11
64 Kirkabister ......E 7
43 Kirkandrews .....G 7
44 Kirkandrews upon
Eden ....G 2

44 Kirkbampton .....G 1
43 Kirkbank ....C 11
43 Kirkbean ....F 10
64 Kirkbrae ....A 2
44 Kirkbride, Cumb. .G 1
43 Kirkbride, Dumf. &
Gall. ....C 9
53 Kirkbuddo ....C 9
48 Kirkburn, Borders .F 5
37 Kirkburn, Humber. .B 7
35 Kirkburton ......F 10
34 Kirkby, Merseyside .G 3
33 Kirkby, Lincs. ...A 8
40 Kirkby, N. Yorks. .E 5
40 Kirkby Fleetham ..F 3
33 Kirkby Green .....D 8
32 Kirkby in Ashfield .E 2
24 Kirkby le Thorpe .A 2
39 Kirkby Lonsdale ..G 8
35 Kirkby Malham ...A 7
23 Kirkby Mallory ...B 8
40 Kirkby Malzeard ..H 2
41 Kirkby Mills .....G 7
33 Kirkby on Bain ...D 9
39 Kirkby Stephen ..D 10
39 Kirkby Thore .....C 9
24 Kirkby Underwood .C 2
36 Kirkby Wharf .....C 3
41 Kirkbymoorside ...F 7
53 Kirkcaldy ....H 7
44 Kirkcambeck .....F 4
43 Kirkcarswell .....G 8
42 Kirkcolm ....E 1
47 Kirkconnel ......H 12
43 Kirkconnell,
Dumf. & Gall. ..E 10
43 Kirkconnell,
Dumf. & Gall. ..F 7
42 Kirkcowan ....E 4
43 Kirkcudbright ...F 8
30 Kirkdale ....A 2
42 Kirkdale House ...F 6
49 Kirkdean ....E 4
48 Kirkfieldbank ....E 1
43 Kirkgunzeon .....E 9
34 Kirkham, Lancs. ..D 3
36 Kirkham, N. Yorks. .A 5
35 Kirkhamgate ....E 11
45 Kirkharle ....E 8
45 Kirkheaton,
Nothumb. ....E 8
35 Kirkheaton,
W. Yorks. ......E 10
56 Kirkhill, Highland .E 1
48 Kirkhill, Lothian .C 5
59 Kirkhill, Tayside .L 4
58 Kirkhill of
Kennethmont .....E 3
48 Kirkhope ....G 6
48 Kirkhouse ....A 6
62 Kirkioost, Highland
...........F 5
63 Kirkibost, W. Isles .C 3
53 Kirkinch ....F 5
42 Kirkinner ....F 5
47 Kirkintilloch ...B 11
39 Kirkland, Cumb. ..B 9
38 Kirkland, Cumb. ..C 3
43 Kirkland, Dumf. &
Gall. ....C 9
43 Kirkland, Dumf. &
Gall. ....C 11
47 Kirkland, Dumf. &
Gall. ....H 2
42 Kirkland, Dumf. &
Gall. ....G 5
43 Kirkland Guards .G 12
43 Kirkland of Gelston .F 8
40 Kirkleatham ......C 6
40 Kirklevington ....D 4
26 Kirkley ....F 8
45 Kirkley March ....E 9
31 Kirkleyditch .....B 7
32 Kirklington, Notts. .F 1
40 Kirklington, N. Yorks.
...........G 3
44 Kirklinton ......F 3
48 Kirkliston ....H 2
42 Kirkmaiden ....H 2
42 Kirkmichael,
Strathclyde .....A 4
52 Kirkmichael,
Tayside ....A 6
47 Kirkmuirhill ....E 12
48 Kirknewton, Lothian
...........C 4
49 Kirknewton,
Northumb. ....F 11
58 Kirkney ....D 3
39 Kirkoswald, Cumb. .A 8
42 Kirkoswald,
Strathclyde .....A 3
43 KirkpatrickDurham .D 8
44 Kirkpatrick-Fleming F 1

38 Kirksanton ....G 4
33 Kirkstead ....D 9
44 Kirkstile, Dumf. &
   Gall. ....D 2
58 Kirkstile, Grampian
   D 3
58 Kirkston of
   Culsalmond ......D 4
61 Kirkstyle ....A 12
44 Kirkton, Borders ...B 4
43 Kirkton, Dumf. &
   Gall. ....C 10
53 Kirkton, Fife .....E 8
58 Kirkton, Grampian .C 6
58 Kirkton, Grampian .E 4
58 Kirkton, Grampian .F 6
58 Kirkton, Grampian .F 4
58 Kirkton, Grampian .C 4
56 Kirkton, Highland ..F 2
56 Kirkton, Highland ..C 3
54 Kirkton, Highland ..F 3
48 Kirkton, Strathclyde
   G 2
53 Kirkton, Tayside ...C 9
59 Kirkton, Tayside ...J 2
48 Kirkton Manor ....D 5
53 Kirkton of Airlie ..B 8
53 Kirkton of
   Auchterhouse ....C 8
56 Kirkton of Barevan .E 4
53 Kirkton of Collace .D 7
53 Kirkton of Craig ..B 11
59 Kirkton of Durris .H 5
58 Kirkton of Glenbuchat
   F 1
53 Kirkton of Glenisla .A 7
53 Kirkton of
   Kingoldrum ......B 8
53 Kirkton of Largo ..G 9
52 Kirkton of Lethendy
   C 6
58 Kirkton of Logie
   Buchan ....E 7
59 Kirkton of Menmuir
   L 3
53 Kirkton of Monikie
   C 10
58 Kirkton of Oyne ...E 4
59 Kirkton of Skene ..G 5
53 Kirkton of
   Strathmartine ...D 8
53 Kirkton of Tealing ..C 9
53 Kirktonbarns ......D 9
58 Kirktown ....B 8
58 Kirktown of Alvah .B 4
58 Kirktown of
   Auchterless ......C 5
58 Kirktown of Bourtie
   E 5
58 Kirktown of Deskford
   B 2
59 Kirktown of Fetteresso
   J 6
58 Kirktown of Mortlach
   D 1
58 Kirktown of Rayne .E 4
58 Kirktown of Slains ..E 8
64 Kirkwall ....D 2
45 Kirkwhelpington ..E 8
37 Kirmington ......F 9
33 Kirmond le Mire ...A 9
47 Kirn ....B 7
43 Kirncleuch ......B 12
53 Kirriemuir ....B 8
26 Kirstead Green ....F 6
44 Kirtlebridge ......F 1
44 Kirtleton ....E 1
25 Kirtling ....J 8
25 Kirtling Green ....K 8
16 Kirtlington ......B 6
61 Kirtomy ....B 7
56 Kirton, Highland ..D 3
24 Kirton, Lincs. ....B 4
32 Kirton, Notts. ....C 4
27 Kirton, Suffolk ....L 6
24 Kirton End ....B 4
24 Kirton Holme .....A 4
37 Kirton in Lindsey .G 7
23 Kislingbury ......F 10
23 Kites Hardwick ....E 8
6 Kittisford ....D 4
13 Kittle ....H 9
31 Kitts Moss ....B 7
59 Kittybrewster .....G 7
9 Kitwood ....C 8
4 Kiverley ....D 4
15 Kivernoll ....A 8
32 Kiveton Park .....B 2
60 Klibreck ....D 6
60 Klibreck Lodge ....D 6
32 Knaith ....B 5
32 Knaith Park ......B 5
7 Knap Corner .....D 11
17 Knaphill ....H 10

6 Knapp, Somerset ...D 6
53 Knapp, Tayside ...D 7
58 Knaps of Auchlee ..C8
26 Knapton, Norfolk ..B 6
36 Knapton, N. Yorks. .B 3
21 Knapton Green ...G 10
25 Knapwell ....J 4
35 Knaresborough ...A 12
44 Knarsdale ....H 5
40 Knayton ....F 4
18 Knebworth ....B 3
36 Knedlington .....D 5
32 Kneesall ....D 4
25 Kneesworth ......L 4
32 Kneeton ....F 4
13 Knelston ....H 8
27 Knettishall ......G 3
4 Knightacott ......B 5
23 Knightcote ......G 7
5 Knighton, Devon ..L 4
7 Knighton, Dorset ..E 9
23 Knighton, Leics. ...B 9
21 Knighton, Powys ...E 8
30 Knighton, Staffs. ..F 6
30 Knighton, Staffs. ..G 6
16 Knighton, Wilts. ..G 4
22 Knightsford Bridge .G 1
21 Knill ....F 8
32 Knipton ....G 5
45 Knitsley ....H 9
31 Kniveton ....E 10
39 Knock, Cumbria ...B 9
58 Knock, Grampian ..B 3
62 Knock, Highland ..G 6
50 Knock, Strathclyde .D 3
63 Knock, W. Isles ...D 6
60 Knockan ....F 3
56 Knockando ......E 7
57 Knockandhu .....G 8
60 Knockanrock .....F 3
61 Knockarthur .....F 7
56 Knockbain ....D 2
62 Knockbreck ......B 2
43 Knockbrex ....G 7
61 Knockdee ....B 11
42 Knockdolian Cas. ..C 2
42 Knockdon ....B 5
46 Knockendon .....D 7
47 Knockenjig ......H 12
46 Knockenkelly ....G 5
47 Knockentiber ....E 9
58 Knockespock Ho. ..E 3
42 Knockgardner ....A 4
42 Knockglass ....F 1
10 Knockholt ....B 3
10 Knockholt Pound ..B 4
55 Knockie Lodge ...H 8
30 Knockin ....H 2
47 Knockinlaw ......E 9
42 Knocklaugh ......B 3
43 Knocklearn ......D 8
42 Knocknain ....E 1
46 Knockrome ......B 1
53 Knockshannoch ...A 7
38 Knocksharry .....G 1
42 Knocksheen .....C 6
43 Knockvennie .....D 8
42 Knockycoid ......D 3
27 Knodishall ......J 7
7 Knole ....D 8
15 Knole Park ......F 9
30 Knolls Green .....B 6
30 Knolton ....F 2
8 Knook ....B 1
23 Knossington .....A 11
34 Knott End-on-Sea ..B 2
25 Knotting ....J 1
25 Knotting Green ...J 1
36 Knottingley ......E 3
39 Knotts ....C 7
30 Knotty Ash ......A 3
17 Knotty Green ....E 10
42 Knowe ....C 6
43 Knowhead, Dumf. &
   Gall. ....C 7
58 Knowhead, Grampian
   F 2
45 Knowesgate .....D 8
47 Knoweside ....H 7
49 Knowetownhead ..G 8
27 Knowl Green .....L 1
19 Knowl Hill ......F 9
15 Knowle, Avon ....G 9
6 Knowle, Devon ...H 4
4 Knowle, Devon ...F 6
4 Knowle, Devon ...B 4
7 Knowle, Somerset ..B 7
22 Knowle, W. Midlands
   D 5
34 Knowle Green ....C 5
8 Knowle, Dorset ...E 2
11 Knowlton, Kent ...C 11
58 Knowsie ....B 8
34 Knowsley ....H 3

4 Knowstone ......D 7
10 Knox Brdige .....D 6
21 Knucklas ....E 8
30 Knutsford ....B 6
31 Knypersley ......E 7
2 Kuggar ....H 4
55 Kyle of Lochalsh ..G 1
55 Kyleakin ....G 1
55 Kylechorky Lodge ..G 8
61 Kyleoag ....G 7
55 Kylerhea ....G 2
63 Kyles Scalpay ....G 3
63 Kyles Stockinish ..G 4
55 Kylesbeg ....M 1
55 Kylesknoydart ....K 2
60 Kylesku ....D 3
55 Kylesmorar ......K 2
60 Kylestrome ......D 4
57 Kyllachy House ...G 3
15 Kymin ....C 8
15 Kynaston ....B 8
21 Kynnersley ......A 12
21 Kyre Park ....F 11
63 Labost ....B 4
37 Laceby ....F 10
17 Lacey Green .....D 9
30 Lach Dennis .....C 5
63 Lackalee ....H 2
40 Lackenby ....C 6
27 Lackford ....H 1
15 Lacock ....G 12
23 Ladbroke ....F 7
11 Laddingford .....C 6
33 Lade Bank ....E 11
2 Ladock ....E 6
63 Ladybank, Fife ...F 8
42 Ladybank, Strathclyde
   A 3
3 Ladycross ....A 10
49 Ladyflat ....D 10
49 Ladykirk ....E 11
55 Ladyleys ....E 6
58 Ladysford ....B 6
43 Lag ....C 9
50 Lagalochan ......F 6
46 Lagg, Strathclyde ..B 1
47 Lagg, Strathclyde ..H 7
47 Lagg, Strathclyde ..G 4
52 Laggan, Central ...F 1
58 Laggan, Grampian ..D 1
47 Laggan, Highland ..K 7
57 Laggan, Highland ..K 2
42 Laggan, Strathclyde .C 2
42 Laggan, Strathclyde .C 3
42 Lagganmullan .....F 6
50 Lagganulva ......C 2
60 Laid ....B 5
60 Laide ....G 1
47 Laigh Braidley ...E 10
47 Laigh Brocklar ...G 10
47 Laigh Cleughearn .D 11
47 Laigh Fenwick ...E 9
47 Laigh Smithstone ..E 8
47 Laighmuir ....E 9
47 Laighstonehall ...D 12
42 Laight ....B 9
19 Laindon ....E 7
57 Laintachan ......H 6
44 Lair ....E 4
60 Lairg ....F 6
60 Lairg Muir ......F 6
60 Lairg Station ....F 6
51 Lairigmor ....A 8
35 Laisterdyke .....D 10
39 Laithes ....B 7
8 Lake ....B 3
44 Lake of Moy .....D 6
38 Lake Side ....F 6
25 Lakenheath ......G 8
24 Lakes End ....F 6
15 Laleham ....G 11
14 Laleston ....F 2
48 Lamancha ....D 5
27 Lamarsh ....L 2
26 Lamas ....C 5
27 Lamb Corner ....M 3
64 Lambaness ......B 4
49 Lambden ....E 10
10 Lamberhurst ....D 5
10 Lamberhurst
   Quarter ....D 5
9 Lambeth ....F 3
32 Lambley, Notts. ...F 3
44 Lambley, Northumb. G 5
9 Lambourn ....F 4
18 Lambourne End ..D 5
10 Lambs Green ....D 1
12 Lambston ....E 3
3 Lamellion ....C 9
5 Lamerton ....H 3
25 Lamesley ....G 10
42 Lamford ....B 6
56 Lamington, Highland
   B 3

48 Lamington, Strathclyde
   F 3
46 Lamlash ....F 5
42 Lamloch ....B 6
38 Lamonby ....B 6
2 Lamorna ....G 2
2 Lamorran ....E 6
12 Lampeter ....B 9
12 Lampeter Velfrey ..F 5
12 Lamphey ....G 4
38 Lamplugh ....C 3
23 Lamport ....E 11
7 Lamyatt ....C 10
4 Lana, Devon .....F 2
4 Lana, Devon .....E 2
48 Lanark ....E 2
34 Lancashire, Co. ...E 5
34 Lancaster ....A 4
45 Lanchester ......H 10
6 Landacre ....H 2
25 Lanbeach ....J 6
4 Landcross ....D 3
59 Landerberry .....G 5
2 Landewednack ...H 4
8 Landford ....D 4
8 Landford Manor ...D 4
13 Landimore ......H 8
4 Landkey ....C 5
13 Landlore ....G 10
3 Landrake, Corn. ..D 10
6 Landrake, Devon ..D 3
12 Landshipping ....F 4
9 Landulph ....D 11
22 Landywood ......B 3
2 Lane ....D 5
17 Lane End, Bucks. ..E 9
38 Lane End, Cumb. ..F 3
9 Lane End, Hants. ..D 7
9 Lane End, Hants. ..G 8
10 Lane End, Kent ...A 4
40 Lane Ends ....B 2
31 Lane Head, Derby .C 10
40 Lane Head, Dur. ..D 1
34 Lane Head, Manchester
   G 5
3 Laneast ....A 9
32 Laneham ....C 5
44 Lanehead ....D 6
35 Laneshaw Bridge ..C 8
32 Langar ....G 4
47 Langbank ....B 8
35 Langbar ....B 9
44 Langburnshiels ...C 4
35 Langcliffe ....A 7
41 Langdale End ...F 9
61 Langdale Lodge ..C 7
2 Langdon, Corn. ...D 5
3 Langdon, Corn. ..A 10
15 Langdon, Heref. &
   Worc. ....A 11
39 Langdon Beck ...B 11
19 Langdon Hills ...E 7
19 Langdyke ....G 8
19 Langenhoe ......B 10
25 Langford, Beds. ...L 3
6 Langford, Devon ..F 4
32 Langford, Essex ...C 8
32 Langford, Notts. ..D 5
16 Langford, Oxon ..D 3
6 Langford Budville ..D 4
25 Langford End ....K 3
27 Langham, Essex ..M 3
23 Langham, Leics. ..A 11
26 Langham, Norf. ...B 3
27 Langham, Suffolk .H 3
34 Langho ....D 6
44 Langholm, Dumf. &
   Gall. ....E 2
48 Langholm, Strathclyde
   F 3
47 Langlands ....D 11
49 Langleeford .....G 12
17 Langley, Berks. ..F 11
31 Langley, Ches. ....C 8
8 Langley, Hants. ..F 6
18 Langley, Herts. ...B 2
11 Langley, Kent ....C 7
44 Langley, Northumb. G 6
6 Langley, Som. ....C 4
22 Langley, War. ....F 5
9 Langley, W. Sussex .C 9
15 Langley Burrell ..G 12
10 Langley Green ...D 1
11 Langley Heath ...C 7
25 Langley Lower
   Green ....M 5
32 Langley Mill .....E 2
40 Langley Moor ....A 3
40 Langley Park ....A 2
26 Langley Street ...E 7
25 Langley Upper
   Green ....M 5
10 Langney ....H 5
32 Langold ....B 3

3 Langore ....A 10
7 Langport ....D 7
33 Langrick ....E 9
15 Langridge ....G 10
4 Langridge Ford ..D 4
33 Langriville ......E 10
35 Langsett ....G 10
49 Langshaw ....E 8
47 Langside, Strathclyde
   D 8
52 Langside, Tayside ..F 3
64 Langskaill ....A 2
9 Langstone ....F 8
40 Langthorne, N. Yorks.
   F 3
40 Langthorpe, N. Yorks.
   H 4
39 Langthwaite .....E 12
41 Langtoft, Humberside
   H 10
24 Langtoft, Lincs. ...D 2
40 Langton, Dur. ....C 2
33 Langton, Lincs. ...C 9
33 Langton, Lincs. ...C 11
41 Langton, N. Yorks. .H 8
33 Langton by Wragby .C 8
10 Langton Green ...D 4
7 Langton Herring ..H 9
8 Langton Matravers .H 2
4 Langtree ....D 3
39 Langwathby .....B 8
60 Langwell ....G 5
61 Langwell Hotel ..E 10
33 Langworth ....C 8
3 Lanivet ....C 7
3 Lank ....B 8
3 Lanlivery ....D 8
2 Lanner ....F 4
3 Lanreath ....D 9
52 Lanrick Castle ...G 2
3 Lansallos ....E 9
15 Lansdown, Avon ..G 10
16 Lansdown, Glos. ..B 3
3 Lanteglos Highway .D 8
49 Lanton, Borders ..G 9
49 Lanton, Northumb. F 11
4 Lapford ....E 6
22 Lapley ....A 2
22 Lapworth ....E 5
50 Larachbeg ....C 4
48 Larbert ....A 1
43 Larbreck ....D 9
58 Largie ....D 4
46 Largiemore .....A 4
53 Largo Ward .....F 9
47 Largs ....C 7
46 Largymore ......G 5
10 Larkfield, Kent ...B 6
47 Larkfield, Strathclyde
   B 7
47 Larkhall ....D 12
8 Larkhill ....B 3
26 Larling ....F 3
51 Laroch ....B 8
44 Larriston ....D 4
39 Lartington ......C 12
59 Lary ....G 1
9 Lasham ....B 8
40 Laskill ....F 6
15 Lassington ......B 11
52 Lassodie ....H 6
41 Lastingham ......F 7
19 Latchingdon &
   Shoreham ......D 8
3 Latchley ....B 11
17 Latchmore Green ..H 7
34 Lately Common ...G 5
23 Lathbury ....H 11
61 Latheron ....D 11
53 Lathockar ......F 9
53 Lathones ....B 8
17 Latimer ....D 10
38 Latterhead ......C 4
15 Latteridge ......F 10
7 Lattiford ....D 10
16 Latton ....E 2
58 Lauchintilly .....F 5
50 Laudale House ...B 5
49 Lauder ....E 8
12 Laugharne ....F 4
32 Laughterton .....C 5
10 Laughton, E. Sussex G 4
36 Laughton, Humber. G 6
23 Laughton, Leics. .C 10
32 Laughton en le
   Morthen ....A 2
4 Launcells ....E 1
3 Launceston .....A 10
7 Launcherley ....B 9
17 Launton ....B 7
38 Laurel Bank .....G 1
59 Laurencekirk ....K 5

48 Laurieston, Central .A 2
43 Laurieston, Dumf. &
   Gall. ....E 7
23 Lavendon ....G 12
27 Lavenham ....K 2
43 Laverhay ....B 12
14 Lavernock ....G 5
8 Laverstock ......C 3
8 Laverstoke ......A 6
16 Laverton, Glos. ...A 2
40 Laverton, N. Yorks. H 2
7 Laverton, Som. ...A 11
30 Lavister ....D 2
48 Law ....D 1
52 Lawers, Tayside ..C 2
52 Lawers, Tayside ..E 3
27 Lawford ....M 4
3 Lawhitton ....A 10
39 Lawkland ....H 10
21 Lawley ....B 12
31 Lawnhead ....H 7
12 Lawrenny ....F 4
27 Lawshall ....K 2
32 Lawton ....F 10
63 Laxay ....E 4
63 Laxdale ....C 5
63 Laxey ....G 2
27 Laxfield ....H 6
64 Laxfirth ....D 7
60 Laxford Bridge ...C 4
64 Laxo ....C 7
64 Laxobigging .....C 7
36 Laxton, Humber. ..E 6
24 Laxton, Northants. .F 1
32 Laxton, Notts. ....D 4
35 Laycock ....C 9
19 Layer Breton ....B 9
19 Layer-de-la-Haye ..B 9
19 Layer Marney ...B 9
27 Layham ....L 3
16 Layland's Green ...G 5
7 Laymore ....F 7
21 Laysters Pole ....F 11
36 Laytham ....C 5
40 Lazenby ....B 3
39 Lazonby ....A 8
31 Lea, Derby ......D 11
15 Lea, Heref. &
   Worc. ....B 10
32 Lea, Lincs. ......B 5
21 Lea, Shropshire ..B 9
21 Lea, Shropshire ..C 9
15 Lea, Wilts. ......F 12
22 Lea Marston .....A 5
34 Lea Town ....D 4
39 Lea Yeat ....F 10
12 Leabrooke ....E 1
55 Leacachan ....G 3
56 Leachkin ....E 2
48 Leadburn ....D 5
18 Leaden Roding ...C 6
33 Leadenham ......E 7
49 Leaderfoot ......F 8
39 Leadgate, Cumb. ..A 9
45 Leadgate, Dur. ...H 9
45 Leadgate, Tyne &
   wear ....G 9
48 Leadhills ....H 2
16 Leafield ....C 4
17 Leagrave ....B 11
6 Leake ....F 4
33 Leake Common
   Side ....E 11
33 Leake Hurn's End .E 11
41 Lealholm ....D 8
62 Leatt ....B 4
23 Leamington ......E 7
23 Leamington Hastings
   E 8
22 Leamonsley .....A 4
45 Leamside ....H 11
51 Leanach ....H 7
56 Leanachan ......L 6
56 Leanaig ....D 1
46 Leargybreck .....B 1
39 Leasgill ....G 7
33 Leasingham ......E 7
40 Leasingthorne ...B 3
17 Leatherhead ....H 12
35 Leathley ....B 11
43 Leaths ....E 8
33 Leaton ....H 3
11 Leaveland ....C 8
36 Leavening ......A 5
18 Leaves Green ....H 4
18 Leavesden Green ..D 1
45 Leazes ....G 10
11 Lebberston ......A 2
16 Lechlade ....D 3
39 Leck ....G 9
15 Leckford ....C 3
61 Leckfurin ....B 7
16 Leckhampstead,
   Berks. ....G 5

23 Leckhampstead,
   Bucks. . . . . H 10
16 Leckhampstead
   Street . . . . F 5
16 Leckhampstead
   Thicket . . . . F 5
15 Leckhampton . . . . B 12
54 Leckie . . . . C 5
60 Leckmelm . . . . G 3
55 Leckroy . . . . K 7
14 Leckwith . . . . G 5
37 Leconfield . . . . C 8
50 Ledaig . . . . D 6
17 Ledburn . . . . B 10
15 Ledbury . . . . A 10
51 Ledcharrie . . . . . . E 12
21 Ledgemoor . . . . . . G 9
54 Ledgowan . . . . D 5
21 Ledicot . . . . F 9
60 Ledmore . . . . F 4
61 Lednagullin . . . . . . B 8
30 Ledsham, Ches. . . . . C 2
36 Ledsham, W. Yorks. D 2
36 Ledston . . . . D 2
16 Ledwell . . . . A 5
50 Lee, Strathclyde . . . E 1
4 Lee, Devon . . . . . . A 4
8 Lee, Hampshire . . . D 5
34 Lee, Lancashire . . . B 4
30 Lee, Shropshire . . . G 3
30 Lee Brockenhurst . . G 4
17 Lee Clump . . . . . . D 10
30 Lee Green . . . . D 5
5 Lee Mill Bridge . . . K 5
5 Lee Mill Estate . . . K 5
5 Lee Moor . . . . J 4
9 Lee-on-the-Solent . . F 7
21 Leebotwood . . . . . C 10
38 Leece . . . . H 5
11 Leeds, Kent . . . . . . C 7
35 Leeds, W. Yorks. . . D 11
1 Leedstown . . . . . . F 3
31 Leek . . . . E 8
22 Leek Wootton . . . . E 6
40 Leeming . . . . F 3
40 Leeming Bar . . . . . F 3
31 Lees, Derby . . . . . . F 11
35 Lees, Manchester . . G 8
44 Lees Hill . . . . F 4
29 Leeswood . . . . . . D 12
30 Leftwich Green . . . C 5
33 Legbourne . . . . . . B 10
49 Legerwood . . . . . . E 8
33 Legsby . . . . B 8
23 Leicester . . . . B 9
23 Leicestershire, Co. . . B 9
23 Leicester For. East. . B 8
7 Leigh, Dorset . . . . E 9
15 Leigh, Glos. . . . . . B 11
10 Leigh, Kent . . . . . C 4
34 Leigh, Manchester . . G 5
21 Leigh, Shropshire . . B 9
10 Leigh, Surrey . . . . . C 1
16 Leigh, Wiltshire . . . E 2
22 Leigh, Heref. &
   Worc. . . . . G 1
19 Leigh Beck . . . . . . F 8
15 Leigh Delamere . . . F 12
11 Leigh Green . . . . . E 8
19 Leigh-on-Sea . . . . . E 8
9 Leigh Park . . . . . . E 8
22 Leigh Sinton . . . . . G 1
7 Leigh upon Mendip
            B 10
6 Leighland Chapel . . C 4
15 Leighterton . . . . . E 11
40 Leighton, N. Yorks. . G 2
21 Leighton, Powys . . . B 8
21 Leighton, Salop . . . B 11
7 Leighton, Som. . . . B 10
25 Leighton Bromswold
            H 2
17 Leighton Buzzard . . B 10
59 Leightonhill . . . . . L 4
15 Leighwoods . . . . . G 9
21 Leinthall Earls . . . . F 10
21 Leinthall Starkes . . E 10
21 Leintwardine . . . . . E 9
23 Leire . . . . C 8
60 Leirinmore . . . . . . A 5
54 Leishmore . . . . . . F 8
27 Leiston . . . . J 7
53 Leitfie . . . . C 7
48 Leith . . . . B 5
49 Leitholm . . . . E 10
2 Lelant . . . . F 3
37 Lelley . . . . D 10
22 Lem Hill . . . . E 1
56 Lemlair . . . . D 1
45 Lemmington Hall . . B 9
41 Lempitlaw . . . . . . F 10
63 Lemreway . . . . . . F 5
18 Lemsford . . . . C 2
58 Lenabo . . . . C 8

22 Lenchwick . . . . . . G 4
42 Lendalfoot . . . . . . C 2
51 Lendrick . . . . G 12
11 Lenham . . . . C 7
11 Lenham Heath . . . . C 8
49 Lennel . . . . E 11
42 Lennies . . . . F 5
47 Lennoxtown . . . . . B 11
17 Lent Rise . . . . F 10
24 Lenton . . . . C 1
41 Lenwade . . . . D 4
47 Lenzie . . . . B 11
58 Leochel-Cushnie . . . F 3
21 Leominster . . . . . . F 10
15 Leonard Stanley . . . D 11
6 Lepe . . . . F 6
62 Lephin . . . . C 1
51 Lephinchapel . . . . H 7
51 Lephinmore . . . . . H 7
36 Leppington . . . . . . A 5
35 Lepton . . . . F 10
50 Lerags . . . . E 6
3 Lerryn . . . . D 8
64 Lerwick . . . . E 7
53 Lesbury . . . . B 10
53 Leslie, Fife . . . . . . G 7
58 Leslie, Grampian . . . E 3
46 Lesmahagow . . . . . E 1
2 Lesnewth . . . . B 2
26 Lessingham . . . . . . C 7
44 Lessonhall . . . . . . H 1
42 Leswalt . . . . E 1
18 Letchmore Heath . . D 2
16 Letchworth . . . . . . M 3
16 Letcombe Bassett . . F 5
16 Letcombe Regis . . . E 5
53 Letham, Fife . . . . . F 8
53 Letham, Tayside . . . B 10
52 Letham, Tayside . . . E 6
53 Letham Grange . . . C 11
56 Lethen House . . . . D 5
57 Lethendryveole . . . H 5
51 Lethenty . . . . D 5
27 Letheringham . . . . J 6
26 Letheringsett . . . . . B 4
5 Lettaford . . . . G 6
64 Lettan . . . . A 4
54 Letterewe . . . . C 3
54 Letterfearn . . . . . . G 3
55 Letterfinlay . . . . . . K 6
55 Lettermorar . . . . . K 1
54 Lettermore . . . . . . C 2
60 Letters . . . . H 3
48 Lettershaws . . . . . G 2
12 Letterston . . . . . . D 3
57 Lettoch, Highland . . H 6
56 Lettoch, Highland . . F 6
21 Letton, Heref. &
   Worc. . . . . E 9
21 Letton, Heref. &
   Worc. . . . . H 9
18 Letty Green . . . . . C 3
32 Letwell . . . . B 3
53 Leuchars . . . . E 9
56 Leuchars House . . . C 8
63 Leurbost . . . . D 5
52 Levedale . . . . A 3
37 Leven, Humberside . C 8
53 Leven, Fife . . . . . . G 8
46 Levencorroch . . . . G 5
39 Levens . . . . G 7
35 Levenshulme . . . . . H 7
64 Levenwick . . . . . . F 7
63 Leverburgh . . . . . . H 1
24 Leverington . . . . . D 5
33 Leverton, Berks. . . . G 4
33 Leverton, Lincs. . . . E 11
33 Leverton Outgate . . E 11
25 Levington . . . . L 5
41 Levisham . . . . F 8
16 Lew . . . . D 4
2 Lewannick . . . . . . B 9
5 Lewdown . . . . G 3
10 Lewes . . . . G 3
44 Lewisham, Borders . . C 2
18 Lewisham . . . . G 3
57 Lewiston . . . . G 1
14 Lewistown . . . . . . E 3
17 Lewknor . . . . D 8
4 Leworthy . . . . B 5
63 Lews Castle . . . . . . D 5
11 Lewson Street . . . . B 8
5 Lewtrenchard . . . . G 3
3 Ley, Cornwall . . . . C 9
58 Ley, Grampian . . . . F 3
10 Leybourne . . . . . . B 5
40 Leyburn . . . . F 1
18 Leycett . . . . E 6
18 Leygreen . . . . B 2
17 Leyhill Com. . . . . . D 10
34 Leyland . . . . E 4
58 Leylodge . . . . F 5
58 Leys . . . . B 7
56 Leys Castle . . . . . . F 2

53 Leys of Cossans . . . . B 8
58 Leys of Dummuies . . D 3
11 Leysdown-on-Sea . . A 9
53 Leysmill . . . . B 10
18 Leyton . . . . E 4
18 Leytonstone . . . . . . E 4
3 Lezant . . . . B 10
54 Liatrie . . . . F 6
14 Libanus . . . . B 3
48 Liberton, Lothian . . B 5
48 Libberton, Strathclyde
            E 3
22 Lichfield . . . . A 5
22 Lickey . . . . E 3
22 Lickey End . . . . E 3
9 Lickfold . . . . D 10
50 Liddesdale . . . . B 5
16 Liddington . . . . F 3
25 Lidgate . . . . J 8
16 Lidlington . . . . L 1
16 Lidstone . . . . B 4
55 Lienassie . . . . G 3
53 Liff . . . . D 8
5 Lifton . . . . G 3
5 Liftondown . . . . . . G 2
23 Lighthorne . . . . G 7
17 Lightwater . . . . H 10
31 Lightwood . . . . F 7
23 Lilbourne . . . . D 9
49 Lilburn Hill . . . . . . G 12
45 Lilburn Tower . . . . . A 8
21 Lilleshall . . . . A 1
16 Lilley, Berks. . . . . . F 5
18 Lilley, Herts. . . . . . A 1
49 Lilliesleaf . . . . G 8
23 Lillingstone Dayrell
            H 10
23 Lillingstone Lovell H 10
7 Lillington, Dorset . . E 9
23 Lillington, War. . . . . E 7
8 Lilliput . . . . G 2
26 Limpenhoe . . . . E 7
15 Limpley Stoke . . . . . H 11
10 Limpsfield . . . . C 3
32 Linby . . . . E 3
9 Linchmere . . . . C 10
43 Lincluden . . . . D 10
33 Lincoln . . . . C 7
22 Lincomb . . . . E 2
62 Lincro . . . . B 3
38 Lindal in Furness . . . H 5
38 Lindale . . . . G 6
49 Lindean . . . . F 7
10 Lindfield . . . . E 2
9 Lindford . . . . C 9
53 Lindifferon . . . . E 8
35 Lindley . . . . E 10
35 Lindley Green . . . . . B 11
53 Lindores . . . . E 7
21 Lindridge . . . . E 12
18 Lindsell . . . . A 6
32 Lindsey . . . . L 3
38 Linefoot . . . . B 3
19 Linford, Essex . . . . . F 7
18 Linford, Hants. . . . . E 3
38 Lingague . . . . H 1
41 Lingdale . . . . D 7
21 Lingen . . . . F 9
10 Lingfield . . . . D 3
10 Lingfield Com. . . . . D 3
30 Lingley Green . . . . . A 4
26 Lingwood . . . . E 7
44 Linhope, Borders . . . C 2
45 Linhope, N'thumb. . . A 8
16 Linkenholt . . . . H 5
3 Linkinhorne . . . . . . B 10
64 Linklater . . . . E 2
53 Linktown . . . . H 7
21 Linley Green . . . . . . G 12
48 Linlithgow . . . . B 3
48 Linlithgow Bridge . . B 3
60 Linneraineach . . . . . F 3
12 Linney . . . . G 2
43 Linns . . . . D 11
63 Linshader . . . . D 3
45 Linshiels . . . . B 7
35 Linsidemore . . . . . . G 8
17 Linslade . . . . B 10
27 Linstead Parva . . . . G 6
44 Linstock . . . . G 3
49 Linthaugh . . . . F 12
12 Linthurst . . . . E 3
35 Linthwaite . . . . F 9

49 Lintlaw . . . . D 11
58 Lintmill . . . . A 3
49 Linton, Borders . . . G 10
25 Linton, Cambs. . . . K 7
22 Linton, Derby . . . . A 6
15 Linton, Heref. &
   Worc. . . . . B 9
10 Linton, Kent . . . . . C 6
35 Linton, N. Yorks. . . A 8
35 Linton, W. Yorks. . . B 12
36 Linton-on-Ouse . . . A 3
8 Linwood, Hants. . . . E 3
33 Linwood, Lincs. . . . B 8
47 Linwood, Strathclyde
            C 9
29 Lioc . . . . C 10
63 Lionel . . . . A 6
9 Liphook . . . . C 9
6 Liscombe . . . . C 2
3 Liskeard . . . . C 9
9 Liss . . . . C 9
9 Liss Forest . . . . . . C 9
37 Lisset . . . . A 9
33 Lissington . . . . . . B 8
14 Lisvane . . . . F 5
15 Liswerry . . . . F 7
23 Litchborough . . . . . G 9
8 Litchfield . . . . A 6
34 Litherland . . . . G 2
25 Litlington, Camb. . . L 4
10 Litlington, E. Sussex
            H 4
25 Little Abington . . . . K 6
25 Little Addington . . . H 1
22 Little Alne . . . . F 5
18 Little Amwell . . . . . C 3
60 Little Assynt . . . . . E 3
17 Little Aston . . . . . . B 4
8 Little Atherfield . . . H 6
64 Little Ayre . . . . E 1
40 Little Ayton . . . . . . D 6
19 Little Baddow . . . . . C 7
15 Little Badminton . . F 11
52 Little Ballinluig . . . . B 4
44 Little Bampton . . . . G 1
25 Little Bardfield . . . . M 8
25 Little Barford . . . . . J 3
26 Little Barningham . . B 4
16 Little Barrington . . . C 3
30 Little Barrow . . . . . C 3
41 Little Barugh . . . . . G 8
45 Little Bavington . . . E 8
27 Little Bealings . . . . K 5
16 Little Bedwyn . . . . . G 4
42 Little Bennane . . . . C 2
19 Little Bentley . . . . . A 11
18 Little Berkhampsted
            C 3
23 Little Billing . . . . . F 11
15 Little Birch . . . . . . A 8
27 Little Blakenham . . K 4
39 Little Blencow . . . . B 7
9 Little Bookham . . . A 12
23 Little Bowden . . . . C 11
25 Little Bradley . . . . . K 8
21 Little Brampton . . . D 9
19 Little Braxted . . . . . B 8
59 Little Brechin . . . . . L 3
7 Little Bredy . . . . . . G 9
17 Little Brickhill . . . . A 10
23 Little Brington . . . . F 10
19 Little Bromley . . . . A 10
30 Little Budworth . . . D 5
18 Little Burstead . . . . E 6
24 Little Bytham . . . . . D 1
42 Little Cairnbrock . . E 1
33 Little Carlton,
   Lincs. . . . . B 11
32 Little Carlton,
   Notts. . . . . D 5
24 Little Casterton . . . E 1
33 Little Cawthorpe . . B 10
17 Little Chalfont . . . . D 11
11 Little Chart . . . . . . D 8
7 Little Cheney . . . . . G 9
25 Little Chesterford . . L 6
8 Little Cheverell . . . A 2
25 Little Chishill . . . . . L 5
19 Little Clacton . . . . . B 11
38 Little Clifton . . . . . B 3
58 Little Colp . . . . . . C 5
22 Little Comberton . . H 3
16 Little Compton . . . A 4
27 Little Cornard . . . . L 2
21 Little Cowarne . . . . G 11
16 Little Coxwell . . . . E 4
26 Little Crakehall . . . F 3
26 Little Cressingham . . E 2
34 Little Crosby . . . . . G 2
23 Little Dalby . . . . . . A 11
58 Little Dens . . . . . . C 8
15 Little Dewchurch . . A 8
37 Little Driffield . . . . A 8

26 Little Dunham . . . . D 2
52 Little Dunkeld . . . . C 5
18 Little Dunmow . . . . B 6
18 Little Easton . . . . . B 6
31 Little Eaton . . . . . . F 12
26 Little Ellingham . . . E 3
7 Little Elm . . . . B 10
18 Little End . . . . D 5
25 Little Eversden . . . . K 5
27 Little Fakenham . . . H 2
16 Little Faringdon . . . D 3
40 Little Fencote . . . . . F 3
36 Little Fenton . . . . . D 3
26 Little Fransham . . . D 2
17 Little Gaddesden . . C 11
15 Little Garway . . . . . B 8
25 Little Gidding . . . . G 2
27 Little Glemham . . . J 6
25 Little Gransden . . . K 4
7 Little Green . . . . . A 10
33 Little Grimsby . . . . A 10
60 Little Gruinard . . . . G 1
18 Little Hadham . . . . B 4
24 Little Hale . . . . B 2
18 Little Hallingbury . . B 5
17 Little Hampden . . . D 9
23 Little Harrowden . . E 12
17 Little Haseley . . . . . D 7
37 Little Hatfield . . . . C 9
12 Little Haven . . . . . F 2
22 Little Hay . . . . B 5
31 Little Hayfield . . . . A 9
31 Little Haywood . . . H 8
21 Little Hereford . . . F 11
27 Little Horkesley . . . M 2
18 Little Hormead . . . . A 4
10 Little Horsted . . . . . F 3
35 Little Horton . . . . . D 10
17 Little Horwood . . . . A 9
23 Little Houghton . . . F 11
31 Little Hucklow . . . . B 10
34 Little Hulton . . . . . G 6
17 Little Hungerford . . G 8
23 Little Irchester . . . . E 12
17 Little Kelk . . . . A 8
17 Little Kimble . . . . . C 9
17 Little Kingshill . . . . D 10
38 Little Langdale . . . . E 5
8 Little Langford . . . . C 2
19 Little Leighs . . . . . . B 7
34 Little Lever . . . . . . F 6
23 Little Linford . . . . . H 11
10 Little Londond,
   E. Sussex . . . . F 4
8 Little London, Hants. A 5
17 Little London, Hants. H 7
24 Little London, Lincs. C 5
35 Little London,
   W. Yorks. . . . . C 10
31 Little Longstone . . . C 10
58 Little Lynturk . . . . F 3
22 Little Malvern . . . . H 1
27 Little Maplestead . . M 1
22 Little Marcle . . . . . A 10
17 Little Marlow . . . . . E 9
26 Little Massingham . . C 1
26 Little Melton . . . . . E 5
12 Little Milford . . . . . F 3
14 Little Mill . . . . D 6
17 Little Milton . . . . . D 7
17 Little Missenden . . D 10
30 Little Ness . . . . H 3
30 Little Neston . . . . . C 2
12 Little Newcastle . . . D 3
40 Little Newsham . . . C 1
19 Little Oakley,
   Essex . . . . A 12
23 Little Oakley,
   Northants. . . . . . . D 12
44 Little Orton . . . . . . G 2
36 Little Ouseburn . . . A 2
25 Little Paxton . . . . . J 3
2 Little Petherick . . . B 6
42 Little Pinmore . . . . C 3
26 Little Plumstead . . . D 6
32 Little Ponton . . . . . G 6
4 Little Potheridge . . . E 4
25 Little Raveley . . . . . G 4
35 Little Ribson . . . . . B 12
16 Little Rissington . . . B 3
30 Little Ryburgh . . . . C 3
45 Little Ryle . . . . B 8
39 Little Salkeld . . . . . B 8
8 Little Samborne . . . C 5
25 Little Sampford . . . M 7
25 Little Shelford . . . . K 5
44 Little Scatwell . . . . D 7
6 Little Silver, Devon . F 7
6 Little Silver, Devon . E 3

36 Little Smeaton . . . . E 3
26 Little Snoring . . . . . B 2
15 Little Sodbury . . . . F 10
16 Little Somerford . . . E 1
40 Little Stainton . . . . C 4
30 Little Stanney . . . . . C 3
25 Little Staughton . . . J 2
33 Little Steeping . . . . D 11
27 Little Stonham . . . . J 4
23 Little Stretton,
   Leics. . . . . B 10
21 Little Stretton,
   Shropshire . . . . . . C 10
39 Little Strickland . . . C 8
25 Little Stukeley . . . . H 3
45 Little Swinburne . . . E 8
49 Little Swinton . . . . E 11
16 Little Tew . . . . A 5
25 Little Thetford . . . . H 6
25 Little Thurlow . . . . K 8
18 Little Thurrock . . . . F 6
42 Little Torhouse . . . . E 3
4 Little Torrington . . . D 4
45 Little Tosson . . . . . C 8
19 Little Totham . . . . . C 9
38 Little Town . . . . . . C 5
56 Little Urchany . . . . E 4
38 Little Urswick . . . . H 5
19 Little Wakering . . . . E 9
27 Little Waldingfield . . L 2
26 Little Walsingham . . B 2
19 Little Waltham . . . . C 7
18 Little Warley . . . . . E 6
37 Little Weighton . . . D 7
27 Little Welnetham . . J 2
21 Little Wenlock . . . . B 12
27 Little Whittingham
   Green . . . . H 6
45 Little Whittington . . F 8
25 Little Wilbraham . . J 6
8 Little Wishford . . . . B 2
22 Little Witley . . . . . F 1
16 Little Wittenham . . E 6
16 Little Wolford . . . . A 3
23 Little Woolstone . . H 12
25 Little Wymington . . J 1
18 Little Wymondley . . A 2
22 Little Wyrley . . . . . B 4
27 Little Yeldam . . . . . L 1
64 Little-ayre . . . . C 6
41 Littlebeck . . . . E 9
35 Littleborough,
   Manchester . . . . . F 8
32 Littleborough,
   Notts. . . . . B 5
11 Littlebourne . . . . . B 10
25 Littlebury . . . . L 6
34 Littledale . . . . A 4
15 Littledean . . . . C 10
61 Littleferry . . . . G 8
4 Littleham, Devon . . D 3
6 Littleham, Devon . . H 4
9 Littlehampton . . . . F 11
5 Littlehempston . . . . J 7
45 Littlehoughton . . . . A 10
59 Littlemill, Grampian H 1
56 Littlemill, Highland . E 5
45 Littlemill,
   Northumb. . . . . . . A 10
47 Littlemill,
   Strathclyde . . . . . . H 9
16 Littlemore . . . . D 6
31 Littleover . . . . G 11
25 Littleport . . . . G 7
25 Littleport Bridge . . G 7
11 Littlestone-on-Sea . . F 9
40 Littlethorpe, Ches. . . H 3
30 Littleton, Ches. . . . . D 3
43 Littleton, Dumf. &
   Gall. . . . . F 7
8 Littleton, Hants. . . . C 4
7 Littleton, Som. . . . . C 8
9 Littleton, Surrey . . . A 11
17 Littleton, Surrey . . . G 11
53 Littleton, Tayside . . D 7
15 Littleton Drew . . . . F 11
8 Littleton Panell . . . . A 2
15 Littleton upon
   Severn . . . . E 9
40 Littletown . . . . A 4
17 Littlewick Green . . . F 9
15 Littleworth, Glos. . . D 11
16 Littleworth, Oxon . . D 4
22 Littleworth, Heref. &
   Worc. . . . . G 2
22 Littleworth, Staffs. . A 4
31 Littleworth, Staffs. . H 8
10 Littleworth,
   W. Sussex . . . . . . F 1
31 Litton, Derby . . . . . C 10
39 Litton, N. Yorks. . . H 11
7 Litton, Som. . . . . . A 9
30 Liverpool . . . . A 2
35 Liversedge . . . . E 10

41 Liverton, Cleveland . D 7
5 Liverton, Devon .... H 7
48 Livingston ....C 3
48 Livingston Station .. C 3
29 Lixwm ....C 11
2 Lizard ....H 4
28 Llaingoch ....B 2
20 Llaithddu ....D 6
20 Llan................B 4
14 Llan-Rumney ....F 5
28 Llanaber ....H 5
28 Llanaelhaearn ....F 3
28 Llanafan ....E 2
20 Llanafan-fawr ....G 5
20 Llanafan-fechan .....G 5
28 Llanallgo ....B 4
29 Llanarmon Dyffryn
   Ceiriog ....G 10
29 Llanarmon-yn-lal . .E 11
13 Llanarth, Dyfed ....A 7
15 Llanarth, Gwent ....C 7
14 Llanarthney ....C 7
29 Llanasa.............B 10
28 Llanbabo ....B 3
20 Llanbadarn Fawr ...D 2
20 Llanbadarn Fynyda .E 6
21 Llanbadarn-y-
   garreg ....G 7
15 Llanbadoc ....D 7
28 Llanbadrig ....A 3
15 Llanbeder ....E 7
28 Llanbedr,
   Gwynedd ....H 5
14 Llanbedr, Powys ....B 6
21 Llanbedr, Powys ....H 7
29 Llanbedr-Dyffryn-
   Clwyd ....D 10
28 Llanbedr-goch ......B 4
28 Llanbedrog ....G 3
29 Llanbedr-y-cennin . .C 7
28 Llanberis ....D 5
14 Llanbethery ....G 4
20 Llanbister ....E 6
14 Llanblethian ....G 3
12 Llanboidy ....E 5
14 Llanbradach ....E 5
56 Llanbryde ....D 8
20 Llanbrynmair ....B 5
14 Llancadle ....G 4
14 Llancaiach ....E 4
14 Llancarfan ....G 4
15 Llancayo ....D 7
15 Llancloudy ....B 8
21 Llancoch ....E 7
14 Llandaff ....F 5
28 Llandanwg ....G 5
13 Llandarcy ....G 10
12 Llandawke ....F 6
28 Llanddaniel Fab ....C 4
13 Llanddarog ....E 8
20 Llanddeiniol ....E 1
28 Llanddeiniolen .....D 5
29 Llandderfel ....F 9
13 Llanddeusant,
   Dyfed ....E 11
28 Llanddeusant,
   Gwynedd ....B 3
14 Llanddew ....A 4
13 Llanddewi ....H 8
20 Llanddewi-Brefi ....G 2
15 Llanddewi
   Rhydderch ....C 7
12 Llanddewi Velfrey . .E 5
20 Llanddewi'r Cwm . .G 6
29 Llanddoget ....D 7
28 Llanddona ....B 5
12 Llanddowror ....F 6
29 Llanddulas ....B 8
28 Llanddyfnan ....B 4
14 Llandefaelog Fach . .A 4
14 Llandefaelog
   ter-graig ....A 4
14 Llandefalle ....A 4
28 Llandegai ....C 5
28 Llandegfan ....C 5
15 Llandegfedd ....E 7
29 Llandegla ....E 11
21 Llandegley ....F 7
13 Llandeilo ....E 9
20 Llandeilo Graban ..H 6
14 Llandeilo'r Fan ....A 2
12 Llandeloy ....D 2
13 Llandenny ....D 7
15 Llandevenny ....F 7
12 Llandewi Velfrey . .E 5
20 Llandewi
   Ystradenny ......E 6
12 Llandilo ....D 4
20 Llandinabo ....B 8
20 Llandinam ....D 6
12 Llandissilio ....E 5
15 Llandogo ....D 8
14 Llandough, S. Glam. G 5
14 Llandough, S. Glam. G 3

13 Llandovery ....D 11
14 Llandow ....G 3
20 Llandre, Dyfed .....D 2
13 Llandre, Dyfed ....C 10
29 Llandrillo ....F 9
29 Llandrillo-yn-Rhos. .B 7
20 Llandrindod Wells ..F 6
21 Llandrinio ....A 8
29 Llandudno ....B 7
29 Llandudno Junc. ....B 7
28 Llandwrog ....E 4
12 Llandybie ....E 9
13 Llandyfaelog ....F 7
13 Llandyfan ....E 9
14 Llandyfodwg ....F 3
13 Llandyfriog ....C 7
28 Llandyfrydog ....B 4
12 Llandygwydd ....C 6
29 Llandyrnog ....D 10
29 Llandysilio ....H 12
21 Llandyssil ....C 7
13 Llandyssul ....C 7
14 Llanedeyrn ....F 5
20 Llaneglwys ....H 6
20 Llanegryn ....B 2
13 Llanegwad ....E 8
28 Llaneilian ....A 4
29 Llanelian-y-Rhos ..B 7
29 Llanelidan ....E 10
14 Llanelieu ....A 5
14 Llanellen ....C 6
13 Llanelli, Dyfed ....G 8
14 Llanelli, Gwent ....C 5
28 Llanelltyd ....H 6
28 Llanelwedd ....G 6
28 Llanenddwyn ....H 5
28 Llanengan ....G 2
28 Llanerchymedd ......B 4
20 Llanerfyl ....A 6
28 Llanfachraeth ......B 3
28 Llanfachreth ....H 7
28 Llanfaelog ....C 3
28 Llanfaelrhys ....G 2
15 Llanfaenor ....C 7
28 Llanfaes, Gwynedd .C 5
14 Llanfaes, Powys ....B 4
28 Llanfaethlu ....B 3
28 Llanfalgan ....D 4
28 Llanfair ....G 5
20 Llanfair-Caereinion .B 6
20 Llanfair-Clydogau . .G 2
29 Llanfair Dyffryn
   Clwyd ....E 10
12 Llanfair
   Nant-Gwyn .....C 5
29 Llanfair Talhaiarn . .C 8
21 Llanfair Waterdine E 8
28 Llanfairfechan .....C 6
28 Llanfair-P.G. ....C 5
28 Llanfair-y-
   Cwmmwd ....D 4
28 Llanfairynghornwy .A 3
28 Llanfair-yn-
   Neubwll ....C 2
12 Llanfallteg ....E 5
12 Llanfallteg West ....E 5
20 Llanfaredd ....G 6
20 Llanfarian ....E 2
29 Llanfechain ....H 11
28 Llanfechell ....A 3
20 Llanfendigaid ......B 1
29 Llanferres ....D 11
28 Llanfflewyn ....A 3
28 Llanfigael ....B 3
20 Llanfihangel ....A 6
14 Llanfihangel
   Crucorney ....B 6
29 Llanfihangel Glyn
   Myfyr ....E 9
14 Llanfihangel
   Llantarnam ......E 6
14 Llanfihangel Nant
   Bran ....A 3
21 Llanfihangel
   Rhydithon ....F 7
15 Llanfihangel Rogiet .F 8
14 Llanfihangel
   Tal-y-llyn ....A 4
13 Llanfihangel
   ar-arth ....C 8
21 Llanfihangel-nant-
   Melan ....G 7
13 Llanfihangel-
   uwch-Gwili ......E 8
20 Llanfihangel-y-.
   Creuddyn ....E 2
20 Llanfihangel yn
   Nhowyn ....C 3
20 Llanfihangel-y-.
   Pennant ....B 2
28 Llanfihangel-y-
   pennant ....F 5
21 Llanfihangel-y-
   traethau ....G 5

14 Llanfilo ....A 4
14 Llanfoist ....C 6
29 Llanfor ....G 8
14 Llanfrechfa ....E 6
28 Llanfrothen ....F 5
14 Llanfrynach ....B 4
29 Llanfwrog, Clwyd .D 10
28 Llanfwrog,
   Gwynedd ....B 2
29 Llanfyllin ....H 10
29 Llanfynydd, Clwyd .E 12
13 Llanfynydd, Dyfed . .D 9
12 Llanfyrnach ....D 6
20 Llangadfan ....A 6
13 Llangadog, Dyfed .D 10
13 Llangadog, Dyfed . .F 7
29 Llangadwaladr,
   Clwyd ....G 11
28 Llangadwaladr,
   Gwynedd ....C 3
28 Llangaffo ....C 4
28 Llangain ....E 7
20 Llangammarch
   Wells ....H 5
14 Llangan ....G 3
15 Llangarron ....B 8
14 Llangasty-Tal-y-
   llyn ....B 5
13 Llangathen ....E 9
14 Llangattock ....C 5
15 Llangattock
   Lingoed ....B 7
14 Llangattock nigh
   Usk ....C 6
15 Llangattock Vibon-
   Avel ....C 8
29 Llangedwyn ....H 11
28 Llangefni ....C 4
14 Llangeinor ....F 2
20 Llangeinwen ....D 4
20 Llangeitho ....F 2
13 Llangeler ....C 7
13 Llangelynin ....B 1
13 Llangendeirne ......F 8
13 Llangennech ....G 9
13 Llangennith ....H 7
14 Llangenny ....C 6
14 Llangenyw ....C 8
28 Llangian ....G 2
13 Llangiwg ....F 10
28 Llangoed ....B 5
12 Llangoedmor ....B 5
29 Llangollen ....F 11
12 Llangolman ....D 5
14 Llangorse ....B 4
15 Llangoven ....D 8
29 Llangower ....G 8
29 Llangranog ....B 6
28 Llangristiolus .....C 4
15 Llangrove ....B 8
15 Llangua ....B 7
21 Llangunllo ....E 7
13 Llangunnor ....E 8
20 Llangurig ....D 5
29 Llangwm, Clwyd . .F 9
12 Llangwm, Dyfed ...F 3
13 Llangwm, Gwent ...D 7
13 Llangwm-isaf ......D 7
28 Llangwnnadl ....G 2
29 Llangwyfan ....D 10
28 Llangwyfanisaf .....C 3
28 langwyllog ....B 4
20 Llangwyryfon ......E 2
12 Llangybi, Dyfed ...G 2
15 Llangybi, Gwent ...E 7
28 Llangybi, Gwynedd .F 4
13 Llangyfelach ......G 10
20 Llangynfelyn ......C 2
20 Llangynhafal ......D 10
14 Llangynidr ....B 5
12 Llangynin ....E 6
10 Llangynllo ....C 7
13 Llangynog, Dyfed . .E 7
29 Llangynog, Powys . .H 9
14 Llangynwyd ....E 2
14 Lanhamlach ....B 4
14 Llanharan ....F 3
15 Llanharry ....F 3
15 Llanhennock ....E 7
14 Llanhilleth ....D 5
28 Llaniestyn ....G 2
21 Llanigan ....H 7
20 Llanilar ....E 2
14 Llanilid ....F 3
14 Llanilterne ....F 4
15 Llanishen, Gwent ..D 8
14 Llanishen, S. Glam. .F 5
28 Llanllawddog ......D 8
20 Llanllechid ....C 5
20 Llanllugan ....B 6
21 Llanllwchaiarn .....C 7

13 Llanllwch ....E 7
28 Llanllyfni ....E 4
15 Llanllywel ....D 7
14 Llanmadoc ....H 8
15 Llanmaes ....G 3
15 Llanmartin ....E 7
14 Llanmerewig ....C 7
14 Llanmihangel ......G 3
12 Llanmiloe ....F 6
15 Llanmorlais ....G 8
29 Llannefydd ....C 9
13 Llannon ....F 9
20 Llannor ....F 3
20 Llanon ....F 1
13 Llanpumsaint ......D 7
28 Llanreithan ....D 2
29 Llanrhaeadr ....D 10
29 Llanrhaeadr-ym-
   Mochnant ....H 10
13 Llanrhidian ....H 8
29 Llanrhos ....B 7
14 Llanrhyddlad ......A 3
20 Llanrhystyd ....E 1
12 Llanrian ....D 2
13 Llanrug ....D 5
29 Llanrwst ....D 7
12 Llansadurnen ......F 6
13 Llansadwrn,
   Dyfed ....D 10
28 Llansadwrn,
   Gwynedd ....C 5
13 Llan-saint ....F 7
13 Llansamlet ....G 10
14 Llansannan ....G 3
14 Llansantffraed .....B 5
20 Llansantffraed
   Cwmdeuddwr .....F 5
20 Llansantffraed-in-
   Elvel ....G 6
20 Llansantffraid ......F 1
29 Llansantffraid Glan
   Conway ....C 7
29 Llansantffraid-ym-
   Mechain ....H 11
29 Llansilin ....G 11
15 Llansoy ....D 7
14 Llanspyddid ....B 3
12 Llanstadwell ......F 3
13 Llanstephan ....F 7
14 Llanteg ....F 5
14 Llanthony ....B 6
15 Llantilio Crossenny . C 7
15 Llantilio Pertholey ..C 6
12 Llantood ....C 5
15 Llantrisant, Gwent .E 7
14 Llantrisant,
   Mid Glam. ......F 4
14 Llantrithyd ....G 4
14 Llantwit Fardre ...F 4
14 Llantwit-Major .....G 3
29 Llanuwchllyn ......G 8
15 Llanvaches ....E 7
15 Llanvair Discoed ..E 8
15 Llanvapley ....C 7
15 Llanvetherine .....C 7
14 Llanveynoe ....A 6
15 Llanvihangel
   Gobion ....C 7
14 Llanvihangel
   Pontymoel ....D 6
15 Llanvihangel Ystern-
   Llewern ....C 7
14 Llanwarne ....B 8
29 Llanwddyn ....H 9
14 Llanwenarth ....C 6
13 Llanwenog ....B 8
15 Llanwern ....E 7
12 Llanwinio ....D 6
12 Llanwnda, Dyfed ..C 3
28 Llanwnda,
   Gwynedd ....D 4
13 Llanwnen ....B 8
20 Llanwnog ....C 6
13 Llanwrda ....D 10
20 Llanwrin ....B 3
14 Llanwrthwl ....F 5
20 Llanwrtyd ....H 4
20 Llanwrtyd Wells ...H 4
14 Llanwyddelan ......B 6
30 Llanybiodwel ......H 1
13 Llanybri ....F 6
12 Llanybyther ....C 8
12 Llanycefn ....E 4
13 Llanychaer Birdge . .C 3
29 Llanymawddwy ....H 8
20 Llanymynech ......H 1
28 Llanynghenedl .....B 3
29 Llanynys ....D 10
30 Llan-y-pwll ....E 2
21 Llanyre ....F 6
28 Llanystumdwy .....F 4
14 Llanywern ....A 4

12 Llawhaden ....E 4
30 Llawnt ....G 1
20 Llawr-y-glyn ......C 5
30 Llay ....E 2
14 Llechfaen ....A 4
12 Llechryd, Dyfed . .C 5
14 Llechryd, Mid Glam. C 4
29 Llechrydau ....G 11
13 Llethrid ....H 8
20 Lledrod ....E 2
29 Llidiad-Nenog .....C 9
28 Llidiardau,
   Gwynedd ....G 1
29 Llidiardau,
   Gwynedd ....F 8
29 Llidiart-y-parc ....F 10
14 Llithfaen ....F 3
29 Llong ....D 12
21 Llowes ....H 7
13 Llundain-fach .....G 1
14 Llwydcoed ....D 3
13 Llwyn-Celyn ......A 8
29 Llwyn Dafydd .....B 7
21 Llwynderw, Powys ..B 7
20 Llwynderw, Powys . .D 5
12 Llwyn-drain ....D 6
20 Llwyngwril ....A 2
13 Llwyn-hendy ....G 9
29 Llwyn-mawr ....G 11
14 Llwyn-on ....C 3
20 Llwyn-y-groes .....G 2
20 Llwyn-y-pia ....E 3
30 Llynclys ....H 1
28 Llynfaes ....B 3
29 Llysfaen ....C 8
14 Llyswen ....A 4
14 Llysworney ....G 3
12 Llys-y-fran ....E 4
14 Llywel ....A 2
20 Llywernog ....D 3
49 Loanend ....D 12
48 Loanhead, Lothian . .C 5
47 Loanhead,
   Strathclyde ....D 9
48 Loanhead,
   Strathclyde ....F 3
58 Loanhead of
   Fedderate ....C 6
47 Loans ....F 8
45 Loansdean ....E 10
4 Lobb ....B 3
61 Loch Choire Lodge .D 7
42 LochHead ....G 4
60 Loch Loyal Lo. ....C 6
55 Lochailort ....L 2
50 Lochaline ....C 4
42 Lohans ....F 2
43 Locharbriggs ......D 10
43 Locharwoods ......E 11
60 Lochassynt Lodge . .D 3
51 Lochawe ....E 8
50 Lochboisdale .....E 3
57 Lochcallater ....L 7
54 Lochcarron ....F 3
61 Lochdhu Lodge ...C 9
51 Lochdochart Ho. . .E 11
50 Lochdonhead ......D 5
54 Lochdrum ....B 6
46 Lochead,
   Strathclyde ....B 3
46 Lochead,
   Strathclyde ....A 5
52 Lochearnhead .....E 1
53 Lochee ....D 8
43 Lochend, Dumf. &
   Gall. ....F 9
52 Lochend, Fife .....H 6
56 Lochend, Highland . F 2
61 Lochend, Highland A 11
43 Lochend, Highland .D 8
43 Lochfoot ....D 9
50 Lochgair ....H 6
57 Lochgarthside ......H 1
47 Lochgate ....F 11
53 Lochgelly ....H 7
46 Lochgoilhead ......A 4
51 Lochgoilhead ......G 9
56 Loch-hill ....C 8
47 Lochhill ....H 11
56 Lochindorb Lo. ....F 5
47 Lochingirrcoh .....H 11
60 Lochinver ....E 3
48 Lochlycock ....F 2
43 Lochmaben ....C 11
60 Lochmore Lodge ...D 4
52 Lochore ....G 6
46 Lochranza ....A 4
47 Lochridge ....E 9
58 Lochs Crofts ......B 1
59 Lochside, Grampian L 5
56 Lochside, Highland .B 8
61 Lochside, Highland .D 8
60 Lochstack Lodge ...C 4

61 Lochstrathy ....C 8
59 Lochton ....H 5
59 Lochton of Leys ...H 4
53 Lochty, Fife ....F 10
59 Lochty, Tayside ...L 3
50 Lochuisge ....B 5
43 Lochurr ....C 8
47 Lochwinnoch ......C 8
43 Lochwood ....B 11
55 Lochy Brdige ......M 5
44 Lock Hills ....H 3
3 Lockengate ....D 7
43 Lockerbie ....C 12
16 Lockeridge ....G 3
8 Lockerley ....C 4
16 Locking ....H 7
16 Lockinge ....E 5
37 Lockington, Humber. B 7
32 Lockington, Leics. ..B 7
30 Lockleywood ......G 5
8 Lock's Heath ......E 6
4 Lockshill ....E 4
41 Lockton ....F 8
23 Loddington, Leics. .B 11
23 Loddington,
   Northants. ......D 11
5 Loddiswell ....L 6
26 Loddon ....F 6
25 Lode ....J 6
7 Loders ....G 8
9 Lodsworth ....D 10
40 Lofthouse, N. Yorks. H 1
35 Lofthouse,
   W. Yorks. ......E 12
41 Loftus ....C 7
47 Logan ....G 10
42 Logan Mains ......G 2
53 Logie, Fife ....E 7
53 Logie, Fife ....E 9
56 Logie Hill ....B 3
58 Logie Newton ......D 4
59 Logie Pert ....L 4
52 Logiealmond Lo. ..D 4
52 Logierait ....B 5
12 Login ....E 5
25 Lolworth ....J 5
54 Lonbain ....D 1
36 Londesborough ....C 6
18 London ....F 3
3 London Apprentice .F 4
18 London Colney ....D 2
40 Londonderry ....F 3
33 Londonthorpe ......F 7
54 Londubh ....B 2
60 Lone ....C 4
15 Long Ashton ....G 9
32 Long Bennington ..F 5
7 Long Bredy ....G 9
23 Long Buckby ......E 11
7 Long Burton ....E 10
32 Long Clawson .....G 4
8 Long Common .....E 6
31 Long Compton,
   Staffordshire .....H 7
16 Long Compton,
   Warwickshire ....A 4
17 Long Crendon ......C 8
8 Long Crichel ......E 1
17 Long Ditton ....G 12
36 Long Drax ....D 5
32 Long Duckmanton . .C 2
32 Long Eaton ....G 2
30 Long Green ....C 3
16 Long Hanborough ..C 5
48 Long Hermiston ...B 4
23 Long Itchington ...F 7
23 Long Lawford ......D 8
7 Long Load ....D 8
17 Long Marston, Herts. C 9
36 Long Marston,
   N. Yorks. ....B 3
22 Long Marston,
   Warwick ....G 5
39 Long Marton ....C 9
27 Long Melford ......K 2
15 Long Newnton ....E 12
40 Long Newton ......D 4
35 Long Preston ......A 7
37 Long Riston ....C 9
36 Long Sandall ......F 4
25 Long Stanton All
   Sainsts ....J 5
25 Long Stanton
   St. Michael ......J 5
26 Long Stratton .....F 5
23 Long Street ....G 11
9 Long Sutton, Hants. A 9
24 Long Sutton, Lincs. .C 5
7 Long Sutton, Som. . D 8
21 Long Waste ....A 11
32 Long Whatton .....H 2
41 Long Whins ....G 11
16 Long Wittenham ...E 6

47 Longbar ....D 8
45 Longbenton ....F 11
16 Longborough ......A 3
22 Longbridge, War. ...F 6
22 Longbridge, W. Midlands ......D 3
7 Longbridge Deverill ....B 11
54 Longbridgemuir ....E 11
44 Longbyre ....F 5
42 Longcastle ....G 5
31 Longcliffe ....E 10
16 Longcot ....E 4
49 Longcroft, Borders .D 8
48 Longcroft, Central ..A 1
17 Longcross ....H 10
21 Longden ....B 10
22 Longdon ....A 4
22 Longdon Green ....A 4
21 Longdon upon Tern ....A 11
6 Longdown ....G 2
2 Longdowns ....F 4
45 Longdyke ....B 10
10 Longfield ....A 5
10 Longfield Hill ....A 5
31 Longford, Derby ...F 10
15 Longford, Glos. ...B 11
18 Longford, London ..F 1
30 Longford, Salop ...G 5
23 Longford, W. Midlands ......D 7
53 Longforgan ....D 8
49 Longformacus ......D 9
45 Longframlington ...C 9
8 Longham, Dorset ..F 2
26 Longham, Norf. ....D 2
58 Longhill ....B 7
45 Longhirst ....D 10
15 Longhope ....B 10
45 Longhorsley ....D 9
45 Longhoughton ...B 10
38 Longlands ....B 5
16 Longlane, Berks. ..G 6
31 Longlane, Derby .F 11
15 Longlevens .....B 11
22 Longley Green .....G 1
58 Longmanhill ......A 5
9 Longmoor Camp ...C 9
56 Longmorn ....D 8
49 Longnewton ....G 8
15 Longney ......C 11
49 Longniddry ......B 7
31 Longnor ....D 9
21 Longnot ....B 10
8 Longparish ....B 6
34 Longridge, Lancs. ..D 5
48 Longridge, Lothian .C 2
48 Longriggend ......B 1
31 Longsdon ....E 8
58 Longside ....C 8
30 Longslow ....G 5
8 Longstock ....B 5
3 Longstone ....B 7
25 Longstowe ....K 4
24 Longthorpe ....F 3
34 Longton, Lancs. ....E 4
31 Longton, Staffs ...F 7
44 Longtown, Cumb. ..F 2
14 Longtown, Heref. & Worc. ....A 6
21 Longville in the Dale ....C 11
15 Longwell Green ...G 10
17 Longwick ....D 8
45 Longwitton ....D 9
21 Longwood .....B 11
16 Longworth ....D 5
49 Longyester ....C 8
62 Lonmore ....D 2
10 Loose ....C 6
17 Loosley Row ......D 9
58 Lootcherbrae ....B 3
8 Lopcombe Corner ..C 4
7 Lopen ....E 8
30 Loppington ....G 3
45 Lorbottle ....B 8
45 Lorbottle Hall .....B 8
9 Lordington ....E 9
44 Lordsgate ....F 3
43 Lorg ....B 7
32 Loscoe ....E 2
56 Lossiemouth ....C 8
30 Lostock Gralam ...C 5
30 Lostock Green .....C 5
34 Lostock Junction ...F 5
3 Lostwithiel ....D 8
61 Lothbeg ....F 9
35 Lothersdale ......C 8
61 Lothmore ....F 9
7 Lottisham ....C 9
17 Loadwater ......E 10
32 Loughborough ....H 3
13 Loughor ....G 9

23 Loughton, Bucks. .H 11
18 Loughton, Essex ...D 4
21 Loughton, Salop ..D 11
24 Lound, Lincs. ....D 2
32 Lound, Notts. ......B 4
26 Lound, Suffolk ....E 8
31 Lount ....H 12
33 Louth ....B 10
35 Love Clough ......D 7
9 Lovedean ....E 8
4 Loveacott ....C 4
4 Lover ....D 4
36 Loversall ....G 4
18 Loves Green ....C 6
40 Lovesome Hill .....E 4
12 Loveston ....F 4
7 Lovington ....C 9
42 Low Ardwell .....G 2
43 Low Barlay ....F 7
35 Low Bradfield ...H 11
35 Low Bradley .....B 9
38 Low Braithwaite ....A 6
45 Low Brunton ......F 7
36 Low Burnham ....G 5
40 Low Burton ....G 3
45 Low Buston .....B 10
36 Low Catton ......B 5
40 Low Coniscliffe ....D 3
42 Low Craighead .....A 3
44 Low Cranecleugh ..D 5
44 Low Crosby ....G 3
41 Low Dalby ....F 8
40 Low Dinsdale .....D 4
36 Low Eggborough ...E 3
40 Low Etherley ......B 2
44 Low Geltbridge ....G 4
47 Low Grange ....H 8
22 Low Habberley ..D 2
7 Low Ham ....C 8
45 Low Hedgeley ....A 9
39 Low Hesket ......A 7
45 Low Hesleyhurst ...C 9
41 Low Hutton ......H 8
42 Low Knockbrex ...E 5
31 Low Leighton .....B 8
38 Low Lorton ......C 4
42 Low Malzie ....F 4
41 Low Marishes ...G 8
32 Low Marnham ....C 5
41 Low Mill ....F 7
34 Low Moor ......C 6
45 Low Moorsley ...H 11
45 Low Newton-by-the-Sea ....A 10
44 Low Row, Cumb. ...G 4
38 Low Row, Cumb. ...B 6
39 Low Row, N. Yorks. ....E 12
42 Low Salchrie ......E 1
37 Low Santon ......F 7
47 Low Shawsburn ...D 12
26 Low Street ....C 6
26 Low Thurlton ....E 7
48 Low Torry ....A 3
45 Low Town ......C 9
47 Low Waters .....D 12
40 Low Worsall ....D 4
38 Low Wray ....E 6
39 Lowbridge House ...E 7
38 Lowca ....C 2
32 Lowdham ....F 4
30 Lowe ....G 4
6 Lower Aisholt ......C 5
7 Lower Ansty ......F 11
6 Lower Ashton ....H 2
17 Lower Assendon ....F 8
63 Lower Bayble ......D 6
10 Lower Beeding .....E 1
39 Lower Bentham ...H 9
7 Lower Bockhampton ....G 10
23 Lower Boddington ..G 8
2 Lower Boscaswell ...C 1
9 Lower Bourne ....B 10
22 Lower Brailes .....H 6
62 Lower Breakish ....F 2
22 Lower Broadheath ..F 2
15 Lower Bullingham ...A 8
25 Lower Caldecote ...F 3
15 Lower Cam ....D 10
14 Lower Chapel ....A 4
8 Lower Chicksgrove .C 1
8 Lower Chute .....A 4
10 Lower Cokeham ...H 1
31 Lower Crossings ...B 9
35 Lower Cumberworth ....F 11
14 Lower Cwm-twrch ...C 1
34 Lower Darwen ....E 6
25 Lower Dean .....H 2
54 Lower Diabaig ...D 2
10 Lower Dicker ...G 4
21 Lower Dinchope ..D 10
61 Lower Dounreay ...A 9

21 Lower Down ......D 9
2 Lower Drift ....G 2
36 Lower Dunsforth ...A 2
8 Lower Everleigh ...A 3
15 Lower Failand ....G 8
9 Lower Farringdon ..C 8
38 Lower Foxdale ...G 1
12 Lower Freystrop ...F 3
9 Lower Froyle .....B 9
60 Lower Gledfield ...G 6
10 Lower Green, Kent .D 5
26 Lower Green, Norf. .B 3
27 Lower Hacheston ...J 6
62 Lower Halistra ....B 2
11 Lower Halstow ....A 7
11 Lower Hardres ...C 10
56 Lower Hempriggs ...C 7
21 Lower Hergest ....G 8
16 Lower Heyford ....B 6
10 Lower Higham ....A 6
10 Lower Hordley ....G 3
10 Lower Horsebridge .G 4
51 Lower Kinchrackine E 8
7 Lower Kingcombe ...F 9
10 Lower Kingswoood ..C 1
30 Lower Kinnerton ...D 2
15 Lower Langford ...H 8
8 Lower Largo ......G 9
31 Lower Leigh .....G 8
57 Lower Lenie ......G 1
20 Lower Llanfadog ...F 5
4 Lower Loxhore ...B 5
15 Lower Lydbrook ...C 9
21 Lower Lye ....F 9
14 Lower Machen ....E 5
15 Lower Maes-coed ...A 7
19 Lower Mayland ...D 9
62 Lower Milovaig ...C 1
34 Lower Moor ....G 3
18 Lower Nazeing ....C 4
52 Lower Oakfield ...H 6
62 Lower Ollach ....D 4
14 Lower Penarth ....G 5
22 Lower Penn ......C 2
8 Lower Pennington .G 5
30 Lower Peover ....C 6
35 Lower Place ......F 8
22 Lower Quinton ...G 5
21 Lower Rochford ...F 11
34 Lower Salter .....A 5
6 Lower Seagry .....F 1
63 Lower Shader ....A 5
25 Lower Shelton ....L 1
17 Lower Shiplake ...F 8
23 Lower Shuckburgh ..F 8
16 Lower Slaughter ...B 3
16 Lower Stanton St. Quintin ......F 12
11 Lower Stoke ......A 7
26 Lower Street ......B 6
22 Lower Strensham ...H 3
17 Lower Sundon ....A 11
8 Lower Swanwick ....E 6
16 Lower Swell ......B 3
62 Lower Tote ....B 1
12 Lower Town ......C 3
23 Lower Tysoe ......H 7
9 Lower Upham .....D 7
6 Lower Vexford ...C 5
34 Lower Walton .....H 5
7 Lower Waterston ..G 10
7 Lower Weare .....A 7
21 Lower Welson .....G 8
30 Lower Whitley ....B 5
9 Lower Wield .....B 8
17 Lower Winchendon .C 8
17 Lower Woodend ...E 9
8 Lower Woodford ...C 3
22 Lower Wyche .....H 1
23 Lowesby ....A 10
26 Lowestoft ....F 8
26 Lowestoft End ....F 8
38 Loweswater ....C 4
10 Lowfield Heath ...D 2
34 Logwill, Lancs. ...A 5
39 Lowgill, Cumbria ...E 8
25 Lowick, Northants. .G 1
45 Lowick, Northumb. B 11
38 Lowick Green .....E 6
14 Lowlands ....E 6
22 Lowsonford ....E 5
39 Lowther ....C 8
37 Lowthorpe ....A 8
34 Lowton, Manchester ....G 5
6 Lowton, Som. .....D 5
34 Lowton Common ..G 5
6 Loxbeare ....E 3
9 Loxhill ....B 11
4 Loxhore ....B 5
22 Loxley ....G 6
7 Loxton ....A 7
9 Loxwood ....C 11
60 Lubachoinnich ...G 5

60 Lubcroy ....F 4
23 Lubenham ....C 10
51 Lubnaclach .....A 11
54 Lubriach ....B 7
6 Luccombe ....B 3
9 Luccombe Village ..H 7
45 Lucker ....D 11
3 Luckett ....B 11
15 Luckington ......F 11
53 Lucklawhill ......E 9
6 Luckwell Bridge ...B 2
21 Lucton ....F 10
37 Ludborough ....H 10
12 Ludchurch ....F 5
35 Luddenden ......E 9
35 Luddenden Foot ...E 9
10 Luddesdown .....B 5
36 Luddington, Humberside ......E 6
22 Luddington, War. ...G 5
25 Luddington in the Brook ....G 2
21 Ludford ....E 10
33 Ludford Magna ...A 9
33 Ludford Parva ...A 9
17 Ludgershall ....B 7
8 Ludgershall ......A 4
2 Ludgvan ....F 2
26 Ludham ....D 7
21 Ludlow ....E 4
26 Ludney Green ....E 4
57 Ludwell ....D 12
40 Ludworth ....A 4
7 Luffincott ......F 2
4 Lugar ....G 10
49 Lugate ....E 7
49 Luggate Burn ....B 8
49 Luggiebank ....B 12
47 Lugton ....D 9
21 Lugwardine ....H 11
62 Luib ....E 5
51 Luib Hotel .....E 12
21 Luibeilt ....A 9
21 Lulham ....H 9
22 Lullington, Derby ..A 6
7 Lullington, Som. ...A 11
22 Lulsey ....G 1
15 Lulsgate Bottom ...H 8
35 Lumb ....E 9
35 Lumbutts ....E 8
36 Lumby ....D 3
47 Lumloch ....B 11
59 Lumphanan ......G 3
52 Lumphinnans ....H 6
49 Lumsdaine .....B 11
58 Lumsden ....E 2
53 Lunan ....B 11
53 Lunanhead ....B 9
52 Luncarty ....D 6
37 Lund, Humberside .B 7
36 Lund, N. Yorks. ...D 4
51 Lundavra ....A 8
26 Lunderton ......C 8
55 Lundie, Highland ..H 5
53 Lundie, Tayside ...D 8
53 Lundin Links .....G 9
50 Lungar (Hotel) ...G 5
64 Lunna ....C 7
47 Lunning ....C 7
13 Lunnon ....H 9
10 Lunsford ....B 6
6 Lunsford's Cross ..G 6
34 Lunt ....G 2
21 Luntley ....G 9
6 Luppitt ....F 5
35 Lupset ....E 11
39 Lupton ....G 8
21 Lurgashall ......C 10
56 Lurgmore ....F 1
33 Lusby ....C 10
9 Luss ....H 10
62 Lusta ....C 2
5 Lustleigh ....H 6
58 Luston ....F 10
17 Luthermuir ......K 4
53 Luthrie ....E 8
17 Luton, Beds. ....B 12
5 Luton, Devon ...H 8
10 Luton, Kent .....A 6
13 Lutterworth .....D 9
5 Lutton, Devon ...K 5
24 Lutton, Lincs. ...C 5
25 Lutton, Northants. .G 2
6 Luxborough ......B 3
3 Luxulyan ....D 7
61 Lybster ....D 11
21 Lydbury North ...D 9
11 Lydd ....F 9
11 Lydd-on-Sea ....G 9
11 Lydden ....D 11
23 Lyddington .....B 12
17 Lyde Green .....H 8
6 Lydeard St. Lawrence ......C 4
5 Lydford ....G 4

35 Lydgate ....E 8
21 Lydham ....C 9
16 Lydiard Millicent ...F 2
34 Lydiate ....G 2
7 Lydlinch ....E 10
15 Lydney ....D 9
12 Lydstep ....G 4
22 Lye ....D 3
15 Lye Cross ....H 8
17 Lye Green, Bucks. .D 10
10 Lye Green, E Sussex ....E 4
16 Lyford ....E 5
47 Lylestone, Strathclyde ....E 8
49 Lylestone, Borders .D 8
11 Lymbridge Green .D 10
7 Lyme Regis ......G 7
11 Lyminge ....D 10
8 Lymington ......F 4
9 Lyminster ......F 11
30 Lymm ....B 5
8 Lymore ....G 4
11 Lympne ....E 10
15 Lympsham ......A 6
6 Lympstone ......H 3
57 Lynaberack ......K 3
57 Lynachlaggan ....J 4
6 Lynch ....B 3
26 Lynch Green ....E 4
57 Lynchat ....J 3
8 Lyndhurst ......E 4
23 Lyndon ....B 12
48 Lyne, Borders ...E 5
17 Lyne, Surrey ...G 11
15 Lyne Down ......A 9
57 Lyne of Gorthleck .H 1
58 Lyne of Skene ...F 5
30 Lyneal ....G 3
62 Lynedale House ...C 3
16 Lyneham, Oxon ...B 4
16 Lyneham, Wilts. ...F 1
44 Lyneholmeford ...F 4
57 Lynmore ....G 6
45 Lynemouth .....D 11
64 Lyness ....E 1
26 Lyng, Norfolk ...D 4
7 Lyng, Somerset ...C 7
4 Lynmouth ......A 6
11 Lynsted ....B 8
4 Lynton ....A 6
7 Lyon's Gate .....F 10
21 Lyonshall ....G 9
8 Lytchett Matravers .G 1
8 Lytchett Minster ...G 1
61 Lyth ....B 11
34 Lytham ....D 3
34 Lytham St Anne's ..D 2
41 Lythe ....D 8
34 Lythes ....E 3
63 Maaruig ....F 3
2 Mabe Burnthouse ..F 5
33 Mabie ....D 10
33 Mablethorpe ...B 12
48 Mabiehill ....D 4
31 Macclesfield .....C 7
31 Macclesfield For. ..C 8
58 Macduff ....A 4
52 Machany ....F 4
14 Machen ....E 5
46 Machrihanish ....G 1
50 Machrins ....H 1
20 Machynlleth ......B 3
31 Mackworth .....F 11
49 Macmerry ....B 7
52 Madderty ....E 4
48 Maddiston ....B 2
9 Madehurst ....E 11
21 Madeley, Salop ...B 12
30 Madeley, Staffs. ...F 6
30 Madeley Heath ...F 6
25 Madingley ....J 5
21 Madley ....H 9
21 Madresfield ......G 2
2 Madron ....F 2
28 Maenaddwyn ....B 4
20 Maenclochog .....D 4
14 Maendy ....G 3
28 Maentwrog ....F 6
28 Maen-y-groes ....A 7
30 Maer ....F 6
29 Maerdy, Clwyd ...F 7
15 Maerdy, Dyfed ...D 10
15 Maerdy, Gwent ...B 7
13 Maerdy, Mid Glam. .D 3
30 Maesbrook Green ..H 2
30 Maesbury ....H 2
30 Maesbury Marsh ...H 2
14 Maesgwynne .....E 5
29 Maeshafn ....D 11
21 Maesllyn ....C 7
20 Maesmynis ....H 6
14 Maesteg ....E 2
13 Maestir ....B 9

13 Maestwynog .....C 10
13 Maes-y-bont .....E 9
13 Maesycrugiau ....C 8
14 Maes-y-cwmmer ...E 5
13 Maesymeillion ....B 7
18 Magdalen Laver ...C 5
58 Maggieknockater ..C 1
10 Magham Down ....G 5
34 Maghull ....G 3
15 Magor ....E 10
7 Maiden Bradley ...B 11
45 Maiden Law .....H 10
7 Maiden Newton ...F 9
12 Maiden Wells ....G 3
5 Maidencombe .....J 8
48 Maidencots ......C 2
17 Maidenhead .....F 10
39 Maidenhill ....B 7
45 Maidens ....A 3
17 Maiden's Green ...G 9
33 Maidenwell .....B 10
23 Maidford ....G 9
17 Maid's Moreton ...A 8
5 Maidstone ....C 6
23 Maidwell ....D 10
64 Mail ....E 7
14 Maindee ....E 6
61 Mains, Highland ...F 8
47 Mains, Strathclyde .D 11
52 Mains, Tayside ...B 6
42 Mains of Airies ...E 1
59 Mainsof Allardice ..K 6
58 Mains of Altries ...H 6
58 Mains of Annochie ..C 7
53 Mains of Ardestie .D 10
58 Mains of Arnage ...D 7
58 Mains of Auchindachy ......C 2
58 Mains of Auchmedden .....A 6
53 Mains of Balgavies B 10
53 Mains of Ballindarg .B 9
59 Mains of Balnakettle ......K 4
58 Mains of Birness ...D 7
56 Mains of Bunachton .F 2
58 Mains of Cairnborrow ......D 2
58 Mains of Cardno ...A 7
58 Mains of Crichie ...C 7
56 Mains of Dalvey ...F 7
59 Mains of Drum ...G 5
59 Mains of Drummuir .C 2
56 Mains of Drynie ...E 2
58 Mains of Edingight .B 3
58 Mains of Esslemont .E 7
59 Mains of Glenfarquhar ....J 5
59 Mains of Haulkerton ....K 5
58 Mains of Inkhorn ..D 7
58 Mains of Keithfield .D 6
58 Mains of Kirkhall ..F 6
58 Mains of Logie ...C 5
59 Mains of Melgund .L 3
56 Mains of Newhall ..C 3
43 Mains of Terregles .D 10
59 Mains of Thornton .K 4
52 Mains of Throsk ...H 3
56 Mains of Tore ...D 2
58 Mains of Towie ...C 5
58 Mains of Usan ...B 12
40 Mainsforth ......B 3
43 Mainsriddle ......F 10
21 Mainstone ....D 8
15 Maisemore .....B 11
6 Malborough ......M 6
18 Malden Rushett ...H 2
19 Maldon ....A 8
35 Malham ....A 8
55 Mallaig ....K 1
55 Mallaigvaig ......K 1
48 Malleny Mills .....C 4
52 Malling ....G 1
28 Malltraeth ....C 3
20 Mallwyd ....A 4
15 Malmesbury ....F 12
4 Malmsmead ......A 7
30 Malpas, Cheshire ..E 5
2 Malpas, Corn. ...E 5
14 Malpas, Gwent ...E 6
58 Malt Land ....F 7
40 Maltby, Cleveland .D 5
32 Maltby, S. Yorks. ..A 3
33 Maltby le Marsh ..B 11
11 Maltman's Hill ...D 8
41 Malton ....H 8
21 Malvern Link ....G 1
21 Malvern Wells ...H 1
21 Mamble ....E 12
14 Mamhilad ....D 6
2 Manaccan ....G 5
21 Manafon ....B 7
5 Manaton ....H 6

33 Manby B 11
22 Mancetter C 6
35 Manchester G 7
29 Mancot D 12
24 Manea F 6
42 Maneight A 6
40 Manfield D 2
64 Mangaster C 7
63 Mangersta D 1
44 Mangertton D 3
15 Mangotsfield G 10
12 Manian Fawr B 5
63 Manish H 2
30 Manley C 4
14 Manmoel D 5
16 Manningford Bohune H 2
16 Manningford Bruce H 2
35 Manningham D 10
10 Mannings Heath E 1
8 Mannington F 2
27 Manningtree M 4
59 Mannofield G 6
12 Manorbier G 4
12 Manorbier Newton G 4
49 Manorhill F 9
12 Manorowen C 3
43 Mansefield B 9
13 Manselfield H 9
21 Mansell Gamage H 9
21 Mansell Lacy H 9
39 Mansergh G 8
47 Mansfield, Strathclyde H 11
32 Mansfield, Notts. D 3
32 Mansfield Woodhouse D 3
38 Mansriggs G 5
7 Manston, Dorset E 11
11 Manston, Kent B 12
8 Manswood E 2
37 Manton, Humber. G 7
23 Manton, Leics. B 12
24 Manthorpe, Lincs. D 2
32 Manthorpe, Lincs. F 6
16 Manton, Wilts. G 3
18 Manuden A 5
50 Maolachy F 6
7 Maperton D 10
17 Maple Cross E 11
32 Maplebeck D 4
17 Mapledurham F 7
9 Mapledurwell A 8
10 Maplehurst F 1
10 Maplescombe B 4
31 Mapleton E 10
32 Mapperley F 2
32 Mapperley Park F 3
7 Mapperton, Dorset F 12
7 Mapperton, Dorset F 8
22 Mappleborough Green E 4
37 Mappleton C 10
35 Mapplewell F 12
7 Mappowder F 10
57 Mar Lodge K 7
2 Marazion G 2
30 Marbury F 4
24 March, Cambs. F 5
48 March, Strathclyde H 3
16 Marcham D 5
30 Marchamley G 4
43 Marchbankwood B 11
47 Marchburn H 11
31 Marchington G 9
31 Marchington Woodlands G 9
30 Marchwiel E 2
8 Marchwood E 5
14 Marcross G 3
21 Marden, Heref. & Worc. H 10
10 Marden, Kent D 6
16 Marden, Wilts. H 2
10 Marden Beech D 6
10 Marden Thorn D 6
14 Mardy C 6
7 Mare Green D 7
17 Marefield, Bucks. E 9
23 Marefield, Leics. A 11
33 Mareham le Fen D 10
33 Mareham on the Hill C 10
32 Marehey E 1
10 Maresfield F 3
37 Marfleet D 9
30 Marford E 2
13 Margam H 11
7 Margaret Marsh D 11
18 Margaret Roding C 6
18 Margaretting D 6
11 Margate A 12
46 Margnaheglish F 5
24 Marham D 8
4 Marhamchurch F 1
24 Marholm E 2
28 Marianglas B 4
4 Mariansleigh D 6
59 Marionburgh G 5
62 Marishader B 4
63 Mariveg E 5
43 Marjoriebanks C 11
43 Mark, Dumf. & Gall. F 7
42 Mark, Strathclyde D 2
7 Mark, Somerset A 7
7 Mark Causeway B 7
10 Mark Cross E 5
10 Markbeech D 4
33 Markby B 12
23 Market Bosworth B 7
24 Market Deeping E 2
30 Market Drayton G 5
23 Market Harborough C 10
8 Market Lavington A 2
23 Market Overton A 12
33 Market Rasen A 8
33 Market Stainton B 9
26 Market Street C 6
36 Market Weighton C 6
27 Market Weston G 3
23 Markfield A 8
14 Markham D 5
32 Markham Moor C 4
53 Markinch G 8
35 Markington A 10
49 Markle B 8
19 Marks Tey B 9
15 Marksbury H 10
17 Markyate C 11
48 Marlage D 1
16 Marlborough G 3
21 Marlbrook, Heref. & Worc. G 10
22 Marlbrook, Heref. & Worc. E 3
22 Marlcliff G 4
5 Marldon J 7
27 Marlesford J 6
30 Marley Green F 4
45 Marley Hill G 10
8 Marley Mount F 4
49 Marleyknowe F 12
26 Marlingford E 4
12 Marloes F 1
17 Marlow, Bucks. E 9
21 Marlow, Heref. & Worc. E 9
17 Marlow Bottom E 9
10 Marlpit Hill C 3
7 Marnhull D 11
58 Marnoch C 3
31 Marple A 8
36 Marr G 3
61 Marrel E 9
40 Marrick E 1
12 Marros F 5
45 Marsden, Tyne & Wear G 12
35 Marsden, W. Yorks. F 9
39 Marsett F 11
6 Marsh, Devon E 6
6 Marsh, Somerset C 4
16 Marsh Baldon D 6
16 Marsh Benham G 5
37 Marsh Chapel G 11
17 Marsh Gibbon B 7
6 Marsh Green, Devon G 4
10 Marsh Green, Kent D 3
21 Marsh Green, Shropshire A 11
6 Marsh Street B 3
18 Marshall's Heath B 2
26 Marsham C 5
34 Marshaw B 5
11 Marshborough B 11
21 Marshbrook C 10
15 Marshfield, Avon G 11
14 Marshfield, Gwent F 6
2 Marshgate B 2
32 Marshland B 1
34 Marshside E 2
7 Marshwood F 7
40 Marske E 1
40 Marske-by-the-Sea C 6
30 Marston, Ches. C 5
21 Marston, Heref. & Worc. G 9
32 Marston, Lincs. F 6
16 Marston, Oxon C 6
22 Marston, Staffs. A 2
31 Marston, Staffs. G 8
16 Marston, Wilts. H 1
22 Marston Green D 5
7 Marston Magna D 9
16 Marston Meysey D 2
31 Marston Montgomery F 10
25 Marston Moretaine L 1
31 Marston on Dove G 11
23 Marston St. Lawrence H 8
21 Marston Stannett G 11
23 Marston Trussell D 10
15 Marstow B 9
17 Marsworth C 10
16 Marten H 4
30 Marthall C 6
26 Martham D 8
8 Martin, Hants. D 2
11 Martin, Kent C 12
33 Martin, Lincs. D 8
8 Martin Drove End D 2
22 Martin Hussingtree F 2
4 Martinhoe A 5
4 Martinhoe Cross A 6
30 Martinscroft A 5
44 Martinshouse B 3
7 Martinstown G 10
27 Martlesham K 6
12 Martletwy F 4
22 Martley F 1
7 Martock D 8
31 Marton, Ches. C 7
40 Marton, Cleveland D 5
37 Marton, Humber. C 9
32 Marton, Lincs. B 5
41 Marton, N. Yorks. G 7
36 Marton, N. Yorks. A 2
21 Marton, Salop B 8
23 Marton, War. E 7
40 Marton le Moor H 4
40 Marton-in-the-Forest H 6
8 Martyr Worthy C 6
17 Martyr's Green H 11
43 Marwhirn B 8
64 Marwick C 1
4 Marwood B 4
4 Marwood Middle B 4
5 Mary Tavy H 4
54 Marybank D 8
56 Maryburgh D 1
59 Maryculter G 6
49 Marygold C 10
58 Maryhill, Grampian C 6
47 Maryhill, Strathclyde B 10
59 Marykirk L 4
56 Marypark F 7
38 Maryport, Cumb. B 3
42 Maryport, Dumf. & Gall. H 2
53 Maryton, Tayside B 8
53 Maryton, Tayside B 11
59 Marywell, Grampian H 3
59 Marywell, Grampian G 7
53 Marywell, Tayside C 11
40 Masham G 2
45 Mason F 10
32 Mastin Moor C 2
59 Mastrick G 6
18 Matching C 5
18 Matching Green C 5
18 Matching Tye C 5
45 Matfen F 8
10 Matfield D 5
15 Mathern E 8
22 Mathon H 1
12 Mathry D 2
26 Matlask B 5
31 Matlock D 11
31 Matlock Bath D 11
15 Matson C 11
38 Matterdale End C 6
32 Mattersey A 4
32 Mattersey Thorpe A 4
17 Mattingley H 8
26 Mattishall D 4
26 Mattishall Burgh D 4
53 Mattocks C 9
47 Mauchline G 10
58 Maud C 7
13 Maudsland D 7
16 Maugersbury B 3
38 Maughold G 3
54 Mauld F 8
25 Maulden L 2
39 Maulds Meaburn D 8
40 Maunby F 4
21 Maund Bryan G 11
6 Maundown C 4
26 Mautby D 8
22 Mavesyn Ridware A 4
33 Mavis Enderby D 10
56 Maviston D 5
22 Maw Green B 4
43 Mawbray G 11
52 Mawcarse G 6
34 Mawdesley F 4
14 Mawdlam F 1
2 Mawgan G 4
2 Mawla E 4
2 Mawnan G 5
2 Mawnan Smith G 5
24 Maxey E 2
22 Maxstroke C 6
49 Maxton, Borders F 8
11 Maxton, Kent D 11
49 Maxwellheugh F 10
42 Maxwellston B 4
43 Maxwellstown D 10
5 Maxworthy G 1
31 May Bank E 7
13 Mayals H 9
47 Maybole H 8
17 Maybury H 11
10 Mayfield, E. Sussex E 5
31 Mayfield, Staffs. F 10
17 Mayford H 10
19 Mayland D 9
10 Maynard's Green F 5
15 Maypole, Gwent C 8
2 Maypole, Is. of Scilly D 2
26 Maypole Green F 7
64 Maywick E 7
4 Mead D 1
15 Meadgate H 10
47 Meadowfoot E 11
21 Meadowtown B 8
39 Meal Bank F 8
37 Meals G 11
38 Mealsgate A 4
35 Mearbeck A 7
7 Meare B 8
6 Meare Green D 6
47 Mearns D 10
23 Mears Ashby E 11
23 Measham A 7
10 Meath Green D 2
39 Meathop G 7
63 Meavag G 3
5 Meavy J 4
23 Medbourne C 11
45 Medburn F 9
4 Meddon D 2
17 Medmenham F 9
45 Medomsley H 9
9 Medstead B 8
22 Meer End E 6
31 Meerbrook D 8
33 Meers Bridge B 12
25 Meesden M 5
4 Meeth E 4
44 Megdale C 1
48 Meggethead G 4
12 Meidrim E 6
21 Meifod A 7
53 Meigle C 7
43 Meikle Barncleugh D 10
43 Meikle Beoch D 9
47 Meikle Carco H 12
47 Meikle Earnock D 12
59 Meikle Fiddes J 5
52 Meikle Forter A 6
61 Meikle Gluich H 7
46 Meikle Grenach C 6
47 Meikle Hareshaw E 11
47 Meikle Ittington E 7
56 Meikle Kildrummie D 4
49 Meikle Pinkerton B 9
59 Meikle Strath K 4
58 Meikle Tarty E 7
58 Meikle Wartle D 5
43 Meikleholm C 11
47 Meiklelaught E 7
52 Meikleour C 6
58 Meikleton C 3
28 Meillteyrn G 2
43 Meinbank D 12
13 Meinciau F 8
31 Meirheath F 8
63 Melbost D 6
63 Melbost Borve A 5
25 Melbourn L 5
31 Melbourne, Derby H 12
36 Melbourne, Humberside C 5
48 Melbourne, Strathclyde E 4
7 Melbury Abbas D 12
7 Melbury Bubb F 9
7 Melbury Osmond E 9
7 Melbury Sampford F 9
64 Melby D 6
25 Melchbourne J 1
7 Melcombe Regis H 10
5 Meldon, Devon G 4
45 Meldon, N'thumb. E 9
25 Meldreth L 5
58 Meldrum House E 6
50 Melfort F 5
55 Melgarve K 8
29 Meliden B 10
14 Melin Court D 2
20 Melin-byrhedin C 4
29 Melin-y-coed D 7
20 Melin-y-grug B 6
29 Melin-y-wig E 9
39 Melkinthorpe C 8
44 Melkridge G 5
15 Melksham H 12
54 Mellanguan A 2
46 Melldalloch B 4
39 Melling, Lancs. H 8
34 Melling, Merseyside G 3
34 Melling Mount G 3
27 Mellis H 4
60 Mellon Charles G 1
60 Mellon Udrigle G 1
31 Mellor, Manchester A 8
34 Mellor, Lancs. D 5
34 Mellor Brook D 5
7 Mells A 10
39 Melmerby, Cumb. B 8
40 Melmerby, N. Yorks. G 4
40 Melmerby, N. Yorks. G 1
7 Melplash F 8
49 Melrose F 8
64 Melsetter E 1
40 Melsonby D 2
35 Meltham F 9
35 Meltham Mills F 10
37 Melton, Humber. D 7
27 Melton, Suffolk K 6
26 Melton Constable B 3
32 Melton Mowbray H 5
37 Melton Ross F 8
36 Meltonby B 6
54 Melvaig A 1
21 Melverley A 9
61 Melvich B 8
6 Membury F 6
58 Memsie A 7
59 Memus L 2
3 Menabilly E 8
28 Menai Bridge C 5
27 Mendham G 6
27 Mendlesham J 4
27 Mendlesham Green J 4
3 Menheniot C 10
43 Mennock A 9
35 Menston C 10
52 Menstrie G 3
36 Menthorpe D 5
17 Mentmore B 10
55 Meoble L 2
21 Meole Brace A 10
9 Meonstroke D 7
10 Meopham B 5
10 MeophamGreen B 5
10 Meopham Station A 5
25 Mepal G 5
25 Meppershall L 2
21 Merbach H 8
30 Mere, Cheshire B 6
7 Mere, Wilts. C 11
34 Mere Brow E 3
35 Mere Clough D 7
11 Meresborough B 7
34 Mereside D 2
30 Meretown H 6
10 Mereworth C 5
59 Mergie H 5
22 Meriden D 6
62 Merkadale E 3
43 Merkland D 8
60 Merkland Lodge D 5
12 Merlin's Bridge F 3
30 Merrington H 3
12 Merrion G 3
7 Merriot E 8
5 Merrivale H 4
9 Merrow A 11
44 Merrylaw C 2
3 Merrymeet C 10
34 Merseyside, Co. H 3
11 Mersham D 9
10 Merstham C 2
9 Merston F 10
8 Merstone H 6
2 Merther E 6
13 Merthyr E 7
14 Merthyr Cynog A 3
14 Merthyr Mawr F 2
14 Merthyr Tydfil D 4
14 Merthyr Vale D 4
4 Merton, Devon E 4
18 Merton, London G 3
26 Merton, Norfolk F 2
17 Merton, Oxon B 7
44 Mervinslaw B 5
4 Meshaw D 6
19 Messing B 9
37 Messingham G 7
27 Metfield G 6
33 Metheringham D 8
53 Methil G 8
28 Methlem G 1
35 Methley D 12
58 Methlick D 6
52 Methven E 5
24 Methwold F 8
24 Methwold Hythe F 8
26 Mettingham F 6
26 Metton B 5
3 Mevagissey E 7
36 Mexborough G 3
61 Mey A 12
16 Meysey Hampton D 2
63 Miavaig C 2
58 Michael Muir D 6
15 Michaelchurch B 8
14 Michaelchurch Escley A 6
21 Michaelchurch-on-Arrow G 8
14 Michaelston-le-Pit G 5
14 Michaelston-super-Ely G 4
14 Michaelstone-y-Fedw F 6
3 Michaelstow B 8
8 Michelmersh C 5
27 Mickfield J 4
30 Mickle Trafford C 3
36 Micklebring H 3
41 Mickleby D 8
36 Micklefield D 2
10 Mickleham C 1
31 Mickleover G 11
44 Micklethwaite H 1
39 Mickleton, Dur. C 12
22 Mickleton, Glos. H 5
35 Mickletown D 12
40 Mickley G 3
45 Mickley Square G 9
58 Mid Ardlaw A 7
59 Mid Beltie G 4
59 Mid Cairncross J 2
48 Mid Calder C 3
61 Mid Clyth D 11
58 Mid Cowbog B 6
54 Mid Crochail F 7
58 Mid Culsh C 6
47 Mid Drumloch D 11
14 Mid Glamorgan, Co. E 4
48 Mid Hartwood C 3
43 Mid Laggan D 8
9 Mid Lavant E 10
54 Mid Mains F 8
46 Mid Sannox E 5
54 Mid Strom F 2
46 Mid Thundergay E 4
64 Mid Yell B 7
64 Midbea A 2
17 Middle Assendon F 8
16 Middle Aston A 6
16 Middle Barton B 5
15 Middle Bridge G 8
7 Middle Chinnock E 8
59 Middle Drums L 3
58 Middle Essie B 8
32 Middle Handley B 1
17 Middle Claydon B 8
22 Middle Littleton G 4
12 Middle Mill D 2
49 Middle Ord D 12
33 Middle Rasen A 8
52 Middle Rigg F 5
15 Middle Street D 11
23 Middle Tysoe H 7
8 Middle Wallop B 4
8 Middle Winterslow C 4
8 Middle Woodford C 3
43 Middlebie D 12
57 Middlebridge M 4
49 Middlefield D 10
43 Middlegill A 11
40 Middleham F 2
21 Middlehope D 10
7 Middlemarsh E 10
58 Middlemuir C 5
58 Middlemuir House E 7
40 Middlesbrough C 5
39 Middleshaw, Cumb. F 8
43 Middleshaw, Dumf. & Gall. D 12
44 Middlesknowes B 6
40 Middlesmoor H 1
40 Middlestone B 3
40 Middlestone Moor B 3
35 Middlestown E 11
49 Middlethird E 9
15 Middleton, Avon G 8

31 Middleton, Derby .E 11
31 Middleton, Derby .D 10
27 Middleton, Essex ..L 2
58 Middleton, Grampian ......E 6
35 Middleton, Manchester ......F 7
8 Middleton, Hants. ..B 6
21 Middleton, Heref. & Worc. ..E 11
34 Middleton, Lancs. ..A 3
48 Middleton, Lothian .D 6
24 Middleton, Norf. ...D 8
41 Middleton, N. Yorks. ....G 8
35 Middleton, N. Yorks. ....B 10
25 Middleton, Northants. ......C 11
45 Middleton, Northumberland ..E 9
45 Middleton, Northumb. ......B 12
21 Middleton, Salop .E 11
30 Middleton, Salop ...G 2
47 Middleton, Strathclyde ......E 8
27 Middleton, Suffolk .H 7
52 Middleton, Tayside .F 6
52 Middleton, Tayside .B 6
22 Middleton, War. ...B 5
13 Middleton, W. Glam. H 7
35 Middleton, W. Yorks. ...D 11
23 Middleton Cheney ..H 8
31 Middleton Green ...G 8
49 Middleton Hall ....G 12
39 Middleton in Teesdale ....C 11
58 Middleton of Rora ..C 8
9 Middleton-on-Sea .F 11
21 Middleton on the Hill ....F 11
37 Middleton-on-the Wolds ....B 7
58 Middleton One Row ....D 4
21 Middleton Priors ..C 11
40 Middleton Quernhow ....G 3
40 Middleton St. George ....D 4
21 Middleton Scriven .D 12
16 Middleton Stoney ..B 6
40 Middleton Tyas .....E 3
21 Middletown ....A 8
30 Middlewich ....D 6
27 Middlewood Green ..J 4
47 Middleyard ....F 10
7 Middlezoy ....C 7
40 Middridge ....C 3
60 Midfield ....A 6
15 Midford ....H 10
34 Midge Hall ....E 4
44 Midgeholme ....G 5
35 Midgeley ....F 11
16 Midgham ....G 6
35 Midgley ....D 9
35 Midhopestones ...G 11
9 Midhurst ....D 10
49 Midlem ....G 8
48 Midlock ....G 2
7 Midsomer Norton A 10
60 Midtown ....B 6
54 Midtown Brae .....A 2
59 Midtown of Barras .J 6
58 Midtown of Buchromb ....C 1
33 Midville ....E 11
43 Miefield ....F 7
61 Migdale ....G 7
59 Migvie ....G 2
7 Milborne Port .....D 10
7 Milborne St. Andrew ....F 11
7 Milborne Wick ...D 10
45 Milbourne ....E 9
50 Milbuie ....H 1
39 Milburn ....B 9
15 Milbury Heath ....E 10
40 Milby ....H 4
16 Milcombe ....A 5
27 Milden ....K 3
25 Mildenhall, Suff. .H 8
16 Mildenhall, Wilts. .G 3
16 Mile Elm ....G 1
19 Mile End, Essex ....A 9
26 Mile End, Suffolk ..F 6
21 Milebrook ....E 8
26 Mileham ....D 2
15 Miles End ....C 9
30 Miles Green ....E 6
21 Miles Hope ....F 11
52 Milesmark ....H 5

49 Milfield ....F 12
31 Milford, Derby ....F 12
4 Milford, Devon ...D 1
31 Milford, Staffs. ...H 8
9 Milford, Surrey ....B 11
8 Milford, Wilts. ....C 3
12 Milford Haven .....F 4
8 Milford on Sea ....G 4
47 Milhall ....D 10
15 Milkwall ....C 9
8 Milkwell ....D 1
8 Mill Bank ....D 6
31 Mill Brow ....A 8
27 Mill Common ......G 7
17 Mill End, Bucks. ...F 9
25 Mill End, Cambs. ..G 4
17 Mill End, Herts. ...E 11
18 Mill End, Herts. ...M 4
18 Mill Green, Essex .D 6
27 Mill Green, Suffolk .L 3
18 Mill Hill ....E 2
39 Mill Houses ......H 8
9 Mill Lane ....A 9
58 Mill of Ardo, Grampian ....E 7
58 Mill of Ardo, Grampian ....D 6
58 Mill of Carden ....E 4
59 Mill of Culfork ....F 2
59 Mill of Gellan ....G 3
59 Mill of Mondynes ..J 5
59 Mill of Monquich ..H 6
58 Mill of Muiresk ...C 4
58 Mill of Pot ....C 5
59 Mill of Uras ......J 6
31 Mill Street ....D 3
26 Millbeck ....C 5
38 Millbeck ....C 5
64 Millbounds ....B 3
58 Millbreck ....C 7
58 Millbrex ....C 6
9 Millbridge ....B 10
25 Millbrook, Beds. ..L 1
3 Millbrook, Corn. ..D 11
4 Millbrook, Devon ..C 6
8 Millbrook, Hants. ..E 5
47 Millburn ....F 9
5 Millcombe ....L 7
11 Millcorner ....F 7
31 Milldale ....E 10
59 Millden Lodge .....J 3
53 Milldens ....B 10
58 Millerhill ....B 6
31 Miller's Dale .....C 10
31 Millers Green ....E 11
59 Millfield ....H 2
30 Millgreen ....G 5
31 Millhalf ....H 8
6 Millhayes ....E 5
49 Millheugh, Borders .G 9
47 Millheugh, Strathclyde ......D 12
35 Millholme ....F 8
38 Millhouse, Cumb. ..B 6
35 Millhouse, S. Yorks. ....G 11
46 Millhouse, Strathclyde ....B 4
43 Millhousebridge ...C 11
32 Millhouses ....B 1
43 Milliganton ......C 10
47 Millikenpark .....C 9
36 Millington ....B 6
49 Millknowe ....C 9
38 Millmeece ....G 7
38 Millom ....G 4
3 Millpool ....C 8
46 Millport ....D 6
43 Millquarter ......C 7
31 Millthorpe ....C 11
31 Millthrop ....F 9
59 Milltimber ....G 6
53 Millton ....C 8
57 Milltown of Auchriachan .....H 7
58 Milltown, Grampian .F 2
58 Milltown, Grampian .F 7
59 Milltown, Grampian G 4
58 Milltown, Grampian C 3
32 Milltown, Derby ...D 1
4 Milltown, Devon ...B 4
54 Milltown, Highland .D 7
41 Milltown, Tayside ..K 5
52 Milltown of Aberdalgie ....E 5
58 Milltown of Auchindown .....D 1
59 Milltown of Campfield ......G 4
56 Milltown of Edinvillie ....F 8
58 Milltown of Minnes .E 7
58 Milltown of Towie .F 2

47 Millwell ....D 11
53 Milnacraig ....B 7
52 Milnathort ....G 6
4 Milne ....B 12
47 Milngavie ....B 10
43 Milnmark ....C 7
35 Milnrow ....F 8
39 Milnthorpe ....G 7
21 Milson ....E 11
11 Milstead ....B 7
8 Milston ....B 3
14 Milton, Avon .....H 6
25 Milton, Cambs. ....J 6
51 Milton, Central ...G 12
44 Milton, Cumb. .....G 4
31 Milton, Derby ....G 11
43 Milton, Dumf. & Gall. ....C 9
43 Milton, Dumf. & Gall. ....D 9
42 Milton, Dumf. & Gall. ....F 3
12 Milton, Dyfed .....G 4
58 Milton, Grampian ..E 1
58 Milton, Grampian ..A 3
9 Milton, Hants. ....F 8
61 Milton, Highland .C 12
57 Milton, Highland .H 5
57 Milton, Highland ..G 1
56 Milton, Highland ..D 2
56 Milton, Highland ..E 1
56 Milton, Highland ..B 3
54 Milton, Highland ..E 1
16 Milton, Oxon .....E 6
16 Milton, Oxon .....A 5
7 Milton, Som. ......D 8
42 Milton, Strathclyde .B 4
42 Milton, Strathclyde .A 3
47 Milton, Strathclyde .B 9
59 Milton, Tayside ...J 2
52 Milton, Tayside ...A 6
7 Milton Abbas .....F 11
5 Milton Abbot .....H 3
48 Milton Bridge .....C 5
25 Milton Bryna .....M 1
7 Milton Clevedon ..C 10
58 Milton Coldwells ..D 7
4 Milton Damerel ...E 3
16 Milton End ....D 2
25 Milton Ernest ....K 1
30 Milton Green .....D 3
16 Milton Hill ....E 6
23 Milton Keynes ....H 12
16 Milton Lilbourne ..K 3
23 Milton Malsor ....G 10
58 Milton of Ardlethen D 6
59 Milton of Auchinhove ......G 3
53 Milton of Balgonie .G 8
56 Milton of Braicklaich ......D 3
47 Milton of Campsie .B 11
58 Milton of Cushnie ..E 3
59 Milton of Dillavaird .J 5
56 Milton of Farr ....F 2
58 Milton of Fishrie ..B 5
58 Milton of Lesmore .E 2
59 Milton of Logie ...G 2
59 Milton of Murtle ..G 6
58 Milton of Noth ....E 2
46 Milton of Smerby ..G 2
59 Milton of Tullich ..H 1
7 Milton on Stour ..C 11
11 Milton Regis .....B 7
16 Milton under Wychwood ....B 4
5 Miltoncombe .....J 4
56 Miltonduff ....D 7
42 Miltonise ....D 3
6 Milverton ....D 4
31 Milwich ....G 8
51 Minard ....H 7
12 Minchinhampton ..D 12
49 Mindrum ....F 11
49 Mindrummill .....F 11
6 Minehead ....B 3
29 Minera ....E 12
16 Minety ....E 1
23 Minffordd ....F 5
50 Mingarrypark .....A 4
33 Miningsby ....D 10
31 Minions ....C 9
47 Minishant ....H 8
57 Minmore ....G 7
58 Minnigaff ....E 5
58 Minnonie ....B 5
38 Minorca ....G 2
44 Minsca ....E 1
36 Minskip ....A 2
8 Minstead ....E 4
11 Minster, Kent ....B 11
11 Minster, Kent ....A 8
16 Minster Lovell ....C 4
45 Minsteracres .....G 8

21 Minsterley ....B 9
15 Minsterworth .....C 11
7 Minterne Magna ..F 10
33 Minting ....C 9
58 Mintlaw ....C 7
49 Minto ....G 8
43 Minto Cott ....F 7
21 Minton ....C 9
12 Minwear ....F 4
22 Minworth ....C 5
64 Mirbister ....C 1
38 Mirehouse ....D 2
61 Mireland ....B 12
35 Mirfield ....E 10
58 Miserden ....C 12
14 Miskin, Mid Glam. .F 4
14 Miskin, Mid Glam. .D 4
36 Misson ....H 5
36 Misterton, Notts. .H 5
7 Misterton, Som. ...E 8
23 Misterton, War. ...D 9
27 Mistley ....M 4
18 Mitcham ....G 3
15 Mitcheldean ......B 9
8 Mitcheldever ......B 6
15 Mitchel Troy .....C 8
2 Mitchell ....D 6
15 Mitcheltroy Com. ..C 8
45 Mitford ....D 10
2 Mithian ....E 4
22 Mitton ....A 2
17 Mixbury ....A 7
31 Mixon ....D 9
53 Moanzie ....E 8
44 Moat Common ....F 3
30 Mobberley ....B 6
9 Moccas ....H 9
29 Mochdre, Clwyd ..B 7
28 Mochdre, Powys ..D 6
42 Mochrum ....G 4
10 Mockbeggar, Kent .C 6
10 Mockbeggar, Kent ..A 6
38 Mockerkin ....C 3
5 Modbury ....K 5
31 Moddershall .....G 8
61 Modsarie ....B 7
29 Moelfre, Clwyd ...G 11
28 Moelfre, Gwynedd ..B 4
43 Moffat ....A 11
25 Moggerhanger ...K 2
60 Moin House ......B 6
22 Moira ....A 6
11 Molash ....C 9
62 Mol-chlach ....G 4
35 Mold ....D 11
35 Moldgreen ....F 10
18 Molehill Green ....A 5
37 Molescroft ....C 8
45 Molesden ....E 9
25 Molesworth ....H 2
4 Molland ....C 7
4 Molland Cross ....C 6
30 Mollington, Ches. ..C 2
23 Mollington, Oxon ..G 8
47 Mollinsburn ......B 12
19 Molting Green ....B 9
13 Monachty ....A 8
51 Monachylemore ...F 11
46 Monamore Bridge ..F 5
21 Monaughty ....F 8
59 Monboddo House ..J 5
51 Monevechadan ...G 9
27 Moneyden ....J 5
52 Moneydie ....D 5
43 Moniaive ....C 8
53 Monifieth ....D 9
53 Monikie ....C 9
53 Monimail ....F 8
12 Monington ....C 5
35 Monk Bretton ....F 12
36 Monk Fryston ....D 3
17 Monk Sherborne ..H 7
27 Monk Soham .....C 5
45 Monk-Wearmouth .G 12
21 Monkhide ....H 11
21 Monkhopton .....C 11
21 Monkland ....G 10
4 Monkleigh ....D 3
14 Monknash ....G 3
4 Monkokehampton ..E 5
45 Monkridge ....D 7
27 Monks Eleigh ....K 3
10 Monk's Gate .....E 1
31 Monks' Heath ....C 7
23 Monks Kirby .....D 8
17 Monks Risborough .D 9
58 Monkshill ....D 5
6 Monksilver ....C 4
22 Monkspath Street .D 5
15 Monkswood ....D 7
10 Monkton, Devon ..F 5
12 Monkton, Dyfed ...G 3
11 Monkton, Kent ....B 11
6 Monkton, Som. ...C 6

47 Monkton, Strathclyde ....G 8
15 Monkton Coombe .H 11
7 Monkton Deverill .B 11
15 Monkton Farleigh .H 11
6 Monkton Heathfield ....D 6
8 Monkton Up Wimborne ......E 2
47 Monkton Wyld ....F 7
47 Monktonhill ......F 8
9 Monkwood ....C 8
15 Monmouth ....C 8
15 Monmouth Cap ...B 7
21 Monnington on Wye ....H 9
53 Monorgan ....D 8
41 Monreith ....G 4
42 Monreith Mains ...G 4
7 Montacute ....E 8
58 Montcoffer House .B 4
21 Mountford ....A 9
21 Montford Bridge ..A 9
58 Montgarrie ......F 3
21 Montgomery ......C 8
47 Montgreenan .....E 8
59 Montrose ....L 5
8 Monxton ....B 5
31 Monyash ....D 10
58 Monymusk ....F 4
52 Monzie, Tayside ..E 4
59 Monzie, Tayside ..M 5
47 Moodiesburn .....B 11
35 Moor Allerton ...C 11
8 Moor Crichel .....E 2
36 Moor Ends ....F 5
36 Moor Monkton ....B 3
56 Moor of Granary ..D 6
38 Moor Row ....D 3
11 Moor Street ......B 7
8 Moordown ....G 3
30 Moore ....B 4
15 Moorend ....D 10
8 Moorgreen ....E 6
31 Moorhall ....C 11
21 Moorhampton ....H 9
44 Moorhouse, Cumb. .G 2
32 Moorhouse, Notts. ..D 5
7 Moorlinch ....C 7
41 Moorsholm ....D 7
5 Moorshop ....H 4
35 Moorside, Manchester ....F 8
33 Moorside, Lincs. ...D 9
8 Moortown, Hants. ..F 3
8 Moortown, I. o. W. .H 6
37 Moortown, Lincs. ..G 8
55 Morar ....K 1
24 Morborne ....F 2
4 Morchard Bishop ..E 6
23 Morcott ....B 12
30 Morda ....G 2
7 Morden, Dorset ...G 12
18 Morden, London ..G 2
15 Mordiford ....A 9
49 Mordington Mains ....D 12
40 Mordon ....C 3
21 More ....C 9
6 Morebath ....D 3
49 Morebattle ....G 10
34 Morecambe ......A 3
7 Morecombelake ...G 7
60 Morefield ....G 3
39 Moreland ....F 8
5 Moreleigh ....K 6
52 Morenish ....D 1
38 Moresby ....C 2
8 Morestead ....D 6
35 Moreton, Derby ...F 1
40 Moreton, Dur. ....B 3
17 Moreton, Essex ...C 5
30 Moreton, Merseyside ....A 1
17 Moreton, Oxon ...D 8
16 Moreton-in-Marsh .A 3
21 Moreton Jeffries ..G 11
22 Moreton Morrell ..F 6
21 Moreton on Lugg ..H 10
23 Moreton Pinkney ..G 9
30 Moreton Say .....G 5
15 Moreton Valence ..C 11
5 Moretonhampstead .G 6
21 Morfa ....F 9
28 Morfa'Bychan ....F 5
14 Morfa Glas ....D 2
28 Morfa-Nefyn .....F 2
8 Morgan's Vale ....D 4
32 Morley, Derby ....F 1
40 Morley, Dur. .....E 4
35 Morley, W. Yorks. .D 11
31 Morley Green ....B 7
26 Morley St. Botolph .E 4

26 Morning Thorpe ...F 5
48 Morningside, Lothian ....B 5
48 Morningside, Strathclyde ......D 1
45 Morpeth ....D 10
31 Morrey ....H 10
43 Morrington ....C 9
25 Morris Green .....M 8
42 Morriston, Strathclyde ......A 3
13 Morriston, W. Glam. ....G 10
26 Morston ....A 3
4 Mortehoe ....B 3
32 Morthen ....A 2
17 Mortimer Com. ...H 7
17 Mortimer West End .H 7
21 Mortimer's Cross ...F 9
18 Mortlake ....F 2
15 Morton, Avon .....E 9
44 Morton, Cumb. ....H 2
32 Morton, Derby ....D 1
24 Morton, Lincs. ....C 2
32 Morton, Lincs. ....A 5
30 Morton, Salop ....H 2
22 Morton Bagot ....F 4
40 Morton-on-Swale ..E 3
40 Morton Tinmouth ..C 2
2 Morvah ....F 1
3 Morval ....D 9
55 Morvich ....G 3
61 Morvich Lodge ...F 8
21 Morville ....C 12
4 Morwenstow ......D 1
32 Mosborough .....B 2
44 Moscow, Cumb. ...F 4
47 Moscow, Strathclyde F 9
38 Mosedale ....B 6
35 Moselden Height ..F 9
22 Moseley, Heref. & Worc. ....F 2
22 Moseley, W. Midlands ....D 4
29 Moss, Clwyd ....E 12
50 Moss, Highland ...A 4
36 Moss, S. Yorks. ...F 4
34 Moss Bank ....G 4
17 Moss End ....G 9
56 Moss of Barmuckity ......D 8
58 Mossat ....F 2
64 Mossbank ....C 7
44 Mossburnford ....A 5
43 Mossdale ....D 7
26 Mossend ....C 12
38 Mosser ....C 4
47 Mossgiel ....F 9
49 Mosshouses ......E 8
43 Mosslands ....B 11
31 Mossley, Ches. ...D 7
35 Mossley, Manchester ....G 8
30 Mossley Hill .....B 3
44 Mosspeeble ......D 2
56 Moss-side ....D 4
58 Mosstodloch .....B 1
7 Mosterton ....F 8
29 Mostyn ....B 11
6 Motcombe ....D 11
5 Mothecombe .....L 5
47 Motherwell ......D 12
18 Mottingham .....G 4
8 Mottisfont ....C 5
8 Mottistone ....H 5
35 Mottram ....H 8
30 Mouldsworth ....C 4
52 Moulin ....A 4
58 Moulinearn ......B 4
17 Moulsford ....F 7
25 Moulsoe ....H 12
30 Moulton, Ches. ...C 5
24 Moulton, Lincs. ...C 4
26 Moulton, Norf. ....E 7
40 Moulton, N. Yorks. .E 3
23 Moulton, Northants. ....E 11
14 Moulton, S. Glam. .G 4
25 Moulton, Suffolk ..J 8
24 Moulton Chapel ..D 4
25 Moulton St. Michael F 5
24 Moulton Seas End .C 4
3 Moulzie ....L 8
44 Mounces ....D 5
58 Mounie Castle ....E 5
2 Mount ....C 8
21 Mount Ambrose ..E 4
27 Mount Bures .....M 2
2 Mount Hawke ....E 4
48 Mount Lothian ...D 5
49 Mount Pleasant, Borders ....D 10

31 Mount Pleasant, Derbyshire ......E 11
29 Mount Pleasant, Clwyd ......C 11
14 Mount Pleasant, Mid Glam. ....D 4
8 Mount Pleasant, Hampshire ......F 4
17 Mount Pleasant, Hampshire ......H 7
22 Mount Pleasant, Heref. & Worc. ....F 3
27 Mount Pleasant, Suffolk ......G 8
8 Mount Sorrel ......D 2
35 Mount Tabor ......D 9
45 Mountain ......B 8
14 Mountain Ash ......D 4
48 Mountain Cross ......E 4
12 Mountain Water ......E 3
48 Mountbenger .....G 6
58 Mountblairy ......B 4
10 Mountfield ......F 6
56 Mountgerald ......D 1
2 Mountjoy ......D 6
18 Mountnessing ......D 6
15 Mounton ......E 8
58 Mountsolie ......B 7
23 Mountsorrel ......A 9
2 Mousehole ......G 2
43 Mouswald ......D 11
31 Mow Cop ......D 7
49 Mowhaugh ......G 10
23 Mowsley ......C 10
59 Mowtie ......H 6
55 Moy, Highland ....L 5
55 Moy, Highland ....L 8
56 Moy, Highland ....F 3
56 Moy Hall ......F 3
56 Moy House ......D 6
55 Moy Lodge ......L 8
8 Moyle ......H 3
8 Moyles Court ......E 3
12 Moylgrove ......C 5
46 Muasdale ......E 2
15 Much Birch ......A 8
21 Much Cowarne ....H 11
15 Much Dewchurch ....A 8
18 Much Hadham ......B 4
34 Much Hoole ......E 3
15 Much Marcle ......A 10
21 Much Wenlock ......B 11
59 Muchalls ......H 6
7 Muchelney ......D 8
3 Muchlarnick ......D 9
54 Muchrachd ......F 6
56 Muckernich ......D 2
42 Muckfoot ......C 3
19 Mucking ......F 7
7 Muckleford ......G 9
30 Mucklestone ......F 6
30 Muckleton ......H 4
58 Muckletown ......E 3
22 Muckley Corner ......B 4
33 Muckton ......B 10
60 Mudale ......D 6
4 Muddiford ......B 4
10 Muddles Green ......G 4
8 Mudeford ......G 3
7 Mudford ......D 9
7 Mudgley ......B 8
47 Mugdock ......B 10
62 Mugeary ......D 4
31 Mugginton ......F 11
45 Muggleswick ......H 9
61 Muie ......F 7
57 Muir ......K 6
54 Muir of Fairburn ......D 8
58 Muir of Fowlis ......F 3
56 Muir of Ord ......E 1
58 Muirden ......B 4
48 Muirfoot ......D 2
53 Muirhead, Fife ......E 9
53 Muirhead, Fife ......G 7
59 Muirhead, Grampian ......L 5
47 Muirhead, Strathclyde ......B 11
53 Muirhead, Tayside ..D 8
48 Muirhouses, Lothian ......A 3
47 Muirhouses, Strathclyde ....D 11
47 Muirkirk ......G 11
47 Muirmill ......A 12
53 Muirdrum ......C 10
55 Muirshearlich ....L 5
47 Muirshield ......D 10
59 Muirskie ......H 6
58 Muirtack, Grampian ....C 5
58 Muirtack, Tayside .D 7
56 Muirton, Highland ..C 3
59 Muirton, Tayside ..L 4

52 Muirton, Tayside ...E 6
54 Muirton Mains ....D 8
52 Muirton of Ardblair .C 6
52 Muirtown ......F 4
58 Muiryfold ......C 5
43 Muiryhill ......A 9
39 Muker ......E 11
26 Mulbarton ......E 5
58 Mulben ......C 1
41 Mulgrave ......D 8
2 Mullion ......H 4
55 Mullochbuie ......L 1
13 Mumbles ......H 9
33 Mumby ......C 12
21 Munderfield Row .G 12
21 Munderfield Stocks ......G 12
26 Mundesley ......B 6
26 Mundford ......F 1
26 Mundham ......F 6
19 Mundon Hill ......D 8
55 Munerigie ......J 6
60 Mungasdale ......G 2
38 Mungrisdale ......B 6
56 Munlochy ......D 2
47 Munnoch ......E 7
21 Munsley ......H 12
21 Munslow ......D 10
21 Munslow Aston ...D 10
5 Murchington ......G 6
17 Murcott ......C 7
61 Murkle ......A 11
55 Murlaggan, Highland ......K 4
55 Murlaggan, Highland ......L 7
48 Murrayfield, Lothian ......B 5
52 Murrayfield, Tayside ......D 5
43 Murraythwaite ...D 12
24 Murrow ......E 5
17 Mursley ......A 9
59 Murthil ......L 2
52 Murthly ......C 6
52 Murthly Castle ....C 5
39 Murton, Cumbria ...C 9
45 Murton, Dur. ......H 12
49 Murton, Northumb. E 12
36 Murton, N. Yorks. ....B 4
40 Murton Grange ....F 5
6 Musbury ......G 6
41 Muscoates ......G 7
48 Musselburgh ......B 6
32 Muston, Leics. ....F 5
41 Muston, N. Yorks. .G 11
22 Mustow Green ....E 2
43 Mutehill ......G 7
27 Mutford ......G 8
52 Muthill ......E 4
6 Mutterton ......F 4
21 Muxton ......A 12
61 Mybster ......B 11
13 Myddfai ......D 11
30 Myddle ......H 3
13 Mydroilyn ......B 8
2 Mylor Bridge ......F 5
12 Mynachlog-ddu ...D 5
21 Myndtown ......C 9
20 Mynydd-bach, Dyfed ......E 8
15 Mynydd-bach, Gwent ......E 8
13 Mynyddgarreg ....F 7
28 Myntho ......G 3
58 Myre of Bedlam ....C 6
59 Myrebird ......G 5
9 Mytchett ......A 10
35 Mytholmroyd ......E 9
34 Mythop ......D 2
40 Myton-on-Swale ...H 4
36 Naburn ......C 4
11 Nackington ......C 10
27 Nacton ......L 5
37 Nafferton ......A 8
15 Nailbridge ......C 9
15 Nailsea ......G 8
23 Nailstone ......A 7
15 Nailsworth ......D 11
56 Nairn ......D 4
10 Nalderswood ......D 1
2 Nancegollan ......F 3
2 Nancledra ......F 2
9 Nanhurst ......B 11
29 Nannerch ......C 11
32 Nanpantan ......H 2
3 Nanpean ......D 7
3 Nanstallon ......C 7
28 Nant Peris ......D 5
14 Nant-ddu ......C 3
13 Nanteris ......A 7
13 Nantgaredig ......E 8
14 Nantgarw ......F 4
20 Nant-glâs ......F 5

29 Nantglyn ......D 9
20 Nantgwyn ......E 5
28 Nantlle ......E 4
30 Nantmawr ......H 1
20 Nantmel ......F 6
28 Nantmor ......F 5
30 Nantwich ......E 5
13 Nantybai ......C 11
14 Nant-y-Bwch ......C 5
14 Nant-y-cafn ......D 2
14 Nant-y-derry ......D 6
13 Nant-y-ffin ......D 9
14 Nantyffyllon ......E 2
14 Nantyglo ......C 5
21 Nant-y-Meichiaid ...A 7
14 Nant-y-moel ......E 3
28 Nant-y-pandy ......C 6
17 Naphill ......D 9
35 Nappa ......B 7
23 Napton on the Hill ..F 8
12 Narberth ......E 4
23 Narborough, Leics. ..B 8
24 Narborough, Norf. ..D 8
3 Narkurs ......D 10
50 Narrachan ......F 6
28 Nasareth ......E 4
23 Naseby ......D 10
17 Nash, Bucks. ......A 8
21 Nash, Heref. & Worc. ......F 8
15 Nash, Gwent ......F 7
21 Nash, Salop ......E 11
24 Nassington ......F 2
18 Nasty ......B 4
4 Natcott ......D 2
39 Nateby, Cumbria ..D 10
34 Nateby, Lancs. ....C 3
39 Natland ......F 7
27 Naughton ......K 3
16 Naunton, Glos. ....B 2
22 Naunton, Heref. & Worc. ......H 2
22 Naunton, Beauchamp ......G 3
54 Naust ......B 2
33 Navenby ......D 7
18 Navestock ......D 5
18 Navestock Side ....D 5
61 Navidale ......E 10
41 Nawton ......G 7
41 Nayland ......M 3
19 Naze Park ......B 12
18 Nazeing ......C 4
8 Neacroft ......F 3
64 Neap ......D 7
38 Near Sawrey ......F 6
40 Neasham ......D 4
13 Neath ......G 11
13 Neath Abbey ......G 10
31 Neather Heage ....E 12
26 Neatishead ......C 6
20 Nebo, Dyfed ......F 1
28 Nebo, Gwynedd ....A 4
28 Nebo, Gwynedd ....E 4
29 Nebo, Gwynedd ....E 7
27 Necton ......E 2
60 Nedd ......D 3
27 Nedging ......K 3
27 Nedging Tye ......K 3
27 Needham ......G 5
27 Needham Market ...K 4
25 Needingworth ......H 4
31 Needlewood ......H 10
21 Neen Savage ......E 12
21 Neen Sollars ......E 12
21 Neenton ......D 11
28 Nefyn ......F 3
23 Nelly Andrews Green ......A 8
35 Nelson, Lancs. ....C 7
14 Nelson, Mid Glam. ......E 4
45 Nelson Village ....E 10
48 Nemphlar ......E 1
15 Nempnett Thrubwell ......H 8
39 Nenthall ......A 10
39 Nenthead ......A 10
49 Nenthorn ......F 9
29 Nercwys ......D 11
29 Nerston ......D 11
35 Nesfield ......B 9
49 Nesbit ......F 12
30 Ness ......C 2
30 Nesscliffe ......H 3
30 Neston, Ches. ....B 2
15 Neston, Wilts. ....G 11

39 Nether Burrow ......H 8
44 Nether Cassock ....C 1
7 Nether Cerne ......F 10
59 Nether Contlaw ....G 6
43 Nether Craigenputtock ...C 9
58 Nether Crimond ....E 6
48 Nether Dalgliesh ..H 5
58 Nether Dallachy ...A 1
6 Nether Exe ......F 3
48 Nether Fingland ....H 2
58 Nether Glasslaw ....B 6
58 Nether Gribton ....D 10
53 Nether Handwick ..C 8
36 Nether Haugh ......G 2
23 Nether Hayford ....F 10
44 Nether Hindhope ..B 6
48 Nether Howcleugh ..H 3
58 Nether Kellet ......H 7
58 Nether Kinmundy ..C 8
47 Nether Kirkton ....D 9
32 Nether Langwith ...C 3
58 Nether Leask ......D 8
47 Nether Newton ....E 10
31 Nether Padley ......B 11
58 Nether Park ......B 7
59 Nether Pitforthie ...J 6
36 Nether Poppleton ..B 3
40 Nether Silton ......F 5
6 Nether Stowey ....B 5
59 Nether Thaneston ..K 4
53 Nether Urquhart ...F 7
8 Nether Wallop ....B 5
22 Nether Whitacre ...C 6
48 Nether Whitecleuch ......G 1
16 Nether Worton ....A 5
8 Netheravon ......A 3
58 Netherbrae ......B 5
48 Netherburn ......E 1
7 Netherbury ......F 8
47 Netherby, Cumb. ...F 2
35 Netherby, N. Yorks. ......C 11
4 Nethercott ......B 4
15 Netherend ......D 9
10 Netherfield ......F 6
8 Netherhampton ....C 3
49 Netherhowden ....D 7
43 Netherlaw ......G 8
47 Netherley ......H 6
43 Nethermill, Dumf. & Gall. ......C 11
58 Nethermill, Grampian ......D 8
43 Nethermiln ......A 11
21 Nethermuir ......C 7
47 Netherplace ......D 10
22 Netherseal ......A 6
16 Netherstreet ......H 1
43 Netherthird, Dumf. & Gall. ......F 8
47 Netherthird, Strathclyde ....G 10
35 Netherthong ......F 10
45 Netherwitton ......D 9
47 Netherwood ......F 11
47 Netherton, Central A 10
5 Netherton, Devon ..J 8
6 Netherton, Hants. ..H 5
22 Netherton, Heref. & Worc. ..H 3
34 Netherton, Merseyside ......G 2
45 Netherton, Northumb. ......B 8
47 Netherton, Strathclyde ....D 12
59 Netherton, Tayside .L 3
52 Netherton, Tayside .B 6
22 Netherton, W. Midlands ....C 3
35 Netherton, W. Yorks. ......F 10
35 Netherton, W. Yorks. ......F 11
64 Nethertown, Highland ......F 2
38 Nethertown, Cumb. .D 2
57 Nethy Bridge ......G 6
8 Netley ......E 5
8 Netley Marsh ......E 5
17 Nettlebed ......E 8
8 Nettlebridge ......A 10
7 Nettlecombe, Dorset ......G 8
9 Nettlecombe, I.o.W. H 7
6 Nettlecombe, Som. .C 4
17 Nettleden ......C 11
33 Nettleham ......C 7
10 Nettlestead ......C 6
10 Nettlestead Green ..C 5

9 Nettlestone ....G 8
45 Nettlesworth ....H 10
37 Nettleton, Lincs. ...G 9
15 Nettleton, Wilts. ...F 11
5 Netton, Devon ....L 4
8 Netton, Wilts. ....B 3
14 Neuadd, Powys ....C 4
20 Neuadd, Powys ....B 6
20 Neuadd-ddu ......E 5
19 Nevendon ......E 7
12 Nevern ......C 4
43 New Abbey ....E 10
58 New Aberdour ....A 6
18 New Addington ....H 4
9 New Alresford ....C 7
53 New Alyth ......B 7
32 New Annesley ....E 2
10 New Ash Green ....B 5
18 New Barnet ......D 3
49 New Belses ......G 8
23 New Bilton ......F 8
33 New Bolingbroke ..D 10
23 New Bradwell ......H 11
32 New Brampton ....C 1
40 New Brancepeth ...A 2
43 New Bridge, Dumf. & Gall. ...D 10
36 New Bridge, Humberside ......E 4
29 New Brighton, Clwyd ......D 11
30 New Brighton, Merseyside ....A 2
32 New Brinsley ......E 2
26 New Buckenham ...F 4
58 New Byth ......B 6
26 New Catton ......E 5
32 New Clipstone ....D 3
26 New Costessey ....D 5
43 New Cowper ......G 12
20 New Cross ......E 2
47 New Cumnock ....H 11
58 New Deer ......C 6
45 New Delaval ......E 11
17 New Denham ......F 11
2 New Downs ......E 4
23 New Duston ......F 10
36 New Earswick ....B 4
36 New Edlington ....G 3
22 New End ......F 4
30 New Ferry ......B 2
36 New Fryston ......D 2
43 New Galloway ....D 7
2 New Grimsby ......C 7
45 New Haggerston ..B 11
45 New Hartley ......E 11
12 New Hedges ......G 5
45 New Herrington ...H 11
35 New Hey ......F 8
16 New Hinksey ......D 6
26 New Holkham ....B 2
37 New Holland ......E 8
38 New Hotel ......E 5
45 New Horton Grange ......E 10
32 New Houghton, Derbyshire ....D 2
26 New Houghton, Norfolk ......C 1
39 New Houses ......H 10
39 New Hutton ......F 8
10 New Hythe ......B 6
15 New Inn, Dyfed ...C 8
15 New Inn, Gwent ...D 8
39 New Inn, N. Yorks. ......H 10
21 New Invention ....E 8
54 New Kelso ......E 3
58 New Kendal ......E 6
45 New Lambton ....H 11
48 New Lanark ......E 2
34 New Lane ......F 3
33 New Leake ......D 11
58 New Leeds ......B 7
34 New Longdon ....E 4
42 New Luce ......E 3
49 New Mains, Lothian A 8
48 New Mains, Strathclyde ......F 1
59 New Mains of Ury .J 6
18 New Malden ......G 2
40 New Marske ......C 6
30 New Marton ......G 2
59 New Mill, Grampian .J 6
35 New Mill, W. Yorks. ......F 10
16 New Mill, Wilts. ...H 3
2 New Mills, Corn. ...D 6
31 New Mills, Derby ..B 8
20 New Mills, Powys ..B 6
8 New Milton ......F 4

27 New Mistley ......M 4
12 New Moat ......D 4
47 New Monkland ....C 12
45 New Mousen ......C 12
58 New Pitsligo ......B 6
2 New Polzeath ......B 6
47 New Prestwick ....G 8
13 New Quay ......A 7
21 New Radnor ......F 7
39 New Rent ......B 7
11 New Romney ......F 9
36 New Rossington ...G 4
20 New Row ......E 3
8 New Sarum ......C 3
52 New Sauchie ......H 4
52 New Scone ......E 6
50 New Selma ......D 6
63 New Shawbost ....B 4
45 New Shoreston ....D 12
47 New Stevenston ...C 12
8 New Swanage ....H 2
63 New Tolsta ......B 6
17 New Town, Berks. ..G 7
8 New Town, Dorset .D 2
7 New Town, Dorset .D 1
10 New Town, E. Sussex F 3
49 New Town, Lothian .B 7
17 New Town, Hants. ..H 5
16 New Town, Wilts. ...G 4
14 New Tredegar ....D 5
48 New Trows ......F 1
32 New Tupton ......D 1
63 New Valley ......C 5
37 New Waltham ......G 10
25 New Wimpole ......K 4
49 New Winton ......B 7
16 New Yatt ......C 5
33 New York, Lincs. ...E 9
45 New York, Tyne & Wear ...F 11
64 Newark ......A 4
24 Newark, Cambs. ...E 3
32 Newark, Notts. ....E 5
48 Newarthill ......C 1
48 Newbattle ......C 6
39 Newbiggin, Cumb. ..B 7
44 Newbiggin, Cumbria H 4
38 Newbiggin, Cumbria B 5
39 Newbiggin, Cumbria B 8
39 Newbiggin, Dur. ...B 11
45 Newbiggin, Dur. ...H 9
45 Newbiggin, Northumb. ...G 8
39 Newbiggin, N. Yorks. ......F 11
39 Newbiggin, N. Yorks. ......G 12
45 Newbiggin-by-the Sea ......D 11
39 Newbiggin on Lune .E 9
49 Newbigging, Borders ......D 8
48 Newbigging, Strathclyde ....E 3
59 Newbigging, Tayside ......K 1
32 Newbold, Derby ...C 1
32 Newbold, Leics. ....H 1
23 Newbold on Avon ..D 8
22 Newbold on Stour .G 6
22 Newbold Pacey ....F 6
23 Newbold Verdon ..B 8
24 Newborough, Cambs. E 3
28 Newborough, Gwynedd ......D 4
31 Newborough, Staffordshire ...H 10
23 Newbottle, Northants. ......H 8
45 Newbottle, Tyne & Wear ....H 11
27 Newbourn ......L 6
29 Newbridge, Clwyd .F 12
2 Newbridge, Corn. ...F 1
3 Newbridge, Corn. ..C 10
12 Newbridge, Dyfed ..D 3
14 Newbridge, Gwent ..E 5
15 Newbridge, Gwent ..E 7
8 Newbridge, Hants. ..E 4
8 Newbridge, I.o.W. ..E 6
48 Newbridge, Lothian .B 4
20 Newbridge on Wye .F 6
45 Newbrough ......F 6
48 Newburgh, Borders .G 6
53 Newburgh, Fife ....E 7
58 Newburgh, Grampian ......B 7
58 Newburgh, Grampian ......E 7
40 Newburgh Priory ...G 5
49 Newburn, Northumb. ......E 11
45 Newburn, Tyne & Wear ....G 10

16 Newbury ....G 5
39 Newby, Cumbria ....C 8
40 Newby, N. Yorks. ....D 5
41 Newby, N. Yorks. ...F 10
39 Newby, N. Yorks. ...H 9
38 Newby Bridge ......G 6
44 Newby East ....G 3
44 Newby West ....H 2
40 Newby Wiske ......F 4
15 Newcastle, Gwent ...C 7
21 Newcastle, Salop ...D 8
12 Newcastle Emlyn ...C 6
31 Newcastle-under-Lyme
    F 7
45 Newcastle upon Tyne
    F 10
44 Newcastleton ......D 3
12 Newchapel, Dyfed ..C 6
31 Newchapel, Staffs. ..E 7
10 Newchapel, Surrey ..D 2
13 Newchurch, Dyfed ..E 7
15 Newchurch, Gwent...E 8
9 Newchurch, I.o.W...H 7
11 Newchurch, Kent ...E 9
35 Newchurch, Lancs...C 7
35 Newchurch, Lancs. ..E 7
21 Newchurch, Powys ..G 7
31 Newchurch, Staffs. .H 10
6 Newcott ....E 6
10 Newdigate ....D 1
17 Newell Green ......G 9
11 Newenden ....E 7
15 Newent ....B 10
15 Newerne ....D 9
43 Newfield,
    Dumf. & Gall. ..E 12
43 Newfield,
    Dumf. & Gall ...E 9
40 Newfield, Dur. ......B 2
45 Newfield, Dur. ....H 10
56 Newfield, Highland .B 3
9 Newfound ....A 7
12 Newglae ....E 2
26 Newgate ....A 3
18 Newgate Street .....C 3
64 Newgord ....A 8
48 Newhall, Borders ...F 6
30 Newhall, Ches. .....F 4
31 Newhall, Derby ...H 11
56 Newhallpoint ....C 3
18 Newham, London ...F 4
45 Newham,
    Northumb. ......E 12
45 Newham Hall ....D 12
10 Newhaven ....H 3
31 Newhaven House ..D 10
41 Newholm ....D 8
48 Newhouse ....C 1
45 Newhouses ....E 8
10 Newick ....F 3
11 Newingreen ......D 10
11 Newington, Kent ...B 7
11 Newington, Kent ..D 10
32 Newington, Notts. ..A 4
17 Newington, Oxen ...D 7
21 Newington, Salop ..D 9
59 Newkirk ....G 2
15 Newland, Glos. ....C 9
22 Newland,
    Heref. & Worc. ...G 2
37 Newland, Humber. .D 8
36 Newland, N. Yorks. E 5
6 Newland, Som. ....B 2
53 Newlandhead ......C 9
44 Newlands, Borders .D 3
43 Newlands,
    Dumf. & Gall. ..C 10
56 Newlands, Grampian E 8
45 Newlands,
    Northumb. ......G 9
47 Newlands,
    Strathclyde ......G 8
47 Newlands,
    Strathclyde ....D 11
61 Newlands of Geise .A 10
2 Newlyn ....G 2
58 Newmachar ....F 6
48 Newmains ....D 1
25 Newmarket, Suff. ..J 7
63 Newmarket,
    W. Isles. ....C 5
44 Newmill, Borders ..B 3
2 Newmill, Corn. .....F 2
58 Newmill, Grampian .B 2
59 Newmill of
    Inshewan ....L 2
35 Newmillerdam .....F 12
48 Newmills, Fife .....A 3
15 Newmills, Gwent ...D 8
56 Newmills, Highland .C 2
48 Newmills, Lothian ..C 4
58 Newmills of Boyne .B 3
52 Newmiln ....D 6
47 Newmilns ....F 10

15 Newnham, Glos....C 10
9 Newnham, Hants. ..A 8
25 Newnham, Herts. ...L 3
11 Newnham, Kent ....B 8
23 Newnham, Northants
    F 9
21 Newnham Bridge ..E 11
53 Newpark ....F 9
4 Newport, Devon ....C 4
12 Newport, Dyfed ....C 4
25 Newport, Essex ....M 6
15 Newport, Glos. ....E 10
30 Newport, Gwent ....H 6
14 Newport, Gwent ...F 6
61 Newport, Highland
    E 10
36 Newport, Humber...D 6
8 Newport, I.o.W. ...G 6
26 Newport, Norfolk ..D 8
30 Newport, Salop ....H 6
53 Newport-on-Tay ...D 9
23 Newport Pagnell ..H 12
9 Newpound Com. ..C 11
2 Newquay ....D 5
52 Newrow ....H 4
35 Newsam Green ...D 12
58 Newseat ....D 4
34 Newsham, Lancs. ...D 4
40 Newsham, N. Yorks. D 1
40 Newsham,
    N. Yorks. ....G 4
36 Newsholme,
    Humberside ......D 5
35 Newsholme, Lancs. .B 7
35 Newsholme,
    W. Yorks. ....C 9
49 Newstead, Borders ..F 8
45 Newstead,
    Northumb. ......E 12
32 Newstead, Notts. ...E 2
36 Newthorpe ....D 3
49 Newton, Borders ...G 8
25 Newton, Cambs. ...K 5
30 Newton, Ches. .....B 4
30 Newton, Ches. .....C 4
30 Newton, Ches. ...'..D 4
35 Newton, Ches. .....E 5
40 Newton, Cleveland .D 6
38 Newton, Cumbria .H 5
32 Newton, Derby ....D 2
7 Newton, Dorset ...E 11
43 Newton,
    Dumf. & Gall. ..B 12
58 Newton, Grampian .C 8
56 Newton, Grampian ..C 7
15 Newton,
    Heref. & Worc. ...A 7
21 Newton,
    Heref. & Worc. ..G 10
61 Newton, Highland .C 12
56 Newton, Highland ..E 3
56 Newton, Highland ..C 3
56 Newton, Highland ..E 1
60 Newton, Highland ..D 4
34 Newton, Lancs. ....D 2
34 Newton, Lancs. ....D 3
39 Newton, Lancs. ....H 8
34 Newton, Lancs. ....B 6
24 Newton, Lincs. ....B 1
48 Newton, Lothian ...B 4
14 Newton, Mid Glam. .G 2
24 Newton, Norfolk ..D 5
26 Newton, Norfolk ...D 1
41 Newton, N. Yorks. .H 9
23 Newton, Northants.
    D 12
45 Newton, Northumb. .B 8
45 Newton, Northumb. .G 8
32 Newton, Notts. .....F 4
6 Newton, Som. .....B 5
31 Newton, Staffs. ....H 9
47 Newton, Strathclyde
    C 11
48 Newton, Strathclyde F 2
27 Newton, Suffolk ...L 2
52 Newton, Tayside ...D 4
23 Newton, War. ......D 8
13 Newton, W. Glam. .H 9
36 Newton, W. Yorks. .D 2
8 Newton, Wilts. ....D 4
5 Newton Abbot .....J 7
43 Newton Arlosh ...F 12
40 Newton Aycliffe ...C 3
40 Newton Bewley ....C 5
23 Newton Blossomville
    G 12
25 Newton Bromswold .J 1
23 Newton Burgoland .A 7
33 Newton by Toft ....B 7
5 Newton Ferrers ....L 4
26 Newton Flotman ...F 5
23 Newton Harcourt ..A 8
58 Newton House .....E 4
34 Newton-le-Willows,
    Lancashire ....H 4

40 Newton-le-Willows,
    N. Yorkshire .....F 2
36 Newton Kyme ......C 2
17 Newton Longville ..A 9
47 Newton Mearns ...D 10
40 Newton Morrell ...D 3
41 Newton Mulgrave ..D 8
12 Newton Mountain ..F 3
50 Newton of Ardtoe ..A 4
52 Newton of
    Balcanquhal ......F 6
53 Newton of Falkland .F 7
58 Newton of Murcar ..F 7
60 Newton of Ochtow .G 5
52 Newton of Pitcairns .F 5
36 Newton-on-Ouse ...A 3
41 Newton-on-Rawcliffe
    F 8
45 Newton-on-the-Moor
    C 10
32 Newton on Trent ...C 5
6 Newton Poppleford .G 4
17 Newton Purcell ....A 7
22 Newton Regis ......A 6
39 Newton Reigny ....B 7
49 Newton St. Boswells .F 8
4 Newton St. Cyres ...D 7
26 Newton St. Faith ...D 5
15 Newton St. Loe ...H 10
4 Newton St. Petrock .E 3
31 Newton Solney ...H 11
8 Newton Stacey ....B 6
42 Newton Stewart ....E 5
8 Newton Toney .....B 4
4 Newton Tracey ....C 4
47 Newton upon Ayr ..G 8
36 Newton upon
    Derwent ....B 5
30 Newton Valence ...C 8
43 Newtonairds ....D 9
58 Newtongarry Croft .D 3
48 Newtongrange .....C 6
59 Newtonmill ....L 3
57 Newtonmore ....J 3
31 Newtown, Ches. ....B 8
30 Newtown, Ches. ....E 5
2 Newtown, Corn. ....G 4
44 Newtown, Cumb. ..G 2
44 Newtown, Cumb. ..G 3
39 Newtown, Cumbria .C 7
4 Newtown, Devon ...C 6
8 Newtown, Dorset ..G 2
15 Newtown, Glos. ...A 12
15 Newtown, Glos. ...D 10
56 Newtown, Grampian
    C 7
8 Newtown, Hants. ..D 4
9 Newtown, Hants. ..D 7
8 Newtown, Hants. ..E 4
8 Newtown, Hants. ..E 7
16 Newtown, Hants. ..H 6
21 Newtown,
    Heref. & Worc. ..G 10
21 Newtown,
    Heref. & Worc. ..H 11
55 Newtown,
    Highland ....J 7
38 Newtown, I.o.M. ...H 2
8 Newtown, I.o.W. ..G 5
34 Newtown, Lancs. ...E 4
45 Newtown,
    Northumb. ......A 8
45 Newtown,
    Northumb. ......C 8
49 Newtown,
    Northumb. .....F 12
20 Newtown, Powys ..C 6
30 Newtown, Salop ...G 3
31 Newtown, Staffs. ...D 7
31 Newtown, Staffs. ..H 9
7 Newtown, Wilts. ..C 12
23 Newtown Linfold ..A 8
48 Newtown of
    Covington ....E 3
58 Newtown of
    Melrose ....A 5
53 Newtyle ....C 8
12 Neyland ....F 3
15 Nibley ....F 10
36 Nicholashayne .....E 5
13 Nicholaston ......H 8
44 Nickie's Hill ......H 4
35 Nidd ....A 11
59 Nigg, Grampian ....G 7
56 Nigg, Highland ....C 4
56 Nigg Station ......B 4
6 Nightcott ....D 2
9 Nine Ashes ......C 6
48 Nine Mile Burn ....D 4
44 Ninebanks ....H 6
10 Ninfield ....G 6
8 Ningwood ....G 5
49 Nisbet ....G 9
43 Nithside ....D 10

8 Niton ....H 6
30 No Man's Heath,
    Cheshire ....E 4
22 No Man's Heath,
    Warwickshire ....A 6
2 No Man's Land,
    Cornwall ....C 6
4 No Man's Land,
    Devon ....E 7
18 Noak Hill ....E 5
48 Noblehall ....E 4
48 Noblehouse ....D 5
3 Nobold ....A 10
23 Nobottle ....F 10
33 Nocton ....D 8
6 Noke ....C 6
12 Nolton ....E 2
12 Nolton Haven .....E 2
9 Noneley ....G 3
39 Nook ....G 8
56 Norbury, Ches. ....E 4
31 Norbury, Derby ....F 9
21 Norbury, Salop ....C 9
31 Norbury, Staffs. ...H 6
24 Nordelph ....E 7
35 Norden ....F 7
56 Norden Heath .....H 1
21 Nordley ....C 12
16 Nore Marsh ....F 2
26 Norfolk, Co. ......D 4
49 Norham ....E 11
30 Norley ....C 4
8 Norley Wood .....F 5
24 Norman Cross ....F 3
36 Normanby, Humber. E 6
41 Normanby ....G 7
33 Normanby-by-Spital A 7
37 Normanby le Wold .B 9
9 Normandy ....A 10
10 Norman's Bay ....G 6
6 Norman's Green ...F 4
8 Normansland .....D 4
31 Normanton,
    Derbyshire .....G 11
32 Normanton, Leics. .F 5
32 Normanton, Lincs. .F 6
32 Normanton, Notts. .E 4
36 Normanton,
    W. Yorks. ....E 2
23 Normanton le
    Heath ....A 7
32 Normanton on
    Soar ....H 2
32 Normanton on the
    Wolds ....G 3
32 Normanton on
    Trent ....C 5
34 Normoss ....C 2
9 Norney ....B 10
15 Norrington Com. ..H 12
31 Norris Hill ....H 11
32 North Anston .....B 2
34 North Ashton .....G 4
16 North Aston ......A 6
9 North Atrochie ....D 7
8 North Baddesley ..D 5
51 North Ballachulish ..B 8
7 North Barrow .....C 9
26 North Barsham ....B 2
19 North Benfleet ....E 7
9 North Bersted ....F 10
49 North Berwick ....A 8
9 North Boarhunt ...E 7
5 North Bovey .....G 6
47 North Brackenridge
    E 12
7 North Bradley ...A 12
5 North Brentor ....H 4
7 North Brewham ..C 10
7 North Buckland ...B 4
26 North Burlingham .D 7
7 North Cadbury ....D 9
32 North Carlton,
    Lincolnshire .....B 6
32 North Carlton, Notts.
    B 3
46 North Carrine ....H 2
36 North Cave ......D 6
16 North Cerney .....C 1
9 North Chapel .....C 11
8 North Charford ...D 3
45 North Charlton ...A 10
7 North Cheriton ...D 10
7 North Chideock ...G 8
36 North Cliffe ......C 6
32 North Clifton .....C 5
33 North Coates .....G 11
33 North Cockerington
    A 10
7 North Coker .....E 9
32 North Collingham .D 5
10 North Common ...F 3
14 North Cornelly ....F 2

50 North Corry ......B 5
58 North Cottown ....F 5
26 North Cove ....F 8
43 North Cowshaw ..C 11
40 North Cowton ....E 3
44 North Craigs .....E 1
23 North Crawley ...H 12
18 North Cray ......G 5
26 North Creake .....B 2
7 North Curry ......D 7
37 North Dalton .....B 7
3 North Darley .....B 10
35 North Deighton ..B 12
47 North Drumboy ..D 10
36 North Duffield ....C 5
33 North Elkington ..A 10
26 North Elmham ....C 3
36 North Elmsall ....F 3
15 North End, Avon ..G 11
15 North End, Avon ..H 7
17 North End, Bucks. .A 9
17 North End, Bucks. .E 8
7 North End, Dorset .D 11
18 North End, Essex ..B 6
9 North End, Hants. .F 8
16 North End, Hants. .H 5
37 North End,
    Humberside .....D 10
24 North End, Lincs. ...B 3
34 North End,
    Merseyside ....G 2
45 North End,
    Northumb. ....C 9
6 North End, Som. ..D 6
9 North End,
    W. Sussex .....E 12
54 North Erradale ....B 1
6 North Esworthy ...D 2
19 North Fambridge ..D 8
46 North Feorline ....F 4
37 North Ferriby ....E 7
37 North Frodingham .B 8
63 North Galson .....A 5
64 North Gluss ......C 7
8 North Gorley .....E 3
58 North Gorrachie ..B 5
26 North Green ......F 5
44 North Greenhill ...F 4
41 North Grimston ..H 8
10 North Halling ....B 6
47 North Halls ......F 11
9 North Hayling ....F 9
45 North Hazelrigg ..C 12
9 North Heath ....D 12
3 North Hill ....B 9
16 North Hinksey ...D 6
10 North Holmwood ..C 1
47 North Hourat ....D 8
5 North Huish ......K 6
32 North Hykeham ..D 6
12 North Johnston ...F 3
37 North Kelsey .....G 8
56 North Kessock ....E 2
37 North Killingholme .E 9
40 North Kilvington ..G 4
23 North Kilworth ...D 9
58 North Kinmundy ..F 6
58 North Kirkton ....C 8
33 North Kyme ......E 8
10 North Lancing ....G 1
40 North Lees ......H 3
23 North Luffenham .B 12
16 North Leigh ......C 5
32 North Leverton with
    Habblesthorpe ...B 5
22 North Littleton ...G 4
27 North Lopham ...G 3
45 North Lyham ....C 12
9 North Marden ....D 9
17 North Marston ...B 8
48 North Middleton,
    Lothian ....C 6
49 North Middleton,
    Northumb. .....G 12
4 North Molton ....G 6
58 North Monkshill ..C 5
41 North Moor ......H 12
16 North Moreton ...E 6
9 North Mundham ..F 10
32 North Muskham ..D 5
37 North Newbald ...C 7
23 North Newington .H 7
16 North Newton ...H 2
6 North Newton ...C 6
15 North Nibley .....E 10
9 North Oakley .....A 7
18 North Ockendon ..E 6
40 North Ormesby ...A 10
33 North Ormsby ....A 10
40 North Otterington .F 4
37 North Owersby ...H 8
7 North Perrott ....E 8
6 North Petherton ..C 6
3 North Petherwin ..A 10

26 North Pickenham ..E 1
22 North Piddle .....G 3
7 North Poorton ....F 8
6 North Quarme ....C 2
48 North Queensferry .A 4
4 North Radworthy ..C 6
33 North Rauceby ...F 7
35 North Rigton ....B 11
31 North Rode ......D 7
64 North Roe ....B 7
24 North Runcton ...D 7
64 North Sandwick ...B 8
38 North Scale ......H 4
32 North Scarle .....D 6
45 N. Seaton Colliery .D 11
63 North Shawbost ...B 4
50 North Shian ......C 6
45 North Shields ....F 11
19 North Shoebury ...D 9
34 North Shore ......D 2
40 North Shortcleugh .H 2
38 North Side, Cumb. .B 2
24 North Side, Cambs. .E 4
41 North Skelton ....C 7
37 North Somercotes .G 12
40 North Stainley ...G 3
39 North Stainmore ..D 10
15 North Stoke, Avon
    G 10
17 North Stoke, Oxon .F 7
9 North Stoke, W. Sussex
    E 11
17 North Street, Berks.
    G 7
9 North Street, Hants. .C 8
45 North Sunderland .D 12
4 North Tamerton ..F 5
4 North Tawton .....F 5
37 North Thoresby ...G 10
45 North Tidworth ...A 4
45 North Togston ...C 10
63 North Tolsta ......B 6
26 North Tuddenham .D 3
45 North Walbottle ...F 10
26 North Walsham ...C 6
9 North Waltham ...B 7
9 North Warnborough
    A 9
59 North Water Bri. ..L 4
61 North Watten ....B 11
18 North Weald Bassett
    D 5
32 North Wheatley ...B 5
15 North Wick ......H 9
5 North Whilborough .J 7
33 North Willingham ..A 8
32 North Wingfield ...D 1
32 North Witham ....H 6
7 North Wootton,
    Dorset ....E 10
24 North Wootton,
    Norfolk ....C 7
7 North Wootton,
    Somerset ....B 9
15 North Wraxall ...G 11
16 North Wroughton .F 3
45 North Yardhope ..C 7
40 North Yorkshire, Co.
    F 5
40 Northallerton .....F 4
4 Northam, Devon ..C 3
8 Northam, Hants. ..E 6
23 Northampton ....F 11
23 Northamptonshire,
    County ....E 11
18 Northaw ....D 3
24 Northborough
    Peakirk ....E 3
11 Northbourne ....C 12
8 Northbrook ......B 6
17 Northchurch .....C 10
5 Northcott ....G 2
23 Northend ....G 7
49 Northfield, Borders
    C 11
59 Northfield, Grampian
    G 6
22 Northfield,
    W. Midlands ....D 4
10 Northfleet ....A 5
11 Northiam ....F 7
25 Northill ....K 3
9 Northington .....B 7
33 Northlands ......E 10
16 Northleach ......C 2
16 Northleigh ......G 5
4 Northlew ....F 4
16 Northmoor ......H 7
6 Northmoor Green or
    Moorland ......C 6
53 Northmuir ....B 8
9 Northney ....F 9
18 Northolt ....E 1
29 Northop ....C 11

29 Northophall ....C 12
24 Northorpe, Lincs. ...B 3
24 Northorpe, Lincs. ...D 2
37 Northorpe, Lincs. ...G 7
7 Northover, Som. ...B 8
7 Northover, Som. ....D 8
35 Northowram .....D 10
15 Northport ....G 1
8 Northport ....G 1
26 Northrepps ....B 5
63 Northton ....H 1
64 Northtown ....D 3
45 Northumberland,
 County ....D 8
15 Northway, Glos. ...A 12
6 Northway, Som. ....C 5
30 Northwich ....C 5
15 Northwick ....F 9
24 Northwold ....F 8
8 Northwood, I.o.W. ..G 6
18 Northwood, Lond. ..E 1
30 Northwood, Salop ..G 3
25 Northwood End ....C 5
15 Northwood Green .C 10
30 Northwood, Ches. ..B 4
40 Norton, Cleveland ..C 5
15 Norton, Glos. .....B 11
15 Norton, Gwent .....B 7
22 Norton, Heref. &
 Worc. ....G 2
22 Norton, Heref. &
 Worc. ....G 4
8 Norton, I.o.W. .....G 5
41 Norton, N. Yorks. ...H 8
23 Norton, Northants. ..F 9
32 Norton, Notts. .....C 3
21 Norton, Powys .....F 8
21 Norton, Salop ....A 11
21 Norton, Salop .....B 1
21 Norton, Salop ....D 10
36 Norton, S. Yorks. ...H 9
27 Norton, Suffolk ....J 3
15 Norton, Wilts. ....F 12
8 Norton Bavant ....B 8
31 Norton Bridge ....G 7
22 Norton Canes .....A 4
21 Norton Canon ....H 9
32 Norton Disney ....D 6
22 Norton East ....A 4
7 Norton Ferris ....C 11
6 Norton Fitzwarren .D 5
8 Norton Green .....G 5
15 Norton Hawkfield ..H 9
18 Norton Heath .....D 6
30 Norton in Hales ....F 5
31 Norton in the
 Moors ....E 7
23 Norton Juxta
 Twycross ......A 7
40 Norton-le-Clay ....H 4
22 Norton Lindsey ....F 6
15 Norton Malreward ..H 9
7 Norton St. Philip .A 11
7 Norton sub Hamdon E 8
26 Norton Subcourse ..F 7
32 Norton Woodseats ..B 1
32 Norwell ....D 5
32 Norwell Woodhouse
 ....D 5
26 Norwich ....E 5
64 Norwick ....A 8
32 Norwood ....B 2
10 Norwood Hill .....D 1
23 Noseley ....B 10
5 Noss Mayo ....L 4
40 Nosterfield ....G 3
55 Nostie ....G 2
16 Notgrove ....B 2
14 Nottage ....F 1
32 Nottingham ....F 3
32 Nottinghamshire,
 County ....D 4
35 Notton, W. Yorks. .F 12
15 Notton, Wilts. .....G 12
19 Nounsley ....C 8
22 Noutard's Green ...E 2
56 Novar House ......C 2
21 Nox ....A 9
17 Nuffield ....E 7
57 Nuide ....K 3
36 Nun Monkton .....A 3
36 Nunburnholme ....B 6
32 Nuncargate ....E 2
23 Nuneaton ....C 7
16 Nuneham Courtenay
 ....D 6
49 Nunlands ....D 12
38 Nunnery Howe ....H 2
7 Nunney ....B 10
41 Nunnington ....G 7
45 Nunnykirk ....D 9
37 Nunsthorpe ......F 10
40 Nunthorpe ....D 5
8 Nunton ....C 3
40 Nunwick ....H 3

43 Nunwood ....D 10
8 Nursling ....D 5
9 Nutbourne ....F 9
9 Nutbourne ......D 12
10 Nutfield ....C 2
32 Nuthall ....F 2
25 Nuthampstead ...M 5
9 Nuthurst ....E 1
10 Nutley, E. Sussex ..E 3
9 Nutley, Hants. ....B 7
36 Nutwell ....G 4
9 Nyetimber ......F 10
9 Nyewood ....D 9
4 Nymet Rowland ..E 6
4 Nymet Tracey ....F 6
15 Nympsfield .....D 11
6 Nynehead ....D 5
7 Nythe ....C 7
6 Nyton ....E 10
11 Oad Street ......B 7
23 Oadby ....B 9
31 Oakamoor ....F 9
48 Oakbank ....C 4
14 Oakdale ....D 5
5 Oake ....D 5
22 Oaken ....B 2
34 Oakenclough .....B 4
29 Oakengates ....A 12
29 Oakenholt ......C 12
40 Oakenshaw, Dur. ..A 2
35 Oakenshaw, W. Yorks.
 ....D 10
14 Oakfield, Gwent ...E 6
15 Oakfield, Hants. ...C 5
6 Oakford, Devon ...D 3
13 Oakford, Dyfed ...A 8
6 Oakfordbridge ....D 3
31 Oakgrove ....C 8
23 Oakham ....A 12
9 Oakhanger ....C 9
7 Oakhill ....B 9
25 Oakington ....J 5
15 Oaklands ....D 7
15 Oakle Street ....C 10
25 Oakley, Beds. ....K 1
17 Oakley, Bucks. ...C 7
8 Oakley, Dorset ...F 2
52 Oakley, Fife .....H 5
9 Oakley, Hants. ...A 7
27 Oakley, Suffolk ...H 5
17 Oakley Green ...F 10
20 Oakleypark ......D 5
15 Oakridge Lynch ..D 12
16 Oaksey ....E 1
32 Oakthorpe ....A 6
40 Oaktree Hill .....E 4
45 Oakwood, Northumb.
 ....F 8
49 Oakwood, Borders ..G 7
9 Oakwoodhill ....B 12
35 Oakworth ....C 9
11 Oar ....B 9
16 Oare, Berks. .....G 6
16 Oare, Som. ....B 2
16 Oare, Wilts. .....H 3
6 Oareford ....B 2
33 Oasby ....F 7
59 Oathlaw ....M 2
50 Oban, Highland ...K 2
50 Oban, Strathclyde ..E 6
58 Obliston ....B 1
7 Oborne ....D 10
56 Obsdale ....C 2
30 Occlestone Green ..D 5
27 Occold ....H 5
52 Ochil Hills Hosp. ...F 6
47 Ochiltree ....G 10
58 Ochtermuthill ....E 3
52 Ochtrelure ....F 2
32 Ockbrook ....G 2
17 Ockham ....H 11
10 Ockle ....A 3
21 Ocle Pychard ...H 11
9 Ocley ....B 12
41 Octon ....H 10
7 Odcombe ....E 8
15 Odd Down ......H 10
39 Oddendale ....D 8
22 Oddingley ....F 3
16 Oddington, Glos. ..B 3
16 Oddington, Oxon ..C 6
25 Odell ....J 1
64 Odie ....C 3
9 Odiham ....A 9
8 Odstock ....C 3
23 Odstone ....A 7
23 Offchurch ....F 7
22 Offenham ....G 4
15 Offerton ....G 11
10 Offham, E. Sussex .G 3
10 Offham, Kent ....B 5
25 Offord Cluny ....J 3
25 Offord D'Arcy ...J 3
27 Offton ....K 4

6 Offwell ....F 5
16 Ogbourne Maizey ..G 3
16 Ogbourne St. Andrew
 ....G 3
16 Ogbourne St. George
 ....G 3
45 Ogle ....E 9
14 Ogmore ....G 2
14 Ogmore-by-Sea ...G 2
14 Ogmore Vale .....G 2
7 Okeford Fitzpaine .E 11
4 Okehampton .....F 5
59 Old Aberdeen ....G 7
9 Old Alresford ....C 7
53 Old Balkello .....C 8
45 Old Berwick .....A 9
52 Old Blair ....A 4
33 Old Bolingbroke ..D 10
35 Old Bramhope ...C 11
31 Old Brampton ...C 11
43 Old Bridge of Urr ..E 8
26 Old Buckenham ...F 4
16 Old Burghclere ...H 6
40 Old Byland ....G 6
37 Old Clee ....F 10
6 Old Cleeve ....B 4
43 Old Clouden .....D 9
29 Old Colwyn .....B 8
43 Old Craighouse ..C 12
42 Old Dailly ....B 3
32 Old Dalby ....H 4
58 Old Deer ....C 7
60 Old Drumrunie Lo...F 3
49 Old Dryburn ....E 12
36 Old Edlington ....G 3
40 Old Eldon ....B 3
37 Old Ellerby ......C 9
24 Old Fletton ......F 3
36 Old Goole ....E 5
44 Old Graitney ....F 2
37 Old Hall ....E 10
19 Old Heath ......B 10
10 Old Heathfield ....F 5
25 Old Hurst ....H 4
39 Old Hutton ......F 8
2 Old Kea ....E 5
47 Old Kilpatrick ....B 9
18 Old Knebworth ...B 2
26 Old Lakenham ...E 5
38 Old Laxey ....G 2
33 Old Leake ......E 11
45 Old Lyham .....C 12
41 Old Malton ......H 8
36 Old Micklefield ...D 2
16 Old Milton ....G 4
22 Old Milverton ....E 6
47 Old Monkland ...C 12
19 Old Montsale ...D 10
45 Old Mousen ....C 12
8 Old Netley ....E 6
27 Old Newton ......J 4
43 Old Orchardton ...F 9
48 Old Philpstoun ...B 3
40 Old Quarrington ..A 3
32 Old Radford ......F 3
21 Old Radnor ......F 8
58 Old Rattray .....B 8
58 Old Rayne ....E 4
11 Old Romney ......E 9
52 Old Scone ....D 6
36 Old Snydale ......E 2
15 Old Sodbury ....F 10
33 Old Somerby .....G 7
23 Old Stratford ...H 11
30 Old Swan ....A 3
39 Old Tebay ....E 8
40 Old Thirsk ....G 4
39 Old Town, Cumb. ..A 7
39 Old Town, Cumbria .G 8
2 Old Town,
 Is. of Scilly .....D 2
45 Old Town,
 Northumb. ...D 7
35 Old Trafford .....G 7
32 Old Tupton ......D 1
25 Old Warden ......L 2
25 Old Weston ......A 2
17 Old Windsor .....G 10
11 Old Wives Lees ...C 9
17 Old Woking ....H 11
60 Oldany ....D 3
22 Oldberrow ....F 5
4 Oldborough ......E 6
21 Oldbury, Salop ..C 12
22 Oldbury, War. ....C 6
22 Oldbury, W. Midlands
 ....C 3
15 Oldbury on the Hill
 ....E 11
15 Oldbury-upon-Severn
 ....E 9
14 Oldcastle, Gwent ..A 11
14 Oldbury, Mid Glam. .F 2
32 Oldcotes ....A 3

22 Oldfield, Heref. &
 Worc. ....F 2
35 Oldfield, W. Yorks. .C 8
7 Oldford ....A 11
35 Oldham ....G 8
49 Oldhamstocks ...B 10
15 Oldland ....G 10
58 Oldmeldrum .....E 6
58 Oldnoth ....D 3
21 Oldpark ....A 12
60 Oldshore Beg ....B 3
60 Oldshore More ...B 3
40 Oldstead ....G 5
58 Oldtown of Ord ...B 4
14 Oldway ....H 9
4 Oldways End ....D 7
58 Oldwhat ....C 6
48 Oliver ....G 4
8 Oliver's Battery ...C 7
64 Ollaberry ....C 7
30 Ollerton, Ches. ...C 6
32 Ollerton, Notts. ...E 5
30 Ollerton, Salop ...H 5
20 Olmarch ....G 2
23 Olney ....G 12
22 Olton ....D 5
15 Olveston ....F 9
22 Ombersley ....F 2
32 Ompton ....D 4
38 Onchan ....H 2
31 Onecote ....E 9
15 Onen ....C 7
18 Ongar ....D 5
29 Onger Hill ......C 7
21 Onibury ....D 10
51 Onich ....A 7
14 Onllwyn ....C 2
30 Onneley ....F 6
9 Onslow Village ..A 11
47 Onthank ....E 9
35 Openshaw ....G 7
32 Openwoodgate ....E 1
54 Opinan, Highland ..C 1
60 Opinan, Highland ..F 3
49 Orange Lane .....E 10
62 Orbost ....D 2
33 Orby ....C 12
46 Orcadia ....C 6
4 Orchard Hill ....C 3
6 Orchard Portman ..D 6
8 Orcheston ....B 2
15 Orcop ....B 8
15 Orcop Hill ......A 8
62 Ord ....G 5
58 Ordens ....B 4
58 Ordhead ....F 4
59 Ordie ....G 2
58 Ordiequish ......B 1
32 Ordsall ....B 4
1 Ore ....G 7
30 Orford, Cheshire ..A 5
21 Oreton, Salop ..D 12
27 Orford, Suffolk ...K 7
8 Organ Ford ......D 6
64 Orgill ....D 1
32 Orgreave ....A 8
64 Orkney, Co. .....C 2
11 Orlestone ....E 8
21 Orleton, Heref. &
 Worc. ....F 10
21 Orleton, Heref. &
 Worc. ....F 12
23 Orlingbury ......E 12
40 Ormesby ....C 5
26 Ormesby St. Margaret
 ....D 8
26 Ormesby St. Michael
 ....D 8
60 Ormiscaig ....G 1
49 Ormiston ....B 7
38 Ormely Hall .....F 2
50 Ormsaigbeg .....A 2
50 Ormsaigmore ....A 2
49 Ormsary House ...B 2
34 Ormskirk ....F 3
63 Orosay ....F 5
64 Orphir ....D 2
18 Orpington ....G 5
34 Orrell, Merseyside .G 2
34 Orrell, Manchester .G 4
34 Orrell Post ......G 4
53 Orrock ....H 7
43 Orroland ....G 8
18 Orsett ....F 6
18 Orsett Heath ....F 6
22 Orslow ....A 2
32 Orston ....F 5
38 Orthwaite ....B 5
39 Orton, Cumbria ...D 8
23 Orton, Northants. .D 11
32 Orton on the Hill ..B 1
58 Orton Station ....B 1
24 Orton Waterville .F 3

25 Orwell ....K 5
34 Osbaldeston .....D 5
36 Osbaldwick ......B 4
23 Osbaston ....B 7
24 Osbournby ....D 4
30 Oscroft ....D 4
62 Ose ....D 3
32 Osgathorpe ......H 2
33 Osgodby, Lincs. ...A 8
36 Osgodby, N. Yorks. .D 4
41 Osgodby, N. Yorks.
 ....G 10
62 Oskaig ....D 5
50 Oskamuil ....D 2
31 Osmaston ....F 10
7 Osmington ......H 10
7 Osmington Mills ..H 10
29 Osmondthorpe ..D 12
40 Osmotherley .....E 5
11 Ospringe ....B 8
32 Ossett ....E 11
32 Ossington ....D 5
19 Ostend ....D 9
30 Oswaldkirk ......G 6
34 Oswaldtwistle ....D 6
30 Oswestry ....G 2
10 Otford ....B 4
11 Otham ....C 7
7 Othery ....C 7
27 Otley, Suffolk ...K 5
35 Otley, W. Yorks. .C 10
46 Otter Ferry ......A 4
6 Otterburn ....D 6
45 Otterburn, Northumb.
 ....D 7
35 Otterburn, N. Yorks.
 ....A 7
45 Otterburn Camp ...C 7
6 Otterham ....B 2
6 Otterhampton ...B 6
17 Ottershaw ......H 11
64 Otterswick ......B 7
6 Otterton ....H 4
6 Ottery St. Mary ..G 5
11 Ottinge ....D 10
37 Ottringham .....E 10
39 Oughtershaw ...G 11
43 Oughterside ....H 12
35 Oughtibridge ...H 11
40 Oulston ....H 6
44 Oulton, Cumb. ...H 1
26 Oulton, Norfolk ..C 4
31 Oulton, Staffs. ...G 7
26 Oulton, Suffolk ..F 8
35 Oulton, W. Yorks. .D 12
26 Oulton Broad ....F 8
26 Oulton Street ....C 5
25 Oundle ....G 1
39 Ousby ....B 8
15 Ousdale ....E 10
25 Ousden ....J 8
36 Ousefleet ....E 5
40 Ouston, Dur. ...H 10
45 Ouston, Northumb. .F 9
44 Ouston, Northumb. .H 6
38 Out Gate ....E 6
37 Out Newton ....E 11
34 Out Rawcliffe ....C 3
45 Outchester .....C 12
64 Outertown ......D 1
35 Outhgill ....E 10
16 Outlane ....E 9
24 Outwell ....E 6
8 Outwick ....D 3
10 Outwood, Surrey .D 2
35 Outwood, W. Yorks.
 ....E 12
35 Ovenden ....D 9
49 Ovenscloss ......F 7
25 Over, Cambs. .....H 5
30 Over, Cheshire ...D 5
15 Over, Glos. ......F 9
43 Over Cleuchbrae .B 11
16 Over Compton ...E 9
48 Over Dalgleish ...H 5
31 Over Haddon ...D 10
43 Over Hazlefield ..G 8
39 Over Kellet .....H 7
16 Over Kiddington ..B 5
16 Over Norton ....A 4
40 Over Silton ......F 5
6 Over Stowey .....B 5
7 Over Stratton ....E 8
30 Over Tabley .....B 6
8 Over Wallop .....B 3
22 Over Whitacre ...C 6
49 Over Whitton ...G 10
7 Over Woodhouse ..C 2
64 Overbister ....B 4
22 Overbury ....H 3
58 Overhall ....C 5
58 Overhill ....D 4
7 Overleigh ....C 8

22 Overley Green ....F 4
50 Overpool ....C 3
22 Overseal ....A 6
58 Overside ....B 8
11 Oversland ....B 9
30 Overstone ......E 11
26 Overstrand ......B 5
23 Overthorpe .....H 8
30 Overton, Ches. ...C 4
30 Overton, Clwyd ...F 2
43 Overton, Dumf. &
 Gall. ....E 10
58 Overton, Grampian .F 6
8 Overton, Hants. ...A 6
34 Overton, Lancs. ...A 3
36 Overton, N. Yorks. .B 3
21 Overton, Salop ...E 10
47 Overton, Strathclyde
 ....D 8
48 Overton, Strathclyde
 ....D 1
13 Overton, W. Glam. .H 8
29 Overton Bridge ..F 12
30 Overton Green ...D 6
58 Overtown, Grampian
 ....D 7
48 Overtown, Strathclyde
 ....D 1
39 Overtown, Lancs. .H 8
16 Overtown, Wilts. ...F 3
58 Overtown of Memsie
 ....B 7
26 Overy Staithe .....A 1
17 Oving, Bucks. .....B 8
9 Oving, W. Sussex .F 10
10 Ovingdean ....H 2
40 Ovingham ....G 9
40 Ovington, Durham
 ....D 2
9 Ovington, Essex ..L 1
9 Ovington, Hants. ..C 7
26 Ovington, Norfolk ..E 2
45 Ovington, Northumb.
 ....G 9
8 Ower ....D 5
7 Owermoigne .....H 11
31 Owler Bar ....B 11
32 Owlerton ....A 1
17 Owlswick ....C 8
33 Owmby-by-Spital ..B 7
8 Owslebury ....D 6
23 Owston, Leics. ..A 11
36 Owston, S. Yorks. .F 3
36 Owston Ferry ....G 6
33 Owstwick ......D 10
32 Owthorpe ....G 4
24 Oxborough ......E 8
24 Oxen Park ....F 5
38 Oxenholme ....F 8
35 Oxenhope ....D 9
26 Oxenrig ....E 11
16 Oxenton ....A 1
16 Oxenwood ....H 4
16 Oxford ....C 5
4 Oxford Cross ....B 3
16 Oxfordshire, Co. ...C 5
18 Oxhey ....D 1
22 Oxhill ....G 6
22 Oxley ....B 2
19 Oxley Green .....C 9
49 Oxnam ....G 9
17 Oxshott ....H 12
35 Oxspring ....G 11
10 Oxted ....C 3
49 Oxton, Borders ...D 7
32 Oxton, Notts. ....E 3
36 Oxton, N. Yorks. ...C 3
13 Oxwich ....H 8
13 Oxwich Green ....H 8
60 Oykel Bridge ....G 5
58 Oyne ....E 4
13 Oystermouth ....H 9
7 Packers Hill ....E 10
23 Packington ......A 7
22 Packington Park ...D 5
53 Padanaram ......B 9
7 Padbury ....A 8
18 Paddington ......F 3
11 Paddlesworth ...D 10
29 Paddock Wood ...D 5
56 Paddockhaugh ...D 8
44 Paddockhole .....E 1
30 Padogreen ....G 4
35 Padfield ....G 9
30 Padgate ....A 5
35 Padiham ....D 7
29 Padog ....E 8
35 Padside ....A 10
6 Padstow ....B 6
9 Padworth ....G 7
40 Page Bank ......B 3
9 Pagham ....F 10
19 Paglesham ......E 9
63 Paible ....G 1

5 Paignton ... K 8
23 Pailton ... D 8
21 Painscastle ... H 7
45 Painshawfield ... G 9
15 Painswick ... C 12
11 Painter's Forstal ... B 8
47 Paisley ... C 9
58 Paithnick ... B 2
26 Pakefield ... F 8
27 Pakenham ... J 2
29 Pale ... G 9
10 Palehouse Com. ... F 4
8 Palestine ... H 5
17 Paley Street ... G 9
42 Palgowan ... C 5
27 Palgrave ... G 4
11 Palmarsh ... E 10
18 Palmers Green ... E 3
43 Palnackie ... F 9
42 Palnure ... E 5
32 Palterton ... C 2
17 Pamber End ... H 7
17 Pamber Green ... H 7
17 Pamber Heath ... H 7
8 Pamphill ... F 1
25 Pampisford ... K 6
7 Panborough ... B 8
53 Panbride ... D 10
4 Pancrasweek ... E 2
29 Pandy, Clwyd ... G 11
15 Pandy, Gwent ... B 7
20 Pandy, Gwynedd ... B 2
20 Pandy, Powys ... B 5
29 Pandy Tudor ... D 8
19 Panfield ... A 7
17 Pangbourne ... F 7
43 Panlands ... C 11
35 Pannal ... B 11
59 Pannanich ... H 1
30 Pant ... H 1
20 Pant Mawr ... D 4
28 Pant-glas, Gwynedd ... E 4
21 Pantglas, Salop ... C 8
13 Pantgwyn, Dyfed ... D 9
12 Pantgwyn, Dyfed ... B 6
13 Pant-lasau ... G 10
33 Panton ... B 9
20 Pant-perthog ... B 3
20 Pant-y-dwr ... E 5
21 Pant-y-ffrid ... B 7
13 Pantyffynnon ... F 9
14 Pantygasseg ... D 5
15 Pant y Goitre ... C 7
12 Pantymenyn ... D 5
29 Pantymwyn ... D 11
14 Pant-yr-awel ... E 3
26 Panxworth ... D 6
38 Papcastle ... B 3
49 Papple ... B 8
32 Papplewick ... E 3
25 Papworth Everard ... J 4
25 Papworth St. Agnes ... J 4
3 Par ... D 8
7 Parbrook ... C 9
29 Parc ... G 8
12 Parc-llyn ... B 6
38 Pardshaw ... C 3
27 Parham ... J 6
43 Park, Dumf. & Gall. ... B 10
59 Park, Grampian ... G 5
50 Park, Strathclyde ... C 6
17 Park Corner, Berks. ... F 9
10 Park Corner, E. Sussex ... D 4
17 Park Corner, Oxon ... E 8
40 Park End, Cleveland ... C 5
45 Park End, Northumb. ... E 7
9 Park Gate ... E 7
44 Park Nook ... F 4
58 Parkdargue ... C 4
38 Parkend, Cumb. ... A 5
15 Parkend, Glos. ... C 5
27 Parkeston ... M 5
30 Parkgate, Ches. ... B 1
43 Parkgate, Dumf. & Gall. ... C 11
10 Parkgate, Surrey ... D 1
48 Parkgatestone ... F 4
4 Parkham ... D 3
4 Parkham Ash ... D 2
56 Parkhead ... F 8
58 Parkhill House ... F 6
15 Parkhouse ... D 8
8 Parkhurst ... G 6
13 Parkmill ... H 9
59 Parkneuk ... K 5
30 Parkside ... E 3
8 Parkstone ... G 2
8 Parley Cross ... F 2
4 Parracombe ... B 5

30 Parrah Green ... F 6
12 Parrog ... C 4
24 Parson Drove ... E 5
19 Parson's Heath ... A 10
31 Partick ... C 10
34 Partington ... H 6
33 Partney ... C 11
38 Parton, Cumb. ... C 2
43 Parton, Dumf. & Gall. ... E 8
15 Parton, Glos. ... B 12
10 Partridge Green ... F 1
31 Parwich ... E 10
23 Passenham ... H 11
9 Passfield ... C 9
26 Paston Street ... B 6
43 Patchacott ... F 3
10 Patcham ... G 2
9 Patching ... E 12
4 Patchole ... B 5
15 Patchway ... F 9
35 Pateley Bridge ... A 10
19 Paternoster Heath ... B 9
52 Path of Condie ... F 5
7 Pathe ... C 7
53 Pathead, Fife ... H 8
48 Pathead, Lothian ... C 6
47 Pathhead ... H 11
52 Pathstruie ... F 5
47 Patna ... H 9
16 Patney ... H 2
38 Patrick ... G 1
40 Patrick Brompton ... F 2
34 Patricroft ... G 6
37 Patrington ... E 10
17 Patrixbourne ... C 10
38 Patterdale ... D 6
44 Pattieshill ... F 3
22 Pattingham ... B 2
23 Pattishall ... G 10
19 Pattiswick Green ... B 8
2 Paul ... G 2
23 Paulerspury ... G 10
37 Paull ... E 9
22 Paulton ... A 10
45 Pauperhaugh ... C 9
25 Pavenham ... K 1
6 Pawlett ... B 6
49 Pawston ... F 11
22 Paxford ... H 5
12 Paxton ... D 12
6 Payhembury ... F 4
35 Paythorne ... B 7
22 Peacehaven ... H 3
22 Peachley ... F 2
31 Peak Dale ... C 9
31 Peak Forest ... B 9
58 Peaknowe ... B 4
55 Peanmeanach ... L 1
9 Pearsie ... L 1
10 Pearsons Green ... D 6
10 Pease Pottage ... E 1
7 Peasedown St. John ... A 10
16 Peasemore ... F 5
21 Peasenhall ... H 7
9 Peaslake ... B 12
34 Peasley Cross ... H 4
11 Peasmarsh ... F 7
49 Peaston Bank ... C 7
53 Peat Inn ... F 9
8 Peathill ... A 7
23 Peatling Magna ... C 9
23 Peatling Parva ... C 9
27 Peaton ... D 10
27 Pebmarsh ... M 2
22 Pebworth ... G 5
35 Peckett Well ... D 8
30 Peckforton ... E 4
18 Peckham ... F 3
23 Peckleton ... B 8
44 Pedderhill ... F 3
11 Pedlinge ... E 10
22 Pedmore ... D 3
7 Pedwell ... C 8
25 Peebles ... E 5
38 Peel ... G 1
9 Peel Common ... F 7
25 Pegsdon ... M 2
45 Pegswood ... D 10
62 Peinaha ... B 4
62 Peinchorran ... E 4
62 Peinlick ... B 3
62 Peinmore ... C 4
12 Pelcomb Cross ... C 4
19 Peldon ... B 9
22 Pelsall ... B 4
45 Pelton ... H 10
45 Pelton Fell ... H 10
43 Pelutho ... G 12
9 Pelynt ... D 9
13 Pemberton, Dyfed ... G 8
34 Pemberton, Manchester ... G 4

13 Pembrey ... G 7
21 Pembridge ... G 9
12 Pembroke ... G 3
12 Pembroke Dock ... G 3
10 Pembury ... D 5
13 Pen Rhiwfawr ... F 10
11 Pen-Sarn ... E 7
15 Penalt ... C 8
12 Penally ... G 5
15 Penalt ... A 9
3 Penare ... F 7
14 Penarth ... G 5
20 Pen-bont-rhyd-y-beddau ... D 2
12 Penbryn ... B 6
12 Pencader ... C 8
13 Pen-cae ... A 7
28 Pencaenewydd ... F 3
28 Pencarnisiog ... C 3
12 Pencarreg ... C 8
14 Pencelli ... B 4
13 Penclawdd ... G 9
15 Pencoed, Heref. & Worc. ... B 8
14 Pencoed, Mid Glam. ... F 3
21 Pencombe ... G 11
15 Pencraig, Heref. & Worc. ... B 9
29 Pencraig, Powys ... G 9
2 Pendeen ... F 1
14 Penderyn ... C 3
12 Pendine ... F 6
34 Pendlebury ... G 6
34 Pendleton, Lancs. ... C 6
35 Pendleton, Manchester ... G 7
15 Pendock ... A 11
3 Pendoggett ... B 7
3 Pendomer ... E 8
14 Pendoylan ... G 4
14 Pendre ... F 2
20 Penegoes ... B 3
12 Penfeidir ... D 2
13 Pen-ffordd, Dyfed ... C 8
12 Pen-ffordd, Dyfed ... E 4
14 Pengam ... D 5
18 Penge ... G 3
13 Pengelly ... A 8
14 Pengenffordd ... A 5
3 Pengover Green ... C 10
14 Pen-groes oped ... D 6
2 Penhale ... H 4
2 Penhalurick ... F 4
16 Penhill ... E 2
15 Penhow ... E 7
10 Penhurst ... F 6
20 Peniarth ... B 2
28 Penicuik ... C 5
13 Peniel ... E 8
62 Penifiler ... D 4
46 Peninver ... G 4
28 Penisar-waum ... D 5
35 Penistone ... G 11
30 Penketh ... A 4
42 Penkill ... B 3
42 Penkiln ... G 6
22 Penkridge ... A 3
30 Penley ... F 3
13 Penllergaer ... G 9
13 Pen-llyn, Gwynedd ... B 3
14 Penllyn, S. Glam. ... G 3
29 Penmachno ... E 7
13 Penmaen ... H 8
28 Penmaenan ... C 6
28 Penmaenmawr ... C 6
28 Penmaenpool ... H 6
29 Penmaenrhos ... B 8
14 Penmark ... G 4
28 Penmon ... B 6
50 Penmore Mill ... B 1
28 Penmorfa ... F 5
28 Penmynydd ... C 4
17 Penn ... E 10
17 Penn Street ... E 10
20 Pennal ... B 3
29 Pennan ... A 6
13 Pennant, Clwyd ... G 9
13 Pennant, Dyfed ... A 8
29 Pennant, Gwynedd ... D 7
20 Pennant, Powys ... C 4
29 Pennant-Melangell ... H 9
13 Pennard ... H 9
21 Pennerley ... C 9
38 Pennington, Cumb. ... G 5
8 Pennington, Hants. ... G 4
14 Pennorth ... B 4
38 Penny Bridge ... G 5
14 Penny Hill ... C 5
50 Pennyghael ... E 3
14 Pennyglen ... H 7
50 Pennygown ... C 3
4 Pennymoor ... E 7
45 Pennywell ... G 11

12 Penparc, Dyfed ... B 5
12 Penparc, Dyfed ... D 2
20 Penparcau ... D 2
14 Penpelleni ... D 6
13 Penpillick ... D 8
3 Penpoint ... B 8
2 Penpol ... F 5
43 Penpont, Dumf. & Gall. ... B 9
14 Penpont, Powys ... A 3
12 Pen-y-bryn ... C 5
12 Penrherber ... C 6
14 Penrhiw ... C 6
14 Penrhiwceiber ... E 4
13 Penrhiw-goch ... E 9
13 Pen-rhiw-llan ... C 7
14 Penrhiwpal ... B 7
15 Penrhos, Gwent ... C 7
28 Penrhos, Gwynedd ... G 3
14 Penrhos, Powys ... C 1
28 Penrhos,garnedd ... C 5
28 Penrhyn ... A 3
29 Penrhyn Bay ... B 7
20 Penrhyn-coch ... D 2
28 Penrhyndeudraeth ... F 5
28 Penrhynside ... B 7
13 Penrice ... H 8
21 Penrieth ... C 6
39 Penrith ... A 11
2 Penrose ... C 6
38 Penruddock ... B 6
2 Penryn ... F 5
29 Pensarn ... B 9
21 Pensax ... E 1
30 Pensby ... B 1
7 Penselwood ... C 10
15 Pensford ... H 9
45 Penshaw ... H 11
10 Penshurst ... D 4
3 Pensilva ... C 10
49 Penston ... B 7
3 Pentewan ... E 7
28 Pentir ... D 5
2 Pentire ... D 5
2 Pentireg ... B 6
12 Pentlepoir ... F 5
27 Pentlow ... L 1
24 Pentney ... D 8
2 Penton Mewsey ... A 5
28 Pentraeth ... B 5
29 Pentre, Clwyd ... D 10
29 Pentre, Clwyd ... F 12
14 Pentre, Mid Glam. ... E 3
21 Pentre, Powys ... B 8
21 Pentre, Powys ... C 8
20 Pentre, Powys ... D 6
21 Pentre, Salop ... A 9
28 Pentre Berw ... C 4
20 Pentre Dolau-Honddu ... H 5
13 Pentre Gwenlais ... E 9
28 Pentre Gwyffryn ... G 5
29 Pentre Halkyn ... C 11
21 Pentre-Isaf ... C 8
14 Pentre Meyrick ... G 3
29 Pentre-bach, Clwyd ... G 10
13 Pentrebach, Dyfed ... B 9
14 Pentrebâch, Mid Glam. ... D 4
14 Pentre-bach, Powys ... A 2
13 Pentrebach, W. Glam. ... F 9
21 Pentrebeirdd ... A 7
29 Pentre-bont ... E 7
13 Pentre-cagal ... C 7
29 Pentre-celyn ... E 10
13 Pentre-cwrt ... C 7
29 Pentre-dwfr ... F 11
13 Pentre-dwr ... G 10
13 Pentrefelin, Dyfed ... E 9
28 Pentrefelin, Gwynedd ... A 4
29 Pentrefoelas ... E 8
12 Pentre-galar ... D 5
13 Pentregat ... B 7
20 Pentre-llwyn-llwyd ... G 5
14 Pentre-poeth ... F 6
13 Pentre'r-felin, Dyfed ... B 9
28 Pentre'r felin, Gwynedd ... F 5
14 Pentrer-felin, Powys ... A 3
29 Pentre-tafarn-y-fedw ... D 7
13 Pentre-ty-gwyn ... C 11
29 Pentre-uchaf ... C 10
32 Pentrich ... E 1
8 Pentridge ... D 2
15 Pen-twyn, Gwent ... C 8
14 Pentwyn, Mid Glam. ... D 4
14 Pentyrch ... F 4
12 Penuchadre ... G 2

20 Penuwch ... F 2
3 Penwithick Stents ... D 7
16 Penwood ... H 5
14 Penwylit ... C 2
13 Pen-y-banc, Dyfed ... E 9
13 Pen-y-banc, Dyfed ... F 9
21 Penybont, Powys ... F 7
29 Pen-y-bont, Clwyd ... H 11
29 Pen-y-bont-fawr ... H 10
14 Pen-y-cae, Powys ... C 2
29 Pen-y-cae, Clwyd ... F 12
14 Pen-y-cae-mawr ... E 7
15 Pen-y-clwdd ... D 7
14 Pen-y-coedcae ... F 4
14 Pen-y-cwm ... E 2
14 Pen-y-fai ... F 2
29 Penyffordd ... D 12
14 Pen-y-garnedd ... H 10
14 Pen-y-graig ... E 3
13 Pen-y-groes, Dyfed ... F 9
12 Penygroes, Dyfed ... C 5
28 Penygroes, Gwynedd ... E 4
14 Pen-y-groes, S. Glam. ... F 5
28 Pen-y-groeslon ... G 2
28 Pen-y-Gwyrd ... E 6
14 Penyrheol ... E 5
14 Pen-yr-Heolgerrig ... D 4
14 Penyrynys ... B 2
28 Penysarn ... A 4
29 Pen-y-stryt ... E 11
29 Penywaun ... D 3
2 Penzance ... G 2
22 Peopleton ... G 3
30 Peover Heath ... C 6
30 Peover Superior ... C 6
9 Peper Harow ... B 10
45 Peplow ... H 5
17 Peppard Common ... F 8
45 Peppermoor ... B 10
47 Perceton ... E 8
59 Percie ... H 3
22 Percyhorner ... A 7
45 Perkinsville ... H 10
32 Perlethorpe ... C 4
2 Perranarworthal ... F 5
2 Perranporth ... D 5
2 Perranuthnoe ... G 3
2 Perranwell ... F 5
2 Perranwell Station ... F 5
2 Perranzabuloe ... D 5
22 Perry Barr ... C 4
18 Perry Green ... B 4
10 Perry Street ... A 5
22 Pershore ... G 3
59 Pert ... L 4
21 Pertenhall ... J 2
52 Perth ... E 6
22 Perton ... B 2
45 Pertwood ... C 12
5 Peter Tavy ... H 4
24 Peterborough ... F 3
57 Peterburn ... B 1
21 Peterchurch ... H 9
59 Petercutter ... G 6
28 Peterhead ... C 8
40 Peterlee ... A 4
18 Peter's Green ... B 2
3 Peters Marland ... A 3
9 Petersfield ... D 9
14 Peterstone Wentlooge ... F 6
14 Peterston-super-Ely ... G 4
15 Peterstow ... B 9
4 Petrockstow ... E 4
11 Pett ... G 7
27 Pettaugh ... J 5
53 Petterden ... C 9
48 Pettinain ... E 2
27 Pettistree ... K 6
6 Petton, Devon ... D 4
30 Petton, Salop ... G 3
14 Petts Wood ... G 4
58 Petty ... D 5
48 Pettycur ... A 5
58 Pettymuck ... C 6
9 Petworth ... D 11
10 Pevensey ... H 5
10 Pevensey Bay ... H 5
16 Pewsey ... H 3
17 Pheasants ... E 9
17 Pheasant's Hill ... F 8
4 Philham ... D 1
49 Philiphaugh ... F 3
17 Phillack ... F 3
2 Philleigh ... F 6
48 Phil-stoun ... B 3
15 Phocle Green ... A 11
17 Phoenix Green ... H 8
57 Phoines ... K 3

38 Phurt ... F 2
38 Pica ... C 3
17 Piccott's End ... C 11
36 Pickburn ... F 3
41 Pickering ... G 8
8 Picket Piece ... A 5
8 Picket Post ... E 3
40 Pickhill ... G 4
21 Picklescott ... B 10
53 Pickletillem ... E 9
30 Pickmere ... C 5
6 Pickney ... C 5
4 Pickwell, Devon ... C 5
23 Pickwell, Leics. ... A 11
24 Pickworth, Lincs. ... B 1
24 Pickworth, Leics. ... D 1
30 Picton, Cheshire ... C 3
40 Picton, N. Yorks. ... D 4
10 Piddinghoe ... H 3
17 Piddington, Bucks. ... E 9
23 Piddington, Northants. ... G 11
17 Piddington, Oxon ... B 7
7 Piddlehinton ... F 10
7 Piddletrenhide ... F 10
25 Pidley ... H 4
40 Piercebridge ... D 2
64 Pierowall ... A 2
9 Pigdon ... D 9
31 Pikehall ... D 10
18 Pilgrims Hatch ... D 6
15 Pilham ... A 6
15 Pill ... G 8
3 Pillaton ... C 10
22 Pillerton Hersey ... G 6
22 Pillerton Priors ... G 6
21 Pilleth ... F 8
8 Pilley, Hants. ... F 5
35 Pilley, S. Yorks. ... G 12
14 Pillgwenlly ... F 6
4 Pillhead ... C 3
34 Pilling ... B 3
34 Pilling Lane ... B 3
15 Pillowell ... D 9
11 Pillwell ... D 11
44 Pilmuir, Borders ... B 3
59 Pilmuir, Grampian ... H 5
31 Pilsbury ... D 9
7 Pilsdon ... F 7
31 Pilsley, Derby ... C 11
32 Pilsley, Derby ... D 2
23 Pilton, Northants. ... G 1
23 Pilton, Leics. ... B 12
7 Pilton, Somerset ... B 9
13 Pilton Green ... H 8
7 Pimperne ... E 12
24 Pinchbeck ... C 3
24 Pinchbeck Bars ... C 3
24 Pinchbeck West ... C 3
42 Pinclanty ... C 3
34 Pinfold ... F 3
6 Pinhoe ... G 3
17 Pinkneys Green ... F 9
22 Pinley Green ... E 5
42 Pinminnoch ... B 3
2 Pinmoee ... B 3
42 Pinmore Mains ... C 3
6 Pinn ... G 4
18 Pinner ... E 1
22 Pinvin ... G 3
42 Pinwherry ... C 3
42 Pinxton ... E 2
21 Pipe and Lyde ... H 10
30 Pipe Gate ... F 6
22 Piphill ... A 4
56 Piperhill ... E 4
3 Pipers Pool ... A 9
23 Pipewell ... D 11
4 Pippacott ... B 4
14 Pipton ... A 5
17 Pirbright ... H 10
49 Pirnie ... G 9
46 Pirnmill ... E 4
22 Pirton, Heref. & Worc. ... G 2
18 Pirton, Herts. ... A 2
15 Pishill ... E 8
28 Pistyll ... F 3
52 Pitagowan ... A 3
58 Pitblae ... A 7
53 Pitcairlie Farm ... F 7
52 Pitcairn ... B 4
52 Pitcairngreen ... D 5
58 Pitcaple ... E 5
53 Pitcarity ... A 8
6 Pitch Green ... D 8
9 Pitch Place ... A 11
15 Pitchcombe ... D 11
17 Pitchcott ... B 8
21 Pitchford ... B 10
7 Pitcombe ... C 10
53 Pitcorthie ... F 10
49 Pitcox ... B 9
59 Pitdrichie ... J 5

58 Pitfichie . . . . F 4
53 Pitfour Castle . . . . . . E 7
53 Pitkevy . . . . G 7
53 Pitlessie . . . . F 8
52 Pitlochry . . . . A 4
58 Pitmachie . . . . E 4
57 Pitmain . . . . J 3
58 Pitmedden . . . . E 6
6 Pitminster . . . . D 5
53 Pitmuies . . . . B 10
58 Pitmunie . . . . F 4
7 Pitney . . . . C 8
53 Pitroddie . . . . E 7
53 Pitscottie . . . . F 9
19 Pitsea . . . . E 7
23 Pitsford . . . . E 11
17 Pitstone . . . . C 10
17 Pitstone Green . . . . C 10
59 Pittarrow . . . . K 5
56 Pittendreich . . . . . . D 7
61 Pittenraill . . . . F 7
53 Pittenweem . . . . . . G 10
40 Pittington . . . . A 3
58 Pittodrie . . . . E 4
8 Pitton . . . . C 4
10 Pittswood . . . . C 5
58 Pittulie . . . . A 7
40 Pity Me, Durham . . . A 3
45 Pity Me, Northumb. . E 7
27 Pixey Green . . . . H 5
10 Pixham . . . . C 1
21 Pixley . . . . H 12
58 Plaidy . . . . B 5
12 Plain Dealings . . . . E 4
48 Plains . . . . C 1
Plainsfield . . . . C 5
21 Plaish . . . . C 10
9 Plaistow . . . . C 11
10 Plaistow Street . . . . D 3
8 Plaitford . . . . D 4
20 Plas Llysyn . . . . C 5
29 Plas Newydd . . . . . F 11
44 Plashetts . . . . D 5
16 Plastow Green . . . . H 6
29 Plas-yn-Cefn . . . . . . C 9
10 Platt . . . . B 5
34 Platt Bridge . . . . . . G 5
45 Plawsworth . . . . . . H 11
10 Plaxtol . . . . C 5
17 Play Hatch . . . . F 8
11 Playden . . . . F 8
27 Playford . . . . K 5
2 Playing Place . . . . . . E 5
15 Playley Green . . . . A 10
21 Plealey . . . . B 9
52 Plean . . . . H 3
53 Pleasance . . . . F 7
34 Pleasington . . . . E 5
32 Pleasley . . . . D 2
44 Plenmeller . . . . G 5
18 Pleshey . . . . B 6
45 Plessey Checks . . . E 10
54 Plockton . . . . F 2
21 Ploughfield . . . . H 9
49 Ploughlands . . . . . E 10
21 Plowden . . . . D 9
21 Ploxgreen . . . . B 9
11 Pluckley . . . . D 8
11 Pluckley Thorne . . . D 8
43 Plumbland . . . . H 12
30 Plumley . . . . C 6
10 Plumpton . . . . G 2
39 Plumpton Foot . . . . A 7
10 Plumpton Green . . . F 2
39 Plumpton Head . . . . B 7
39 Plumpton Wall . . . . B 7
26 Plumstead . . . . B 4
32 Plumtree . . . . G 3
32 Plungar . . . . B 5
7 Plush . . . . F 10
13 Plwmp . . . . B 7
5 Plymouth . . . . K 4
5 Plympton . . . . K 4
5 Plympton St. Maurice
K 3
5 Plymstock . . . . K 4
4 Plymtree . . . . F 4
40 Pockley . . . . G 6
36 Pocklington . . . . B 6
24 Pode Hole . . . . C 3
7 Podimore . . . . D 9
23 Podington . . . . F 12
40 Podmore . . . . G 6
24 Pointon . . . . B 2
8 Pokesdown . . . . G 3
32 Polbae . . . . D 4
40 Polbain . . . . F 2
8 Polbathic . . . . D 10
8 Polbeth . . . . B 11
3 Poldean . . . . B 11
8 Poldullie Bridge . . . F 1
5 Pole Moor . . . . E 9
5 Polebrook . . . . G 2
10 Polegate . . . . G 5

30 Polelane Ends . . . . . B 5
22 Polesworth . . . . B 6
60 Polglass . . . . F 2
3 Polgooth . . . . E 7
9 Poling . . . . F 11
9 Poling Corner . . . . E 11
3 Polkerris . . . . D 8
60 Polla . . . . B 5
36 Pollington . . . . E 4
50 Polloch . . . . A 5
47 Pollockshaws . . . . C 10
47 Pollokshields . . . . . C 10
54 Polmaddie . . . . C 7
54 Polmaily . . . . F 8
3 Polmassick . . . . E 7
48 Polmont . . . . B 2
48 Polmoody . . . . H 4
47 Polnessan . . . . H 9
55 Polnish . . . . L 1
9 Polperro . . . . E 9
3 Polruan . . . . E 8
43 Polsham . . . . B 8
43 Polskeoch . . . . A 8
27 Polstead . . . . L 3
6 Poltimore . . . . G 3
48 Polton . . . . C 5
49 Polwarth . . . . D 10
1 Polyphant . . . . B 9
2 Polzeath . . . . B 6
24 Pondersbridge . . . . F 4
9 Pondtail . . . . A 9
1 Ponsanooth . . . . . . F 5
5 Ponsworthy . . . . . . H 6
29 Pont Cyfyngf . . . . . D 7
14 Pont Ebbw . . . . F 6
12 Pont Hentry . . . . . . F 8
14 Pont Hirwaun . . . . . B 2
20 Pont-Llogel . . . . . . A 6
28 Pont Pen-y-benglog . D 6
20 Pont-Robert . . . . . . B 5
13 Pont Yates . . . . F 8
13 Pontamman . . . . . . F 9
14 Pont ar Hydfer . . . . B 2
13 Pontardawe . . . . . . G 10
13 Pontardulais . . . . . . G 9
13 Pontargothi . . . . E 8
13 Pont-ar-llechau . . . E 10
13 Pont-ar-Sais . . . . . . D 8
29 Pontblyddyn . . . . . D 12
14 Pontbren Llwyd . . . D 3
36 Pontefract . . . . E 2
45 Ponteland . . . . F 10
20 Ponterwyd . . . . D 3
21 Pontesbury . . . . B 9
21 Pontesford . . . . B 9
29 Pontfadog . . . . F 11
12 Pontfaen, Dyfed . . . D 4
14 Pont-faen, Powys . . A 3
13 Pontgarreg . . . . B 7
14 Pont-hir . . . . E 6
14 Pont-llan-fraith . . . . E 5
13 Pontlliw . . . . G 9
14 Pontlottyn . . . . D 4
28 Pont-lyfni . . . . E 4
14 Pontneddfechan . . . D 2
14 Pontnewydd . . . . . . E 6
20 Pontrhydfendigaid . . F 3
13 Pont-rhyd-y-fen . . G 11
20 Pont-rhyd-y-groes . . E 3
14 Pontrhydyrun . . . . . E 6
15 Pontrilas . . . . B 7
28 Pont-rug . . . . D 4
10 Ponts Green . . . . . . F 5
13 Pontshaen . . . . B 8
15 Pontshill . . . . B 9
14 Pontsticill . . . . C 4
13 Pont-tywely . . . . . . C 7
13 Pontyberem . . . . . . F 8
29 Pont-y-bodkin . . . D 12
29 Pont y Clogwyn . . . E 8
14 Pontyclun . . . . E 2
14 Pontycymer . . . . . . E 2
12 Pontyglazier . . . . . . C 5
14 Pont-y-gwaith . . . . E 3
29 Ponty-y-pant . . . . . E 7
14 Pontypool . . . . D 6
14 Pontypool Road . . . D 6
14 Pontypridd . . . . E 4
12 Pont-yr-hafod . . . . . D 3
21 Pont-ysgawrhyd . . . A 7
14 Pont-y-waun . . . . . . E 5
8 Pooksgreen . . . . E 5
2 Pool, Cornwall . . . . E 4
21 Pool Heref. & Worc.
H 10
35 Pool, W. Yorks . . . C 11
34 Pool Hay . . . . F 2
34 Pool Head . . . . G 11
52 Pool of Muckhart . . G 5
21 Pool Quay . . . . A 8
27 Pool Street . . . . L 1
8 Poole . . . . G 2
30 Poole Green . . . . . . E 5

16 Poole Keynes . . . . . E 1
31 Poolend . . . . D 8
54 Poolewe . . . . B 2
39 Pooley Bridge . . . . A 1
19 Poolhill . . . . A 10
32 Poolsbrook . . . . C 2
38 Poortown . . . . G 1
17 Pootings . . . . C 3
17 Popeswood . . . . G 9
27 Popham . . . . B 7
18 Poplar . . . . F 4
8 Porchfield . . . . G 6
54 Porin . . . . D 7
1 Porkellis . . . . F 4
6 Porlock . . . . B 2
6 Porlock Weir . . . . . . B 2
53 Port Allen . . . . E 7
50 Port Appin . . . . C 6
44 Port Bannatyne . . . . C 6
40 Port Carlisle . . . . . . G 1
40 Port Clarence . . . . . C 5
20 Port Dinorwic . . . . . C 5
46 Port Driseach . . . . . B 5
58 Port Elphinstone . . . F 5
58 Port Erin . . . . H 1
58 Port Erroll . . . . D 8
13 Port Eynon . . . . H 8
47 Port Glasgow . . . . . B 8
54 Port Henderson . . . . B 1
3 Port Isaac . . . . B 7
50 Port Lamont . . . . . . B 6
42 Port Logan . . . . H 2
41 Port Mulgrave . . . . C 8
52 Port of Menteith . . . G 1
63 Port of Ness . . . . . . A 6
3 Port Quin . . . . B 7
50 Port Ramsay . . . . . . C 6
38 Port St. Mary . . . . . H 1
51 Port Sonachan . . . . . E 7
30 Port Sunlight . . . . . . B 2
13 Port Talbot . . . . . . H 10
13 Port Tennant . . . . . H 10
42 Port William . . . . . . G 4
46 Portachoillan . . . . . D 3
46 Port an Eilein . . . . . B 5
46 Portavadie . . . . B 4
15 Portbury . . . . G 8
9 Portchester . . . . F 7
47 Portencross . . . . D 7
7 Portesham . . . . H 9
58 Portessie . . . . A 2
38 Port e Vullen . . . . . G 3
12 Portfield Gate . . . . . E 3
3 Portgate . . . . G 3
58 Portgordon . . . . A 1
61 Portgower . . . . E 9
14 Porth . . . . E 4
2 Porth Mellin . . . . . . H 4
2 Porth Navas . . . . . . G 5
3 Porthallow, Corn. . . D 9
2 Porthallow, Corn. . . G 5
14 Porthcawl . . . . G 1
2 Porthcothan Bay . . . C 6
2 Porthcurno . . . . G 1
28 Porthdafarch . . . . . . B 2
12 Porthgain . . . . D 2
2 Porthilly . . . . B 6
14 Porthkerry . . . . H 4
2 Porthleven . . . . G 3
28 Porthmadog . . . . . . F 5
2 Porthmeor . . . . F 2
11 Portholland . . . . . . F 7
2 Porthoustock . . . . . G 5
2 Porthowann . . . . . . E 4
3 Porthpean . . . . E 7
13 Porth-y-rhyd, Dyfed E 8
13 Porth-y-rhyd, Dyfed
C 10
51 Portincaple . . . . H 9
36 Portington . . . . D 6
51 Portinnisherrich . . . F 7
38 Portinscale . . . . C 5
15 Portishead . . . . G 8
58 Portknockie . . . . . . A 2
59 Portlethen . . . . H 7
2 Portloe . . . . F 6
16 Portmahomack . . . . H 9
28 Portmeirion . . . . . . F 5
3 Portmellon . . . . E 7
8 Portmore . . . . F 5
62 Port na Long . . . . . . E 3
63 Portnaguiran . . . . . . C 6
63 Portnaluchaig . . . . . K 1
60 Portnancon . . . . B 5
51 Portnellan, Central E 11
51 Portnellan, Central . F 11
50 Portnocroish . . . . . . C 6
48 Portobello . . . . B 6
8 Porton . . . . B 3
42 Portpatrick . . . . F 1
2 Portreath . . . . E 4
62 Portree . . . . D 4
47 Portrye . . . . D 7
2 Portscatho . . . . F 6

9 Portsea . . . . F 8
61 Portskerra . . . . A 8
15 Portskewett . . . . . . E 8
10 Portslade, Surrey . . G 1
10 Portslade, Surrey . . G 2
42 Portslogan . . . . F 1
9 Portsmouth, Hants . . F 8
35 Portsmouth, W.Yorks
E 7
58 Portsoy . . . . A 3
8 Portswood . . . . E 6
50 Portuairk . . . . A 2
63 Portvoller . . . . C 6
63 Portway, Heref. &
Worc. . . . . A 8
22 Portway, War. . . . . . E 4
3 Portwrinkle . . . . . . D 10
42 Portyerrock . . . . . . H 5
2 Postbridge . . . . H 5
17 Postcombe . . . . D 8
11 Postling . . . . D 10
26 Postlingford . . . . . . K 1
26 Postwick . . . . E 6
59 Potarch . . . . H 3
47 Poteath . . . . D 7
44 Potholm . . . . D 2
17 Potsgrove . . . . A 10
24 Pott Row . . . . C 8
31 Pott Shrigley . . . . . . B 8
17 Potten End . . . . C 11
41 Potter Brompton . . G 10
26 Potter Heigham . . . . D 7
18 Potter Street . . . . . . C 5
33 Potterhanworth . . . . C 7
33 Potterhanworth Booths
C 8
16 Potterne . . . . H 1
16 Potterne Wick . . . . . H 1
18 Potters Bar . . . . D 3
22 Potters Cross . . . . . . D 2
23 Potterspury . . . . . . H 11
40 Potto . . . . E 5
25 Potton . . . . K 3
4 Poughill, Corn. . . . . E 1
4 Poughill, Devon . . . E 7
16 Poulshot . . . . H 1
30 Poulton, Ches. . . . . D 3
16 Poulton, Glos. . . . . D 2
34 Poulton-Le-Fylde . . C 2
14 Pound . . . . F 1
2 Pound Bank . . . . . . E 1
10 Pound Green, E.Sussex
F 4
8 Pound Green, I.o.W.
G 5
10 Pound Hill . . . . D 2
41 Poundland, Dumf. &
Gall. . . . . C 9
42 Poundland, Strathclyde
C 3
17 Poundon . . . . B 7
10 Poundsbridge . . . . . D 4
5 Poundsgate . . . . J 6
2 Poundstock . . . . A 2
53 Pourie . . . . D 9
45 Powburn . . . . A 9
6 Powderham . . . . . . H 3
7 Powerstock . . . . G 8
43 Powfoot . . . . E 12
53 Powgavie . . . . E 7
22 Powick . . . . G 2
4 Powler's Piece . . . . D 2
52 Powmill . . . . G 5
20 Powys, Co . . . . E 6
7 Poxwell . . . . H 11
17 Poyle . . . . F 11
10 Poynings . . . . G 1
17 Poyntington . . . . . D 10
31 Poynton . . . . B 8
30 Poynton Green . . . . H 4
27 Poys Street . . . . H 6
12 Poyston Cross . . . . . E 3
27 Poystreet Green . . . J 3
3 Praa Sands . . . . G 3
62 Prabost . . . . C 3
18 Pratt's Bottom . . . . H 5
11 Pratt's Heath . . . . . H 7
2 Praze . . . . F 3
2 Praze-an-Beeble . . . F 3
2 Predannack Manor
Farm . . . . H 4
30 Prees . . . . G 4
34 Preesall . . . . B 2
34 Preesall Park . . . . . C 2
12 Prendergast . . . . . . E 3
45 Prendwick . . . . B 8
13 Pren-gwyn . . . . C 7
28 Prenteg . . . . F 5
30 Prenton . . . . B 2
30 Prescot . . . . A 3
30 Prescott . . . . H 3
29 Presen . . . . F 11
30 Pressgreen . . . . G 4
27 Pulham Market . . . . G 5

31 Prestbury, Ches. . . . C 7
15 Prestbury, Glos. . . . B 12
21 Presteigne . . . . F 8
21 Presthope . . . . C 11
21 Prestleigh . . . . B 9
49 Preston, Borders . . D 10
5 Preston, Devon . . . . H 7
21 Preston, Dorset . . . H 10
10 Preston, E. Sussex . . G 2
27 Preston, Essex . . . . . K 2
15 Preston, Glos . . . . A 10
16 Preston, Glos . . . . . D 2
18 Preston, Herts . . . . . A 2
37 Preston, Humber . . . D 9
11 Preston, Kent . . . . . B 9
11 Preston, Kent . . . . . B 11
34 Preston, Lancs . . . . . D 4
45 Preston, Northumb.
E 12
48 Preston, Lothian . . . B 6
49 Preston, Lothian . . . B 8
16 Preston, Wilts . . . . . F 1
22 Preston Bagot . . . . . E 5
17 Preston Bissett . . . . A 7
6 Preston Bowyer . . . D 5
30 Preston Brockhurst . H 4
30 Preston Brook . . . . . B 4
9 Preston Candover . . B 7
23 Preston Capes . . . . . G 9
17 Preston Crowmarsh . E 7
3 Preston Gubbals . . . H 4
22 Preston on Stour . . . G 5
30 Preston on the Hill . B 4
21 Preston on Wye . . . . H 9
7 Preston Plucknett . . E 8
21 Preston upon the
Weald Moors . . . A 12
21 Preston Wynne . . . H 11
43 Prestonmill . . . . . . F 10
48 Prestonpans . . . . . . B 8
40 Preston-under-Scar . F 1
35 Prestwich . . . . G 7
47 Prestwick, Northumb.
F 10
47 Prestwick, Strathclyde
G 8
17 Prestwood . . . . D 9
14 Price Town . . . . E 3
25 Prickwillow . . . . . . G 7
7 Priddy . . . . A 8
39 Priest Hulton . . . . . H 7
44 Priesthaugh . . . . . . C 3
47 Priesthill . . . . C 10
47 Priestland . . . . F 10
21 Priestweston . . . . . . C 8
23 Primethorpe . . . . . . C 8
24 Primrose Hill, Cambs.
F 5
32 Primrose Hill, Notts.
D 2
49 Primrosehill, Borders
D 10
17 Primrosehill, Herts
D 11
49 Primsidemill . . . . . G 10
13 Princes Gate . . . . . . F 5
17 Princes Risborough . D 9
23 Princethorpe . . . . . . E 7
5 Princetown, Devon . H 5
14 Princetown, Mid Glam.
C 4
49 Printonan . . . . E 10
29 Prion . . . . D 10
21 Priors Frame . . . . . H 11
23 Priors Hardwick . . . G 8
23 Priors Marston . . . . F 8
21 Priorslee . . . . A 12
21 Priory Wood . . . . . H 8
15 Priston . . . . H 10
19 Prittlewell . . . . E 8
10 Privett . . . . C 8
4 Prixford . . . . B 4
2 Probus . . . . E 6
43 Prospect . . . . G 12
58 Protstonhill . . . . A 6
45 Prudhoe . . . . G 9
51 Ptarmigan Lodge . . G 10
51 Pubil . . . . C 11
15 Publow . . . . H 9
18 Puckeridge . . . . B 4
7 Puckington . . . . D 7
15 Pucklechurch . . . . . G 10
5 Pucknall . . . . D 5
30 Puddington, Ches. . . C 2
4 Puddington, Devon . E 7
26 Puddledock . . . . F 4
7 Puddletown . . . . . . G 10
21 Pudlestone . . . . F 11
35 Pudsey . . . . D 11
9 Pulborough . . . . . . D 12
30 Puleston . . . . H 6
30 Pulford . . . . D 2
7 Pulham . . . . E 10
27 Pulham Market . . . . G 5

27 Pulham St. Margaret
G 5
25 Pulloxhill . . . . M 2
48 Pumpherston . . . . . . B 3
13 Pumpsaint . . . . C 10
12 Puncheston . . . . D 3
7 Puncknoll . . . . G 9
19 Punnett's Town . . . . F 5
9 Purbrook . . . . E 8
44 Purdomstone . . . . . . E 1
8 Purewell . . . . G 3
18 Purfleet . . . . F 5
7 Puriton . . . . B 7
19 Purleigh . . . . D 8
17 Purley, Berks . . . . . F 7
18 Purley, London . . . . H 3
25 Purls Bridge . . . . . . G 6
7 Purse Caundle . . . . D 10
21 Purslow . . . . D 9
36 Purston Jaglin . . . . . E 2
16 Purtington . . . . E 7
15 Purton, Glos . . . . . . D 10
16 Purton, Wilts . . . . . E 2
16 Purton Stoke . . . . . . E 2
49 Purvishaugh . . . . . . E 8
23 Pury End . . . . H 10
16 Pusey . . . . D 4
4 Putford . . . . D 2
15 Putley . . . . A 9
18 Putney . . . . F 2
4 Putsborough . . . . . . B 3
17 Puttenham, Bucks. . . C 9
10 Puttenham, Surrey . A 10
15 Puxton . . . . H 7
13 Pwll . . . . G 8
14 Pwllcrochan . . . . . . G 3
28 Pwlldefaid . . . . H 1
14 Pwllgloyw . . . . A 3
13 Pwllheli . . . . G 3
14 Pwll-Meyric . . . . . . E 8
12 Pwlltrap . . . . E 6
13 Pwll-y-glaw . . . . . H 11
29 Pydew . . . . B 7
32 Pye Bridge . . . . E 2
14 Pye Corner, Gwent . F 7
18 Pye Corner, Herts . . C 4
22 Pye Green . . . . A 3
10 Pyecombe . . . . G 2
8 Pyle, I.o.W. . . . . . . H 6
14 Pyle, Mid Glam. . . . F 2
7 Pylle . . . . B 9
25 Pymore . . . . G 6
17 Pyrford . . . . H 11
24 Pyrgad . . . . C 4
17 Pyrton . . . . E 8
23 Pytchley . . . . E 12
4 Pyworthy . . . . F 2
21 Quabbs . . . . D 7
24 Quadring . . . . B 3
17 Quainton . . . . B 8
8 Quarley . . . . B 4
31 Quarndon, Derby . F 11
23 Quarndon, Leics. . . A 9
47 Quarrier's Homes . . C 8
24 Quarrington . . . . . . A 2
40 Quarrington Hill . . . A 4
22 Quarry Bank . . . . . . C 3
54 Quarrybank . . . . D 4
58 Quarryburn . . . . A 6
56 Quarryhill . . . . B 3
56 Quarrywood . . . . . . C 7
47 Quarter . . . . D 12
6 Quartley . . . . D 3
22 Quat . . . . C 1
22 Quatford . . . . C 1
40 Quebec . . . . A 2
23 Quedgeley . . . . C 11
25 Queen Adelaide . . . G 7
15 Queen Charlton . . . H 9
4 Queen Dart . . . . . . D 7
7 Queen Oak . . . . . . C 11
10 Queen Street . . . . . . D 6
11 Queensborough . . . . A 8
9 Queens Camel . . . . . D 9
30 Queens Head . . . . . G 2
30 Queen's Park . . . . . G 2
35 Queensbury . . . . . . D 9
29 Queensferry, Clwyd
C 12
48 Queensferry, Lothian
B 4
34 Queenstown . . . . . . D 2
47 Queenzieburn . . . . . B 11
16 Quemerford . . . . . . G 1
64 Quendale . . . . F 7
25 Quendon . . . . M 6
16 Quenington . . . . . . D 2
34 Quernmore . . . . A 4
3 Quethiock . . . . C 10
27 Quidenham . . . . G 3
8 Quidhampton, Hants.
A 6

8 Quidhampton, Wilts. C 3
58 Quilquox ....D 6
38 Quine's Hill ....H 2
50 Quinish House ......B 2
23 Quinton ....G 11
2 Quintrel Downs ...D 5
49 Quixwood ....C 10
4 Quoditch ....F 3
52 Quoig ....E 3
48 Quothquan ....E 3
64 Quoys ....D 7
62 Rassay House (Hotel)
  D 5
4 Rabscott ....C 6
30 Raby ....B 2
9 Rackenford ....D 7
9 Rackham ....E 11
26 Rackheath Com. ...D 6
43 Racks ....D 11
64 Rackwick, Orkney .D 1
64 Rackwick, Orkney ..A 2
31 Radbourne ....G 11
34 Radcliffe, Manchester
  F 6
45 Radcliffe, Northumb.
  C 11
32 Radcliffe on Soar ...G 2
32 Radcliffe on Trent ..F 4
17 Radclive ....A 7
16 Radcot ....D 4
56 Raddery House ....D 3
23 Radford Semele ...F 7
7 Radpole ....H 10
18 Radlett ....D 2
16 Radley ....D 6
17 Radnage ....D 8
7 Radstock ....A 10
23 Radstone ....H 9
23 Radway ....G 7
30 Radway Green ....E 6
25 Radwell ....J 1
25 Radwinter ....L 7
14 Radyr ....F 5
48 Raecleugh ....H 3
63 Raerinish ....D 5
60 Raffin ....D 2
56 Rafford ....D 6
32 Ragdale ....H 4
53 Ragfield ....F 10
15 Raglan ....D 7
32 Ragnall ....C 5
34 Rainford ....G 4
18 Rainham, Essex .....F 5
11 Rainham, Kent ....B 7
11 Rainham Mark .....A 7
30 Rainhill ....A 4
30 Rainhill Stoops ....A 4
31 Rainow ....C 8
40 Rainton ....H 4
32 Rainworth ....D 3
39 Raisbeck ....D 9
44 Raise ....H 5
36 Raisthorpe ....A 6
53 Rait ....D 7
33 Raithby, Lincs. ....C 10
33 Raithby, Lincs. ....B 10
9 Rake ....C 9
11 Ram Lane ....C 8
62 Ramasaig ....D 1
3 Rame, Corn. .....E 11
2 Rame, Corn. .....F 4
7 Rampisham ......F 9
34 Rampside ....A 1
25 Rampton, Cambs. ..H 5
32 Rampton, Notts. ...B 5
35 Ramsbottom .....E 7
16 Ramsbury ....G 4
61 Ramscraigs ......D 10
9 Ramsdean ....D 8
17 Ramsdell ....H 7
16 Ramsden ....C 3
19 Ramsden Bellhouse .E 7
19 Ramsden Heath ....D 7
25 Ramsey, Cambs. ...G 4
27 Ramsey, Essex ....M 5
38 Ramsey, I.O.M. ...G 2
19 Ramsay Island .....G 2
25 Ramsay St. Mary's .G 4
48 Ramseycleuch ....H 5
11 Ramsgate ....B 12
26 Ramsgate Street ...B 4
40 Ramsgill ....H 1
45 Ramshaw ....H 8
44 Ramshope ....C 6
31 Ramshorn ....F 9
5 Ramsley ....C 3
9 Ramsnest Com. ...C 11
32 Ranby ....B 4
33 Rand ....B 8
15 Randwick ....D 11
47 Ranfurly ....C 9
31 Rangemore ......H 10
15 Rangeworthy .....F 10
47 Rankinston ....H 9

9 Ranmore Com. ....A 12
34 Rann ....E 6
38 Rannerdale ......C 4
51 Rannoch Station ..B 11
55 Ranochan ....L 2
6 Ranscombe ......B 3
32 Ranskill ....A 4
31 Ranton ....H 7
26 Ranworth ....D 7
64 Rapness ....B 3
55 Rarsaidh ....H 2
43 Rascarre ....G 9
58 Rashiereive ......E 7
40 Raskelf ....H 5
14 Rassau ....C 5
35 Rastrick ....E 10
55 Ratagan ....H 3
23 Ratby ....B 8
23 Ratcliffe Culey ....B 7
23 Ratcliffe on the
  Wreake ....A 9
58 Rathen ....B 7
53 Rathillet ....E 8
35 Rathmell ....A 7
48 Ratho ....B 4
48 Ratho Station .....B 4
58 Rathven ....A 2
23 Ratley ....G 7
21 Ratlinghope ......C 9
61 Rattar ....A 11
5 Rattery ....K 6
27 Rattlesden ....J 3
53 Rattray ....C 7
38 Raughton Head ...A 6
25 Raunds ....H 1
49 Ravelaw ....D 11
36 Ravenfield ....H 3
38 Ravenglass ....F 3
26 Raveningham ......F 7
41 Ravenscar ....E 10
38 Ravensdale ....G 2
25 Ravensden ....K 2
32 Ravenshead ......E 3
30 Ravensmoor ......E 5
23 Ravensthorpe,
  Northants. ....E 10
35 Ravensthorpe,
  W. Yorks. ....E 10
23 Ravenstone, Bucks.
  G 11
23 Ravenstone, Leics. ..A 7
39 Ravenstonedale ...E 9
48 Ravenstruther .....E 2
40 Ravensworth ......D 2
41 Raw ....E 9
49 Rawburn ....D 9
36 Rawcliffe, Humber. .E 5
36 Rawcliffe, N. Yorks. B 4
36 Rawcliffe Bridge ....E 5
35 Rawdon ....C 11
36 Rawmarsh ....G 2
22 Rawnsley ....A 4
19 Rawreth ....E 8
6 Rawridge ....F 5
47 Raws ....E 9
35 Rawtenstall ......E 7
47 Rawyards ....C 12
58 Raxton ....D 6
27 Raydon ....L 3
19 Rayleigh ....E 8
7 Raymond's Hill ...F 7
19 Rayne ....E 8
25 Reach ....J 7
34 Read ....D 6
19 Reading ....G 8
11 Reading Street ....E 8
39 Reagill ....C 8
61 Rearquhar ....G 7
23 Rearsby ....A 10
61 Reaster ....A 11
49 Reaveley ....A 8
64 Reawick ....D 6
61 Reay ....B 9
11 Reculver ....A 11
6 Red Ball ....E 4
44 Red Dial ....H 1
16 Red Hill ....G 2
5 Red Post ....J 7
34 Red Rock ....F 5
5 Red Roses ....F 5
45 Red Row ....C 10
31 Red Street ....E 7
28 Red Wharf ....B 5
12 Redberth ....G 4
17 Redbourn ....C 12
58 Redbourne ....G 7
18 Redbridge ....E 4
30 Redbrook, Clwyd ..F 4
15 Redbrook, Gwent ..C 8
11 Redbrook Street ....D 8
56 Redburn, Highland .E 5
56 Redburn, Highland .C 1
44 Redburn, Northumb. G 6
40 Redcar ....C 8

56 Redcastle, Highland
  E 1
53 Redcastle, Tayside .B 11
15 Redcliffe Bay ......G 7
47 Redcraig ....G 9
49 Redden ....F 10
48 Redding ....B 2
48 Reddingmuirhead ..B 2
35 Reddish ....H 8
26 Redditch ....E 4
47 Reddochbraes ....F 12
27 Redenhall ....G 6
44 Redesdale Camp ...C 6
45 Redesmouth ......E 7
53 Redford, Tayside .C 10
53 Redford, Tayside ..K 5
48 Redfordgreen .....H 6
52 Redgorton ....D 6
27 Redgrave ....G 3
59 Redheugh ....L 2
15 Redhill, Avon ......H 8
58 Redhill, Grampian .D 4
58 Redhill, Grampian .G 5
10 Redhill, Surrey ....C 2
45 Redhouse ....C 3
27 Redisham ....G 7
15 Redland, Avon .....G 9
64 Redland, Orkney ..C 2
27 Redlingfield ....H 5
8 Redlynch, Dorset ..D 4
13 Redlynch, Som. ...C 10
39 Redmain ....B 4
15 Redmarley D'Abitot
  A 10
40 Redmarshall ......A 4
32 Redmile ....G 5
40 Redmire ....F 1
3 Redmoor ....D 8
59 Redmyre ....K 5
49 Rednal ....G 2
49 Redpath ....F 8
54 Redpoint ....C 1
2 Redruth ....E 4
48 Redscarhead ......E 5
15 Redwick, Avon ....F 8
15 Redwick, Gwent ...F 7
40 Redworth ....C 3
25 Reed ....L 5
26 Reedham ....E 7
36 Reedness ....E 6
60 Reedy Loch ....D 11
63 Reef ....C 2
33 Reepham, Lincs. ...C 7
26 Reepham, Norf. ...C 4
40 Reeth ....E 1
38 Regaby ....F 2
56 Rehaurie ....E 5
61 Reidhbreac ....G 7
60 Reiff ....E 2
10 Reigate ....C 2
41 Reighton ....H 11
41 Reighton Gap .....G 11
61 Reisque ....E 6
61 Reiss ....B 12
2 Rejerrah ....D 5
2 Releath ....E 4
43 Relief ....D 12
2 Relubbus ....F 3
5 Relugas ....E 5
17 Remenham ....F 8
17 Remenham Hill ....F 9
29 Remony ....C 3
32 Rempstone ....H 3
16 Rendcomb ....C 1
27 Rendham ....J 6
47 Renfrew ....C 10
25 Renhold ....K 2
29 Renishaw ....E 2
45 Rennington ......A 10
47 Renton ....B 9
28 Renwick ....A 8
26 Repps ....D 7
31 Repton ....G 11
28 Reraig ....B 10
53 Rescobie ....B 10
50 Resipol ....A 4
28 Resolis ....C 3
14 Resolven ....D 2
55 Resourie ....M 2
49 Reston ....C 11
2 Retew ....D 6
2 Rettendon ....D 7
19 Rettendon Place ...D 7
2 Retyn ....D 6
50 Reudle ....C 1
33 Revesby ....D 10
8 Rew Street ....G 6
6 Rewe ....F 3
26 Reymerston ......E 3
12 Reynalton ....F 4
13 Reynoldston ......D 3
2 Rezare ....B 10
15 Rhadyr ....D 7

13 Rhandir-mwyn ....C 11
20 Rhayader ....F 5
60 Rhegreanoch .....E 3
56 Rheindown ....E 1
60 Rhemore ....C 3
29 Rhewl, Clwyd ....D 10
29 Rhewl, Clwyd ....F 11
28 Rhicarn ....E 2
60 Rhiconich ....B 4
60 Rhicullen ....C 3
60 Rhidorroch ....G 3
60 Rhidorroch Old Lodge
  G 4
28 Rhid-y-sarn ......F 6
61 Rhifail ....C 7
29 Rhigos ....D 3
60 Rhimichie ....B 4
56 Rhinduie ....E 1
60 Rhiroy ....G 3
28 Rhiw ....G 2
28 Rhiwbryfdir ......F 6
28 Rhiwderyn ....F 6
29 Rhiwlas, Clwd ....G 11
28 Rhiwlas, Gwynedd .D 5
29 Rhiwlas, Gwynedd .F 8
6 Rhode ....C 6
11 Rhodes Minnis ....D 10
32 Rhodesia ....B 3
12 Rhodiad ....D 1
14 Rhoose ....H 4
13 Rhos, Dyfed .....E 5
13 Rhos, W. Glam. ..G 10
13 Rhos Amman .....F 10
13 Rhos-Hill ....C 5
28 Rhoscolyn ....C 2
12 Rhoscrowther .....G 3
29 Rhosesmor ......C 11
13 Rhosfach ....D 5
28 Rhos-fawr ....B 4
28 Rhosgadfan ......D 4
28 Rhosgoch, Gwynedd
  A 3
21 Rhos goch, Powys ..H 7
28 Rhos-lan ....F 4
20 Rhoslefain ....C 6
28 Rhosllanerchrugog .F 12
13 Rhosmaen ....E 9
28 Rhos-meirch ......B 4
28 Rhosneigr ....C 3
28 Rhos-on-Sea .....B 8
13 Rhossili ....H 7
12 Rhosson ....D 1
28 Rhostryfan ....D 4
30 Rhostyllen ....E 2
28 Rhosybol ....A 4
29 Rhos-y-gwaliau ...G 9
28 Rhos-y-llan ......F 2
46 Rhu, Strathclyde ..C 3
47 Rhu, Strathclyde ..A 7
54 Rhu Noa ....C 4
28 Rhualt ....C 10
46 Rhubodach ....B 5
30 Rhuddall Heath ...D 4
29 Rhuddlan ....B 9
4 Rhude Cross ......E 1
21 Rhulen ....G 7
46 Rhunahaorine ....E 2
28 Rhyd, Gwynedd ..F 6
20 Rhyd, Powys .....B 5
29 Rhyd-Ddu ....E 5
13 Rhyd-Lewis ....B 7
29 Rhyd-Lydan ......E 8
28 Rhydargaeau ......D 8
14 Rhydberry ....A 3
13 Rhydcymerau .....C 9
28 Rhydd ....H 2
13 Rhydding ....G 10
13 Rhyddlan ....C 6
28 Rhyd-leos ....G 11
28 Rhydlios ....G 1
20 Rhydlydan ....C 6
13 Rhydlydan ....C 6
13 Rhydowen ....C 8
20 Rhydrosser ....F 1
21 Rhydspence ......H 8
29 Rhydtalog ....E 11
28 Rhydwyn ....A 3
13 Rhyd-y-croesau ...G 11
28 Rhydyelafdy ......G 3
14 Rhydyfelin ....E 4
13 Rhyd-y-felin ......D 2
13 Rhyd-y-fro ....F 10
21 Rhyd-y-groes .....B 8
28 Rhydymain ....H 7
14 Rhyd-y-meirch ....D 6
29 Rhydymwyn ......D 11
28 Rhyd-yr-onnen ...B 2
20 Rhyfud ....F 2
29 Rhyl ....B 9
14 Rhymney ....D 4
53 Rhynd, Fife ......E 9
52 Rhynd, Tayside ...E 6
28 Rhynie ....E 2
22 Ribble ....E 1

39 Ribblehead ....G 10
34 Ribbleton ....D 4
34 Ribby ....D 3
34 Ribchester ....D 5
60 Ribigill ....B 6
37 Riby ....F 9
37 Riby Cross Roads ..F 9
36 Riccall ....C 4
47 Riccarton ....F 9
44 Riccarton Junction ..C 4
21 Richards Castle ...E 10
17 Richings Park .....F 11
18 Richmond, London .F 2
40 Richmond, N. Yorks.
  E 2
54 Rickarton ....H 5
31 Rickerscote ......H 7
27 Rickinghall Inferior .H 3
27 Rickinghall Superior
  H 3
25 Rickling ....M 6
18 Rickling Green ....A 5
17 Rickmansworth ...E 11
44 Riddings, Cumb. ..E 3
32 Riddings, Derby ...E 2
4 Riddlecombe .....E 5
35 Riddlesden ....C 9
8 Ridge, Dorset .....G 1
8 Ridge, Hants. ....D 5
18 Ridge, Herts. .....D 2
8 Ridge, Wilts. .....C 1
10 Ridge Green ......C 2
28 Ridgebourne ......F 6
15 Ridgehill ....H 8
32 Ridgeway ....B 1
21 Ridgeway Cross ..H 12
25 Ridgewell ....L 8
10 Ridgewood ....F 3
25 Ridgemont ....L 1
45 Riding Mill ....G 8
13 Ridley, Kent ......B 5
44 Ridley, Northumb..G 6
30 Ridley Green ......E 4
23 Ridlington, Leics. .B 11
26 Ridlington, Norf. ..B 6
45 Ridsdale ....E 7
52 Riechip ....B 5
52 Riemore ....B 5
60 Rienachait ....D 2
40 Rievaulx ....G 6
55 Rifern ....K 2
47 Rigfoot ....D 9
44 Rigg ....F 1
47 Riggend ....B 12
47 Righead ....F 10
56 Righoul ....E 4
39 Rigmaden Park ...G 8
33 Rigsby ....C 11
48 Rigside ....F 2
22 Rileyhill ....A 5
3 Rilla Mill ....B 10
41 Rillington ....H 8
35 Rimington ....C 7
7 Rimpton ....D 9
61 Rimsdale ....C 7
37 Rimswell ....D 10
12 Rinaston ....D 3
43 Ringford ....F 8
31 Ringinglow ....B 11
26 Ringland ....D 4
10 Ringles Cross .....F 3
10 Ringmer ....G 3
5 Ringmore, Devon ..J 8
5 Ringmore, Devon ..L 5
56 Ringorm ....E 5
24 Ring's End ....E 5
27 Ringsfield ....G 7
27 Ringsfield Corner ..G 7
17 Ringshall, Bucks. ..C 10
27 Ringshall, Suffolk ..K 3
27 Ringshall Stocks ...K 4
24 Ringstead, Norf. ..B 8
25 Ringstead, Northants.
  H 1
8 Ringwood ....F 3
11 Ringwould ....C 12
58 Ringmore ....F 2
64 Rinnigill ....E 2
2 Rinsey ....G 3
10 Ripe ....G 4
32 Ripley, Derby .....E 1
8 Ripley, Hants. ....F 3
35 Ripley, N. Yorks. .A 11
10 Ripley, Surrey ....H 11
37 Riplingham ......D 4
40 Ripon ....H 3
24 Rippingale ....C 2
21 Ripple, Heref. &
  Worcs. ....H 2
11 Ripple, Kent ......C 12
35 Ripponden ....E 4
21 Risbury ....G 11
37 Risby, Humberside .F 7

27 Risby, Suffolk .....J 1
14 Risca ....E 6
37 Rise ....C 9
24 Risegate ....C 3
33 Riseholme ....C 7
25 Riseley, Beds. ....J 1
17 Riseley, Berks. ...H 8
27 Rishangles ....H 4
34 Rishton ....D 6
28 Rishworth ....E 9
32 Risley ....G 2
40 Risplith ....H 3
60 Rispond ....A 5
16 Rivar ....H 4
19 Rivenhall End .....B 8
15 River Bank ....H 6
10 Riverhead ....B 4
4 Riverton ....C 5
34 Rivington ....F 5
4 Roachill ....D 7
23 Roade ....G 11
44 Roadhead ....F 4
48 Roadmeetings ....D 1
61 Roadside, Highland
  B 11
47 Roadside, Strathclyde
  H 10
59 Roadside of Catterline
  J 6
59 Roadside of Kinneff
  K 6
6 Roadwater ....B 4
62 Roag ....D 2
42 Roan of Craigoch ..A 4
44 Roansgreen ......E 3
14 Roath ....F 5
43 Roberthill ....D 12
44 Roberton, Borders .B 3
48 Roberton, Strathclyde
  F 2
10 Robertsbridge ....F 6
35 Roberttown ......E 10
12 Robeston Cross ...F 2
12 Robeston Wathen .E 4
31 Robin Hood .....D 11
31 Robin Hood Inn ..C 11
41 Robin Hood's Bay .E 9
24 Roborough ....D 4
30 Roby ....A 3
34 Roby Mill ....F 4
31 Rocester ....F 9
12 Roch ....E 2
12 Roch Gate ....E 2
35 Rochdale ....F 7
3 Roche ....D 7
10 Rochester, Kent ..A 6
44 Rochester, Northumb.
  C 6
10 Rochford ....E 8
2 Rock, Cornwall ...B 6
45 Rock, Northumb. .A 10
22 Rock, Heref. & Worcs.
  E 1
9 Rock, W. Sussex ..E 12
2 Rock Ferry ......B 2
22 Rock Hill ....E 3
6 Rockbeare ....G 4
44 Rockcliffe, Cumb. .G 2
43 Rockcliffe, Dumf. &
  Gall. ....F 9
15 Rockfield, Gwent ..C 8
61 Rockfield, Highland
  H 9
8 Rockford ....E 3
29 Rockhampton ....E 9
26 Rockheath ....D 6
23 Rockingham .....C 12
26 Rockland All Saints .F 3
26 Rockland St. Mary .E 6
26 Rockland St. Peter .F 3
9 Rockley ....G 3
17 Rockwell End ....E 9
6 Rockwell Green ...D 5
16 Rodborough .....D 11
16 Rodbourne, Wilts. .F 2
15 Rodbourne, Wilts. .F 12
16 Rodbourne Cheney .E 2
21 Rodd ....F 8
49 Roddam ....G 12
40 Roddam Rigg ...G 12
7 Rodden ....H 9
7 Rode ....A 11
31 Rode Heath ......D 6
31 Rodeheath ....H 1
63 Rodel ....H 1
6 Roden ....A 11
6 Rodhuish ....B 4
21 Rodington ....C 10
15 Rodley ....C 10
15 Rodmarton ......D 12
10 Rodmell ....G 3
11 Rodmersham .....B 8
7 Rodney Stoke ....A 8
31 Rodsley ....F 10

6 Rodway ... B 6
7 Rodwell ... H 7
35 Roecliffe ... A 12
18 Roehampton ... G 2
64 Roesound ... C 7
10 Roffey ... E 1
61 Rogart ... F 7
9 Rogate ... D 9
14 Rogerstone ... E 6
47 Rogerton ... D 11
15 Rogiet ... E 8
26 Rollesby ... D 7
23 Rolleston, Leics. ... B 10
32 Rolleston, Notts. ... C 6
31 Rolleston, Staffs. ... G 10
37 Rolston ... C 10
11 Rolvenden ... E 7
11 Rolvenden Layne ... E 7
39 Romaldkirk ... C 12
26 Roman Hill ... F 8
40 Romanby ... F 4
48 Romannobridge ... E 4
4 Romansleigh ... D 6
62 Romesdal ... C 3
18 Romford ... E 5
31 Romiley ... A 8
8 Romsey ... D 5
22 Romsley, Salop. ... D 1
22 Romsley, Salop. ... D 3
38 Ronague ... H 1
41 Rookdale ... H 9
39 Rookhope ... A 11
8 Rookley ... H 6
7 Rooks Bridge ... A 7
4 Rook's Nest ... C 4
37 Roos ... D 10
48 Rootpark ... D 2
9 Ropley ... C 8
9 Ropley Dean ... C 7
33 Ropsley ... G 7
58 Rora ... C 8
58 Rorandle ... F 4
21 Rorrington ... B 8
2 Rose ... D 5
4 Rose Ash ... D 7
10 Rose Hill ... F 3
10 Roseacre, Kent ... C 6
34 Roseacre, Lancs. ... C 3
48 Rosebank ... D 1
45 Rosebrough ... C 12
12 Rosebush ... D 4
2 Rosecare ... B 2
41 Rosedale Abbey ... F 7
45 Roseden ... A 8
60 Rosehall ... F 5
58 Rosehearty ... A 7
30 Rosehill ... G 5
56 Roseisle ... C 7
2 Rosemarket ... F 3
56 Rosemarkie ... D 3
6 Rosemary Lane ... E 5
47 Rosemount, Strathclyde ... F 8
53 Rosemount, Tayside ... C 7
2 Rosenannon ... C 6
2 Rosewarne ... F 3
48 Rosewell ... C 5
40 Roseworth ... C 4
2 Roseworthy ... F 3
39 Rosgill ... D 8
55 Roshven ... L 1
62 Roskhill ... D 2
38 Rosley ... A 6
48 Roslin ... C 5
31 Rosliston ... H 11
47 Rosneath ... A 7
43 Ross, Dumf. & Gall. ... G 7
45 Ross, Northumb. ... B 12
15 Ross-on-Wye ... B 9
30 Rossett ... D 2
52 Rossie Ochill ... F 6
36 Rossington ... G 4
56 Rosskeen ... C 2
47 Rossland ... B 9
61 Roster ... C 11
30 Rostherne ... B 6
38 Rosthwaite ... D 5
31 Roston ... F 10
2 Rosudgeon ... G 3
48 Rosyth ... A 4
45 Rothbury ... C 9
23 Rotherby ... A 10
10 Rotherfield ... E 4
17 Rotherfield Greys ... F 8
17 Rotherfield Peppard ... F 8
32 Rotherham ... A 2
23 Rothersthorpe ... F 10
17 Rotherwick ... H 8
56 Rothes ... E 8
46 Rothesay ... C 6
58 Rothiebrisbane ... D 5
58 Rothienorman ... D 5

64 Rothiesholm ... C 4
45 Rothill ... B 9
23 Rothley ... A 9
58 Rothmaise ... D 4
37 Rothwell, Lincs. ... G 9
23 Rothwell, Northants. ... D 11
35 Rothwell, W. Yorks. ... D 12
35 Rothwell Haigh ... D 12
37 Rotsea ... B 8
59 Rottal ... K 1
10 Rottingdean ... H 3
38 Rottington ... D 2
43 Roucan ... D 11
8 Roud ... H 6
31 Rough Close ... F 8
11 Rough Common ... B 10
31 Rough Hay ... H 10
26 Rougham ... C 1
27 Rougham Green ... J 2
55 Roughburn ... L 7
35 Roughlee ... C 7
22 Roughley ... B 5
44 Roughsike ... E 3
33 Roughton, Lincs. ... D 9
26 Roughton, Norf. ... B 5
22 Roughton, Salop. ... C 1
47 Roughwood ... D 8
17 Round Oak ... H 7
7 Roundham ... E 7
35 Roundhay ... C 12
43 Roundstonefoot ... A 12
9 Roundstreet Com. ... C 12
16 Roundway ... H 1
22 Rous Lench ... G 4
6 Rousdon ... G 6
47 Routdaneburn ... D 7
37 Routh ... C 8
61 Rovie Lodge ... F 7
8 Row, Cornwall ... B 8
39 Row, Cumbria ... F 7
44 Rowanburn ... E 2
51 Rowardennan Hotel ... H 10
31 Rowarth ... A 8
16 Rowde ... H 1
15 Rowden Down ... G 12
29 Ro-wen ... C 7
44 Rowfoot ... G 5
19 Rowhedge ... B 10
9 Rowhook ... C 12
22 Rowington ... E 5
31 Rowland ... C 10
9 Rowland's Castle ... G 12
45 Rowland's Gill ... G 10
9 Rowledge ... B 9
37 Rowley, Humber. ... D 7
21 Rowley, Salop. ... B 8
22 Rowley Regis ... C 3
15 Rowlstone ... B 7
9 Rowly ... B 11
22 Rowney Green ... E 4
8 Rownhams ... D 5
17 Rowsham ... B 9
31 Rowsley ... D 11
33 Rowston ... E 8
30 Rowton, Ches. ... D 3
30 Rowton, Salop. ... H 5
49 Roxburgh ... F 9
49 Roxburgh Newtown ... F 9
37 Roxby, Humber. ... E 7
41 Roxby, N. Yorks. ... D 7
25 Roxton ... K 3
18 Roxwell ... C 6
34 Royal Oak ... G 3
55 Roybridge ... L 6
18 Roydon, Essex ... C 4
27 Roydon, Norfolk ... C 4
24 Roydon, Norfolk ... C 8
25 Royston, Herts. ... L 5
35 Royston, S. Yorks. ... F 12
35 Royton ... F 8
29 Ruabon ... F 12
2 Ruan High Lanes ... F 6
2 Ruan Lanihorne ... E 6
2 Ruan Minor ... H 4
15 Ruardean ... C 9
15 Ruardean Woodside ... C 9
22 Ribery ... D 3
39 Ruckcroft ... A 8
21 Ruckhall Com. ... H 10
11 Ruckinge ... E 9
33 Ruckland ... B 10
21 Ruckley ... B 10
40 Rudby ... F 5
45 Rudchester ... F 9
32 Ruddington ... G 3
15 Rudford ... B 11
7 Rudge ... A 11
15 Rudgeway ... F 9
9 Rudgwick ... C 12
15 Rudhall ... B 9

14 Rudry ... F 5
41 Rudston ... H 11
31 Rudyard ... D 8
49 Ruecastle ... G 8
34 Rufford ... F 3
36 Rufforth ... B 3
45 Ruffside ... H 8
23 Rugby ... E 8
31 Rugeley ... H 9
56 Ruilick ... E 1
6 Ruishton ... D 6
18 Ruislip ... E 1
18 Ruislip Common ... E 1
44 Ruletownhead ... B 4
49 Rumbletonlaw ... E 9
52 Rumblingbridge ... G 5
27 Rumburgh ... G 6
2 Rumford ... C 6
14 Rumney ... F 5
52 Runacraig ... F 1
30 Runcorn ... B 4
9 Runcton ... F 10
24 Runcton Holme ... D 6
5 Rundlestone ... H 4
9 Runfold ... A 10
26 Runhall ... E 4
26 Runham ... D 7
6 Runnington ... D 5
19 Runsell Green ... C 8
41 Runswick ... D 8
57 Runtaleave ... M 8
19 Runwell ... C 8
17 Ruscombe ... F 9
56 Rosehaugh House ... D 2
19 Rush Green ... B 11
15 Rushall, Heref. & Worcs. ... A 9
27 Rushall, Norfolk ... G 5
22 Rushall, W. Midlands ... B 4
8 Rushall, Wilts. ... A 3
27 Rushbrooke ... J 2
21 Rushbury ... C 10
25 Rushden, Herts. ... M 4
25 Rushden, Northants. ... J 1
27 Rushford ... G 2
10 Rushlake Green ... F 5
27 Rushmere ... G 8
27 Rushmere St. Andrew ... K 5
27 Rushmere Street ... K 5
9 Rushmoor, Surrey ... B 10
8 Rushmore, Wilts. ... D 1
22 Rushock ... C 9
35 Rusholme ... H 7
30 Rushton, Ches. ... D 4
23 Rushton, Northants. ... D 11
21 Rushton, Salop. ... B 11
31 Rushton Spencer ... D 8
22 Rushwick ... G 2
40 Rushyford ... B 3
52 Ruskie ... G 1
33 Ruskington ... E 8
43 Rusko ... F 7
38 Rusland ... F 6
10 Rusper ... D 1
15 Ruspidge ... C 9
10 Russell's Green ... G 6
17 Russell's Water ... E 8
9 Rustington ... F 11
41 Ruston ... G 9
37 Ruston Parva ... A 8
41 Ruswarp ... D 9
47 Rutherford ... F 9
47 Rutherglen ... C 11
3 Ruthernbridge ... C 7
31 Ruthin ... D 10
59 Ruthrieston ... G 7
49 Ruthven, Borders ... E 10
58 Ruthven, Grampian ... C 3
56 Ruthven, Highland ... F 4
57 Ruthven, Highland ... J 3
53 Ruthven, Tayside ... B 7
53 Ruthven House ... B 8
2 Ruthvoes ... D 6
43 Ruthwell ... E 11
15 Ruxton Green ... B 8
30 Ruyton Eleven Towns ... H 3
45 Ryal ... F 8
7 Ryall ... G 7
10 Ryarsh ... B 5
38 Rydal ... E 6
9 Ryde ... G 7
4 Rydon ... F 2
11 Rye ... F 8
11 Rye Foreign ... F 7
11 Rye Harbour ... F 8
43 Ryemuir ... D 11
15 Ryhall ... D 1
37 Ryhill, Humber. ... E 10
36 Ryhill, W. Yorks. ... F 2

45 Ryhope ... H 12
33 Ryland ... B 7
35 Rylstone ... A 8
7 Ryme Intrinseca ... E 9
36 Ryslaw ... E 10
36 Ryther ... C 3
15 Ryton, Glos. ... A 10
41 Ryton, N. Yorks. ... H 8
21 Ryton, Salop. ... B 10
22 Ryton, Salop. ... B 1
45 Ryton, Tyne & Wear ... G 9
23 Ryton-on-Dunsmore ... E 7
34 Sabden ... C 6
18 Sacombe ... B 3
45 Sacriston ... H 10
40 Sadberge ... C 4
46 Saddell ... F 3
52 Saddington ... C 10
24 Saddle Bow ... D 7
8 Saddle Heath ... E 3
55 Saddleworth ... F 9
39 Sadgill ... E 7
25 Saffron Walden ... L 6
8 Sageston ... G 4
26 Saham Hills ... E 2
26 Saham Toney ... E 2
30 Saighton ... D 3
50 Sailean ... C 6
49 St. Abbs ... C 11
2 St. Agnes, Corn. ... E 4
2 St. Agnes, Is. of Scilly ... D 2
18 St. Albans ... C 2
2 St. Allen ... E 5
53 St. Andrews ... E 10
14 St. Andrews Major ... G 5
34 St. Anne's ... D 2
43 St. Ann's ... B 11
3 St. Ann's Chapel, Cornwall ... C 11
5 St. Ann's Chapel, Devon ... L 5
2 St. Anthony ... G 5
10 St. Anthony's Hill ... H 5
15 St. Arvans ... E 8
29 St. Asaph ... C 9
14 St. Athan ... G 3
3 St. Austell ... D 7
7 St. Bartholomew's Hill ... D 12
38 St. Bees ... D 2
3 St. Blazey ... D 8
3 St. Blazey Gate ... D 7
49 St. Boswells ... F 8
3 St. Breock ... C 7
3 St. Breward ... B 8
15 St. Briavels ... D 9
12 St. Brides ... F 2
14 St. Brides Major ... G 2
15 St. Brides Netherwent ... E 7
14 St. Bride's-super-Ely ... G 4
14 St. Bride's Wentlooge ... F 6
38 St. Bridget Beckermet ... E 3
5 St. Budeaux ... K 3
3 St. Buryan ... G 1
15 St. Catherine ... G 11
51 St. Catherines ... G 8
3 St. Clears ... E 6
3 St. Cleer ... C 9
2 St. Clement ... E 5
3 St. Clether ... A 9
46 St. Colmac ... C 5
2 St. Columb Major ... C 6
2 St. Columb Minor ... C 5
2 St. Columb Porth ... C 5
2 St. Columb Road ... D 6
58 St. Combs ... A 8
27 St. Cross South Elmham ... G 6
49 St. Cuthberts ... E 11
12 St. David's, Dyfed ... D 1
52 St. David's, Tayside ... E 4
15 St. Day ... E 4
6 St. Decumans ... B 4
2 St. Dennis ... D 6
15 St. Devereux ... A 7
12 St. Dogmaels ... B 5
12 St. Dogwells ... D 3
3 St. Dominick ... C 11
14 St. Donats ... G 3
16 St. Edith's Marsh ... H 1
3 St. Endellion ... B 7
2 St. Enoder ... D 6
2 St. Erme ... E 5
3 St. Erney ... D 10
2 St. Erth ... F 3
2 St. Ervan ... C 6
2 St. Ewe ... E 7

14 St. Faggans ... F 4
58 St. Fergus ... B 8
52 St. Fillans ... E 2
12 St. Florence ... G 4
2 St. Gennys ... B 2
29 St. George ... C 9
15 St. George's, Avon ... H 7
14 St. George's, S. Glam. ... G 4
3 St. Germans ... D 10
4 St. Giles in the Wood ... D 4
5 St. Giles on the Heath ... G 2
20 St. Harmon ... E 5
26 St. Helena ... D 5
9 St. Helens, I. o. W. ... G 7
34 St. Helens, Merseyside ... G 4
2 St. Hilary, Corn. ... F 3
14 St. Hilary, S. Glam. ... G 3
10 Saint Hill ... D 3
14 St. Illtyd ... D 5
12 St. Ishmael's ... F 2
2 St. Issey ... C 6
3 St. Ive ... C 10
3 St. Ive Cross ... C 10
25 St. Ives, Cambs. ... H 4
2 St. Ives, Corn. ... F 2
8 St. Ives, Dorset ... F 3
27 St. James South Elmham ... G 6
8 St. Joan à Gores Cross ... A 2
3 St. John ... D 11
38 St. John Beckermet ... D 3
22 St. John's, Heref. & Worcs. ... G 2
38 St. John's, I.o.M. ... G 1
4 St. John's Chapel, Devon ... C 4
39 St. John's Chapel, Durham ... A 11
24 St. John's Fen End ... D 6
24 St. John's Highway ... D 6
38 St. Judas ... F 2
2 St. Just ... G 1
2 St. Just Lane ... F 6
58 St. Katherines ... D 5
2 St. Keverne ... G 5
3 St. Kew ... B 7
3 St. Kew Highway ... B 7
3 St. Keyne ... D 9
3 St. Lawrence, Corn. ... C 7
19 St. Lawrence, Essex ... C 9
9 St. Lawrence, I. o. W. ... H 7
17 St. Leonards, Bucks. ... C 10
8 St. Leonards, Dorset ... F 3
11 St. Leonards, E. Sussex ... G 7
2 St. Levan ... G 1
14 St. Lythans ... G 4
3 St. Mabyn ... B 7
6 St. Margaret ... D 4
27 St. Margaret South Elmham ... G 6
15 St. Margarets, Heref. & Worcs. ... A 7
18 St. Margarets, Hertfordshire ... C 4
11 St. Margaret's at Cliffe ... D 12
64 St. Margaret's Hope ... E 2
38 St. Mark's ... H 1
3 St. Martin ... D 9
52 St. Martins, Tayside ... D 6
30 St. Martin's, Salop. ... G 2
2 St. Martin's Green ... G 4
8 St. Mary Bourne ... A 6
14 St. Mary Church ... G 3
18 St. Mary Cray ... G 5
11 St. Mary in the Marsh ... E 9
18 St. Marylebone ... F 3
64 St. Marys ... D 3
11 St. Mary's Bay ... E 9
15 St. Mary's Grove ... G 8
19 St. Mary's Hoo ... C 8
15 St. Maughans ... C 8
2 St. Mawes ... F 5
2 St. Mawgan ... C 6
3 St. Mellion ... C 11
14 St. Mellons ... F 6
3 St. Merryn ... B 7
3 St. Mewan ... E 7
3 St. Michael Caerhays ... E 7
2 St. Michael Penkevil ... E 6
27 St. Michael South Elmham ... G 6

11 St. Michaels, Kent ... E 7
21 St. Michaels, Heref. & Worcs. ... F 11
34 St. Michaels on Wyre ... C 3
3 St. Minver ... B 7
53 St. Monans ... G 10
3 St. Neot ... C 9
25 St. Neots ... J 3
2 St. Newlyn East ... D 5
12 St. Nicholas, Dyfed ... C 2
14 St. Nicholas, S. Glam. ... G 4
31 St. Nicholas at Wade ... A 11
52 St. Ninians ... H 3
26 St. Olaves ... E 8
19 St. Osyth ... B 11
15 St. Owen's Cross ... B 8
18 St. Pancras ... F 3
18 St. Paul's Cray ... G 5
18 St. Paul's Walden ... B 2
11 St. Peters ... A 12
3 St. Petrox ... G 3
47 St. Quivox ... G 8
2 St. Stephen ... D 6
3 St. Stephens, Corn. ... A 10
3 St. Stephens, Corn. ... D 11
3 St. Teath ... B 7
3 St. Tudy ... B 8
12 St. Twynnells ... G 3
3 St. Veep ... D 8
53 St. Vigeans ... C 11
3 St. Wenn ... C 7
15 St. Weonards ... B 8
22 Saintbury ... H 5
51 Salachail ... B 8
5 Salcombe ... M 6
6 Salcombe Regis ... G 5
19 Salcott ... C 9
35 Sale ... H 7
22 Sale Green ... F 3
33 Saleby ... B 11
10 Salehurst ... F 6
20 Salem, Dyfed ... D 2
12 Salem, Dyfed ... D 9
28 Salem, Gwynedd ... E 5
50 Salen, Highland ... A 4
50 Salen, Mull, Strathclyde ... C 3
34 Salesbury ... D 5
23 Salford, Beds. ... H 12
35 Salford, Manchester ... G 7
16 Salford, Oxon. ... A 4
22 Salford Priors ... G 4
10 Salfords ... C 2
26 Salhouse ... D 6
52 Saline ... H 5
8 Salisbury ... C 3
26 Sall ... C 4
51 Sallachan ... B 8
55 Sallachy, Highland ... G 3
60 Sallachy, Highland ... F 6
3 Salmonby ... C 10
43 Salmond's Muir ... C 10
21 Salop, Co. ... B 10
16 Salperton ... B 2
25 Salph End ... K 2
48 Salsburgh ... C 1
3 Salt ... G 8
3 Saltash ... D 11
56 Saltburn ... C 3
41 Saltburn-by-the Sea ... C 7
32 Saltby ... H 5
47 Saltcoats ... E 7
35 Salterforth ... C 7
24 Salters Lode ... E 7
30 Satterswall ... D 5
33 Saltfleet ... A 11
33 Saltfleetby St. Clements ... A 11
33 Saltfleetby St. Peter ... A 11
33 Saltfleetby Saints ... A 11
15 Saltford ... G 10
37 Salthaugh Grange ... E 10
26 Salthouse ... A 4
36 Saltmarshe ... E 6
30 Saltney ... D 3
41 Salton ... D 7
4 Saltren's ... D 3
45 Saltwick ... E 10
11 Saltwood ... D 10
9 Salvington ... F 12
22 Salwarpe ... F 3
7 Salway Ash ... F 8
22 Sambourne ... F 4
30 Sambrook ... H 6
34 Samlesbury ... D 5
34 Samlesbury Bottoms ... D 5
6 Sampford ... B 4
6 Sampford Arundel ... D 5

4 Sampford Courtenay ......F 5
6 Sampford Peverell ..E 4
5 Sampford Spinney ..H 4
19 Samuel's Corner ...E 9
49 Samuelston ....B 7
54 Sanachan ....F 2
51 Sancton ....G 7
2 Sancreed ....G 1
37 Sancton ....C 7
64 Sand ....D 7
36 Sand Hutton ......A 5
38 Sand Side ....G 5
55 Sandaig, Highland ...J 1
55 Sandaig, Highland ..H 1
35 Sandal Magna .....E 12
38 Sandale ....A 5
30 Sandbach ....D 6
46 Sandbank ....A 6
8 Sandbanks ....G 2
58 Sandend ....A 3
18 Sanderstead ......H 3
15 Sandford, Avon ....H 7
39 Sandford, Cumbria .D 9
4 Sandford, Devon ...F 7
8 Sandford, Dorset ...G 1
9 Sandford, I.o.W. ...H 7
30 Sandford, Salop ...H 2
47 Sandford, Strathclyde ......E 12
16 Sandford-on-Thames ....D 6
7 Sandford Orcas ....D 9
16 Sandford St. Martin .B 5
58 Sandfordhill ....C 8
64 Sandgarth ....C 3
11 Sandgate ....E 10
58 Sandhaven ....A 7
42 Sandhead ....G 2
47 Sandhill ....H 9
45 Sandhoe ....F 8
44 Sandholm ....D 3
36 Sandholme, Humber. ....D 6
24 Sandholme, Lincs. ..B 4
17 Sandhurst, Berks. ..H 4
15 Sandhurst, Glos. ..B 11
11 Sandhurst, Kent ...E 7
10 Sandhurst Cross ...E 6
40 Sandhutton ....G 4
32 Sandiacre ....G 2
33 Sandilands ......B 12
30 Sandiway ....C 5
16 Sandleigh ....D 6
10 Sandling ....B 6
64 Sandness ....D 6
19 Sandon, Essex .....C 7
25 Sandon, Herts. .....M 4
31 Sandon, Staffs. ...G 8
9 Sandown ....H 7
3 Sandplace ....D 9
18 Sandridge, Herts. ..C 2
15 Sandridge, Wilts. ..H 12
41 Sandsend ....D 8
64 Sandside ....D 1
61 Sandside Hotel .....A 9
64 Sandsound ....D 7
36 Sandtoft ....F 5
11 Sandway, Kent .....C 7
6 Sandway, Som. ....C 2
22 Sandwell ....C 4
38 Sandwick, Cumbria .C 6
64 Sandwick, Orkney Is. ....E 2
63 Sandwick, Highland .D 5
64 Sandwick, Shetland Is. ......E 7
38 Sandwith ....D 2
25 Sandy ....K 3
30 Sandy Bank ....G 4
10 Sandy Cross ......F 5
12 Sandy Haven ......F 2
16 Sandy Lane, Wilts. ..G 1
35 Sandy Lane, W. Yorks. ....D 9
29 Sandycroft ....D 12
43 Sandyford, Dumf. & Gall. ....B 12
47 Sandyford, Strathclyde ......G 9
38 Sandygate ....F 2
43 Sandyhills ....F 9
34 Sandylands ....A 3
4 Sandymoor Cross ..F 3
5 Sandypark ....G 6
44 Sandysike ....F 2
49 Sandystones ......G 8
15 Sandyway ....B 8
50 Sanna ....A 2
47 Sanquhar ....H 12
38 Santon Bridge .....E 4
27 Santon Downham ...G 1
23 Sapcote ....C 8
21 Sapey Common ...F 12

27 Sapiston ....H 2
15 Sapperton, Glos. ..D 12
33 Sapperton, Lincs. ..G 7
24 Saracen's Head ....C 4
61 Sarclet ....C 12
12 Sardis ....F 3
12 Sardis Mountain ...F 5
8 Sarisbury ....E 6
28 Sarn, Gwynedd ....G 2
14 Sarn, Mid Glam. ...F 2
21 Sarn, Powys ......C 7
12 Sarnau, Dyfed .....B 6
13 Sarnau, Dyfed .....D 8
29 Sarnau, Gwynedd ..F 9
14 Sarnau, Powys ....A 3
21 Sarnau, Powys ....A 8
28 Sarn-back ....H 2
21 Sarnesfield ....G 9
13 Saron, Dyfed ......C 7
13 Saron, Dyfed ......F 9
28 Saron, Gwynedd ...D 5
17 Sarratt ....D 11
11 Sarre ....B 11
16 Sarsden ....B 4
8 Sarson ....B 4
60 Sausthorpe ....C 11
60 Savalmore ....F 6
31 Saverley Green ....F 8
50 Savory ....C 4
41 Sawbridgeworth ...B 5
41 Sawdon ....G 9
32 Sawley, Derby .....G 2
32 Sawley, Lancs. ....C 6
25 Sawston ....K 6
25 Sawtry ....G 3
32 Saxby, Leics. .....H 5
33 Saxby, Lincs. .....B 7
32 Saxby All Saints ...E 7
32 Saxelby ....H 4
32 Saxilby ....C 6
26 Saxlingham ....B 3
26 Saxlingham Nethergate ....F 5
25 Saxmundham .....J 7
25 Saxon Street .....J 8
32 Saxondale ....F 4
27 Saxtead ....J 6
27 Saxtead Green ....J 6
26 Saxthorpe ....C 4
35 Saxton ....C 3
10 Sayers Common ...F 2
48 Scabcleuch ....H 5
34 Scackleton ....H 6
63 Scadabay ....H 3
32 Scaftworth ....A 4
32 Scagglethorpe ....H 8
50 Scalasaig ....H 1
36 Scalby, Humber. ..D 6
41 Scalby, N. Yorks. ..F 10
23 Scaldwell ....E 11
44 Scaleby ....G 3
44 Scalebyhill ....G 3
38 Scales, Cumb. ....C 6
38 Scales, Cumbria ...H 5
44 Scales, Lans. .....D 3
39 Scales Houses .....A 8
32 Scalford ....H 5
44 Scaling ....D 7
50 Scallastle ....D 4
64 Scalloway ....E 7
62 Scalpay House ....E 5
55 Scamadale ....K 1
55 Scamodale ....M 2
41 Scampston ....H 8
33 Scampton ....B 7
56 Scaniport ....F 2
64 Scapa ....D 2
64 Scar ....A 4
39 Scar End ....B 11
41 Scarborough ......F 10
43 Scarbrae ....C 9
32 Scarcliffe ....C 12
35 Scarcroft ....C 12
54 Scardroy ....D 6
44 Scare ....F 3
61 Scarfskerry ....A 11

40 Scargill ....D 1
34 Scarisbrick ....F 3
26 Scarning ....D 2
32 Scarrington ....F 4
34 Scarth Hill ....F 3
37 Scartho ....G 10
64 Scarwell ....C 1
56 Scatraig ....F 3
64 Scatsta ....C 7
37 Scawby ....G 7
37 Scawby Brook ....F 7
40 Scawton ....G 6
10 Scayne's Hill .....F 3
14 Scethrog ....B 4
47 Schaw ....G 9
31 Scholar Green ....E 7
35 Scholes, W. Yorks. .F 10
35 Scholes, W. Yorks. .E 10
36 Scholes, W. Yorks. .D 2
40 School Aycliffe ....C 3
35 Scissett ....F 11
12 Scleddau ....D 3
26 Sco Ruston ....C 6
12 Scole ....G 4
59 Scolly's Cross .....J 4
12 Scolton ....E 3
62 Sconser ....E 4
53 Scoonie ....G 8
50 Scoor ....F 2
33 Scopwick ....D 8
60 Scoraig ....G 2
37 Scorborough .....C 8
47 Scorrieholm ......F 12
2 Scorrier ....E 4
5 Scorriton ....J 6
40 Scorton ....E 3
34 Scot Lane End ....F 5
44 Scotby ....G 3
40 Scotch Corner ....E 2
34 Scotforth ....A 4
33 Scothern ....B 7
45 Scots' Gap ....D 8
33 Scots Hole ....D 8
56 Scotsburn ....D 6
61 Scotscalder Sta. ...B 10
53 Scotscraig ....D 9
44 Scotsdike ....F 2
59 Scotston, Grampian .K 5
52 Scotston, Tayside ..C 4
50 Scotstown ....A 5
45 Scotswood ....G 10
53 Scottas ....J 1
36 Scotter ....G 6
36 Scotterthorpe .....G 6
37 Scotton, Lincs. ....G 7
40 Scotton, N. Yorks. ..F 2
35 Scotton, N. Yorks. .A 12
49 Scoughall ....A 8
26 Scoulton ....E 3
60 Scourie ....E 3
60 Scourie More .....C 3
64 Scousburgh ....F 7
61 Scrabster ....A 10
49 Scraesburgh .....G 9
33 Scrafield ....C 10
45 Scrainwood ....B 8
33 Scramblesby ......B 10
24 Scrane End ....A 5
23 Scraptoft ....B 10
26 Scratby ....D 8
36 Scrayingham .....A 5
24 Scredington ......B 2
6 Screedy ....D 4
43 Screel ....F 9
33 Scremby ....C 11
49 Scremerston .....D 12
32 Screveton ....F 4
61 Scriberscross .....F 8
33 Scrivelsby ....B 9
35 Scriven ....A 12
43 Scroggs ....C 12
32 Scrooby ....A 4
31 Scropton ....G 10
33 Scrub Hill ....E 9
40 Scruton ....F 3
33 Sculcoates ....D 8
26 Sculthorpe ....B 2
37 Scunthorpe ......F 7
31 Scurlage ....H 8
26 Sea Palling ......C 7
7 Seaborough ......F 8
39 Seacombe ....A 2
33 Seacroft, Lincs. ...D 12
35 Seacroft, W. Yorks. ....D 12
48 Seafield, Lothian ..C 3
47 Seafield, Strathclyde ....G 8
10 Seaford ....H 4
34 Seaforth ....G 2
63 Seaforth Head ....E 4
45 Seaham ....H 12
45 Seahouses ....D 12
10 Seal ....B 4

30 Sealand ....C 2
9 Seale ....A 10
41 Seamer, N. Yorks. .G 10
40 Seamer, N. Yorks. .D 5
47 Seamill ....E 7
37 Searby ....G 8
11 Seasalter ....B 9
38 Seascale ....E 3
33 Seathorne ....D 12
38 Seathwaite, Cumb. .D 5
38 Seathwaite, Cumb. .F 5
38 Seatoller ....D 5
3 Seaton, Corn. ....D 10
38 Seaton, Cumb. ...B 3
6 Seaton, Devon ...G 6
45 Seaton, Dur. .....H 12
23 Seaton, Leics. ...B 12
37 Seaton, Humber. .B 9
45 Seaton, Northumb. E 11
45 Seaton Burn ......F 10
40 Seaton Carew ....B 5
45 Seaton Delaval ..E 11
36 Seaton Ross .....C 6
45 Seaton Sluice ....E 11
58 Seatown, Grampian .A 3
58 Seatown, Grampian ..B 4
7 Seatown, Dorset ..G 7
40 Seave Green .....E 6
45 Seaview ....G 8
43 Seaville ....F 12
7 Seavington St. Mary .E 7
7 Seavington St. Michael ....E 7
19 Seawick Sands ...C 11
15 Sebastopol, Gwent .E 6
14 Sebastopol, Mid Glam. ....D 5
38 Sebergham ....A 6
22 Seckington ....A 6
60 Second Coast .....G 1
39 Sedbergh ....F 9
15 Sedbury ....E 9
39 Sedbusk ....F 11
22 Sedgeberrow .....H 4
32 Sedgebrook ......F 6
40 Sedgefield ....B 4
24 Sedgeford ....B 8
7 Sedgehill ....C 12
22 Sedgley ....C 2
39 Sedgwick ....F 7
10 Sedlescombe .....F 6
10 Sedlescombe St. ..F 6
15 Seend ....H 12
15 Seende Cleeve ...H 12
25 Seer Green ....E 10
26 Seething ....F 6
34 Sefton ....G 2
45 Seghill ....F 11
31 Seighford ....H 7
63 Seilebost ....G 2
22 Seisdon ....C 2
30 Selattyn ....G 1
9 Selborne ....C 9
35 Selby ....D 4
9 Selham ....D 10
49 Selkirk ....G 7
55 Sellack ....B 9
38 Sellafield Station ..E 3
64 Sellafirth ....B 7
15 Sellindge ....D 9
11 Sellindge Lees ....D 9
11 Selling ....B 9
55 Sells Green ......H 12
22 Selly Oak ....D 4
10 Selmeston ....G 4
18 Selsdon ....H 4
15 Selsey ....D 11
10 Selsfield Common ..E 2
39 Selside ....H 10
11 Selstead ....D 10
32 Selston ....E 2
6 Selworthy ....B 3
64 Semblister ....D 6
27 Semer ....K 3
15 Semington ....H 12
9 Semley ....D 12
11 Send ....A 11
9 Sendmarsh ......A 11
14 Senghenydd .....E 4
2 Sennen ....G 1
2 Sennen Cove .....G 1
14 Sennybridge .....B 3
24 Setchey ....D 7
8 Setley ....F 5
64 Setter, Bressay Shetland Is. .....E 7
64 Setter, Zetland Shetland Is. .....D 6
64 Setter, Zetland Shetland Is. .....D 7
35 Settle ....A 7

45 Settlingstones .....F 7
41 Settrington ....H 8
2 Seven Ash ....C 5
18 Seven Kings .....E 4
14 Seven Sisters .....C 2
16 Seven Wells ......A 2
16 Sevenhampton, Glos. ....B 1
16 Sevenhampton, Wilts. ....E 3
10 Sevenoaks ....C 4
10 Sevenoaks Weald ..C 4
15 Severn Beach .....F 8
16 Severn Stoke .....H 2
11 Sevington, Kent ...D 9
15 Sevington, Wilts. ..F 11
45 Sewards End .....L 7
41 Sewerby ....H 12
2 Seworgan ....G 4
56 Sewstern ....H 6
10 Seyning ....G 1
17 Shabbington .....C 7
22 Shackerstone .....A 7
27 Shadingfield .....G 7
9 Shackleford ......B 10
50 Shadforth ....A 4
11 Shadoxhurst .....D 8
27 Shadwell, Norfolk .G 2
35 Shadwell, W. Yorks. ....C 12
7 Shaftesbury .....D 12
36 Shafton ....F 2
16 Shalbourne ......H 4
8 Shalcombe ....G 5
9 Shalden ....B 8
9 Shaldon ....J 8
8 Shalfleet ....G 5
19 Shalford, Essex ..A 11
9 Shalford, Surrey ..A 11
19 Shalford Green ...A 7
52 Shalloch ....B 3
4 Shallowford ......B 6
11 Shalmsford Street .C 9
23 Shalstone ....H 9
46 Shalunt ....B 5
9 Shamley Green ...B 11
43 Shancastle ....C 9
47 Shandon ....A 7
56 Shandwick ....B 4
32 Shangton ....C 10
45 Shankhouse .....E 11
45 Shanklin ....H 7
46 Shannochie ......G 5
53 Shanzie ....B 7
39 Shap ....D 8
26 Shapwick, Dorset .F 1
7 Shapwick, Som. ..B 7
22 Shardlow ....G 2
22 Shareshill ....B 3
35 Sharlston, W. Yorks. ....E 12
36 Sharlston, W. Yorks. ....E 2
11 Sharnal Street ....A 7
25 Sharnbrook ......J 1
23 Sharnford ....C 8
56 Sharoe Green ....D 4
40 Sharow ....H 3
25 Sharpenhoe ......M 2
45 Sharperton ......C 8
15 Sharpness ....D 10
10 Sharpthorne .....E 3
40 Sharrington .....D 1
22 Shatterford ......D 1
5 Shaugh Prior .....J 4
15 Shave Cross .....F 7
30 Shavington ....E 6
16 Shaw, Berks. .....G 6
35 Shaw, Lancs. .....A 8
15 Shaw, Wilts. .....H 12
34 Shaw Green .....E 4
35 Shaw Mills ......A 11
30 Shawbury ....H 4
45 Shawdon Hill ....B 9
23 Shawell ....D 9
31 Shawford ....D 6
35 Shawforth ....E 7
43 Shawhill ....E 12
47 Shawood ....G 10
47 Shawton ....D 11
7 Shear Cross .....B 11
43 Shearington .....E 11
23 Shearsby ....C 9
4 Shebbear ....E 3
30 Shebdon ....H 6
61 Shebster ....B 9
9 Shedfield ....E 7
31 Sheen ....D 9
21 Sheephouse ......F 12
15 Sheepscombe ....C 12
5 Sheepstor ....J 4
4 Sheepwash, Devon ..E 4
4 Sheepwash, Devon ..C 7

45 Sheepwash, Northumb. ......D 10
15 Sheepway ....G 8
23 Sheepy Magna ...B 7
23 Sheepy Parva ....B 7
18 Sheering ....C 5
11 Sheerness ....A 8
9 Sheet, Hants. ....D 9
21 Sheet, Salop .....E 10
32 Sheffield ....B 1
25 Sheffield ....L 2
16 Shefford Woodlands ....G 4
60 Sheigra ....B 3
43 Sheillahill ....F 8
21 Sheinton ....B 11
11 Shelderton ....E 9
31 Sheldon ....C 10
6 Sheldon, Devon ...E 5
22 Sheldon, War. ....D 5
11 Sheldwich ....B 9
35 Shelf ....D 10
27 Shelfanger ....H 7
22 Shelfield, W. Midlands ....B 4
22 Shelfield, War. ....F 5
32 Shelford ....F 4
49 Shellacres ....E 11
18 Shelley, Essex ....C 5
35 Shelley, W. Yorks. .F 10
16 Shellingford ......E 4
18 Shellow Bowells ..C 6
22 Shelsley Beauchamp ....F 1
21 Shelsley Walsh ...F 12
32 Shelthorpe ......H 3
26 Shelton, Norfolk ..F 5
25 Shelton, Northants. .H 1
32 Shelton, Notts. ...F 5
21 Shelton, Salop ...A 10
21 Shelve ....C 9
21 Shelwick ....H 10
21 Shelwick Green ..H 10
56 Shenachie ....F 4
18 Shenfield ....D 6
23 Shenington ......H 7
18 Shenley ....D 2
17 Shenley Brook End .A 9
23 Shenley Church End ....H 11
15 Shenmore ....A 7
42 Shennanton ......E 4
22 Shenstone, Heref. & Worcs. ....E 2
22 Shenstone, Staffs. ..B 4
57 Shenval ....G 8
24 Shepeu Stow .....D 4
18 Shephall ....B 3
18 Shepherd's Bush ..F 2
18 Shepherd's Green ..F 8
11 Shepherdswell ...C 11
35 Shepley ....F 10
15 Shepperdine .....E 9
17 Shepperton ......G 11
17 Shepperton Grn. ..G 11
25 Shepreth ....K 5
32 Shepshed ....H 2
7 Shepton Beauchamp ....D 7
7 Shepton Mallet ...B 9
7 Shepton Montague .C 10
10 Shepway ....C 6
40 Sheraton ....B 5
7 Sherborne, Dorset .E 10
16 Sherborne, Glos. ...C 3
9 Sherborne St. John .A 8
22 Sherbourne ......F 6
40 Sherburn, Dur. ...A 3
41 Sherburn, N. Yorks. .G 9
40 Sherburn Hill ....A 4
36 Sherburn in Elmet ..D 3
9 Shere ....A 12
26 Shereford ....C 2
8 Sherfield English ...D 4
17 Sherfield on Loddon ....H 7
5 Sherford ....L 6
36 Sheriff Hutton ....A 3
26 Sheringham ......A 4
23 Sherington ......G 12
24 Shernborne ......B 8
21 Sherriffhales ......A 1
8 Sherrington ......B 1
15 Sherston ....F 11
4 Sherwood Green ..D 4
63 Sheshader ....C 6
22 Shettleston ......C 11
34 Shevington ......F 4
34 Shevington Moor ..F 4
3 Sheviock ....D 10
55 Shewglie ....G 8
52 Shian ....C 3
49 Shidlaw ....F 10
43 Shiel, Dumf. & Gall. .A 8

43 Shiel, Dumf. & Gall. D 7
55 Shiel Bridge H 3
45 Shiel Dykes B 9
54 Shieldaig D 2
54 Shieldaig Lodge (Hotel) C 2
48 Shieldhill, Central B 2
43 Shieldhill, Dumf. & Gall. C 10
43 Shieldhill, Dumf. & Gall. C 11
47 Shieldmuir D 12
50 Shielfoot A 4
58 Shielhill, Grampian B 8
59 Shielhill, Tayside L 2
47 Shieloans F 11
16 Shifford D 5
22 Shifnal B 1
45 Shilbottle B 10
44 Shilburn Haugh D 5
40 Shildon C 3
47 Shillford D 9
6 Shillingford, Devon D 3
17 Shillingford, Oxon. E 7
43 Shillingford Abbot G 2
6 Shillingford St. George G 2
7 Shillingstone E 11
25 Shillington M 2
45 Shillmoor B 7
63 Shiltenish E 4
16 Shilton, Oxon. C 4
23 Shilton, War. D 7
7 Shilvinghampton H 9
27 Shimpling, Norf. G 4
27 Shimpling, Suffolk K 2
27 Shimpling Street K 2
40 Shincliffe A 3
40 Shincliffe Colliery A 3
45 Shiney Row H 11
17 Shinfield G 8
59 Shinfur J 2
43 Shinnelhead B 8
5 Shinner's Bridge J 7
10 Shipbourne C 5
26 Shipdham E 3
7 Shipham A 8
5 Shiphay J 8
17 Shiplake F 8
48 Shiplaw D 5
45 Shipley, Northumb. A 9
22 Shipley, Salop. C 2
9 Shipley, W. Sussex D 12
35 Shipley, W. Yorks. C 10
10 Shipley Bridge D 2
26 Shipmeadow F 7
25 Shippea Hill Sta. G 7
16 Shippon D 6
22 Shipston on Stour H 6
16 Shipton, Glos. B 1
21 Shipton, Salop. C 11
36 Shipton, N. Yorks. A 3
8 Shipton Bellinger B 4
7 Shipton Gorge G 8
7 Shipton Green F 9
15 Shipton Moyne E 12
16 Shipton-on-Cherwell B 6
16 Shipton-under-Wychwood B 4
36 Shiptonthorpe C 6
17 Shirburn E 8
34 Shirdley Hill F 2
22 Shire Oak B 4
32 Shirebrook C 3
32 Shiregreen A 1
15 Shirehampton B 9
45 Shiremoor F 11
15 Shirenewton E 8
32 Shireoaks B 3
4 Shirewell Cross B 5
21 Shirl Heath F 10
32 Shirland D 1
31 Shirley, Derby F 10
8 Shirley, Hants. E 5
22 Shirley, W. Midlands D 5
9 Shirrell Heath E 7
4 Shirwell B 5
46 Shishkine F 4
21 Shobdon F 9
5 Shobrooke F 7
30 Shocklach E 3
19 Shoeburyness E 9
8 Sholden C 12
8 Sholing E 6
4 Shop, Cornwall D 1
4 Shop, Cornwall B 6
27 Shop Street H 5
44 Shopford F 4
18 Shoreditch F 3
10 Shoreham B 4
10 Shoreham-by-Sea G 1

56 Shoremill C 3
49 Shoresdean E 12
49 Shoreswood E 12
56 Shoretown D 2
16 Shornecote E 1
10 Shorne Ridgeway A 6
22 Short Heath, Leics. A 6
22 Short Heath, W. Midlands B 3
22 Short Heath, W. Midlands C 4
5 Shortacombe G 4
10 Shortgate G 4
2 Shortlanesend E 5
47 Shortlees F 9
15 Shortwood G 10
8 Shorwell H 6
7 Shoscombe A 10
30 Shotatton H 2
26 Shotesham F 6
19 Shotgate E 7
45 Shotley Bridge H 9
27 Shotley Gate M 5
27 Shotley Street M 5
45 Shotleyfield H 9
11 Shottenden C 9
9 Shottermill C 10
22 Shottery G 5
23 Shotteswell H 8
27 Shottisham L 6
31 Shottle E 11
29 Shotton, Clwyd C 12
40 Shotton, Durham A 4
49 Shotton, Northumb. F 11
40 Shotton Colliery A 4
48 Shotts C 1
30 Shotwick C 2
38 Shoughlaige-e-Caine G 1
56 Shougle D 8
24 Shouldham E 8
24 Shouldham Thorpe E 8
22 Shoulton F 2
10 Shover's Green E 5
21 Shrawardine A 9
22 Shrawley F 2
17 Shreding Green F 11
22 Shrewley E 5
21 Shrewsbury A 10
8 Shrewton B 2
9 Shripney F 10
16 Shrivenham E 3
26 Shropham F 3
19 Shrub End B 9
21 Shrucknall H 11
25 Shady Camps L 7
63 Shulishader C 6
38 Shundraw C 5
15 Shurdington B 12
17 Shurlock Row G 9
61 Shurrery Lodge B 10
6 Shurton B 5
22 Shustoke C 6
22 Shut End C 2
4 Shute, Devon F 8
6 Shute, Devon F 6
23 Shutford H 7
15 Shuthonger A 12
23 Shutlanger G 10
22 Shuttington B 6
32 Shuttlewood C 2
43 Sibbaldbie C 12
23 Sibbertoft D 10
21 Sibdon Carwood D 9
23 Sibford Ferris H 7
23 Sibford Gower H 7
27 Sible Hedingham M 1
33 Sibsey E 10
24 Sibson, Cambs. F 2
23 Sibson, Leics. B 7
32 Sibthorpe F 5
27 Sicklesmere J 2
35 Sicklinghall B 12
6 Sid G 5
57 Sidbury, Devon G 5
21 Sidbury, Salop. D 12
18 Sidcup G 5
38 Siddick B 2
31 Siddington, Ches. C 7
16 Siddington, Glos. D 1
32 Sidemoor E 3
6 Sidford G 5
9 Sidlesham F 10
10 Sidley G 6
10 Sidlow Bridge C 1
6 Sidmouth H 4
5 Sigford H 6
14 Siggiston G 3
37 Sigglesthorne C 9
17 Silchester H 7
38 Sileby A 9
38 Silecroft G 4
20 Silian G 1

24 Silk Willoughby A 2
35 Silkstone G 11
35 Silkstone Com. G 11
44 Silloans C 6
43 Silloth F 11
58 Sillyearn B 3
13 Siloh C 10
41 Silpho F 9
35 Silsden C 9
25 Silsoe M 2
25 Silver End, Beds. L 2
19 Silver End, Essex B 8
11 Silver Street B 7
48 Silverburn C 5
39 Silverdale, Lancs. H 7
31 Silverdale, Staffs. F 7
23 Silverstone H 10
6 Silverton, Devon F 3
47 Silverton, Strathclyde B 9
21 Silvington D 11
45 Simonburn F 7
6 Simonsbath B 1
34 Simonstone D 6
44 Simprim E 11
23 Simpson, Bucks. H 12
12 Simpson, Dyfed E 2
49 Sinclair's Hill D 10
47 Sinclairston H 9
40 Sinderby Quernhow G 4
45 Sinderhope H 7
17 Sindlesham G 8
44 Singdean C 4
17 Singleborough A 8
34 Singleton, Lancs. C 3
9 Singleton, W. Sussex E 10
10 Singlewell or Ifield A 5
30 Singret F 2
58 Sinnahard F 2
41 Sinnington G 7
22 Sinton Green F 2
18 Sipson F 1
14 Sirhowy C 5
7 Sissinghurst D 7
49 Sisterpath E 10
15 Siston G 10
2 Sithney G 3
11 Sittingbourne B 8
58 Sittyton E 6
22 Six Ashes C 2
32 Six Hills H 4
15 Six Mile Bottom J 7
31 Six Roads End G 10
33 Sixhills B 9
27 Sizewell J 8
61 Skail C 7
64 Skail, Egilsay, Orkney Is. B 3
64 Skaill, Mainland, Orkney Is. D 3
64 Skaill, Mainland, Orkney Is. C 1
47 Skares H 10
59 Skateraw, Grampian H 7
49 Skateraw, Lothian B 10
62 Skeabost C 3
25 Skeeby E 2
23 Skeffington B 11
37 Skeffling E 11
35 Skegby D 2
33 Skegness D 12
61 Skelbo G 8
36 Skelbrooke F 3
24 Skeldyke B 4
32 Skellingthorpe C 6
64 Skellister D 7
36 Skellow F 3
35 Skelmanthorpe F 11
34 Skelmersdale F 4
58 Skelmonae D 6
47 Skelmorlie C 7
58 Skelmuir D 7
61 Skelpick B 7
39 Skelton, Cumb. B 7
40 Skelton, Cleveland C 6
36 Skelton, Humber. E 5
36 Skelton, N. Yorks. B 3
36 Skelton, N. Yorks. E 1
40 Skelton, N. Yorks. H 4
38 Skelwirth Bridge E 6
64 Skelwick A 3
33 Skendleby C 11
58 Skene House F 5
15 Skenfrith B 8
37 Skerne B 8
46 Skeroblingarry G 2
61 Skerray B 7
60 Skerricha C 4
23 Skerton A 4
23 Sketchley C 7
13 Sketty H 9
13 Skewen G 10

40 Skewsby H 6
26 Skeyton C 5
60 Skiag Bridge E 4
61 Skibo Castle G 7
33 Skidbrooke A 11
37 Skidby D 8
63 Skigersta A 6
6 Skilgate D 3
32 Skillington H 6
43 Skinburness F 12
25 Skinidin C 1
41 Skinningrove C 7
46 Skipness D 4
9 Skipsea B 9
37 Skipsea Brough B 9
40 Skipton-on-Swale G 4
36 Skipwith C 4
24 Skirbeck A 4
48 Skirling E 3
17 Skirmett E 8
45 Skirpenbeck A 5
39 Skirwith, Cumb. B 8
39 Skirwith, N. Yorks. H 9
61 Skirza A 12
62 Skitby F 3
62 Skulamus F 6
60 Skullomie B 6
57 Skye of Curr G 5
35 Slack D 8
58 Slackhall B 9
58 Slackhead A 2
43 Slacks of Cairnbanno C 6
15 Slad D 12
18 Slade B 4
18 Slade Green F 5
3 Sladesbridge C 7
44 Slaggyford H 5
34 Slaidburn B 6
59 Slains Park K 6
49 Slainsfield E 12
45 Slaithwaite F 9
45 Slaley G 8
48 Slamannan B 1
17 Slapton, Bucks. B 10
5 Slapton, Devon L 7
23 Slapton, Northants. G 9
54 Slattadale C 3
35 Slattcks F 7
16 Slaugham E 1
30 Slaughter Hill E 6
3 Slaughterbridge A 8
15 Slaughterford G 11
23 Slawston C 11
9 Sleaford, Hants. B 9
24 Sleaford, Lincs. A 2
39 Sleagill C 8
21 Sleap A 11
4 Sleap A 11
15 Sledge Green A 11
37 Sledmere A 7
44 Sleetbeck E 3
39 Sleightholme D 11
41 Sleights D 8
8 Slepe G 1
4 Slerra D 2
46 Sliddery G 4
62 Sligachan E 4
51 Sligrachan H 9
38 Slimbridge D 10
31 Slindon, Staffs. G 7
9 Slindon, W. Sussex E 11
9 Slinfold C 12
9 Sling D 5
41 Slingsby H 7
58 Slioch D 3
25 Slip End, Beds. B 11
25 Slip End, Herts. L 4
26 Slipper's Bottom D 6
31 Slipton D 12
31 Slitting Mill H 9
57 Slochd G 4
57 Slochnacraig M 7
50 Slockavullin H 5
43 Slogarie E 7
35 Sloothby C 12
17 Slough F 10
6 Slough Green D 6
34 Slyne A 4
49 Smailholm F 9
45 Smaithwaite C 5
10 Small Dole G 1
11 Small Hythe E 7
35 Smallbridge F 8
26 Smallburgh C 6
58 Smallburn, Grampian D 8
47 Smallburn, Strathclyde G 11

32 Smalley F 1
10 Smallfield D 2
43 Smallholm D 11
6 Smallridge F 6
8 Smannel A 5
39 Smardale D 9
11 Smarden D 7
6 Smeatharpe E 5
11 Smeeth, Kent D 9
24 Smeeth, Norfolk E 6
23 Smeeton Westerby C 10
35 Smelthouses A 10
61 Smerral D 11
22 Smethwick C 4
31 Smisby H 12
34 Smith Green B 4
44 Smithfield F 3
6 Smithincott E 4
18 Smith's Green B 6
47 Smithston H 9
54 Smithstown B 2
56 Smithton E 3
32 Smithy Houses E 1
45 Snableazes B 10
43 Snade C 9
21 Snailbeach B 9
25 Snailwell H 7
41 Snainton G 9
36 Snaith E 4
33 Snape, Suffolk J 7
40 Snape, N. Yorks. G 3
34 Snape Green F 3
27 Snape Street J 7
23 Snarestone A 7
33 Snarford B 7
11 Snargate E 8
11 Snave E 9
21 Snead C 8
41 Sneaton D 9
41 Sneaton Thorpe E 9
33 Snelland B 8
31 Snelston F 10
24 Snettisham B 8
45 Snitter C 8
33 Snitterby A 7
22 Snitterfield F 5
21 Snitton E 11
21 Snodhill H 8
10 Snodland B 6
11 Snowdown C 11
16 Snowshill A 2
5 Soar, Devon M 6
13 Soar, Dyfed D 9
14 Soar, Powys A 3
9 Soberton D 7
9 Soberton Heath E 7
25 Soham H 7
12 Solbury F 2
4 Soldon Cross E 2
9 Soldridge C 8
10 Sole Street A 5
11 Solestreet C 9
22 Solihull D 5
21 Sollers Dilwyn G 9
15 Sollers Hope A 9
34 Sollom E 3
12 Solva E 2
44 Solwaybank E 1
21 Somerby, Leics. A 11
37 Somerby, Lincs. F 8
32 Somercotes E 2
8 Somerford G 3
16 Somerford Keynes E 1
9 Somerley F 9
26 Somerleyton F 8
31 Somersal Herbert G 10
33 Somersby C 10
6 Somerset, Co. C 6
25 Somersham, Cambs. H 5
27 Somersham, Suff. K 4
16 Somerton, Oxon. A 6
7 Somerton, Som. C 8
27 Somerton, Suffolk K 1
10 Sompting G 1
17 Sonning G 8
17 Sonning Common A 9
17 Sonning Eye F 8
59 Sootywells K 5
8 Sopley F 3
15 Sopworth F 11
44 Sorbie, Dumf. & Gall. D 2
42 Sorbie, Dumf. & Gall. G 5
44 Sorbietrees D 10
61 Sordale B 10
47 Sorn G 10
47 Sornbeg F 10
48 Sornfallow F 2
47 Sornhill F 10
50 Soroba Farm D 8
61 Sortat B 12
33 Sotby B 9

17 Sotwell E 7
29 Soughton D 11
17 Soulbury A 9
39 Soulby D 9
16 Souldern A 6
25 Souldrop J 1
64 Sound, Zetland, Shetland Is. D 7
64 Sound, Zetland, Shetland Is. E 7
49 Sourhope G 11
64 Sourin B 2
6 Sourton G 4
38 Soutergate G 5
26 South Acre D 1
5 South Allington M 7
52 South Alloa H 4
9 South Ambersham D 10
32 South Anston B 2
17 South Ascot G 10
8 South Baddesley F 5
50 South Balloch C 9
7 South Barrow C 9
28 South Beach G 3
48 South Bellsdyke A 2
19 South Benfleet E 7
9 South Bersted F 10
36 South Bramwith F 4
5 South Brent K 6
7 South Brewham C 10
52 South Bridge-end E 3
45 South Broomhill C 10
26 South Burlingham E 7
7 South Cadbury D 9
42 South Cairn E 1
33 South Carlton C 7
46 South Carrine H 2
37 South Cave D 7
16 South Cerney D 2
7 South Chard D 5
45 South Charlton A 9
7 South Cheriton D 10
36 South Cliffe D 6
32 South Clifton C 5
33 South Cockerington A 11
32 South Collingham D 5
14 South Cornelly F 1
27 South Cove G 8
51 South Creagan C 7
26 South Creake B 1
23 South Croxton A 10
37 South Dalton C 7
10 South Darenth A 4
63 South Dell A 6
58 South Denmore F 7
46 South Druimachro E 2
36 South Duffield C 4
33 South Elkington A 10
36 South Elmsall F 3
17 South End, Berks. B 7
17 South End, Bucks. B 9
34 South End, Cumb. A 1
37 South End, Humber. E 9
54 South Erradale C 1
19 South Fambridge D 8
16 South Fawley F 5
46 South Feorline G 4
37 South Ferriby E 7
58 South Fornet F 5
63 South Galson A 5
46 South Garrochty D 6
14 South Glamorgan, Co. G 4
8 South Gorley E 3
58 South Gorrachie B 5
19 South Green, Essex E 7
11 South Green, Kent B 7
46 South Hall B 5
19 South Hanningfield D 7
9 South Harting D 9
9 South Hayling F 8
45 South Hazelrigg C 11
17 South Heath D 10
10 South Heighton H 3
40 South Hetton A 4
36 South Hiendley F 2
3 South Hill, Corn. B 10
7 South Hill, Som. D 8
16 South Hunksey D 6
4 South Hole D 1
41 South Holme G 7
10 South Holmwood D 1
18 South Hornchurch F 5
47 South Hourat D 8
32 South Hykeham D 6
45 South Hylton G 11
60 South Keanchulish G 3
37 South Kelsey G 8
37 South Killingholme F 9
47 South Kilrusken D 7
40 South Kilvington G 4
23 South Kilworth D 9

36 South Kirkby ....F 2
59 South Kirktown ....G 5
33 South Kyme ....E 9
10 South Lancing ......H 1
16 South Leigh ....C 5
32 South Leverton .....B 5
47 South
    Limmerhaugh ..G 11
22 South Littleton .....G 4
27 South Lopham ......G 3
23 South Luffenham ..B 12
53 South Mains .....B 11
10 South Malling ......G 3
16 South Marston ......E 3
49 South Middleton ..G 12
36 South Milford ......D 3
5 South Milton ....L 6
18 South Mimms ......D 2
4 South Molton ......C 6
16 South Moreton .....E 6
9 South Mundham ...F 10
32 South Muskham ...E 5
37 South Newbald .....D 7
16 South Newington ...A 5
8 South Newton ......C 2
32 South Normanton ..E 2
18 South Norwood ....G 3
10 South Nutfield .....C 2
18 South Ockendon ...F 6
33 South Ormsby .....C 10
40 South Otterington ..F 4
33 South Owersby .....A 8
18 South Oxhey ....E 1
7 South Perrott ......F 8
7 South Petherton ...D 8
3 South Petherwin ..B 10
26 South Pickenham ...E 1
5 South Pool ....M 6
4 South Radworthy ..C 6
33 South Rauceby .....F 7
26 South Raynham ...C 2
33 South Reston .....B 11
24 South Runcton ....E 7
32 South Scarle ......D 6
63 South Shawbost ...B 3
45 South Shields ....F 12
34 South Shore ....D 2
37 South Skirlaugh ...C 7
33 South Somercotes .A 11
35 South Stainley .....A 1
18 South Stifford ....F 6
15 South Stoke, Avon
              H 10
17 South Stoke, Oxon. .F 7
9 South Stoke,
    W. Sussex ....E 11
11 South Street, Kent ..B 9
18 South Street,
    London ....H 4
10 South Street
    E. Sussex ....F 3
4 South Tawton ......F 5
33 South Thoresby ...C 11
8 South Tidworth ...A 4
9 South Town ....B 8
26 South Walsham ...D 7
9 S. Warnborough ..A 8
18 South Weald ....E 6
17 South Weston ....D 8
5 South Wheatley, Corn.
              G 1
32 South Wheatley, Notts.
              B 5
7 South Widcombe ....A 9
23 South Wigston ....B 9
33 South Willingham ..B 9
32 South Wingfield ....E 1
32 South Witham .....H 6
8 South Wonston .....B 6
19 South Woodham
    Ferrers ....D 6
24 South Wootton ....C 7
15 South Wraxall ...H 11
36 South Yorkshire, Co.
              G 2
4 South Zeal ....F 5
18 Southall F1
16 Southam, Glos B1
23 Southam, War. .....F 7
8 Southampton ......E 5
10 Southborough .....E 5
8 Southbourne, Dorset
              G 3
9 Southbourne,
    W. Sussex ....E 9
26 Southburgh ....E 3
37 Southburn ....B 7
19 Southchurch ......E 9
4 Southcott, Devon ..D 3
16 Southcott, Wilts ...H 3
44 Southdean ....G 5
10 Southease ....G 5
46 Southend, Strathclyde
              H 2

16 Southend, Wilts ....G 3
19 Southend-on-Sea ...E 8
14 Southerndown ......G 2
43 Southerness ......F 10
24 Southery ....F 7
41 Southfield ....G 7
41 Southfleet ....A 5
18 Southgate, London ..E 3
24 Southgate, Norfolk .B 8
26 Southgate, Norfolk ..C 4
13 Southgate, W. Glam H 9
25 Southill ....L 3
6 Southleigh ....G 5
19 Southminster ......D 9
45 Southmoor ....B 10
27 Southoe ....J 3
27 Southolt ....H 5
35 Southorpe ....E 2
35 Southowram ......E 10
34 Southport ....E 2
26 Southrepps ....B 6
33 Southrey D8
16 Southrop ....D 3
9 Southrope ....D 8
9 Southsea ....F 8
64 Southtown ....E 3
18 Southwark ....E 3
9 Southwater ....D 12
15 Southway ....B 8
7 Southwell, Dorset ..H 7
32 Southwell, Notts ...E 4
45 Southwick, Tyne
    & Wear ....G 12
9 Southwick, Hants ..E 8
24 Southwick,
    Northants ....F 1
10 Southwick,
    W. Sussex ....G 1
5 Southwick, Wilts ..A 11
27 Southwold ....H 8
26 Southwood, Norf ...E 7
7 Southwood, Som. ..C 9
49 Soutra Mains .....C 7
63 Soval Lodge ....D 4
35 Sowerby, N. Yorks. .G 4
35 Sowerby, W. Yorks. .E 9
35 Sowerby Bridge ...E 9
38 Sowerby Row ......A 6
6 Sowton ....G 3
44 Spadeadam ....F 4
36 Spalding ....C 3
36 Spaldington ....D 5
25 Spaldwick ....H 2
53 Spalefield ....F 10
32 Spalford ....C 5
24 Spanby ....B 2
26 Sparham ....D 4
38 Spark Bridge .....G 5
7 Sparkford ....D 9
38 Sparklow ....D 9
5 Sparkwell ....K 4
31 Sparrowpit ....B 9
16 Sparsholt, Hants. ..C 6
16 Sparsholt, Oxon ..E 4
45 Spartylea ....H 7
41 Spaunton ....F 7
6 Spaxton ....C 6
55 Spean Bridge .....L 6
8 Spearywell ....C 4
43 Speddoch ....C 9
16 Speen, Berks. .....G 5
17 Speen, Bucks. .....D 9
41 Speeton ....H 11
30 Speke ....B 3
10 Speldhurst ....D 4
18 Spellbrook ....B 5
18 Spelsbury ....B 4
14 Spelter ....E 2
17 Spencers Wood ...G 8
41 Spennithorne .....F 2
40 Spennymoor ....B 3
22 Spetchley ....G 2
7 Spetisbury ......F 12
27 Spexhall ....G 7
58 Spey Bay ....A 1
37 Speybridge ....G 6
56 Speyview ....E 8
33 Spilsby ....D 11
45 Spindlestone ....D 11
32 Spinkhill ....B 2
35 Spinney Hills .....B 9
61 Spinningdale ......G 7
61 Spital ....B 11
33 Spital in the Street ..B 8
21 Spitalford ....A 10
10 Spithurst ....F 3
49 Spittal, Dumf. &
    Gall. ....E 5
42 Spittal, Dumf. &
    Gall. ....F 4
12 Spittal, Dyfed ....E 3
49 Spittal, Lothian ...B 7
49 Spittal, Northumb. .D 12

36 Spittal, Humberside .B 5
59 Spittal of Glenmuick .J 1
57 Spittal of Glenshee .M 7
59 Spittalburn ....J 4
52 Spittalfield ....C 6
26 Spixworth ....D 5
35 Spofforth ....B 12
29 Spon Green ......D 12
32 Spondon ....G 1
26 Spooner Row .....F 4
26 Sporle ....D 2
49 Spott ....B 9
49 Spottiswoode ....D 8
23 Spratton ....E 10
18 Spreakley ....B 9
4 Spreyton ....F 6
10 Splayne's Green ...F 3
35 Spofforth ....B 12
29 Spon Green ......D 12
33 Spridlington ....B 7
38 Spring Valley .....H 2
47 Springburn ......C 10
44 Springfield, Dumf. &
    Gall. ....F 2
19 Springfield, Essex ...C 7
53 Springfield, Fife ...F 8
56 Springfield,
    Grampiam ......D 6
22 Springfield, W.
    Midlands ....D 4
33 Springhill ....B 3
43 Springholm ....E 9
44 Springkell ....E 1
47 Springside ....E 8
32 Springthorpe .....A 6
32 Springthorpe .....A 6
45 Springwell ....G 11
37 Sproatley ....D 9
30 Sproston Green ...C 6
36 Spotbrough ....G 3
27 Sproughton ......L 4
49 Sprouston ....F 10
26 Sprowston ....D 6
32 Sproxton, Leics. ...H 6
40 Sproxton, N. Yorks .G 6
30 Spurstow ....E 4
57 Sronlairig Lodge ...J 1
57 Sronpadruig ......L 3
57 Stackhouse ....A 7
12 Stackpole ....G 3
35 Stacksteads ....E 7
5 Staddiscombe ....K 4
36 Staddlethorpe ....E 6
17 Stadhampton .....D 7
39 Staffield ....A 8
62 Staffin ....A 4
31 Stafford ....H 8
31 Staffordshire, Co ..H 8
49 Stagehall ....E 7
24 Stag's Holt ....E 5
25 Stagsden ....K 1
25 Stagsden W. End ..K 1
35 Stainburn ....B 11
32 Stainby ....H 6
35 Staincross ....F 12
17 Staines ....G 11
33 Stainfield, Lincs. ..C 8
24 Stainfield, Lincs. ...C 2
39 Stainforth,
    N. Yorks. ....H 10
36 Stainforth, S. Yorks. .F 4
34 Staining ....D 2
35 Stainland ....E 9
41 Stainsacre ....D 9
40 Stainton, Cleveland .D 5
39 Stainton, Cumb. ...B 7
39 Stainton, Cumbria .G 7
40 Stainton, Dur. .....C 1
40 Stainton, N. Yorks. .F 1
32 Stainton, S. Yorks. .A 3
33 Stainton by
    Langworth ......B 8
37 Stainton le Vale ..H 9
38 Stainton with
    Agarley ....H 5
41 Staintondale .....E 10
38 Stair, Cumb. ......C 5
47 Stair, Strathclyde ...G 9
41 Staithes ....C 8
34 Stake Pool ....B 3
45 Stakeford ....D 11
45 Stakeford ....D 11
26 Stalham ....C 7
26 Stalham Green ...C 7
11 Stalisfield Green ..C 8
39 Stalling Busk ....G 11
37 Stallingborough ...F 9
34 Stalmine ....C 3
35 Stalybridge .....G 8
25 Stambourne ....L 8
24 Stamford, Lincs. ..E 1
45 Stamford,
    Northumb. ......A 10

36 Stamford Bridge ....B 5
45 Stamfordham .....F 9
38 Stanah ....C 6
38 Stanborough ......C 2
17 Stanbridge, Beds. ..B 10
8 Stanbridge, Dorset ..F 2
35 Stanbury ....C 9
47 Stand ....C 12
48 Standburn ....B 2
40 Standeford ....A 3
11 Standen ....D 7
7 Standerwick ....A 11
29 Standford ....C 9
34 Standish ....F 4
16 Standlake ....D 5
8 Standon, Hants. ...C 6
18 Standon, Herts ....B 4
30 Standon, Staffs. ...G 6
30 Standon Massey ..D 6
27 Standwell Green ...H 4
48 Stane ....C 2
26 Stanfield ....C 2
25 Stanford, Beds. ...L 3
11 Stanford, Kent ...D 10
21 Stanford Bishop ..G 12
22 Stanford Bridge ...F 1
16 Stanford Dingley ..G 6
19 Stanford le Hope ...F 7
23 Stanford on Avon ..D 9
32 Stanford on Soar ..H 3
21 Stanford on Teme .F 12
18 Stanford Rivers ...D 5
16 Stanford the Vale ..E 4
10 Stnaford's End ....D 3
24 Stranground ......H 2
26 Stanhoe ....B 1
39 Stanhope ....A 12
23 Stanion ....C 12
52 Stank ....F 1
32 Stanley, Derby ....F 1
45 Stanley, Dur. .....H 10
31 Stanley, Staffs. ...E 8
32 Stanley, Tayside ...D 6
16 Stanley, Wilts .....G 1
35 Stanley, W. Yorks. .E 12
32 Stanley Common ...F 1
21 Stanley Hill .....H 12
35 Stanley Lane Ends .E 12
10 Stanmer ....G 2
16 Stanmore, Berks. ..F 6
8 Stanmore, Hants. ...C 6
18 Stanmore, London ..E 2
44 Stannersburn .....D 5
45 Stannington,
    Northumb. ......E 10
31 Stannington,
    S. Yorks ....A 11
21 Stansbatch ....F 9
27 Stansfield ....K 1
27 Stanshope ....C 7
27 Stanstead ....K 1
18 Stanstead Abbots ..C 4
27 Stanstead Street ...K 1
10 Stansted ....B 5
18 Stansted
    Mountfitchet ....A 5
31 Stanton, Derby ..H 11
16 Stanton, Glos .....A 2
14 Stanton, Gwent ...E 3
45 Stanton,Northumb. .D 9
31 Stanton, Staffs. ...F 9
27 Stanton, Suffolk ...H 2
31 Stanton by Bridge .G 12
15 Stanton by Dale ...F 2
15 Stanton Drew .....H 9
16 Stanton Fitzwarren .E 3
16 Stanton Harcourt ..D 5
32 Stanton Hill ......D 2
31 Stanton in Peak ..D 11
21 Stanton Lacy ....E 10
21 Stanton Long ....C 11
32 Stanton on the
    Wolds ....G 3
15 Stanton Prior ....H 10
16 Stanton St. Bernard .H 2
17 Stanton St. John ...C 7
15 Stanton St.
    Quintin ....F 12
27 Stanton Street ....J 3
23 Stanton under
    Bardon ....A 8
30 Stanton upon Hine
    Heath ....H 4
15 Stanton Wick ......H 9
30 Stanwardine in the
    Fields ....H 3
19 Stanway, Essex ...B 9
16 Stanway, Glos. ....A 2
17 Stanwell ....G 11
17 Stanwell Moor ...G 11
25 Stanwick ....H 1
41 Stape ....F 8
8 Stapehill ....F 2
30 Stapeley ....E 5

31 Stapenhill ......H 11
11 Staple, Kent .....B 11
6 Staple, Somerset ..B 4
6 Staple Cross, Devon D 4
10 Staple Cross, E. Sussex
              F 6
6 Staple Fitzpaine ..D 6
15 Staple Hill ....G 9
10 Staplefield ....E 2
25 Stapleford, Cambs. .K 6
18 Stapleford, Heref.
    & Worc. ....B 3
32 Stapleford, Leics. ..H 5
32 Stapleford, Lincs. .D 6
32 Stapleford, Notts. ...F 2
8 Stapleford, Wilts. ..B 2
18 Stapleford Abbotts .D 5
18 Stapleford Tawney ..D 5
6 Staplegrove ....D 6
6 Staplehay ....D 5
10 Staplehurst ....D 6
44 Stapleton, Cumb. ...F 3
21 Stapleton, Heref.
    & Worc. ....F 9
23 Stapleton, Leics. ...B 8
40 Stapleton, N. Yorks.
              D 3
21 Stapleton, Salop ..B 10
7 Stapleton, Som ....D 8
44 Stapleton Grange ..F 1
6 Stapley ....E 5
25 Staploe ....J 2
12 Star, Dyfed ......C 6
53 Star, Fife ....G 8
15 Star, Somerset ....H 7
39 Starbottom ......H 11
64 Starcross ....H 3
64 Starkigarth ....E 7
25 Starlings Green ...M 6
15 Starston ....G 5
39 Starforth ....D 12
15 Startley ....F 12
30 Statham ....B 5
7 Stathe ....C 7
32 Stathern ....G 5
40 Station Town .....B 4
25 Staughton Green ..J 2
25 Staughton Highway .J 2
15 Staunton, Glos. ...C 9
15 Staunton, Glos. ..A 11
31 Staunton Harold
    Hall ....H 12
32 Staunton in the Vale .F 5
21 Staunton on Arrow .F 9
21 Staunton on Wye ...H 9
38 Staveley, Cumbria ..G 6
38 Staveley, Cumbria ..E 7
32 Stavely, Derby .....C 2
35 Staveley, N. Yorks. .A 12
5 Staverton, Devon ..J 7
15 Staverton, Glos. ..B 12
23 Staverton, Northants.F 9
15 Staverton, Wilts. .H 11
15 Staverton Bridge ..B 12
7 Stawell ....B 7
6 Stawford ....G 3
6 Stawley ....D 4
64 Staxigoe ....B 12
41 Staxton ....G 10
20 Staylittle ....C 4
32 Staynall ....C 2
32 Staythorpe ....E 5
40 Stean ....H 1
40 Stearsby ....H 6
6 Steart ....B 6
18 Stebbing ....B 6
64 Stebbligrind ......H 7
11 Stedham ....D 10
45 Steel Rigg ....E 8
44 Steele Road ......B 6
21 Steen's Bridge ...G 11
9 Steep ....D 9
7 Steeple, Dorset ..H 12
19 Steeple, Essex ....D 9
7 Steeple Ashton ...A 12
16 Steeple Aston .....B 6
16 Steeple Barton ...B 5
25 Steeple Bumpstead .L 8
17 Steeple Claydon ...A 8
25 Steeple Gidding ...G 2
8 Steeple Langford ..B 2
16 Steeple Morden ...L 4
35 Steeton ....C 9
62 Stein ....C 2
45 Stelling Hall .....F 8
11 Stelling Minnis ...C 10
35 Stenalees ....D 7
48 Stenhousemuir ....A 2
64 Stenness ....C 6
62 Stenscholl ....A 4
31 Stenson ....G 11
64 Stenswall ....D 7

49 Stenton ....B 9
12 Stepaside ....F 5
43 Stepends ....C 9
18 Stepney ....F 4
25 Steppingley ......M 1
47 Stepps ....C 11
27 Sternfield ....J 7
16 Stert ....H 1
25 Stetchworth .....J 7
18 Stevenage ....B 2
47 Stevenston ......E 7
9 Steventon, Hants. .A 7
16 Steventon, Oxon. ..E 5
25 Stevington ....K 1
25 Stewarby ....L 1
46 Stewarton,
    Strathclyde ......G 2
47 Stewarton,
    Strathclyde ......E 9
17 Stewkley ....B 9
33 Stewton ....B 10
12 Steynton ....F 4
4 Stibb ....E 1
4 Stibb Cross ......D 3
16 Stibb Green ......H 3
26 Stibbard ....C 3
24 Stibbington ......F 2
49 Stichill ....F 9
3 Sticker ....E 7
33 Stickford ....D 10
3 Sticklepath, Devon .F 5
6 Sticklepath, Som. ..E 6
33 Stickney ....D 10
26 Stiffkey ....A 3
18 Stifford ....F 6
22 Stifford's Bridge ..G 1
10 Stile Bridge ......C 6
36 Stillingfleet ......C 4
40 Stillington,
    Cleveland ....C 4
40 Stillington,
    N. Yorks. ....H 6
24 Stilton ....E 3
31 Stinchcombe ....D 10
7 Stinsford ....G 10
21 Stirchley ....B 12
61 Stirkoke House ...C 12
52 Stirling, Central ...H 3
38 Stirling, Grampian ..C 8
19 Stisted ....A 8
16 Stitchcombe ......G 3
3 Stithians ....F 4
56 Stittenham ......B 2
23 Stivichall ....D 7
33 Stixwould ....D 9
30 Stoak ....C 3
48 Stobo ....F 4
7 Stoborough ......H 12
7 Stoborough Grn. ..H 12
35 Stobs Castle ......B 3
49 Stobswood, Borders D 9
45 Stobswood,
    Northumb. ......D 10
48 Stobwood ....D 2
19 Stock ....D 7
22 Stock Wood ....F 3
58 Stockbridge,
    Grampian ....C 8
8 Stockbridge, Hants. .C 5
43 Stockbridgehill ....D 12
47 Stockbriggs .....F 12
11 Stockbury ....B 7
16 Stockcross ....G 5
38 Stockdale Wath ....A 6
23 Stockerston .....B 11
9 Stockholm ....B 11
47 Stockiemuir ......A 10
18 Stocking Pelham ..A 4
23 Stockingford .....C 7
6 Stockland ....F 6
6 Stockland Bristol ..B 6
4 Stockleigh English .E 7
4 Stockleigh Pomeroy .F 7
16 Stockley ....G 1
7 Stocklinch ....E 7
31 Stockport ....A 7
35 Stocksbridge .....G 11
45 Stocksfield ......G 9
21 Stockton, Heref.
    & Worcs. ....F 10
26 Stockton, Norfolk ..F 7
21 Stockton, Salop ...B 8
22 Stockton, Salop ...B 1
23 Stockton, War. ....F 8
8 Stockton, Wilts. ..B 1
30 Stockton Heath ...B 5
40 Stocktonon-Tees ..C 4
22 Stockton on Teme ..E 1
36 Stockton-on-the-
    Forest ....B 4
18 Stodmarsh ......B 11
26 Stody ....B 4
60 Stoer ....D 2
7 Stoford, Som. .....E 9

ST		GREAT BRITAIN INDEX	SY

8 Stoford, Wilts.......C 2
6 Stogumber........C 4
6 Stogursey.........B 5
4 Stoke, Devon.....D 1
8 Stoke, Hants......A 5
9 Stoke, Hants......F 8
11 Stoke, Kent.......A 7
27 Stoke, Suffolk...L 5
7 Stoke Abbott......F 8
23 Stoke Albany....C 11
27 Stoke Ash........H 4
32 Stoke Bardolph....F 4
21 Stoke Bliss.......F 12
23 Stoke Bruerne....G 10
25 Stoke-by-Clare.....L 8
27 Stoke-by-Nayland..L 3
6 Stoke Canon......F 3
8 Stoke Charity.....B 6
8 Stoke Climsland..B 10
21 Stoke Cross......G 11
17 Stoke D`Abernon..H 12
25 Stoke Doyle......G 1
23 Stoke Dry.......B 12
21 Stoke Edith......H 11
8 Stoke Farthing....D 2
24 Stoke Ferry......E 8
5 Stoke Fleming....L 7
5 Stoke Gabriel.....K 7
15 Stoke Gifford....F 9
23 Stoke Golding.....B 7
23 Stoke Goldington.G 11
17 Stoke Green.....F 10
17 Stoke Hammond...A 9
26 Stoke Holy Cross..E 5
21 Stoke Lacy......G 11
16 Stoke Lyne......A 6
17 Stoke Mandeville..C 9
18 Stoke Newington..E 3
31 Stoke-on-Trent....F 7
15 Stoke Orchard...A 12
6 Stoke Pero......B 2
17 Stoke Poges.....F 10
21 Stoke Prior,
    Heref. & Worcs..G 10
22 Stoke Prior,
    Heref. & Worcs...E 3
4 Stoke Rivers......C 5
32 Stoke Rochford...G 6
17 Stoke Row......F 8
7 Stoke St. Gregory...D 7
6 Stoke St. Mary...D 6
7 Stoke St. Michael..B 10
21 Stoke
    St. Milborough..D 11
7 Stoke sub Hamdon..D 8
17 Stoke Talmage...D 7
7 Stoke Trister....C 10
30 Stoke upon Tern...G 5
30 Stoke Wake.....F 11
7 Stokeford.......G 12
32 Stokeham.......C 5
5 Stokeinteignhead..J 8
17 Stokenchurch....D 8
5 Stokenham.......L 7
21 Stokesay.......D 10
26 Stokesby.......D 1
40 Stokesley.......D 5
6 Stolford.........B 5
7 Ston Easton......A 9
17 Stone, Bucks....C 8
15 Stone, Glos......E 10
22 Stone, Heref.
    & Worc.......E 2
10 Stone,Kent.......A 4
11 Stone, Staffs....G 7
7 Stone Allerton...A 7
24 Stone Bridge Corner E 4
35 Stone Chair.....D 10
4 Stone Cross, Devon .C 5
11 Stone Cross, Kent .D 9
10 Stone Cross,
    W. Sussex......H 5
39 Stone House......G 10
10 Stone Street.....C 4
26 Stonebridge, Norf..B 6
22 Stonebridge,
    W. Midlands....D 5
32 Stonebroom......D 1
10 Stonecrouch......E 6
15 Stone-edge Batch..G 8
37 Stoneferry......D 8
47 Stonefield......D 11
46 Stonefield Castle
    Hotel.........B 4
44 Stonegarthside....E 3
10 Stonegate, E. Sussex E 5
41 Stonegate, N. Yorks D 8
58 Stonegate Crofts...D 8
41 Stonegrave......G 7
44 Stonehaugh......E 6
59 Stonehaven.......J 6
5 Stonehouse, Devon .K 3
43 Stonehouse, Dumf.
    & Gall.........E 9

15 Stonehouse, Glos. .D 11
44 Stonehouse,
    Northumb......G 5
47 Stonehouse,
    Strathclyde.....E 12
23 Stoneleigh.......E 7
25 Stonely.........J 2
19 Stone's Green....A 11
32 Stonesby.......H 5
16 Stonesfield......B 5
38 Stonethwaite.....D 5
8 Stoney Cross.....E 4
31 Stoney Middleton..C 10
23 Stoney Stanton....C 8
7 Stoney Stoke....C 10
7 Stoney Stratton...B 10
21 Stoney Stretton...A 9
48 Stoneyburn, Lothian C 2
48 Stoneyburn,
    Strathclyde.....G 2
23 Stoneygate.......B 9
19 Stoneyhills......D 9
42 Stoneykirk......F 2
58 Stoneywood......F 6
27 Stonham Aspal....J 4
17 Stonor.........E 8
23 StontonWyville...C 10
4 Stony Cross, Devon .C 4
22 Stony Cross,
    Heref. & Worc...G 1
34 Stony Hill......D 2
23 Stony Stratford...H 11
4 Stoodleigh, Devon ..C 5
6 Stoodleigh, Devon .D 3
9 Stopham........D 11
17 Stopsley.......B 12
30 Storeton.......B 2
35 Storiths........B 9
63 Stornoway......D 5
22 Storridge.......G 1
9 Storrington.....E 12
39 Storth.........G 7
36 Storwood.......C 5
56 Stotfield........C 8
25 Stotfold........L 3
21 Stottesdon......D12
23 Stoughton, Leics...B 9
9 Stoughton, Surrey .A 11
9 Stoughton,
    W.Sussex......E 9
55 Stoul..........K 1
22 Stourlton.......G 3
7 Stour Provost....D 11
7 Stour Row......D 11
22 Stourbridge.....D 2
7 Stourpaine......E 12
22 Stourport-on-
    Severn........D 2
22 Stourton, Staffs....D 2
22 Stourton, War....H 6
7 Stourton, Wilts...C 11
7 Stourton Caundle..E 10
64 Stove..........B 3
27 Stoven.........G 7
24 Stow Bardolph....E 7
26 Stow Bedon.....F 3
25 Stow cum Quy...J 6
22 Stow Longa.....H 2
19 Stow Maries.....D 8
16 Stow-on-the-Wold..B 3
24 Stowbridge......E 7
21 Stowe, Salop....E 8
31 Stowe-by-Chartley .H 8
15 Stowe Green....D 9
7 Stowell........D10
27 Stowlangtoft.....H 3
27 Stowmarket.....J 3
11 Stowting.......D 10
22 Stowupland.....J 4
46 Straad.........C 5
57 Straanruie......H 6
59 Strachan.......H 4
51 Strachur.......G 8
27 Stradbroke......H 5
25 Stradishall......K 8
24 Stradsett.......E 8
32 Stragglethorpe...E 6
43 Strahanna......B 7
42 Straid.........C 2
43 Straith.........C 9
42 Straiton.......A 5
58 Stralock, Grampian .E 6
52 Straloch, Tayside ..A 5
31 Stramshall......G 9
59 Stranathro......H 6
49 Stranghow......D 7
51 Stranog........H 6
42 Stranraer.......E 1

20 Strata Florida......F 3
17 Stratfield Mortimer .H 7
17 Stratfield Saye....H 8
17 Stratfield Turgis...H 8
18 Stratford.......F 4
27 Stratford St. Andrew J 6
27 Stratford St. Mary .M 3
8 Stratford sub Castle .C 3
8 Stratford Tony...C 2
22 Stratford-upon-
    Avon.........G 5
52 Strathallan Castle..F 4
55 Strathan, Highland .K 3
60 Strathan, Highland .E 2
60 Strathan, Highland .A 6
47 Strathaven.....E 12
47 Strathblane.....B 10
54 Strathcarron.....E 3
50 Strathcoil.......D 4
58 Strathdon.......F 1
60 Strathkanaird....F 3
53 Strathkinness....F 7
57 Strathmashie Ho...K 2
53 Strathmiglo......F 7
61 Strathmore Hotel ..C 10
54 Strathpeffer......D 8
54 Strathrannoch....B 8
54 Strathvaich Lo....B 7
61 Strathy.........A 8
61 Strathy Inn......A 8
52 Strathyre.......E 1
4 Stratton, Corn....E 1
7 Stratton, Dorset...G 10
16 Stratton, Glos....D 1
17 Stratton Audley...B 7
7 Stratton-on-the-
    Fosse........A 10
16 Stratton
    St. Margaret.....E 3
26 Stratton St. Michael .F 5
26 Stratton Strawless...C 5
53 Stravithie......F 10
10 Streat.........F 2
18 Streatham......G 3
17 Streatley, Beds ...A 11
17 Streatley, Berks....F 7
7 Street, Somerset...C 8
41 Street, Yorks......E 7
30 Street Dinas.....F 2
11 Street End, Kent ...C 10
9 Street End,
    W. Sussex......F 10
36 Street Houses......C 3
57 Street of
    Kincardine.....H 5
22 Streethay.......A 5
36 Streethouse.....E 2
40 Streetlam.......E 3
22 Streetly.........B 4
21 Strefford.......D 10
32 Strelley.........F 2
36 Strensall.......A 4
25 Strethall.......L 6
25 Stretham.......H 6
30 Stretton, Cheshire..B 5
30 Stretton, Cheshire..B 5
32 Stretton, Derby...D 1
23 Stretton, Leics.....A 12
22 Stretton, Staffs....A 2
31 Stretton, Staffs...G 11
22 Stretton en le Field .A 6
21 Stretton
    Grandison......H 11
21 Stretton Heath....A 9
23 Stretton-on-
    Dunsmore......E 7
22 Stretton on Fosse..H 6
21 Stretton Sugwas...H 10
23 Stretton-under-
    Fosse.........D 8
58 Strichen........B 7
6 Stringston......B 5
23 Strixton.......F 12
15 Stroat.........E 9
54 Stromeferry.....F 2
54 Stromemore.....F 2
64 Stromness......D 1
55 Stronachlachar...F 11
55 Stronchreggan Ho..M 4
63 Strond.........H 1
55 Strone, Highland..L 5
57 Strone, Highland..G 1
47 Strone, Strathclyde .A 7
51 Strone, Strathclyde H 10
60 Stronechrubie....E 4
55 Stronenaba......L 6
57 Stronetoper.....K 4
51 Stronmilchan....E 8
50 Strontian......A 5
50 Strontoiller.....E 6
51 Stronuich......C 12
10 Strood.........A 6

10 Strood Green.......C 1
15 Stroud, Glos. ....D 11
9 Stroud, Hants....D 8
17 Stroud Green....E 8
17 Stroude.......G 11
32 Stroxton.......G 6
33 Struan.........D 3
33 Strubby........B 11
26 Strumpshaw....E 6
54 Struy..........F 8
58 Stuartfield......C 7
38 Stub Place......F 3
35 Stubbington.....F 7
35 Stubbins.......E 7
11 Stubbs Cross....D 8
44 Stubbyknowe....F 2
28 Stubhampton....E 1
44 Stublick........G 6
32 Stubshaw Cross...G 5
32 Stubton.......E 6
46 Stuck..........B 5
52 Stuckgowan.....G 10
51 Stuckindroin....F 10
8 Stuckton.......E 3
9 Stud Green......F 9
45 Studdon........H 7
39 Studfold.......E 9
17 Studham......C 11
8 Studland.......H 2
17 Studley, Oxon....C 7
22 Studley, War.....F 4
16 Studley, Wilts....G 1
40 Studley Roger....H 3
25 Stump Cross.....L 6
25 Stuntney.......G 7
10 Stunts Green.....G 5
7 Sturbridge......G 7
25 Sturmer.......L 8
7 Sturminster Com. .E 11
8 Sturminster
    Marshall.......F 1
7 Sturminster
    Newton.......E 11
11 Sturry ....B 10
37 Sturton.........G 7
32 Sturton le Steeple..B 5
27 Stuston.........H 4
27 Stutton, Suffolk...M 4
36 Stutton, N. Yorks...C 3
31 Styal..........B 7
31 Styrrup........A 3
58 Succoth, Grampian .D 2
51 Succoth, Highland .G 10
21 Suckley........G 12
25 Sudborough.....G 1
27 Sudbourne......K 7
15 Sudbrook, Gwent..F 8
33 Sudbrook, Lincs...F 7
33 Sudbrooke......C 7
31 Sudbury, Derby ...G 10
18 Sudbury, London...E 2
27 Sudbury, Suffolk..L 2
56 Suddie.........D 2
15 Sudgrove......D 12
26 Suffield, Norfolk...B 5
41 Suffield, N. Yorks. F 10
27 Suffolk, County...J 4
30 Sugnall........G 6
61 Suisgill.........E 9
62 Suisnish.......E 5
30 Sulby.........G 2
23 Sulgrave.......H 9
17 Sulham........G 7
17 Sulhamstead.....G 7
17 Sulhamstead
    Abbots.......G 7
62 Sulishaderbeg....D 4
9 Sullington......E 12
64 Sullom........C 7
14 Sully..........G 5
29 Summer Hill....E 12
35 Summerbridge ...A 10
2 Summercourt....D 6
40 Summerhouse....C 2
15 Summerleaze....F 7
17 Summerseat.....F 7
16 Summertown....C 2
35 Summit, Lancs...F 8
35 Summit, Lancs...E 8
17 Sunbury on
    Thames.........G 11
43 Sundaywell.....C 9
38 Sunderland, Cumb. B 4
34 Sunderland, Lancs .B 3
45 Sunderland, Tyne
    & Wear.......G 12
40 Sunderland Bridge .A 3
18 Sundon Park.....B 11
10 Sundridge......C 4
50 Sunipol.........G 1
37 Sunk Island.....E 10
17 Sunningdale......G 10

17 Sunninghill ....G 10
16 Sunningwell ....D 6
40 Sunniside, Dur....A 2
45 Sunniside, Tyne
    & Wear.......G 10
38 Sunny Bank.....F 5
56 Sunnyhillock....D 4
52 Sunnylaw.......G 3
10 Sunnyside......D 3
8 Sunton.........A 4
49 Sunwick......D 11
18 Surbiton.......G 2
38 Surby.........H 1
24 Surfleet.........C 3
24 Surfleet Seas End ...C 4
26 Surlingham......E 6
10 Surrey, County...C 2
26 Sustead........B 5
36 Susworth......G 6
4 Sutcombe......E 2
64 Sutherland......E 2
26 Suton..........E 5
56 Sutors of Cromarty ..C 4
33 Sutterby.......C 11
24 Sutterton......B 4
17 Sutton, Beds....K 3
17 Sutton, Berks....F 11
25 Sutton, Cambs....G 5
24 Sutton, Cambs....F 2
11 Sutton, Kent....C 12
18 Sutton, London...H 3
24 Sutton, Norfolk...C 7
32 Sutton, Notts....B 4
32 Sutton, Notts....F 5
16 Sutton, Oxon....C 5
22 Sutton, Salop....C 1
30 Sutton, Salop....G 5
7 Sutton, Som.....C 9
36 Sutton, S. Yorks...F 3
30 Sutton, Staffs....H 6
27 Sutton, Suffolk...H 6
10 Sutton, Surrey...B 12
9 Sutton, W. Sussex .E 11
23 Sutton Basset....C 11
10 Sutton at Hone....A 4
15 Sutton Benger....F 12
32 Sutton Bonington..H 2
24 Sutton Bridge....C 6
23 Sutton Cheney...B 7
22 Sutton Coldfield...B 5
16 Sutton Courtenay..C 6
24 SuttonCrosses....C 5
40 Sutton Grange....H 3
9 Sutton Green....A 11
40 Sutton Howgrave .G 3
32 Sutton in Ashfield ..D 2
23 Sutton in the Elms..C 8
31 Sutton Lane Ends...C 8
21 Sutton Maddock...B 12
7 Sutton Mallet....C 7
8 Sutton Mandeville .C 1
7 Sutton Montis....D 9
37 Sutton-on-Hull...D 9
33 Sutton on Sea....B 12
36 Sutton-on-the-
    Forest........A 4
31 Sutton on the Hill .G 11
32 Sutton on Trent...D 5
24 Sutton St. Edmund .D 5
24 Sutton St. James...D 5
21 Sutton St. Michael .H 10
21 Sutton St. Nicholas H 10
8 Sutton Scotney....B 6
22 Sutton-under-
    Brailes........H 6
40 Sutton-under-
    Whitestonecliffe .G 5
36 Sutton upon
    Derwent.......B 5
11 Sutton Valence...C 7
7 Sutton Veny....B 11
7 Sutton Waldron ..E 12
15 Sutton Wick.....H 9
33 Swaby.........B 11
31 Swadlincote.....H 11
26 Swaffham......E 1
25 Swaffham Bulbeck .J 7
25 Swaffham Prior...J 7
26 Swafield........B 6
40 Swainby.......E 5
26 Swainsthorpe....E 5
15 Swainswick.....G 10
33 Swalcliffe......H 7
11 Swalecliffe.....A 10
37 Swallow........G 9
17 Swallowcliffe....C 1
17 Swallowfield....H 8
32 Swallownest.....B 2
15 Swalwell......G 10
30 Swan Green.....C 6
8 Swanage......H 2

64 Swanbister.........D 2
17 Swanbourne.....A 9
63 Swanibost......A 6
37 Swanland......D 7
10 Swanley........A 4
10 Swanley Village...A 4
9 Swanmore......D 7
23 Swannington, Leics. A 7
26 Swannington, Norf. D 4
10 Swanscombe....A 5
13 Swansea......H 10
26 Swanton Abbott..C 6
26 Swanton Morley..D 3
26 Swanton Novers..B 3
32 Swanwick......E 1
24 Swarby.........B 1
26 Swardeston.....E 5
31 Swarkestone....G 12
45 Swarland......C 10
45 Swarland Estate ..C 10
9 Swarraton......B 7
32 Swaton........B 2
25 Swavesey......H 5
8 Sway..........F 4
33 Swayfield.......H 7
9 Swaythling.....D 6
21 Sweet Green....F 12
7 Sweetham......F 7
39 Sweetholme....C 8
49 Sweethope......E 9
3 Sweethouse....C 8
27 Swefling........J 6
23 Swepstone......A 7
16 Swerford......A 5
30 Swettenham....C 6
27 Swilland.......K 5
36 Swillington.....D 2
4 Swimbridge.....C 5
4 Swimbridge
    Newland......C 5
16 Swinbrook.....C 4
32 Swinderley.....D 6
15 Swindon, Glos....B 12
22 Swindon, Staffs....C 2
16 Swindon, Wilts ....F 3
37 Swine.........D 9
36 Swinefleet......E 5
15 Swineford......G 10
25 Swineshead, Beds...J 2
24 Swineshead, Lincs..B 3
24 Swineshead Bridge .A 3
61 Swiney.........D 11
23 Swinford, Leics....D 9
16 Swinford, Oxon....C 5
11 Swingfield Minnis .D 10
11 Singfield Street...D 11
47 Swinhill.......D 12
45 Swinhoe......E 12
37 Swinhope......G 9
40 Swinithwaite....F 1
44 Swinnie........A 5
31 Swinscoe.......E 9
44 Swinside Hall....A 5
24 Swinstead......C 1
49 Swinton, Borders ..E 11
34 Swinton,
    Manchester....G 6
41 Swinton, N. Yorks. H 7
40 Swinton, N. Yorks. G 2
36 Swinton, S. Yorks. G 2
49 Swinton Quarter ...E 11
49 Swintonmill.....E 10
23 Swithland.......A 9
56 Swordale, Highland .C 1
63 Swordale, W. Isles .D 6
55 Swordland......K 2
61 Swordly........B 7
30 Sworton Heath...B 5
43 Swydd-ffynnon...F 3
31 Swynnerton.....G 7
7 Swyre..........G 8
20 Sychnant.......E 5
20 Sychtyn.......B 5
15 Syde..........C 12
17 Sydenham......D 8
5 Sydenham Damerel .H 3
26 Syderstone......B 1
7 Sydling St. Nicholas F 10
16 Sydmonton......H 6
32 Syerston.......E 5
35 Syke..........F 8
36 Sykehouse......E 4
34 Sykes..........B 5
64 Symbister......D 8
47 Symington,
    Strathclyde.....F 8
48 Symington,
    Strathclyde.....F 3
15 Symonds Yat....C 9
7 Symondsbury....G 8
13 Synod Inn......B 7
49 Synton Parkhead ..G 7
61 Syre..........C 7
23 Syresham......H 9

23 Syston, Leics ......A 9
32 Syston, Lincs.......F 6
22 Sytchampton.......F 2
23 Sywell ....E 11
54 Taagan ....C 4
47 Tackhouse ....E 11
16 Tackley ....B 6
26 Tacolneston ....F 4
36 Tadcaster ....C 3
31 Taddington ......C 10
4 Taddiport ....D 4
17 Tadley ....H 7
25 Tadlow ....K 4
23 Tadmarton ......H 7
15 Tadwick ....G 10
10 Tadworth ....B 1
14 Tafarnau-bach ...C 4
29 Tafarn-gelyn ....D 11
12 Tafarn-y-bwlch ...D 4
14 Taffs Well ......F 5
20 Tafolwern ....B 4
29 Tai ....D 7
29 Tai-bach, Clwyd ..G 10
13 Taibach, W. Glam .H 11
29 Tai-mawr ....F 9
61 Tain, Highland ...A 11
56 Tain, Highland ...B 3
29 Tainant ....F 12
13 Tairgwaith ....F 10
28 Tai'r-lon ....E 4
18 Takeley ....B 5
18 Takeley Street ...B 5
14 Talachddu ....A 4
29 Talacre ....B 10
6 Talaton ....F 4
12 Talbenny ....F 2
14 Talbot Green ....F 4
8 Talbot Village ...G 2
20 Talerddig ......B 5
13 Talgarreg ......B 7
14 Talgarth ....A 5
20 Taliesin ....C 2
62 Talisker ....E 3
31 Talke ....E 7
44 Talkin ....G 4
48 Talla Linnfoots ..G 4
54 Talladale ....C 3
29 Tallard ....G 8
30 Tallarn Green ...F 3
38 Tallentire ......B 3
13 Talley ....D 9
24 Tallington ......E 2
60 Talmine ....B 6
13 Talog ....D 7
20 Talsarn ....G 1
28 Talsarnau ......G 5
2 Talskiddy ......C 6
28 Talwrn, Gwynedd ..C 4
29 Talwrn, Clwyd ...E 12
20 Talybont, Dyfed ..C 2
28 Tal-y-bont,Gwynedd H 5
28 Tal-y-bont,Gwynedd C 5
29 Tal-y-bont,Gwynedd C 7
14 Talybont, Powys ..B 4
29 Tal-y-cafn ......C 7
15 Tal-y-coed ......C 7
14 Tal-y-garn ......F 4
20 Tal-y-llyn, Gwynedd A 3
14 Tal-y-llyn, Powys ..B 4
18 Tal-y-sarn ......E 4
14 Talywain ....D 6
20 Tal-y-wern ......B 4
40 Tame ....D 5
5 Tamerton Foliot ..K 3
22 Tamworth ....B 5
39 Tan Hill ....E 11
12 Tancredston .....D 2
11 Tanden ....D 8
47 Tandlemuir ......C 8
10 Tandridge ....C 3
45 Tanfield ....G 10
45 Tanfield Lea ....H 10
8 Tangley ....A 5
9 Tangmere ....E 10
64 Tankerness ......D 3
35 Tankersley .....G 12
28 Tan-lan ....F 5
61 Tannach ....C 12
59 Tannachie ....J 5
59 Tannadice ....L 2
27 Tannington .....H 5
31 Tansley ....D 11
31 Tansley Knoll ...D 11
24 Tansor ....F 2
45 Tantobie ....H 10
40 Tanton ....D 5
40 Tanworth in Arden .E 5
28 Tan-y-bwlch .....F 6
29 Tan-y-fron .....D 9
20 Tan-y-graig, Dyfed .E 3
28 Tan-y-graig, Gwynedd ....F 3
28 Tan-y-grisiau ...F 6
12 Tan-y-groes .....B 6

29 Tan-y-pistyll ....G 10
17 Taplow ....F 10
46 Tarbert, Strathclyde A 1
46 Tarbert, Strathclyde .C 4
63 Tarbert, W. Isles ..F 2
55 Tarbet, Highland ..K 2
60 Tarbet, Highland ..C 3
51 Tarbet, Strathclyde G 10
47 Tarbolton ......G 9
47 Tarbrax ....D 3
30 Tarbuck Green ...A 3
44 Tarcoon ....E 2
22 Tardebigge .....E 3
59 Tarfside ....J 2
59 Tarland ....G 2
34 Tarleton ....E 3
34 Tarlscough .....F 3
15 Tarlton ....D 12
34 Tarnbrook ......B 5
30 Tarporley ......D 4
6 Tarr ....C 4
8 Tarrant Crawford ..E 1
8 Tarrant Gunville ..E 1
8 Tarrant Hinton ..E 1
8 Tarrant Keyneston .F 1
8 Tarrant Launceston .E 1
8 Tarrant Monkton ..E 1
8 Tarrant Rawston ..E 1
8 Tarrant Rushton ..E 1
10 Tarring Neville ..H 3
21 Tarrington .....H 11
62 Tarskavaig .....G 5
58 Tarves ....D 6
54 Tarvie ....D 8
30 Tarvin ....D 4
26 Tasburgh ....F 5
21 Tasley ....C 12
16 Taston ....B 5
31 Tatenhill ......H 10
43 Tath Hill ......B 11
39 Tatham ....H 8
33 Tathwell ....B 10
17 Tatling End ....E 11
10 Tatsfield ......B 3
30 Tattenhall .....D 3
26 Tatterford .....C 2
26 Tattersett .....C 1
33 Tattershall ....D 9
33 Tattershall Bridge .D 9
33 Tattershall Thorpe ..D 9
27 Tattingstone ...L 4
27 Tattingstone Whitehorse ....L 4
6 Tatworth ....F 6
58 Tauchers ....C 1
6 Taunton ....D 6
26 Taverham ....D 5
12 Tavernspite ....F 5
5 Tavistock ......H 3
4 Taw Green, Devon .E 5
4 Taw Green, Devon .F 5
4 Tawstock ....C 4
31 Taxal ....B 8
47 Tayburn ....E 10
51 Taychreggan ....E 7
46 Tayinloan ......E 2
52 Taymouth Castle ..C 3
51 Taynafead ......F 8
15 Taynton, Glos. ...B 10
16 Taynton, Oxon ...C 3
51 Taynuilt ....D 7
53 Tayport ....D 9
46 Tayvallich .....A 2
33 Tealby ....A 8
62 Teangue ....G 6
39 Tebay ....E 8
17 Tebworth ....A 10
4 Tedburn St. Mary ..E 7
16 Teddington, Glos. ..A 1
18 Teddington, London ....G 2
21 Tedstone Delamere ....F 12
21 Tedstone Wafre ..F 12
23 Teeton ....E 10
8 Teffont Evias ...C 1
8 Teffont Magna ..C 2
12 Tegryn ....D 6
23 Teigh ....A 12
5 Teigncrace .....H 7
5 Teignmouth .....H 8
56 Teindland ......D 8
44 Teindside ......B 3
21 Telford ....B 12
10 Telham ....G 6
7 Tellisford .....A 11
10 Telscombe .....H 3
43 Templand, Cornwall .C 11
3 Temple, Cornwall ..B 8
13 Temple Bar, Dyfed .B 8
13 Temple Bar, Dyfed ..E 9
48 Temple, Lothian ..B 5
22 Temple Ballsall ..E 5
7 Temple Cloud ....A 9

11 Temple Ewell ...D 11
22 Temple Grafton ..G 5
16 Temple Guiting ..A 2
36 Temple Hirst ....E 4
39 Temple Sowerby ..C 8
7 Templecombe ....D 10
53 Templehall .....H 7
6 Templeton, Devon ..E 2
12 Templeton, Dyfed ..F 4
4 Tempelton Bridge ..E 7
25 Tempsford ......K 3
24 Ten Mile Bank ...F 1
21 Tenbury Wells ...F 11
12 Tenby ....G 5
19 Tendring ....B 11
19 Tendring Green ..A 11
64 Tenston ....C 1
11 Tenterden ......E 7
42 Terally ....G 2
19 Terling ....B 7
30 Ternhill ....G 5
2 Terras ....D 6
17 Terrick ....C 9
41 Terrington .....H 7
24 Terrington St. Clement D 6
24 Terrington St. John .D 6
10 Teston ....C 6
8 Testwood ....E 5
15 Tetbury ....E 12
15 Tetbury Upton ...E 12
30 Tetchill ....G 3
4 Tetcott ....F 2
33 Tetford ....C 10
37 Tetney ....G 10
37 Tetney Lock ....G 11
17 Tetsworth ......D 8
22 Tettenhall .....B 2
58 Teuchan ....D 8
58 Teuchar ....C 5
53 Teuchatcroft ...B 9
32 Teversal ....D 2
25 Teversham ......J 6
44 Teviothead .....C 2
59 Tewel ....J 6
18 Tewin ....B 3
15 Tewkesbury .....A 12
11 Teynham ....B 8
11 Teynham Street ..B 8
38 Thackthwaite, Cumb. ....C 4
38 Thackthwaite, Cumb. ....C 6
9 Thakeham ....D 12
17 Thame ....D 8
17 Thames Ditton ...G 12
11 Thanington .....B 10
48 Thankerton .....F 2
26 Tharston ....F 5
16 Thatcham ....H 5
34 Thatto Heath ...H 4
25 Thaxted ....M 7
62 The Aird ....C 3
21 The Bage ....H 8
43 The Barony, Dumf. & Gall. ......C 11
64 The Barony, Orkney B 1
31 The Blythe .....G 9
62 The Braes ......E 4
21 The Broad ......F 10
15 The Camp ....C 12
10 The Chart ......C 3
17 The City ....D 8
15 The Cleaver ....A 8
8 The Common .....C 4
21 The Corner .....D 10
60 The Craigs .....G 5
38 The Cronk ......F 2
47 The Den ....D 8
24 The Engine .....E 4
44 The Fauld ......F 2
44 The Flatt ......E 4
11 The Forstal ....E 7
38 The Green, Cumbria G 4
7 The Green, Wilts ..C 12
43 The Grove ......D 10
49 The Hardens ....D 10
9 The Haven ......C 12
27 The Heath ......L 2
10 The Hermitage ..C 1
46 The Highland Hotel .A 5
38 The Howe ....H 1
19 The Hythe ......B 10
43 The Lake ....G 7
11 The Leacon .....E 8
17 The Lee ....D 10
38 The Lhen ....F 2
21 The Marsh ......B 5
45 The Middles ....H 10
10 The Moor ....E 6
61 The Mound ......G 8
47 The Murray .....D 11
64 The Ness ....A 8

59 The Neuk ....H 5
15 The Oval ....H 10
15 The Pill ....F 8
58 The Pole of Itlaw ..B 4
21 The Pound ......E 7
15 The Quarry .....D 10
12 The Rhos ....F 4
9 The Sands ......B 10
16 The Slade ......G 6
11 The Stocks .....E 8
19 The Stone ......C 9
17 The Throat .....G 9
2 The Towans .....C 5
21 The Vauld ......G 10
22 The Wyke ....B 1
59 Theakston ......G 3
37 Thealby ....E 7
17 Theale, Berks. ...G 7
17 Theale, Somerset ..B 8
17 Theale Green ...G 7
37 Thearne ....C 8
37 Theberton ....J 7
23 Theddingworth ...D 10
33 Theddlethorpe All Saints ......A 11
33 Theddlethorpe St. Helen ....A 11
4 Thelbridge Cross ..E 7
27 Thelnetham .....G 3
30 Thelwall ....B 5
30 Themelthorpe ...C 4
23 Thenford ....H 8
25 Therfield ......L 4
27 Thetford ....G 2
18 Theydon Bois ...D 4
15 Thickwood ......G 11
33 Thimbleby, Lincs. ..C 9
40 Thimbleby, N. Yorks. ....F 5
40 Thirkleby ......G 5
40 Thirlby ....G 5
49 Thirlestane ....E 8
38 Thirlspot ......C 5
40 Thirn ....G 2
40 Thirsk ....G 4
34 Thistlebottom ..A 5
34 Thistleton, Lancs. ..C 3
32 Thistleton,Leics. ..H 6
25 Thistley Green ..H 8
36 Thixendale .....A 6
45 Thockrington ...E 8
24 Tholomas Drove ..E 5
40 Tholthorpe .....H 5
12 Thomas Chapel ...F 4
34 Thomas Close ...A 7
22 Thomas Town ....F 4
58 Thomastown .....D 3
56 Thompson ....F 2
56 Thomshill ......D 8
10 Thong ....A 5
33 Thoock ....A 5
39 Thoralby ....F 12
37 Thoresway .....G 9
37 Thorganby, Lincs. ..G 9
36 Thorganby, N. Yorks. ....C 5
41 Thorgill ....E 7
27 Thorington ....H 7
27 Thorington Street ..L 3
35 Thorlby ....B 8
18 Thorley, Herts. ..B 5
8 Thorley, I.o.W. ..G 5
18 Thorley Street, Herts. B 5
8 Thorley Street, I.o.W. G 5
40 Thormanby .....H 5
33 Thorn ....F 7
40 Thornaby-on-Tees .C 5
26 Thornage ......B 4
17 Thornborough, Bucks. A 8
40 Thornborough, N. Yorks. .....G 3
15 Thornbury, Avon ..E 9
4 Thornbury, Devon .E 3
21 Thornbury, Heref. & Worc. .....F 11
23 Thornby ....E 10
31 Thorncliff ....D 8
7 Thorncombe ....F 7
9 Thorncombe Street B 11
25 Thorncote Green ..K 3
8 Thorncross ....H 6
4 Thorndon ......H 4
4 Thorndon Cross ..F 4
6 Thorne, Somerset ..D 4
36 Thorne, S. Yorks. ..F 5
35 Thorner ....C 12
24 Thorney, Cambs. ..E 4
33 Thorney, Notts. ..C 6
7 Thorney, Somerset .D 7
37 Thorney Crofts ..E 9

8 Thorney Hill ....F 4
58 Thorneybank ....D 4
6 Thornfalcor ....D 6
7 Thornford ......E 9
44 Thorngrafton ...F 6
7 Thorngrove .....C 7
37 Thorngumbald ...D 9
24 Thornham ....A 8
27 Thornham Magna ..H 4
27 Thornham Parva ..H 4
24 Thornhaugh .....E 2
52 Thornhill, Central .G 2
38 Thornhill, Cumb. ..D 3
31 Thornhill, Dumf. & Gall. ....B 9
8 Thornhill, Hants. ..E 6
14 Thornhill, Mid Glam. ....F 5
35 Thornhill, W. Yorks. E 11
37 Thornholme .....A 9
49 Thornielaw .....F 8
49 Thornington ....F 11
40 Thornley, Dur. ...A 4
40 Thornley, Dur. ...B 1
47 Thornliebank ...D 10
25 Thorns ....K 8
35 Thornseat .....H 11
31 Thornsett ......B 8
38 Thornthwaite, Cumb. C 5
35 Thornthwaite, N. Yorks. .....A 10
17 Thornton, Bucks. ...A 8
40 Thornton, Cleveland ......D 5
12 Thornton, Dyfed ..F 2
53 Thornton, Fife ...G 7
36 Thornton, Humber. .C 5
34 Thornton, Lancs. ..C 2
23 Thornton, Leics. ..A 8
33 Thornton, Lincs. ..C 9
34 Thornton, Merseyside ......G 2
49 Thornton, Northumb. E 12
53 Thornton, Tayside ..C 9
35 Thornton, W. Yorks. D 9
37 Thornton Curtis ..E 8
18 Thornton Heath ..G 3
30 Thornton Hough ..B 2
35 Thornton in Craven .B 8
39 Thornton in Lonsdale H 9
40 Thornton-le-Beans .F 4
36 Thornton-le-Clay ..A 5
41 Thornton-le-Dale .G 8
37 Thornton le Moor, Lincolnshire ..G 8
40 Thornton-le-Moor, N. Yorks. ....F 4
30 Thornton-le-Moors .C 3
40 Thornton-le-Street .G 4
47 Thornton Mains ..E 12
39 Thornton Rust ...F 12
40 Thornton Steward ..F 2
40 Thornton Watlass ..G 3
47 Thorntonhall ...D 10
49 Thorntonloch ...B 10
49 Thorntonpark ...E 12
18 Thornwood Com ..C 5
49 Thorndykes .....E 9
38 Thornythwaite ..C 6
32 Thoroton ....F 5
36 Thorp Arch .....C 2
27 Thorp Green ....K 2
31 Thorpe, Derby ...E 10
37 Thorpe, Humberside B 7
33 Thorpe, Lincs. ...B 12
26 Thorpe, Norf. ...F 7
35 Thorpe, N. Yorks. ..A 9
32 Thorpe, Notts. ...E 5
17 Thorpe, Surrey ...G 11
27 Thorpe Abbotts ..G 5
36 Thorpe Acre ....H 2
32 Thorpe Arnold ..H 5
36 Thorpe Audlin ..F 3
41 Thorpe Bassett ..H 8
19 Thorpe Bay .....E 9
23 Thorpe by Water ..E 12
22 Thorpe Constantine .A 6
26 Thorpe End Garden Village ......D 6
35 Thorpe Hesley ...G 12
36 Thorpe in Balne ..F 4
32 Thorpe in the Fallows B 6
23 Thorpe Langton ..C 10
40 Thorpe Larches ..C 5
19 Thorpe-le-Soken ..B 11
36 Thorpe le Street ..C 6
23 Thorpe Malsor ...D 11
42 Thorpe Mandeville H 9
26 Thorpe Market ...B 5

27 Thorpe Morieux ...K 2
32 Thorpe on the Hill ..D 6
26 Thorpe St. Andrew .D 6
33 Thorpe St. Peter ...D 11
32 Thorpe Salvin ...B 2
23 Thorpe Satchville .A 10
40 Thorpe Thewles ..C 4
36 Thorpe Underwood .A 3
25 Thorpe Waterville .G 1
26 Thorpe Willoughby .D 3
27 Thorpeness ......J 8
19 Thorrington ....B 10
7 Thorverton .....F 3
27 Thrandeston ....H 4
25 Thrapston ......G 1
38 Threapland .....A 4
30 Threapwood .....F 3
42 Threave ....A 4
10 Three Bridges ...D 2
2 Three Burrows ...E 4
11 Three Chimneys ..D 7
14 Three Cocks .....A 5
13 Three Crosses ...H 9
10 Three Cups Corner .F 5
40 Three Gates, Cleveland ......B 5
7 Three Gates, Dorset E 9
24 Three Holes .....E 6
8 Three Legged Cross .E 3
11 Three Oaks ......G 7
24 Threekingham ....B 2
10 Threelag Cross ..E 9
31 Threelows ......E 9
17 Threemile Cross ..G 8
2 Threemilestone ..E 5
49 Threepwood .....E 8
38 Threlkeld ......C 6
35 Threshfield ....A 8
26 Thrigby ....D 7
39 Thringarth .....C 11
32 Thringstone ....H 2
40 Thrintoft ......F 3
25 Thriplow ....K 5
24 Throckenholt ...E 5
25 Throcking ......M 4
45 Throckley ......F 9
22 Throckmorton ...G 3
45 Throphill ......D 9
45 Thropton ....C 8
43 Throughgate ....C 9
5 Throwleigh .....G 5
11 Throwley ....C 8
11 Throwley Forstal .C 8
32 Thrumpton .....G 2
61 Thrumster .....C 12
37 Thrunscoe ......F 10
45 Thrunton ......B 9
7 Thrupe ....B 9
15 Thrupp, Glos. ...D 11
16 Thrupp, Oxon ...C 6
5 Thruselton ....G 3
18 Thrushesbush ...C 5
34 Thrushgill .....A 5
23 Thrussington ...A 10
8 Thruxton, Hants. ..B 4
15 Thruxton, Heref. & Worc. .....A 7
36 Thrybergh ......H 3
23 Thurcaston .....A 9
32 Thurcroft ......A 2
4 Thurdon ....E 2
26 Thurgarton, Norf. .B 5
32 Thurgarton, Notts. .E 4
35 Thurgoland ....G 1
23 Thurlaston, Leics. .B 8
23 Thurlaston, War. ..E 8
6 Thurlbear ......D 6
24 Thurlby, Lincs. ...D 2
32 Thurlby, Lincs. ...D 6
25 Thurleigh ......J 2
5 Thurlestone ....L 5
6 Thurloxton .....C 6
32 Thurlston .....G 1
35 Thurlstone ....G 11
26 Thurlton ......D 7
23 Thurmaston ....A 9
21 Thurnby ....B 10
26 Thurne ....D 7
11 Thurnham, Kent ..B 7
34 Thurnham, Lancs. .B 3
26 Thurning, Norf. ..C 4
25 Thurning, Northants. G 2
36 Thurnscoe .....G 2
44 Thursby ....H 2
26 Thursford Green ..B 3
9 Thursley ......B 10
61 Thurso ....A 10
61 Thurso East ...A 10
30 Thurstaston ...B 1
27 Thurston ......J 2
44 Thurstonfield ...G 2
35 Thurstonland ...F 10
26 Thurton ....E 6
31 Thurvaston ....F 11

26 Thuxton ....E 3
27 Thwaite, Suffolk ...H 4
39 Thwaite, N. Yorks. .E 11
26 Thwaite St. Mary ...F 6
41 Thwing ....H 10
52 Tibbermore ....E 5
43 Tibbers ....B 9
15 Tibberton ....B 10
22 Tibberton, Heref.
& Worc. ....F 3
30 Tibberton, Salop ...H 5
26 Tibenham ....F 4
32 Tibshelf ....D 2
37 Tibthorpe ....B 7
10 Ticehurst ....E 6
9 Tichborne ....C 7
9 Tichfield ....F 7
24 Tickencote ....E 1
15 Tickenham ....G 8
32 Tickhill ....A 3
21 Ticklerton ....C 10
31 Ticknall ....H 12
37 Tickton ....C 8
22 Tidbury Green .....E 4
16 Tidcombe ....H 4
17 Tiddington, Oxon ..D 7
22 Tidington, War. ....F 6
10 Tidebrook ....E 5
3 Tideford ....D 10
3 Tideford Cross ...D 10
15 Tidenham ....E 9
31 Tideswell ....C 10
17 Tidmarsh ....G 7
22 Tidmington ....H 6
8 Tidpit ....D 2
2 Tiers Cross ....F 3
23 Tiffield ....G 10
58 Tifty ....D 5
59 Tigerton ....L 3
54 Tighchuig ....F 8
52 Tighnablair ....E 3
46 Tighnabruaich .....B 5
51 Tigh-na-criche ....G 8
60 Tighnafiline ......C 1
5 Tigley ....K 6
25 Tilbrook ....H 2
18 Tilbury ....F 6
22 Tile Cross ....C 5
17 Tilehurst ....G 7
9 Tilford ....B 10
10 Tilgale ....E 2
58 Tillathrowie ....D 2
30 Tilley ....G 4
52 Tillicoultry ....G 4
19 Tillingham ....D 10
21 Tillington, Heref.
& Worc. ....H 10
9 Tillington,
W. Sussex ......D 11
21 Tillington Com ...H 10
59 Tillyarblet ....L 3
59 Tillybardine ......K 2
58 Tiliycorthie ......E 7
59 Tillydrine House ..H 4
58 Tillyfar ....E 7
58 Tillyfourie ....F 4
58 Tillygrieg ....E 6
58 Tillyminnate ......D 2
11 Tilmanstone ......C 11
24 Tilney All Saints ..D 7
24 Tilney High End ...D 7
24 Tilney St. Lawrence .D 7
8 Tilshead ....A 2
30 Tilstock ....F 4
30 Tilston ....E 3
30 Tilstone Fearnall ..D 4
17 Tilsworth ....B 10
23 Tilton on the Hill ..B 10
15 Tiltups End ....E 11
33 Timberland ....D 2
31 Timbersbrook .....D 7
6 Timbercombe ......B 3
35 Timble ....B 10
49 Timpendean ....G 9
30 Timperley ....A 6
15 Timsbury, Avon ...H 10
8 Timsbury, Hants. ..D 5
27 Timworth Green ...H 2
7 Tincleton ....G 11
44 Tindale ....G 4
35 Tingewick ....A 7
35 Tingley ....D 11
25 Tingrith ....M 1
3 Tinhay ....G 3
48 Tinnis ....F 6
35 Tinshill ....C 11
3 Tintagel ....A 7
15 Tintern Parva .....D 8
7 Tintinhull ....D 8
35 Tintwistle ....G 9
43 Tinwald ....C 11
24 Tinwell ....E 1
57 Tippacott ....A 6
58 Tipperty, Grampian .E 7
58 Tipperty, Grampian .B 4

24 Tipp's End ....F 6
8 Tiptoe ....F 4
22 Tipton ....C 3
6 Tipton St. Johns ...G 4
19 Tiptree ....B 9
50 Tirghoil ....E 1
15 Tirley ....A 11
14 Tir-Phil ....D 4
39 Tirril ....C 7
8 Tisbury ....C 1
9 Tisman's Com .....C 12
31 Tissington ....E 10
4 Titchberry ....C 1
26 Titchmarsh ....G 1
26 Titchwell ....A 1
32 Tithby ....F 4
45 Titlington ....B 9
21 Titley ....F 9
10 Titsey ....C 3
31 Tittensor ....F 7
26 Tittleshall ....C 2
15 Tittups End ....E 11
30 Tiverton, Ches. ...D 4
6 Tiverton, Devon ...E 3
6 Tiverton Junction .E 4
27 Tivetshall St. Margaret
G 4
27 Tivetshall St. Mary .G 4
22 Tividale ....C 3
6 Tivington ....B 3
31 Tixall ....H 8
24 Tixover ....E 1
64 Toab ....D 3
31 Toadmoor ....E 12
50 Tobermory ....B 2
50 Toberonochy ......G 5
63 Tobson ....C 2
58 Tocher ....D 4
16 Tockenham ....F 2
16 Tockenham Wick ...F 1
34 Tockholes ....E 5
15 Tockington ....F 9
36 Tockwith ....B 3
7 Todber ....D 11
17 Toddington, Beds. .A 11
16 Toddington, Glos. ..A 1
22 Todenham ....H 6
53 Todhall ....E 8
44 Todhills ....G 2
35 Todmorden ....E 8
49 Todrig ....G 7
32 Todwick ....B 2
40 Toft Hill ....B 2
26 Toft, Cambs. ......K 5
32 Toft, Lincs. ....D 2
40 Toft Hill ....B 2
26 Toft Monks ....F 7
33 Toft Next Newton ..A 7
26 Toftbarns ....G 8
26 Toftrees ....C 2
61 Tofts ....A 12
26 Toftwood Com .....D 3
45 Togston ....C 10
55 Toigal ....K 1
50 Tokavaig ....G 5
17 Tokers Green ......F 8
36 Toll Bar ....F 3
36 Toll End ....C 3
58 Toll of Birness ....D 7
6 Tolland ....C 4
8 Tollard Royal .....D 1
7 Toller Fratrum ....F 9
7 Toller Porcorum ...F 9
32 Tollerton, Notts. ..G 3
36 Tollerton, N. Yorks. A 3
19 Tollesbury ....C 9
19 Tolleshunt D'Arcy .C 9
19 Tolleshunt Major ..C 9
56 Tollie ....D 1
63 Tolmachan ....F 2
64 Tolob ....F 7
7 Tolpuddle ....G 11
62 Tolstachaolais ....C 3
57 Tolvah ....J 4
10 Tolworth ....B 1
57 Tomatin ....G 4
57 Tombain ....J 4
56 Tombreck ....F 2
57 Tomcrasky ....H 6
55 Tomdoun ....J 5
56 Tomich, Highland ..E 1
56 Tomich, Highland ..G 7
56 Tomich, Highland ..C 3
60 Tomich, Highland ..F 6
57 Tomintoul,
Grampian ....K 7
57 Tomintoul,
Grampian ....H 7
57 Tomintoul,
Highland ....G 2
58 Tomnaven ....D 2
57 Tomnavoulin ......G 8
52 Tomphibil ....B 3
44 Tomishielburn .....E 2

14 Ton ....D 6
14 Ton-Pentre ....E 3
10 Tonbridge ....C 5
14 Tondu ....F 2
14 Ton-fanau ....B 1
63 Tong, W. Iles ......C 5
22 Tong, Salop ....A 2
35 Tong, W. Yorks. ...D 10
32 Tonge ....H 2
9 Tongham ....A 10
43 Tongland ....F 8
60 Tongue ....B 6
60 Tongue House .....B 6
14 Tongwynlais ....F 5
13 Tonna ....G 11
14 Ton-teg ....F 4
18 Tonwell ....B 3
14 Tonypandy ....E 3
14 Tonyrefail ....E 3
6 Toot Baldon ......D 6
18 Toothill ....D 5
35 Top of Hebers .....F 7
40 Topcliffe ....H 4
26 Topcroft ....F 6
26 Topcroft Street ....F 5
25 Toppesfield ....L 8
34 Toppings ....F 6
6 Topsham ....G 3
57 Torbain ....H 7
46 Torbeg, Arran I. ...F 4
59 Torbeg, Grampian
G 1
61 Torboll ....G 7
56 Torbreck ....F 3
5 Torbryan ....J 7
55 Torcastle ....L 5
57 Torcross ....L 7
57 Torcroy ....J 3
55 Torcuileann ......J 2
5 Tore ....D 2
55 Torgyle Bridge ....H 7
46 Torinturk ....C 3
32 Torksey ....B 5
55 Torlundy ....M 5
15 Tormarton ....F 11
42 Tormitchell ....B 3
46 Tormore ....F 4
56 Tornagrain ....E 3
57 Tornahaish ....J 8
59 Tornaveen ....G 4
57 Torness ....G 1
40 Toronto ....B 2
38 Torpenhow ....A 4
48 Torphichen ....B 2
59 Torphins ....G 4
3 Torpoint ....D 11
5 Torquay ....J 8
49 Torquhan ....E 7
62 Torran, Highland ..C 5
56 Torran, Highland ..B 3
47 Torrance ....B 11
50 Torraneidhinn .....B 3
50 Torrans ....E 2
47 Torranyard ....A 8
5 Torre, Devon ......J 8
6 Torre, Somerset ...B 4
54 Torridon ....D 3
54 Torridon House ....D 2
62 Torrin ....F 5
61 Torrisdale ....B 7
34 Torrisholme ....A 3
55 Torrlaoighseach ...H 3
60 Torroboll ....F 6
58 Torry, Grampian ...D 2
59 Torry, Grampian ...G 7
48 Torryburn ....A 3
58 Torterston ....C 8
43 Torthorwald ......D 11
9 Tortington ....F 11
38 Torver ....F 5
48 Torwood ....A 1
32 Torworth ....B 4
4 Tosberry ....D 1
54 Toscaig ....F 1
52 Toseland ....J 3
34 Tosside ....B 6
50 Tostarie ....C 1
27 Tostock ....J 3
62 Totaig, Highland ..C 1
55 Totaig, Highland ..G 2
62 Tote ....C 3
61 Totegan ....A 8
8 Totland ....G 5
31 Totley ....B 11
7 Totnell ....E 9
5 Totnes ....K 7
62 Totscore ....B 3
18 Tottenham ....E 3
24 Tottenhill ....D 7
18 Totteridge ....E 2
17 Totternhoe ....B 10
34 Tottington ....F 6
8 Totton ....E 5
17 Touchen-end ....F 9

59 Toucks ....J 6
56 Toulton ....C 5
56 Toulvaddie ....B 4
58 Toux ....C 7
40 Tow Law ....A 1
46 Toward ....C 6
46 Toward Quay ......C 6
23 Towcester ....G 10
2 Towednack ....F 2
18 Tower Hamlets .....F 4
10 Tower Hill ....E 1
17 Towersey ....D 8
58 Towie ....F 2
56 Towiemore ....C 1
39 Town End ....G 7
34 Town Green ....G 3
10 Town Row ....E 4
27 Town Street ....G 1
49 Town Yetholm ....G 10
43 Townfoot ....B 10
43 Townhead, Dumf.
& Gall. ....C 10
43 Townhead, Dumf.
& Gall. ....G 8
59 Townhead,
Grampian ....K 5
45 Townhead, Northumb.
F 7
42 Townhead,
Strathclyde .....A 3
47 Townhead of Aber .A 9
47 Townhead of Gree .E 9
43 Town head of
Greenlaw ....E 8
52 Townhill ....H 6
16 Townsend, Oxon ...E 5
7 Townsend, Som. ...A 8
2 Townshend ....F 3
36 Towthorpe ....A 4
30 Towton ....C 3
14 Towyn ....B 9
33 Toynton All Saints .D 11
33 Toynton Fen Side .D 11
33 Toynton St. Peter ..D 11
10 Toy's Hill ....C 3
47 Trabboch ....G 9
47 Trabboch Mains ...G 9
47 Trabbochburn .....G 9
2 Traboe ....D 4
56 Tradespark ....D 4
35 Trafford Park .....H 7
9 Traigh House ......K 1
43 Trailtrow ....D 12
14 Trallong ....A 3
30 Tranmere ....A 2
9 Tranent ....B 7
30 Tranmere ....A 2
61 Trantlemore ......B 8
14 Tranwell ....E 10
13 Trapp ....E 10
14 Trawdon ....C 8
35 Trawden ....C 8
14 Trawscoed ....A 4
28 Trawsfynydd ......G 6
13 Tre-Herbert ....B 9
14 Trelaw ....E 3
34 Treales ....D 3
28 Trearddur Bay ....B 2
62 Treaslane ....B 7
14 Trebanog ....E 3
3 Trebartha ....B 9
3 Trebarwith ....A 7
2 Trebetheric ....B 6
6 Treborough ....C 3
2 Trebudannon .....D 6
3 Trebullett ....B 10
3 Treburley ....B 10
2 Trebyan ....D 7
14 Trecastle ....A 2
14 Trecenydd ....F 5
3 Trecwn ....D 3
14 Trecynon ....D 3
30 Tredaule ....B 9
14 Tre-ddiog ....D 2
14 Tredegar ....D 4
22 Tredington ....H 6
3 Tredizzick ....B 6
14 Tredomen ....A 4
12 Tredrissi ....C 2
14 Tredunnock ....E 7
14 Tredustan ....A 5
2 Treen ....G 1
32 Treeton ....A 2
12 Trefasser ....C 2
28 Trefdraeth ....C 3
14 Trefecca ....A 5
12 Trefeglwys ....C 5
20 Trefenter ....E 2
12 Treffgarne ....E 3
12 Treffgarne Owen ..D 2
12 Treffynnon, Dyfed .D 2
28 Treffynnon,
Gwynedd ......B 3

14 Trefil ....C 4
12 Trefilan ....G 1
29 Trefnant ....C 10
30 Trefonen ....G 1
28 Trefor ....B 3
14 Treforest Industrial
Estate ....F 4
12 Trefriw ....D 7
29 Tref-y-nant ....F 12
3 Tregadillet ......A 10
28 Tregaian ....B 4
15 Tregare ....C 7
20 Tregaron ....F 2
28 Tregarth ....C 5
29 Tregeare ....A 9
29 Tregeiriog ....G 11
28 Tregele ....A 3
2 Tregeseal ....F 1
12 Treglemais ....D 2
2 Tregonetha ....C 6
2 Tregony ....E 6
3 Tregoss ....D 7
2 Tregowris ....G 5
14 Tregoyd ....A 5
13 Tre-groes ....C 7
20 Tregynon ....C 6
14 Trehafod ....E 4
14 Treharris ....E 4
14 Treherbert ....D 3
3 Trekenner ....B 10
3 Treknow ....A 7
3 Trelash ....A 9
2 Trelassick ....B 6
12 Trelech ....D 6
12 Tre-lech-a'r-Betws .D 6
12 Treleddyd fawr ....D 1
14 Trelewis ....E 4
3 Treligga ....A 7
3 Trelights ....B 7
3 Trelill ....B 7
2 Trelissick ....F 5
15 Trelleck ....D 8
15 Trelleck Grange ...D 8
29 Trelogan ....B 10
28 Tremadog ....F 5
12 Tremail ....A 8
14 Tremain ....B 6
2 Tremaine ....A 9
3 Tremar ....C 9
3 Trematon ....D 11
29 Tremeirchion .....C 10
3 Tremore ....C 7
2 Trenance, Corn. ...C 5
2 Trenance, Corn. ...C 6
2 Trenance, Corn. ...H 4
2 Trenarren ....E 7
21 Trench ....A 12
2 Trenear ....F 4
3 Treneglos ....A 9
2 Trenewan ....D 9
2 Trengune ....B 2
7 Trent Nether Compton
D 2
31 Trentham ....F 7
4 Trentishoe ....A 5
14 Treoes ....F 3
14 Treorchy ....E 3
20 Tre'r-ddol ....C 2
3 Trerule Foot .....D 10
12 Tresaith ....B 6
3 Tresayes ....D 7
22 Trescott ....B 2
2 Trescowe ....G 3
15 Tresham ....E 11
2 Tresillian ....E 6
12 Tresinwen ....C 2
2 Treskinnick Cross ..A 2
3 Tresmeer ....A 9
3 Tresparrett ....B 2
3 Tresparrett Posts ..B 2
52 Tressait ....A 3
64 Tresta, Zetland ...B 8
64 Tresta, Zetland ...D 7
32 Treswell ....B 5
3 Trethosa ....D 7
3 Trethurgy ....D 7
3 Tretio ....D 1
15 Tretire ....B 8
14 Tretower ....B 5
29 Treuddyn ....D 11
3 Trevadlock ....B 9
3 Trevalga ....D 3
2 Trevalyn ....D 3
3 Trevanson ....B 7
3 Trevarrack ....C 5
3 Trevarrian ....D 6
3 Trevarrian ....C 5
3 Trevarrick ....E 7
12 Trevaughan, Dyfed .E 5
13 Trevaughan, Dyfed .E 7
3 Trevellas ....D 5
3 Trevelmond ....C 9

2 Treverva ....F 5
14 Trevethin ....D 6
2 Trevigro ....C 10
12 Trevine ....D 2
2 Treviscoe ....D 6
2 Trevivian ....A 9
2 Trevoll ....D 5
2 Trevone ....B 6
28 Trevor ....F 3
2 Trevose ....B 6
3 Trewarmett ......A 8
3 Trewassa ....A 8
2 Trewellard ....F 1
2 Trewen ....A 9
2 Trewennack ....G 4
21 Trewern ....A 8
3 Trewerthern ....B 7
3 Trewetha ....B 7
3 Trewidland ....D 9
12 Trewilym ....C 5
3 Trewint ....B 2
2 Trewithian ....F 6
2 Trewoon ....D 7
35 Triangle ....E 9
8 Trickett's Cross ...F 3
44 Triermain ....F 4
40 Trimdon ....B 4
40 Trimdon Colliery ..B 4
40 Trimdon Grange ..B 4
26 Trimingham ....B 6
27 Trimley ....L 6
27 Trimley Heath ....L 6
31 Trimpley ....D 1
12 Trimsaran ....F 8
4 Trimstone ....B 4
14 Trinant ....D 5
17 Tring ....C 10
17 Tring Wharf .....C 10
6 Trinity, Devon ....F 3
59 Trinity, Tayside ...L 4
6 Triscombe ....C 5
55 Trislaig ....M 5
2 Trispen ....E 5
45 Tritlington ......D 10
52 Trochrie ....C 5
13 Troedyraur ....B 7
13 Troed-y-rhiw,
Dyfed ....B 8
14 Troedyrhiw,
Mid Glam. ......D 4
47 Troon, Strathclyde .F 8
2 Troon, Cornwall ...F 4
43 Troqueer ....D 10
51 Trossachs Hotel ..G 12
27 Trostan ....H 2
10 Trottiscliffe .....B 5
3 Trotton ....D 9
45 Troughend ....D 7
38 Troutbeck, Cumbria .C 6
38 Troutbeck, Cumbria .E 6
38 Troutbeck Bridge ..E 6
15 Trow Green ....D 9
32 Troway ....B 1
15 Trowbridge ......H 11
32 Trowell ....F 2
15 Trowle Common ..H 11
17 Trowley Botton ...C 11
49 Trows ....F 9
26 Trowse Newton ...E 5
7 Trudoxhill ....B 10
3 Trull ....D 6
62 Trumpan ....B 2
21 Trumpet ....H 12
25 Trumpington ......K 6
6 Trumps ....E 4
26 Trunch ....B 6
2 Truro ....E 5
3 Truscott ....A 10
3 Trusham ....H 2
31 Trusley ....G 11
33 Trusthorpe ......B 12
22 Trysull ....C 2
16 Tubney ....D 5
5 Tuckenhay ....K 7
2 Tuckingmill ......F 4
27 Tuddenham, Suff. .H 8
27 Tuddenham, Suff. .K 5
10 Tudeley ....D 5
15 Tudorville ....B 9
28 Tudweiliog ....G 2
9 Tuesley ....B 11
15 Tuffley ....C 11
12 Tufton ....D 4
3 Tugby ....B 11
21 Tugford ....D 11
45 Tughall ....E 12
54 Tuirnaig ....B 3
57 Tulchan ....M 7
52 Tullibody ....H 3
56 Tullich, Central .D 12
57 Tullich, Highland ..G 2

54 Tullich, Highland ...E 3	13 Tycroes, Dyfed ....F 9	38 Ulpha ....F 4	35 Upper Cumberworth
51 Tullich, Strathclyde .F 8	28 Ty-croes, Gwynedd .C 3	37 Ulrome ....B 9	F 10
56 Tullich Muir ....B 3	29 Tycrwyn ....H 10	64 Ulsta ....C 7	14 Upper Cwmbran ...E 6
52 Tulliemet ....B 5	20 Tydd Gote ....D 5	49 Ulsoon ....G 9	13 Upper Cwm-twrch .F 11
59 Tullo of Benholm ..K 5	24 Tydd St. Giles .....D 5	50 Ulva House ....D 2	58 Upper Dallachy ...A 1
58 Tulloch, Grampian .D 5	24 Tydd St. Mary .....D 5	38 Ulverston ....G 5	43 Upper Dalveen ...A 9
55 Tulloch, Highland ..L 7	29 Tyddininco ....G 9	43 Ulzieside ....A 8	25 Upper Dean ......H 1
52 Tullochan ....D 1	19 Tye Green, Essex ..B 7	62 Umachan ....C 5	35 Upper Denby .....F 11
51 Tullochgorm ....H 7	25 Tye Green, Essex ..L 7	4 Umberleigh ......D 5	44 Upper Denton ....G 4
57 Tullochmacarrick ...J 8	12 Ty-hen ....E 6	60 Unapool ....D 4	56 Upper Derraid ....F 6
58 Tullochs ....C 2	17 Tylers Green, Bucks.	44 Under Burnmouth ..E 3	54 Upper Diabaig ....D 2
59 Tullochvenus ....G 3	E 10	10 Under River ......C 4	10 Upper Dicker .....G 4
52 Tullybannocher ....E 2	10 Tyler's Grn., Surrey .C 2	39 Underbarrow ......F 7	61 Upper Dournreay ..A 9
53 Tullyfergus ....B 7	14 Tylorstown ....E 3	36 Undercliffe ....D 10	50 Upper Druimfin ...B 2
53 Tullymurdoch .....B 7	20 Tylwch ....D 5	47 Underhills ....F 9	31 Upper Elkstone ...D 9
58 Tullynessle ....F 3	29 Ty-nant, Clwyd ...F 9	64 Underhoull ....A 8	31 Upper End ....C 9
13 Tumble ....F 9	29 Ty-nant, Gwynedd ..H 8	32 Underwood ....E 2	56 Upper Ethie ......C 3
33 Tumby ....D 9	24 Tyncwm ....D 4	15 Undy ....F 7	15 Upper Framilode ..C 10
33 Tumby Woodside ..D 9	51 Tyndrum ....E 10	64 Unifirth ....D 6	22 Upper Gornal .....C 3
18 Tumford ....C 4	11 Tyneham ....H 12	59 Union Croft ....H 6	25 Upper Gravenhurst .L 2
52 Tummel Bridge ....A 3	45 Tyne & Wear, Co. .F 10	38 Union Mills ....H 2	16 Upper Green ......H 5
10 Tunbridge Wells ...D 5	48 Tynehead ....C 6	32 Unstone ....C 1	15 Upper Grove Com .B 9
15 Tunley ....H 10	44 Tynemouth ....F 11	32 Unstone Green ....C 1	9 Upper Hale ......A 10
37 Tunstall, Humber. .D 10	14 Tynewydd ....D 3	35 Unsworth ....F 7	62 Upper Halistra ....B 2
11 Tunstall, Kent .....B 7	49 Tyninghame ....B 8	44 Unthank, Cumb. ...H 2	17 Upper Halliford ..G 11
39 Tunstall, Lancs. ...H 8	50 Tynribbie ....C 6	39 Unthank, Cumb. ...A 8	10 Upper Halling.....B 6
40 Tunstall, N. Yorks. .F 2	43 Tynron ....B 9	39 Unthank, Cumb. ...B 7	23 Upper Hambleton .A 12
31 Tunstall, Staffs. ....F 2	20 Tynswydd ....F 2	49 Unthank, Northumb.	11 Upper Hardress Court
27 Tunstall, Suffolk ...K 6	20 Ty'n-y-ffridd .....G 10	E 12	C 10
45 Tunstall, Tyne	7 Up Cerne ....F 10	39 Unthank End ......B 7	10 Upper Hartfield ...E 3
& Wear ....H 12	6 Up Exe ....F 3	7 Up Cerne ....F 10	36 Upper Haugh .....G 2
26 Tunstall St. Mary ..E 7	15 Up Hatherley .....B 12	6 Up Exe ....F 3	21 Upper Heath .....D 11
9 Tunworth ....A 8	34 Up Holland ....G 4	15 Up Hatherley .....B 12	26 Upper Helmsley ...A 5
21 Tupsley ....H 10	9 Up Marden ....E 9	34 Up Holland ....G 4	36 Uper Helmsley ...A 5
23 Tur Langton ......C 10	9 Up Nately ....A 8	9 Up Marden ....E 9	21 Upper Hergest ....G 8
17 Turgis Green ......H 8	8 Up Somborne .....C 5	9 Up Nately ....A 8	23 Upper Heyford,
53 Turin ....B 10	9 Up Sydling ....F 9	8 Up Somborne .....C 5	Northants ....F 10
16 Turkdean ....B 2	8 Upavon ....A 3	9 Up Sydling ....F 9	16 Upper Heyford, Oxon
15 Turleigh Freshford H 11	11 Upchurch ....A 7	8 Upavon ....A 3	B 6
15 Turnastone ....A 7	4 Upcott, Devon .....E 4	11 Upchurch ....A 7	21 Upper Hill ....G 10
42 Turnberry ....A 3	21 Upcott, Heref.	4 Upcott, Devon .....E 4	44 Upper Hindhope ..B 6
31 Turnditch ....F 11	& Worc. ....G 8	21 Upcott, Heref.	35 Upper Hopton ....E 10
10 Turner's Hill ......E 2	6 Upcott, Somerset ...D 3	& Worc. ....G 8	10 Upper Horsebridge .G 5
7 Turners Puddle ....G 11	17 Updown Hill ......H 10	6 Upcott, Somerset ...D 3	31 Upper Hulme .....D 8
48 Turnhouse ....B 4	47 Uphall ....B 3	17 Updown Hill ......H 10	16 Upper Inglesham ..D 3
7 Turnworth ....E 11	48 Uphall Station .....B 3	47 Uphall ....B 3	57 Upper Inverbrough .G 4
58 Turriff ....C 5	4 Upham, Devon .....E 7	48 Uphall Station .....B 3	58 Upper Ironside ....B 6
34 Turton Bottoms ....F 6	9 Upham, Hants .....D 7	4 Upham, Devon .....E 7	53 Upper Kenley .....F 10
49 Turvelaws ....F 12	21 Uphampton, Heref.	9 Upham, Hants .....D 7	13 Upper Killay ......H 9
23 Turvey ....G 12	& Worc. ....F 9	21 Uphampton, Heref.	58 Upper Kinkell .....E 5
17 Turville ....E 8	22 Uphampton, Heref.	& Worc. ....F 9	19 Upper Kirby ......B 11
17 Turville Heath .....E 8	& Worc. ....F 2	22 Uphampton, Heref.	58 Upper Knaven .....C 6
23 Turweston ....H 9	14 Uphill ....H 6	& Worc. ....F 2	56 Upper Knockando ..E 7
48 Tushielaw ....G 6	49 Uplawmoor ....D 9	14 Uphill ....H 6	16 Upper Lambourn ..F 4
31 Tutbury ....G 10	15 Upleadon ....B 10	49 Uplawmoor ....D 9	15 Upper Langford ...H 8
22 Tutnall ....E 3	40 Upleatham ....C 6	15 Upleadon ....B 10	32 Upper Langwith ...C 2
15 Tutshill ....E 8	11 Uplees ....B 8	40 Upleatham ....C 6	31 Upper Leigh ......F 8
26 Tuttington ....C 5	7 Uploders ....G 8	11 Uplees ....B 8	59 Upper Lochton ....H 4
17 Tutts Clump ......G 7	6 Uplowman ....E 4	7 Uploders ....G 8	22 Upper Longdon ...A 4
3 Tutwell ....B 11	6 Uplyme ....G 6	6 Uplowman ....E 4	61 Upper Lybster ....D 11
32 Tuxford ....C 4	18 Upminster ....E 6	6 Uplyme ....G 6	15 Upper Lydbrook ..C 9
64 Twatt, Orkney Is. ...C 1	6 Upottery ....E 5	18 Upminster ....E 6	21 Upper Lye ....F 9
64 Twatt, Shetland Is. .D 7	21 Uppat ....F 2	6 Upottery ....E 5	62 Upper Milovaig ....C 1
47 Twechar ....B 11	21 Upper Affcott .....D 10	21 Uppat ....F 2	16 Upper Minety .....E 1
48 Tweddaleburn .....D 5	60 Upper Ardchronie ..G 6	21 Upper Affcott .....D 10	35 Upper Moor Side .D 11
49 Tweedmouth ......D 12	22 Upper Arley ......D 1	60 Upper Ardchronie ..G 6	15 Upper Morton .....E 9
48 Tweedshaws ....H 3	17 Upper Arncott ....B 7	22 Upper Arley ......D 1	58 Upper Mulben .....B 1
48 Tweedsmuir ....G 4	23 Upper Astrop .....H 8	17 Upper Arncott ....B 7	44 Upper Mumble ....E 2
2 Twelveheads ......E 5	42 Upper Barr ....E 5	23 Upper Astrop .....H 8	49 Upper Nisbet .....G 9
30 Twemlow Green ....C 6	63 Upper Barvas .....B 5	42 Upper Barr ....E 5	17 Upper North Dean .D 9
24 Twenty ....C 3	17 Upper Basildon ...F 7	63 Upper Barvas .....B 5	52 Upper Obney .....C 5
15 Twerton ....H 10	63 Upper Bayble .....D 6	17 Upper Basildon ...F 7	62 Upper Ollach .....E 4
44 Twice Brewed .....F 6	10 Upper Beeding ....G 1	63 Upper Bayble .....D 6	22 Upper Penn ....C 3
18 Twickenham ......G 2	24 Upper Benefield ...F 1	10 Upper Beeding ....G 1	36 Upper Poppleton ..B 3
15 Twigworth ....B 11	23 Upper Bentley ....E 3	24 Upper Benefield ...F 1	21 Upper Pulley .....B 10
10 Twineham ....F 1	58 Upper Boddam ....E 4	23 Upper Bentley ....E 3	22 Upper Quinton ....G 5
15 Twinhoe ....H 10	23 Upper Boddington .G 8	58 Upper Boddam ....E 4	8 Upper Ratley .....D 5
27 Twinstead ....L 2	20 Upper Borth ......D 2	23 Upper Boddington .G 8	21 Upper Rochford ...F 11
27 Twinstead Green ...L 2	9 Upper Bourne .....B 9	20 Upper Borth ......D 2	42 Upper Rusko ......E 6
4 Twitchen, Devon ..B 4	58 Upper Boyndie ....A 6	9 Upper Bourne .....B 9	55 Upper Sandaig ....H 2
4 Twitchen, Devon ..C 7	22 Upper Brailes .....H 6	58 Upper Boyndie ....A 6	21 Upper Sapey ......F 12
21 Twitchen, Salop ...D 9	62 Upper Breakish ...F 6	22 Upper Brailes .....H 6	46 Upper Scoulag ....C 6
5 Two Bridges ......H 5	21 Upper Breinton ...H 10	62 Upper Breakish ...F 6	16 Upper Seagry .....F 1
31 Two Dales ....D 11	32 Upper Broughton ..H 4	21 Upper Breinton ...H 10	63 Upper Shader .....B 5
22 Two Gates ....B 5	16 Upper Bucklebury ..G 6	32 Upper Broughton ..H 4	25 Upper Shelton ....L 1
4 Two Pots ....B 4	8 Upper Burgate ....D 3	16 Upper Bucklebury ..G 6	26 Upper Sheringham .A 4
23 Twycross ....B 7	59 Upper Burnhaugh ..H 6	8 Upper Burgate ....D 3	48 Upper Side ....D 6
17 Twyford, Berks. ...G 9	37 Ulceby Skitter .....F 9	59 Upper Burnhaugh ..H 6	47 Upper Skelmorlie ..C 7
17 Twyford, Bucks. ...B 7	11 Ulcombe ....C 7	25 Upper Caldecote ..L 3	16 Upper Slaughter ...B 3
31 Twyford, Derby ...G 11	38 Uldale ....B 5	8 Upper Canterton ..E 4	51 Upper Sonachan ..E 8
8 Twyford, Hants ...D 6	39 Uldale House ......F 9	23 Upper Catesby ....F 8	15 Upper Soudley ....C 9
23 Twyford, Leics. ...A 10	15 Uley ....D 11	20 Upper Chapel ....H 6	15 Upper Stanton Drew
26 Twyford, Norf. ....C 3	45 Ulgham ....D 10	6 Upper Cheddon ...C 6	H 9
15 Twyford Com ......A 8	60 Ullapool ....G 3	8 Upper Chicksgrove .C 1	25 Upper Stondon ....M 3
13 Twyn Llanan ......E 11	22 Ullingswick ......G 11	14 Upper Church Village	22 Upper Stonnal .....B 4
14 Twyncarno ....C 4	62 Ullinish ....D 2	F 4	23 Upper Stowe .....F 10
43 Twynholm ....F 7	38 Ullock ....C 3	8 Upper Chute ......A 4	8 Upper Street, Hants. D 3
15 Twyning ....A 12	8 Ullwell ....H 2	8 Upper Clatford ....B 5	26 Upper Street, Norf. .D 7
22 Twyning Green ....F 3		43 Upper Clifton .....F 10	22 Upper Strensham ..F 3
13 Twyn-mynydd .....F 10		28 Upper Clynnog ....F 4	17 Upper Sundon ....A 11
15 Twyn-y-Sheriff ....D 7		59 Upper Coll ....C 5	16 Upper Swell ......B 3
23 Twywell ....D 12		20 Upper Corris .....B 3	26 Upper Tasburgh ...F 5
28 Ty-Hen ....G 1		42 Upper Graigenbay .D 6	31 Upper Tean ....F 8
21 Tyberton ....H 9			52 Upper Tillyrie ....F 6

62 Upper Tote ....B 4	13 Velindre, Dyfed ....C 7	
15 Upper Town, Avon .H 8	12 Velindre, Dyfed ....C 4	
21 Upper Town,	14 Velindre, Powys ...A 5	
Heref. & Worc. ..G 11	6 Yellow ....B 4	
23 Upper Tysoe ......H 7	64 Vementry ....D 6	
16 Upper Upham .....F 3	64 Veness ....B 3	
10 Upper Upnor ......A 6	6 Venn Ottery ......G 4	
23 Upper Wardington ..G 8	21 Vennington ....A 9	
23 Upper Weald ......H 11	6 Venny Tedburn ...F 7	
23 Upper Weedon .....F 9	9 Ventnor ....H 7	
17 Upper Winchendon .C 8	16 Vernham Dean ....H 4	
8 Upper Woodford ..B 3	16 Vernham Street ...H 4	
58 Upper Woodhead ...F 4	12 Verwig ....B 5	
9 Upper Wootton ...A 9	8 Verwood ....E 2	
22 Upper Wyche .....H 1	6 Veryan ....F 6	
44 Upperby ....H 2	6 Vicarage ....G 5	
35 Uppermill ....G 8	38 Vickerstown ......H 4	
58 Uppertack of	6 Victoria, Corn. ....D 7	
Gressiehill ....B 6	14 Victoria, Gwent ...D 5	
35 Upperthong ......F 10	64 Vidlin ....C 7	
59 Upperton, Grampian K 5	10 Vinehall Street ....F 6	
9 Upperton, W. Sussex	10 Vine's Cross ....F 5	
D 11	15 Viney Hill ....C 9	
64 Uppertown ....F 2	17 Virginia Water ....G 10	
21 Uppington ....A 11	5 Virginstow ....G 3	
40 Upsall ....F 5	2 Vobster ....A 10	
18 Upshire ....D 4	64 Voe ....C 7	
11 Upstreet ....B 11	15 Vowchurch ....A 7	
17 Upton, Berks. ....F 10	64 Voxter ....C 7	
24 Upton, Cambs. ....E 2	64 Voy ....C 1	
25 Upton, Cambs. ....G 3	40 Wackerfield ......C 2	
30 Upton, Cheshire ...C 3	26 Wacton ....F 5	
4 Upton, Cornwall ..E 1	22 Wadborough .....G 3	
6 Upton, Devon ....F 4	17 Waddesdon ......B 8	
8 Upton, Dorset ....B 5	22 Waddingham .....G 7	
7 Upton, Dorset ...H 11	34 Waddington Lancs. .C 6	
8 Upton, Hants. ....D 5	33 Waddington, Lincs. .D 7	
32 Upton, Lincs. .....B 6	3 Wadebridge ......B 7	
30 Upton, Merseyside .A 1	6 Wadeford ....E 6	
26 Upton, Norfolk ...D 7	25 Wadenhoe ....G 1	
23 Upton, Northants ..F 10	18 Wadesmill ....B 4	
32 Upton, Notts. ....C 5	10 Wadhurst ....E 5	
32 Upton, Notts. ....A 5	31 Wadshelf ....C 11	
16 Upton, Oxon .....E 6	32 Wadsley ....A 11	
6 Upton, Somerset ..C 3	32 Wadsley Bridge ...A 1	
7 Upton, Somerset ..D 8	15 Wadswick ....G 11	
22 Upton, War. .....F 5	36 Wadworth ....F 6	
36 Upton W. Yorks. ..F 3	29 Waen Fach ....H 11	
15 Upton Bishop .....B 9	61 Wag ....E 9	
15 Upton Cheyney ...G 10	33 Wainfleet All Saints	
9 Upton Cressett ...C 12	D 12	
9 Upton Grey ......A 8	33 Wainfleet Bank ...D 11	
4 Upton Hellions ....F 7	45 Wainfordrigg .....C 7	
8 Upton Lovel ......B 1	32 Waingroves ......E 1	
21 Upton Magna ....A 11	2 Wainhouse Corner .B 2	
7 Upton Noble .....B 10	10 Wainscott ....A 6	
6 Upton Pyne ......F 3	35 Wainstalls ....D 9	
15 Upton St. Leonards	37 Waitby ....D 10	
C 11	35 Wakefield ....E 12	
7 Upton Scudamore .A 12	24 Wakerley ....F 1	
22 Upton Snodsbury ..G 3	19 Wakes Colne .....A 9	
22 Upton upon Severn .H 2	27 Walberswick ......H 8	
22 Upton Warren .....E 3	9 Walberton ....E 11	
9 Upwaltham ....E 10	45 Walbottle ....F 10	
25 Upware ....H 6	33 Walcot, Lincs. ....B 2	
24 Upwell ....E 6	33 Walcot, Lincs. ....E 8	
7 Upwey ....H 10	21 Walcot, Salop ...A 11	
25 Upwood ....G 4	21 Walcot, Salop ...D 9	
64 Urafirth ....C 6	22 Walcot, War. ....F 5	
56 Urchal ....E 3	16 Walcot, Wilts. ....F 3	
56 Urchany ....E 4	23 Walcote ....D 9	
16 Urchfont ....H 2	26 Walcott ....B 7	
63 Urgha Beag ....G 3	39 Walden Head ....G 12	
40 Urlay Nook ....D 4	36 Walden Stubbs ...E 3	
34 Urmston ....A 3	10 Walderslade ......B 6	
56 Urquhart, Grampian C 8	9 Walderton ....E 9	
56 Urquhart, Highland .D 1	7 Walditch ....G 8	
40 Urra ....E 6	31 Waldley ....F 9	
56 Urray ....D 1	45 Waldridge ....H 10	
40 Ushaw Moor ......A 3	27 Waldringfield .....L 6	
13 Usk ....D 7	10 Waldron ....F 4	
37 Usselby ....H 8	32 Wales ....B 2	
56 Ussie ....D 1	33 Walesby, Lincs. ....A 8	
64 Ustaness ....D 7	32 Walesby, Notts.....C 4	
45 Usworth ....G 11	15 Walford, Heref.	
35 Utley ....C 9	& Worc. ....B 9	
4 Uton ....D 7	21 Walford, Heref.	
37 Utterby ....H 10	& Worc. ....E 9	
31 Uttoxeter ....G 9	30 Walford, Salop ...H 3	
28 Uwchmynydd .....H 1	30 Walford Heath ...H 3	
18 Uxbridge ....F 1	30 Walghampton ....E 5	
64 Uyeasound ....B 8	23 Walgrave ....E 11	
12 Uzmaston ....F 3	8 Walhampton .....F 5	
12 Vachelich ....D 1	34 Walk Mill ....D 7	
28 Valley ....B 2	34 Walkden ....G 6	
3 Valley Truckle ....A 8	45 Walker ....G 11	
62 Valtos, Skye ......B 4	34 Walker Fold ......C 5	
63 Valtos, W. Isles ...C 2	48 Walkerburn ......F 6	
20 Van ....D 5	32 Walkeringham ....A 5	
19 Vange ....E 7	18 Walkern ....A 3	
14 Varteg Hill ....D 6	21 Walker's Green ...H 10	
62 Vatten ....D 2	53 Walkerton ....G 7	
14 Vaynor ....C 4	8 Walkford ....G 4	

5 Walkhampton ....J 4
37 Walkington ....C 8
32 Walkley ....A 1
45 Wall, Northumb. ....F 7
22 Wall, Staffs. ......B 4
44 Wall Bowers ....G 4
21 Wall under Heywood
   C 10
43 Wallaceton ....C 9
42 Wallacetown,
   Strathclyde .....A 4
47 Wallacetown,
   Strathclyde .....G 8
30 Wallasey ....A 2
38 Wallend, Cumbria .G 5
19 Wallend, Kent .....F 8
17 Wallingford ....E 7
9 Wallington, Hants. .E 7
25 Wallington, Herts. .M 4
18 Wallington, London H 3
9 Walliswood ....B 12
64 Walls ....D 6
45 Wallsend ....F 11
38 Wallthwaite ....C 6
48 Wallyford ....B 6
11 Walmer ....C 12
34 Walmer Bridge .....E 3
35 Walmersley ....F 7
22 Walmley ....C 5
27 Walpole ....H 7
24 Walpole Crosskeys .D 6
24 Walpole Highway ...D 6
24 Walpole Island ....D 6
24 Walpole St. Andrew D 6
24 Walpole St. Peter ..D 6
22 Walsall ....B 4
22 Wallsall Wood .....B 4
35 Walsden ....E 8
23 Walsgrave on Sowe .D 7
27 Walsham le Willows H 3
34 Walshaw ....F 6
35 Walshford ....B 12
48 Walston ....E 3
18 Walsworth ....A 2
17 Walter's Ash ......D 9
14 Walterston ....G 4
15 Walterstone ....B 7
11 Waltham, Kent .....C 6
37 Waltham, Humber. G 10
18 Waltham Abbey ....D 4
9 Waltham Chase .....E 7
18 Waltham Cross .....D 4
18 Waltham Forest ....E 4
32 Waltham on the Wolds
   H 2
17 Waltham St. Lawrence
   F 9
18 Walthamstow ......E 3
23 Walton, Bucks. , ..H 12
24 Walton, Cambs. ....E 3
44 Walton, Cumb. .....G 3
32 Walton, Derby .....C 1
23 Walton, Leics .....C 9
21 Walton, Powys .....F 8
30 Walton, Salop .....H 4
7 Walton, Som. ......C 8
27 Walton, Suffolk ...L 6
22 Walton, War. ......G 6
36 Walton, W. Yorks. .B 2
35 Walton, W. Yorks. .E 12
15 Walton Cardiff ....A 12
7 Walton Elm ....D 11
12 Walton East ....E 4
15 Walton-in-Gordano G 7
34 Walton-Le-Dale ....D 4
17 Walton-on-Thames
   G 12
34 Walton on the Hill,
   Merseyside ....H 3
31 Walton-on-the-Hill,
   Staffordshire ....H 8
10 Walton on the Hill,
   Surrey ....C 1
19 Walton on the Naze
   B 12
32 Walton on the Wolds
   H 3
15 Walton Park ....G 7
31 Walton upon Trent
   H 10
12 Walton West ....F 2
29 Walwen ....C 11
45 Walwick ....F 7
45 Walwick Grange ....F 7
40 Walworth ....C 3
12 Walwyn's Castle ...F 2
6 Wambrook ....E 6
43 Wamphraygate ......H 7
9 Wanborough, Surrey
   A 10
16 Wanborough, Wilts. .F 3
48 Wandel ....G 2
45 Wandon ....C 11
18 Wandsworth ....F 3

45 Wandylaw ....A 9
27 Wangford ....G 8
23 Wanlip ....A 9
48 Wanlockhead ....H 2
10 Wannock ....H 4
24 Wansford, Cambs. ..F 2
37 Wansford, Humber.
   B 8
18 Wanstead ....E 4
7 Wanstrow ....B 10
15 Wanswell ....D 10
16 Wantage ....E 5
23 Wappenbury ....E 7
23 Wappenham ....H 9
36 Warcop ....D 9
10 Warbleton ....F 5
9 Warblington ....E 8
17 Warborough ....E 7
25 Warboys ....G 4
34 Warbreck ....C 2
2 Warbstow ....B 2
30 Warburton ....A 5
27 Ward Green ....J 4
11 Warden ....A 9
23 Wardington ....G 8
48 Wardlaw, Borders ..H 5
47 Wardlaw,
   Strathclyde .....E 8
30 Wardle, Ches. .....E 5
35 Wardle, Lancs. ....E 8
23 Wardley ....B 11
31 Wardlow ....C 10
45 Wardon ....F 7
25 Wardy Hill ....G 6
18 Ware, Herts. ......C 4
11 Ware, Kent ....B 11
8 Wareham ....G 1
11 Warehorne ....E 8
45 Waren Mill ....C 12
45 Warenford ....C 12
45 Warenton ....C 12
18 Wareside ....B 4
25 Waresley, Cambs. ..K 3
22 Waresley, Heref.
   &Worc. ....E 2
17 Warfield ....G 9
5 Warfleet ....L 7
24 Wargate ....C 3
17 Wargrave ....F 9
26 Warham All Saints ..A 3
26 Warham St. Mary ...A 2
45 Wark, Northumb ....E 7
49 Wark, Northumb. ..E 11
4 Warkleigh ....D 5
23 Warkton ....D 12
23 Warkwork ....H 8
45 Warkworth ....B 10
40 Warlaby ....F 4
35 Warland ....E 8
3 Warleggan ....C 8
22 Warley ....C 3
10 Warlingham ....B 2
35 Warmfield ....E 12
30 Warmingham ....D 5
24 Warmington, Cambs. F 2
23 Warmington, War...G 7
7 Warminster ....B 11
11 Warmlake ....C 7
15 Warmley ....G 10
15 Warmley Tower ...G 10
36 Warmsworth ....G 3
7 Warmwell ....H 11
22 Warndon ....F 2
9 Warnford ....D 8
10 Warnham ....E 1
9 Warningcamp .....E 11
10 Warninglid ....E 1
31 Warren, Ches. ....C 7
12 Warren, Dyfed ....G 3
5 Warren House Inn .H 5
17 Warren Row ....F 9
11 Warren Street ....C 8
23 Warrington, Bucks.
   G 12
30 Warrington, Ches. ..A 5
8 Warsash ....E 6
31 Warslow ....D 9
32 Warsop ....C 3
36 Warter ....B 6
40 Warthermaske ....G 2
36 Warthill ....B 4
10 Wartling ....G 5
32 Wartnaby ....H 4
34 Warton, Lancs. ....D 3
39 Warton, Lancs. ....H 7
45 Warton, Northumb. .C 8
22 Warton, War. .....B 6
44 Warwick, Cumb. ...G 3
22 Warwick, War. .....F 6
44 Warwick Bridge ...G 3
22 Warwickshire, Co. ..F 6
44 Warwicksland ......E 3
64 Wasbister ....B 2
38 Wasdale Head ......D 4

16 Wash Common .....H 5
3 Washaway ....C 7
5 Washbourne ....K 7
31 Washerwall ....E 8
6 Washfield ....E 3
40 Washfold ....E 1
6 Washford ....B 4
4 Washford Pyne ....E 7
33 Washingborough ...C 7
45 Washington,
   Tyne & Wear ....G 11
9 Washington,
   W. Sussex ....E 12
17 Wasing ....H 7
40 Waskerley ....A 1
22 Wasperton ....F 6
40 Wass ....G 6
6 Watchet ....B 4
16 Watchfield, Oxon ..E 3
7 Watchfield, Som. ..B 7
39 Watchgate ....E 9
43 Watchill ....G 12
38 Watendlath ....D 5
5 Water, Devon .....H 6
35 Water, Lancs. ....E 7
18 Water End, Herts. ..C 2
36 Water End, Humber. C 6
24 Water Newton .....F 2
22 Water Orton ......C 5
17 Water Stratford ...A 7
14 Water Street ......F 1
38 Water Yeat ....F 5
25 Waterbeach ....J 6
44 Waterbeck ....E 1
26 Waterden ....B 2
17 Waterend ....E 9
31 Waterfall ....E 9
35 Waterfoot, Lancs. ..E 7
47 Waterfoot,
   Strathclyde .....D 10
8 Waterford, Hants. ..G 5
18 Waterford, Herts. ..B 3
38 Waterhead, Cumb. ..E 6
43 Waterhead, Dumf.
   & Gall. ....B 12
43 Waterhead, Dumf.
   & Gall. ....C 8
47 Waterford,
   Strathclyde .....H 10
48 Waterheads ....D 5
45 Waterhouses, Dur ..A 5
31 Waterhouses, Staffs. E 9
33 Watering Dyke Houses
   B 7
10 Wateringbury .....C 6
64 Wateringhouse ....E 2
15 Waterlane ....D 12
32 Waterloo, Derby ...D 1
8 Waterloo, Dorset ..G 2
12 Waterloo, Dyfed ...G 3
34 Waterloo,
   Merseyside ......G 2
26 Waterloo, Norf. ...D 5
62 Waterloo, Skye ...F 6
48 Waterloo,
   Strathclyde .....D 1
52 Waterloo, Tayside ..C 5
6 Waterloo Cross ....E 4
9 Waterlooville .....E 8
48 Watermeetings ....H 2
17 Waterperry ....C 7
5 Waterrow ....D 4
30 Waters Upton .....H 5
18 Watersfield ......E 11
43 Waterside, Dumf.
   & Gall. ....D 12
58 Waterside Grampian E 7
42 Waterside,
   Strathclyde .....A 5
47 Waterside
   Strathclyde .....E 9
47 Waterside,
   Strathclyde .....B 11
17 Waterstock ....D 7
13 Waterston ....F 3
18 Watford, Herts. ...D 1
23 Watford, Northants. E 9
7 Wath, N. Yorks. ...G 3
40 Wath, N. Yorks. ...H 2
38 Wath Brow ....D 3
36 Wath upon Dearne .G 2
15 Watley's End .....F 9
24 Watlington, Norf. ..D 7
17 Watlington, Oxon ..E 8
32 Watnall Chaworth ..F 2
61 Watten ....B 11
22 Wattisfield ......H 3
27 Wattisham ....K 3
37 Watton, Humberside B 8
26 Watton, Norf. .....E 2
18 Watton-at-Stone ..B 3
47 Wattston ....B 12
14 Wattstown ....E 3

55 Wauchan ....L 3
37 Wauldby ....D 7
20 Waun Fawr ....D 2
13 Waunarlwydd .....G 9
13 Waun-deg ....D 7
28 Waunfawr ....D 5
13 Waunlwyd ....D 5
23 Wavendon ....H 12
44 Waverbridge ......H 1
30 Waverton, Ches. ...D 3
44 Waverton, Cumb. ..H 1
37 Wawne ....C 8
26 Waxham ....C 7
37 Waxholme ....D 11
6 Way Village ....E 3
7 Wayfield ....B 6
7 Wayford ....F 7
7 Waytown ....F 8
6 Weacombe ....B 5
18 Wealdstone ....E 2
35 Weardley ....C 11
4 Weare ....A 7
4 Weare Giffard ....D 3
39 Weasdale ....E 9
26 Weasenham All Saints
   C 1
26 Weasenham St. Peter
   C 1
30 Weaverham ....C 5
41 Weaverthorpe .....H 9
22 Webheath ....E 4
5 Webton ....A 7
58 Wedderlairs ......D 6
49 Wedderlie ....D 9
23 Weddington ......C 7
16 Wedhampton ......H 2
7 Wedmore ....A 8
22 Wednesbury ....C 3
22 Wednesfield ......B 3
17 Weedon ....B 9
23 Weedon Bec ....F 9
23 Weedon Lois ......G 9
22 Weeford ....B 5
4 Week, Devon ......C 4
4 Week, Devon ......D 6
4 Week St. Mary ....F 1
4 Weeke ....C 6
23 Weekely ....D 12
37 Weel ....C 8
19 Weeley ....B 11
19 Weeley Heath .....B 11
52 Weem ....B 3
21 Weeping Cross,
   Shropshire ......A 10
31 Weeping Cross,
   Staffordshire ...H 8
27 Weeting ....G 1
34 Weeton, Lancs. ....D 3
35 Weeton, N. Yorks. .B 11
49 Weetwoodhill ....F 12
35 Weir ....E 7
15 Weirend ....B 9
32 Welbeck Abbey ...C 3
32 Welbeck Colliery ..C 3
26 Welborne ....E 4
33 Welbourn ....E 7
41 Welburn, N. Yorks. .G 7
41 Welburn, N. Yorks. .H 7
40 Welbury ....E 4
33 Welby ....F 7
25 Welches Dam ......G 6
4 Welcombe ....D 1
23 Weldon ....C 12
45 Weldon Bridge ....C 9
16 Welford, Berks. ...G 5
23 Welford, Northants. B 9
22 Welford-on-Avon ..G 5
23 Welham ....C 11
18 Welhamgreen .....C 2
9 Well, Hants. ......A 9
33 Well, Lincs. ......C 11
40 Well, N. Yorks. ...G 3
7 Well Bottom ......E 12
17 Well End ....E 9
10 Well Hill ....B 4
6 Well Town ....E 3
22 Welland ....H 2
53 Wellbank ....D 9
43 Welldale ....E 12
22 Wellesbourne Hastings
   G 6
22 Wellesbourne
   Mountford ......G 6
40 Wellfields ....A 4
59 Wellford ....L 2
18 Welling ....F 5
22 Wellingborough ..E 12
26 Wellingham ....C 2
33 Wellingore ....E 7
38 Wellington, Cumb. ..E 3
21 Wellington, Heref.
   & Worc. ....H 10
21 Wellington, Salop .A 12

6 Wellington, Som. ...D 5
21 Wellington Heath .H 12
21 Wellington Marsh .H 10
15 Wellow, Avon .....H 10
8 Wellow, I.o.W. ....G 5
32 Wellow, Notts. ....D 4
7 Wells ....B 9
26 Wells-next-the-Sea .A 2
58 Wells of Ytham ...D 4
23 Wellsborough .....B 7
5 Wellswood ....J 8
52 Wellwood ....H 6
24 Welney ....F 6
4 Welsford ....D 1
15 Welsh Bicknor ....C 9
30 Welsh Frankton ...G 2
12 Welsh Hook ....D 3
15 Welsh Newton .....B 8
14 Welsh St. Donats ..G 4
30 Welshampton .....G 3
21 Welshpool ....B 8
7 Welton, Avon .....A 10
38 Welton, Cumb. .....A 6
37 Welton, Humberside D 7
33 Welton, Lincs. ....B 7
23 Welton, Northants .E 9
33 Welton le Marsh ..C 11
33 Welton le Wold ...B 10
37 Welwick ....E 11
18 Welwyn ....B 2
18 Welwyn Garden City
   C 2
30 Wem ....G 4
6 Wembdon ....C 6
18 Wembley ....E 2
5 Wembury ....L 4
4 Wembworthy ......E 5
2 Wendron ....G 4
25 Wendy ....K 4
27 Wenhaston ....H 7
25 Wennington, Cambs.
   G 3
39 Wennington, Lancs. H 8
18 Wennington, London
   F 5
31 Wensley, Derby. ..D 11
40 Wensley, N.Yorks. ..F 1
36 Wentbridge ......E 3
21 Wentnor ....C 9
26 Wentworth, Cambs. G 6
35 Wentworth, S. Yorks
   G 12
14 Wenvoe ....G 4
21 Weobley ....G 9
21 Weobley Marsh ...G 9
24 Wareham ....E 8
22 Wergs ....B 2
14 Wern ....C 4
13 Wernffrwd ....H 8
15 Wernyrheolydd ....C 7
24 Werrington, Cambs. E 3
3 Werrington, Corn. A 10
31 Werrington, Suffolk .E 8
30 Wervin ....C 3
34 Wesham ....D 3
32 Wessington ......D 1
26 West Acre ....D 1
16 West Adderbury ..A 5
6 West Adsborough ..C 6
49 West Allerdean ..E 12
45 West Allotment ..F 11
5 West Alvington ...L 6
8 West Amesbury ...B 3
4 West Anstey .....C 7
4 West Ash ....D 2
33 West Ashby ....C 9
9 West Ashling .....E 9
7 West Ashton .....A 12
40 West Auckland ...C 2
41 West Ayton ......G 10
59 West Balhagarty ..K 5
6 West Bagborough ..C 5
33 West Barkwith ...B 8
41 West Barnby .....D 8
49 West Barns ....B 9
42 West Barr ....G 4
7 West Bay ....G 8
26 West Beckham ....B 4
17 West Bedfont ...G 11
45 West Benridge ...D 10
19 West Bergholt ....A 9
7 West Bexington ..H 9
24 West Bilney ......D 8
49 West Blackadder .D 11
10 West Blatchington G 2
48 West Bold ....F 6
45 West Boldon .....G 11
43 West Bowhill ....D 12
35 West Bowling ....D 10

26 West Bradenham ...E 2
34 West Bradford ....C 6
7 West Bradley .....C 9
59 West Braidieston ..K 5
35 West Bretton ....F 11
32 West Bridgford ...G 3
22 West Bromwich ....C 4
47 West Browncastle .E 11
4 West Buckland,
   Devon ....C 5
6 West Buckland, Som. D 5
64 West Burrafirth ..D 6
9 West Burton,
   W. Sussex ....E 11
39 West Burton,
   N. Yorks. ....F 12
40 West Butsfield ....A 1
36 West Butterwick ..B 8
17 West Byfleet .....H 11
49 West Byres ....C 7
26 West Caister .....D 8
48 West Calder ......C 3
7 West Camel ....D 9
58 West Cannahars ...E 7
47 West Carberth ....B 10
36 West Carr ....F 5
47 West Cauldcoats ..E 11
7 West Chaldon .....H 11
16 West Challow .....E 4
7 West Chelborough .F 9
45 West Chevington ..C 10
9 West Chiltington .D 12
9 West Chiltington
   Common ....D 12
7 West Chinnock ....E 8
8 West Chisenbury ..A 3
9 West Clandon ....A 11
11 West Cliffe ......D 12
61 West Clyth ....D 11
7 West Coker ....E 8
7 West Compton,
   Dorset ....G 9
7 West Compton, Som. B 9
36 West Cowick ......E 4
7 West Cranmore ...B 10
27 West Creeting Grn. .J 4
13 West Cross ....H 9
44 West Curthwaite ..H 2
46 West Darlochan ...G 2
8 West Dean, Hants. ..C 4
9 West Dean, Sus. ...E 10
24 West Deeping .....E 2
30 West Derby ....A 3
24 West Dereham ....E 7
45 West Ditchburn ...A 9
4 West Down ....B 4
18 West Drayton, London
   F 1
32 West Drayton, Notts.
   C 4
45 West Edington ....E 9
37 West Ella ....D 8
15 West End, Avon ...G 8
17 West End, Berks. ..G 9
28 West End, Gwynedd G 3
8 West End, Hants. ..E 6
18 West End, Herts. ..C 3
37 West End, Humber. D 7
33 West End, Lincs. .G 11
26 West End, Norf. ...D 8
48 West End,
   Strathclyde .....E 2
17 West End, Surrey ..H 10
8 West End, Wilts. ..D 1
45 West Fallodon ...A 10
10 West Farleigh ....C 6
30 West Felton ......H 2
10 West Firle ....G 3
36 West Garforth ....D 2
16 West Ginge ....E 5
13 West Glamorgan, Co.
   G 10
16 West Grafton .....H 3
17 West Green ....H 8
8 West Grimstead ...D 4
10 West Grinstead ...F 1
36 West Haddlesey ...D 3
23 West Haddon ......E 9
16 West Hagbourne ..E 6
22 West Hagley ......D 3
44 West Hall ....F 4
32 West Hallam ......F 2
37 West Halton ......E 7
18 West Ham ....F 4
16 West Hanney .....E 5
19 West Hanningfield .D 7
36 West Hardwick ....E 2
24 West Harnham .....C 3
7 West Harptree ....A 9
21 West Harrington .H 11
40 West Hartlepool ..B 5
6 West Hatch ....D 6
15 West Hay ....H 8
24 West Head ....E 7

17 West Heath ....H 9	4 West Sandford ......F 7	48 Wester Ochiltree ..B 3
61 West Helmsdale ...E 9	64 West Sandwick .....B 7	49 Wester Pencaitland .C 7
16 West Hendred ......E 5	40 West Scrafton ......C 9	64 Wester Quarff ......E 7
41 West Heslerton ....H 9	48 West Sidewood ....D 3	56 Wester Rarichie ....B 4
15 West Hill, Avon ...G 8	43 West Skelston ......C 9	57 Wester Shennach ..G 7
6 West Hill, Devon. .G 4	45 West Sleekburn ...E 11	54 Wester Slumbay ....F 3
10 West Hoathly .....E 2	26 West Somerton ....D 7	56 Wester Teaninch ...C 2
7 West Holme ......H 12	7 West Stafford ....G 10	61 Westerdale,
49 West Hopes ......C 8	36 West Stockwith ....E 9	Highland ....C 10
18 West Horndon .....E 6	9 West Stoke ....E 9	41 Westerdale,
7 West Horrington ...A 9	39 West Stonesdale ..E 11	N. Yorks ....E 7
9 West Horsley .....A 12	7 West Stoughton ...A 7	27 Westerfield ....K 5
45 West Horton ......C 11	7 West Stour ....D 11	9 Westergate ....F 10
11 West Hougham ...D 11	11 West Stourmouth ..B 11	10 Westerham ....C 3
10 West Humble .....C 1	27 West Stow ....H 1	45 Westerhope ....F 10
6 West Huntspill ....B 6	16 West Stowell ......H 2	15 Westerleigh ....F 10
17 West Hyde ....E 11	60 West Strathan .....B 6	64 Westermill ....E 3
11 West Hythe ......E 10	8 West Stratton .....B 6	40 Westerton, Dur. ...B 3
16 West Ilsley ....F 6	11 West Street ....C 8	58 Westerton,
9 West Itchenor ....F 9	40 West Summer Side ..G 2	Grampian ....C 3
33 West Keal ....D 10	10 West Sussex, Co. ..E 1	53 Westerton,
16 West Kennett .....G 2	40 West Tanfield ......G 3	Tayside ....B 11
47 West Kilbride .....E 7	3 West Tapnouse ....C 8	9 Westerton,
10 West Kingsdown ..B 5	46 West Tarbert ......B 1	W. Sussex .....E 10
15 West Kington .....F 11	49 West Third ....F 9	58 Westertown ....C 3
58 West Kinharrachie ..D 7	45 West Thirston .....C 10	58 Westfield, Cumb. ..B 2
58 West Kinnernie ...F 5	9 West Thorney .....F 9	11 Westfield, E. Sussex .F 7
30 West Kirby ....B 1	18 West Thurrock ....F 6	58 Westfield, Grampian
41 West Knapton ....H 9	9 West Tisted ....C 8	E 7
7 West Knighton ...G 10	52 West Tofts ....D 6	22 Westfield, Heref.
7 West Knoyle .....C 11	33 West Torrington ...B 8	& Worc. ....G 1
45 West Kyloe ......B 11	15 West Town, Avon ..G 8	61 Westfield,
7 West Lambrook ...D 7	15 West Town, Avon ..H 8	Highland ....B 10
11 West Langdon ...C 11	9 West Town, Hants ..F 8	26 Westfield, Norf. ...D 3
61 West Langwell ....F 7	21 West Town, Heref.	45 Westfield, Northumb.
9 West Lavington,	& Worc. ....F 10	D 12
W. Sussex ......D 10	8 West Tytherley ....C 4	7 Westfields ....F 10
8 West Lavington,	16 West Tytherton ...G 1	52 Westfields of Rattray
Wiltshire ....A 2	24 West Walton ......D 6	C 6
40 West Layton ......D 2	24 West Walton	39 Westgate, Dur. ....A 11
32 West Leake ......G 3	Highway ....D 6	36 Westgate, Lincs. ...F 5
49 West Learmouth ..F 11	4 West Warlington ...E 6	26 Westgate, Norf. ...B 3
26 West Lexham .....D 1	53 West Wemyss .....H 8	11 Westgate on Sea ...A 11
36 West Lilling ......A 4	15 West Wick ....H 7	44 Westgillsyke ......F 2
45 West Linkhall ....A 10	25 West Wickham,	27 Westhall ....G 7
48 West Linton ......D 4	Cambs. ....K 7	7 Westham, Dorset ..H 10
9 West Liss ....C 9	18 West Wickham,	10 Westham, E. Sussex .H 5
15 West Littleton ....G 11	London ....G 4	7 Westham, Som. ...B 7
3 West Looe ....D 9	12 West Williamston ..F 4	9 Westhampnett ....E 10
6 West Luccombe ...B 2	8 West Willow ......D 4	58 Westhaugh ....E 4
7 West Lulworth ...H 11	24 West Winch ......D 7	7 Westhay ....B 8
41 West Lutton ......H 9	8 West Winterslow ...C 4	34 Westhead ....F 3
7 West Lydford ....C 9	9 West Wittering ....F 9	21 Westhide ....H 11
45 West Lyham .....C 12	40 West Witton ......F 1	59 Westhill ....G 6
7 West Lyng ....C 7	45 West Woodburn ...D 7	21 Westhope, Heref.
24 West Lynn ......D 7	16 West Woodhay ....H 5	& Worc. ....G 10
45 West Mains,	7 West Woodlands ..B 11	31 Westhope, Salop ..D 10
Northumb. ....B 12	9 West Worldham ...B 9	24 Westhorpe, Lincs. ..B 3
47 West Mains,	25 West Wratting .....K 7	27 Westhorpe, Suff. ..H 3
Strathclyde ....D 8	17 West Wycombe ...E 9	34 Westhoughton ....G 5
48 West Mains,	64 West Yell ....C 7	39 Westhouse ....H 9
Strathclyde ....D 2	35 West Yorkshire, Co.	32 Westhouses ......D 2
10 West Malling .....B 5	D 10	4 Westleigh, Devon ..C 3
22 West Malvern .....G 1	4 Westacott ....C 5	6 Westleigh, Devon ..D 4
9 West Marden .....E 9	11 Westbere ....B 10	34 Westleigh,
32 West Markham ....C 4	32 Westborough ......F 6	Gtr. Manchester ..G 5
37 West Marsh ......F 10	8 Westbourne, Dorset .F 2	27 Westleton ....H 7
35 West Marton .....B 8	27 Westbourne, Suff. ..K 5	21 Westley, Salop ....B 9
9 West Meon ....D 8	9 Westbourne,	27 Westley, Suffolk ...J 1
19 West Mersea .....C 10	W. Sussex .....E 9	25 Westley Waterless .K 7
22 West Midlands, Co. .C 4	16 Westbrook ....G 5	17 Westlington ......C 8
7 West Milton ......G 8	17 Westbury, Bucks. ..A 7	44 Westlinton ....G 2
11 West Minster .....A 8	21 Westbury, Salop ...A 9	11 Westmarsh ......B 11
17 West Molesey ....G 12	7 Westbury, Wilts. ..A 12	10 Westmeston ......G 2
8 West Moors ......F 2	7 Westbury Leigh ..A 12	18 Westmill ....A 4
7 West Morden ....G 12	15 Westbury on Trym .G 9	18 Westminster ......F 3
49 West Morrison ....F 8	15 Westbury-on-Severn	53 Westmuir ....B 8
41 West Ness ....G 7	C 10	64 Westness ....B 2
37 West Newton,	7 Westbury-sub-Mendip	43 Westnewton, Cumb.
Humberside ......C 9	A 8	G 12
24 West Newton, Norfolk	34 Westby ....D 3	49 Westnewton,
C 8	12 Westcatt ....A 12	Northumb. ....F 11
5 West Ogwell .....J 7	19 Westcliff on Sea ..E 8	15 Weston, Avon .....H 10
7 West Orchard ....E 11	7 Westcombe ....B 10	30 Weston, Ches. ....E 6
16 West Overton .....G 2	17 Westcote ....B 3	30 Weston, Ches. ....B 4
59 West Park ....H 5	17 Westcott, Bucks. ..B 8	6 Weston, Devon ...F 5
8 West Parley ......F 2	6 Westcott, Devon ..F 4	6 Weston, Devon ...G 5
5 West Panson .....G 2	15 Westcott Barton ..B 5	7 Weston, Dorset ...H 7
49 West Peaston ....C 7	10 Westdean ....H 4	9 Weston, Hants. ...D 8
10 West Peckham ....C 5	57 Wester Aviemore ..H 4	18 Weston, Herts. ...A 3
45 West Pelton .....H 10	52 Wester Balgedie ..G 6	24 Weston, Lincs. ....C 4
7 West Pennard ....B 9	48 Wester Causewayend	35 Weston, N. Yorks. .B 10
2 West Pentire .....D 5	C 3	23 Weston, Northants .G 9
6 West Porlock .....B 2	52 Wester Clunie .....A 4	32 Weston, Notts. ....C 5
4 West Putford .....D 2	49 Wester Essenside ..G 7	21 Weston, Salop ...C 11
6 West Quantoxhead ..B 6	58 Wester Fintray .....F 6	21 Weston, Salop ....E 9
45 West Rainton ....H 11	57 Wester Fodderletter	30 Weston, Salop ....G 4
33 West Rasen ......A 8	G 7	31 Weston, Staffs. ...G 8
26 West Raynham ...C 2	60 Wester Greenyards .G 6	48 Weston, Strathclyde
40 West Rounton ....E 4	49 Wester Happrew ...E 4	E 3
25 West Row ....H 8	49 Wester Housebryres .F 8	7 Weston Bampfylde .D 9
26 West Rudham .....C 1	56 Wester Lamington ..B 3	21 Weston Beggard ..H 11
26 West Runton .....A 5	56 Wester Milton .....D 5	23 Weston by Welland
49 West Saltoun .....C 7	53 Wester Newburn ...G 9	C 11

25 Weston Colville ....K 7	22 Whateley ....B 6	48 Whitecraig ....B 6
31 Weston Coyney ....F 8	27 Whatfield ....K 3	15 Whitecroft ....D 9
23 Weston Favell ....F 11	10 Whatlington ......F 6	42 Whitecrook ....F 3
25 Weston Green ....K 7	31 Whatstandwell ...E 11	48 Whitecross, Central .B 2
15 Weston Heath ....A 1	32 Whatton ....F 5	3 Whitecross, Corn. ..B 7
15 Weston-in-Gordano	42 Whauphill ....G 5	61 Whiteface ....G 7
G 8	26 Wheatacre ....F 8	42 Whitefarland .....A 4
30 Weston Jones ....H 6	18 Wheathampstead ..C 2	42 Whitefaulds ......A 4
26 Weston Longville ..D 4	9 Wheatley, Hants. ..B 9	35 Whitefields,
30 Weston Lullingfields H 3	17 Wheatley, Oxon. ..D 7	Manchester .....G 7
22 Weston-on-Avon ..A 3	40 Wheatley Hill .....A 4	52 Whitefield, Tayside .D 6
16 Weston-on-the-Grn .B 6	30 Wheatley Lane ....C 7	6 Whitefirld, Som. ..C 4
9 Weston Patrick ...B 8	22 Wheaton Aston ...A 2	58 Whiteford ....E 5
30 Weston Rhyn .....G 1	6 Wheddon Cross ...B 3	6 Whitehall, Devon .E 5
15 Weston Road .....G 8	58 Wheedlemont .....E 2	64 Whitehall, Orkney .B 4
22 Weston Sudedge ..H 5	17 Wheeler's Green ..G 8	43 Whitehaugh ......B 3
14 Weston-super-Mare H 4	9 Wheelerstreet ....B 11	38 Whitehaven ......C 2
17 Weston Turville ...C 9	30 Wheelock ....D 6	43 Whitehill, Dumf.
15 Weston under Penyard	30 Wheelock Heath ..D 6	& Gall. ....D 12
B 9	34 Wheelton ....E 5	58 Whitehill, Grampian B 3
23 Weston under	59 Wheen ....K 1	9 Whitehill, Hants. ..C 9
Wetherley ....E 7	36 Wheldrake ....C 4	47 Whitehill,
23 Weston Underwood,	16 Whelford ....D 3	Strathclyde ....D 7
Bucks. ....G 12	38 Whelpo ....A 5	58 Whitehills, Grampian
31 Weston Underwood,	40 Whenby ....H 6	A 4
Derbyshire ......F 11	27 Whepstead ....J 1	47 Whitehills,
32 Weston Upon Trent .G 1	27 Wherstead ....L 5	Strathclyde ....D 11
22 Weston-under-Lizard	8 Wherwell ....B 5	58 Whitehouse,
A 2	31 Wheston ....C 10	Grampian ....F 4
15 Westonbirt ......E 11	10 Whetsted ....C 5	46 Whitehouse,
25 Westoning ....M 1	23 Whetstone ....B 9	Strathclyde ....C 3
7 Westonzoyland ...C 7	16 Whichford ....A 4	49 Whitekirk ....A 8
36 Westow ....A 5	38 Whicham, Cumb. ..G 4	59 Whiteknowes .....G 3
7 Westport, Som. ...D 7	45 Whickham,	7 Whitelackington ..E 7
46 Westport,	& Wear ....G 10	49 Whitelaw ....D 11
Strathclyde ......G 2	5 Whiddon Down ...G 6	49 Whitelee ....F 8
16 Westridge Green ..F 6	53 Whigstreet ....C 9	36 Whiteley ....F 3
48 Westrigg ....C 2	23 Whilton ....F 9	9 Whiteley Bank ....H 7
49 Westruther ....D 9	4 Whimble ....F 2	31 Whitlcey Green ...B 9
24 Westry ....F 5	6 Whimple ....F 4	17 Whiteley Village ..H 11
38 Westville ....E 2	26 Whimpwell Green ..C 7	10 Whitemans Green ..E 2
4 Westward Ho .....C 3	26 Whinburgh ....E 3	56 Whitemire ....D 5
4 Westwater ....E 1	49 Whinkerstones ...E 10	3 Whitemoor ....D 7
11 Westwell, Kent ...C 8	43 Whinnie Liggate ..F 8	31 Whitemore ....D 7
16 Westwell, Oxon ...C 3	58 Whinnyfold ......D 8	8 Whitenap ....D 5
11 Westwell Leacon ..C 8	9 Whippingham ....G 6	8 Whiteparish ......D 4
25 Westwick, Cambs. ..J 5	17 Whipsnade ....B 11	58 Whiterashes ......E 6
40 Westwick, Dur. ...D 1	25 Whissendine ......A 11	48 Whiteside, Lothian ..C 1
6 Westwood, Devon .F 4	26 Whissonsett ......C 2	44 Whiteside, Northumb.
45 Westwood, Dur,. ..C 9	17 Whistley Green ...G 9	F 5
47 Westwood,	23 Whiston, Northants.	10 Whitesmith ......G 4
Strathclyde ......D 11	F 11	6 Whitestaunton ....E 6
15 Westwood, Wilts. .H 11	30 Whiston, Merseyside A 3	4 Whitestone, Devon .A 4
16 Westwoodside ....G 5	32 Whiston, S. Yorks. .A 2	4 Whitestone, Devon ..F 7
40 Wether Cote .....F 4	22 Whiston, Staffs. ...A 2	59 Whitestone,
44 Wetheral ....H 3	31 Whiston, Staffs. ...F 8	Grampian ....H 4
35 Wetherby ....B 12	30 Whiston Lane Ends .A 3	58 Whitestones ......B 6
27 Wetherden ....J 3	38 Whitbeck ....G 3	15 Whiteway ....C 12
27 Wetheringsett ....J 4	21 Whitbourne ......G 12	6 Whiteway House ..H 2
25 Wethersfield .....M 8	21 Whitbourne Ford ..F 1	34 Whitewell ....B 5
64 Wethersta ....C 7	48 Whitburn, Lothian .C 2	5 Whiteworks ....J 5
27 Wetherup Street ..J 4	45 Whitburn, Tyne	56 Whitewreath ......D 8
31 Wetley Rocks .....E 8	& Wear ....G 12	15 Whitfield, Avon ...E 10
30 Wettenhall ....D 5	45 Whitburn Colliery .G 12	48 Whitfield, Borders .D 4
31 Wetton ....E 9	30 Whitby, Cheshire ..C 3	11 Whitfield, Kent ...D 11
30 Wetwang ....G 6	41 Whitby, N. Yorks. .D 9	23 Whitfield, Northants.
30 Wetwood ....G 6	44 Whitcastles ......D 1	H 9
16 Wexcombe ....H 4	15 Whitchurch, Avon ..G 9	44 Whitfield, Northumb.
27 Wexham Street ..F 10	17 Whitchurch, Bucks. .B 9	G 6
26 Weybourne ......A 4	5 Whitchurch, Devon .H 4	29 Whitford, Clwyd ..B 10
27 Weybread ....G 5	12 Whitchurch, Dyfed .D 2	6 Whitford, Devon ..G 6
17 Weybridge ......H 11	8 Whitchurch, Hants. .A 6	36 Whitgift ....E 6
6 Weycroft ....F 6	15 Whitchurch, Heref.	31 Whitgreave ......G 7
61 Weydale ....A 10	& Worc. ....C 8	42 Whithorn ....G 5
8 Weyhill ....B 5	17 Whichurch, Oxon ..F 7	46 Whiting Bay .....G 5
7 Weymouth ....G 7	30 Whitchurch, Salop .F 4	24 Whitington ......E 8
17 Whaddon, Bucks. ..A 9	14 Whitchurch, S. Glam. F 5	12 Whitland ....E 5
25 Whaddon, Cambs. ..K 4	17 Whitchurch Hill ...F 7	44 Whitlaw ....B 3
15 Whaddon, Glos. ..C 11	7 Whitcombe ......G 10	47 Whitletts ....G 8
8 Whaddon, Wilts. ..C 3	21 Whitcott Keysett ..D 8	17 Whitley, Berks. ...G 8
39 Whale ....C 7	34 White Chapel ....C 4	15 Whitley, Wilts. ...H 12
32 Whaley ....C 2	34 White Coppice .....E 5	45 Whitley Bay .....F 11
31 Whaley Bridge ....B 8	7 White Cross, Avon .A 9	45 Whitley Chapel ...G 7
32 Whaley Thorns ...C 3	6 White Cross, Devon.	35 Whitley Lower ...E 11
34 Whalley ....D 6		22 Whitlock's End ...D 4
45 Whalton ....E 9	7 White Lackington ..F 10	15 Whitminster .....D 11
34 Wham ....A 6	22 White Ladies Aston .G 3	31 Whitmore ....F 7
24 Whaplode ....C 4	13 White Mill ....E 8	6 Whitnage ....E 4
24 Whaplode Drove ..D 4	19 White Notley .....B 8	21 Whitney ....H 8
24 Whaplode	33 White Pit ....B 11	38 Whitrigg, Cumb. ..A 4
St. Catherine ....D 4	18 White Roding .....C 5	44 Whitrigg, Cumb. ..G 1
39 Wharfe ....H 10	21 White Stone .....H 11	44 Whitriggs ....B 4
34 Wharles ....D 3	17 White Waltham ...F 9	8 Whitsbury ....D 3
45 Wharmley ....F 7	56 Whiteacre ....E 8	4 Whitsleigh Barton .D 4
35 Wharncliffe Side .H 11	22 Whiteacre Heath ..C 5	6 Whitsome ....D 4
30 Wharram-le-Street .A 5	55 Whitebridge ......H 8	49 Whitsomehill ....D 11
30 Wharton, Ches. ...D 5	15 Whitebrook ......D 8	15 Whitson ....F 7
21 Wharton, Heref.	49 Whiteburn ....E 8	15 Whitson Common .F 7
& Worc. ....G 10	42 Whitecairn ....F 3	11 Whitstable ......A 9
40 Whashton ....E 2	58 Whitecairns ......F 7	4 Whitstone ....F 1
39 Whasset ....G 7	48 Whitecastle ....E 3	45 Whittingham .....B 9
22 Whatcote ....H 6	7 Whitechurch	21 Whittingslow .....D 9
	Canonicorum .....G 7	32 Whittington, Derby. .C 1

16 Whittington, Glos. ..B 1
22 Whittington, Heref.
& Worc. ....G 2
39 Whittington, Lancs. ..H 8
30 Whittington, Salop .G 2
22 Whittington, Staffs. .A 5
22 Whittington, Staffs. .D 2
34 Whittle-le-Woods ...E 5
23 Whittlebury ....H 10
24 Whittlesey ....F 4
25 Whittlesford ......K 6
34 Whittlestone Head ..E 6
49 Whitton, Borders ..G 10
40 Whitton, Cleveland .C 4
37 Whitton, Humber. ..E 7
45 Whitton, Northumb.
C 9
21 Whitton, Powys ....F 8
21 Whitton, Salop ....E 11
27 Whitton, Suffolk ..K 4
16 Whittonditch ......G 4
45 Whittonstall ......G 9
16 Whitway ....H 6
32 Whitwell, Derby. ..C 3
18 Whitwell, Herts. ..B 2
9 Whitwell, I.o.W. ..H 7
23 Whitwell, Leics. ..A 12
40 Whitwell, N. Yorks. .E 3
41 Whitwell-on-the-
Hill ....H 7
23 Whitwick ....A 8
36 Whitwood ....E 2
35 Whitworth ....E 7
30 Whixal ....G 4
36 Whixley ....A 2
22 Whoberly ....D 6
40 Whorlton, Dur. ...D 1
40 Whorlton, N. Yorks. E 5
44 Whygate ....E 6
21 Whyle ....F 11
10 Whyteleafe ....B 2
15 Wibdon ....E 9
23 Wibtoft ....C 8
11 Wichling ....B 8
15 Wick, Avon ....G 10
8 Wick, Dorset .....G 3
22 Wick, Heref.
& Worc. ....H 3
61 Wick, Highalnd ...C 12
14 Wick, Mid Glam. ..G 3
6 Wick, Som. ....B 5
7 Wick, Som. ....D 7
9 Wick, W. Sussex .F 11
8 Wick, Wilts. .....D 3
17 Wick Hill ....H 9
16 Wick Rissington ...B 3
15 Wick St. Lawrence .H 7
25 Wicken, Cambs. ...H 7
23 Wicken, Northants. H 10
45 Wicken Bonhunt ...M 6
33 Wickenby ....B 8
22 Wichenford ....F 1
32 Wickersley ....A 2
19 Wickford ....E 7
16 Wickham, Berks. ..G 5
9 Wickham, Hants. ..E 7
19 Wickham Bishops ..C 8
16 Wickham Heath ....G 5
27 Wickham Market ...K 6
27 Wickham St. Paul ..L 1
27 Wickham Skeith ...H 4
27 Wickham Street,
Suffolk ....H 4
27 Wickham Street,
Suffolk ....K 1
11 Wickhambreaux ....B 10
25 Wickhambrook ....K 8
22 Wickhamford ......H 4
26 Wickhampton .....E 7
26 Wicklewood ......E 4
26 Wickmere ....B 5
10 Wickstreet ....G 4
15 Wickwar ....E 10
22 Widdington ....M 6
45 Widdrington ......C 10
45 Widdrington Sta. ..D 10
45 Wide Open ....F 10
5 Widecombe in the
Moor ....H 6
3 Widegates ....D 10
2 Widemouth ....A 2
64 Widewall ....E 2
19 Widford, Essex ...C 7
18 Widford,
Hertford ......B 4
17 Widmere ....E 9
17 Widmer End ....D 9
32 Widmerpool ......G 4
30 Widnes ....B 4
6 Widworthy ....F 5
8 Wield ....B 7
34 Wigan ....F 5
8 Wigbeth ....E 2
6 Wiggaton ....G 5

24 Wiggenhall
St. Germans ....D 7
24 Wiggenhall St. Mary
Magdalen .....D 7
24 Wiggenhall St. Mary
the Virgin .....D 7
36 Wigginton ....A 4
17 Wigginton, Herts. ..C 10
16 Wigginton, Oxon ...A 5
22 Wigginton, Staffs. ..A 6
35 Wiggleworth ......A 7
44 Wiggonby ....H 1
9 Wiggonholt ....D 11
36 Wighill ....B 3
26 Wighton ....B 2
8 Wigley ....D 5
21 Wigmore, Heref.
& Worc. ....E 9
11 Wigmore, Kent ....B 7
32 Wigsley ....C 6
25 Wigsthorpe ....G 1
23 Wigston Magna ....B 9
24 Wigtoft ....B 4
44 Wigton ....H 1
42 Wigtown ....F 5
35 Wigtwizzle ....G 11
35 Wike ....C 12
23 Wilbarston ....C 11
36 Wilberfoss ....B 5
25 Wilburton ....H 6
26 Wilby, Norfolk ...F 3
23 Wilby, Northants. .E 12
27 Wilby, Suffolk ...H 5
16 Wilcot ....H 2
30 Wilcott ....H 2
15 Wilcrick ....E 7
31 Wildboarclough ...C 8
25 Wilden ....K 2
8 Wildhern ....A 5
36 Wildsworth ....G 6
32 Wilford ....F 3
30 Wilkesley ....F 5
61 Wilkhaven ....H 9
48 Wilkieston ....C 4
18 Wilkin's Green ...C 2
6 Willand ....E 4
30 Willaston, Ches. ..B 2
30 Willaston, Ches. ..E 5
23 Willen ....H 12
22 Willenhall,
W. Midlands ...B 3
23 Willenhall,
W. Midlands ...E 7
37 Willerby, Humber. .D 8
41 Willerby, N. Yorks. G 10
22 Willersley ....H 4
21 Willersley ....H 8
11 Willesborough ....D 9
18 Willesden ....E 2
4 Willesleigh ......C 5
23 Willey Leics. ....D 8
21 Willey, Salop ....C 12
9 Willey Green .....A 11
23 Williamscot ......H 8
18 Willian ....A 2
18 Willingale ....C 6
4 Willingcott ......B 4
10 Willingdon ....H 4
25 Willingham, Cambs. H 5
32 Willingham, Lincs. .B 6
25 Willingham, Beds. ..K 2
31 Willington, Derby. .G 11
40 Willington, Dur. ..B 2
22 Willington, War. ..H 6
30 Willington Corner ..D 4
36 Willitoft ....D 5
6 Williton ....B 5
44 Willmontswick ....G 6
33 Willoughby, Lincs. .C 11
23 Willoughby, War. ..E 8
32 Willoughby on the
Wolds ....H 4
23 Willoughby Waterleys
C 9
32 Willoughton ......A 6
19 Willows Green ....B 7
15 Willsbridge ......G 10
5 Willsworthy ......H 4
22 Wilmcote ....F 5
6 Wilmington, Devon. F 5
10 Wilmington, Kent .A 4
10 Wilmington, E. Sussex
H 4
31 Wilmslow ....B 7
22 Wilnecote ....B 6
34 Wilpshire ....D 5
35 Wilsden ....D 9
33 Wilsford, Lincs. ..F 7
8 Wilsford, Wilts. ..B 3
16 Wilsford, Wilts. ..H 2
25 Wilshamstead .....L 2
35 Wilsill ....A 10
10 Wilsley Pound ....D 6

15 Wilson, Heref.
& Worc. ....B 9
32 Wilson, Leics. ...H 1
48 Wilsontown ....D 2
24 Wilsthorpe ....D 2
17 Wilstone ....C 10
34 Wilton, Borders ..B 3
40 Wilton, Cleveland .C 6
38 Wilton, Cumb. ....D 3
16 Wilton, Hants. ...H 4
15 Wilton, Heref.
& Worc. ....B 9
41 Wilton, N. Yorks. ..G 8
8 Wilton, Wilts. ...C 3
16 Wiltshire, Co. ...G 2
25 Wimbish ....L 7
25 Wimbish Green ....M 7
18 Wimbledon ....G 2
24 Wimblington ......F 5
8 Wimborne Minster .F 1
9 Wimborne St. Giles .E 2
24 Wimbotsham ......E 7
25 Wimpole Lodge ....K 4
22 Wimpstone ....G 5
7 Wincanton ....C 10
9 Winchfield ....A 9
30 Wincham ....C 5
48 Winchburgh ......B 4
16 Winchcombe ......C 6
11 Winchelsea ......F 8
11 Winchelsea Beach ..F 8
8 Winchester ......C 6
10 Winchet Hill ....D 8
17 Winchmore Hill ...E 10
31 Wincle ....D 8
38 Windermere ......E 5
23 Winderton ....H 7
17 Windlesham ......H 10
31 Windley ....F 11
31 Windmill ....B 10
10 Windmill Hill,
E. Sussex ....G 5
6 Windmill Hill, Som. .E 6
16 Windrush ....C 3
44 Windshielknowe ...C 4
17 Windsor ....G 10
15 Windsoredge .....D 11
47 Windy Yet ....D 9
59 Windyedge ....H 6
53 Windygates ......G 8
49 Windywalls ......H 9
10 Wineham ....F 1
37 Winestead ....E 10
35 Winewall ....C 8
27 Winfarthing .....G 4
15 Winford, Avon ...H 8
9 Winford, I.o.W. ..H 7
21 Winforton ....H 8
7 Winfrith Newburgh
H 11
17 Wing, Bucks. ....B 9
23 Wing, Leics. ....B 12
40 Wingate ....A 4
34 Wingates,
Manchester ....F 5
45 Wingates, Northumb.
D 9
32 Wingerworth .....C 1
17 Wingfield, Beds. ..B 11
27 Wingfield, Suffolk .H 5
7 Wingfield, Wilts. ..A 11
11 Wingham ....B 11
11 Wingmore ....C 10
17 Wingrave ....B 9
32 Winkburn ....D 4
17 Winkfield ....G 9
17 Winkfield Row ...G 10
17 Winkfield Street ..G 10
31 Winkhill ....E 9
11 Winklebury ......A 7
4 Winkleigh ....E 5
40 Winksley ....H 3
8 Winkton ....F 3
45 Winlaton ....G 10
45 Winlaton Mill ...G 10
61 Winless ....B 12
34 Winmarleigh .....B 3
8 Winnall, Hants. ..C 6
8 Winnall, Heref.
& Worc. ......A 7
2 Winnard's Perch ..C 6
17 Winnersh ....G 8
38 Winscales ....C 3
15 Winscombe ....H 7
30 Winsford, Ches. ..D 5
6 Winsford, Som. ..C 3
7 Winsham ....F 7
31 Winshill ....H 11
13 Winsh-wen ....G 10
39 Winskill ....B 8
10 Winslade ....A 8
15 Winsley ....H 11
17 Winslow ....A 8
16 Winson ....C 2

8 Winsor ....E 5
38 Winster, Cumbria ..F 6
31 Winster, Derby. ..D 11
27 Winston, Dur. ....D 2
27 Winston, Suff. ...J 5
15 Winstone ....C 12
4 Winswell ....E 4
7 Winterborne Clenston
F 11
7 Winterborne
Herrington ....G 10
7 Winterborne
Houghton .....F 11
7 Winterborne Kingston
F 11
7 Winterborne Monkton
G 10
7 Winterborne Stickland
F 11
7 Winterborne
Whitechurch ..F 11
7 Winterborne Zelston
F 12
15 Winterbourne,
Avon ....F 9
16 Winterbourne, Berks.
G 5
7 Winterbourne Abbas
G 9
16 Winterbourne Bassett
G 2
8 Winterbourne
Dauntsey .....C 3
15 Winterbourne Down
F 10
8 Winterbourne Earls .C 3
8 Winterbourne Gunner
C 3
16 Winterbourne
Monkton ....G 2
7 Winterbourne
Steepleton ....G 9
8 Winterbourne Stoke B 2
35 Winterburn ......A 8
35 Wintercleugh .....H 2
37 Winteringham ....E 7
30 Winterley ....E 6
35 Wintersett ......F 12
44 Wintershields ...F 4
8 Winterslow ......C 4
37 Winterton ......E 7
26 Winterton-on-Sea .D 8
33 Winthorpe, Lincs. .D 12
32 Winthorpe, Notts. .E 5
39 Winton, Cumbria ..D 10
8 Winton, Dorset ...G 2
41 Winton, N. Yorks. ..F 4
41 Wintringham ......H 9
25 Winwick, Cambs. ..G 2
30 Winwick, Cheshire .H 5
23 Winwick, Northants. E 9
31 Wirksworth ......E 11
33 Wirswall ....F 4
24 Wisbech ....E 6
24 Wisbech St. Mary ..E 5
47 Wisborough Green C 11
47 Wishaw,
Strathclyde ...D 12
22 Wishaw, War. ....H 5
17 Wisley ....H 11
33 Wispington ......C 9
27 Wissett ....H 5
21 Wistanstow ......D 10
33 Wistanswick .....G 5
30 Wistaston ....E 5
30 Wistaston Green ..E 5
25 Wistow, Cambs. ...G 4
12 Wiston, Dyfed ...E 4
36 Wistow, N. Yorks. ..D 4
48 Wiston, Strathclyde .F 2
34 Wiswell ....C 6
25 Witcham ....G 6
25 Witchampton .....E 1
25 Witchford ....G 6
19 Witham ....B 8
7 Witham Friary ...B 11
24 Witham on the Hill .D 2
33 Withcall ....B 10
11 Witherenden Hill ..E 5
4 Witheridge ......E 7
23 Witherley ....B 7
23 Withern ....B 11
37 Withernsea ......D 11
37 Withernwick .....C 9
37 Withersdale Street .G 6
25 Withersfield ....K 7
39 Witherslack .....G 7
6 Withiel ....C 7
6 Withiel Florey ..C 3
16 Withington, Glos. ..C 1
21 Withington, Heref.
& Worc. .....H 11
35 Withington,
Manchester ...H 7

21 Withington, Salop .A 11
31 Withington, Staffs. ..G 9
30 Withington Green ..C 6
21 Withington Marsh .H 11
6 Withleigh ....E 3
34 Withnell ....E 5
23 Withybrook ......D 8
6 Withycombe ......B 3
6 Withycombe Raleigh
H 4
10 Withyham ....E 4
6 Withypool ....C 2
22 Witley ....B 11
16 Witney ....C 5
22 Witton, Heref.
& Worc. ......F 2
59 Witton, Tayside ..K 3
45 Witton Gilbert ..H 10
40 Witton le Wear ..B 2
40 Witton Park ....B 2
6 Wiveliscombe ....C 4
10 Wivelrod ....B 8
10 Wivelsfield .....F 2
10 Wivelsfield Green .F 2
19 Wivenhoe ....B 10
19 Wivenhoe Cross ..B 10
26 Wiverton ....A 3
19 Wix ....A 11
22 Wixford ....G 4
25 Wixoe ....L 8
23 Woburn ....A 10
23 Woburn Sands ...H 12
17 Woking ....H 11
17 Wokingham ......G 9
5 Wolborough .....J 7
37 Wold Newton,
Humberside ...G 10
41 Wold Newton,
Humberside ...H 10
10 Woldingham .....C 3
48 Wolfclyde ......F 3
24 Wolferton ......C 7
52 Wolfhill ....D 6
12 Wolf's Castle ...D 3
23 Wolfsdale ......E 3
49 Woll ....G 7
23 Wollaston, Northants.
F 12
21 Wollaston, Salop .A 9
30 Wollerton ......G 5
22 Wolseley ....H 9
21 Wolsingham ....A 1
31 Wolstanton ....E 7
23 Wolston ....E 7
16 Wolvercote ....C 6
22 Wolverhampton ..B 2
22 Wolverley, Heref.
& Worc. ......D 2
30 Wolverley, Salop ..G 3
23 Wolverton, Bucks. .H 11
16 Wolverton, Hants. .H 6
22 Wolverton, War. ..F 5
16 Wolverton Com ...H 6
15 Wolvesnewton ...D 8
23 Wolvey ....C 8
40 Wolviston ......C 5
41 Wombleton .....G 7
22 Wombourn ......C 2
36 Wombwell ......G 2
11 Womenswold ....C 11
36 Womersley .....E 3
9 Wonersh ....B 11
5 Wonson ....G 5
17 Wooburn ....E 10
17 Wooburn Green ..E 10
17 Wooburn Moor ..E 10
26 Wood Dalling ...C 4
25 Wood End, Beds. ..K 1
25 Wood End, Beds. ..K 2
18 Wood End, Herts. .A 3
22 Wood End, War. ..B 6
22 Wood End, War. ..E 4
33 Wood Enderby ...D 10
18 Wood Green ....E 3
22 Wood Hayes ....B 3
26 Wood Norton ...C 3
25 Wood Walton ...G 3
4 Woodacott .....E 3
39 Woodale ......G 12
32 Woodall ....B 2
26 Woodbastwick ..D 6
32 Woodbeck ......B 5
7 Woodbridge, Dorset.
E 10
27 Woodbridge, Suff. .K 6
32 Woodborough, Notts.
E 3
16 Woodborough, Wilts.
H 2
6 Woodbury, Devon. .G 4
7 Woodbury, Som. ..B 9

6 Woodbury Salterton G 4
15 Woodchester ....D 11
11 Woodchurch .....E 8
6 Woodcombe .....B 3
17 Woodcote, Oxon. ..F 7
22 Woodcote, Salop ...A 1
8 Woodcott ....A 6
15 Woodcroft ......E 8
8 Woodcutts ......D 1
25 Woodditton .....J 8
16 Woodeaton .....C 6
38 Woodend, Cumb. ..F 4
59 Woodend,
Grampian .....H 3
48 Woodend,
Strathclyde ...F 2
23 Woodend, Northants.
G 9
8 Woodfalls ......D 3
44 Woodfield, Dumf.
& Gall. ....F 1
47 Woodfield,
Strathclyde ...G 8
10 Woodfield, Surrey ..B 1
4 Woodford, Corn. ..E 1
15 Woodford, Glos. ..E 10
31 Woodford,
Manchester ...B 7
18 Woodford, London .E 4
25 Woodford, Northants.
H 1
7 Woodford, Som. ..B 9
23 Woodford Halse ..G 9
26 Woodgate, Norf. ..D 3
22 Woodgate, Heref.
& Worc. ......E 3
9 Woodgate,
W. Sussex ....F 10
9 Woodgreen .....D 3
49 Woodhall, Lothian ..B 9
45 Woodhall, Northumb.
B 9
39 Woodhall,
N. Yorks. .....F 12
33 Woodhall Spa ...D 9
17 Woodham ....H 11
19 Woodham Ferrers ..D 8
19 Woodham Mortimer C 8
19 Woodham Walter ..C 8
53 Woodhaven .....D 9
35 Woodhead, Derby ..G 9
58 Woodhead,
Grampian .....D 5
58 Woodhead House ..C 5
49 Woodheads ......E 8
15 Woodhill, Avon ..G 8
22 Woodhill, Salop ..D 1
56 Woodholme .....D 2
45 Woodhorn ......D 11
45 Woodhorn Demesne
D 11
32 Woodhouse, Derby .B 1
23 Woodhouse, Leics. .A 9
35 Woodhouse,
W. Yorks. .....D 11
23 Woodhouse Eaves ..A 8
5 Woodhuish .....K 8
25 Woodhurst .....H 4
10 Woodingdean ...G 2
5 Woodland, Devon ..J 7
40 Woodland, Dur. ..C 1
58 Woodland,
Grampian .....E 6
58 Woodland,
Grampian .....F 6
8 Woodlands, Dorset .E 2
43 Woodlands, Dumf.
& Gall. ....D 11
59 Woodlands,
Grampian .....H 5
8 Woodlands, Hants. .E 4
56 Woodlands,
Highland .....D 1
17 Woodlands Park ..F 9
16 Woodlands St. Mary
G 4
31 Woodlane ......H 10
43 Woodlea ....C 8
5 Woodleigh .....L 6
35 Woodlesford ....D 12
17 Woodley, Berks. ..G 8
35 Woodley,
Manchester ...H 8
16 Woodmancote, Glos.
A 1
16 Woodmancote, Glos.
C 1
9 Woodmancote,
W. Sussex ....E 9
9 Woodmancott ...B 7
37 Woodmansey ....C 10
9 Woodmansgreen ..C 10
10 Woodmansterne ..B 2
8 Woodminton .....D 2

No.	Place	Ref.
11	Woodnesborough	B 11
24	Woodnewton	F 1
34	Woodplumpton	D 4
26	Woodrising	E 3
10	Wood's Green	E 5
30	Woodseaves, Salop	G 5
30	Woodseaves, Staffs.	H 6
16	Woodsend	F 3
32	Woodsetts	B 3
7	Woodside, Berks.	G 10
43	Woodside, Dumf. & Gall.	D 11
53	Woodside, Fife	F 9
59	Woodside, Grampian	G 7
49	Woodside, Northants.	E 12
53	Woodside, Tayside	C 7
59	Woodside of Arbeadie	H 5
44	Woodslee	F 2
16	Woodstock	B 5
12	Woodstock Cross	D 4
12	Woodstock Slop	D 4
32	Woodthorpe, Derby.	C 2
32	Woodthorpe, Leics.	H 3
26	Woodton	F 6
4	Woodtown, Devon.	C 4
4	Woodtown, Devon.	D 3
59	Woodtown, Grampian	K 3
34	Woodvale	F 2
31	Woodville	H 11
8	Woodyates	D 2
21	Woofferton	F 10
7	Wookey	B 8
7	Wookey Hole	A 9
7	Wool	H 11
4	Woolacombe	B 3
11	Woolage Green	C 11
15	Woolaston	D 9
7	Wollavington	B 7
9	Woolbeding	D 10
6	Woolbrook	G 5
6	Woolcotts	C 3
35	Wooldale	F 10
49	Wooler	G 12
7	Woolfardisworthy	E 7
48	Woolfords Cotts	D 3
8	Woolgarston	H 2
17	Woolhampton	G 7
15	Woolhope	A 9
7	Woolland	F 11
15	Woollard	H 9
4	Woollaton	E 3
4	Woolley, Corn.	D 1
15	Woolley, Avon	G 10
25	Woolley, Cambs.	H 3
35	Woolley, S. Yorks.	F 11
18	Woolmer Green	B 3
22	Woolmere Green	F 3
27	Woolpit	J 3
27	Woolpit Green	J 3
23	Woolscott	E 8
4	Woolsey	D 2
21	Woolstaston	C 10
32	Woolsthorpe, Lincs.	G 5
32	Woolsthorpe, Lincs.	H 6
30	Woolston, Cheshire	A 5
5	Woolston, Devon	L 6
8	Woolston, Hants.	E 6
21	Woolston, Salop	D 9
30	Woolston, Salop	H 2
5	Woolston Green	J 6
16	Woolstone	E 4
30	Woolton	B 3
16	Woolton Hill	H 5
27	Woolverstone	L 5
7	Woolverton	A 11
18	Woolwich	F 4
21	Woonton	G 9
45	Wooperton	A 8
49	Wooplaw	E 7
30	Woore	F 6
25	Wootton, Beds.	L 1
8	Wootton, Hants.	F 4
37	Wootton, Humber.	E 8
11	Wootton, Kent	C 11
23	Wootton, Northants.	F 11
16	Wootton, Oxon.	B 5
16	Wootton, Oxon.	D 6
21	Wootton, Salop	E 10
31	Wootton, Staffs.	F 9
31	Wootton, Staffs.	G 7
16	Wootton Bassett	F 2
9	Wootton Bridge	G 7
9	Wootton Com.	G 7
6	Wootton Courtenay	B 3
7	Wootton Fitzpaine	G 7
16	Wootton Rivers	H 3
9	Wootton St. Lawrence	A 7
22	Wootton Wawen	F 5
22	Worcester	G 2
22	Wordsley	C 2
22	Worfield	C 1
64	Work	C 3
38	Workington	B 2
32	Worksop	B 3
37	Worlaby	F 8
16	World's End, Berks.	F 6
9	World's End, Hants.	E 8
15	Worle	H 7
30	Worleston	E 5
26	Worlingham	F 7
25	Worlington	H 8
27	Worlingworth	H 5
27	Wormald Green	A 11
15	Wormbridge	A 7
24	Wormegay	D 8
15	Wormelow Tump	A 8
31	Wormhill	C 9
53	Wormiehills	C 11
27	Wormingford	M 2
17	Worminghall	C 7
16	Wormington	A 1
7	Worminster	B 9
48	Wormiston	E 5
53	Wormit	E 9
23	Wormleighton	G 8
18	Wormley, Herts.	C 4
9	Wormley, Surrey	B 10
11	Wormshill	B 7
21	Wormsley	H 9
9	Worplesdon	A 11
35	Worral	H 11
35	Worsbrough	G 12
34	Worsley	G 6
26	Worstead	C 6
25	Worsted Lodge	K 6
35	Worsthorne	D 7
34	Worston	C 6
5	Worswell	L 4
11	Worth, Kent	C 12
10	Worth, W. Sussex	D 2
8	Worth Matravers	H 1
27	Wortham	H 4
21	Worthen	B 9
30	Worthenbury	F 3
26	Worthing, Norf.	D 3
9	Worthing, W. Sussex	F 12
32	Worthington	H 1
6	Worthy	A 2
9	Worting	A 7
35	Wortley, S. Yorks.	G 11
35	Wortley, W. Yorks.	D 11
16	Worton	H 1
27	Wortwell	G 6
5	Wotter	J 4
9	Wotton	A 12
15	Wotton-under-Edge	E 11
17	Wotton Underwood	C 8
23	Woughton on the Green	H 12
10	Wouldham	B 6
27	Wrabness	M 5
58	Wraes	D 3
4	Wrafton	C 4
33	Wragby, Lincs.	B 8
36	Wragby, W. Yorks.	E 2
36	Wragholme	G 11
26	Wramplingham	E 4
36	Wrangbrook	F 3
58	Wrangham, Grampian	D 4
49	Wrangham, Northumb.	F 12
33	Wrangle	E 11
33	Wrangle Com.	E 11
33	Wrangle Lowgate	E 11
6	Wrangway	D 5
6	Wrantage	D 6
15	Wraxall, Avon	G 8
7	Wraxall, Dorset.	F 9
7	Wraxhall, Som.	C 9
39	Wray	H 8
5	Wrayland	H 7
17	Wraysbury	G 11
34	Wrea Green	D 3
39	Wreay, Cumb.	C 7
44	Wreay, Cumb.	H 3
9	Wrecclesham	B 9
45	Wrekenton	G 11
41	Wrelton	F 8
30	Wrenbury	E 4
26	Wreningham	F 4
27	Wrentham	G 8
35	Wrenthorpe	E 11
21	Wrentnall	B 9
36	Wressle	D 5
25	Wrestlingworth	K 4
24	Wretton	F 8
30	Wrexham	E 2
30	Wrexham Industrial Estate	E 2
22	Wribbenhall	E 2
34	Wrightlington Bar	F 4
30	Wrinehill	E 6
15	Wrington	H 8
7	Writhlington	A 10
19	Writtle	C 7
21	Wrockwardine	A 11
36	Wroot	G 5
10	Wrotham	B 5
10	Wrotham Heath	B 5
16	Wroughton	F 3
22	Wroxall	E 6
21	Wroxeter	B 11
9	Wroxhall	H 7
26	Wroxham	D 6
31	Wroxton	H 7
31	Wyaston	F 10
24	Wyberton	B 4
25	Wyboston	K 3
30	Wybunbury	E 5
10	Wych Cross	E 3
22	Wychbold	F 3
22	Wychnor	A 5
22	Wychnor Bridges	A 5
22	Wyck	B 9
40	Wycliffe	D 1
17	Wycombe Marsh	E 10
25	Wyddial	M 5
11	Wye	C 9
17	Wyerstone	H 3
27	Wyerstone Street	H 3
15	Wyesham	C 8
7	Wyke, Dorset	D 11
21	Wyke, Salop	B 12
9	Wyke, Surrey	A 10
35	Wyke, W. Yorks.	D 10
17	Wyke Champflower	C 10
7	Wyke Regis	H 7
41	Wykeham, N. Yorks.	G 9
41	Wykeham, N. Yorks.	H 8
30	Wykey	H 3
35	Wylam	G 9
22	Wylde Green	C 5
14	Wyllie	E 5
8	Wylye	B 2
9	Wymering	E 8
32	Wymeswold	H 3
32	Wymondham, Leics.	H 6
26	Wymondham, Norf.	E 4
7	Wynford Eagle	G 9
40	Wynyard Forest	C 4
9	Wyre Piddle	G 3
32	Wysall	G 3
22	Wythall	E 4
16	Wytham	C 6
38	Wythburn	D 6
31	Wythenshawe	A 7
9	Wyton	H 4
32	Wyville	G 6
54	Wyvis Lodge	B 8
36	Yaddlethorpe	F 6
8	Yafford	H 6
40	Yafforth	F 4
5	Yalberton	K 7
10	Yalding	C 6
16	Yanworth	C 2
36	Yapham	B 6
9	Yapton	F 11
33	Yarburgh	A 10
6	Yarcombe	D 6
4	Yard	D 6
4	Yard Gate	C 6
22	Yardley	G 7
23	Yardley Gobion	H 11
23	Yardley Hastings	F 12
21	Yardro	H 11
31	Yarlet	G 7
7	Yarlington	C 10
40	Yarm	D 4
8	Yarmouth	G 5
4	Yarnacott	C 5
21	Yarnbrook	A 12
31	Yarnfield	G 7
4	Yarnscombe	D 4
16	Yarnton	C 6
21	Yarpole	F 10
48	Yarrow	G 6
48	Yarrow Feus	G 6
21	Yarsop	H 9
24	Yarwell	F 2
15	Yate	F 10
17	Yateley	H 9
16	Yatesbury	G 2
16	Yattendon	G 6
15	Yatton, Avon	H 7
15	Yatton, Heref. & Worc.	A 9
21	Yatton, Heref. & Worc.	F 9
15	Yatton Keynell	G 12
9	Yaverland	H 7
26	Yaxham	D 3
24	Yaxley, Cambs.	F 3
27	Yaxley, Suffolk	H 4
23	Yazor	H 9
35	Yeadon	C 10
39	Yealand Conyers	H 7
39	Yealand Redmayne	H 7
5	Yealmpton	K 4
6	Yearby	C 6
40	Yearsley	H 6
30	Yeaton	H 3
16	Yelford	D 4
25	Yelling	J 4
11	Yelsted	B 7
23	Yelvertoft	E 9
5	Yelverton, Devon	K 4
26	Yelverton, Norfolk	E 6
7	Yenston	D 10
4	Yeo Mill	C 7
16	Yeoford	F 6
3	Yeolmbridge	A 10
7	Yeovil	D 9
7	Yeovil Marsh	D 9
7	Yeovilton	D 9
12	Yerbeston	F 4
12	Yerbeston Mountain	F 4
64	Yesnaby	C 1
49	Yetholm Mains	F 11
45	Yetlington	B 8
7	Yetminster	E 9
47	Yett, Strathclyde	G 9
47	Yett, Strathclyde	C 12
6	Yettington	H 4
52	Yetts of Muckhart	G 5
25	Yielden	J 1
48	Yieldshields	D 2
18	Yiewsley	F 1
20	Ynys	F 2
20	Ynys Tachwedd	C 2
14	Ynys-boeth	E 4
14	Ynysbwl	E 4
14	Ynysddu	E 5
14	Ynyshir	E 4
13	Ynstawe	G 10
39	Yockenthwaite	G 11
21	Yockleton	A 9
36	Yokefleet	E 6
47	Yoker	C 10
58	Yonder Bognie	C 3
36	York	B 3
17	York Town	H 9
11	Yorkletts	B 9
39	Yockenthwaite	G 11
21	Yockleton	A 9
36	Yokefleet	E 6
47	Yoker	C 10
58	Yonder Bognie	C 3
36	York	B 3
17	York Town	H 9
11	Yorkletts	B 9
15	Yorkley	D 9
48	Yorkeston	D 6
4	Youldonmoor Cross	E 2
31	Youlgreaves	D 10
36	Youlthorpe	B 5
34	Youlton	A 3
19	Young's End	B 7
31	Yoxall	H 10
7	Yoxford	H 7
29	Ysbyty Ifan	E 8
20	Ysbyty Ystwyth	E 3
20	Yspytty Cynfyn	D 3
37	Ysceifog	C 10
13	Yspitty	G 9
14	Ystalyfera	F 11
14	Ystrad	E 3
13	Ystrad Aeron	A 8
20	Ystrad Meurig	F 3
14	Ystradfellte	C 3
14	Ystrad-ffin	B 11
14	Ystradgynlais	C 1
14	Ystrad-mynach	E 5
13	Ystradowen, Dyfed	F 10
14	Ystradowen, S. Glam.	G 3
20	Ystumtuen	D 3
58	Ythsie	D 6
4	Zeal Monachorum	F 6
7	Zeals	C 11
2	Zelah	D 5
2	Zennor	F 2
64	Zetland, Co.	D 7

INDEX TO LONDON MAPS

ABBREVIATIONS

App. – *Approach*
Av. – *Avenue*
Bdy. – *Broadway*
Bldg. – *Building(s)*
Br. – *British*
Bri. – *Bridge*
Ch. – *Church*
Cl. – *Close*
Cnr. – *Corner*
Coll. – *College*
Con. – *Convent*
Cres. – *Crescent*
Ct. – *Court*
Dri. – *Drive*
Ex. – *Exchange*
F.C. – *Football Club*
Gdns. – *Gardens*
Gro. – *Grove*
Gt. – *Great*
Ho. – *House*
Hosp. – *Hospital*
Hot. – *Hotel*
Inst. – *Institute*
La. – *Lane*
Lit. – *Little*
Min. – *Ministry*
Mkt. – *Market*
Mt. – *Mount*
Mus. – *Museum*
Nat. – *National*
Nth. – *North*
Pal. – *Palace*
Pk. – *Park*
Pl. – *Place*
Pol. – *Police*
Poly. – *Polytechnic*
Pr. – *Prince*
R.C. – *Roman Catholic*
Rd. – *Road*
Sanct. – *Sanctuary*
Sch. – *School*
Soc. – *Society*
Sq. – *Square*
St. – *Street, Saint*
Sta. – *Station*
Sth. – *South*
Ter. – *Terrace*
Th. – *Theatre*
Wk. – *Walk*
Yd. – *Yard*

The normal abbreviations for the London Postal Districts have been used throughout, e.g., NW10.

73 Abbey Gdns......C 3
73 Abbey Gdns Mews.C 3
79 Abbey Orchard St.D 7
73 Abbey Rd........B 3
80 Abbey St.........D 4
67 Abbey Wood....G 12
80 Abbots La........B 4
76 Abchurch La.....H 3
73 Abercorn Close...C 4
73 Abercorn Pl.......C 3
73 Aberdeen Place....E 5
80 Aberdour St.......E 3
77 Abingdon Rd......D 1
79 Abingdon St......D 8
77 Abingdon Villas...E 1
67 Abridge..........A 1
68 Abridge Rd......A 12
73 Acacia Gdns......B 5
73 Acacia Pl.........B 5
73 Acacia Rd.........B 5
67 Academy Rd.....H 11
70 Acre La. SW2.....B 6
70 Acre La., Carshalton......F 5
66 Acton............F 3
66 Acton Central Sta..G 3
66 Acton La.........F 3
66 Acton (Main Line) Sta............F 3
66 Acton Park.......G 3
75 Acton St..........D 9
66 Acton Town Sta...G 2
75 Adam St.........J 9
77 Adam & Eve Mews D 2
74 Adams Row......J 4
71 Addington........F 8
71 Addington G.C.....F 8
71 Addington Palace G.C...........F 8
71 Addington Rd., Sanderstead.....G 7
71 Addington Rd., W. Wickham.....E 9
80 Addington Square..J 2
79 Addington St.....C 10
71 Addington Village Rd............F 8
71 Addiscombe.......E 7
71 Addiscombe Rd...E 7
71 Addiscombe Sta...E 7
69 Addlestone.......F 2
66 Adelaide Rd.......E 5
75 Adelaide St........J 8
75 Adelphi Ter.........J 9
75 Adelphi Theatre....J 9
76 Adler St..........G 6
79 Admiralty.........B 8
79 Admiralty Arch...B 8
73 Adpar St..........F 5
74 Æolian Hall.......H 5
75 Agar St...........J 8
75 Agdon St........E 12
77 Airways Terminal (Europe)..........E 3
78 Airways Terminal..F 4
79 Alaska St........B 11
71 Albany Park Sta..C 12
80 Albany Rd.......H 3
74 Albany St.........C 5
74 Albermarle St.....J 5
78 Albert Bridge......J 1
78 Albert Bridge Rd..J 1
77 Albert Court......D 4
79 Albert Embank.....F 9
78 Albert Gate......C 3
77 Albert Memorial..C 4
77 Albert Place......D 3
67 Albert Rd.......G 11
74 Albert St.........B 5
74 Albert Ter........A 3
74 Albert Ter. Mews..A 3
79 Alberta St.......G 12
75 Albery Theatre....J 8
73 Albion Close.....H 6
73 Albion Gate......H 6
73 Albion Mews.....H 6
73 Albion St.........H 6
67 Aldborough Hatch..........C 12
67 Aldborough Rd..C 12
80 Aldbridge St......G 4
66 Aldenham Park...A 2
66 Aldenham Res.....A 2
65 Aldenham Rd., Bushey..........A 5
66 Aldenham Rd., Watford..........A 2
74 Aldenham St......C 7
76 Aldermanbury....G 2
80 Alderminster Rd...F 6
78 Alderney St.......F 5
67 Aldersbrook.....D 10
67 Aldersbrook Rd..D 10
75 Aldersgate St.....F 13
78 Aldford St.........A 3
76 Aldgate..........H 4
76 Aldgate High St...G 5
75 Aldwych.........H 9
75 Aldwych Theatre..H 9
65 Alexander Ave....D 6
77 Alexander Place....E 6
77 Alexander Square..E 6
73 Alexander St......G 2
77 Alexandra Gate....C 5
66 Alexandra Palace..C 6
66 Alexandra Park...C 6
66 Alexandra Park Rd C 6
80 Alexis St..........E 6
74 Alfred Mews......F 7
74 Alfred Place......F 7
73 Alfred Rd.........F 1
80 Alice St...........E 3
76 Alie St...........H 6
70 All England Lawn Tennis Club....C 4
70 All Saints Rd......E 4
75 All Saints St.......B 9
66 All Souls Ave.....E 4
77 Allen St..........D 1
76 Allhallows La......J 2
75 Allingham Ter....B 13
78 Allington St.......D 5
73 Allitsen Rd.......B 6
74 Allsop Place......E 3
66 Allum La..........A 2
66 Alma Grove......F 6
73 Alma Sq...........C 4
66 Alperton.........E 2
77 Alpha Place......H 6
80 Alscot Rd.........E 5
80 Alvey St..........F 5
75 Ambassadors Th...H 8
79 Ambergate St....G 12
73 Amberley Rd.....E 2
70 Amberwood Rise..E 3
78 Ambrosden Av....E 6
79 Amelia St........F 13
67 Amhurst Park....D 7
75 Ampton St........D 9
75 Amwell St.......D 11
78 Anderson St.......F 2
73 Andover Pl........C 2
75 Anerley Rd.......D 7
71 Anerley Sta.......D 7
70 Angel Hill........E 4
67 Angel Rd..........B 8
67 Angel Road Sta...B 8
75 Angel St.........G 13
76 Anglesea St.......E 7
77 Ann La...........J 4
76 Anning St.........E 4
77 Ansdell St........D 3
77 Ansdell Ter........D 2
77 Anselm Rd........H 1
66 Apex Corner.......B 3
78 Apple Tree Yard..A 7
76 Appleby St........B 5
76 Appolo St.........F 4
78 Apsley House.....C 4
78 Apsley Way......C 4
71 Aquarius G.C.....B 8
73 Aquila St.........B 5
79 Aquinas St.......B 11
80 Arch St...........E 1
79 Archbishop's Pk..D 10
74 Archer St.........H 7
74 Archery Close....H 2
66 Archway Rd......D 6
68 Ardleigh Green...C 3
68 Ardleigh Green Rd.C 3
77 Argyll Rd, W8....D 1
66 Argyle Rd, W13...F 1
75 Argyle Square.....D 9
74 Argyll St, W1.....H 6
75 Argyle St. WC1....D 9
66 Arkley...........A 4
66 Arkley La.........A 4
74 Arlington Av......B 2
74 Arlington Rd......B 5
76 Arlington Sq......B 2
78 Arlington St......B 6
75 Arlington Way...C 11
77 Armadale Rd......J 1
75 Arne St..........H 9
76 Arnold Circus.....D 5
72 Arnolds La.......C 3
66 Arnos Grove Sta...B 6
80 Arnside St........H 2
67 Arsenal F.C.......E 7
73 Artesian Rd.......H 1
76 Arthur St.........J 3
76 Artillery Ground...E 2
76 Artillery La.......F 4
79 Artillery Row.....D 7
73 Arts Theatre......H 8
75 Arundel St.......H 10
72 Ash..............F 5
73 Ashbridge St......E 6
77 Ashburn Gdns.....E 3
77 Ashburn Mews....E 3
77 Ashburn Place.....F 3
75 Ashby St........D 12
69 Ashford Hospital..B 3
69 Ashford La........D 3
69 Ashford Manor G.C.............C 3
69 Ashford Rd, Feltham..........C 4
69 Ashford Rd, Laleham........D 3
69 Ashley Rd., Walton E 4
74 Ashland Place.....F 3
69 Ashley Park.......E 4
78 Ashley Place......E 6
70 Ashley Rd, Epsom.........G 3
73 Ashmill St........F 6
79 Ashmole St......H 10
70 Ashtead..........H 2
70 Ashtead Common.G 1
70 Ashtead Park.....H 2
70 Ashtead Sta.......H 1
73 Ashworth Rd.....D 3
77 Astell St..........G 6
65 Aston Rd..........B 4
77 Astwood Mews....F 3
77 Atherstone Mews..E 4
79 Atterbury St.......F 8
75 Attneave St......D 10
79 Auckland St......G 9
78 Audley St.........B 4
76 Audrey St.........B 6
74 Augustus St.......C 5
76 Austin St..........D 5
76 Austin Friars.....G 3
79 Austral St.......E 12
75 Australia House..H 10
75 Ave Maria La....H 12
76 Avebury Estate...D 6
76 Avebury St........A 3
68 Aveley............G 4
68 Aveley Rd........E 4
79 Aveline St.......G 10
80 Avely St..........F 3
76 Avenue, The EC3..H 4
70 Avenue, The SW4..B 5
69 Avenue, The, Sunbury.......D 5
66 Avenue Rd. N14...A 6
73 Avenue Rd. NW8..B 6
68 Avenue Rd, Bexleyheath....H 1
74 Avery Row........H 5
71 Averyhill Rd.....B 11
80 Avon Place.......C 2
80 Avondale Square..G 6
79 Avonmouth St....D 13
74 Aybrook St........F 3
80 Aylesbury Rd......G 3
75 Aylesbury St.....E 12
78 Aylesford St.......G 7
80 Ayres St...........C 1
76 Bache's St........D 3
76 Back Church La...H 6
75 Back Hill........E 11
68 Back La...........G 5
80 Bacon Gr..........E 5
76 Bacon St..........E 6
72 Badger's Mount...G 1
80 Bagshot St........G 4
75 Bainbridge St.....G 8
74 Baker St..........F 3
74 Baker's Mews.....G 3
75 Baker's Row.....E 11
80 Balaclava Rd......F 6
74 Balcombe St.......E 2
74 Balderton St......H 4
75 Baldwin Ter......B 13
75 Baldwin's Gdns...F 11
65 Baldwin's La.......A 4
80 Balfour St.........E 2
68 Balgores La.......C 3
70 Balham...........B 5
70 Balham High Rd...C 5
70 Balham Hill.......B 5
70 Balham Sta........B 5
66 Ballards La.......C 5
67 Balls Pond Rd.....E 7
76 Baltic Shipping Exchange......G 4
76 Baltic St..........E 1
67 Banbury Res.......C 8
80 Bank End.........A 2
76 Bank of England..G 3
75 Bankruptcy Court H 10
79 Bankside........A 13
79 Bankside Power Station........A 13
76 Banner St.........E 2
70 Banstead..........G 4
70 Banstead Downs..G 4
70 Banstead Downs G.C.............G 4
70 Banstead Hospital.G 4
70 Banstead Rd......G 3
70 Banstead Road South.........F 5
76 Barbican.........F 1
75 Barbican Sta.....F 13
75 Barford St.......B 11
79 Barge House St...A 11
71 Baring Rd.........C 9
76 Baring St.........A 2
73 Bark Place........J 2
67 Barking..........E 11
67 Barking Park....E 11
67 Barking Rd......F 10
67 Barking Sta.......E 11
67 Barkingside......C 11
77 Barkston Gdns.....F 2
75 Barlett Court....G 11
67 Barley La.......D 12
80 Barlow St..........F 3
66 Barn Hill Park....D 2
74 Barnby St.........C 6
72 Barnehurst........A 1
70 Barnes............A 3
70 Barnes Bridge.....A 3
70 Barnes Bridge Sta..A 3
70 Barnes Common..A 3
70 Barnes Sta........A 3
66 Barnet...........B 4
66 Barnet Bypass.....A 3
66 Barnet Gate......A 3
76 Barnet Grove.....D 6
66 Barnet La, Elstree.A 2
66 Barnet La, Totteridge......A 4
66 Barnet Rd.........A 3
66 Barnet Way.......A 3
70 Barnetwood La....H 1
80 Barnham St.......C 4
75 Barnsbury Rd....B 11
75 Baron St.........B 11
76 Baroness Rd.......C 5
79 Baron's Place....C 11
76 Barrett St.........H 4
73 Barrie St..........H 4
73 Barrow Hill Rd....C 6
67 Barrowell Green...B 7
75 Barter St..........G 9
75 Bartholomew Cl...F 13
76 Bartholomew La...G 3
80 Bartholomew St....E 3
78 Basil St...........D 2
80 Basing Place......C 4
76 Basinghall Av.....G 2
76 Basinghall St......G 2
75 Bastwick St......E 13
72 Bat & Ball Sta.....H 2
75 Batchelor St......B 11
65 Batchworth.......B 3
65 Batchworth Hth...B 4
65 Batchworth Heath Hill.............B 4
74 Bateman St.......H 7
76 Bateman's Row...D 4
65 Bath Rd, Cranford.H 5
65 Bath Rd, Colnbrook.....H 2
76 Bath St...........D 2
80 Bath Ter..........D 1
66 Bathurst Gdns.....F 4
73 Bathurst Mews....H 5
73 Bathurst St.......H 5
70 Battersea.........A 5
77 Battersea Bridge...J 5
70 Battersea Bridge Rd...............A 5
70 Battersea Park....A 5
70 Battersea Park Rd..A 5
70 Battersea Rise.....B 5
80 Battle Bridge La...B 3
75 Battle Bridge Rd...C 8
75 Battlebridge Basin.B 9
75 Batty St..........G 7
76 Baxendale St......C 6
74 Bayham Place.....B 6
74 Bayham St........B 6
65 Bayhurst Wood...C 3
74 Bayley St.........F 7
79 Baylis Rd........C 11
66 Bayswater........F 5
73 Bayswater Rd.....J 4
68 Beacontree Hth....D 1
74 Beak St...........H 6
72 Bean.............C 4
80 Bear Gdns.........A 1
79 Bear La..........B 12
75 Bear St...........J 8
74 Beatty St.........B 5
74 Beauchamp Place.D 2
75 Beauchamp St....F 11
78 Beaufort Gdns.....D 2
77 Beaufort St.......H 5
74 Beaumont Mews..F 4
74 Beaumont Place...E 6
74 Beaumont St......F 4
71 Beckenham.......D 8
71 Beckenham Hill Rd. C 9
71 Beckenham Hill Sta. C 9
71 Beckenham Junc. Sta. D 8
71 Beckenham Place Park C 9
71 Beckenham Place & Foxgrove G.C...C 9
71 Beckenham Rd.....D 8
67 Beckton.........F 11
67 Beckton Rd......F 10
68 Becontree........D 1
68 Becontree Ave.....D 1
68 Becontree Sta.....E 1
80 Bedale St.........B 2
70 Beddington........F 6
70 Beddington Corner E 5
70 Beddington La.....E 6
70 Beddington Lane Sta. E 5
70 Beddington Park..E 5
71 Beddlestead La....H 9
69 Bedford Rd, Feltham C 4
69 Bedfont Rd, Stanwell B 3
75 Bedford Av.......G 7
74 Bedford College..D 3
77 Bedford Gdns.....B 2
70 Bedford Hill......C 5
75 Bedford Place.....F 8
75 Bedford Row.....F 10
75 Bedford Square...F 7
75 Bedford St........J 8
75 Bedford Way......E 8
75 Bedfordbury......J 8
68 Bedford's Park....B 3
72 Bedonwell Rd.....A 1
71 Beech Farm Rd...H 9
76 Beech St..........F 1
72 Beechen Wood....F 1
72 Beechenlea La.....D 2
78 Beeston Place.....D 5
78 Belgrave Mews North D 3
78 Belgrave Mews South D 4
78 Belgrave Mews West D 3
78 Belgrave Place....D 4
78 Belgrave Rd.......F 6
78 Belgrave Square...D 3
66 Belgravia.........G 5
75 Belgrove St.......C 8
68 Belhus Park.......F 4
76 Bell La...........G 5
73 Bell St............F 6
76 Bell Wharf La......J 2
75 Bell Yard.......H 11
71 Belle Grove Rd...A 11
71 Bellingham........C 8
71 Bellingham Rd....C 9
66 Belmont..........C 1
66 Belmont G.C......C 1
70 Belmont Rise......F 4
70 Belmont Sta.......F 4
68 Belvedere.........G 2
79 Belvedere Rd.....B 10
75 Bemerton St.......A 9
75 Benjamin St......F 12
70 Benhill Av........F 4
70 Benhill Rd.........E 5
68 Bennet Castle La...E 1
74 Bentinck St.......G 4
68 Beredens La.......C 5
78 Berkeley Hotel....B 5
74 Berkeley Mews....G 3
74 Berkeley Square...J 5
75 Berkeley St........A 5
67 Bermondsey.......G 8
80 Bermondsey Leather Market........C 3

80 Bermondsey St. ...C 4	67 Blackheath Rd. ...H 9	68 Bramble La.......E 4	80 Brockham St......D 2	76 Bunhill Fields.....E 2	70 Cambridge Park. Twickenham....B 1
80 Bermondsey Wall East...........C 7	71 Blackheath Royal G.C. B 10	77 Bramerton St. ....H 6	66 Brockley Hill.....B 2	76 Bunhill Row......E 2	77 Cambridge Place..D 3
80 Bermondsey Wall West..........C 6	78 Blacklands Ter....F 2	77 Bramham Gdns ...F 2	71 Brockley Rise.....B 8	72 Bunker's Hill La...F 5	70 Cambridge Rd. ...D 2
75 Bernard St.......E 8	67 Blackwall.........F 9	66 Bramley Rd.......A 6	71 Brockley Rd.......B 8	80 Burbage Close....D 2	73 Cambridge Sq.....G 6
74 Berners Mews ...G 6	67 Blackwall Reach ..G 9	71 Brampton Rd. ....A 12	71 Brockley Sta. .....A 8	70 Burgh Heath .....H 4	78 Cambridge St.....F 5
74 Berners Place ...G 6	67 Blackwall Tunnel..G 9	76 Branch Place......A 3	70 Brockwell Park...B 6	70 Burgh Heath Rd...G 3	66 Camden..........E 6
75 Berners Rd......B 12	80 Blackwood St......G 2	70 Brand Drive......D 3	80 Brockworth Close .J 4	75 Burgh St.........B 13	75 Camden High St..B 5
74 Berners St. ......G 6	67 Blake Hall.......D 10	80 Brandon St.......G 2	75 Bromfield St. ....B 11	79 Burhill G.C.......F 4	66 Camden St.......A 6
75 Berry St. ...E 12	80 Blake's Rd.......J 4	72 Brands Hatch .....F 4	71 Bromley ....D 9	71 Burleigh St. ......H 9	74 Camden St........A 6
79 Berryfield Rd. ...G 13	74 Blandford Estate ..E 1	72 Brands Hatch Motor Racing Circuit....F 4	67 Bromley, Tower Hamlets.......F 9	71 Burling La........H 11	66 Camden Town ....E 6
70 Berrylands Sta. ...D 2	74 Blandford Place...G 3	71 Brasted Hill......H 12	67 Bromley-by-Bow ..F 9	74 Burlington Arcade.J 6	75 Camden Walk ...B 12
71 Berry's Green Rd. ...H 11	74 Blandford Square..E 1	71 Brasted La.......H 12	71 Bromely Common E 10	74 Burlington Gdns...J 6	77 Camera Place....H 4
71 Berry's Hill......G 11	74 Blandford St......F 3	67 Bravel La.........B 12	71 Bromley Hill......C 9	73 Burne St.........F 6	76 Camlet St.........D 5
68 Berwick Pond Rd...E 3	77 Blantyre St.......J 4	78 Bray Place.......F 2	71 Bromely North Sta. D 9	77 Burnsall St.......F 6	75 Camley St. ....B 7
74 Berwick St.......H 6	71 Blendon Rd......B 12	76 Bread St..........H 2	71 Bromley Rd. SE6..C 9	71 Burnt Ash La.....C 9	76 Camomile St......G 4
79 Bessborough Gdns.G 7	80 Blendon Row......F 2	65 Breakspear Rd. North C 3	71 Bromley Rd. Beckenham..D 9	66 Burnt Oak.......C 3	77 Campden Grove ..C 1
79 Bessborough Pl...G 7	73 Blenheim Rd......B 4	65 Breakspear Rd. South D 3	71 Bromley Rd. Chislehurst....D 11	66 Burnt Oak Sta....C 3	77 Campden Hill Rd..C 1
69 Bessborough Res...D 5	73 Blenheim Ter......B 3	75 Bream's Buildings G 11	71 Bromley South Sta. D 9	71 Burntash Hill.....B 9	77 Campden St.......B 2
78 Bessborough St. ...G 7	76 Bletchley St.......C 2	77 Brechin Place .....F 4	77 Brompton ....G 5	71 Burntash Rd......B 9	76 Camrose Ave.....C 2
71 Bethlehem Royal Hospital........E 8	77 Blithfield St. ....E 2	66 Brecknock Rd.....E 6	77 Brompton Cemetery H 2	70 Burntwood La. SW17 C 5	79 Canada House....A 8
67 Bethnal Green......E 8	73 Blomfield Rd......F 3	77 Bremner Rd.......D 4	79 Brompton Hospital F 5	71 Burntwood La. Coulsdon.......H 7	80 Canal St..........H 3
76 Bethnal Green Rd...E 5	76 Blomfield St. .....G 3	74 Brendon St........G 1	78 Brompton Place...D 2	79 Burrell St........B 12	70 Cane Hill Hospital H 5
67 Bethnal Green Sta..F 8	73 Blomfield Vil.....F 3	66 Brent............D 2	77 Brompton Square .D 6	78 Burton Court.....G 2	67 Cann Hall........D 10
80 Bethwin Rd. ......J 1	78 Bloomfield Ter....F 4	66 Brent Reservoir...D 3	77 Brompton Rd......E 6	80 Burton Grove.....G 3	77 Canning Place....D 3
72 Betsham ....C 5	66 Bloomsbury.......F 6	66 Brent Sta.........D 4	66 Brondesbury Park .E 4	78 Burton St.........D 8	67 Canning Town ...F 10
75 Betterton St.......G 9	75 Bloomsbury Sq....F 9	66 Brent St..........C 4	66 Brondesbury Park Sta. E 4	69 Burtons Rd........C 5	67 Canning Town Sta..F 9
71 Beulah Hill.......C 7	75 Bloomsbury St....G 8	66 Brentford.........G 2	66 Brondesbury Sta...E 4	73 Burwood Place....G 6	76 Cannon St.........H 2
76 Bevan St.......B 2	75 Bloomsbury Way..G 8	70 Brentford Central Sta. A 1	80 Bronti Close......G 2	69 Burwood Rd......F 4	76 Cannon Street Sta..J 2
76 Bevenden St......C 3	76 Blossom St........E 4	66 Brentford F.C.....H 2	79 Brook Drive ....E 11	76 Bury Court.......G 4	79 Cannon Row .....C 8
80 Bevington St......D 7	69 Blundell La........G 6	68 Brentwood.......B 5	71 Brook Fever Hospital A 10	75 Bury Place ......G 8	76 Canon St..........A 1
76 Bevis Marks......G 4	79 Boadicea St.......B 9	68 Brentwood Bypass.B 5	66 Brook Green .....G 4	76 Bury St. EC3.....G 4	67 Canonbury.......E 7
72 Bexley ....B 1	69 Board La.........C 6	68 Brentwood Rd.....D 3	73 Brook Mews North H 4	67 Bury St. N9......A 7	67 Canonbury Sta....E 7
71 Bexley Heath G.C.B 12	70 Bolingbroke Grove B 6	68 Brentwood & Warley Sta..........B 5	74 Brook St. ....H 4	78 Bury St. SW1.....B 6	66 Canons Park......B 2
72 Bexley Hospital ...C 1	74 Bolsover St........F 5	78 Bressenden Place..D 5	75 Brooke St. ......F 11	65 Bury St. Ruislip..D 4	66 Canon's Park Sta..C 2
71 Bexley La.......C 12	70 Bolters La........G 4	69 Bretlands.........E 2	69 Brooklands Rd....F 3	77 Bury Walk........F 6	73 Capel Rd.........E 10
71 Bexley Rd. SE9...B 11	79 Bolton Cres.......J 12	74 Brewer St.........H 7	74 Brook's Mews.....H 5	67 Bury Wood......A 10	73 Capland St.......E 5
72 Bexley Rd. Erith...A 1	77 Bolton Gdns......F 3	76 Brick La..........E 5	66 Brookshill ....B 1	76 Busby St.........E 6	74 Capper St.........E 6
72 Bexley Sta.......B 1	78 Bolton St.........B 5	78 Brick St..........B 4	70 Broom Rd........C 1	67 Bush Hill.........A 7	74 Carburton St......F 5
72 Bexleyheath......B 1	77 Boltons, The......G 3	75 Bride La..........H 12	66 Broomfield Park..B 6	67 Bush Hill G.C.....A 7	73 Cardigan Rd......D 1
80 Bianca Rd.......H 6	76 Bondway.........H 9	75 Bridewell Place...H 12	76 Broomfield Wood .F 4	76 Bush La..........H 2	79 Cardigan St......G 11
74 Bickenhall St......F 3	76 Bonhill St.........E 3	74 Bridford Mews....F 5	74 Brown Hart Gdns. H 4	65 Bushey...........A 6	74 Cardington St.....D 6
71 Bickley ....D 10	76 Bonnington Sq...H 9	69 Bridge Rd. Chertsey E 2	74 Brown St.........G 2	67 Bushey Hall G.C..A 5	76 Carey La.........G 1
75 Bidborough St. ...D 8	76 Boot St..........D 3	69 Bridge Rd. Esher..D 6	71 Brownhill Rd......B 9	66 Bushey Heath.....A 1	75 Carey St. ....G 10
73 Biddulph Rd.......D 2	67 Borders La.......A 11	70 Bridge Rd. Chessington F 2	75 Brownlow Mews .E 10	70 Bushey Rd........D 3	74 Carlisle Av.......H 4
71 Biggin Hill .....H 10	66 Borehamwood ...A 3	79 Bridge St. ....C 8	80 Browning St.......F 2	65 Bushey & Oxhey Sta. A 5	79 Carlisle La........D 10
71 Biggin Hill Airport G 10	72 Borough Green ...H 5	79 Bridgefoot.......G 8	75 Brownlow St. ...F 10	69 Bushy Park.......D 6	78 Carlisle Place ....E 6
67 Billet Rd. E17.....C 8	80 Borough High St...C 2	73 Bridgeman St......C 6	69 Brox.............B 2	76 Bute St. ....F 5	74 Carlisle St........G 7
68 Billet Rd., Chadwell Heath..........C 1	80 Borough Market...B 2	66 Bridgewater Rd....E 2	68 Broxhill Rd.......B 3	80 Buttesland St......D 3	74 Carlos Place......J 4
77 Billing Place......J 3	79 Borough Polytechnic D 12	74 Bridgeway St......C 7	67 Broxwood Way ...B 1	72 Button St.........D 2	74 Carlow St.........B 5
77 Billing Rd.......J 3	79 Borough Rd......D 12	65 Bridle Rd.........D 5	67 Bruce Castle Park .C 7	68 Butts La..........D 3	66 Carlton Ave. East .D 2
77 Billing St.......J 3	79 Borrett Rd........G 13	76 Bridport Place....B 3	67 Bruce Grove Sta. .C 7	71 Buxton La........H 7	78 Carlton Gdns. ...B 7
76 Billingsgate Market.J 3	73 Boscobel St. ......E 5	67 Bridport Rd .....B 7	76 Brune St..........F 5	76 Buxton St........E 6	73 Carlton Hill......B 3
76 Billiter St.........H 4	80 Boss St...........C 5	73 Bridstow Place....G 1	73 Brunel Estate ....F 1	69 Byfleet..........G 3	79 Carlton House Ter.B 7
71 Bina Gdns........F 3	78 Bostall Hill Rd...G 12	70 Brighton Rd. Coulsdon H 5	65 Brunel University..F 3	76 Byfleet Rd........G 4	73 Carlton Vale......C 1
68 Bind La.........C 4	67 Bostall Woods....H 12	70 Brighton Rd. Croydon G 6	77 Brunswick Centre .E 8	69 Byfleet & New Haw Sta...........F 3	77 Carlyle Square ...G 5
74 Bingham Place....F 3	66 Boston Manor....G 1	70 Brighton Rd. Sutton F 4	80 Brunswick Court..C 4	73 Byng Place ....E 7	77 Carlyle's House...H 6
71 Bingham Rd. Sta...E 7	66 Boston Manor Sta.G 1	70 Brigstock Rd......D 6	77 Brunswick Gdns...B 2	76 Byward St........J 4	75 Carmelite St. ....H 11
74 Binney St.........H 4	76 Boston Place.....E 2	67 Brimsdown Sta....A 8	66 Brunswick Park..B 6	78 Bywater St.......F 2	74 Carnaby St. ......H 6
72 Birches, The .....F 2	66 Boston Rd........G 1	75 Bristol St. ....F 12	76 Brunswick Place ..D 3	76 Cabbel St.........G 6	75 Carnegie St. ....B 10
76 Birchin La.......H 3	75 Boswell St........F 9	73 Bristol Gdns......F 3	75 Brunswick Square .E 9	76 Cable St..........H 6	73 Caroline Place....J 2
72 Birchwood Rd....C 1	78 Botanic Gdns.....H 2	73 Bristol Mews......E 3	76 Brushfield St......F 4	71 Cackets La......G 11	78 Caroline Ter. .....F 3
74 Bird St...........H 4	69 Botleys..........E 1	75 Britannia St.......C 9	74 Bruton La........J 5	68 Cadbury Rd.......E 6	65 Carpenders Park ..B 5
78 Birdcage Walk...C 7	76 Botolph La........J 3	75 British Council...F 10	74 Bruton Place.....J 5	80 Cadiz St..........G 2	65 Carpenders Park Sta. B 5
80 Bird-in-Bush Rd..J 6	67 Bounces Rd.......B 8	75 British Medical Association....D 8	74 Bruton St.........J 5	78 Cadogan Gdns....E 2	67 Carpenters Rd.....E 9
80 Birdlip Close......J 4	80 Boundary La......H 2	75 British Museum...F 8	74 Bryanston Mews East G 2	78 Cadogan Gate....E 3	78 Carriage Drive East J 4
74 Birkbeck Coll......E 7	71 Boundary Rd......G 9	77 Britten St.........G 6	74 Bryanston Mews West G 2	78 Cadogan La.......E 3	78 Carriage Drive Nth.H 4
71 Birkbeck Sta.......D 8	79 Boundary Row....C 11	75 Britton St........F 12	74 Bryanston Place...G 2	78 Cadogan Pier.....H 1	74 Carriage Rd., The .C 2
75 Birkenhead St.....C 9	76 Boundary St......D 5	70 Brixton ....A 6	74 Bryanston Square .G 2	78 Cadogan Place....E 3	79 Carroun Rd......J 10
66 Bishops Ave. The..D 5	66 Bounds Green Rd. C 6	70 Brixton Hill......B 6	74 Bryanston St......H 2	78 Cadogan Square..E 2	70 Carshalton ....E 5
73 Bishop's Bridge Rd. G 3	74 Bourdon St......J 5	70 Brixton Prison....B 6	68 Bryant Ave. ......C 3	78 Cadogan St.......F 2	70 Carshalton Beeches Sta. F 5
79 Bishop's Ter. ....E 11	66 Bourne, The ......B 6	79 Brixton Rd.......J 11	80 Brymer Rd........G 5	78 Cadogan Ter......E 9	70 Carshalton Ho....F 5
70 Bishopsford Rd...E 4	66 Bourne Hill.......B 6	70 Brixton Sta.......B 6	76 Buckfast St.......D 6	76 Caesar St.........C 4	70 Carshalton on the Hill F 5
76 Bishopsgate .....G 4	78 Bourne St........F 3	67 Broad La. N15....C 8	67 Buckhurst Hill ...B 10	80 Caldew St........J 2	70 Carshalton Rd. Wallington .....F 5
69 Bittams La.......E 2	73 Bourne Ter.......F 2	72 Broad La. Dartford C 2	71 Buckhurst Rd....H 11	76 Cale St. ....F 6	70 Carshalton Rd. Woodmansterne G 5
67 Black Horse La...C 8	68 Bournebridge ....A 2	67 Broad Mead Rd. .C 10	78 Buckingham Gate.D 6	75 Caledonia St......C 9	75 Carter La........H 13
67 Black Horse Rd. Sta. C 8	68 Bournebridge La...A 2	79 Broad Sanctuary..D 8	78 Buckingham Palace C 5	75 Caledonian Rd....B 9	80 Carter Place......G 1
73 Black Lion Gate..J 3	75 Bouverie St.......H 11	76 Broad Street Sta...F 3	78 Buckingham Palace Gdns...........C 5	66 Caledonian Rd. & Barnsbury Sta...E 6	79 Carter St. ....G 13
65 Black Park ....E 1	67 Bow ....F 9	77 Broad Walk, The..C 3	78 Buckingham Palace Rd............E 5	77 Callow St. ....H 4	78 Carteret St........D 7
79 Black Prince Rd. .F 10	67 Bow Bridge.......F 9	74 Broadcasting House G 5	78 Buckingham Place.D 6	80 Calmington Rd....H 4	75 Carthusian St.....F 13
76 Blackall St........E 3	67 Bow Common.....F 9	73 Broadley St.......F 5	79 Buckingham St. ...A 9	75 Calshot St. ....B 9	75 Carting La........J 9
66 Blackbird Hill....D 3	67 Bow La...........H 2	73 Broadley Ter......E 6	76 Buckland St......C 3	75 Calthorpe St. ...E 10	74 Carton St.........G 3
74 Blackburnes Mews.J 3	67 Bow Rd..........F 9	76 Broadstone Place..F 3	76 Buckle St.........G 6	78 Calvert Av.......D 4	75 Cartwright Gdns. .D 8
71 Blackfen ....B 11	75 Bow St...........H 9	78 Broadway, SW1...D 7	76 Bucklersbury .....H 2	76 Calvin St.........E 5	76 Cassiobury Park ..A 4
71 Blackfen Rd.......B 11	66 Bowes Park Sta...C 6	70 Broadway, SW19..C 4	76 Bucknall St........G 8	71 Camberwell.......A 7	76 Casson St.........F 6
75 Blackfriars Bridge.J 12	80 Bowles Rd........H 6	65 Broadway, Southall G 2	71 Bug Hill ....H 8	79 Camberwell New Rd. J 11	73 Castellan Rd......E 3
75 Blackfriars La....H 12	75 Bowling Green La.E 11	74 Broadwick St......H 6	67 Bugsby's Reach .G 10	80 Camberwell Rd....J 2	70 Castelnau ....A 3
79 Blackfriars Rd....C 12	79 Bowling Green St.H 11		75 Bulinga St. ....F 8	75 Cambridge Circus.H 8	66 Castle Bar Park Sta.F 1
75 Blackfriars Sta. ..H 12	76 Bowling Green Walk D 3		68 Bull La..........D 2	67 Cambridge Heath Sta. F 8	75 Castle Baynard St.H 13
71 Blackheath ....A 9	76 Boyd St..........H 6		74 Bulstrode St. .....G 4	67 Cambridge Park. E11 D 10	66 Cat Hill ....A 5
67 Blackheath Hill...H 9	79 Boyfield St.......C 12				80 Catesby St........F 3
	76 Brackley St.......F 1				71 Catford ....B 9
	76 Brad St..........B 11				71 Catford Bridge ...B 8
	73 Braden St.........E 2				
	79 Braganza St......G 12				
	80 Braham St........G 5				
	80 Braidwood St......B 4				

71 Catford Hill .....B 8
71 Catford Sta. .....B 8
77 Cathcart Rd. ....H 3
78 Catherine Place ..D 6
75 Catherine St. .....H 9
74 Cato St. ....G 1
80 Cator St. ....J 5
69 Catos Hill ....E 6
75 Catton St. ....G 9
79 Causton St. ......F 7
77 Cavaye Place .....G 4
73 Cavendish Av. ....C 5
73 Cavendish Cl. .....C 5
78 Cavendish Hotel ..B 6
74 Cavendish Place ..G 5
66 Cavendish Rd. NW6 .....E 4
70 Cavendish Rd. SW12 .....B 5
74 Cavendish Square .G 5
76 Cavendish St. .....C 2
78 Caversham St. ....H 2
78 Caxton Hall ......D 7
78 Caxton St. ....D 7
76 Cayton St. ....D 2
70 Caesar's Camp ...C 3
79 Cenotaph ....C 8
79 Centaur St. ....D 10
75 Central Criminal Court .....G 12
71 Central Hill .....C 7
68 Central Park......D 2
70 Central Rd. ....D 4
75 Central St. ....D 13
68 Chadwell Heath...D 1
68 Chadwell Hth La..D 1
75 Chadwell St. ......C 11
78 Chadwick St. .....E 7
74 Chagford St. ......E 2
65 Chalfont Common B 1
65 Chalfont Park ....C 1
65 Chalfont St. Peter .C 1
66 Chalk Farm Rd. ..E 6
70 Chalk La. ....G 3
71 Chalky Hill .....G 11
74 Chalton St. ....C 7
76 Chamber St.......H 6
80 Chambers St. .....C 6
76 Chambord St. .....D 5
79 Chancel St. ......B 12
73 Chancery La....G 10
75 Chandos Place ....J 8
74 Chandos St. ......G 5
75 Chantry St. ......B 13
80 Chapel Court ....C 2
67 Chapel End.......C 9
75 Chapel Market...B 11
73 Chapel Side. ......J 2
73 Chapel St. NW1 ..F 6
78 Chapel St. SW1...D 4
79 Chapter Rd. .....G 13
78 Chapter St. ....F 7
79 Charing Cross Pier.B 9
75 Charing Cross Rd..H 8
79 Charing Cross Sta..A 9
73 Charlbert St. ......B 6
73 Charles La. ....B 6
76 Charles Square....D 3
78 Charles St. ....B 4
78 Charles II St. ......A 7
80 Charleston St......F 2
74 Charlotte Mews ..F 6
76 Charlotte Rd. .....D 4
74 Charlotte St. ......F 6
75 Charlotte Ter...B 10
67 Charlton ....G 10
67 Charlton F.C. ...G 10
69 Charlton La. ......B 7
67 Charlton Park...H 10
75 Charlton Place ..B 12
67 Charlton Rd. SE7 H 10
69 Charlton Rd. Shepperton .....D 4
67 Charlton Way ...H 9
78 Charlwood Place .F 6
78 Charlwood St. ....G 6
71 Charmwood La..F 12
74 Charrington St. ..B 7
76 Chart St. ....D 3
75 Charterhouse .....F 12
75 Charterhouse Sq. .F 13
75 Charterhouse St. .F 12
66 Chase Rd. ....A 6
66 Chase Side. ....A 6
80 Chatham St. ......E 3
74 Cheam ....F 4
70 Cheam Rd. ....F 3
70 Cheam Sta. ....F 4
76 Cheapside.........H 2

78 Chelsea Barracks..G 4
78 Chelsea Bridge...H 4
78 Chelsea Bridge Rd. G 4
78 Chelsea Embank..H 2
77 Chelsea Hospital for Women ....G 5
77 Chelsea Manor Gdns. .....C 6
77 Chelsea Manor St..G 6
77 Chelsea Park Gdns.H 5
77 Chelsea PolytechnicG 5
78 Chelsea Reach....H 3
77 Chelsea Square ...G 5
71 Chelsfield Hill...F 12
71 Chelsfield La. Orpington.....E 12
72 Chelsfield La. Orpington......F 1
71 Chelsfield Rd....E 12
71 Chelsfield Sta...F 12
71 Chelsfield Village .F 12
71 Chelsham ....H 8
71 Chelsham Ct. Rd..H 9
71 Chelsham Rd. .....H 8
78 Cheltenham Ter...F 2
75 Cheney Rd........C 8
74 Chenies Mews ....E 7
74 Chenies St. ......F 7
77 Cheniston Gdns...D 2
73 Chepstow Cres...H 1
73 Chepstow Place ..H 1
73 Chepstow Rd. ....G 1
73 Chepstow Villas..H 1
76 Chequer St. ......E 2
68 Chequers Rd. ....B 3
76 Cherbury St......C 3
69 Chertsey ....E 2
69 Chertsey Bridge..E 3
69 Chertsey G.C. ....D 2
69 Chertsey La......D 2
69 Chertsey Rd. Byfleet .....G 3
69 Chertsey Rd. Feltham .....C 4
69 Chertsey Rd. Shepperton.....E 3
78 Chesham Mews...D 3
78 Chesham Place...D 3
78 Chesham St. ......E 3
76 Cheshire St. ......E 6
78 Chester Close....D 4
74 Chester Gate ....D 5
78 Chester Mews ...D 4
74 Chester Place...C 5
74 Chester Rd. ......D 4
78 Chester Row .....F 3
78 Chester Square...E 4
78 Chester St. ....D 4
74 Chester Terrace ..D 5
79 Chester Way .....F 11
78 Chesterfield Hill..A 4
78 Chesterfield St....B 4
77 Cheval Place......D 6
71 Chevening Park ..H 12
76 Cheyne Gdns. ....H 6
77 Cheyne Hospital ..H 6
77 Cheyne Row .....H 6
77 Cheyne Walk ....H 6
79 Chicheley St. ....C 10
73 Chichester Rd.....F 3
78 Chichester St. ....G 6
76 Chicksand St. .....F 6
67 Chigwell ....B 11
67 Chigwell La......A 11
67 Cigwell Rise .....B 11
67 Chigwell Rd. ....C 10
67 Chigwell Row ...B 12
68 Childerditch La...D 6
77 Child's Place .....F 2
77 Child's St. ....F 2
70 Chiltern Rd. .....F 4
74 Chiltern St. ......F 3
76 Chilton St. ....E 6
73 Chilworth Mews ..H 4
73 Chilworth St......H 4
67 Chingford ....B 9
67 Chingford Hatch ..B 9
67 Chingford La......B 10
67 Chingford Mount Rd. .....B 9
67 Chingford Rd.....C 9

73 Chippenham Mews E 1
73 Chippenham Rd...E 1
70 Chipstead ....H 5
70 Chipstead Valley Rd. .....H 5
71 Chislehurst ......D 11
71 Chislehurst Common .....C 11
71 Chislehurst G.C. ..C 11
71 Chislehurst Rd. Bromley.......D 10
71 Chislehurst Rd. Orpington.....E 11
71 Chislehurst Sta...D 10
71 Chislehurst West .C 10
76 Chiswell St.......F 2
66 Chiswick ....G 3
70 Chiswick Bridge..A 2
66 Chiswick High Rd. G 2
66 Chiswick House ...A 3
66 Chiswick Park Sta.G 3
70 Chiswick Sta. .....A 2
66 Chiswick Steps....H 3
63 Chitty St.........F 6
65 Chorleywood Rd. .A 3
66 Christchurch Ave..C 1
67 Christchurch Rd...B 6
78 Christchurch St....G 2
76 Christian St.......H 7
73 Christina St. ......E 4
76 Christopher St.....F 3
80 Chumleigh St. ....H 4
68 Church Elm La....E 2
66 Church End ....C 4
72 Church Hill, Dartford .....C 2
67 Church Hill, Loughton .....A 11
69 Church Hill, Pyrford .....H 2
66 Church Hill Rd....A 5
79 Church House ...D 9
71 Church La........H 9
71 Church Rd. SE19..D 7
70 Church Rd. SW19 .C 4
69 Church Rd. Addlestone .....F 2
69 Church Rd. Ashford .....C 3
69 Church Rd. Byfleet G 3
71 Church Rd. Chelsfield .....F 12
68 Church Rd. Noak Hill .....A 3
65 Church Rd. Northolt .....E 5
72 Church Rd. Sutton-at-Hone..........D 2
70 Church Rd. Teddington......C 1
73 Church St. NW8...F 5
67 Church St. Edmonton .....B 7
67 Church St. Enfield .A 7
70 Church St. Epsom.G 3
69 Church St. Walton.E 4
78 Churchill Gardens Estate ....G 6
78 Churchill Gardens Rd...........G 5
74 Churchill Hotel ...G 3
77 Churchway ....D 7
77 Churchyard Row .E 12
78 Churton St.......F 6
73 Circus Rd. ....E 6
75 City Garden Row C 13
75 City of London School .....H 12
75 City Rd. EC1 ...C 12
76 City Rd. EC1.....D 3
76 City Road Basin ..C 13
75 City University ..D 12
77 City & Guilds College .....D 5
74 Civil Service Commission ....J 6
78 Clabon Mews.....E 2
73 Clanricarde Gdns..J 2
70 Clapham ....A 6
70 Clapham Common B 5
70 Clapham Common North Side .....B 5
70 Clapham Common South Side .....B 5
66 Clapham Junc. Sta. H 5
70 Clapham Park Rd. B 6
70 Clapham Rd. .....A 6
70 Clapham Sta. .....A 6
67 Clapton Common .D 8

67 Clapton Sta.......D 8
75 Claremont Close .C 11
75 Claremont Square C 11
74 Clarence Gate.....E 3
74 Clarence Gardens .D 5
78 Clarence House...C 6
73 Clarendon Gdns...E 4
73 Clarendon Grove .C 7
73 Clarendon Place ..H 4
78 Clarendon St......G 5
77 Clareville Grove..F 4
77 Clareville St. ......F 4
78 Clarges Mews.....B 5
78 Clarges St. ....B 5
74 Claridge's Hotel ..H 4
78 Claverton St. .....G 6
73 Clay St. ....F 3
70 Claybury Hosp...C 11
70 Claygate..........F 1
67 Clayhall..........C 11
67 Clayhall Av.......C 11
67 Clayhall Park.....C 11
79 Claylands Place ..J 10
79 Claylands Rd....J 10
65 Claypit La........B 4
73 Clayton St. ......H 11
79 Cleaver Square...G 11
79 Cleaver St. ......G 11
76 Clement St. ....C 2
76 Clement's La......H 3
79 Cleopatra's Needle A 9
76 Clere Place ....E 3
76 Clere St. ....E 3
75 Clerkenwell Close E 11
76 Clerkenwell Green E 12
75 Clerkenwell Rd...E 11
73 Cleveland Gdns...H 3
78 Cleveland Row....B 6
74 Cleveland Square .H 3
74 Cleveland St. .....F 6
74 Cleveland Terrace .G 4
74 Clifford St. ....J 5
73 Clifton Gdns......E 3
73 Clifton Hill.......B 3
73 Clifton Place .....H 5
73 Clifton Rd. ....E 4
73 Clifton St. ....F 3
80 Clink St. ....A 2
75 Clipstone St......F 5
67 Clissold Park ....D 7
78 Cliveden Place ...E 3
76 Cloak La.........H 3
69 Clockhouse La....C 3
74 Cloth Fair........F 13
75 Cloudesley Place .B 11
75 Cloudesley Rd....B 11
75 Cloudesley Sq.....A 11
75 Cloudesley St. ....B 11
76 Club Row ....D 5
75 Coalbrookdale Gt .C 5
76 Coate St. ....C 7
76 Cobb St. ....G 5
69 Cobham ....H 5
69 Cobham Park ....H 5
69 Cobham Rd. .....H 6
72 Cobham Terrace Rd. .....B 4
69 Cobham & Stoke D'Abernon Sta..H 5
80 Cobourg Rd. .....H 5
73 Cochrane St.......C 5
73 Cock Hill ....G 4
75 Cock La..........G 12
76 Cockfosters.......A 5
66 Cockfosters Sta...A 6
79 Cockspur St.......B 8
76 Code St. ....E 6
76 Coin St. ....B 11
77 Colbeck Mews ...F 3
68 Colchester Rd.....C 3
72 Coldblow Maypole B 1
70 Coldharbour La. SE5 .....B 6
65 Coldharbour La. Hayes.........G 5
70 Cole Park ....B 1
80 Cole St. ....H 3
75 Colebrooke Row .B 12
80 Colegrove Rd......J 6
77 Coleherne Mews .G 2
77 Coleherne Rd. ....G 2
80 Coleman Rd.......J 4
76 Coleman St. ......G 3
75 Coley St. ....E 10
65 Colham Green ....F 4
66 Colin Deep La....C 3

70 Colindale.........C 3
66 Colindale Av......C 3
66 Colindale Sta. ....C 3
77 Coliseum Theatre..J 8
76 College Hill ......H 2
75 College of Arms ..H 13
70 College Place .....A 6
71 College Rd. SE21..B 7
71 College Rd. Bromley .....D 9
72 College Rd. Dartford .....D 1
70 College Rd. Epsom .....G 3
76 College St. ....H 2
68 Collier Row ......C 2
68 Collier Row La....C 2
68 Collier Row Rd...C 2
76 Collier St. ....C 9
70 Collier's Wood....C 5
77 Collingham Gdns..F 3
77 Collingham Place .F 2
77 Collingham Rd...F 3
75 Collinson St.......C 13
65 Colnbrook ....H 2
65 Colnbrook Bypass .H 2
65 Colnbrook St. ....D 12
65 Colney Butts......A 5
66 Colney Hatch ....B 5
66 Colney Hatch La...C 6
79 Colombo St. ......B 12
75 Colonnade........E 8
75 Columbia Rd. ....D 5
74 Colville Place ....F 7
75 Compton St.......E 12
79 Concert Hall Approach .....B 10
73 Conduit Mews....H 4
73 Conduit Place ....H 5
74 Conduit St. ......H 5
80 Congreve St.......F 4
74 Connaught Place..H 2
74 Connaught Sq.....H 2
74 Connaught St.....H 6
79 Cons St. ....C 11
78 Constitution Hill..C 5
76 Content St. ....F 2
69 Convent Rd.......C 4
74 Conway St........E 6
73 Cooks St. ....H 12
75 Coombe Hill G.C. .C 2
70 Coombe La........D 3
70 Coombe Rd., Kingston.......D 2
70 Coombe Rd. New Malden........D 3
71 Coombe Rd. Sta...E 7
70 Coombe Wood G.C. .....C 2
75 Coomb's St. ......C 13
80 Cooper's Rd. .....G 5
80 Cooper's Wood ...G 4
77 Cope Place ....D 1
75 Copenhagen St....A 9
65 Copperfield St.....C 13
70 Copse Hill ....D 3
65 Copse Wood......C 4
76 Copsem La........F 6
76 Copthall Av.......G 3
76 Copthall Court ...G 3
75 Coptic St. ....G 8
79 Coral St. ....C 11
75 Coram St. ....E 8
75 Coram's Field Playground .....E 9
76 Corbet Place......F 5
76 Corbets Tey .....E 4
68 Corbets Tey Rd...E 4
74 Cork St. ....J 6
76 Corn Exchange...H 4
76 Cornhill ....H 3
77 Cornwall Gdns...E 3
77 Cornwall Rd. ....B 11
76 Coronet St. ......D 3
75 Corporation Row.E 11
76 Corsham St. ......D 3
79 Cosser St. ....D 10
73 Cosway St. ....F 6
76 Cotham St. ......F 2
77 Cottage Place ....D 6
78 Cottage Walk.....D 3
70 Cottenham Park ..D 3

70 Cottenham Park Rd. .....D 3
77 Cottesmore Gdns..D 3
79 Cottington St.....F 12
70 Coulsdon ....H 6
70 Coulsdon Court G.C. .....G 6
70 Coulsdon La......H 5
70 Coulsdon North Sta. .....G 6
70 Coulsdon Rd. ....H 6
78 Coulson St. ......F 2
79 County Hall .....C 9
80 County St.........E 2
71 Court La. ....B 7
77 Courtenay St. ....G 10
77 Courtfield Gdns...F 2
77 Courtfield Rd. ....F 3
75 Covent Garden ...H 9
79 Covent Garden Market .....H 8
74 Coventry St. ......J 7
80 Cowan St. ....H 4
75 Cowcross St......F 12
65 Cowley..........F 3
79 Cowley St. ....D 8
70 Cowper St. ....D 3
67 Craddocks Av....H 2
80 Crail Row ....F 3
74 Cramer St........F 4
79 Crampton St. ....F 13
75 Cranbourn St. ...H 8
67 Cranbrook Rd. ..C 11
65 Cranford.........H 4
65 Cranford La......H 5
68 Cranham ....D 5
77 Cranleigh St. .....C 6
77 Cranley Gdns. ....G 4
77 Cranley Mews....F 4
77 Cranley Place ....F 5
76 Cranwood St......D 3
73 Craven Hill Gdns..H 3
73 Craven St. ....B 8
73 Craven Terrace ...H 4
74 Crawford Place ...G 1
74 Crawford St. .....F 2
72 Crayford.........A 2
72 Crayford Rd......B 2
76 Creechurch La....H 4
75 Creed La. ....H 12
67 Creekmouth .....F 12
77 Cremer St. ....C 5
77 Crescent Place ...E 6
77 Cresswell Gdns. ..F 3
77 Cresswell Place ..G 4
75 Crestfield St......C 9
66 Cricklewood .....E 4
66 Cricklewood La. ..D 4
66 Cricklewood Sta...E 4
80 Crimscott St. .....E 4
79 Crinan St. ....B 9
78 Cringle St.........J 6
76 Cripplegate Institute .....F 1
74 Criterion Theatre..J 7
72 Crockenhill ......E 1
75 Crofton Heath ...E 10
71 Crofton Park Sta. .B 8
71 Crofton Rd. ......C 11
71 Croham Hurst G.C. F 7
71 Croham Rd.......F 7
75 Cromer St. ....D 9
71 Crompton St. ....E 4
77 Cromwell Cres....F 1
77 Cromwell Gdns...E 5
77 Cromwell Mews ..E 5
77 Cromwell Place ..E 5
77 Cromwell Rd. SW5 & SW7..........E 3
69 Cromwell Rd. Hounslow......B 6
76 Crondall St. ......C 3
76 Cropley St........B 2
80 Crosby Row......C 3
74 Crosby Square....G 4
68 Cross La. ....D 3
70 Crossdeep........C 1
75 Crosswall ....H 5
66 Crouch End ......D 6
66 Crouch Hill ......D 6
66 Crouch Hill Sta. ..D 6
68 Crow La..........D 2
75 Crown Dale ......C 6
79 Crown Office Row H 11
80 Crown St. ....J 2
74 Crowndale Rd.....B 6
65 Croxley Green ...A 4
65 Croxley Green Sta. A 4
65 Croxley Sta.......A 4

71 Croxted Rd.....B 7
71 Croydon.......E 7
70 Croydon La.....G 5
71 Croydon Rd. SE20 D 7
71 Croydon Rd.
  Beckenham.....D 8
71 Croydon Rd. Bromley
  E 10
71 Croydon Rd.
  Chelsham.....H 9
70 Croydon Rd. Croydon
  E 6
70 Croydon Rd. Mitcham
  D 5
80 Crucifix La......C 4
75 Cruden St.......B 12
75 Cruickshank St..C 10
71 Crutched Friars..F 4
71 Crystal Palace F.C. D 7
71 Crystal Palace Sta..C 7
71 Crystal Palace Park C 7
75 Cubit St.........D 10
70 Cuddington G.C...G 4
71 Cudham.......G 11
71 Cudham La. Cudham
  G 11
71 Cudham La. Green
  Street Green...F 11
71 Cudham La. Horns
  Green.......H 11
71 Cudham Rd.....G 11
78 Culford Gdns....F 2
76 Culham St.......H 4
74 Culross St.......J 3
73 Culworth St......C 6
74 Cumberland Gate .H 2
74 Cumberland Hotel H 3
74 Cumberland Market
  D 5
78 Cumberland St...G 5
74 Cumberland Ter...C 5
75 Cumming St....C 10
80 Cunard St.......H 3
78 Cundy St........F 4
73 Cunningham Pl...E 5
79 Cureton St.......F 8
80 Curlew St........C 5
75 Cursitor St.......G 11
76 Curtain Rd......E 4
80 Curtis St........E 5
78 Curzon Gate.....B 4
78 Curzon St.......B 4
76 Custom House...J 4
67 Custom House Sta.F 10
79 Cut, The........C 11
73 Cuthbert St......F 5
74 Cutler St........G 4
75 Cynthia St......C 10
74 Cypress Place....F 6
75 Cyrus St........D 12
78 Dacre St........D 7
68 Dagenham......E 2
68 Dagenham Av....E 1
68 Dagenham Dock Sta.
  F 1
68 Dagenham Heathway
  Sta.........E 1
68 Dagenham Rd...D 2
68 Dagenham Park..B 4
75 Dallington St....E 12
67 Dalston........E 7
67 Dalston Junc. Sta. .E 7
67 Dalston La......E 8
72 Daltons Rd......E 1
75 Dame St........B 13
75 Danbury St.....B 12
75 Dane St........F 9
71 Danson Park....D 7
79 Danson Rd. SE17 G 13
71 Danson Rd. Bexley
  Heath......B 12
77 Danvers St......H 5
74 D'Arblay St......H 6
76 Darby St........J 6
72 Darenth........C 3
72 Darenth Rd......B 3
72 Dartford........B 2
72 Dartford G.C. ...C 2
72 Dartford Heath ..B 2
72 Dartford-Purfleet
  Tunnel......A 3
72 Dartford Rd. Dartford
  B 2
72 Dartford Rd. Hextable
  C 2
66 Dartmouth Park Hill
  D 6
71 Dartmouth Rd....C 8

78 Dartmouth St....D 7
80 Dartnell Rd......H 4
80 Darwin St.......F 3
65 Datchet.........H 1
80 Date St.........G 2
76 Davenant St......F 6
73 Daventry St......F 6
80 Davey St........H 5
71 Davidson Rd.....E 7
74 Davies Mews....H 4
74 Davies St.......H 4
66 Dawes Rd.......H 4
80 Dawes St.......F 3
65 Dawley Rd......G 4
67 Daws Hill......A 9
75 Dawson Place...H 1
71 Days La.......B 11
79 De Laune St.....G 12
77 De Vere Gdns....D 3
74 De Walden St....F 4
80 Deacon St.......E 1
80 Deacon Way.....E 1
76 Deal St.........F 6
79 Dean Bradley St..E 8
79 Dean Farrar St...D 7
79 Dean Ryle St....E 8
79 Dean Stanley St..E 8
74 Dean St.........H 7
78 Deanery St......B 4
80 Dean's Buildings..F 3
75 Dean's Court....H 13
66 Dean's La.......B 3
79 Dean's Yard.....D 8
66 Deansbrook Rd...B 3
67 Debden Sta.....A 11
80 Decima St.......D 4
70 Deer Park......D 4
79 Defence, Ministry of
  B 8
65 Delaford Park....F 2
73 Delamere Terrace.F 3
74 Delancey St.....B 5
73 Delaware Rd.....E 2
75 Delhi St.........A 9
78 Denbigh Place...F 6
78 Denbigh St......F 6
65 Denham........D 2
65 Denham Aerodrome
  C 2
74 Denman St......J 7
75 Denmark Grove..B 11
71 Denmark Hill....B 7
71 Denmark Hill Sta..A 7
75 Denmark St......G 8
70 Denning Avenue..F 6
68 Dennises La.....E 4
79 Denny Crescent ..F 11
79 Denny St........F 11
78 Denyer St.......F 2
80 Depot St........J 2
67 Deptford........H 8
67 Deptford Sta.....H 9
76 Derbyshire St....D 7
76 Dereham Place...D 4
74 Dering St.......H 5
71 Derry Downs....E 12
77 Derry St........D 2
80 Deverell St......E 2
75 Devonia Rd.....B 12
67 Devons Rd......F 9
74 Devonshire Close..F 5
74 Devonshire Mews
  South........F 4
74 Devonshire Mews
  West........F 4
74 Devonshire Place..F 4
74 Devonshire Plce. Mews
  F 4
76 Devonshire Row ..G 4
76 Devonshire Square G 4
74 Devonshire St....F 4
73 Devonshire Ter....H 4
75 Dewey Rd.......B 11
74 Dial Walk, The ...C 3
80 Dickens Square...D 2
75 Dignum St.......B 11
78 Dilke St........H 2
76 Dingley Place....D 2
76 Dingley Rd......D 1
76 Diss St.........C 5
76 Distaff La.......H 1
79 Distin St........F 11
70 Ditton Hill......E 1
65 Ditton Park .....G 1
70 Ditton Rd.......E 2
76 Dock St.........J 6
80 Dockhead.......C 6
80 Dockley Rd......D 6

79 Doddington Gr....G 12
78 Dolben St.......B 12
79 Dolland St......G 10
66 Dollis Hill La.....D 4
66 Dollis Hill Sta....E 3
78 Dolphin Square...G 7
75 Dombey St......F 9
76 Dominion St.....F 3
80 Domville Grove...G 5
75 Donegal St......C 10
78 Donne Place.....E 1
79 Doon St........B 10
78 Dorchester Hotel..B 4
74 Doric Way......D 7
76 Dorking Rd......G 2
75 Dorrington St....F 11
74 Dorset Close.....F 2
78 Dorset Estate....C 5
78 Dorset Mews....D 4
78 Dorset Place.....F 7
78 Dorset Rise.....H 12
70 Dorset Rd. SW19 .D 4
79 Dorset Rd. SW8...J 9
78 Dorset Square....E 2
74 Dorset St.......F 3
75 Doughty Mews...E 10
75 Doughty St......E 10
78 Douglas St.......F 7
77 Douro Place.....D 3
76 Dove Mews......F 4
76 Dove Row......B 6
77 Dovehouse St....G 5
78 Dover House Rd..B 3
78 Dover St........A 5
76 Dowgate Hill....H 2
78 Down St........B 4
71 Downe.........G 10
71 Downham Estate..C 9
71 Downham Way...C 9
79 Downing St......C 8
70 Downs Rd. Epsom G 3
70 Downs Rd. Sutton G 4
72 Downs Rd.
  Swanscombe....C 6
72 Downs Wood....G 6
69 Downside.......H 5
69 Downside Rd....H 5
79 Draco St.......H 13
76 Drant St........F 5
79 Draper St.......E 13
79 Drapers Hall....G 3
78 Draycott Avenue..F 1
78 Draycott Place...F 2
78 Draycott Terrace..F 2
77 Drayson Mews...C 2
77 Drayton Gdns....G 4
66 Drayton Green...F 1
67 Drive, The......D 11
80 Druid St........C 5
74 Drummond Cres..C,7
74 Drummond St....D 6
75 Drury La.......H 9
76 Dryden St.......H 9
76 Drysdale St......D 4
77 Duchess of Bedford's
  Walk.........C 1
74 Duchess St......F 5
75 Duchess Theatre ..H 9
75 Duchy St.......B 11
65 Ducks Hill......C 4
65 Ducks Hill Rd....C 4
66 Dudden Hill La...E 3
76 Dufferin St......E 2
78 Duke of York St...A 6
78 Duke of York's
  H.Q.........F 3
75 Duke of York's Th. J 8
74 Duke St. SW1....A 6
74 Duke St. W1....H 4
80 Duke Street Hill...B 3
76 Duke's La.......C 2
76 Duke's Place....G 4
75 Duke's Rd.......D 7
72 Dulwich........B 7
71 Dulwich College .C 7
71 Dulwich Common .B 7
71 Dulwich Park....B 7
71 Dulwich Village...B 7
71 Dulwich Wood Pk. C 7
71 Dulwich & Sydenham
  Hill G.C......C 7
76 Dunbridge St.....E 7
75 Duncan St......B 12
75 Duncan Terrace ..B 12
76 Dunloe St.......C 5
80 Dunlop Place....C 6
68 Dunning's La....D 6
70 Dunstans Hill....F 4

76 Dunston Rd......A 5
72 Dunton Green ...H 1
80 Dunton Rd......F 5
78 Duplex Ride.....C 3
76 Durant St.......C 6
67 Durants Park....A 8
76 Durham Rd......D 3
79 Durham St......G 10
73 Durham Terrace ..G 2
66 Durnsford Rd. N11
  C 6
70 Durnsford Rd. SW19
  C 4
78 Dyley St........E 3
75 Dyott St........G 8
78 Dysart St.......E 3
75 Eagle St........F 9
75 Eagle Wharf Rd...B 2
66 Ealing.........F 2
66 Ealing Broadway Sta.
  F 2
66 Ealing Common ..G 2
66 Ealing Common Sta.
  G 2
66 Ealing G.C......F 1
76 Ealing Rd. Brentford
  G 2
65 Ealing Rd. Greenford
  E 6
66 Ealing Rd. Wembley
  E 2
73 Eamont St.......B 6
66 Eardley Cres.....G 1
80 Earl Rd.........F 5
76 Earl St.........F 3
74 Earlham St......H 8
77 Earl's Court.....G 1
77 Earl's Court Gdns. F 2
77 Earl's Court Rd...E 1
77 Earl's Court Sq...G 2
77 Earl's Court Sta...F 2
77 Earl's Path .....A 10
77 Earl's Walk......E 1
70 Earlsfield Rd.....B 4
70 Earlsfield Sta.....B 4
75 Earlstoke St. ...D 12
75 Earnshaw St.....G 8
66 East Acton......G 3
66 East Acton Sta...F 3
66 East Barnet......A 6
69 East Bedfont....B 4
71 East Croydon Sta. .E 7
71 East Dulwich ....B 7
71 East Dulwich Rd..B 7
71 East Dulwich Sta..B 7
66 East End Rd.....C 5
70 East Ewell......F 4
66 East Finchley ....C 5
66 East Finchley Sta. .C 5
71 East Hall Rd.....E 12
67 East Ham.......F 11
75 East Harding St...G 11
72 East Hill, Dartford .B 3
70 East Hill, SW18...B 4
67 East India Dock Rd.
  F 9
66 East La.........D 2
69 East Moseley....D 6
70 East Putney Sta...B 4
76 East Rd.........D 3
70 East Sheen......B 12
70 East Sheen Gate..B 2
76 East Smithfield ...J 6
80 East St. SE17 ....F 4
70 East St., Epsom ..G 3
70 East Tenter St....H 6
67 East Wickham ...H 12
73 Eastbourne Mews .G 4
73 Eastbourne Ter...G 4
65 Eastbury........B 4
74 Eastcastle St.....G 6
76 Eastcheap......H 3
65 Eastcote.......D 6
65 Eastcote La......E 5
67 Eastern Avenue ..D 10
68 Eastern Avenue East
  C 2, C 3
68 Eastern Avenue West
  C 1
68 Easthall La......F 3
67 Eastham Manor
  Way.........F 11
75 Eastman Dental
  Hospital......D 10
75 Easton St.......D 11
69 Eastworth.......E 2

69 Eastworth Rd.....E 2
78 Eaton Gate......E 3
78 Eaton La........E 3
78 Eaton Mews North E 3
78 Eaton Mews South.E 4
78 Eaton Mews West .E 4
78 Eaton Place.....E 3
78 Eaton Row......D 4
78 Eaton Square....E 4
78 Eaton Terrace....E 3
76 Ebenezer St.....D 2
76 Ebor St........E 5
78 Ebury Bridge....F 4
78 Ebury Bridge Rd...G 4
78 Ebury Mews.....E 4
78 Ebury Mews East .E 4
78 Ebury Square....F 4
78 Ebury St........E 4
78 Eccleston Bridge ..E 5
78 Eccleston Mews...D 4
78 Eccleston Square .E 5
78 Eccleston Street Mews
  F 5
78 Eccleston Place...E 5
73 Edbrooke Rd.....E 1
71 Eden Park ......D 8
70 Edge Hill Rd.....F 6
78 Edge St.........B 2
66 Edgware.......B 3
66 Edgware Rd., NW2
  D 3
66 Edgware Rd. NW9 C 3
73 Edgware Rd. W2..F 5
78 Edinburgh Gate...C 2
77 Edith Grove .....J 4
77 Edith Terrace ....J 3
80 Edmund St......J 3
70 Eel Pie Is........B 1
70 Effra Rd........B 6
77 Egerton Crescent .E 6
77 Egerton Gardens ..E 6
77 Egerton Place....E 6
77 Egerton Terrace ..E 6
69 Egham.........C 1
80 Elba Place......E 2
71 Elder Rd........C 7
76 Elder St........E 4
77 Eldon Rd........D 3
76 Eldon St........F 3
80 Elephant Rd.....E 1
80 Elephant & Castle Sta.
  E 1
73 Elgin Avenue....D 2
75 Elia St........C 12
78 Elizabeth Bridge...F 5
78 Elizabeth St.....E 4
77 Ellen St........H 6
78 Elliott's Row ....E 12
78 Ellis St........E 3
65 Elm Avenue.....D 5
68 Elm Park........D 3
77 Elm Park Gdns...G 5
77 Elm Park La.....G 4
77 Elm Park Rd. SW3 H 4
65 Elm Park Rd., Pinner
  C 5
77 Elm Place.......G 5
75 Elm St.........E 10
73 Elm Tree Rd.....C 5
71 Elmers End......D 8
73 Elms Mews......J 4
71 Elmstead.......C 10
71 Elmstead La.....C 10
71 Elmstead Wood ..C 10
69 Elmwood Avenue .C 5
77 Elnathan Mews ..E 3
66 Elstree Aerodrome .A 2
66 Elstree Aerodrome. A 1
66 Elstree Hill South..A 2
66 Elstree Rd., Bushey A 1
66 Elstree Rd., Stanmore
  B 2
66 Elstree & Boreham-
  wood Sta......A 2
66 Elthorne Heights ..F 1
77 Elvaston Mews ...D 4

77 Elvaston Place....D 4
70 Elvers Way......H 3
78 Elverton St......E 7
76 Elwin St........E 5
75 Ely Place.......F 11
78 Elystan Place ....F 2
77 Elystan St.......F 6
78 Embankment Gdns.
  H 3
69 Ember La.......E 6
75 Emerald St......F 10
68 Emerson Park ...D 3
80 Emerson St......A 1
78 Emery Hill St....E 6
77 Emperor's Gate...E 3
66 Empire Pool.....E 2
75 Endell St........G 8
77 Endlebury Rd....B 9
78 Endsleigh Gdns...D 7
74 Endsleigh Place ..E 7
74 Endsleigh St.....D 7
71 Endwell Rd......A 8
67 Enfield.........A 7
67 Enfield Chase Sta. A 7
67 Enfield G.C......A 7
66 Enfield G.C......A 6
67 Enfield Town Sta..A 7
74 Enford St.......F 2
80 Enid St........D 6
77 Ennismore Gdns...D 6
77 Ennismore Gardens
  Mews.......D 5
77 Ennismore Mews..D 6
77 Ennismore St ....D 6
76 Ensign St.......J 6
79 Environment, Dept. of
  B 13
70 Epsom.........G 2
70 Epsom Common ..G 2
70 Epsom District
  Hospital ......G 2
70 Epsom Downs Race
  Course.......H 3
70 Epsom Downs Sta. G 3
70 Epsom G.C......G 3
70 Epsom La.......H 3
70 Epsom Rd., Croydon
  E 6
70 Epsom Rd., Ewell .G 3
70 Epsom Rd.,
  Leatherhead....H 1
70 Epsom Rd., Morden
  E 4
67 Epping Forest
  A 10, C 9
67 Epping New Rd...A 10
67 Epworth St......E 3
79 Erasmus St......F 8
72 Erith..........A 2
68 Erith Marshes ...G 1
68 Erith Reach .....G 2
68 Erith Rd., Belvedere
  G 2
68 Erith Rd.,
  Northumberland
  Heath.........H 2
74 Eros..........J 7
76 Errol St.........E 2
69 Esher..........F 6
69 Esher Common ..E 6
69 Esher La........E 6
69 Esher Rd........F 5
69 Esher Sta.......E 6
80 Esmeralda Rd....F 7
68 Essendine Rd.....D 1
75 Essex Rd.......A 12
75 Essex St........H 10
77 Essex Villas.....D 1
77 Eustace Rd......J 1
74 Euston Centre ...E 5
74 Euston Square...D 7
74 Euston Sta......D 6
74 Euston Station
  Colonnade....D 7
74 Euston Rd.......D 6
74 Euston Rd.......D 6
74 Euston Tower....E 6
77 Evelyn Gdns.....G 4
67 Evelyn St.......G 8
74 Everilda St.....A 10
74 Eversholt St.....C 6
70 Ewell.........F 3
70 Ewell Bypass....F 3
70 Ewell East Sta...F 3
70 Ewell West Sta...F 3
79 Ewer St.......B 13
75 Exeter St.......H 9
77 Exhibition Rd.....D 5
75 Exmouth Market.D 11

80 Exon St.........F 4
79 Exton St.........B 11
72 Eynsford.........E 3
79 Eyre Street Hill..E 11
76 Ezra St.........C 6
69 Faggs Rd.........B 4
80 Fair St.........C 4
76 Fairchild St.......E 4
71 Fairchildes Rd....G 9
71 Fairclough St....H 7
80 Faircombe St....C 7
67 Fairlop Sta......C 11
67 Fairmead Rd....A 10
69 Fairmile.........G 5
69 Fairmile La......G 5
70 Fairoak La.......G 1
72 Fairseat.........G 5
71 Falconwood Sta..B 11
71 Falkirk St.......C 4
65 Falling La.......F 3
80 Falmouth Rd....E 2
76 Fann St.........E 1
76 Fanshaw St......C 4
80 Faraday St......H 3
71 Farleigh........G 8
71 Farleigh Court Rd.G 8
71 Farley Rd........F 7
77 Farm La. SW6....J 1
70 Farm La., Epsom.H 2
74 Farm St.........J 4
71 Farnborough....F 11
71 Farnborough
    Bypass........F 11
71 Farnborough Common
        E 10
79 Farnham Place...B 13
79 Farnham Royal..G 10
72 Farningham.....E 3
72 Farningham Rd...D 3
72 Farningham Rd. &
    Sutton-at-Hone Sta.
        D 3
72 Farningham Wood D 2
75 Farringdon Rd...E 11
75 Farringdon Sta..F 12
75 Farringdon St...G 12
76 Fashion St......F 5
79 Faunce St.......G 12
77 Fawcett St......H 3
72 Fawkham Green...E 4
71 Featherbed La....F 8
76 Featherstone St...E 2
69 Feltham.........C 4
69 Feltham Rd......C 4
76 Felthamhill.....C 5
69 Felthamhill Rd...C 4
68 Fen La.........E 6
76 Fencepiece Rd...E 5
76 Fenchurch Avenue H 4
76 Fenchurch Bldgs..H 4
76 Fenchurch St....H 4
76 Fenchurch Street Sta.
        H 5
80 Fendall St.......E 2
79 Fentiman Rd.....J 9
75 Fernsbury St....D 11
77 Fernshaw Rd....J 3
67 Ferry La. N17....C 8
68 Ferry La., Rainham F 2
76 Fetter La.......G 11
71 Fickleshole.....G 9
75 Field Court......F 10
65 Field End Rd.....D 5
75 Field Place.....C 11
75 Field St.........C 9
75 Fieldgate St.....G 7
72 Filston La.......G 2
77 Finborough Rd...H 3
76 Finch La........H 3
66 Finchley........C 5
66 Finchley Central Sta.
        C 5
66 Finchley G.C....B 4
66 Finchley Rd......E 5
73 Finchley Rd......B 4
66 Finchley Rd......D 4
66 Finchley Road &
    Frognall Sta.....E 5
79 Finck St.........D 10
67 Finsbury........F 7
71 Finsbury Circus..F 3
67 Finsbury Park...D 7
67 Finsbury Park Sta.D 7
76 Finsbury Pavement F 3
76 Finsbury Square..F 3
76 Finsbury St......F 2
76 Fire Brigade H.Q..F 9
67 Firs La.........B 7
78 First St.........E 1

80 Firtree Rd.......G 4
76 Fish Street Hill...J 3
75 Fisher St........F 9
73 Fisherton St.....E 5
76 Fishmongers' Hall J 3
79 Fitzalan St......E 10
74 Fitzhardinge St...G 3
66 Fitzjohn's Avenue E 5
78 Fitzmaurice Place.A 5
74 Fitzroy Square...E 6
74 Fitzroy St.......E 6
75 Flaxman Terrace..D 8
75 Fleet La........G 12
75 Fleet St.........H 11
79 Fleming Rd.....H 12
76 Fleur de Lis St....E 4
80 Flint St.........F 3
80 Flinten St.......F 4
78 Flood St.........G 1
76 Flood Walk......G 6
75 Floral St........H 8
76 Florida St.......D 7
76 Flower Walk, The .C 4
76 Flower & Dean St..F 5
76 Fochelle St......D 5
76 Foley St........F 6
76 Folgate St.......F 4
71 Foots Cray......C 12
71 Foots Cray La....C 12
71 Foots Cray Rd....B 10
76 Forbes St.......H 6
69 Ford Bridge Rd...C 3
69 Fordbridge Rd....D 4
76 Fore St. EC2.....F 2
76 Fore St. N18.....B 8
65 Fore St., Ruislip..C 5
79 Foreign Office....C 8
70 Forest Gate.....E 10
71 Forest Hill......C 7
71 Forest Hill Sta....C 8
71 Forest Hospital..B 10
67 Forest La.......E 10
67 Forest Rd. E17...C 9
75 Farringdon Rd...E 12
70 Forest Rd., Sutton.E 4
67 Forest Side......A 10
73 Formosa St.....E 3
76 Fornier St.......F 5
74 Forston St.......B 2
80 Fort Rd. ....F 6
66 Fortis Green Rd...C 5
66 Fortress Rd......E 6
74 Fortune St......E 2
66 Forty Avenue....D 2
66 Forty La........D 3
76 Foster La........G 1
74 Foubert's Place...H 6
77 Foulis Terrace ...F 5
76 Fountain St......D 5
76 Fox Court.......F 11
69 Fox Hill Rd......F 1
76 Fox La.........B 6
68 Foxburrow Wood A 1
69 Foxoak Hill .....F 4
73 Frampton St.....E 5
76 Francis St.......E 6
78 Franklin's Row...G 3
79 Frazier St.......C 11
80 Frean St........D 6
75 Frederick St.....D 9
80 Fremantle St....F 4
66 French St.......D 5
80 Frensham St.....H 6
80 Friary Rd.......J 7
75 Friend St. ....C 12
74 Friends House...D 7
66 Friern Barnet....B 5
75 Frith St.........H 7
71 Frith Wood .....G 8
75 Frome St........B 13
68 Front La........D 4
66 Fryent Way .....D 2
70 Fulham F.C......A 3
74 Fulham Palace...A 4
66 Fulham Palace Rd. H 4
70 Fulham Rd. SW6..A 4
77 Fulham Rd. SW10.G 5
76 Fuller St.........D 6
65 Fulmer.........E 1
69 Fulwell G.C......C 5
75 Furnival St. .....G 11
70 Furze Hill.......H 4
66 Furzehill Rd......A 3
78 Fynes St........E 7
80 Gainsford St.....C 5
68 Gale St.........E 1
71 Gallery Rd.......B 7

72 Galley Hill ......B 5
67 Galliard Rd......A 8
67 Gallions Reach ..G 11
68 Gallows Corner...C 3
79 Gambia St.......B 12
70 Gander Green La. .E 4
74 Ganton St.......H 6
67 Gants Hill Sta....D 11
74 Garbutt Place....F 4
73 Garden Rd......C 4
79 Garden Row ....D 12
76 Garden Walk....D 4
76 Garlick Hill.....H 2
70 Garratt La.......C 4
76 Garrett St.......E 1
75 Garrick St.......H 8
75 Garrick Theatre ..J 8
80 Garth Rd........E 3
73 Garway Rd.......H 2
74 Gascogne Place ..D 5
79 Gasholder Place..G 12
69 Gaston Bridge Rd..D 4
75 Gate St.........G 9
73 Gateforth St.....E 6
67 Gates Corner...C 10
80 Gateway........H 2
78 Gatliff Rd.......G 4
79 Gaunt St........D 13
79 Gayfere St......E 8
79 Gaywood St.....E 12
79 Gaza St.........G 12
75 Gee St.........E 13
76 Geffrye Museum ..C 4
76 Geffrye St.......B 5
75 General Post Office
        G 13
77 Geological Museum
        E 5
80 George Row......C 6
74 George St. ......G 2
74 George Yard .....H 4
65 George V Avenue .C 6
79 Geraldine Mary
    Harmsworth Park
        E 11
79 Geraldine St.....E 12
68 Gerpins La......E 4
75 Gerrard Rd......B 12
74 Gerrard St.......H 7
65 Gerrards Cross ...D 1
79 Gerridge St......D 11
77 Gertrude St......H 4
68 Gidea Park......C 3
68 Gidea Park Sta....C 3
75 Gilbert Place ....G 8
79 Gilbert Rd......F 11
74 Gilbert St.......H 4
72 Gildenhill Rd....D 3
78 Gillingham St....E 5
76 Gilston Rd......G 4
75 Giltspur St. .....G 12
66 Gladstone Park ..E 3
70 Gladstone St....D 12
79 Glass Hill St.....C 13
74 Glasshouse St. ...J 6
74 Glasshouse Walk..G 6
75 Glasshouse Yard .E 13
77 Glebe Place .....H 6
77 Gledhow Gdns. ...F 3
80 Glengall Rd......H 6
80 Glengall Terrace..H 5
74 Glentworth St....E 7
67 Globe Rd........F 8
80 Globe St. ....D 2
80 Globe Theatre, SE1 E 3
74 Globe Theatre, W1 H 7
74 Globe Yard .....H 5
74 Gloucester Avenue A 4
74 Gloucester Gate..B 4
73 Gloucester Mews..H 4
73 Gloucester Mews West
        H 4
74 Gloucester Place..F 2
74 Gloucester Place Mews
        G 3
77 Gloucester Rd.....E 3
73 Gloucester Square.H 5
78 Gloucester St....G 6
73 Gloucester Terrace G 3
77 Gloucester Walk ..C 1
75 Gloucester Way ..D 11
79 Glyn St. ....G 9
76 Godfrey St.......G 6
79 Goding St. ......G 9
75 Godson St.......B 11
73 Goldstone Rd....H 7
76 Golden La.......E 1
74 Golden Square....H 6

66 Golders Green ....D 4
66 Golders Green Rd. D 4
66 Golders Green Sta. D 5
74 Goldhawk Rd.....G 4
74 Goldington Cres...B 7
74 Goldington St.....B 7
76 Goldman St. ....H 13
73 Goldney Rd......E 1
74 Goodge Place ....F 6
74 Goodge St. ......F 6
76 Goodman St.....H 5
76 Goodmans Yard ..H 5
67 Goodmayes .....D 12
67 Goodmayes Hospital
        D 12
67 Goodmayes La...D 12
76 Gopsall St.......B 3
77 Gordon Place....C 2
74 Gordon Square ...E 7
74 Gordon St. ......E 7
72 Gore Hill.......C 3
74 Gore St.........D 4
71 Gorse Rd........E 12
68 Goresbrook Rd...E 1
67 Gorsuch St......C 5
74 Gosfield St......F 5
66 Gospel Oak Sta...E 6
76 Gosset St.......D 6
75 Goswell Rd......D 12
75 Goswell Terrace..D 12
76 Goulston St......G 5
75 Gough Square ...G 11
75 Gough St.......E 10
74 Gower Mews ....F 7
74 Gower Place.....E 7
74 Gower St........E 7
76 Gowers Walk.....H 6
76 Gracechurch St...H 3
74 Grafton Mews ...E 6
74 Grafton Place....D 7
74 Grafton St. ......J 5
74 Grafton Way .....E 6
76 Graham Rd......E 8
78 Graham Terrace..F 3
72 Granby St. ......D 6
79 Granby Terrace...C 6
70 Grandstand Rd...H 3
78 Grange, The.....D 5
67 Grange Hill.....B 11
67 Grange Park Sta...A 7
80 Grange Rd. SE1...D 4
71 Grange Rd. SE25..D 7
76 Grange St.......B 3
80 Grange Walk.....D 4
80 Grange Yard ....D 5
71 Grangewood....D 7
73 Grantbridge St....B 12
73 Grantully Rd.....D 2
74 Granville Place ...H 3
73 Granville Rd.....C 1
75 Granville Square .D 10
75 Grape St. ....G 8
76 Gravel La., Abridge
        A 12
72 Gravesend G.C....C 6
79 Gray St. ....C 11
68 Grays ....H 6
75 Gray's Inn Gardens
        F 10
75 Grays Inn Rd.....D 9
75 Grays Inn Rd....H 11
69 Great Bookham
    Common.......H 6
67 Great Cambridge Rd.
        A 8
74 Great Castle St...G 5
74 Great Central St...F 2
74 Great Chapel St...G 7
70 Great Chertsey Rd.A 2
73 Great College St...D 8
74 Great Cumberland
    Place..........H 2
80 Great Dover St....D 2
76 Great Eastern St...E 4
79 Great George St...C 8
79 Great Guildford St.
        B 13
75 Great James St....F 10
74 Great Marlborough St.
        H 6
66 Great North Rd...A 5
76 Great North Way .C 4
75 Great Ormond St..F 9
75 Great Percy St....C 10

79 Great Peter St....D 8
74 Great Portland St..F 5
74 Great Pulteney St..H 6
75 Great Queen St...G 9
75 Great Russell St...G 8
76 Great St. Helens...G 4
79 Great Scotland Yd. B 8
79 Great Smith St...D 8
69 Great South West Rd.
        B 4
79 Great Suffolk St. .C 13
75 Great Sutton St...E 12
76 Great Swan Alley .G 3
70 Great Tattenhams.H 3
74 Great Titchfield St..F 6
74 Great Tower St....J 4
68 Great Warley.....C 5
69 Great West Rd....A 5
76 Great Winchester St.
        G 3
74 Great Windmill St. H 7
48 Great Wood ......A 1
72 Great Wood......G 6
72 Greatness ....H 2
75 Greatorex St. ....F 6
75 Greek St.........H 7
65 Green, The.......G 5
67 Green Court......E 1
80 Green Hundred Rd.
        H 7
71 Green La. SE9 ...C 11
70 Green La. SW16...D 6
69 Green La., Addlestone
        E 2
68 Green La., Goodmayes
        D 1
69 Green La., Hatton.B 5
67 Green La., Ilford .D 12
70 Green La., Morden E 4
65 Green La., Northwood
        B 4
69 Green La., Shepperton
        D 4
67 Green Lanes, N4 &
    N16........B 7, D 7
78 Green Park......C 5
72 Green Rd.......C 3
74 Green St. W1....H 3
72 Green St., Dartford C 3
67 Green St., Newham
        E 10
69 Green St., Sunbury D 4
72 Green Street Green,
    Dartford........C 4
71 Green Street Green,
    Farnborough....F 11
75 Green Terrace ...D 11
70 Green Wrythe La. .E 5
73 Greenberry St....C 6
78 Greencoat Place..E 6
76 Greencoat Row ..E 6
76 Greenfield Rd....G 7
65 Greenford.......F 6
76 Greenford Avenue .F 1
65 Greenford Green ..E 6
65 Greenford Rd.....F 6
65 Greenford Sta....E 6
66 Greenhill.......D 1
72 Greenhithe......B 4
74 Greenwell St.....E 5
67 Greenwich ......H 9
67 Greenwich High Rd.
        H 9
67 Greenwich Park..H 9
67 Greenwich Reach .G 9
67 Greenwich Sta....H 9
79 Greet St........B 11
73 Grendon St......E 6
73 Grenville Place...E 3
75 Grenville St......E 9
76 Gresham St......G 2
75 Gresse St........G 7
75 Greville St......F 11
78 Greycoat Place...E 7
78 Greycoat St......E 7
76 Greyeagle St.....E 5
76 Grimsby St......E 6
73 Grittleton Rd.....E 1
78 Groom Place ....D 4
78 Grosvenor Bridge .H 5
78 Grosvenor Cres...C 4
78 Grosvenor Crescent
    Mews..........C 3
78 Grosvenor Gdns...D 5
74 Grosvenor Hill...J 5
74 Grosvenor House
    Hotel ....J 3
80 Grosvenor Park ...J 1

78 Grosvenor Place...D 4
78 Grosvenor Rd.....H 6
74 Grosvenor Square .H 4
74 Grosvenor St.....H 5
80 Grosvenor Terrace H 1
73 Grove End Rd.....C 4
71 Grove Park......C 10
71 Grove Park Hospital
        C 10
67 Grove Rd. E2....F 8
67 Grove Rd. E18...C 10
70 Grove Rd., Mitcham
        D 5
67 Grove Rd., Romford
        D 12
67 Grovegreen Rd....D 9
68 Gubbins La.......C 4
69 Guildford Rd......F 2
76 Guildhall........G 2
78 Guildhouse St....F 6
75 Guilford St.......E 9
79 Gundulf St......F 10
71 Gunnersbury....G 3
66 Gunnersbury Ave..G 2
66 Gunnersbury Park G 2
74 Gunter Grove ...J 3
80 Guy St.........C 3
80 Guy's Hospital...C 2
79 Gye St.........G 9
71 Gypsey Hill Sta...C 7
76 Haberdasher St....C 3
67 Hackbridge......E 5
67 Hackney........E 8
67 Hackney Downs ..E 8
67 Hackney Downs Sta.
        E 8
67 Hackney Marsh ..E 8
76 Hackney Rd......C 5
67 Hackney Wick....E 9
68 Hacton La.......E 4
80 Hadden Hall St....E 3
76 Haggerston Park ..B 6
76 Haggerston Rd....A 5
67 Hainault.......C 12
67 Hainault Estate ..B 12
68 Hainault Forest...B 1
67 Hainault Rd., Chigwell
        B 11
67 Hainault Rd., Hainault
        C 12
76 Halcomb St......B 4
67 Hale End.......B 9
75 Half Moon Cres..B 10
78 Half Moon St.....B 5
77 Halford Rd......H 1
68 Halfway Reach ...F 2
71 Halfway St......B 11
70 Haling Park Rd...F 6
78 Halkin Place.....D 3
78 Halkin St.......D 4
73 Hall Gate.......D 4
68 Hall La. E4......B 9
68 Hall La., Upminster
        D 4
68 Hall La........D 6
73 Hall Place, W2...F 5
72 Hall Place, Bexley .B 1
73 Hall Rd. NW8....D 4
71 Hall Rd., Eltham .B 10
75 Hall St.........C 12
68 Hall Wood, Brentwood
        B 6
72 Hall Wood, Fairseat
        G 6
74 Hallam St.......F 5
73 Hallfield Estate...G 3
69 Halliford Rd.....D 4
78 Halsey St.......E 2
72 Halstead........G 1
70 Ham...........C 1
70 Ham Common....C 2
70 Ham Cross ......C 2
70 Ham Gate.......C 2
70 Ham House ......B 1
73 Hamilton Close...C 4
73 Hamilton Gdns...C 4
78 Hamilton Place...C 3
73 Hamilton Terrace..C 3
66 Hammersmith ....G 4
66 Hammersmith Bri..G 4
66 Hammersmith Rd. G 4
66 Hampden Way ...B 6
65 Hampermill La...A 5
66 Hampstead......C 3
66 Hampstead Heath .D 5
66 Hampstead Heath Sta.
        E 5
66 Hampstead La. ...D 5
66 Hampstead Ponds .E 5

74 Hampstead Rd. . . . C 6
69 Hampton . . . . D 6
69 Hampton Court Bridge D 6
70 Hampton Court G.C. D 1
70 Hampton Court Palace D 1
70 Hampton Court Park D 1
69 Hampton Court Rd. D 6
69 Hampton Court Way E 6
69 Hampton Rd., Feltham C 5
69 Hampton Rd., Twickenham . . . . C 6
79 Hampton St. . . . . F 13
70 Hampton Wick . . . D 1
71 Hamsey Green . . . . G 8
76 Hanbury St. . . . . . . F 5
75 Handel St. . . . . E 8
69 Hangar Hill . . . . . . F 4
66 Hanger Hill . . . . F 2
66 Hanger La. . . . . F 2
66 Hanger Lane Sta. . . F 2
80 Hankey St. . . . . D 3
79 Hanover Gdns. . . H 10
74 Hanover Gate . . . . D 1
74 Hanover Square . . H 5
74 Hanover St. . . . . . . H 5
74 Hanover Terrace . . D 2
74 Hanover Terrace Mews D 2
78 Hans Crescent . . . . D 2
78 Hans Place . . . . D 2
78 Hans Rd. . . . . D 2
78 Hans St. . . . . D 2
74 Hanson St. . . . . F 6
74 Hanway Place . . . . G 7
74 Hanway St. . . . . . . G 7
66 Hanwell . . . . G 1
69 Hanworth . . . . C 5
69 Hanworth Park . . . C 5
69 Hanworth Rd., Hanworth . . . . . . C 5
69 Hanworth Rd., Hounslow . . . . . . B 6
73 Harbet Rd. . . . . F 5
74 Harcourt St. . . . . . . F 1
77 Harcourt Terrace . . G 3
69 Hardwick La. . . . . . E 2
75 Hardwick St. . . . . D 11
69 Hare Hill . . . . F 2
70 Hare La. . . . . F 1
68 Hare Street . . . . C 3
76 Hare Walk . . . . B 4
65 Harefield . . . . C 3
65 Harefield Hospital . C 3
65 Harefield Place G.C. D 3
65 Harefield Rd. . . . . . B 3
74 Harewood Avenue . E 1
68 Harewood Hall La. E 4
74 Harewood Place . . H 5
73 Harewood Row . . . F 6
66 Harlesden . . . . E 3
66 Harlesden Sta. . . . . F 3
77 Harley Gdns. . . . . . G 4
74 Harley Place . . . . . . G 4
74 Harley St. . . . . F 4
79 Harleyford Rd. . . . . H 9
79 Harleyford St. . . . H 11
65 Harlington . . . . H 4
65 Harlington Rd. . . . . F 4
69 Harlington Road East B 5
65 Harmondsworth . . H 3
65 Harmondsworth La. H 3
79 Harmsworth St. . . G 12
68 Harold Hill . . . . B 3
79 Harold Place . . . . G 10
68 Harold Wood . . . . . C 4
80 Harper Rd. . . . . D 2
75 Harper St. . . . . F 9
67 Harringay Stadium D 7
67 Harringay Stadium Sta. . . . . D 7
67 Harringay West Sta. D 7
77 Harrington Gdns. . F 3
77 Harrington Rd. . . . E 5
74 Harrington Square . B 6
74 Harrington St. . . . . C 6
75 Harrison St. . . . . . . D 9
66 Harrow . . . . C 1
66 Harrow on the Hill D 1
66 Harrow on the Hill Sta. D 1
76 Harrow Place . . . . . G 4
73 Harrow Rd. W9 . . . F 1
71 Harrow Rd., Chelsham G 8
66 Harrow Rd., Wembley E 2
66 Harrow School . . . D 1
66 Harrow Weald . . . . C 1
66 Harrow & Wealdstone Sta. . . . . C 1
74 Harrowby St. . . . . . G 2
76 Hart St. . . . . H 4
72 Hartley . . . . E 5
72 Hartley Wood . . . . D 5
65 Hartsbourne G.C. . B 6
76 Harvey St. . . . . A 3
65 Harvil Rd. . . . . D 3
78 Hasker St. . . . . E 2
67 Haslebury Rd. . . . . B 7
65 Haste Hill G.C. . . . C 4
75 Hastings St. . . . . . . D 8
65 Hatch End . . . . C 6
65 Hatch End Sta. . . . C 6
67 Hatch La. . . . . B 9
69 Hatchord Park . . . . H 4
76 Hatfield St. . . . . E 1
79 Hatfields . . . . B 12
73 Hatherley Grove . . G 2
69 Hatton . . . . B 4
69 Hatton Cross Sta. . . B 4
75 Hatton Garden . . . F 11
69 Hatton Rd. . . . . B 4
73 Hatton St. . . . . E 5
75 Hatton Wall . . . . . F 11
75 Havelock St. . . . . . . A 9
68 Havering . . . . D 3
68 Havering Park . . . . B 2
68 Havering Rd. . . . . . . B 2
68 Havering-atte-Bower B 2
66 Haverstock Hill . . . E 5
75 Haverstock St. . . . C 13
72 Hawley . . . . C 3
72 Hawley Rd. . . . . C 3
71 Hawsted La. . . . . . F 12
74 Hay Hill . . . . J 5
70 Haydon's Rd. Sta. . C 4
65 Hayes . . . . G 4
71 Hayes, Bromley . . . E 9
71 Hayes Common . . . E 9
65 Hayes End . . . . F 4
71 Hayes La., Beckenham D 9
71 Hayes La., Bromley E 9
70 Hayes La., Coulsdon H 6
73 Hayes Place . . . . F 6
65 Hayes Rd. . . . . G 5
65 Hayes & Harlington Sta. . . . . G 4
79 Hayles St. . . . . E 12
65 Hayling Rd. . . . . B 5
74 Haymarket . . . . J 7
75 Haymarket Theatre J 7
80 Haymerle Rd. . . . . H 6
75 Hayne St. . . . . . . F 13
78 Hay's Mews . . . . . . A 4
75 Hayward's Place . E 12
71 Hazel Wood . . . . . G 11
75 H.Q.S. Wellington J 10
78 Headfort Place . . . . D 4
70 Headley Rd. . . . . . . H 2
65 Headstone . . . . C 6
66 Headstone Drive . . C 1
65 Headstone La. . . . . C 6
65 Headstone La. Sta. C 6
76 Hearn St. . . . . E 4
72 Heath La. . . . . C 2
68 Heath Park . . . . D 3
68 Heath Park Rd. . . . D 3
69 Heath Rd. . . . . B 6
69 Heath Row . . . . F 3
68 Heath Way . . . . E 1
66 Heathbourn Rd. . . . B 1
75 Heathcote St. . . . . . D 9
69 Heathrow Airport London . . . . A 3
72 Heaverham . . . . H 4
74 Heddon St. . . . . J 6
67 Hedge La. . . . . B 7
68 Hedgemans Rd. . . . E 1
79 Heiron St. . . . . H 13
75 Hemingford Rd. . A 10
76 Hemming St. . . . . . E 7
80 Hemp Row . . . . F 3
76 Hemsworth St. . . . . B 4
77 Hemus Place . . . . . G 6
66 Hendon . . . . C 4
66 Hendon Central Sta. . . . . D 4
66 Hendon G.C. . . . . . C 4
66 Hendon Way . . . . . D 4
66 Hendon Wood La. A 3
80 Hendre Rd. . . . . F 4
76 Heneage . . . . F 6
76 Heneage La. . . . . . . G 4
77 Henniker Mews . . . H 4
74 Henrietta Place . . . G 4
75 Henrietta St. . . . . . . J 9
76 Henriques St. . . . . . H 7
80 H.M.S. *Belfast* . . . . B 4
75 H.M.S. *Chrysanthemum* . J 11
75 H.M.S. *Discovery* . J 10
75 H.M.S. *President* . . J 11
75 Herbal Hill . . . . . . E 11
76 Herbrand St. . . . . . . E 8
79 Hercules Rd. . . . . D 10
77 Hereford Square . . . F 4
73 Hereford Rd. . . . . . G 1
76 Hereford St. . . . . . . E 6
75 Hermes St. . . . . . . C 10
75 Hermit St. . . . . C 12
80 Hermitage Wall . . . B 7
71 Herne Hill . . . . B 7
70 Herne Hill Sta. . . . . B 6
79 Herrick St. . . . . F 8
69 Hersham . . . . F 5
69 Hersham Rd. . . . . . E 5
69 Hersham Sta. . . . . . E 5
67 Hertford Rd. . . . . . . A 8
78 Hertford St. . . . . . . B 4
71 Heseirs Hill . . . . . . H 9
71 Heseirs Rd. . . . . . . H 9
77 Hesper Mews . . . . . F 2
65 Heston . . . . H 5
65 Heston Rd. . . . . H 5
76 Hewett St. . . . . E 4
71 Hewitts Rd. . . . . . . F 12
72 Hextable . . . . D 2
79 Heyford Avenue . . . J 9
80 Heygate St. . . . . F 1
78 Hide Place . . . . F 7
66 High Barnet Sta. . . A 4
75 High Holborn . . . G 10
66 High Rd. N2 . . . . . C 5
67 High Rd. N17 . . . . C 7
66 High Rd. N20 . . . . A 5
66 High Rd. NW10 . . E 3
69 High Rd., Byfleet . G 3
67 High Rd., Chigwell B 11
72 High Rd., Dartford C 2
65 High Rd., Eastcote D 5
67 High Rd., Ilford . D 12
67 High Rd., Leytonstone D 9
67 High Rd., Loughton A 10
71 High Rd., Orpington E 11
67 High Rd., Woodford Bridge . . . . C 10
67 High Rd., Woodford Green . . . . B 10
67 High St. E11 . . . . . D 10
67 High St. E15 . . . . . F 9
66 High St. N8 . . . . . C 6
67 High St. SE15 . . . . H 8
67 High St. SE27 . . . . C 6
70 High St. SW18 . . . . B 4
70 High St., Merton, SW19 . . . . D 4
70 High St. SW19 . . . . C 4
68 High St., Aveley . . G 4
70 High St., Banstead . G 4
71 High St., Beckenham D 8
71 High St., Bexley Heath A 12
65 High St., Bushey . . A 6
70 High St., Carshalton F 5
71 High St., Croydon . E 7
70 High St., Epsom . . G 2
69 High St., Feltham . . C 4
65 High St., Harlington G 4
66 High St., Harrow . . C 1
68 High St., Hornchurch D 3
69 High St., Hounslow A 6
70 High St., New Malden D 3
67 High St., Ponders End A 8
65 High St., Rickmansworth . A 3
69 High St., Shepperton E 4
71 High St., Sidcup . C 12
69 High St., Stanwell . B 3
70 High St., Sutton . . . F 4
70 High St., Teddington C 1
69 High St., Walton . . E 4
65 High St., Watford . A 5
71 High St., West Wickham . . . . E 8
70 High St., Colliers Wood . . . . C 5
67 High St. North . . . E 10
67 High St. South . . . F 11
67 Higham Hill . . . . . . C 8
67 Highams Park . . . . B 9
67 Highams Park, Hale End Sta. . . . . B 9
67 Highbury . . . . E 7
67 Highbury & Islington Sta. . . . . E 7
66 Highgate . . . . D 6
66 Highgate G.C. . . . . D 5
66 Highgate Ponds . . . D 5
66 Highgate Rd. . . . . . E 6
66 Highgate Sta. . . . . . D 6
66 Highgate Wood . . . D 6
76 Highway, The . . . . . J 7
66 Highwood Hill . . . . B 3
77 Hildyard Rd. . . . . . H 1
66 Hilfield La. . . . . A 1
66 Hilfield Reservoir . . A 1
65 Hill End . . . . B 3
65 Hill End Rd. . . . . . C 3
73 Hill Rd. . . . . C 4
78 Hill St. . . . . A 4
80 Hillery Rd. . . . . F 3
77 Hillgate Place . . . . B 2
77 Hillgate St. . . . . B 2
65 Hillingdon . . . . E 4
65 Hillingdon G.C. . . . F 3
65 Hillingdon Heath . . F 4
65 Hillingdon Hill . . . . F 3
65 Hillingdon Rd. . . . . E 3
65 Hillingdon Sta. . . . . E 4
79 Hillingdon St. . . . H 13
67 Hillreach . . . . G 10
71 Hilly Fields . . . . B 8
78 Hilton Hotel . . . . B 4
70 Hinchley Wood . . . E 1
74 Hinde St. . . . . G 4
71 Hither Green . . . . . B 9
78 Hobart Place . . . . . D 4
76 Hobury St. . . . . H 4
77 Hocker St. . . . . D 5
68 Hoe La. . . . . A 1
67 Hoe Street . . . . D 9
66 Hogarth House . . . H 3
77 Hogarth Rd. . . . . . . F 2
71 Hogtrough Hill . . H 11
78 Holbein Mews . . . . F 3
78 Holbein Place . . . . . F 3
75 Holborn . . . . G 11
75 Holborn Circus . . G 11
75 Holborn Viaduct . G 12
75 Holborn Viaduct Sta. G 12
68 Holden's Wood . . . C 5
66 Holders Hill . . . . . . C 4
66 Holders Hill Rd. . . . C 4
75 Holford Gdns. . . . . C 10
66 Holland Avenue . . G 4
66 Holland Rd. . . . . G 4
77 Holland St. . . . . C 1
74 Hollen St. . . . . G 7
74 Holles St. . . . . G 5
67 Hollow Pond . . . . . D 9
66 Holloway Rd. . . . . D 6
76 Holloway St. . . . . . G 6
72 Hollows Wood . . . . F 1
70 Holly La. . . . . H 4
77 Hollywood Rd. . . . H 3
71 Holmwood Park . . F 10
79 Holyoake Rd. . . . . F 12
80 Holyrood St. . . . . . B 4
76 Holywell La. . . . . . . E 4
76 Holywell Row . . . . E 3
79 Home Office . . . . . . C 8
72 Home Rd. . . . . C 2
74 Homer Row . . . . . . F 1
74 Homer St. . . . . F 1
67 Homerton . . . . E 8
67 Homerton High St. E 8
67 Homerton Rd. . . . . E 8
79 Hone Parade . . . . E 10
66 Honeypot La. . . . . . C 2
71 Honor Oak Park . . . B 8
71 Honor Oak Park Sta. B 8
71 Honor Oak & Forest Hill G.C. . . . . B 8
70 Hook . . . . E 2
72 Hook Green, Meopham . . . . . . E 6
72 Hook Green, Southfleet . . . . . . C 5
72 Hook Green . . . . . . E 6
72 Hook Green . . . . . . C 5
72 Hook Green Rd. . . C 2
71 Hook La., Bexley Hth B 11
68 Hook La., Stapleford Abbotts . . . . A 2
70 Hook Rise . . . . E 2
70 Hook Rd., Chessington E 2
70 Hook Rd., Epsom . G 2
70 Hook Rd., Horton F 2
71 Hookwood Rd. . . G 12
76 Hooper St. . . . . H 6
76 Hopetown St. . . . . . F 6
74 Hopkins St. . . . . . . H 7
79 Hopton St. . . . . . . A 12
76 Horatio St. . . . . C 6
66 Horn La. . . . . G 3
68 Hornchurch . . . . . . D 3
68 Hornchurch Marshes F 2
68 Hornchurch Rd. . . D 3
68 Hornchurch Stadium E 4
71 Horns Green . . . . H 11
67 Horns Rd. . . . . . . D 11
66 Hornsey . . . . D 6
66 Hornsey La. . . . . . . D 6
66 Hornsey Rise . . . . . D 6
66 Hornsey Rd. . . . . D 6
77 Hornton Place . . . . C 2
77 Hornton St. . . . . . . C 1
79 Horse Guards . . . . . B 8
79 Horseferry Rd. . . . . E 7
79 Horseguards Av. . . B 8
80 Horselydown La. . . B 5
66 Horsenden Hill . . . . E 1
80 Horsley St. . . . . H 2
77 Hortensia Rd. . . . . . J 3
70 Horton, Ewell . . . . . F 2
69 Horton, Staines . . . A 1
70 Horton Hospital . . G 2
72 Horton Kirby . . . . . D 3
70 Horton La. . . . . G 2
69 Horton Rd., Horton A 1
69 Horton Rd., Stanwell B 2
75 Hosier La. . . . . . . G 12
69 Hospital Bridge Rd. B 6
74 Hospital for Nervous Diseases . . . . G 4
75 Hospital for Sick Children . . . . E 9
73 Hospital of St. John C 5
79 Hotspur St. . . . . . . F 10
75 Houghton St. . . . . H 10
76 Hounsditch . . . . G 4
69 Hounslow . . . . A 6
69 Hounslow Central Sta. B 6
69 Hounslow East Sta. B 6
69 Hounslow Heath . . B 5
69 Hounslow Rd. . . . . C 5
69 Hounslow Sta. . . . . B 6
69 Hounslow West Sta. A 5
79 Houses of Parliament D 9
70 Howell Hill . . . . G 3
78 Howick Place . . . . . E 6
73 Howland St. . . . . . . F 6
73 Howley Place . . . . . F 4
76 Hows St. . . . . B 5
67 Hoxton . . . . E 7
76 Hoxton Square . . . D 4
76 Hoxton St. . . . . B 4
78 Hugh Mews . . . . . . F 5
78 Hugh St. . . . . F 5
76 Hull St. . . . . D 1
80 Humphrey St. . . . . G 5
79 Hungerford Railway Bridge . . . . B 9
74 Huntley St. . . . . E 7
65 Huntsmoor Park . . F 3
74 Huntsworth Mews . E 2
76 Hunton St. . . . . E 6
79 Hurlbutt Place . . . F 13
70 Hurlingham House A 4
69 Hurst Rd., Molesey D 5
71 Hurst Rd., Sidcup B 12
66 Hyde, The . . . . C 3
78 Hyde Park Barracks C 3
78 Hyde Park Corner . C 4
73 Hyde Park Cres. . . . H 6
73 Hyde Park Gdns. . . H 5
73 Hyde Park Gdns. Mews . . . . H 5
77 Hyde Park Gate . . D 4
78 Hyde Park Hotel . . C 2
73 Hyde Park Square . H 6
73 Hyde Park St. . . . . . H 6
76 Hyde Rd. . . . . B 3
69 Hythe . . . . C 2
69 Hythe End . . . . C 1
65 Ickenham . . . . D 4
76 Idol La. . . . . J 4
77 Ifield Rd. . . . . H 3
72 Ightham . . . . H 5
73 Ilchester Gdns. . . . D 11
67 Ilford . . . . E 11
67 Ilford Football Club D 11
67 Ilford G.C. . . . . . . D 11
67 Ilford La. . . . . E 11
79 Iliffe St. . . . . F 13
76 Imber St. . . . . B 2
77 Imperial College . . D 5
77 Imperial College of Science . . . . D 5
65 Imperial Drive . . . . D 6
75 Imperial Hotel . . . F 8
77 Imperial Institute . . D 5
77 Imperial Institute Rd. D 4
79 Imperial War Museum E 11
76 India St. . . . . H 5
74 Ingestre Place . . . . . H 6
75 Inglebert St. . . . . . C 11
68 Ingrave . . . . B 6
68 Ingrave Green . . . . B 6
74 Inner Circle . . . . . . D 3
77 International Hotel E 2
73 Inverness Place . . . H 3
73 Inverness Terrace . H 3
73 Inverness Terrace Gate J 3
80 Inville Rd. . . . . G 3
76 Ironmonger La. . . . G 2
76 Ironmonger Row . . D 1
76 Ironmonger St. . . . . D 2
76 Ironmonger's Hall . F 1
75 Irving St. . . . . J 8
79 Isabella St. . . . . . B 12
69 Island Barn Res. . . . E 6
67 Isle of Dogs . . . . . . G 9
70 Isleworth . . . . B 1
70 Isleworth Sta. . . . . . A 1
67 Islington . . . . E 7
75 Islington Green . . B 12
75 Islington High St. . B 12
79 Italian Walk . . . . . . G 9
65 Iver . . . . F 2
65 Iver Heath . . . . E 2
65 Iver La. . . . . F 2
77 Iverna Court . . . . . D 2
77 Iverna Gdns. . . . . . D 2
66 Iverson Rd. . . . . . . E 4
78 Ives St. . . . . E 1
74 Ivor Place . . . . E 2
76 Ivy St. . . . . B 4
72 Ivyhouse La. . . . . . H 1
77 Ixworth Place . . . . . F 6
71 Jackass La. . . . . . . F 10
80 Jacob St. . . . . C 6
71 Jail La. . . . . G 10
80 Jamaica Rd. . . . . . . D 6
75 James St. WC2 . . . H 9
74 James St. W1 . . . . . G 4
77 Jameson St. . . . . B 2
80 Jardin St. . . . . H 4
77 Jay Mews . . . . D 4
78 Jermyn St. . . . . A 6
73 Jerome Crescent . . . E 6
76 Jerome St. . . . . F 5
69 Jersey Rd. . . . . A 6
76 Jewry St. . . . . H 5
79 Joan St. . . . . B 12
75 Jockey's Fields . . . F 10
65 Joel St. . . . . C 5
75 John Adam St. . . . . J 9
75 John Carpenter St. H 12

76 John Fisher St.....J 6
79 John Islip St. .....F 8
74 John Princess St...G 5
79 John Ruskin St....J 13
75 John St..........E 10
79 Jonathan St.......F 9
75 John's Mews.....E 10
72 Joyce Green Hosp. A 3
72 Joyce Green La....A 3
72 Joyden's Wood....C 1
67 Jubilee Park......A 8
78 Jubilee Place......G 1
75 Judd St...........D 8
73 Junction Mews....G 6
66 Junction Rd.......D 6
77 Justice Walk......H 6
79 Juxon St..........E 10
67 Katherine Rd.....E 10
76 Kay St. ....B 6
75 Kean St..........H 9
75 Keeley St.........G 9
77 Kelso Place.......D 2
75 Kemble St........H 9
77 Kempsford Gdns. .G 2
79 Kempsford Rd. ..F 12
80 Kempshead Rd....G 4
69 Kempton Park Race Course..........C 5
72 Kemsing.........H 3
73 Kendal Street.....H 6
71 Kenley............H 7
79 Kennings Way...G 12
79 Kennington Grove H 10
79 Kennington La...G 10
79 Kennington Oval H 10
79 Kennington Park.H 11
79 Kennington Park Gdns..........H 12
79 Kennington Park Place H 12
79 Kennington Park Rd. G 12
79 Kennington Rd...E 11
74 Kenrick Place.....F 3
66 Kensal Green.....F 4
66 Kensal Green Sta. .F 4
77 Kensington Church St. B 2
77 Kensington Court .C 3
77 Kensington Court Place..........D 3
77 Kensington Gdns. .B 3
73 Kensington Gardens Square.........H 2
77 Kensington Gate..D 3
77 Kensington Gore..C 4
77 Kensington High St. D 1
77 Kensington Mall ..B 2
77 Kensington Palace.B 2
77 Kensington Palace Barracks.......C 2
77 Kensington Palace Gdns...........B 2
77 Kensington Palace Green..........C 2
73 Kensington Park Rd. J 1
77 Kensington Place..B 2
77 Kensington Rd....C 3
77 Kensington Square D 2
66 Kensington & Chelsea G 4
71 Kent House Sta...D 8
76 Kent St...........B 5
74 Kent Terrace. ....D 2
66 Kentish Town.....E 6
66 Kentish Town Sta..E 6
66 Kenton ....D 2
66 Kenton La.........C 2
66 Kenton Rd. ....C 2
75 Kenton St.........E 8
77 Kenway Rd.......F 2
66 Kenwood ....D 5
71 Keston...........F 10
71 Keston Mark ....E 10
70 Kew.............A 2
66 Kew Bridge ......G 2
70 Kew Bridge Rd....A 2
66 Kew Bridge Sta. ..G 2
70 Kew Gardens Sta..A 2
70 Kew Palace.......A 2
70 Kew Rd...........A 2
80 Keyse Rd.........E 5
75 Keystone Crescent.C 9
79 Keyworth St.....D 12
71 Kidbrooke........A 9
71 Kidbrooke Sta. ..A 10
66 Kilburn..........E 4
66 Kilburn High Rd. Sta. E 5
73 Kilburn Park Rd...D 1
66 Kilburn Sta.......E 4
73 Kildare Terrace...G 2
75 Killick St.........C 9
79 King Charles St....C 8
75 King Edward St. .G 13
79 King Edward Walk D 11
67 King George V Dock G 11
69 King George VI Res. B 2
67 King George's Res. A 9
79 King James St...D 12
76 King John's Court .E 4
76 King St. EC2.....G 2
78 King St. SW1.....B 6
75 King St. WC2 ....H 8
66 King St. W6......G 3
76 King William St...H 3
80 King & Queen St...F 2
69 Kingfieldgreen....H 1
80 Kinglake St.......G 4
74 Kingly St.........H 6
76 King's Arms Yard .G 2
79 King's Bench St...C 12
75 King's Bench Walk H 11
75 King's College...H 10
75 King's Cross Rd. .D 10
75 King's Cross Sta...C 8
67 King's Head Hill..A 9
80 King's Head Yard .B 3
75 King's Mews......F 10
80 King's Place.......D 1
78 King's Rd. SW1...E 4
77 King's Rd. SW3 ..G 6
67 King's Rd., Chingford B 9
78 King's Scholars' Passage ....E 6
74 King's Terrace....B 6
66 Kingsbury........C 3
66 Kingsbury Green..D 3
66 Kingsbuıy Rd.....D 3
66 Kingsbury Sta. ...D 2
72 Kingsdown ....F 4
65 Kingshill Avenue..F 5
67 Kingsland.........E 7
67 Kingsland Rd.....C 4
69 Kingsley Rd. .....A 6
73 Kingsmill Terrace .B 5
70 Kingston Bridge ..D 1
70 Kingston Bypass ..D 3
70 Kingston Gate....C 2
70 Kingston Hill.....C 2
65 Kingston Lane....F 3
70 Kingston Rd. SW15 B 3
70 Kingston Rd. SW20 D 4
70 Kingston Rd., Leatherhead....H 1
70 Kingston Rd., New Malden........D 2
69 Kingston Rd., Staines C 3
70 Kingston Rd., Teddington.....C 1
70 Kingston Rd., Tolworth.......F 3
70 Kingston upon Thames D 2
70 Kingston Vale ....C 2
75 Kingsway ....G 9
70 Kingswood Sta....H 4
78 Kinnerton St......C 3
80 Kipling St. ....C 3
79 Kipton St.........D 3
79 Kirby Grove.......C 3
75 Kirby St.........F 11
71 Kirkdale ....C 7
78 Kirtling St........J 6
79 Kirwyn Way .....J 13
80 Kitson Rd. ....J 2
71 Kitto Rd..........A 8
77 Knaresborough Place F 2
70 Knight's Hill......C 6
69 Knights Res. ......D 5
78 Knightsbridge.....C 2
69 Knipp Hill ....G 5
77 Knivet Rd. ....J 1
71 Knockholt ......H 12
71 Knockholt Main Rd. H 11
71 Knockholt Pound G 12
71 Knockholt Rd....G 12
71 Knockholt Sta....F 12
69 Knowle Green ....C 2
74 Knox St..........F 2
77 Kynance Mews....E 3
77 Kynance Place....D 3
76 Laburnum St......B 5
76 Lackington St. ....F 3
66 Ladbroke Grove...F 4
80 Lafone St.........C 5
69 Laleham ....D 3
69 Laleham Rd., Shepperton .....D 3
69 Laleham Rd., Staines C 2
76 Lamb Passage.....E 2
76 Lamb St..........F 5
80 Lamb Walk ......C 4
70 Lambeth ....B 6
79 Lambeth Bridge...E 9
79 Lambeth High St...E 9
79 Lambeth Hospital F 12
79 Lambeth Palace ...E 9
79 Lambeth Palace Rd. D 9
79 Lambeth Pier .....E 9
79 Lambeth Rd. .....E 10
76 Lambeth St.......H 6
79 Lambeth Walk...E 10
75 Lamb's Conduit...E 9
69 Lammas La.......F 6
77 Lamont Rd.......H 4
69 Lampton..........A 6
69 Lampton Rd......A 6
73 Lanark Place .....E 4
73 Lanark Rd.......D 3
73 Lancaster Gate....J 4
78 Lancaster House ..C 6
73 Lancaster Mews ..H 4
73 Lancaster Place....J 9
79 Lancaster St. ....C 12
73 Lancaster Terrace .H 5
78 Lancelot Place....D 2
78 Lancing St........D 7
75 Land Registry Office G 10
70 Landor Rd........A 6
73 Langford Place....B 4
74 Langham Place ...G 5
74 Langham St.......F 5
65 Langley...........G 1
79 Langley La. ......H 9
71 Langley Park, Eden Park...........E 9
65 Langley Park, Slough F 1
71 Langley Park G.C..E 9
75 Langley St........H 8
70 Langley Vale .....H 3
75 Langton Close....D 10
77 Langton St.........J 4
73 Lanhill Rd........E 1
67 Lansdowne Rd....C 8
79 Lant St..........C 13
80 Larcom St. ....F 2
70 Latchmere Rd.....A 5
71 Lathams Rd.......F 9
80 Latona Rd........H 6
79 Laud St. ....G 9
73 Lauderdale Rd....D 2
77 Launceston Place..D 3
68 Launders La. .....F 3
76 Laurence Pountney La. J 3
67 Lausanne Rd. ....H 8
70 Lavender Hill.....B 5
77 Laverton Place....F 2
79 Lavington St.....B 13
75 Lavinia Grove ....B 9
80 Law St...........D 3
79 Lawn La.........H 9
70 Lawn Rd.........H 1
66 Lawrence St. NW7.B 3
77 Lawrence St. SW3 .H 6
79 Layhams Rd......G 9
75 Laystall St.......E 10
70 Layton Rd........F 1
67 Lea Bridge.......D 8
67 Lea Bridge Rd. ...D 8
67 Lea Bridge Sta. ...D 8
67 Lea Valley Rd.....A 9
76 Leadenhall Market H 3
76 Leadenhall St.....H 4
79 Leake St.........C 10
71 Leas Rd..........H 8
75 Leather La.......F 11
70 Leatherhead Bypass H 1
70 Leatherhead Common H 1
70 Leatherhead G.C. G 1
70 Leatherhead Rd., Chessington.....F 1
70 Leatherhead Rd., Leatherhead....H 1
80 Leathermarket St. C 3
71 Leaves Green....G 10
71 Leaves Green Rd..F 10
71 Ledgers Rd.......H 8
71 Lee..............B 9
71 Lee High Rd......B 9
71 Lee Rd...........A 9
75 Leeke St.........C 9
74 Lees Place.......H 3
71 Leesons Rd......D 11
75 Leicester Square...J 7
80 Leigh Hunt St.....C 1
70 Leigham Court Rd. C 6
73 Leinster Gdns.....H 3
73 Leinster Mews ....J 4
73 Leinster Rd.......C 1
73 Leinster Square...H 2
73 Leinster Ter.......J 3
76 Leman St.........H 6
78 Lennox Gdns......E 2
78 Lennox Gardens Mews E 2
76 Leonard St........E 3
79 Leopold Walk ....G 9
80 Leroy St..........E 4
68 Lessness Heath ...G 2
76 Lever St..........D 1
71 Lewisham ....B 8
71 Lewisham High St..B 9
71 Lewisham Rd......A 9
79 Lewisham St.......C 7
77 Lexham Gdns.....E 2
77 Lexham Mews ....E 1
74 Lexington St......H 6
67 Ley St...........D 11
76 Leyden St. ....G 5
67 Leyton...........D 9
67 Leyton High Rd...D 9
67 Leyton Marshes...D 8
67 Leyton Midland Road Sta.............D 9
67 Leytonstone High Rd. Sta.............D 9
67 Leytonstone Rd. ..E 9
69 Liberty La. ....F 2
79 Library St. ......D 12
74 Lidlington Place...C 6
76 Ligonier St. ......D 5
73 Lilestone St.. .....E 6
66 Lillie Rd. ....H 4
78 Lillington Gardens Estate..........F 7
76 Lime St. ....H 4
67 Limehouse........F 9
67 Limehouse Reach .G 9
77 Limerston St......H 4
71 Limpsfield Rd.....G 7
67 Lincoln Rd. ....A 7
78 Lincoln St. ....F 2
75 Lincoln's Inn ....G 10
75 Lincoln's Inn Fields G 10
73 Linden Gdns. .....J 1
75 Lindsey St. ....F 13
74 Linhope St.......E 2
80 Linsey St. ....E 6
76 Linton St.........B 2
74 Lisle St...........H 7
73 Lisson Green Estate E 6
73 Lisson Grove .....E 6
73 Lisson St..........F 6
74 Little Albany St....D 5
77 Little Boltons, The. G 3
75 Little Britain.....G 13
65 Little Bushey La...A 6
78 Little Chester St...D 4
74 Little Edward St...C 5
66 Little Ealing......G 2
68 Little Gaynes La...E 4
79 Little George St...C 8
65 Little Green La....A 4
74 Little Marlborough St. H 6
75 Little New St.....G 11
65 Little Oxhey La....B 6
74 Little Portland St. .G 6
75 Little Russell St....G 8
78 Little St. James's St. B 6
76 Little Trinity La...H 2
70 Little Woodcote ..G 5
70 Little Woodmansterne La.............G 5
69 Littleton ....D 3
69 Littleton La.......D 3
80 Liverpool Grove ..G 2
75 Liverpool Rd.....B 11
76 Liverpool St. .....G 3
76 Liverpool Street Sta. F 4
74 Livonia St........H 6
76 Lizard St.........D 2
80 Llewellyn St.......C 6
75 Lloyd Baker St. .D 10
75 Lloyd Square....D 10
75 Lloyd St.........C 11
76 Lloyd's Avenue...H 4
76 Lloyd's Buildings .H 3
75 Lloyd's Row......D 12
71 Loampit Hill .....A 8
69 Lock La..........H 3
66 Locket Rd.........C 1
71 Locksbottom ....E 10
67 Lockwood Res. ...C 8
67 Lodge Avenue ...E 12
71 Lodge La.........F 9
73 Lodge Rd. ....D 5
80 Loftie St..........C 7
77 Logan Mews......E 1
77 Logan Place ......E 1
76 Lolesworth St.....G 5
79 Lollard Place.....F 11
79 Lollard St........F 10
79 Loman St.........C 13
75 Lombard La......H 11
76 Lombard St.......H 3
80 London Bridge....A 3
80 London Bridge Station B 3
80 London Bridge St. .B 3
74 London Clinic ....E 4
74 London College of Music ....H 6
79 London College of Printing.......E 12
67 London Fields Sta..E 8
74 London Planetarium E 3
79 London Rd. SE1 .D 12
71 London Rd. SE23 .B 7
68 London Rd., Aveley G 4
72 London Rd., Badger's Mount ....G 1
65 London Rd., Batchworth.....B 3
70 London Rd., Croydon E 6
72 London Rd., Dunton Green ....H 1
67 London Rd., Enfield A 7
70 London Rd., Hackbridge......E 5
70 London Rd., Kingston D 2
70 London Rd., Mitcham D 5
70 London Rd., Morden D 4
70 London Rd., Norbury D 6
68 London Rd., Romford D 2
68 London Rd., Shenfield A 6
69 London Rd., Staines C 3
66 London Rd., Stanmore B 2
72 London Rd., Swanscombe....B 4
68 London Rd., W. Thurrock ...H 5
75 London School of Economics ....H 10
70 London School of Hygiene.........F 7
70 London Scottish G.C. C 3
76 London St. EC3 ..H 4
73 London St. W2....G 5
69 London St., Chertsey E 2
68 London Tilbury Rd. G 4, G 5
76 London Wall .....G 3
75 London Weather Centre........G 10
75 Long Acre ....H 8
70 Long Ditton ......E 1
65 Long Elmes.......C 6
70 Long Grove Hospital F 2
70 Long Grove Rd....F 2
75 Long La. EC1 ....F 13
80 Long La. SE1 .....C 3
71 Long La., Bexley Heath.........A 12
71 Long La., Croydon D 8
69 Long La., Staines..B 3
65 Long La., Uxbridge E 4
77 Long Ridge Rd....F 1
76 Long St. ....C 5
80 Long Walk........D 4
77 Long Water, The..B 5
75 Long Yard ....E 9
67 Longbridge Rd. ..E 11
80 Longcroft Rd......H 4
70 Longdown Road North G 3
72 Longfield.........D 5
72 Longfield Hill.....D 6
72 Longfield Rd......D 5
65 Longford ....H 3
74 Longford St.......E 5
71 Longlands........C 11
67 Longleigh La.....H 12
80 Longley St........F 6
66 Longmore Avenue.A 5
78 Longmore St......F 6
67 Longwood Gdns..C 11
73 Lord Hills Bridge..G 2
73 Lord Hills Rd.....F 2
79 Lord North St.....E 8
73 Lord's Cricket Ground D 5
67 Lordship La. N17..C 7
71 Lordship La. SE22.B 7
67 Lordship Rd.......D 7
75 Lorenzo St.......C 10
79 Lorrimore Rd.....H 13
79 Lorrimore Square H 13
76 Lothbury.........G 3
73 Loudon Rd. ......B 4
65 Loudwater La.....A 3
79 Loughborough St. G 10
70 Loughborough Junc. Sta.............A 6
67 Loughton ....A 11
67 Loughton Way...A 10
76 Lovat La..........J 3
76 Love La. EC2.....G 2
70 Love La., Morden .E 4
80 Lovegrove St......G 7
71 Lower Addiscombe Rd...............E 7
70 Lower Ashtead ...H 1
68 Lower Bedford Rd. C 2
78 Lower Belgrave St..E 4
67 Lower Clapton Rd. E 8
67 Lower Edmonton..B 8
69 Lower Feltham ...C 4
69 Lower Green .....E 6
69 Lower Green Rd...E 6
78 Lower Grosvenor Place...........D 5
79 Lower Marsh ....C 11
70 Lower Morden La..E 4
70 Lower Mortlake Rd. B 2
70 Lower Richmond Rd. A 3
67 Lower Rd. ....G 8
78 Lower Sloane St....F 3
69 Lower Sunbury Rd. D 5
71 Lower Sydenham..C 8
71 Lower Sydenham Sta. C 8
76 Lower Thames St...J 3
72 Lowfield St. ......B 3
66 Lowlands Rd. ....D 1
78 Lowndes Place....D 3
78 Lowndes Square ..D 3
78 Lowndes St.......D 3
77 Lucan Place ......F 6
80 Lucey Rd.........E 6
75 Ludgate Circus ..H 12
75 Ludgate Hill.....H 12
76 Luke St...........E 3
72 Lullingstone Castle F 2
72 Lullingstone Park..F 1
74 Lumley St.........H 4
71 Lunghurst Rd.....H 8
78 Lupus St..........G 6
79 Luscombe Way....J 8
71 Lusted La........H 10
73 Luton St..........E 5
74 Luxborough St. ...F 3
71 Luxted Rd.......G 10

78 Lyall St..........E 3
80 Lydney Close.....J 4
80 Lynton Rd.......F 6
73 Lyons Place......E 5
80 Lytham St........G 2
66 Lyttelton Rd.....C 5
75 Mabledon Place..D 8
75 Macclesfield Rd. .D 13
73 Mackennal St....B 6
75 Macklin St.......G 9
80 Macks Rd.......E 6
74 Mackworth St...C 6
80 Macleod St.......G 2
65 Mad Bess Wood..C 4
74 Madame Tussaud's E 3
74 Maddox St.......H 5
80 Madron St........F 4
80 Magdalen St......B 4
79 Magee St........H 11
80 Maguire St........C 5
73 Maida Avenue....F 4
73 Maida Vale......D 3
71 Maiden La........J 9
71 Maidstone Rd....C 12
71 Main Rd., Biggin Hill
          H 10
71 Main Rd., Sidcup.C 11
72 Main Rd., Sutton-at-
      Hone.........D 3
78 Makins St........F 1
70 Malden..........E 3
70 Malden Manor Sta. E 3
70 Malden Rd., Cheam
          F 4
70 Malden Rd., New
      Malden........D 3
70 Malden Rushett...G 1
70 Malden Way......E 3
74 Malet Place......E 7
74 Malet St........E 7
78 Mall, The ....B 7
77 Mallord St........H 5
73 Mallory St.......E 6
76 Mallow St.......E 2
80 Malt St..........H 6
75 Malta St.........D 12
80 Maltby St........D 5
73 Malvern Mews...D 1
73 Malvern Rd......D 1
67 Manchester Rd...G 9
74 Manchester Square G 4
74 Manchester St....G 3
80 Manciple St......D 3
74 Mandeville Place ..G 4
75 Manette St.......H 7
80 Mann St.........G 3
71 Manor Avenue....A 8
70 Manor Hospital...G 2
67 Manor Park .....E 11
79 Manor Place......G 13
79 Manor Rd. N16...D 7
67 Manor Rd.,
      Buckhurst Hill..A 10
68 Manor Rd., Hainault
          B 1
70 Manor Rd., Mitcham
          D 5
70 Manor Rd.,
      Wallington....F 5
67 Manor Rd., Woodford
      Bridge........B 11
70 Manor Rd. North .E 1
76 Manresa Rd......G 6
76 Mansell St........H 5
67 Mansfield Hill....B 9
75 Mansfield St......F 5
76 Mansfield St......C 7
71 Mansion, The....B 12
76 Mansion House...H 2
76 Mansion House Place
          H 2
77 Manson Place....F 4
75 Mantell St. .....B 11
72 Maplescombe.....F 3
70 Marble Hill Park ..B 1
75 Marchmont Ter ...E 8
80 Marcia Rd........F 4
74 Margaret St......G 6
77 Margaretta Ter...H 6
75 Margery St.......D 11
76 Mark La.........H 4
76 Mark St.........E 3
78 Market Mews....B 4
74 Market Place.....G 6
78 Markham Square..G 2
78 Markham St......G 2
67 Markhouse Rd....D 9
68 Marks Gate......C 1
68 Marks Gate Rd....C 1

76 Marlborough Av...A 6
73 Marlborough Gate .J 5
80 Marlborough Grove
          G 6
78 Marlborough House
          B 7
73 Marlborough Hill .B 4
73 Marlborough Pl...B 4
78 Marlborough Rd. .B 6
77 Marlborough St..F 6
74 Marle St..........F 6
77 Marloes Rd.......E 2
70 Marlpit La........H 6
66 Marsh La., Highwood
      Hill...........B 3
66 Marsh La., Stanmore
          B 2
65 Marsh Rd........C 5
67 Marsh Side.......B 8
74 Marshall St.......H 6
80 Marshalsea Rd....C 2
78 Marsham St.......E 8
79 Marsland Rd......G 13
75 Mart St..........H 9
78 Martin La........H 3
69 Martindale Rd....B 5
78 Marriet Walk.....D 2
78 Martin Way......D 4
76 Mary St..........A 2
74 Mary Terrace.....B 5
67 Maryland Sta.....E 9
73 Marylands Rd.....E 1
66 Marylebone.......F 6
73 Marylebone Flyover
          F 5
74 Marylebone High St.
          F 4
74 Marylebone La...G 4
74 Marylebone Mews.G 4
74 Marylebone Rd...F 2
74 Marylebone Sta...F 4
74 Marylebone St...F 4
68 Mascalls La.......B 5
80 Mason St.........E 3
71 Masons Hill......D 9
80 Massinger St.....F 4
79 Mathew Parker St..D 8
75 Matilda St.......A 10
74 Maunsel St......E 8
80 Mawbey Place....G 6
69 Maybury........H 1
69 Mayesbrook Park E 12
66 Mayfair..........F 6
78 Mayfair Hotel....A 5
78 Mayfair Place....B 5
75 Maygood St......B 10
68 Mayney Rd.......C 2
71 Maypole Rd......F 12
66 Mays La.........A 4
67 Maze Hill Sta.....H 9
79 Mead Row.......D 11
79 Meadcroft Rd....H 12
79 Meadow Rd..J 9
79 Meadow Row.....E 1
74 Meard St.........H 7
75 Mecklenburg Place E 9
75 Mecklenburg Sq...E 9
75 Medical College of
      St. Bartholomew's
          E 13
78 Medway St.......E 7
75 Melbourne Pl....H 10
74 Melbury Terrace ..E 2
74 Melcombe Place..E 2
74 Melcombe St.....E 2
70 Melfort Rd........D 6
73 Melina Place .....D 4
80 Melior St.........C 3
80 Menshaw St.......E 2
72 Meopham.........E 6
79 Meopham Green .E 6
72 Meopham Sta.....E 6
79 Mepham St......B 10
75 Mercer St........H 8
76 Mercers Hall.....H 2
76 Merchant Taylor's
      Hall...........H 3
75 Meredith St......D 12
75 Merlin St.........D 11
80 Mermaid Court ...C 2
75 Mermaid Theatre H 12
80 Merrick Square..D 2
80 Merrow St........G 3
65 Merry Hill........B 6
65 Merryhill Rd......A 6
70 Merton Park Sta..D 4
70 Merton Rd., SW18 B 4
70 Merton Rd., SW19 C 4
79 Methley St......G 11

78 Metropolitan Police
      H.Q...........D 7
69 Metropolitan Police
      Training School .E 6
79 Metropolitan
      Tabernacle ....E 12
79 Meymott St......B 12
76 Micawber St......C 1
77 Micklethwaite Rd..H 1
75 Middle St........F 13
75 Middle Temple La.
          H 11
74 Middlesex Hosp. ..F 6
76 Middlesex St......G 5
71 Midfield Way....D 12
77 Midland St........C 8
77 Milborne Grove...G 4
69 Milbourne La......F 6
76 Mildmay Forest..G 1
76 Mildmay Miss. Hosp.
          D 5
67 Mile End Rd. ....F 8
69 Miles La. ....G 5
79 Miles Street ......H 8
77 Milford La.......H 10
76 Milk St. ....G 2
66 Mill Hill ....B 3
66 Mill Hill (Broadway)
      Sta............B 3
66 Mill Hill East Sta..C 4
66 Mill Hill G.C. ....A 3
69 Mill La., Chertsey .D 2
68 Mill La., Dagenham
          G 4
76 Mill Row.........B 4
80 Mill St. SE1......C 6
74 Mill St. W1......H 5
79 Millbank.........E 8
79 Millbank Barracks.F 8
74 Miller St.........B 5
67 Millers La. ......B 12
75 Millman St.......E 10
67 Millwall.........G 9
67 Millwall Dock....G 9
67 Millwall F.C......H 8
78 Milmans St.......J 5
78 Milner St........E 2
69 Milton Park......C 1
79 Milton Sta.......F 2
79 Milverton St....G 11
80 Mina Rd.........G 4
76 Mincing La.......H 4
78 Minerva Mews....E 4
80 Minnow St........F 4
76 Minories.........H 5
80 Mint St..........C 1
76 Mintern St.......B 3
70 Mitcham.........D 5
70 Mitcham Common D 5
70 Mitcham G.C. ...D 5
70 Mitcham Junc. Sta.D 5
70 Mitcham La. .....C 5
70 Mitcham Rd. SW17
          C 5
70 Mitcham Rd., Croydon
          E 6
70 Mitcham Sta......D 5
76 Mitchell St.......D 1
71 Mitchley Av......G 7
71 Mitchley Hill.....G 7
79 Mitre Rd........C 11
76 Mitre St.........H 4
76 Moat Mount .....A 3
69 Molesey Rd.......E 5
74 Molyneux St......G 2
79 Monck St.........E 7
79 Monkton St.....E 11
73 Monmouth Rd....H 2
75 Monmouth St.....H 8
80 Monnow Rd......F 6
80 Montagu Close...B 2
73 Montagu Mansions F 3
74 Montagu Mews North
          F 2
74 Montagu Mews South
          G 2
74 Montagu Mews West
          G 2
74 Montagu Place....G 2
74 Montagu Row ....F 3
74 Montagu Square ..G 2
74 Montagu St.......G 3
75 Montague Place ..F 8
76 Montague Rd......B 8
75 Montague St......F 8
80 Montclare St......D 5
79 Montford Place ..G 11
77 Montpelier Place..D 6
77 Montpelier Square.D 6

77 Montpelier St.....D 6
77 Montpelier Walk ..D 6
66 Montrose Avenue .C 3
78 Montrose Place ..D 4
78 Monument St.....J 3
76 Moor La. EC2.....F 2
68 Moor La., Hornchurch
          C 5
65 Moor La.,
      Rickmansworth .B 3
70 Moor La., Surbiton F 2
65 Moor Park G.C...B 4
65 Moor Park Sta. ..B 4
76 Moore St.........E 2
76 Moorfields ....F 2
76 Moorfields Eye Hosp.
          D 2
65 Moorfields Rd. ...D 3
76 Moorgate.........G 2
76 Moorhouse Rd. ...G 1
76 Mora Place.......D 2
72 Morants Ct. Rd...H 1
70 Morden..........E 4
70 Morden G.C. ....E 4
70 Morden Hall Rd...D 4
70 Morden Park.....E 4
70 Morden Rd........D 4
70 Morden Road Halt
          D 4
70 Morden South Sta. D 4
70 Morden Sta.......D 4
80 Morecambe St....F 2
75 Moreland St. ....D 13
78 Moreton Place...G 6
78 Moreton St.......G 6
78 Moreton Terrace..G 6
80 Morgan's La......B 4
70 Morland Rd......E 7
79 Morley St. ......D 11
74 Mornington Cres. .C 6
74 Mornington Place .B 5
74 Mornington St....B 5
74 Mornington Ter. .B 5
80 Morocco St.......C 4
78 Morpeth Ter......E 6
73 Morshead Rd.....D 2
76 Mortimer St......G 6
70 Mortlake.........B 2
70 Mortlake Rd......A 2
74 Morwell St.......G 7
73 Moscow Rd.......J 2
78 Mossop St........E 1
74 Mostyn Rd.......D 4
70 Motspur Park....D 3
71 Mottingham ....C 10
71 Mottingham Rd. .C 10
75 Mount Pleasant, WC1
          E 10
65 Mount Pleasant,
      Southall........F 6
74 Mount Row......J 4
74 Mount Royal Hotel
          H 3
72 Mount Rd........B 4
74 Mount St.........J 4
65 Mount Vernon
      Hospital.......B 4
74 Moxon St........F 3
76 Mulberry St......G 6
77 Mulberry Walk...H 5
70 Mulgrave Rd......F 4
72 Munster Square...D 5
80 Munton Rd.......E 2
75 Muriel St........B 10
79 Murphy St.......D 11
76 Murray Grove....C 2
75 Museum of London
          F 13
75 Museum St.......G 8
66 Muswell Hill......C 6
66 Muswell Hill G.C..C 6
66 Muswell Hill Park Rd.
          C 6
75 Myddleton Passage
          C 11
75 Myddleton Square
          C 11
75 Myddleton St. ...D 11
68 Nags Head La.....C 4
67 Nags Head Rd....A 8
76 Napier Grove.....B 2
71 Nash............F 9
76 Nash Street......D 6
74 Nassau St. ......F 6
74 National Dental
      Hospital.......F 5
79 National Film Theatre
          B 10

79 National Gallery ..A 8
74 National Heart
      Hospital........F 4
77 National History
      Museum.......E 5
75 National Hospital .E 9
67 National Maritime
      Museum.......H 9
79 National Theatre
          B 10
76 Navarre St........D 5
68 Navestock Common
          A 3
75 Neal St..........H 8
66 Neasden..........E 3
66 Neasden Sta......E 3
80 Neate St.........H 4
80 Neckinger.......D 5
75 Nelson Gdns......C 7
75 Nelson Place ....C 12
69 Nelson Rd........B 6
79 Nelson Square ...C 12
75 Nelson Terrace ..C 12
79 Nelson's Column ..A 8
66 Nether St.........C 4
66 Netherland Rd.....A 5
77 Netherton Grove..H 4
74 Netley St.........D 6
77 Nevern Place......F 1
77 Nevern Square....F 1
77 Neville St.........F 5
71 New Addington ...F 9
72 New Barn........D 5
71 New Barn La.,
      Cudham.......H 11
72 New Barn La.,
      Swanley Village .D 2
71 New Beckenham ..C 8
71 New Beckenham Sta.
          C 8
74 New Bond St......H 5
75 New Bridge St...H 12
76 New Broad St....G 3
74 New Burlington St.
          H 6
74 New Cavendish St.
          F 5
76 New Change .....H 1
67 New Charlton ...G 10
80 New Church Rd...J 2
75 New Compton St..H 8
67 New Cross Gate Sta.
          H 8
67 New Cross Rd....H 8
67 New Cross Stadium
          H 8
67 New Cross Sta. ...H 9
72 New Cut........H 1
65 New Denham ....E 3
71 New Eltham .....C 10
75 New Fetter La. ...G 11
69 New Haw........F 3
69 New Haw Rd. ....F 3
76 New Inn St. .....E 4
76 New Inn Yard....E 4
80 New Kent Rd.....E 2
70 New King's Rd....A 4
70 New Malden......D 3
70 New Malden G.C..D 3
76 New North Place ..E 4
76 New North Rd. N1 B 2
67 New North Rd.,
      Hainault.......B 12
75 New North St......F 9
75 New Oxford St...G 8
79 New Palace Yard..C 8
74 New Quebec St...H 3
78 New Ride.........C 2
67 New Rd. E4......B 9
65 New Rd., Croxley
      Green.........A 4
68 New Rd., Dagenham
          F 2
69 New Rd., Littleton D 4
69 New Rd., W. Molesey
          D 6
75 New Row ....J 8
76 New St...........G 4
75 New Wharf Rd....B 9
71 New Years La...G 11
69 Newark La.......H 2
74 Newburgh St.....H 6
75 Newburn St......G 10
67 Newbury Park...D 11

75 Newbury St......F 13
73 Newcastle Place ..F 5
77 Newcombe St.....B 2
80 Newcomen St....C 2
73 Newcourt St......C 6
80 Newent Close....J 4
75 Newgate St.....G 13
67 Newham.........F 10
67 Newham Way....F 10
80 Newhams Row ...D 4
79 Newington Butts .F 12
79 Newington Causeway
          D 13
79 Newington Cres. .F 12
74 Newman Passage..G 7
74 Newman St......G 6
75 Newport Place...H 8
79 Newport St. ....F 10
76 Newton Grove....B 3
70 Newton Rd......G 2
75 Newton St.......G 9
76 Nicholas La......H 3
80 Nicholson St.....B 12
70 Nightingale La....B 5
67 Nightingale Rd.,
      Edmonton.....A 8
70 Nightingale Rd.,
      Wallington.....E 5
76 Nile St..........C 2
80 Nile Terrace......G 5
77 Nine Elms La.....J 7
68 Noak Hill........B 3
68 Noak Hill Rd......B 3
76 Noble St.........G 1
65 Nockhill Wood ..C 4
67 Noel Park........C 7
78 Noel Rd.........B 12
70 Noel St..........G 6
70 Nonsuch Park....F 3
70 Norah St.........D 7
70 Norbiton........D 2
70 Norbiton Sta.....D 2
70 Norbury.........D 6
70 Norbury Cres.....D 6
70 Norbury Hill .....D 6
73 Norfolk Cres.....G 5
73 Norfolk Place.....G 5
79 Norfolk Row ...E 10
73 Norfolk Rd.......A 5
73 Norfolk Square...G 5
76 Norman St. ......D 1
66 North Acton Sta. .D 3
74 North Audley St. .H 3
73 North Bank ......D 6
66 North Circular Rd. N3
          C 5
66 North Circular Rd.
      NW2..........D 3
66 North Circular Rd.
      NW10 ....E 2
67 North Circular Rd.,
      Wood Green....B 7
71 North Cray......C 12
72 North Cray Rd....C 1
74 North Crescent...F 7
75 North Down St....C 9
70 North Cheam.....E 4
66 North Ealing Sta..E 4
71 North End, Croydon
          E 6
72 North End, Erith .A 2
71 North End La....F 10
66 North End Rd., NW11
          D 5
66 North End Rd., W14
          G 4
66 North End Way...D 5
66 North Finchley....B 5
74 North Gower St...D 6
65 North Harrow Sta. D 6
66 North Hill........D 6
65 North Hyde.......C 6
65 North Hyde La....H 5
75 North Mews.....E 10
66 North Middlesex G.C.
          B 5
67 North Middlesex
      Hospital.......E 5
68 North Ockendon..E 5
65 North Orbital Rd. .C 2
76 North Place ......E 6
73 North Ride.......J 4
66 North Rd. N6.....D 6
68 North Rd., Purfleet A 5
68 North Rd., Romford
          B 2
74 North Row.......H 3
70 North Sheen Sta..H 2
68 North St.........C 2

70 North Sugden Rd. .E 1
76 North Tenter St. ..H 5
77 North Terrace ....E 6
65 North View ......D 5
66 North Wembley Sta. E 2
74 North West Poly...A 5
66 North Western Av. A 1
73 North Wharf Rd...G 5
67 North Woolwich.G 11
67 North Woolwich Rd. G 10
75 Northampton Rd. E 11
75 Northampton Sq. D 12
70 Northborough Rd. D 6
75 Northburgh St....E 12
66 Northfields Av. ...G 2
66 Northfields Sta....G 2
72 Northfleet........B 6
75 Northington St. ..F 10
65 Northolt ....E 5
65 Northolt Aerodrome E 4
65 Northolt Park.....E 6
65 Northolt Park Sta. E 6
65 Northolt Rd......E 6
71 Northover Rd.....C 9
76 Northport St......B 3
76 Northumberland Alley H 4
79 Northumberland Av. B 8
72 Northumberland Heath..........A 1
67 Northumberland Park Sta.............C 8
73 Northumberland Place G 1
79 Northumberland St. A 8
73 Northwick Close ..E 5
66 Northwick Park Hospital.......D 1
66 Northwick Park Sta. D 1
73 Northwick Terrace E 4
65 Northwood.......B 4
65 Northwood G.C...C 4
65 Northwood Hills Sta. C 5
65 Northwood Rd....C 3
76 Norton Folgate....F 4
76 Norwich Rd. ....A 6
75 Norwich St. .....G 11
71 Norwood.........C 7
65 Norwood Green...G 6
71 Norwood Junc. Sta. D 7
70 Norwood Rd. SE27 C 6
65 Norwood Rd., Southall G 5
66 Notting Hill ......F 4
77 Notting Hill Gate..A 1
74 Nottingham Place F 3
74 Nottingham St....F 3
74 Nottingham Ter....E 3
73 Nugent Terrace ..C 4
71 Nunhead.........A 8
71 Nunhead La. .....A 7
80 Nursery Row .....F 2
74 Nutford Place ....G 2
76 Nuttall St.........B 4
69 Oak Avenue.....C 5
73 Oak Tree Rd.....D 5
79 Oakden St. ......E 11
70 Oaken La. ......F 1
65 Oakend Wood ...C 1
72 Oakfield La. ......C 2
73 Oakington Rd. ...G 4
66 Oakleigh Park ....A 5
66 Oakleigh Park South B 5
66 Oakleigh Park Sta..A 5
75 Oakley Crescent..C 12
77 Oakley Gdns......H 6
80 Oakley Place .....G 5
74 Oakley Square ....B 6
77 Oakley St.........H 6
67 Oakwood Hill ....A 11
66 Oakwood Park....A 6
66 Oakwood Sta.....A 6
79 Oar St...........B 13
76 Oat La..........G 1
69 Oatlands Av......F 4
69 Oatlands Chase .E 4
69 Oatlands Drive....E 4
69 Oatlands Park ....E 4
79 Occupation Rd. ..G 13
68 Ockendon Rd. ....E 5

69 Ockham Common H 4
69 Ockham La......H 3
69 Ockham Park....H 3
80 Odell St.........G 5
79 Offley Rd.......J 11
74 Ogle St. ....F 6
67 Okehampton Cres. H 12
75 Old Bailey......G 12
74 Old Bond St......J 6
76 Old Broad St......G 3
77 Old Brompton Rd. F 3
74 Old Burlington St. .J 6
76 Old Castle St.....G 5
74 Old Cavendish St. .G 5
67 Old Church Rd. E4 B 9
68 Old Church Rd., Romford........D 2
74 Old Church St. ...G 5
74 Old Compton St...H 7
70 Old Coulsdon ....H 6
77 Old Court Place ...C 2
70 Old Deer Park ....A 1
71 Old Farleigh Rd. ..G 8
67 Old Ford Rd......E 8
75 Old Gloucester St. F 9
80 Old Jamaica Rd...D 6
76 Old Jewry ....G 2
80 Old Kent Rd......F 4
69 Old La...........H 4
73 Old Marylebone Rd. G 6
76 Old Montague St. .F 6
76 Old Nichol St......E 5
79 Old Paradise St.. E 10
78 Old Park La. .....B 4
78 Old Pye St. ......D 7
74 Old Quebec St.....H 3
79 Old Queen St. ....C 7
80 Old Redding......B 6
72 Old Rd...........B 1
67 Old Royal Observatory H 9
75 Old Seacoal La...G 12
76 Old St...........D 3
79 Old Vic Theatre ..C 11
69 Old Woking Rd...G 2
74 Oldbury St.......F 4
76 Oldfield La.......F 6
70 Oldfield Rd.......E 4
80 Olmar St.........H 6
80 Olney Rd.........H 1
66 Olympia ....G 4
80 Omeara St........B 2
77 Onslow Gdns.....F 4
77 Onslow Square...F 5
78 Ontario St........D 13
79 Opal St..........F 12
74 Open Air Theatre..D 3
80 Orange St.........J 7
77 Oratory, The......E 6
80 Orb St...........F 2
74 Orchard St. ......H 3
73 Orchardson St.....E 5
75 Orde Hall St. .....F 9
75 Ordnance Hill.....B 5
67 Orient Football Club D 9
79 Orient St. ....E 12
73 Orme Court......J 2
73 Orme La.........J 2
73 Orme Square.....J 2
73 Orme Square Gate.J 2
78 Ormond Yard ....A 6
78 Ormonde Gate....G 2
76 Ormsby St........B 5
71 Orpington ....E 12
71 Orpington Bypass, Orpington......E 12
71 Orpington Bypass, St. Paul's Cray .D 12
71 Orpington Rd.....D 11
73 Orsett Mews......G 3
79 Orsett St.........F 10
73 Orsett Terrace....G 3
76 Orsman Rd.......A 4
80 Osborn St.........G 6
66 Osidge La........A 6
74 Osnaburgh St.....E 5
73 Ossington St......J 2
80 Ossory Rd........H 6
74 Ossulston St. .....C 7
78 Osten Mews ......A 5
79 Osterley.........A 1
66 Osterley La.......G 1
69 Osterley Park ....G 6
69 Osterley Park Ho. .A 6
79 Oswin St.........E 12

72 Otford...........H 2
72 Otford La. ....G 1
69 Ottershaw ....F 2
70 Ottways La.......H 1
74 Outer Circle B 2, D 2, C 4
75 Outram St.........A 9
70 Outwood La......H 4
79 Oval Cricket Ground, The ....H 10
74 Oval Rd..........A 4
70 Oval Way........G 10
71 Ovenden Rd......H 12
78 Ovington Gdns....D 1
78 Ovington Square ..E 2
78 Ovington St.......E 2
74 Oxendon St. ......J 7
74 Oxford Circus ....G 5
68 Oxford Rd........D 1
73 Oxford Square ....H 6
74 Oxford St.........G 6
65 Oxhey ....A 5
65 Oxhey Drive......B 5
74 Oxhey La. ... A 5, B 6
71 Oxlea Wood......A 11
69 Oxshott ....G 6
69 Oyster La........G 3
75 Packington St.....A 13
66 Paddington ....F 5
73 Paddington General Hospital.........F 1
73 Paddington Green .F 5
73 Paddington Recreation Ground.........C 2
73 Paddington Sta...G 4
73 Paddington St.....F 3
68 Padnall Corner....C 1
79 Page St..........E 7
80 Page's Walk ......A 4
67 Painters Rd......C 12
78 Pakenham St......D 10
73 Palace Court .....J 2
77 Palace Gate ......D 3
77 Palace Gardens Mews B 2
77 Palace Green .....B 2
79 Palace Hotel......H 9
71 Palace Parade.....C 7
70 Palace Rd........B 6
78 Palace St.........D 6
75 Palace Theatre ...H 8
76 Palissy St.........D 5
77 Pall Mall ....B 7
79 Pall Mall East ....A 7
74 Palladium Theatre H 6
78 Palmer St.........D 7
66 Palmer's Green...B 6
67 Palmers Green, Southgate Sta. ..C 7
67 Palmerston Rd. ..B 10
70 Pampisford Rd....F 6
74 Pancras La. ......H 2
75 Pancras Rd.......B 7
74 Panton St........J 7
73 Parade, The......J 3
78 Paradise Walk ...H 2
70 Parchmore Rd....D 6
80 Pardoner St......D 3
73 Parfett St........G 7
79 Paris Garden ....B 12
74 Park Avenue.....A 7
74 Park Crescent ....E 5
74 Park Crescent Mews East ....E 5
74 Park Crescent Mews West...........E 4
68 Park Farm Rd.....A 4
71 Park Hill Rd. ....B 12
71 Park Hospital.....B 9
75 Park La. W1......B 4
70 Park La., Ashtead .H 2
67 Park La., Tottenham C 8
78 Park Lane Hotel...B 5
78 Park Place.......B 6
75 Park Place Villas...F 4
74 Park Rd. NW1 ...D 1
70 Park Rd., Banstead G 4
71 Park Rd., Ficklehole G 9
69 Park Rd., Stanwell.B 3
70 Park Rd., Teddington C 1
69 Park Rd., Twickenham C 6
66 Park Royal.......F 2
66 Park Royal Sta. ..F 2

70 Park Side ....C 3
72 Park Square East ..E 5
74 Park Square West..E 4
80 Park St. SE1.....B 2
74 Park St. W1 .....J 3
74 Park Village East ..B 5
74 Park Village West .B 5
77 Park Walk ....H 4
73 Park West Place ..G 6
65 Park Wood.......C 4
73 Parker St.........G 9
80 Parker's Row.....C 6
75 Parkfield St.......B 11
72 Parkfield Wood ...E 4
80 Parkhouse St......J 3
71 Parklangley ......D 9
74 Parkway ....A 5
65 Parkway, The.....G 5
66 Parliament Hill....E 5
79 Parliament Square.C 8
79 Parliament St.....C 8
76 Parr St..........B 2
79 Parry St.........H 9
68 Parsloes Avenue ..E 1
68 Parsloes Park.....E 1
66 Parson St........C 4
69 Parvis Rd........G 3
79 Pascal St.........J 8
76 Pasley Rd. ......G 13
78 Passmore Terrace..F 3
75 Patent Office.....G 11
75 Pater St. ....D 1
75 Paternoster Square G 13
76 Paton St.........D 1
76 Paul St..........E 3
77 Paulton's Square ..H 5
77 Paultons St.......H 5
73 Paveley St.......D 6
78 Pavilion Rd.......D 2
68 Pea La. ....E 5
78 Peabody Avenue .G 5
76 Peace St.........E 7
75 Peacock St.......F 13
75 Pear Tree Court ..E 11
75 Pear Tree St. ....D 13
79 Pearman St.......D 11
69 Pears Rd. ....A 6
76 Pearson St.......B 5
71 Peckham ....A 7
80 Peckham Hill St...J 6
80 Peckham Park Rd...J 6
71 Peckham Rd......A 7
71 Peckham Rye.....B 7
71 Peckham Rye Common B 7
71 Peckham Rye Park.B 7
71 Peckham Rye Sta. .A 7
76 Pedley St.........E 6
77 Peel St..........B 2
77 Peerless St........D 2
77 Pelham Crescent..F 6
77 Pelham Place ....F 5
77 Pelham St........E 5
80 Pelier St.........H 1
73 Pembridge Gdns. .J 1
73 Pembridge Place ..H 1
73 Pembridge Rd....J 1
73 Pembridge Square.J 1
73 Pembridge Villas..H 1
78 Pembroke Close...C 4
77 Pembroke Place...D 1
77 Pembroke Rd. W8 .E 1
65 Pembroke Rd., Ruislip D 4
77 Pembroke Square..C 1
77 Pembroke Villas..E 1
70 Pen Ponds.......B 2
73 Penfold Place ....F 5
73 Penfold St........E 5
71 Penge...........C 7
71 Penge East Sta....C 8
71 Penge West Sta. ..C 7
71 Penhill Rd.......B 12
76 Penn St..........A 3
80 Pennack Rd.......H 5
77 Pennant Mews ...E 2
76 Pennington St....J 7
79 Penrose Grove....G 13
79 Penrose St.......G 13
74 Penryn St........B 7
79 Penton Place ....G 13
75 Penton Rise......C 10
75 Penton St........B 10
75 Pentonville Rd....C 10
77 Penywern Rd.....F 2
80 Pepler St.........H 2
70 Pepys Rd.........D 3
76 Pepys St.........H 4

75 Percival St......D 12
75 Percy Circus .....C 10
73 Percy Rd. NW6...C 1
69 PercyRd.,HamptonC 6
69 Percy Rd., Twick..B 6
74 Percy St.........G 7
66 Perivale.........E 2
78 Perkins Rents....D 7
71 Perry Hill........C 8
71 Perry St. ....C 11
74 Peter Pan Statue ..A 5
74 Peter St.........H 7
75 Peters La. ......F 12
70 Petersham.......B 2
70 Petersham La. ...D 3
78 Petersham Mews ..E 4
74 Petersham Place..D 4
74 Peto Place ....E 5
76 Petticoat Square ..G 5
71 Petts Wood......D 11
71 Petts Wood Rd. ..D 11
78 Petty France.....D 6
78 Petyward........F 1
80 Phelp St.........H 2
77 Philbeach Gdns...F 1
67 Philip La.........C 7
77 Phillimore Gdns..D 1
77 Phillimore Place ..D 1
77 Phillimore Walk..D 1
76 Philipp St.........B 4
76 Philpot La........H 3
76 Phipp St. ....E 4
75 Phoenix Place....E 10
74 Phoenix Rd.......C 7
75 Phoenix St.......H 8
78 Piccadilly........B 5
74 Piccadilly Circus...J 7
74 Piccadilly Hotel ..J 6
74 Piccadilly Theatre..J 7
75 Pickard St. ......C 13
71 Pickford La......A 12
74 Pickhurst La......E 9
74 Picton Place .....G 4
68 Pike La..........E 5
75 Pilgrim St. ......H 12
80 Pilgrimage St.....D 2
68 Pilgrims Hatch...A 5
71 Pilgrims Way, Knockholt......H 12
72 Pilgrims Way, Otford H 2
78 Pimlico Garden ..H 7
78 Pimlico Rd.......F 4
71 Pinchin St........H 6
76 Pindar St. ....F 4
73 Pindock Mews....E 3
75 Pine St. ....E 11
66 Pinkham Way ....C 6
65 Pinner...........C 5
65 Pinner Green .....C 5
65 Pinner Hill G.C....C 5
65 Pinner Hill Rd....C 5
76 Pinner Rd........D 6
76 Pitfield St........C 3
77 Pitt St...........C 1
75 Pitts Head Mews..B 4
67 Plaistow.........F 10
71 Plaistow La......D 10
71 Plaistow Sta......F 10
72 Platt............H 5
74 Platt St..........B 7
74 Plender Place ....B 6
74 Plender St........B 6
69 Plough La........H 5
74 Plough Yard......E 4
75 Plum Tree Court .G 12
76 Plumbers Row ...G 6
67 Plumstead.......G 11
67 Plumstead Common H 11
67 Plumstead Common Rd.............H 11
67 Plumstead HighSt.G 12
67 Plumstead Marshes G 12
67 Plumstead Rd....G 11
67 Plumstead Sta....G 11
73 Plympton St......E 6
79 Pocock St........C 12
70 Pointers Rd......H 4
72 Pol Hill ....G 1
74 Poland St........H 6
66 Police College....C 3
74 Pollard Row......D 7
74 Polygon Rd.......C 7
74 Polytechnic of London F 3
67 Pomeroy St......H 8
77 Pond Place ......F 6

67 Ponders End.....A 8
79 Ponsonby Place ..F 9
79 Ponsonby Terrace .F 8
78 Pont St.........E 2
76 Poole St.........B 2
80 Pope St.........D 4
74 Poplar...........F 9
67 Poplar High St. ..F 9
73 Poplar Place .....J 2
73 Porchester Gdns...H 3
73 Porchester Place ..H 6
73 Porchester Rd....G 2
73 Porchester Square.G 3
73 Porchester Square Mews..........G 3
73 Porchester Terrace H 3
73 Porchester Terrace Gate...........J 3
73 Porchester Terrace North..........G 3
80 Porlock St........C 3
74 Porters Avenue...E 1
73 Porteus Rd.......F 4
70 Portland Rd......D 7
80 Portland St.......C 5
74 Portman Close...G 3
74 Portman Hotel...G 3
74 Portman Mews South H 3
74 Portman Square...G 3
74 Portman St.......H 3
69 Portmore Park Rd. E 3
76 Portnalls Rd......H 5
75 Portpool La......F 11
74 Portsea Place ....H 2
69 Portsmouth Rd., Esher F 6
70 Portsmouth Rd., Thames Ditton..E 1
69 Portsmouth Rd., Wisley.........H 3
75 Portsmouth St...G 10
76 Portsoken St......H 5
75 Portugal St. .....H 10
74 Post Office Tower .F 6
80 Potier St.........E 3
65 Potter St.........C 5
80 Potter's Fields ...B 4
65 Potterstreet Hill..B 5
76 Poultrey ....H 2
70 Pound La........G 12
71 Poverest Rd......D 11
69 Powdermill La....B 5
76 Pownall Rd.......A 6
69 Poyle ....A 2
70 Poynders Rd......B 6
73 Praed St.........G 5
74 Pratt Mews ......A 6
74 Pratt St..........A 6
77 Pratt Walk ......E 10
71 Pratt's Bottom ...F 12
76 Prebend St.......A 1
76 Prescot St........H 6
66 Preston.........D 2
66 Preston Rd.......D 2
66 Preston Rd. Sta. ..D 2
65 Prestwick Rd.....B 5
79 Price's St........B 12
70 Prideaux Place...D 10
79 Prima Rd.......J 11
66 Primrose Hill ....E 5
66 Primrose Hill Sta..E 5
74 Primrose St.......F 4
74 Prince Albert Rd..B 2
75 Prince Charles Theatre H 7
77 Prince Consort Rd.D 4
77 Prince of Wales Gate C 6
74 Prince of Wales Theatre........J 7
67 Prince Regents La.F 10
76 Princelet St........F 5
70 Princes Coverts ..G 1
73 Prince's Gdns....D 5
77 Prince's Gate ....C 5
77 Prince's Gate Mews D 5
73 Princes Mews....H 2
72 Princes Rd.......B 2
73 Princes Square...H 2
73 Princes St........G 2
77 Princess Beatrice Hospital.......G 2
73 Princess Rd......C 1
75 Princeton St.....F 10
80 Prioress St.......E 3
73 Priory La........B 3
66 Priory Rd........C 6
77 Priory Walk......G 4

76 Pritchards Rd. ...B 7
80 Priter Rd. ....D 6
75 Procter St. ....F 9
75 Provence St. ....B 13
76 Provost St. ....C 2
69 Pryford Rd. ....G 2
75 Public Record Office G 11
75 Public Trustee Office G 9
76 Pudding La. EC3 ..J 3
67 Pudding La., Chigwell A 12
75 Puddle Dock ....H 12
72 Puddledock La. ...C 1
80 Purbrook St. ....D 4
76 Purcell St. ....B 4
74 Purchese Rd. .....C 7
68 Purfleet ....G 4
68 Purfleet Bypass. ...G 4
68 Purfleet Rd. ......G 4
70 Purley ....G 6
71 Purley Downs ....G 7
71 Purley Downs G.C. G 7
71 Purley Downs Rd. .G 7
71 Purley Oaks Sta. .F 7
80 Purley Rd. ....J 7
70 Purley Way ......E 6
70 Putney ....B 3
70 Putney Bridge ....A 4
70 Putney Bridge Rd. .B 4
70 Putney Heath ....B 3
70 Putney High St. ...B 4
70 Putney Hill .....B 4
70 Putney Sta. ......B 4
69 Pyrcroft ....E 2
69 Pyrford ....H 2
69 Pyrford Common Rd. H 2
68 Pyrgo Park ......B 3
76 Quaker St. ....E 5
79 Queen Alexandra Military Hospital F 8
74 Queen Anne Mews G 5
74 Queen Anne St. ...G 4
78 Queen Anne's Gate D 7
77 Queen Elizabeth College ....C 1
79 Queen Elizabeth Hall B 10
70 Queen Elizabeth Hospital ....H 4
80 Queen Elizabeth St. C 5
69 Queen Elizabeth II Res. E 5
69 Queen Mary Res. ..D 3
74 Queen Mary's Gardens D 3
71 Queen Mary's Hospital C 12
70 Queen Mary's Hospital for Children ....F 5
75 Queen Square .....F 9
76 Queen St. EC4 ...H 2
78 Queen St. W1 ....B 5
78 Queen Victoria Memorial ......C 6
75 Queen Victoria St. H 13
74 Queen's College ...G 4
73 Queen's Gdns. ....H 4
77 Queen's Gate .....D 4
77 Queen's Gate Gdns. E 4
77 Queen's Gate Mews D 4
77 Queen's Gate Place E 4
77 Queen's Gate Place Mews ....E 4
77 Queen's Gate Ter. .D 4
73 Queen's Grove ....A 5
75 Queen's Head St. .A 12
73 Queen's Mews ....H 2
66 Queen's Park Rangers F.C. ....G 4
66 Queen's Park Sta. ..F 4
67 Queen's Rd. SE15 .H 8
70 Queen's Rd., Richmond ......B 2
70 Queens Rd., Teddington .....C 1
69 Queens Rd., Weybridge......F 4
67 Queen's Rd., Peckham Sta. ...H 8
70 Queen's Rd. Sta. ..A 5
80 Queen's Row .....E 1
73 Queen's Terrace ..B 5
74 Queen's Theatre ..H 7
66 Queen's Wood ...D 6
77 Queensberry Way .E 5
73 Queensborough Ter. H 3

76 Queensbridge Rd. ..B 6
66 Queensbury.......C 2
77 Queensbury Place .E 4
70 Queensmere Rd. ..C 4
78 Queenstown Rd....J 4
73 Queensway.......H 3
75 Quick St. ....C 12
80 Quilp St. ....C 2
76 Quilter St. ....C 6
77 Racton Rd. ....H 1
77 Radley Mews ......E 2
73 Radnor Mews ....H 5
74 Radnor Place ....H 6
80 Radnor Rd. .....J 6
76 Radnor St. ......D 2
79 Radnor Terrace ..J 9
78 Radnor Walk ....G 2
71 Rag Hill ....H 10
76 Railway Approach.B 3
76 Railway Place ....H 4
75 Railway St. ......C 9
80 Rainbow St. ......J 4
68 Rainham.........F 3
68 Rainham Marshes .F 3
68 Rainham Rd. ......E 2
73 Rainsford St. .....G 6
75 Raleigh St. ......B 13
80 Ralph St. ....D 2
74 Ramillies Place...H 6
74 Ramillies St. .....H 6
74 Rampayne St. ....G 7
76 Ramsey St. ......D 6
79 Randall Road ....F 9
70 Randall Row ....F 9
70 Randalls Rd. .....H 1
73 Randolph Avenue .D 3
73 Randolph Crescent E 3
73 Randolph Gdns. ...C 2
73 Randolph Mews ...E 4
73 Randolph Rd. ....E 4
73 Ranelagh Bridge ..G 3
78 Ranelagh Gardens .G 4
73 Ranelagh Grove ...F 4
67 Rangers Rd. .....A 10
78 Ranston St. ....F 6
78 Raphael St. ....C 2
74 Rathbone Place ...G 7
74 Rathbone St. .....G 7
71 Ravensbourne Sta..D 9
66 Ravenscourt Park G 3
66 Ravenscourt Pk. Sta. G 4
76 Ravenscroft St. ...C 5
79 Ravensdon St. ...G 11
74 Ravey St. ....E 4
78 Rawlings St. ......F 2
75 Rawstorne St. ...D 12
75 Ray St. ....E 11
65 Rayners La.......D 6
70 Raynes Park .....D 3
70 Raynes Park Sta. .D 3
76 Rector St. ....A 1
69 Rectory La., Byfleet G 3
67 Rectory La., Loughton A 11
70 Rectory La., Mitcham C 5
70 Rectory La., Sutton G 5
67 Rectory Rd. Sta. ..E 8
70 Red La. ....F 1
70 Red Lion Row ...H 2
75 Red Lion Square .F 9
75 Red Lion St. .....F 10
71 Red Lodge Rd. ...E 9
74 Red Place ....H 3
73 Redan Place......H 2
67 Redbridge.......C 12
67 Redbridge La. ...D 10
67 Redbridge Sta....D 10
78 Redburn St.......G 2
76 Redchurch St. ....E 5
77 Redcliffe Gdns. ..G 3
77 Redcliffe Mews ...G 3
77 Redcliffe Place ...H 3
77 Redcliffe Rd. .....G 4
77 Redcliffe Square .G 2
77 Redcliffe St. .....H 3
80 Redcross Way ...C 2
77 Redesdale St......G 2
77 Redfield La. ......E 2
69 Redhill Rd.......G 4
75 Redhill St. ....C 5
80 Redmead La.......B 6
77 Reece Mews .....F 4
79 Reede Rd.........E 2
79 Reedworth St.....F 11
76 Rees St..........A 2
74 Reeves Mews ....J 4

74 Regal La. ....A 4
76 Regan Way ......C 4
78 Regency St.......E 7
74 Regent Palace Hotel J 6
75 Regent Square...D 9
74 Regent St........H 6
77 Regent's Park....C 3
74 Regent's Park Barracks ......C 5
66 Regent's Park Rd. N3 C 4
74 Regent's Park Rd. NW1 ....A 4
76 Regents Row .....A 6
70 Reigate Avenue ..E 4
70 Reigate Rd. ......G 3
75 Remington St. ...C 12
74 Remnant St.......G 9
79 Renfrew Rd......F 12
79 Rennie St........A 12
80 Rephidim St......D 3
79 Reston Place .....D 3
80 Reveroy Rd......F 6
74 Rex Place ....A 4
75 Rheidol Terrace ..B 13
78 Richard's Place ...E 1
65 Richings Park ....G 2
70 Richmond ....B 2
70 Richmond Bridge .B 1
70 Richmond Gate ..B 2
70 Richmond G.C....C 2
74 Richmond Mews ..H 7
70 Richmond Park...B 2
70 Richmond Park Public G.C...........B 3
70 Richmond Rd.....C 2
79 Richmond Terrace C 8
77 Rickett St. ......H 1
71 Ricketts Hill Rd. .H 10
65 Rickmansworth ...A 3
65 Rickmansworth Rd., Croxley Green .A 4
65 Rickmansworth Rd.. Harefield.......C 3
70 Riddlesdown Rd..G 6
71 Riddlesdown Sta. .G 7
67 Ridge Avenue.....A 7
70 Ridge Rd........E 4
72 Ridge Wood .....F 6
74 Ridgmount Gdns. .F 7
74 Ridgmount St.....F 7
67 Ridgeway ....B 9
70 Ridgway.........C 3
70 Riding House St. .G 6
80 Riley Rd. ....D 4
77 Riley St.........J 5
69 Ripley ....H 3
68 Ripple Rd. ......E 1
80 Rita Rd.........J 9
75 Ritchie St........B 11
78 Ritz Hotel.......B 6
75 River St. ......C 11
71 Rochester Way, SE9 A 10
72 Rochester Way, Bexley B 1
75 Rockcliffe St......C 12
80 Rockingham St....E 1
67 Roding La. E18 ...C 10
67 Roding La., Buckhurst Hill..........B 11
67 Roding Lane South C 10
67 Roding Valley ...B 10
74 Rodmarton St.....G 3
80 Rodney Place ....E 2
80 Rodney Rd.......F 2
75 Rodney St. ......B 10
70 Roehampton......B 3
70 Roehampton Gate .B 3
70 Roehampton G.C. .B 3
70 Roehampton Vale .C 3
75 Roger St. ....E 10
77 Roland Gdns. ....G 4
77 Roland Way......G 4
80 Rolls Rd.........F 5
72 Roman Villa Rd...C 3

68 Romford.........D 2
68 Romford G.C.....C 3
68 Romford Rd., Aveley F 4
68 Romford Rd., Chadwell Heath D 1
68 Romford Rd., Chigwell Row...B 1
67 Romford Rd., Ilford D 11
67 Romford Rd., Stratford......E 10
75 Romilly St.......H 7
79 Romney St. SW1 ..E 8
72 Romney Street, Kent G 3
76 Rood La. ....H 4
74 Roosevelt Memorial H 4
76 Ropemaker St.....F 2
77 Rosary Gdns. ....F 4
70 Roscoe St........E 2
80 Rose Alley ....A 1
70 Rose Hill........E 4
68 Rose La.........C 1
75 Rosebery Avenue.E 11
78 Rosemoor St......F 2
71 Rosendale Rd.....B 7
75 Rosoman St. ....D 11
74 Rossmore Rd. ...E 1
79 Rotary St........D 12
67 Rotherhithe .....G 8
67 Rotherhithe New Rd. G 8
67 Rotherhithe St....G 8
80 Rothsay St.......D 3
78 Rotten Row .....C 2
80 Rouel Rd........E 6
77 Round Pond......B 3
70 Roundshaw......F 6
67 Roundway, The...C 7
79 Roupell St.......B 11
74 Rousebarn La.....A 4
69 Row Hill........F 2
69 Row Town ....F 2
80 Rowan Rd........D 6
80 Rowcross St......G 5
76 Rowland St......F 7
66 Rowley Bank.....A 3
79 Rowley La.......A 3
66 Roxeth ....D 1
65 Roxeth Green Av..D 6
74 Royal Academy of Arts............J 6
74 Royal Academy of Music.........E 4
66 R.A.F. Museum...C 3
67 Royal Albert Dock G 11
77 Royal Albert Hall .C 4
79 Royal Army Medical College........F 8
78 Royal Automobile Club.........B 7
78 Royal Avenue ...G 2
70 Royal Botanical Gardens ....A 2
77 Royal Cancer Hospital F 5
77 Royal College of Art D 5
77 Royal College of Music D 5
74 Royal College of Physicians......E 5
77 Royal College of Science.........D 5
75 Royal College of Surgeons.......G 10
74 Royal College St..B 7
75 Royal Courts of Justice........H 10
74 Royal Ear Hospital E 7
76 Royal Exchange ..H 3
79 Royal Eye Hospital D 12
79 Royal Festival Hall B 10
75 Royal Free Hospital, N1 ....A 11
75 Royal Free Hospital, WC1 ....D 10
77 Royal Geographical Society.........C 5
78 Royal Horticultural Society Hall ....E 7
78 Royal Hospital....G 3
78 Royal Hospital Rd. G 3

74 Royal Institute of British Architects F 5
73 Royal Lancaster Hotel
78 Royal Mews, The. .D 5
67 Royal Military Academy......H 11
69 Royal Military School of Music......B 6
76 Royal Mint.......J 5
76 Royal Mint St....J 5
67 Royal Naval College G 9
75 Royal Opera House H 9
79 Royal Rd........H 12
74 Royal Society ....J 6
79 Royal St.........D 10
74 Royal Veterinary College ......A 7
67 Royal Victoria Dock G 10
79 Royal Waterloo Hospital ......B 10
70 Royal Wimbledon G.C..........C 3
74 Royle St.........H 6
65 Royston Park ....B 6
67 Ruckholt Rd......E 9
73 Rudolf Rd. ......C 2
70 Rufus St.........D 4
70 Rugby Union Football Ground ......B 1
65 Ruislip ....D 4
65 Ruislip Common. .C 4
65 Ruislip Gardens Sta.E 5
65 Ruislip G.C......D 4
65 Ruislip Lido.....C 4
65 Ruislip Manor Sta. D 5
65 Ruislip Rd.......F 6
80 Runham St.......G 3
74 Rupert St........H 7
68 Rush Green ......D 2
68 Rush Green Rd. ..D 2
70 Rushett La.......G 1
71 Rushey Green....B 8
76 Rushton St.......B 3
79 Rushworth St. ...C 12
71 Ruskin Park .....B 7
75 Russell Hotel .....E 8
66 Russell La........B 5
75 Russell Square ...F 8
75 Rust Square .....J 2
78 Rutherford St.....E 7
77 Rutland Gdns.....C 6
77 Rutland Gate ....C 6
77 Rutland Mews ...D 6
77 Rutland St.......D 6
79 Rutley Close ....H 12
69 Ruxbury Rd. ....E 2
70 Ruxley La. ......F 2
69 Rydens Rd. .....E 5
78 Ryder St.........B 6
73 Ryders Terrace ..B 3
71 Rye La. ....A 7
74 Sackville St. .....J 6
75 Saffron Hill......F 11
75 Saffron St. ......F 11
79 Sail St. ....E 10
79 St. Agnes Place ..H 12
77 St. Alban's Grove .D 3
74 St. Alban's St.....J 7
76 St. Alphage Gdn. .F 2
75 St. Andrew St. ...G 11
75 St. Andrew's Gdns. D 10
75 St. Andrew's Hill .H 12
67 St. Ann's Rd. N15 .D 7
69 St. Ann's Rd., Chertsey......E 2
79 St. Ann's St. .....D 7
73 St. Ann's Terrace B 5
78 St. Barnabas St. ...F 4
75 St. Bartholomew's Hospital ....G 12
66 St. Bernard's Hanwell Hospital ....G 1
76 St. Botolph St....G 5
75 St. Bride St. .....G 12
75 St. Chad St. .....C 9
75 St. Chad's Place ..C 9
76 St. Clare St. .....H 5
75 St. Clement Dane's Church ....H 10
76 St. Clement's Church H 3

75 St. Clement's La. .H 10
75 St. Cross St. .....F 11
71 St. Denham Hill ..C 7
76 St. Dunstan's Hill .J 4
74 St. Edmund's Ter. .B 2
79 St. Gabriel St.....E 12
74 St. George St.....H 5
69 St. George's Av. ..F 4
79 St. George's Cathedral D 11
79 St. George's Circus D 12
78 St. George's Drive .F 5
75 St. George's Gdns. D 9
69 St. George's Hill G.C. F 4
78 St. George's Hospital C 4
79 St. George's Rd. ..D 11
78 St. George's Square G 7
80 St. George's Way. .H 4
75 St. Giles High St.. .G 8
75 St. Helena St.....D 11
76 St. Helen's Place ..G 4
70 St. Helier........E 5
70 St. Helier Avenue .E 4
70 St. Helier Hospital .E 4
70 St. Helier Sta.....E 4
67 St. Jame's Street Sta.
74 St. James's Terrace Mews.........B 2
78 St. James's ....B 6
78 St. James's Drive .B 5
78 St. James's Palace. .B 6
78 St. James's Park ...C 7
78 St. James's Place. .B 6
80 St. James's Rd. SE16 E 7
71 St. James's Rd., Croydon ....E 7
75 St. James's Row ..E 12
75 St. James's Square .B 7
78 St. James's St.....B 6
75 St. John St. ......D 12
70 St. John's Hill ...B 5
75 St. John's La. ....F 12
75 St. John's Square .E 12
67 St. John's Sta.....H 9
66 St. John's Wood ..F 5
73 St. John's Wood Barracks ......B 5
73 St. John's Wood High St.........C 5
73 St. John's Wood Park A 5
73 St. John's Wood Rd. D 5
73 St. John's Wood Terrace ....B 6
80 St. Katherine's Way B 6
67 St. Leonard St.....F 9
76 St. Leonard's Hospital B 4
78 St. Leonard's Ter. .G 2
78 St. Loo Avenue ..H 2
77 St. Luke's Hospital G 6
77 St. Luke's St. ....G 6
79 St. Margaret St....D 8
70 St. Margarets.....B 1
79 St. Margaret's Church D 8
75 St. Mark's Hospital C 13
75 St. Martins in the Fields Church ....J 8
75 St. Martin's La. ...J 8
75 St. Martin's le Grand G 13
79 St. Martin's Place .A 8
75 St. Martin's St. ...J 8
75 St. Martin's Theatre H 8
77 St. Mary Abbots Hospital........E 2
76 St. Mary at Hill ...J 3
76 St. Mary Axe .....G 4
71 St. Mary Cray....D 12
76 St. Mary-le-Bow Church ....H 2
79 St. Mary's Gdns. E 11
73 St. Mary's Hospital, W2..........G 5
68 St. Mary's La. D 4, D 5
70 St. Mary's Rd.....E 1
73 St. Mary's Terrace .F 4
79 St. Mary's Walk...E 11

78 St. Matthew St. ...D 7
76 St. Matthew's Row D 6
73 St. Michael's St. ..G 5
71 St. Mildred's Rd. ..B 9
79 St. Oswald Place .G 10
74 St. Pancras Gardens B 7
74 St. Pancras Hospital B 7
75 St. Pancras Sta...C 8
74 St. Pancras Way ..A 7
76 St. Paul St.......A 1
75 St. Paul's Cathedral H 13
75 St. Paul's Churchyard H 13
71 St. Paul's Cray ...D 12
71 St. Paul's Cray Rd. D 11
75 St. Paul's Pier .J 12
67 St. Paul's Rd.....E 7
79 St. Paul's Terrace H 12
71 St. Paul's Wood Hill D 11
75 St. Peter's Avenue .C 6
76 St. Peter's Close. .C 7
75 St. Peter's St. ....B 12
73 St. Petersburgh Mews J 2
73 St. Petersburgh Pl. .J 2
76 St. Philip Way ....A 2
66 St. Quintin Av. ...F 4
73 St. Stephen's Gdns. G 1
77 St. Stephen's Hospital H 4
65 St. Thomas Drive. .C 5
80 St. Thomas St. ....B 3
79 St. Thomas's Hospital D 9
79 Salamanca St.....F 9
73 Sale Place ....G 6
73 Salem Rd.........H 2
75 Salisbury Court ..H 12
74 Salisbury Place ...F 2
80 Salisbury Row ...F 3
73 Salisbury St. .....E 6
66 Salmon St.........D 3
71 Salmons La.......H 7
73 Samford St. ......E 5
79 Sancroft St......F 10
80 Sanctuary St. ....C 2
71 Sanderstead ......G 7
71 Sanderstead Hill. .G 7
71 Sanderstead Rd. .F 7
71 Sanderstead Sta....F 7
80 Sandford Row ...G 3
71 Sandhurst Rd. ...B 9
75 Sandland St. .....F 10
80 Sandover Rd.......G 4
69 Sandown Park Race
    Course.........E 6
75 Sandwich St. .....D 8
68 Sandy La., Dagenham
    G 4
69 Sandy La., Esher .G 5
70 Sandy La.,
    Twickenham ...D 1
70 Sandy Lane South .F 6
65 Sandy Lodge G.C. B 4
65 Sandy Lodge La.
    B 4
65 Sandy Lodge Rd. ..B 4
76 Sandy Row ......F 4
70 Sandycombe Rd...A 2
71 Sangley Rd. ......B 9
75 Sans Walk......E 12
75 Sardinia St.......G 9
79 Saunders St.....E 10
76 Savage Gdns.....H 4
75 Saville Row ......J 6
75 Savoy Hill.......J 9
75 Savoy Place......J 9
75 Savoy St........J 9
75 Savoy Theatre....J 9
79 Sawyer St........C 13
74 Scala St.........F 6
76 Scarborough St...H 5
80 Scarsdale Rd.....H 4
77 Scarsdale Villas ..E 1
69 School La........F 2
75 School of Arts &
    Crafts.........F 9
77 Science Museum ..D 5
75 Sclater St.......E 5
79 Scoresby St. .....B 12
71 Scotshall La......G 9
75 Scott Ellis Gdns. .D 5
80 Scott Lidgett Cres..D 6

71 Scotts La........D 9
71 Scotts Lodge .....H 11
80 Scovell Rd.......D 1
66 Scratchwood.....A 3
66 Scrubs La........F 4
66 Scrutton St.......E 3
72 Scudders Hill ...D 4
75 Seacoal La......G 12
77 Seagrave Rd......H 1
72 Seal...........H 3
80 Searles Rd.......E 3
80 Sears St.........J 2
75 Sebastian St......D 12
79 Secker St.......B 11
80 Secretan Rd......H 4
78 Sedding St.......F 3
76 Sedlescombe Rd...H 1
75 Sekforde St. ....E 12
76 Selby St. ....E 7
71 Selhurst ....D 7
71 Selhurst Rd.......D 7
79 Sellow Mews.....F 10
74 Selous St. ....A 6
71 Selsdon ....D 7
71 Selsdon Park G.C. .G 7
71 Selsdon Park Rd. .F 8
71 Selsdon Rd.......F 7
71 Selsdon Sta.......F 7
71 Selsdon Wood ....G 8
77 Selwood Place ...G 5
77 Selwood Terrace ..G 5
78 Semley Place.....F 4
75 Senate House ....F 8
73 Senior St.........F 2
75 Serle St.........G 10
77 Serpentine, The ..B 5
77 Serpentine Bridge. .B 5
78 Serpentine Rd.....B 2
80 Setchell Rd. .....E 5
76 Settles Rd........G 7
75 Seven Dials .....H 8
67 Seven Kings ....D 12
67 Seven Sisters Rd...D 7
67 Seven Sisters Sta...C 7
71 Sevenoaks Rd. ..F 12
69 Severnhills Rd....F 4
78 Seville St. ....C 3
73 Sevington St. ....E 2
75 Seward St........D 13
67 Sewardstone Rd. ..A 9
67 Sewardstonebury .A 9
74 Seymour Hall.....G 2
74 Seymour Mews ...G 3
74 Seymour Place ...G 2
74 Seymour St. .....H 2
77 Seymour Walk....H 4
80 Shad Thames.....C 5
76 Shaftesbury Av...H 7
76 Shaftesbury St....C 2
77 Shalcomb St......H 4
80 Shand St.........C 4
79 Sharsted St. .....G 12
71 Shaw La.........H 7
74 Shawfield St. ....G 2
70 Sheen Common...B 2
70 Sheen Rd........B 2
69 Sheerwater Rd....G 2
77 Sheffield Terrace ..B 2
77 Sheldrake Place ..C 1
71 Shelleys Hill ....H 11
75 Shelton St.......H 8
68 Shenfield ....A 6
66 Shenley Rd......A 2
78 Shepherd Market..B 5
78 Shepherd St......B 4
76 Shepherdess Walk .C 2
66 Shepherd's Bush ..G 4
66 Shepherd's Bush Rd.
    G 4
66 Shepherds Hill ...D 6
69 Shepperton.......E 4
69 Shepperton Rd...D 3
74 Sheraton St......H 7
76 Sherborne La.....H 3
71 Sherwood Park Av.
    B 12
71 Ship Hill.......H 10
68 Ship La., Aveley .G 4
72 Ship La., Dartford .D 3
76 Shipton St.......C 6
71 Shire La. ....F 10, F 11
72 Shirehall Rd.. C 2, C 3
73 Shirland Rd......E 2
71 Shirley..........E 8
71 Shirley Park G.C. .E 7
71 Shirley Rd.......E 8
75 Shoe La.........G 11
67 Shooter's Hill....H 11

67 Shooter's Hill G.C.
    H 11
67 Shooter's Hill Rd.H 10
67 Shoreditch.......E 7
76 Shoreditch High St.E 4
76 Shoreditch Park...B 2
72 Shoreham........G 2
80 Shorncliffe Rd...G 5
79 Short St........C 11
71 Shortlands ......D 9
75 Short's Gdns. ...H 8
71 Shortlands G.C. ..D 9
71 Shortlands Rd....D 9
71 Shortlands Sta. ..D 9
74 Shouldham St.....G 2
71 Shrewsbury Mews .G 1
73 Shrewsbury Rd....G 1
73 Shroton St.......F 6
73 Sidcup ....C 11
71 Sidcup Bypass ...C 11
71 Sidcup G.C. .....C 12
70 Sidcup Hill ......C 12
71 Sidcup Rd.......C 11
74 Siddons La.......E 2
79 Sidford Place ....E 10
75 Sidmouth St. ....D 9
70 Sidmouth Wood...B 2
72 Silex St.........C 12
67 Silver St. ....B 7
67 Silver Street Sta...B 7
67 Silver Thorne Rd...A 5
67 Silvertown ......G 10
67 Silvertown Way ..F 10
67 Singer St. ....D 3
71 Single St. ....G 11
65 Sipson ....H 4
65 Sipson Rd........G 4
69 Sixth Cross Rd....C 5
71 Skeet Hill La.....E 12
71 Skibbs La.......E 12
76 Skinner La. ......H 2
75 Skinner St.......D 11
75 Skinners Hall....H 2
72 Slade Green ......A 2
77 Slaidburn St......J 4
71 Slines New Rd...H 8
71 Slines Oak Rd. ..H 8
75 Slingsby Place ...H 8
71 Sloane Avenue...F 1
78 Sloane Court East .G 3
78 Sloane Court West .G 3
78 Sloane Gardens ..F 3
78 Sloane Square....F 3
78 Sloane St........D 2
78 Sloane Terrace ...F 3
65 Slough..........G 1
79 Smith Square ....E 8
79 Smith St........G 2
78 Smith Terrace ...G 2
70 Smitham Sta......G 6
75 Smithfield Central
    Market.........F 12
75 Smithfield St. ...G 12
80 Smyrk's Rd......G 4
67 Snaresbrook ....C 10
67 Snaresbrook Rd...C 9
79 Snow Hill.......G 12
76 Snowden St......F 4
80 Snowfields......C 3
66 Soho...........F 6
74 Soho Square.....G 7
74 Soho St.........G 7
76 Somers Cres.....H 6
73 Somers Mews ...G 2
66 Somers Town ....F 6
77 Somerset House..H 10
80 Sondes St........H 3
66 South Acton Sta...G 3
79 South Africa HouseA 8
74 South Audley St. .J 4
67 South Bermondsey Sta.
    G 8
77 South Bolton Gdns.G 3
74 South Crescent ...F 7
70 South Croydon...F 6
71 South Croydon Sta. F 7
71 South Croxted Rd..C 7
73 South Darenth....D 3
66 South Ealing Rd...G 2
66 South Ealing Sta. .G 2
71 South Eaton Place .E 4
71 South Eden Park .D 8
71 South End, SE9 ..B 11
71 South End, W8....D 2
71 South End, CroydonF 7
68 South End Rd.....E 3
77 South End Row...D 2
66 South Greenford Halt
    F 1

66 South Hampstead Sta.
    E 5
65 South Harrow....D 6
68 South Herts G.C. .A 5
68 South Hornchurch.
    E 3
66 South Kenton Sta. .D 2
79 South Lambeth Rd.H 9
70 South La. ....E 3
70 South Merton Sta. .D 4
75 South Molton La..H 4
74 South Molton St...H 4
71 South Norwood...D 7
71 South Norwood Hill
    D 7
68 South Ockendon ..F 5
65 South Oxhey .....B 5
77 South Parade ....G 5
67 South Park Drive E 12
65 South Place......F 3
78 South St., W1 ....A 4
72 South Street,
    Meopham.....F 6
67 South St., Ponders End
    A 8
68 South St., Romford D 2
76 South Tenter St...H 5
77 South Terrace....E 6
67 South Tottenham Sta.
    D 7
68 South Weald.....B 4
68 South Weald Common
    A 4
73 South Wharf Rd. ..G 5
67 South Woodford Sta.
    C 10
65 Southall.........G 5
65 Southall Green ...G 6
65 Southall La.......H 5
75 Southampton Bldgs.
    G 10
75 Southampton Place G 9
75 Southampton Row.F 9
75 Southampton St. ..J 8
67 Southampton Way H 7
71 Southborough,
    Bromley.......D 10
70 Southborough,
    Surbiton ....E 2
71 Southborough La.D 10
71 Southborough Rd.D 10
67 Southbury Rd.....A 7
70 Southcroft Rd.....C 5
71 Southend......C 9
67 Southend Rd. E18 C 10
68 Southend Rd.,
    Romford.....C 4
75 Southern St. .....B 9
75 Southfields Sta....B 4
72 Southfleet ......C 5
66 Southgate ....A 6
67 Southwark ....G 7
66 Southwark Bridge ..J 2
79 Southwark Bridge Rd.
    C 13
80 Southwark Cathedral
    B 2
67 Southwark Park...B 8
80 Southwark Park Rd.
    E 6
79 Southwark St....B 13
77 Southwell Gdns...E 3
73 Southwick Mews ..G 5
73 Southwick Place ..H 6
73 Southwick St.....G 6
71 Spa Hill.........C 7
66 Spa Rd..........E 5
66 Spaniards Rd.....D 5
65 Sparrowsherne...A 6
77 Spear Mews .....F 1
77 Spelman St.......F 6
75 Spencer St.......D 12
76 Spenser St.......D 6
69 Spinney Hill .....F 2
68 Spital La........B 5
76 Spital Square.....F 4
76 Spital St.........E 6
67 Spitalfields.......F 8
76 Spitalfields Market.F 5
76 Sprimont Place...F 2
79 Spring Gdns. ....B 8
70 Spring Grove ....A 1
73 Spring St. ....H 5
67 Springfield Park...D 8
76 Springfield Rd....E 2
71 Spur Rd.........E 12
80 Spurgeon St......D 2

69 Squires Bridge Rd. D 3
68 Squirrels Heath ...C 3
68 Squirrels Heath Rd.C 4
76 Squirries St......D 6
75 Stacey St. ....H 8
76 Staff St.........D 3
78 Stafford Place....D 6
73 Stafford Rd. NW6.C 1
70 Stafford Rd.,
    Beddington......F 6
68 Stafford St. ......A 5
77 Stafford Terrace..D 1
66 Stag La.........C 3
78 Stag Place ....D 6
69 Staines..........C 2
69 Staines Bridge ...C 2
69 Staines Central Sta.C 2
69 Staines La........D 2
69 Staines Reservoirs .C 2
69 Staines Rd., Hounslow
    B 5
69 Staines Rd., Laleham
    D 2
69 Staines Road East .D 5
69 Staines Rd., West..C 4
77 Stamford Bridge
    Stadium........J 2
66 Stamford Brook Sta.
    G 3
67 Stamford Hill....D 7
67 Stamford Hill Sta..D 7
79 Stamford St......B 11
77 Stanford Rd. .....D 3
77 Stanhope Gdns....E 4
78 Stanhope Gate....B 4
77 Stanhope Mews East
    E 4
77 Stanhope Mews West
    E 4
74 Stanhope Place ..H 2
74 Stanhope Place Gate
    H 2
78 Stanhope Row....B 4
74 Stanhope St......D 6
73 Stanhope Terrace .H 5
70 Stanley Park Rd...F 5
70 Stanley Rd.......C 1
75 Stanley Passage ...C 8
66 Stanmore........B 2
66 Stanmore Hill....B 1
66 Stanmore Sta.....B 2
79 Stannary St......G 11
71 Stanstead Rd. ....B 8
72 Stansted.........F 5
76 Stanway St.......C 4
66 Stanwell ....B 3
69 Stanwell New Rd...C 2
69 Stanwell Rd., Staines
    C 3
69 Stanwell Rd.,
    W. Bedfont...B 4
69 Stanwellmoor ...B 2
80 Staple St. ....D 3
68 Stapleford Abbotts A 2
66 Staples Corner....D 4
73 Star St..........G 5
70 Star & Garter Home
    B 2
72 Star Hill Rd......H 1
74 Starcross St......D 6
68 Station La........D 3
67 Station Rd.......A 9
69 Station Rd.,
    Addlestone.....E 3
66 Station Rd., Harrow
    C 1
65 Station Rd., Hayes G 4
66 Station Rd., New
    Barnet.......A 5
71 Station Rd., Orpington
    E 11
71 Station Rd., Sidcup
    C 11
75 Stationers' Hall ..G 12
80 Stead St.........F 2
79 Steedman St.....F 13
69 Steels La........G 6
74 Stephen St. ......G 7
74 Stephenson Way ..D 6
67 Stepney.........F 8
67 Stepney East Sta...F 8
77 Sterling St.......D 6
80 Sterry St........C 2
76 Steward St.......F 4
77 Stewart's Grove..F 5
68 Stifford ....G 6
68 Stifford Rd.......G 4
78 Stillington St......E 6

76 Stock Exchange...G 3
65 Stockley Rd......G 4
70 Stockwell Rd.....A 6
69 Stoke D'Abernon .H 5
67 Stoke Newington ..D 7
67 Stoke Newington Rd.
    E 7
67 Stoke Newington Sta.
    D 7
69 Stoke Rd........G 5
72 Stone..........B 4
75 Stone Buildings ..G 10
72 Stone Crossing Halt
    B 4
66 Stone Grove......B 2
72 Stone Marshes ...A 3
66 Stonebridge Park Sta.
    E 2
70 Stonecot Hill.....E 4
69 Stonehill Rd......F 1
71 Stonehouse La.,
    Orpington......F 12
69 Stonehouse La.,
    W. Thurrock ...G 4
70 Stoneleigh Sta....F 3
80 Stones End St....D 1
76 Stoney La. ......G 4
80 Stoney St........B 2
72 Stony Corner ....D 6
79 Stopford Rd. ....G 13
70 Store St.........F 7
79 Storey's Gate ....D 8
80 Storks Rd........D 7
67 Stourcliffe St.....G 2
68 Straight Rd.......C 3
75 Strand ....J 9
79 Strand Theatre...H 9
67 Stratford ....E 9
67 Stratford New Town
    E 9
74 Stratford Place...H 4
77 Stratford Rd. ....E 1
67 Stratford Sta. ....E 9
73 Strathearn Place ..H 5
80 Strathnairn St. ...F 7
78 Stratton St. ......B 5
70 Strawberry Hill G.C.
    C 1
70 Strawberry Hill Sta.
    C 1
70 Strawberry Vale...C 1
66 Streatfield Rd. ...C 2
70 Streatham ....C 6
70 Streatham
    Common.........C 6
70 Streatham Common
    North.........C 6
70 Streatham Common
    Sta............C 5
70 Streatham High Rd.
    C 6
70 Streatham Hill ...B 6
70 Streatham Hill Sta. C 6
70 Streatham Rd.....D 5
70 Streatham Sta. ...C 6
75 Streatham St......G 8
70 Streatham Vale ..C 6
70 Street, The ......H 2
66 Stroud Green Rd..D 7
69 Stroude.........D 1
78 Strutton Ground ..D 7
76 Strype St.........G 5
73 Stuart Rd........D 1
68 Stubbers La......E 4
75 Stukeley St.......G 9
79 Sturgeon Rd.....G 13
76 Stutfield St.......H 7
70 Sudbrook Park....C 2
69 Sudbury G.C.....E 2
66 Sudbury Hill Sta...E 1
66 Sudbury Hill &
    Harrow Sta......E 1
66 Sudbury Town Sta. E 2
66 Sudbury & Harrow
    Rd. Sta........E 2
75 Sudeley St.......C 12
79 Sudrey St........C 13
76 Suffolk La.......J 2
76 Suffolk Rd.......A 6
80 Suffolk St. SE1...C 1
79 Suffolk St. SW1 ..H 7
80 Sultan St.........J 1
70 Summer Rd......D 1
66 Summers La......B 5
77 Sumner Place ....F 5
80 Sumner Rd.......J 5
79 Sumner St.......B 13
76 Sun St..........F 3
69 Sunbury ....D 4

69 Sunbury Sta....D 4
73 Sunderland Ter....G 2
71 Sundridge Hill Rd. H 12
71 Sundridge Park G.C. C 10
71 Sundridge Park Sta. D 9
72 Sundridge Rd....H 1
68 Sunnings La....E 4
70 Surbiton....E 2
70 Surbiton G.C....E 1
73 Surrendale Place ..E 2
80 Surrey Canal ...H 4
79 Surrey Row ....C 12
80 Surrey Square....F 4
75 Surrey St....H 10
80 Surrey Terrace ...F 4
73 Sussex Gardens ..H 5
73 Sussex Place....H 5
73 Sussex Square ...H 5
78 Sussex St....H 5
73 Sutherland Avenue E 2
73 Sutherland Place ..G 1
80 Sutherland Square.G 1
78 Sutherland St....G 5
80 Sutherland Walk G 2
70 Sutton...........F 4
72 Sutton-at-Hone ..D 3
72 Sutton at Hone Rd. C 2
68 Sutton Avenue...D 3
70 Sutton Common Rd. E 4
70 Sutton Common Sta. E 4
69 Sutton La., Hounslow A 5
70 Sutton La., Sutton G 4
74 Sutton Row ......G 7
70 Sutton Sta......F 4
65 Swakeleys ......E 4
74 Swallow St.......J 6
80 Swan Mead......E 4
80 Swan St........D 2
78 Swan Walk......H 2
72 Swancombe Marshes A 5
76 Swanfield St......D 5
72 Swanley.........D 2
72 Swanley La......D 2
72 Swanley Village ..D 2
72 Swanley Village Rd. D 2
72 Swanscombe.....B 5
72 Swanscombe Halt .B 5
72 Swanscombe Park .C 5
80 Sweeney Crescent .D 5
75 Swinton St.......D 9
66 Swiss Cottage Sta. .E 5
76 Swithin's Hall ...H 2
72 Sydenham.......C 7
71 Sydenham Hill Sta. C 7
71 Sydenham Rd.....C 8
71 Sydenham Sta.....C 8
77 Sydney Place.....F 5
77 Sydney St........G 6
78 Symons St.......F 3
70 Syon La.........A 1
70 Syon Lane Sta....A 1
70 Syon House ......A 1
80 Tabard St.......D 2
76 Tabernacle St......E 3
78 Tachbrook St......F 6
73 Talbot Rd.......G 1
73 Talbot Square ....H 5
80 Talbot Yard......B 2
75 Tallis St........H 11
77 Tamworth St......H 1
68 Tank La.........G 4
80 Tanner St........C 4
76 Taplow St. ....C 2
79 Tarver Rd.......G 13
79 Tate Gallery.....F 8
71 Tatsfield ....H 10
71 Tatsfield La......H 10
70 Tattenham Corner Rd. H 3
70 Tattenham Corner Sta. H 3
70 Tattenham Way...H 4
80 Tatum St........F 3
74 Taunton Place ...E 2
75 Tavistock Place...E 8
75 Tavistock Square .E 8
75 Tavistock St......H 9
74 Taviton St.......E 7
76 Teale St........B 7
70 Teddington ......C 1
78 Tedworth Square.G 2

75 Temple, The....H 11
75 Temple Avenue ..H 11
75 Temple Bar......H 11
75 Temple Gardens .H 11
75 Temple Place ....H 10
70 Temple Rd.......G 2
77 Templeton Place...F 1
80 Tennis St........C 2
65 Tentelow La. ....G 6
78 Terminus Place....E 5
69 Terrace Rd.......E 5
77 Thackeray St.....D 2
70 Thames Ditton...E 1
70 Thames Ditton Sta. E 1
75 Thames Water Authority .....D 11
68 Thamesmead .....G 1
75 Thavies Inn ....G 11
74 Thayer St........G 4
75 Theatre Royal ...H 9
79 Theed St........B 11
66 Theobald St......A 2
75 Theobald's Rd....F 9
78 Thirleby Rd......E 6
77 Thistlecroft.....F 5
79 Thomas Doyle St. D 12
80 Thomas More St. .A 6
80 Thorburn Square .F 6
76 Thoresby St......C 1
68 Thorndon Park ...C 6
68 Thorndon Park G.C. C 6
65 Thorney La. .....F 2
79 Thorney St.......E 8
73 Thorngate Rd....E 2
70 Thornton Heath ..D 6
74 Thornton Place ...F 2
70 Thornton Rd......E 6
69 Thorpe ....D 2
69 Thorpe Rd., Chertsey D 2
69 Thorpe Rd., Staines A 2
80 Thrale St........B 2
76 Thrawl St........G 5
76 Threadneedle St...H 3
74 Three Kings Yard .H 4
80 Three Oak La.....C 5
76 Throgmorton Avenue G 3
76 Throgmorton St. ..G 3
79 Thrush St.......G 13
80 Thurland Rd......D 6
77 Thurloe Place ....E 5
77 Thurloe Square...E 5
77 Thurloe St.......E 5
80 Thurlow St. ......G 3
76 Thurtle Rd.......B 5
76 Tibbetts Corner ..B 4
78 Tilney St........B 4
79 Tinworth St......F 9
78 Tisdall Place.....F 3
73 Titchborne Row ..H 6
74 Titchfield Rd.....B 2
78 Tite St.........H 2
79 Tiverton St. ....D 13
76 Token House Yard G 3
70 Tollington Park Rd.D 6
74 Tolmers Square ...D 6
65 Tolpits La. ......A 4
70 Tolworth ....E 2
70 Tolworth Rise ...E 2
70 Tolworth Rd......E 2
67 Tomswood Hill ..C 11
75 Tonbridge St.....D 8
80 Tooley St........B 4
70 Tooting Bec Rd...C 5
70 Tooting Bec Sta. ..C 5
70 Tooting Common ..C 5
70 Tooting Graveney .C 5
70 Tooting Graveney Common.....C 5
70 Tooting High St..C 5
70 Tooting Sta......C 5
79 Topaz St........E 10
75 Topham St. ......E 11
77 Tor Gdns.........C 1
73 Torquay St.......G 1
74 Torrens St. ......C 12
74 Torrington Place ..F 7
67 Tottenham ......C 7
74 Tottenham Court Rd. F 6
67 Tottenham Hale...C 7
67 Tottenham Hale Sta. C 8
67 Tottenham Hotspur F.C..........C 8
66 Tottenham La.....D 6

74 Tottenham St......F 6
66 Totteridge ......A 4
66 Totteridge La.....B 4
66 Totteridge & Whetstone Sta..B 5
79 Toulmin St.......C 13
76 Tower, The......J 5
80 Tower Bridge ....B 5
76 Tower Bridge Approach......J 5
80 Tower Bridge Rd. .D 4
67 Tower Hamlets....F 8
76 Tower Hill.......J 5
75 Tower St........H 8
69 Town La. ....B 3
71 Townley Rd......B 12
80 Townsend St......F 3
73 Townshend Rd....B 6
76 Toynbee St.......G 5
79 Trade, Dept. of ..D 7
80 Trafalgar Avenue .H 5
67 Trafalgar Rd......G 9
79 Trafalgar Square ..A 8
80 Trafalgar St......G 3
73 Transept St......F 6
80 Tranton Rd......D 7
67 Traps Hill.......A 11
70 Traps La........D 3
79 Treasury ....C 8
75 Treaty St........B 9
77 Trebovir Rd......F 1
77 Tregunter Rd.....G 3
73 Tresham Crescent .D 6
75 Treveris St.......B 12
78 Trevor Place ....D 1
78 Trevor Square ...D 2
78 Trevor St........C 2
79 Trigon Rd.......J 10
80 Trinity Church Square D 2
76 Trinity House ...H 5
70 Trinity Rd. .....B 5
76 Trinity Square....J 4
80 Trinity St. ......D 2
80 Trothy Rd.......F 7
74 Triton Square.....E 5
72 Trottiscliffe.....G 6
78 Tryon St........F 2
71 Tubbenden La.....E 11
70 Tudor Drive .....E 4
74 Tudor Place .....G 7
69 Tudor Rd........C 6
75 Tudor St........H 11
66 Tufnell Park Rd...E 6
75 Tufton St........E 8
70 Tulse Hill ....B 6
70 Tulse Hill Sta. ...C 6
76 Turin St........D 6
78 Turk's Row .....G 3
66 Turnham Green Sta. G 3
75 Turnmill St......F 12
67 Turnpike La. ....C 7
69 Twickenham .....B 6
70 Twickenham BridgeB 1
70 Twickenham Park .B 1
70 Twickenham Rd., Teddington .....C 1
69 Twickenham Rd., Twickenham....C 5
74 Tyburn Way.....H 2
80 Tyers Gate ......C 4
79 Tyers St.........G 9
75 Tyers Terrace ...G 10
75 Tysoe St........D 11
80 Udall St.........F 6
76 Ufford St. ......C 12
76 Underwood Rd....E 6
76 Underwood St.....C 2
76 Union Square......B 1
79 Union St. ......B 12
76 Union Walk......C 4
74 University College .E 7
74 University College Hospital ......E 6
75 University of London F 8
74 University St......E 6
80 Unwin Close......H 6
73 Upbrook Mews...H 4
68 Upminster........D 4
68 Upminster Bridge Sta. D 4
68 Upminster G.C....D 4
68 Upminster Rd., Rainham......F 3
68 Upminster Rd., Upminster....D 4
67 Upney ....E 12

67 Upney La. ......E 11
67 Upney Sta. .....E 12
78 Upper Belgrave St..D 4
74 Upper Berkeley St..G 2
77 Upper Cheyne RowH 6
67 Upper Clapton...D 8
67 Upper Clapton Rd.D 8
67 Upper Edmonton .B 8
71 Upper Elmer End..E 8
74 Upper Grosvenor St. J 3
79 Upper Ground...A 11
69 Upper Halliford Halt D 4
69 Upper Halliford Rd. D 4
74 Upper Harley St...E 4
66 Upper Holloway Sta. D 6
79 Upper Marsh....D 10
74 Upper Montagu St. F 2
70 Upper Norwood ..D 6
77 Upper Phillimore Gdns..........C 1
68 Upper Rainham Rd. D 3
70 Upper Richmond Rd., East Sheen.....B 2
70 Upper Richmond Rd., Putney........B 3
75 Upper St. Martins La. H 8
75 Upper St. ......D 8
69 Upper Sunbury Rd.D 5
71 Upper Sydenham..C 7
76 Upper Thames St..H 2
70 Upper Tooting Rd.C 5
67 Upper Walthamstow C 9
71 Upper Warlingham Sta..........H 7
71 Upper Wickam La. A 12
74 Upper Wimpole St. F 4
67 Upton ....E 10
67 Upton La........E 10
67 Upton Park Sta...E 10
71 Upton Rd........B 12
80 Urlwin St........H 1
65 Uxbridge ....E 3
66 Uxbridge Rd., Acton G 3
69 Uxbridge Rd., Feltham C 5
65 Uxbridge Rd., Harefield.......D 3
65 Uxbridge Rd., Hatch End .....C 6
66 Uxbridge Rd., Hanwell G 1
65 Uxbridge Rd., Hayes End......F 4
65 Uxbridge Rd., Maple Cross...B 2
65 Uxbridge Rd., Pinner C 5
65 Uxbridge Rd., Southall.......F 5
65 Uxbridge Rd., Stanmore......B 1
77 Uxbridge St.......B 2
77 Vale, The, SW3...H 5
66 Vale, The, W3....G 3
73 Vale Close ....D 3
68 Valence Avenue...D 1
79 Valentine Place ..C 11
67 Valentines Park ..D 11
74 Vallance Rd......E 7
78 Vandon St........D 6
76 Vandy St........E 3
76 Vanston Place....J 1
74 Varndell St......D 6
80 Vauban St. ......E 5
79 Vaudeville Theatre.J 9
79 Vauxhall Bridge ..G 7
78 Vauxhall Bridge Rd. E 6
79 Vauxhall Grove...H 9
79 Vauxhall Park....H 9
79 Vauxhall Sta.....G 8
79 Vauxhall St......G 10
79 Vauxhall Walk...G 9
73 Venables St......H 5
71 Verdant La. .....B 9
74 Vere St.........H 4
74 Vernon Rise .....C 10
75 Verulam St. .....F 11
71 Vesta Rd........A 8

67 Vestry St. ....C 3
67 Vicarage Farm Rd. A 5
77 Vicarage Gate ...B 2
67 Vicarage La., Chigwell .....B 11
68 Vicarage La., South Weald ....B 4
69 Vicarage Rd......C 4
78 Victoria Coach Sta. F 4
67 Victoria Dock Rd. F 10
70 Victoria Drive ...B 4
79 Victoria Embankment J 3
79 Victoria Embankment B 9
79 Victoria Embankment Gdns..........A 9
73 Victoria Gate ....J 5
73 Victoria Grove...D 3
78 Victoria Hospital H 3
78 Victoria Palace Theatre D 5
67 Victoria Park ....E 8
67 Victoria Park Rd...E 8
66 Victoria Rd. NW10 F 3
77 Victoria Rd. W8...D 3
68 Victoria Rd., Romford D 2
65 Victoria Rd., Ruislip D 5
78 Victoria Square...D 5
80 Victory Place ....E 2
80 Victory Square...J 3
78 Victoria Sta......E 5
78 Victoria St........D 6
77 Victoria & Albert Museum ....E 5
74 Vigo St..........J 6
80 Villa St.........G 3
70 Village Way, Enfield A 7
65 Village Way, Harrow D 5
79 Villiers St. ......A 9
76 Vince St.........D 3
79 Vincent Square...E 7
79 Vincent St.......F 7
75 Vincent Terrace ..B 12
75 Vine Hill ......E 11
80 Vine La.........B 4
73 Violet Hill......C 4
79 Virgil St.........D 10
79 Victoria Tower Gardens......D 9
76 Virginia Rd.......D 5
79 Virginia Water Sta. D 1
80 Wadding St. .....F 2
70 Waddington ......H 6
70 Waddon..........E 6
70 Waddon Marsh Halt E 6
67 Wadham Rd......C 9
80 Waite St........H 5
75 Wakefield St.....D 9
75 Wakley St. ......C 12
76 Walbrook ....H 2
79 Walcot Square ...E 11
70 Waldegrave Rd....C 1
71 Waldram Park Rd. B 8
77 Walham Grove...J 1
67 Wallend.........E 11
67 Wallace Collection. G 3
77 Wallgrave Rd.....F 2
77 Wallington ......F 5
79 Walnut Tree Walk E 11
78 Walpole St.......F 2
73 Walterton Rd.....D 1
67 Waltham Forest...C 9
67 Walthamstow.....D 8
67 Walthamstow Avenue C 9
67 Walthamstow Central Sta..........C 9
67 Walthamstow Marshes ....D 8
67 Walthamstow Queen's Rd. Sta........C 9
69 Walton Bridge ...E 4
70 Walton Downs ...H 3
78 Walton Place ....D 2
69 Walton Rd. .....D 5
78 Walton St.......E 1
69 Walton-upon-Thames E 5
67 Walworth.......G 7
80 Walworth Place...G 2
80 Walworth Rd.....F 1
80 Wansey St.......F 1
67 Wanstead ....D 10
67 Wanstead Flats...D 10

67 Wanstead G.C. ..D 10
67 Wanstead Park...E 10
67 Wanstead Park Sta.E 10
67 Wanstead Sta. ...D 10
70 Wandsworth......B 4
70 Wandsworth BridgeA 4
70 Wandsworth Bridge Rd...........A 4
70 Wandsworth Common B 5
70 Wandsworth Common Sta...........B 5
70 Wandsworth PrisonB 5
79 Wandsworth Rd....A 8
70 Wandsworth Rd. Sta. A 6
70 Wandsworth Town Sta...........B 4
67 Wapping.........G 8
80 Wapping High St. .B 6
74 Wardour St......H 7
70 Warham Rd......F 6
78 Warham St.......J 3
68 Warley Barracks ..B 5
68 Warley Rd.   C 4, C 5
71 Warlingham......A 7
75 Warner St. ......E 11
76 Warner Place ....C 6
68 Warren La., W. Thurrock ...G 5
69 Warren La., Woking H 2
71 Warren Rd. F 11, F 12
74 Warren St. ......E 6
73 Warrington Cres...E 3
73 Warwick Avenue ..E 3
73 Warwick Crescent .F 3
73 Warwick Estate...F 2
79 Warwick House St. B 7
75 Warwick La. EC4.G 12
68 Warwick La., Rainham F 4
73 Warwick Place....F 3
67 Warwick Res.....D 8
77 Warwick Rd......F 1
78 Warwick Row ...D 5
78 Warwick Square..F 6
74 Warwick St.......J 6
78 Warwick Way....F 5
71 Wash Pond Rd....H 9
67 Water La........D 12
67 Waterden Rd......E 9
79 Watergate ....H 12
70 Waterhouse La....H 4
75 Waterloo Bridge .J 10
75 Waterloo Pier ...J 10
78 Waterloo Place...B 7
70 Waterloo Rd......C 11
79 Waterloo Sta. ...C 10
66 Waterlow Park ...D 6
76 Waterson St......D 4
69 Watersplash Rd...D 3
65 Watford.........A 5
66 Watford Bypass ..A 2
65 Watford F.C......A 5
65 Watford Heath...A 5
65 Watford High St. Sta. A 5
66 Watford Rd., Harrow E 1
65 Watford Rd., Rickmansworth .A 3
66 Watford Way, NW4 C 4
66 Watford Way, Edgware ......A 5
65 Watford West Sta. A 4
66 Watling Avenue...C 3
76 Watling St. EC4..H 1
72 Watling St., Swanscombe...C 4
72 Watling St.......B 1
71 Watts La. ....D 11
73 Waverley Place...B 4
78 Waverton St. ....E 6
70 Waxwell Terrace .D 10
68 Weald Park ......A 4
66 Wealdstone.......C 1
78 Weaver St. ......E 6
80 Weaver's La. .....B 4
80 Webb St.........B 4
79 Webber Row ....D 11
79 Webber St.......C 12
74 Welbeck St. ......G 4
74 Welbeck Way....G 4
74 Weigh House St...H 4
75 Weirs Passage ...D 8
69 Well Hill ....F 1
76 Wellclose Square..H 6

80 Weller St. . . . . C 1
76 Wellesey Terrace . . C 2
71 Welling . . . . A 12
71 Welling Way . . . . A 11
78 Wellington Arch . . C 4
78 Wellington Barracks
    D 6
73 Wellington Pl. . . . . C 5
73 Wellington Rd. . . . . C 5
69 Wellington Rd. South
    B 5
76 Wellington Row . . D 6
78 Wellington Square . G 2
75 Wellington St. . . . . H 9
74 Wells Mews . . . . . . G 6
74 Wells Rise . . . . B 2
74 Wells St. . . . . G 6
80 Wells Way . . . . . . H 3
80 Welsford St. . . . . . . F 6
66 Wembley . . . . E 2
66 Wembley Central Sta.
    E 2
66 Wembley Hill Sta. . E 2
66 Wembley Stadium . E 2
76 Wenlock Basin . . . . C 1
76 Wenlock Rd. . . . . . C 1
76 Wenlock St. . . . . . . C 2
68 Wennington . . . . F 3
68 Wennington Marshes
    G 3
68 Wennington Rd. . . F 3
76 Wentworth St. . . . . G 5
74 Werrington St. . . . . C 7
76 Wesley's Chapel . . E 3
66 West Acton Sta. . . F 2
69 West Bedfont . . . . B 3
69 West Byfleet . . . . . G 2
69 West Byfleet G.C. . . G 2
69 West Byfleet Sta. . . G 2
75 West Central St. . . G 8
71 West Common Rd. E 9
77 West Cromwell Rd. F 1
71 West Croydon Sta.
    E 7
65 West Drayton . . . . G 3
65 West Drayton Rd. F 4
65 West Drayton &
    Yiewsley Sta. . . G 3
71 West Dulwich Sta. . C 7
66 West Ealing Sta. . . F 1
78 West Eaton Place . E 3
69 West End, Esher . . F 6
65 West End, Southall F 5
66 West End La. . . . . . . G 6
65 West End Rd. D 4, E 5
70 West Ewell . . . . . . F 3
67 West Ferry Rd. . . . G 9
66 West Finchley Sta. . B 5
67 West Green . . . . C 7
67 West Green Rd. . . . C 7
69 West Grove . . . . F 5
78 West Halkin St. . . . D 3
67 West Ham . . . . F 10
67 West Ham F.C. . E 10
67 West Ham Park . . E 10
67 West Ham Stadium
    F 10
66 West Hampstead Sta.
    E 5
65 West Harrow . . . . . D 6
66 West Heath, NW3 . D 5
68 West Heath, SE2. . H 1
72 West Hill . . . . B 2
68 West Horndon Sta. D 6
67 West India Docks . G 9
71 West Kent G.C. . . G 11
77 West Mall . . . . A 1

66 West Middlesex G.C.
    F 1
69 West Molesey . . . . D 6
71 West Norwood . . . . C 7
70 West Norwood Sta. C 6
70 West Park Hospital G 2
78 West Rd. . . . . G 3
65 West Ruislip Sta. . . D 4
75 West Smithfield . . F 12
79 West Square . . . . . E 12
75 West St. . . . . H 8
70 West Sutton Sta. . . F 4
76 West Tenter St. . . . H 5
68 West Thurrock . . H 5
68 West Thurrock
    Marshes . . . . . . H 5
71 West Wickham . . . E 9
71 West Wood La. . . B 11
73 Westbourne Bridge G 3
73 Westbourne Cres. H 4
73 Westbourne Gdns. . G 2
73 Westbourne Gate . . J 5
73 Westbourne Grove H 2
73 Westbourne Park Rd.
    G 1
66 Westbourne Park Sta.
    F 4
73 Westbourne Park
    Villas . . . . G 2
73 Westbourne St. . . H 5
73 Westbourne Ter. . . G 4
73 Westbourne Ter. Rd.
    F 3
74 Westbury Hotel . . . J 5
67 Westcombe Park Sta.
    H 10
79 Westcott Rd. . . . H 12
69 Westend La. . . . . . . F 5
71 Westerham Rd. . . F 10
66 Western Avenue,
    Greenford . . . . . F 1
65 Western Avenue,
    Uxbridge . . . . . E 4
77 Western Hospital . H 2
70 Western Rd., Mitcham
    D 5
65 Western Rd., Southall
    G 5
77 Westgate Terrace . H 3
71 Westhall Rd. . . . . . H 7
71 Westhorne Av. . . B 10
76 Westland Place . . . D 2
70 Westmead Rd. . . . F 5
66 Westminster . . . . . . G 6
79 Westminster Abbey D 8
79 Westminster Bridge C 9
79 Westminster Bridge
    Rd. . . . . D 11
78 Westminster Chapel
    D 6
79 Westminster Hall . D 8
79 Westminster Hospital
    E 8
79 Westminster Pier . . C 9
78 Westminster R.C.
    Cathedral . . . . . E 6
79 Westminster School D 8
78 Westminster Theatre
    D 5
78 Westmoreland Place
    G 5
80 Westmoreland Rd.
    SE17 . . . . H 2
80 Westmoreland Rd.
    SE17 . . . . G 4
71 Westmoreland Rd.,
    Bromley . . . . . . D 9

74 Westmoreland St. . . F 4
78 Westmoreland Ter. G 5
70 Weston Green . . . . E 1
70 Weston Green Rd. . E 1
75 Weston Rise . . . . . C 10
80 Weston St. . . . . C 3
73 Westway . . . . F 3
72 Westwood . . . . C 5
71 Westwood Hill . . . . C 7
77 Wetherby Gdns. . . F 3
77 Wetherby Place . . . F 4
69 Weybridge . . . . E 4
69 Weybridge Rd. . . . . E 3
69 Weybridge Sta. . . . . F 3
74 Weymouth Mews. . F 5
76 Weymouth Ter. . . . B 5
74 Weymouth St. . . . . F 4
68 Whalebone La. . . . . C 1
68 Whalebone La. South
    D 1
75 Wharf Rd. . . . . . . C 13
75 Wharfdale Rd. . . . . B 9
75 Wharton St. . . . . . D 10
66 Wheler St. . . . . E 5
66 Whetstone . . . . B 5
75 Whetstone Park . . G 10
75 Whidborne St. . . . . D 9
67 Whipps Cross . . . . D 9
75 Whiskin St. . . . . . D 12
75 Whiston Rd. . . . . . . B 5
76 Whitby St. . . . . E 5
66 Whitchurch La. . . . C 2
76 White Church Lane G 6
66 White City Stadium F 4
75 White Conduit St. B 11
79 White Hall Place . . B 8
67 White Hart La. N17 C 7
68 White Hart La.,
    Collier Row . . . C 2
67 White Hart Lane Sta.
    C 7
80 White Hart Yard . . C 4
65 White Hill . . . . B 4
73 White Hill La. . . . . F 6
71 White Horse Hill . C 10
78 White Horse St. . . . B 5
76 White Kennett St. . G 4
75 White Lion Hill . . H 13
70 White Lodge . . . . . . B 2
67 Whitechapel . . . . . . F 8
76 Whitechapel High St.
    G 5
76 Whitechapel Rd. . . G 6
76 Whitecross St. . . . . E 2
71 Whitefoot La. . . . . . C 9
75 Whitefriars St. . . . H 11
79 Whitehall . . . . B 8
79 Whitehall Court. . . B 8
79 Whitehall Gdns. . . . B 8
67 Whitehall Rd. . . . . B 9
79 Whitehall Theatre . B 8
79 Whitehart St. . . . . G 11
78 Whiteheads Grove . F 1
71 Whitehorse Rd. . . . D 7
74 Whiteley Village. . F 4
80 White's Grounds . . C 4
76 White's Row . . . . . F 5
74 Whitfield Place . . . E 6
74 Whitfield St. . . . . . F 6
79 Whitgift St. . . . . . . F 9
76 Whitmore Rd. . . . . A 3
78 Whittaker St. . . . . F 3
79 Whittlesey St. . . . B 11
69 Whitton . . . . B 6
65 Whitton Avenue . . E 6
69 Whitton Rd. . . . . . . B 6

71 Whyteleafe . . . . H 7
71 Whyteleafe Rd. . . . H 7
71 Whyteleafe South Sta.
    H 7
67 Wick Rd. . . . . E 8
67 Wickham La. . . . . H 12
67 Wickham Rd. SE4 . A 8
71 Wickham Rd.,
    Beckenham . . . . D 8
71 Wickham Rd.,
    Croydon . . . . . . E 8
79 Wickham St. . . . G 10
71 Wickham Way . . . D 9
75 Wicklow St. . . . . . . C 9
74 Widecroft St. . . . . . F 4
73 Widley Rd. . . . . . . D 1
71 Widmore Rd. . . . D 10
77 Wightman Rd. . . . . D 7
74 Wigmore Hall . . . . G 4
74 Wigmore Place . . . G 5
74 Wigmore St. . . . . . G 4
69 Wisley . . . . G 3
69 Wisley Common . . H 3
69 Wisley La. . . . . G 3
69 Woburn Hill . . . . . E 3
75 Woburn Place . . . . E 8
75 Woburn Square . . . E 8
69 Woking . . . . H 1
71 Woldingham Rd. . H 8
57 Wolseley St. . . . . . C 6
65 Wolsey Way . . . . . B 4
65 Wood End, Hayes . F 4
65 Wood End, S. Harrow
    E 6
67 Wood Grange Park
    Sta. . . . . E 10
66 Wood Green . . . . . . C 6
66 Wood Green Sta. . . C 6
66 Wood La. W12 . . F 4
68 Wood La., Becontree
    E 1
68 Wood La., Dagenham
    E 3
66 Wood La., Stanmore
    B 2
67 Wood St. E17 . . . . C 9
76 Wood St. EC2 . . . G 2
66 Wood St., Barnet . A 4
67 Wood Street Sta. . . C 9
75 Woodbridge St. . . E 12
73 Woodchester Sq. . . F 2
70 Woodcote Grove Rd.
    G 6
70 Woodcote La. . . . . G 5
70 Woodcote Park G.C.
    G 5
70 Woodcote Park G.C.
    (R.A.C.) . . . . . . H 3
70 Woodcote Rd. . . . . F 5
78 Woodfall St. . . . . . G 2
70 Woodfield La. . . . . H 2
67 Woodford . . . . . . C 10
67 Woodford Bridge . B 10
67 Woodford Green . B 10
67 Woodford New Rd. C 9
67 Woodford Wells . B 10
69 Woodham . . . . G 2
69 Woodham La. . . . . G 2
69 Woodland Park . . H 6
72 Woodlands . . . . G 3
69 Woodlands La. . . H 6
70 Woodmansterne . . G 5
70 Woodmansterne La.
    G 5
70 Woodmansterne Rd.
    F 5
70 Woodmansterne Sta.
    G 5
65 Woodridings . . . . . . C 6

70 Wimbledon Sta. . . . C 4
76 Wimbolt St. . . . . . . C 6
76 Wimbourne St. . . . . B 2
71 Woodside . . . . E 7
66 Woodside Avenue . C 5
66 Woodside Park Sta. B 5
70 Woodstock La. . . . . E 1
74 Woodstock St. . . . . H 4
69 Woodthorpe Rd. . . C 3
80 Wooler St. . . . . C 3
67 Woolwich . . . . G 11
67 Woolwich Arsenal Sta.
    G 11
67 Woolwich Church St.
    G 11
67 Woolwich Common
    H 10
67 Woolwich Dockyard
    Sta. . . . . G 11
67 Woolwich Reach . G 11
67 Woolwich Rd. SE7
68 Woolwich Rd.,
    W. Heath . . . . G 1
79 Wootton St. . . . . B 11
70 Worcester Park . . . E 3
70 Worcester Park Sta. E 3
79 Worgan St. . . . . . . G 9
66 Wormwood Scrubs . F 3
76 Wormwood St. . . . G 4
73 Woronzow Rd. . . . A 5
70 Worple Rd. SW19 . D 3
69 Worple Rd., Staines
    D 2
76 Worship St. . . . . . . E 3
69 Wraysbury . . . . B 1
69 Wraysbury Res. . . B 2
75 Wren St. . . . . E 10
80 Wright's Buildings . E 4
77 Wright's La. . . . . . . D 2
72 Wrotham . . . . H 5
72 Wrotham Heath . . H 6
72 Wrotham Heath G.C.
    H 6
72 Wrotham Hill Park G 5
72 Wrotham Rd. C 6, D 6
70 Wrythe, The . . . . . E 5
70 Wrythe La. . . . . . . E 5
74 Wybert St. . . . . D 5
75 Wyclif St. . . . . . . D 12
66 Wyke Green G.C. . G 1
73 Wymering Rd. . . . . D 2
75 Wynatt St. . . . . . D 12
74 Wyndham Place . . F 2
74 Wyndham St. . . . . . F 2
75 Wyndham's Theatre
    J 8
75 Wynford Rd. . . . B 10
77 Wynnstay Gdns. . . D 1
74 Wythburn Place . . G 2
79 Wyvil Rd. . . . . J 8
80 Yalding Rd. . . . . . . E 6
65 Yeading . . . . F 5
65 Yeading La. . . . . . . F 5
77 Yeoman's Row . . . E 6
65 Yiewsley . . . . F 4
74 York Bridge . . . . . E 3
75 York Buildings . . . J 9
74 York Gate . . . . E 3
77 York House Place . C 2
79 York Rd. . . . . . . C 10
74 York St. . . . . F 2
74 York Terrace . . . . E 4
75 York Way . . . . B 9
76 Yorkton St. . . . . . . C 6
77 Young St. . . . . C 2
74 Zoological Gardens
    B 3

PRINTED IN GREAT BRITAIN BY GEORGE PHILIP PRINTERS LTD , LONDON.